Germanic Interrelations

NOWELE Supplement Series (NSS)

ISSN 0900-8675

NOWELE Supplement Series is a book series associated with the journal *NOWELE: North-Western European Language Evolution*. The supplement series is devoted not only to the study of the history and prehistory of a locally determined group of languages, but also to the study of purely theoretical questions concerning historical language development. The series contains publications dealing with all aspects of the (pre-) histories of – and with intra- and extra-linguistic factors contributing to change and variation within – Icelandic, Faroese, Norwegian, Swedish, Danish, Frisian, Dutch, German, English, Gothic and the Early Runic language. The series will publish monographs and edited volumes.

For an overview of all books published in this series, please see
benjamins.com/catalog/nss

Editor

Stephen Laker
Kyushu University, Fukuoka

Co-editor

John Ole Askedal
University of Oslo

Advisory Editors

Michael Barnes
University College London

Rolf H. Bremmer, Jr.
Leiden University

Julia Fernández Cuesta
University of Seville

Volkert F. Faltings
Universität Flensburg

Kurt Gustav Goblirsch
University of South Carolina

Alexandra Holsting
University of Southern Denmark

Christer Lindqvist
Universität Greifswald

Robert Mailhammer
Western Sydney University,
Penrith NSW

Jürg R. Schwyter
University of Lausanne

Arjen P. Versloot
University of Amsterdam

Volume 34

Germanic Interrelations. Studies in memory of Hans Frede Nielsen
Edited by Stephen Laker, Carla Falluomini, Steffen Krogh, Robert Nedoma and Michael Schulte

Germanic Interrelations

Studies in memory of Hans Frede Nielsen

Edited by

Stephen Laker
Kyushu University, Fukuoka

Carla Falluomini
University of Perugia

Steffen Krogh
Aarhus University

Robert Nedoma
Universität Wien

Michael Schulte
University of Agder

John Benjamins Publishing Company
Amsterdam / Philadelphia

The paper used in this publication meets the minimum requirements of the American National Standard for Information Sciences – Permanence of Paper for Printed Library Materials, ANSI Z39.48-1984.

DOI 10.1075/nss.34
Cataloging-in-Publication Data available from Library of Congress:
LCCN 2025003478 (PRINT) / 2025003479 (E-BOOK)

ISBN 978 90 272 2012 7 (HB)
ISBN 978 90 272 4488 8 (E-BOOK)

© 2025 – John Benjamins B.V.
This e-book is Open Access under a CC BY-NC-ND 4.0 license.
https://creativecommons.org/licenses/by-nc-nd/4.0

This license permits reuse, distribution and reproduction in any medium for non-commercial purposes, provided that the original author(s) and source are credited. Derivative works may not be distributed without prior permission.

This work may contain content reproduced under license from third parties. Permission to reproduce this third-party content must be obtained from these third parties directly.

Permission for any reuse beyond the scope of this license must be obtained from John Benjamins Publishing Company, rights@benjamins.nl

John Benjamins Publishing Company · https://benjamins.com

Table of contents

Acknowledgements   VII

Hans Frede Nielsen   1

Publications by Hans Frede Nielsen   9

Ostfries.-nd. *Bau*, *Schuurschott* und *Tiek(e)* — drei friesische Substratnamen
für Insekten: Einige lexikalische Notizen zum Friesischen   19
  Nils Århammar

Towards an edition of the Hildina ballad (*Hildinakvadet*)   34
  Michael P. Barnes

Prosodic complexity and mora counting in North Germanic   50
  Hans Basbøll

The etymology of Old Frisian *ink* 'angry'   72
  Rolf H. Bremmer Jr, Sergio Neri & Roland Schuhmann

Unity and diversity in basic color terms: A comparison of Germanic,
Slavic, and Romance   82
  Bernard Comrie

Of Angles and angels: Philology, history and the representation of identity   103
  John Hines

Old West Frisian *thēia**, Saterlandic *taie* and Modern West Frisian
triuwe 'to push'   126
  Jarich Hoekstra

Deʒsastan   138
  John Insley

Rasmus Rask and Vilhelm Thomsen: The Danish godfathers
of Finnish linguistics   144
  Petri Kallio

Old English breaking: A parallel to Lachmann's Law   157
  Yuri Kleiner

Relativsätze im Saterfriesischen *Stephen Laker & Pyt Kramer*	173
The uses of historical phonology *Anatoly Liberman*	202
Turmbau auf Färöisch: Sprachverwirrung in Rasmus Rasmussens Roman *Bábelstornið* *Christer Lindqvist*	217
The Tienen inscription and the dialectal position of Tungrian *Bernard Mees*	240
Der Name der Insel Thule *Robert Nedoma*	269
Frauennamen in alten niederländischen Ortsnamen *Arend Quak*	287
Latin *brutes, sapo, burdo* *Ludwig Rübekeil*	295
Nochmals zur Metrizität der älteren Runeninschriften *Michael Schulte*	312
Garden, town, villa and *torg*: Four emblematic words that influenced the vocabulary and semantics of European languages *Ingmar Söhrman*	346
The Loveden Hill Urn: Its second runic sequence and an afterthought *Gaby Waxenberger*	356
Subject index	377

Acknowledgements

This book was published with the generous financial support of:

– in Agder, Norway –

University of Agder, Faculty of Humanities and Education
University of Agder Open Access Fund

– in Fukuoka, Japan –

Tanaka Toshiaki German and Dutch Language Fund, Faculty of Languages
and Cultures, Kyushu University
The Dean's Discretionary Fund, Faculty of Languages and Cultures,
Kyushu University

We would like to thank all our sponsors for their generous support.

Hans Frede Nielsen

Hans Frede Nielsen was born on 20 May 1943 in Bramming, Southern Denmark. With two older brothers he grew up in the same Jutlandic village, where his mother, Sonja, and father, Frede, ran a grocery store. In 1959 he became an AFS (American Field Service) exchange student and spent a year in America. He ended up in Arthur, Illinois, a village of less than two thousand people at the time, about three hours' drive south of Chicago. The village was even smaller than Bramming and had the oldest and largest Amish community in Illinois. He stayed with the Jurgens family, whose son Jim was the same age as Hans Frede and became a lifelong friend. After graduating with an American High School Diploma in 1960, he returned to Denmark and continued his studies at the old Cathedral School in Ribe, gaining his *studentereksamen* in 1963.

In autumn 1963 he entered the University of Copenhagen to study English. Among the courses in his first term was one on phonetics. It was during this course that he met his long-time friend, colleague, and also co-founder of NOW-ELE, Erik W. Hansen. The next term they started with Old English, reading prose, followed by further terms studying Old English poetry and other works. Having passed the first part of the English degree programme, he planned on going abroad and was fortunate enough to receive a bursary which enabled him to study two years at Trinity College Cambridge, always among the strongest of Cambridge's colleges academically.

In 1966, Hans Frede enrolled for the Anglo-Saxon, Norse and Celtic Tripos, then part of the Faculty of Archaeology and Anthropology, and one of the smallest subject areas at the university. Interestingly, a short film that was made in anticipation of the arrival of the then Prince Charles's arrival at Trinity College in 1967 shows Hans Frede taking a tutorial with his tutor Dr Denis Marrian.[1] Hans Frede's main interest was Old English, with an emphasis on language. A number of prominent scholars were teaching older Germanic languages at the time, including Dorothy Whitelock, then Elrington and Bosworth Professor of Anglo-Saxon, Peter Clemoes and Ray Page. However, it was Trinity's Dr Dennis Howard

---

1. Footage entitled 'Trinity College Open Day' (British Pathé film ID 2027.23; issued on 30 April 1967) shows Hans Frede taking a tutorial with Dr Denis Marrian (0:20–0:27). It can viewed here https://www.britishpathe.com/asset/88370/ or here https://www.youtube.com/watch?v=fZoJv3K4X78

Green — not yet a professor at the time — who covered the whole breadth of the older Germanic languages and taught him more than anyone else during his two years at Cambridge.

From an obituary in the Independent newspaper (18 December 2008), we learn that Dennis Green was "a demanding and even formidable teacher but also a valued mentor for those willing to keep pace with him". Having already received a grounding in Old English, both at Copenhagen and then at Cambridge, Hans Frede was no doubt well prepared — as he always was with everything he did — to follow Green's one-year course (1967–1968) on Early Germanic languages, or "Teutonic Languages" as it was then called. There were three other students in this course: Bernard Comrie, Robin Cooper and John Hawkins, all of whom went on to become prominent linguists. Due to the small size of the lecture, it allowed for more discussion and special assignments. Bernard Comrie (p.c.), a longtime board member of NOWELE, gives a sense of the course at the time:

> DHG was really the only person who covered the breadth of Germanic linguistics. There were of course specialists in Old English, Old High German, and Old Norse with some knowledge of Germanic linguistics, but I think no one else who was a real specialist across Germanic. So DHG effectively did everything himself, combining lectures with discussion and assignments, and there were no separate supervisions for this subject [...] We had to read certain sections of the Gothic Bible ("set text"), and while we were expected to prepare on our own, we brought questions to class. I still recall one such example, where we were puzzled by a use of the infinitive in Gothic, and DHG explained to us that this was a calque on the Greek, and indeed probably made no sense independently in Gothic. (We also had to show reading knowledge, via set texts, of two of Old English, Old Norse, Old High German, or Old Saxon, but the first three were covered by taking classes in the relevant language/history of the relevant language, while no one in our group did Old Saxon.) In class we went in detail through some aspects of historical phonology and morphology. [...] Students were supposed to wear gowns to lectures, but few did, certainly none of the 4 of us in The Teutonic Languages. (Lecturers were also supposed to wear gowns and nearly always did, including DHG.)

Much of what was taught was later crystallized by Green in his book *Language and History in the Early Germanic World* (1998). Overall the stay in Cambridge was described by Hans Frede as being a lifelong inspiration, not least through the professional contacts he made there and held on to over the years. Thomas L. Markey, a lifelong friend whom Hans Frede met in Cambridge, lamented in an email from 2021, not long before he passed away: "he also sent me a birthday card every year, so I'll miss him this May 29th, a poignant reminder of his loss".

Having earned his BA in Anglo-Saxon Studies from Cambridge in 1968, he returned to Copenhagen to pursue a *magisterkonferens* degree in English philology, which he was duly awarded in 1971. During his studies in Copenhagen, he also took the opportunity to deepen his knowledge of other older Germanic languages, taking Old Danish with Harry Andersen and Old Frisian with Arne Spenter. In order to gain teaching experience, he then decided to get a qualification to teach English, which he completed in 1971–1972 at Nørresundby Gymnasium and Aalborghus State Gymnasium.

Although Hans Frede had embarked on a career as a schoolteacher, he maintained academic contacts and continued to conduct research in an independent capacity. One of these contacts was one of the leading scholars of Frisian at the time, Arne Spenter, who often organized fieldwork trips as part of his teaching. As a result, Hans Frede travelled to Saterland in Lower Saxony, Germany, in June 1972, to help document the Saterland Frisian language together with another student, Flemming Schroller. Maike Lohse (*Us Wurk* vol. 28, 1979: 29) explains how Spenter organized the fieldwork trips.

> Einen besonderen Bestandteil des Unterrichts bildeten die Exkursionen, die man in den Ferien unternahm, und bei denen die Teilnehmer die Hälfte der Unkosten selbst trugen. Spenter reiste dann mit einer kleinen Gruppe Studenten in sprachlich interessante Gebiete und untersuchte verschiedene linguistische Phänomene. Eine der ersten Exkursionen ging nach Nordholland [...] Eine andere Exkursion galt dem Saterländischen. Man suchte in den drei Dörfern Strücklingen, Ramsloh und Scharrel die Friesisch sprechende Bevölkerung auf und ließ die sogenannten Wenkersätze ins Saterländische übertragen; außerdem machte man Tonbandaufnahmen von freier Erzählung. Jeder Teilnehmer arbeitete für sich allein und machte auch selbst seine Informanten ausfindig. Man empfand diese Arbeit nicht nur als Übung, sondern auch als ein sprachwissenschaftlich wichtiges Unternehmen.

Hans Frede admired how Spenter was very experienced with fieldwork, especially when it came to finding and interviewing native speaker informants. Before going to Saterland, he had made contact with the Seelter Buund and also quickly got word out in the local press that there were "Sprachforscher aus Dänemark im Saterland", so that everyone knew they were coming. Spenter then went to Strücklingen, Schroller to Ramsloh, and Hans Frede to Scharrel. Some 45 hours of recordings were made, which largely remained forgotten about for many years (partly as a result of Spenter's untimely death in 1977). However, Pyt Kramer, a native West Frisian speaker and also a specialist in Saterland Frisian, was given the tapes on loan in the 1990s and managed to transcribe them all. These recordings now form a valuable collection of Saterland Frisian speech from that period.

Over the years Hans Frede maintained an interest in Frisian, though less so Modern Frisian. He often published on Frisian runes, Old Frisian phonology, and the phylogeny of Old Frisian. He organized a series of symposia at Odense University in the 1980s and promoted Frisian-related content in the NOWELE journal and book series. Nils Århammar's Festschrift, *A Frisian and Germanic Miscellany* (NOWELE special issue 28/29, 1996), would be one such example, and Nils was determined to write a final article for this volume in appreciation of Hans Frede. He managed to do so, despite failing health, with some extra support from his wife Ritva as well as his former student Jarich Hoekstra. It is a sad circumstance that Jarich — recently honoured with his own Festschrift *From West to North Frisia* (NOWELE Supplement Series vol. 33, 2022) and a contributor to this volume — is also sadly longer with us. At any rate, Hans Frede's contribution to Frisian Studies was recognised, and in 1994 he was made a member of the Fryske Akademy, Leeuwarden.

After his teacher training period at Nørresundby Gymnasium and Aalborghus State Gymnasium (1971–72), Hans Frede took up a post as a full-time English teacher at Aalborg Handelsskole in Jutland. During his pedagogical training and work, Hans Frede again maintained his academic interests and contacts which proved invaluable. Three years into his job at the Aalborg Handelsskole in Jutland, he received an unexpected call from his former classmate Erik W. Hansen, who, after a short stint as a grammar school teacher in Copenhagen, had gained a permanent position at Odense University, a new university founded in 1966 which as of 1998 became known as Syddansk Universitet, or the University of Southern Denmark (SDU) in English. The call was to let him know that a position had become vacant at Odense University's Department of English and that he might like to apply. He did so and was given the post primarily because he had continued to write and publish research articles while having a full-time position as a teacher.

At Odense, Erik W. Hansen had already given the study of language history a new lease of life, for he had developed a new and popular language history course that brought together both theoretical and practical aspects of the study of language. The theoretical basis came from the set textbook, Michael Samuels's *Linguistic Evolution* (1972), which students found stimulating and comprehensible. The practical component came from studying the Old and Middle English texts themselves. With Hans Frede's arrival, a perfect collaboration arose with Erik focusing on the theoretical and conceptual aspects and Hans Frede dealing with the reading of medieval texts and their philological analysis. The symbiosis proved to be very popular with students, but it came by all accounts as something of an irritation to other departmental members who would sometimes complain that students worked so hard on the course that they had no time for other courses. Odense University was going against the trend at other universities in Denmark and around the world at the time where synchronic studies of language, especially generative syntax, were in vogue.

The early years at SDU proved to be very happy and productive. From 1977, Hans Frede was given the opportunity to write a doctoral dissertation under the supervision of Andreas Haarder (this was effectively somewhat like a second doctorate or habilitation since the *Magisterkonferens* degree that he was awarded in 1971 was generally regarded as something similar to a doctoral degree at the time). He submitted his thesis in November 1980 and successfully defended it in February 1982. It was published as a book: *Old English and the Continental Germanic Languages: A Survey of Morphological and Phonological Interrelations* (1981; 2nd edition 1985). This has gone on to be a work of lasting value that is still in good use today, covering the various dialectal features of Old English dialects and their appearance (or not) in Continental Germanic languages and leading to questions about the grouping of the dialects themselves.

While writing his dissertation, he also found time to write another book, *De germanske sprog. Baggrund og gruppering* (1979). Similar to his dissertation, it deals with the grouping of the Germanic languages and the features and arguments that surround the debate but in a more introductory manner. After some encouragement from Elmer H. Antonsen, Hans Frede subsequently translated and revised *De germanske sprog* as *The Germanic Languages: Origins and Early Dialectal Interrelations* in 1989. It should also be noted that 1979 — the year the Danish edition was published — coincided with Hans Frede's marriage to Helene, whom he had met at Odense University. At the time, she was a translator at the European Commission but was taking further studies at Odense University and worked as an English teacher there as well.

Together with Erik W. Hansen, he wrote *Uregelmæssigheder i moderne engelsk* (1980), which was later translated and revised as *Irregularities in Modern English* (1986; 2nd edition revised by Erik W. Hansen 2007). This unique book deals with grammatical as well as sound and spelling irregularities in English, taking Modern English as its starting point but providing historical context where necessary as well as ample comparisons with related Germanic languages. Another highlight of these early years, was hosting the 2nd International Conference of English Historical Linguistics in 1981. The proceedings were co-edited with Erik W. Hansen and Michael Davenport in 1982.

It was also in the early 1980s that Hans Frede and Erik W. Hansen came up with the idea of starting a new linguistics journal that would likewise combine both theoretical and empirical aspects to the study of language change, with a focus on the Germanic languages of northwestern Europe. The history journal *History and Theory* was one of the sources of inspiration for this new linguistics journal. Following a grant of support from Odense University, NOWELE was finally launched in 1983 and is still going strong. There also followed the supplementary book series which started in 1985. Most of the editorial work fell to Hans Frede over the years.

NOWELE seems to have carved out its own niche, broader in scope than journals that focus on a single language, e.g. English or German, yet also narrowly enough defined to contain articles with a great likelihood of being comprehensible to a readership familiar with some of the Germanic languages, especially in its linguistic coverage of a geographically defined set of related yet divergent languages. Neither editor expected that the journal would survive so long, but when it did, both strongly wished it to have a secure future. Its inclusion of theoretical papers has, however, as Erik W. Hansen readily admits not been especially abundant, and this is perhaps another reason why the journal has become so closely connected with Hans Frede over the years. The 1990s saw a merger and reorganization of SDU, also resulting in the foundation of SDU journal Rask, which Hans Frede was editor of for several years. Its last issue appeared in 2022.

In the late 1980s and early 1990s he wrote various research articles, especially on runes, and was involved in projects concerning Otto Jespersen that resulted in two books that he co-edited: *Otto Jespersen: Facets of his Life* (1989) and *A Linguist's Life* (1995). He then followed in Jespersen's footsteps a century earlier by writing his own history of English: *A Journey Through the History of the English Language in England and America*. Work on it started in autumn 1995 and its first volume, *The Continental Backgrounds of English and its Insular Development until 1154*, appeared in 1998. Work on the second volume *From Dialect to Standard: English in England 1154–1776* started in 2000, and it was completed and published in 2004, with the bulk of it written during two separate research stays at Churchill College, Cambridge, in 2000 and 2004, supported by the Carlsberg Foundation. An anticipated third volume that would follow through to the twentieth century was not completed due to health problems, but an article on the development of a spoken standard 1400–1926 appeared in NOWELE in 2017, and this gives a taste of what was planned.

One reason why Hans Frede took a two-year break between writing the first and second volume of his history of English was because in 1997 he was awarded a generous Research Council scholarship to pursue research into early Danish language, which freed him from teaching between August 1997 and December 1999 and gave him opportunity to write *The Early Runic Language of Scandinavia* (2000). This volume focused on the dialectal status of the language of the older runic inscriptions of Scandinavia (AD 200–500). It received positive reviews and has become a valuable and lasting contribution to the field of runology. Shortly before its publication, in 1999, Hans Frede was appointed Professor of Historical

Linguistics with particular reference to the Germanic languages at the University of Southern Denmark. According to Hans Basbøll (p.c.), this involved a special procedure, rather like the German *Ruf*, which is quite exceptional in Denmark:

> The condition for such a *Ruf* at the time was that the person to be "called" should not only (of course) be fully and unquestionably qualified for the position, but should be clearly more qualified than anyone else that might come into consideration. I was chairman of the committee, the two other members were Alfred Bammesberger and Elmar Seebold, both highly qualified specialists.

However, not long after, in 2006, he took early retirement at the age of 63.

In retirement, he remained active at SDU, where he retained an office and came in two or three times a week to work — either to research new articles, manage and edit the NOWELE journal and supplement series, or to organize annual symposia. Generally, it was typical for there to be a symposium on a set theme compatible with the aims and scope of NOWELE that would take place usually each spring in Odense with financial support from SDU. These events were well attended and appreciated by scholars across Europe and throughout the world. They usually lasted one full day and concluded with a visit to the former China Wok House restaurant in the town centre. The papers of these symposia usually resulted in special issues of NOWELE, the last three being *Runic Inscriptions and the Early History of the Germanic Languages* (2020), *Early History of the North Sea Germanic Languages* (2021), and *Historical Germanic Morphosyntax* (2021). It came, however, as a bitter disappointment that the symposium was not supported the last time he applied for funding (though it turned out a blessing in disguise since it would have had to have been cancelled due to the COVID-19 pandemic anyway). At any rate, it was a great uplift for Hans Frede when Robert Nedoma offered to host the event on *Indo-European and Early Germanic Language History*, which was finally held online rather than in Vienna (due to travel restrictions) in 2022. Meanwhile, Carla Falluomini has hosted another successful workshop on *Old Germanic Languages and Latin / Early Romance in Contact* at the University of Perugia in May 2024.

Aside from all his achievements, we can say that Hans Frede was above all else an extremely supportive and generous person. So many friends reached out in a private capacity on his passing to say how much he was always willing to help and support them. I will mention the contents of one email from Jürg Schwyter, formerly Professor of English Linguistics at the University of Lausanne, whose doctoral thesis was revised and published as a volume in the NOWELE Supplement Series: *Old English Legal Language* (1996). In 2009 Jürg Schwyter suffered a severe stroke and fell on hard times. In an email, he emphasized just how much Hans Frede's support meant to him at the time: "Hans Frede never doubted my mental capacities and helped my professional reintegration", and he goes on to say that he "was not only a first-class scholar and editor, but above all, he put people first and was a wonderful friend with most admirable human qualities". Outside of academia, Hans Frede liked to travel by train. He would watch rather than play sports (following European football and cycling closely), and he enjoyed listening to music, especially jazz and Italian opera.

Finally, Hans Frede, despite his departure on 9 January 2021, taken from us by a brain tumor, had a clear vision of NOWELE's future direction. Although he did not live to see this celebratory volume, he knew about its plan and even envisaged some of the authors who might be in it. It is therefore still a great pleasure that we can all show our appreciation in this way and thank him for his outstanding contribution to the field and for all his selfless work on the journal and in organizing enjoyable and stimulating symposia over many decades.

Acknowledgements

I am grateful to Hans Frede's widow Helene for providing personal information on Hans Frede. I am also grateful to NOWELE co-founder Erik W. Hansen, a friend of nearly 60 years, for many details on the early days as students at Copenhagen along with their times in Odense and the foundation of the journal. Bernard Comrie, Thomas L. Markey and Hans Basbøll also provided further helpful information and insights.

SL

Publications by Hans Frede Nielsen

Monographs

Nielsen, Hans Frede. 1979. *De germanske sprog. Baggrund og gruppering.* Odense: Odense Universitetsforlag.

Hansen, Erik W. & Hans Frede Nielsen. 1980. *Uregelmæssigheder i moderne engelsk.* Odense: Odense Universitetsforlag.

Nielsen, Hans Frede. 1981. (2nd, rev. edn 1985). *Old English and the Continental Germanic languages. A survey of morphological and phonological interrelations.* Innsbruck: Institut für Sprachwissenschaft.

Hansen, Erik W. & Hans Frede Nielsen. 1986 (rev. 2nd edn by Erik W. Hansen 2007). *Irregularities in modern English* (= NOWELE Supplement Series, 2). Odense: Odense University Press.

Nielsen, Hans Frede. 1989. *The Germanic languages. Origins and early dialectal interrelations.* Tuscaloosa: University of Alabama Press.

Nielsen, Hans Frede. 1998. *The continental backgrounds of English and its insular development until 1154* (= NOWELE Supplement Series, 19). Odense: Odense University Press.

Nielsen, Hans Frede. 2000. *The Early Runic language of Scandinavia. Studies in Germanic dialect geography.* Heidelberg: Winter.

Nielsen, Hans Frede. 2005. *From dialect to standard. English in England 1154–1776* (= NOWELE Supplement Series, 21). Odense: University Press of Southern Denmark.

Edited volumes / special thematic issues of NOWELE

Bekker-Nielsen, Hans, Peter Foote, Andreas Haarder & Hans Frede Nielsen (eds.). 1977. *Oral tradition — literary tradition: A symposium.* Odense: Odense University Press.

Nielsen, Hans Frede. 1981. *Sammenlignende studier i gotisk* (= Mindre skrifter udgivet af Laboratorium for Folkesproglig Middelalderlitteratur ved Odense Universitet, 5). Odense: Odense University.

Bekker-Nielsen, Hans & Hans Frede Nielsen (eds.). 1982. *Nordboer i Danelagen. Den skandinaviske bosættelsestæthed i Danelagen med udgangspunkt i de sproglige vidnesbyrd.* Odense: Odense Universitet, Engelsk Institut.

Bekker-Nielsen, Hans & Hans Frede Nielsen (eds.). 1985. *Første tværfaglige vikingesymposium. Odense Universitet 1982.* Moesgård: Hikuin.

Danielsen, Niels, Erik W. Hansen, Hans Frede Nielsen & Iørn Piø (eds.). 1980. *Friserstudier.* Odense: Odense Universitetsforlag.

Danielsen, Niels, Erik W. Hansen & Hans Frede Nielsen (eds.). 1982. *Friserstudier II*. Odense: Odense Universitetsforlag.

Davenport, Michael, Erik W. Hansen & Hans Frede Nielsen (eds.). 1983. *Current topics in English historical linguistics* (= Proceedings of the International Conference on English historical linguistics, 2). Odense: Odense University Press.

Danielsen, Niels, Erik W. Hansen, Hans Frede Nielsen & Hans Bekker-Nielsen (eds.). 1983. *Friserstudier III*. Odense: Odense Universitetsforlag.

Bekker-Nielsen, Hans & Hans Frede Nielsen (eds.). 1985. *Fjerde tværfaglige vikingesymposium. Odense Universitet 1985*. Moesgård: Hikuin.

Danielsen, Niels, Erik W. Hansen, Hans Frede Nielsen & Hans Bekker-Nielsen (eds.). 1986. *Friserstudier IV/V*. Odense: Odense Universitetsforlag.

Juul, Arne, Hans Frede Nielsen, & Knud Sørensen (eds.). 1988. *Degeneration on the air?* 2nd edn. Copenhagen: Landscentralen for Undervisningsmidler; Danmarks Laererhojskole.

doi Juul, Arne & Hans Frede Nielsen (eds.). 1989. *Otto Jespersen: Facets of his life and work*. Amsterdam: Benjamins.

Bekker-Nielsen, Hans & Hans Frede Nielsen (eds.). 1989. *Syvende tværfaglige vikingesymposium. Odense Universitet 1988*. Moesgård: Hikuin.

Bekker-Nielsen, Hans & Hans Frede Nielsen (eds.). 1991. *Tiende tværfaglige vikingesymposium. Odense Universitet 1991*. Moesgård: Hikuin.

Juul, Arne, Hans F. Nielsen & Jørgen Erik Nielsen (eds.), with David Stoner (translator) and annotations by Jørgen Erik Nielsen. 1995. *A linguist's life: an English translation of Otto Jespersen's autobiography with notes, photos and a bibliography*. Odense: Odense University Press.

doi Nielsen, Hans Frede & Lene Schøsler (eds.). 1996. *The origins and development of emigrant languages: Proceedings from the Second Rasmus Rask Colloqium, Odense University, November 1994* (= NOWELE Supplement Series, 17; also RASK Supplement, 6). Amsterdam: Benjamins.

Adeline Petersen & Hans Frede Nielsen, with Rolf H. Bremmer, Jr, Erik W. Hansen & Flemming Talbo Stubkjær. 1996. *A Frisian and Germanic miscellany*. Published in honour of Nils Århammar on his sixty-fifth birthday, 7 August 1996 (= NOWELE 28/29). Odense: Odense University Press.

Bekker-Nielsen, Hans & Hans Frede Nielsen (eds.). 1997. *Sekstende tværfaglige vikingesymposium. Odense Universitet 1997*. Moesgård: Hikuin.

Bekker-Nielsen, Hans & Hans Frede Nielsen (eds.). 2001. *Tyvende tværfaglige vikingesymposium. Syddansk Universitet 2001*. Moesgård: Hikuin.

Jørgensen, Jørgen Højgaard & Hans Frede Nielsen (eds.). 2005. *Fireogtyvende tværfaglige vikingesymposium. Syddansk Universitet 2005*. Moesgård: Hikuin.

Bruus, Mette & Hans Frede Nielsen (eds.). 2006. *Goternes sprog, historie og efterliv* (= Mindre Skrifter udgivet af Center for Middelalderstudier ved Syddansk Universitet, 25). Odense: University of Southern Denmark.

Bruus, Mette, Carl-Erik Lindberg & Hans Frede Nielsen (eds.). 2008. *Gotisk workshop. Et uformelt formidlingstræf* (= Mindre Skrifter udgivet af Center for Middelalderstudier, 26). Odense: University of Southern Denmark.

Nielsen, Hans Frede (ed.). 2008. *Early and pre-historic language development in North-Western Europe* (= NOWELE 54/55). Odense: University of Southern Denmark.

Bruus, Mette, Hans Frede Nielsen & Tore Nyberg (eds.). 2010. *Gotisk Workshop 2. Et uformelt formidlingstræf* (= Mindre Skrifter udgivet af Center for Middelalderstudier, 27). Odense: University of Southern Denmark.

Hans Frede Nielsen & Flemming Talbo Stubkjær, with Mette Bruus & Erik W. Hansen. 2010. *The Gothic language. A symposium* (= NOWELE 58/59). Odense: University of Southern Denmark.

Hansen, Erik W., Alexandra Holsting & Hans Frede Nielsen (eds.). 2012. *Ældre germansk sproghistorie: Et uformelt minisymposium.* (= Mindre Skrifter udgivet af Center for Middelalderstudier, 29). Odense: University of Southern Denmark.

Hans Frede Nielsen & Patrick V. Stiles, with Erik W. Hansen, Alexandra Holsting & Flemming Talbo Stubkjaer. 2013. *Unity and diversity in West Germanic, I* (= NOWELE 66(1)). Amsterdam: Benjamins.

Hans Frede Nielsen & Patrick V. Stiles, with Erik W. Hansen, Alexandra Holsting & Flemming Talbo Stubkjaer. 2013. *Unity and diversity in West Germanic, II* (= NOWELE 66(2)). Amsterdam: Benjamins.

Hans Frede Nielsen & Patrick V. Stiles, with Erik W. Hansen, Alexandra Holsting & Flemming Talbo Stubkjaer. 2014. *Unity and diversity in West Germanic, III* (= NOWELE 67(1)). Amsterdam: Benjamins.

Askedal, John Ole & Hans Frede Nielsen (eds.). 2015. *Early Germanic languages in contact* (= NOWELE Supplement Series, 27). Amsterdam: Benjamins.

Alexandra Holsting & Hans Frede Nielsen, with John Ole Askedal, Mette Bruus & Ingmar Söhrman. 2018. *Advances in Gothic philology and linguistics* (= NOWELE 71(1)). Amsterdam: Benjamins.

Nedoma, Robert & Hans Frede Nielsen (eds.). 2020. *Runic inscriptions and the early history of the Germanic languages* (= NOWELE 73(1)). Amsterdam: Benjamins.

Laker, Stephen & Hans Frede Nielsen (eds.). 2021. *Early history of the North Sea Germanic languages* (= NOWELE 74(1)). Amsterdam: Benjamins.

Articles

Nielsen, Hans Frede. 1971. Betragtninger over pronomenet *den. Arkiv för nordisk filologi* 86. 249–254.

Nielsen, Hans Frede. 1975. Morphological and phonological parallels between Old Norse and Old English. *Arkiv för nordisk filologi* 90. 1–18.

Nielsen, Hans Frede. 1976. A list of morphological and phonological parallels between North and West Germanic. *Acta philologica Scandinavica* 31. 96–116.

Nielsen, Hans Frede. 1979. The earliest grouping of the Germanic dialects. *Arkiv för nordisk filologi* 94. 1–9.

Nielsen, Hans Frede. 1981. Old Frisian and the Old English dialects. *Us Wurk* 30. 49–66.

Nielsen, Hans Frede. 1982. On the exceptions to the Germanic and High German consonant shift and *sp, st, sk* in English. *Acta Linguistica Hafniensia* 17(1). 79–85.

Nielsen, Hans Frede. 1982. Final remarks. *Acta Linguistica Hafniensia* 17(1). 96–97.

Nielsen, Hans Frede. 1983. Germanic *ai* in Old Frisian, Old English and Old Norse. *Indogermanische Forschungen* 88. 156–164.

Nielsen, Hans Frede. 1984. On case-form endings in runic Frisian. *Us Wurk* 33(4). 97–99.

Nielsen, Hans Frede. 1984. A note on the origin of Old English breaking and back mutation. *Amsterdamer Beiträge zur älteren Germanistik* 22(1). 73–81.

Nielsen, Hans Frede. 1984. Unaccented vowels in the Frisian runic inscriptions. In Nils Århammar et al. (eds.), *Miscellanea Frisica*, 11–19. Assen: Van Gorcum.

Nielsen, Hans Frede. 1986. Old English, Old Frisian and Germanic. *Philologia Frisica anno 1984*, 168–180. Ljouwert: Fryske Akademy.

Nielsen, Hans Frede. 1986. On the origins of emigrant languages with special reference to the dialectal position of Old English within Germanic. *Journal of English Linguistics* 19. 94–105.

Nielsen, Hans Frede. 1989. On Otto Jespersen's view of language evolution. In Arne Juul & Hans Frede Nielsen (eds.), *Otto Jespersen: Facets of his life and work*, 61–78. Amsterdam: Benjamins.

Nielsen, Hans Frede. 1989. A note on Gothic 2 pt. sg. ind. *saísōst*. *NOWELE* 14. 74–76.

Nielsen, Hans Frede. 1990. The Old English and Germanic decades. In Graham Caie et al. (eds.), *Proceedings from the Fourth Nordic Conference for English Studies (Helsingør, May 11–13, 1989)*, I, 105–117. Copenhagen: Department of English, University of Copenhagen.

Nielsen, Hans Frede. 1990. Jacob Grimm and the 'German' dialects. In Elmer H. Antonsen, James W. Marchand & Ladislav Zgusta (eds.), *The Grimm Brothers and the Germanic past*, 25–32. Amsterdam: Benjamins.

Nielsen, Hans Frede. 1991. The Straubing Heliand-fragment and the Old English dialects. In Per Sture Ureland & George Broderick (eds.), *Language contact in the British Isles*, 243–273. Tübingen: Niemeyer.

Nielsen, Hans Frede. 1991. The Undley bracteate, "Continental Anglian" and the Early Germanic of Schleswig-Holstein. In John Ole Askedal, Harald Bjorvand & Eyvind Fjeld Halvorsen (eds.), *Festskrift til Ottar Grønvik på 75-årsdagen den 21. oktober 1991*, 33–52. Oslo: Universitetsforlaget.

Nielsen, Hans Frede. 1991. Unaccented vowels in Runic Frisian and Ingveonic. In Alfred Bammesberger (ed.), *Old English runes and their continental background*, 299–303. Heidelberg: Winter.

Nielsen, Hans Frede. 1992. Variability in Old English and the Continental Germanic languages. In Matti Rissanen, Ossi Ihalainen, Terttu Nevalainen, & Irma Taavitsainen (eds.), *History of Englishes. New methods and interpretations in historical linguistics*, 640–646. Berlin: De Gruyter.

Nielsen, Hans Frede. 1993. On case-form endings in the earliest runic personal names. In Lena Petersen (ed.), *Personnamn i nordiska och andra germanska fornspråk: Handlingar från NORNA:s artonde symposium i Uppsala 16–19 augusti 1991*, 85–93. Uppsala: NORNA-Förlaget.

Nielsen, Hans Frede. 1993. Runic Frisian *skanomodu* and *aniwulufu* and the relative chronology of monophthongization and *i*-Mutation. *NOWELE* 21/22, 81–88.

Nielsen, Hans Frede. 1994. The beginnings of a "Frisian" runic corpus. In Philippus H. Breuker, Siebren Dijk, Durk Gorter, L. G. Jansma & Willem Visser (eds.), *Philologia Frisica anno 1993*, 210–222. Ljouwert: Fryske Akademy.

Nielsen, Hans Frede. 1994. Ante-Old Frisian: A review. *NOWELE* 24. 91–136. [West Frisian translation: Nielsen 1999; see below.]

Nielsen, Hans Frede. 1994. Ingerid Dal's views on Old Saxon in the light of new evidence. In Toril Swan, Endre Mørck & Old Jansen (eds.), *Language change and language structure*, 195–212. Berlin: De Gruyter.

Nielsen, Hans Frede. 1994. On the dialectal split of Ingvaeonic West Germanic from the Early Runic language of Scandinavia. In Klaus Düwel, with Hannelore Neumann & Sean Nowak (eds.), *Runische Schriftkultur in kontinental-skandinavischer und -angelsächsischer Wechselbeziehung. Internationales Symposium in der Werner-Reimers-Stiftung vom 24.–27. Juni 1992 in Bad Homburg* (= Ergänzungsbände zum Reallexikon der Germanischen Altertumskunde, 10), 117–127. Berlin. De Gruyter.

Nielsen, Hans Frede. 1994. On the origin and spread of initial voiced fricatives and the phonemic split of fricatives in English and Dutch. In Margaret Laing & Keith Williamson (eds.), *Speaking in our tongues*, 7–30. Cambridge: Brewer.

Nielsen, Hans Frede. 1995. Methodological problems in Germanic dialect grouping. In Edith Marold & Christiane Zimmermann (eds.), *Nordwestgermanisch* (= Ergänzungsbände zum Reallexikon der Germanischen Altertumskunde, 13), 115–123. Berlin: De Gruyter.

Nielsen, Hans Frede. 1995. The emergence of the *os* and *ac* runes in the runic inscriptions of England and Frisia: A linguistic assessment. In Volkert F. Faltings, Alastair G. H. Walker & Ommo Wilts (eds.), *Friesische Studien II: Beiträge des Föhrer Symposiums zur Friesischen Philologie vom 7.–8. April 1994*, 19–34. Odense: Odense University Press.

Nielsen, Hans Frede. 1996. Developments in Frisian runology: A discussion of Düwel & Tempel's runic corpus from 1970. In Tineke Looijenga & Arend Quak (eds.), *Frisian Runes and Neighbouring Traditions. Proceedings of the First International Symposium on Frisian runes at the Fries Museum, Leeuwarden 26–29 January 1994* (= Amsterdamer Beiträge zur älteren Germanistik 45), 123–130. Amsterdam: Rodopi.

Nielsen, Hans Frede. 1996. Friesen: The linguistic provenance of the Frisian runic corpus. In Heinrich Beck et al. (eds.), *Reallexikon der Germanischen Altertumskunde*, 2nd ed., vol. 10, 29–35. Berlin: De Gruyter.

Nielsen, Hans Frede. 1996. Gallehus: The linguistic provenance of the inscription. In Heinrich Beck et al. (eds.), *Reallexikon der Germanischen Altertumskunde*, 2nd ed., vol. 10, 336–340. Berlin: De Gruyter.

Nielsen, Hans Frede. 1997. Runologiske forbindelser mellem Frisland og Skandinavien. In Hans Bekker-Nielsen & Hans Frede Nielsen (eds.), *Beretning fra sekstende tværfaglige vikingesymposium. Odense Universitet 1997*, 7–24. Moesgård: Hikuin.

Nielsen, Hans Frede. 1998. The linguistic status of the early runic inscriptions of Scandinavia. In Klaus Düwel, with Sean Nowak (eds.), *Runeninschriften als Quellen interdisziplinärer Forschung. Abhandlungen des Vierten Internationalen Symposiums über Runen und Runeninschriften in Göttingen vom 4.–9. August 1995* (= Ergänzungsbände zum Reallexikon der Germanischen Altertumskunde, 15), 539–555. Berlin: De Gruyter.

Nielsen, Hans Frede. 1998. Det ældste sprog i Danmark. *Humaniora* 13(2). 3–7.

Nielsen, Hans Frede. 1999. Foar-Aldfrysk: In oersjoch. In Anne Dykstra & Rolf H. Bremmer Jr (eds.), *In skiedenis fan 'e Fryske taalkunde*, 34–74. Ljouwert: Fryske Akademy.

Nielsen, Hans Frede. 2000. Ingwäonisch. In Heinrich Beck et al. (eds.), *Reallexikon derGermanischen Altertumskunde*, 2nd ed., vol. 15, 432–439. Berlin: De Gruyter.

Nielsen, Hans Frede. 2001. The dialectal provenance of the Gallehus inscription. In Klaus Düwel, Edith Marold & Christiane Zimmermann, with Lars E. Worgull (eds.), *Von Thorsberg nach Schleswig. Sprache und Schriftlichkeit eines Grenzgebietes im Wandel eines Jahrtausends. Internationales Kolloquium im Wikinger Museum Haithabu vom 29. September — 3. Oktober 1994* (= Ergänzungsbände zum Reallexikon der Germanischen Altertumskunde, 25), 25–36. Berlin: De Gruyter.

Nielsen, Hans Frede. 2001. Frisian and the grouping of the older Germanic languages. In Horst Haider Munske et al. (eds.), *Handbuch des Friesischen / Handbook of Frisian Studies*, 512–523. Tübingen: Niemeyer.

Nielsen, Hans Frede. 2002. Nordic-West Germanic Relations. In Oskar Bandle et al. (eds.), *The Nordic languages: An international handbook of the history of the North Germanic languages* (= Handbücher zur Sprach- und Kommunikationswissenschaft 22), vol. 1, 558–568. Berlin: De Gruyter.

Nielsen, Hans Frede. 2002. Delimitation of Ancient Nordic from Common Germanic and Old Nordic. In Oskar Bandle et al. (eds.), *The Nordic languages: An international handbook of the history of the North Germanic languages* (= Handbücher zur Sprach- und Kommunikationswissenschaft 22), vol. 1, 615–619. Berlin: De Gruyter.

Nielsen, Hans Frede. 2002. The Old English sound system from a North-Sea Germanic perspective. In Yoko Iyeiri & Margaret Connolly (eds.), *And gladly wolde he lerne and gladly teche: Essays on Medieval English presented to Professor Matsuji Tajima on his sixtieth birthday*, 17–38. Tokyo: Kaibunsha.

Nielsen, Hans Frede. 2002. Guldhornsindskriften fra Gallehus. Runer, sprog og politik (= Carl Christian Rafn lecture). Odense: Syddansk Universitetsforlag.

Nielsen, Hans Frede. 2003. On the demise of Old English. In Wilhelm Heizmann & Astrid van Nahl (eds.), *Runica — Germanica — Mediaevalia. Gewidmet Klaus Düwel* (= Ergänzungsbände zum Reallexikon der Germanischen Altertumskunde, 37), 496–508. Berlin: De Gruyter.

Nielsen, Hans Frede. 2003. Rask, Rasmus Kristian. In Heinrich Beck et al. (eds.), *Reallexikon der Germanischen Altertumskunde*, 2nd ed., vol. 24, 143–146. Berlin: De Gruyter.

Nielsen, Hans Frede. 2003. Fransk indflydelse på middelengelsk. In Henrik Galberg Jacobsen, Dorthe Bleses & Pia Thomsen (eds.), *Take Danish — for instance: Linguistic studies in honour of Hans Basbøll presented on the occasion of his 60th birthday 12 July 2003*, 263–272. Odense: Syddansk Universitetsforlag.

Nielsen, Hans Frede. 2004. Friedrich Maurer and the dialectal links of Upper German to Nordic. In Hans-Peter Naumann, with Franziska Lanter & Oliver Szokody (eds.), *Alemannien und der Norden: Internationales Symposium vom 18.–20. Oktober 2001 in Zürich* (= Ergänzungsbände zum Reallexikon der Germanischen Altertumskunde, 43), 12–28. Berlin: De Gruyter.

Nielsen, Hans Frede. 2004. On the terms for Germanic employed by Scandinavian scholars in the 19th and 20th centuries. In Heinrich Beck et al. (eds.), *Zur Geschichte der Gleichung „germanisch–deutsch": Sprache und Namen, Geschichte und Institutionen* (= Ergänzungsbände zum Reallexikon der Germanischen Altertumskunde, 34), 309–323.

Nielsen, Hans Frede. 2004. Multilingualism in England: The French impact on English. In Lennart Elmevik (ed.), *Språkhistoria och flerspråkighet*, 137–144. Uppsala: Kungl. Gustav Adolfs Akademien för svensk folkkultur.

Nielsen, Hans Frede. 2004. Om Danmarks tidligste sproghistorie – i tværvidenskabelig belysning. In Astrid van Nahl et al., Lennart Elmevik & Stefan Brink (eds.), *Namenwelten, Orts- und Personennamen in historischer Sicht. Gewidmet Thorsten Andersson* (= Ergänzungsbände zum Reallexikon der Germanischen Altertumskunde, 44), 638–651. Berlin: De Gruyter.

Nielsen, Hans Frede. 2005. Det frisiske sprog i vikingetiden. In Jørgen Højgaard Jørgensen & Hans Frede Nielsen (eds.), *Beretning fra fireogtyvende tværfaglige vikingesymposium*, 37–47. Moesgård: Hikuin.

Nielsen, Hans Frede. 2006. The vocalism of the Undley runes viewed from a North-Sea Germanic perspective. In Alfred Bammesberger & Gaby Waxenberger (eds.), *Das fuþark und seine einzelsprachlichen Weiterentwicklungen. Akten der Tagung in Eichstätt vom 20. bis 24. Juli 2003* (= Ergänzungsbände zum Reallexikon der Germanischen Altertumskunde, 51), 209–215. Berlin: De Gruyter.

Nielsen, Hans Frede. 2006. Tidlig gotisk sproghistorie. In Mette Bruus & Hans Frede Nielsen (eds.), *Goternes sprog, historie og efterliv* (= Mindre Skrifter udgivet af Center for Middelalderstudier ved Syddansk Universitet, 25), 1–8. Odense: University of Southern Denmark.

Nielsen, Hans F. 2006. The Danish connection. Eller: Dansk indflydelse på det engelske sprogs historie. *Rubicon* 14(2), 47–53.

Nielsen, Hans Frede. 2006. The early runic inscriptions and Germanic historical linguistics. In Marie Stoklund, Michael Lerche Nielsen, Bente Holmberg & Gilliam Fellows-Jensen (eds.), *Runes and their secrets: Studies in runology*, 247–269. Copenhagen: Museum Tusculanum.

Nielsen, Hans Frede. 2007. English and the Jutland dialect; or, the demise of a romantic notion. In Andrew Wawn (ed.), *Constructing nations, reconstructing myth: Essays in honour of T. A. Shippey*, 97–108. Turnhout: Brepols.

Nielsen, Hans Frede. 2007. Wimmer, Ludvig Frands Adalbert. In Heinrich Beck et al. (eds.), *Reallexikon der Germanischen Altertumskunde*, 2nd ed., 34, 125–127. Berlin: De Gruyter.

Nielsen, Hans Frede. 2008. Rasmus Kristian Rask (1787–1832): Liv og Levned. *RASK* 28. 25–42.

Nielsen, Hans Frede. 2008. Fra Østersøen til Sortehavet. Sproglige spor efter goternes vandringer. In Bruus, Mette, Carl-Erik Lindberg & Hans Frede Nielsen (eds.). 2008. *Gotisk workshop. Et uformelt formidlingstræf* (= Mindre Skrifter udgivet af Center for Middelalderstudier, 26), 53–58. Odense: University of Southern Denmark.

Nielsen, Hans Frede. 2008. Dialect in English literature: Chaucer, Shakespeare and Cockney. In Kees Dekker et al. (eds.), *Northern voices: Essays on Old Germanic and related topics: Offered to Professor Tette Hofstra*, 83–98. Leuven: Peters.

Nielsen, Hans Frede. 2009. Forholdet mellem jysk og engelsk: En kritisk vurdering. In Mette Bruus & Lars Bisgaard (eds.), *Beretning fra otteogtyvende tværfaglige vikingesymposium*, 45–56. Moesgård: Hikuin. [Danish translation of T. A. Shippey Festschrift article published in 2007; see above.]

Nielsen, Hans Frede. 2009. Language change in the runic inscriptions of Denmark between 500 and 700. *RASK* 30. 3–15.

Nielsen, Hans Frede. 2010. Gothic and early runic: Two sound systems compared. In Hans Frede Nielsen & Flemming Talbo Stubkjær, with Mette Bruus & Erik W. Hansen (eds.), *The Gothic language: A symposium* (= NOWELE 58/59), 427–442. Odense: University Press of Southern Denmark.

Nielsen, Hans Frede. 2010. The Early Runic Language of Scandinavia: Proto-Norse or North-West Germanic? In John Ole Askedal, Harald Bjorvand, James E. Knirk & Otto Erlend Nordgreen (eds.), *Zentrale Probleme bei der Erforschung der älteren Runen. Akten einer Tagung an der Norwegischen Akademie der Wissenschaften* (= Osloer Beiträge zur älteren Germanistik, 41), 95–114. Frankfurt/Main: Lang.

Nielsen, Hans Frede. 2010. Præteritumsformerne af det gotiske verbum *saian*. In Bruus, Mette, Hans Frede Nielsen & Tore Nyberg (eds.). 2010. *Gotisk Workshop 2. Et uformelt formidlingstræf* (= Mindre Skrifter udgivet af Center for Middelalderstudier, 27), 25–29. Odense: University of Southern Denmark.

Nielsen, Hans Frede. 2011. 'Fremskridt i sproget': Otto Jespersens sprogudviklingsteori, dens tilblivelse og faglige skæbne. *RASK* 33. 109–112.

Nielsen, Hans Frede. 2012. Gothic runic inscriptions in Scandinavia? *Futhark: International Journal of Runic Studies* 2 (2011). 51–61.

Nielsen, Hans Frede. 2012. En fonologisk-typologisk sammenligning mellem vokalsystemerne i oldhøjtysk og gotisk. In Erik W. Hansen, Alexandra Holsting & Hans Frede Nielsen (eds.), *Ældre germansk sproghistorie: Et uformelt minisymposium*, 51–57. Odense: University of Southern Denmark.

doi Nielsen, Hans Frede. 2012. The Germanic roots of the Old English sound system. In Irén Hegedűs & Alexandra Fodor (eds.), *English historical linguistics 2010. Selected papers from the Sixteenth International Conference on English historical linguistics (ICEHL 16), Pécs, 23–27 August 2010*, 43–72. Amsterdam: Benjamins.

Nielsen, Hans Frede. 2013. The Gothic language of bishop Wulfila — phonology, typology and purported linguistic purity. In Anders Kaliff & Lars Munkhammar (eds.), *Wulfila 311–2011: International symposium, Uppsala University June 15–18, 2011*, 179–196. Uppsala: Uppsala University Library.

Nielsen, Hans Frede. 2014. Otto Jespersen's progress in language theory and Georg von der Gabelentz. In Kennosuke Ezawa, Franz Hundsnurscher & Annemete von Vogel (eds.), *Beiträge zur Gabelentz-Forschung*, 199–212. Tübingen: Narr.

doi Nielsen, Hans Frede. 2015. The vowel systems of Old English, Old Norse and Old High German compared. In John Ole Askedal & Hans Frede Nielsen (eds.), *Early Germanic languages in contact* (= NOWELE Supplement Series, 27), 261–276. Amsterdam: Benjamins.

doi Nielsen, Hans Frede. 2017. The phonological systems of Biblical Gothic and Crimean Gothic compared. In Jana Krüger, Vivian Busch, Katharina Seidel, Christiane Zimmermann & Ute Zimmermann (eds.), *Die Faszination des Verborgenen und seine Entschlüsselung — Rāði sāʀ kunni. Beiträge zur Runologie, skandinavistischen Mediävistik und germanischen Sprachwissenschaft* (= Ergänzungsbände zum Reallexikon der Germanischen Altertumskunde, 101), 277–290. Berlin: De Gruyter.

doi Nielsen, Hans Frede. 2017. The emergence and development of a spoken standard in England (1400–1926). *NOWELE* 70(2). 255–266.

Nielsen, Hans Frede. 2019. Tidsskriftet RASK og andre tidlige udgivelsesserier etableret ved Institut for Sprog og Kommunikation, Syddansk Universitet. *RASK* 50. 3–9

Nielsen, Hans Frede. 2021. Deciphering the inscription of the Undley bracteate under the possibilities/restrictions of the Pre-Old English sound system. In Laker, Stephen & Hans Frede Nielsen (eds.), *Early history of the North Sea Germanic languages* (= NOWELE 74(1)), 66–79. Amsterdam: Benjamins.

Reviews

Nielsen, Hans Frede. 1977. Review of Elmer H. Antonsen, *A concise grammar of the older runic inscriptions*, 1975. *Mediaeval Scandinavia* 10, 216–220.

Nielsen, Hans Frede. 1978. Review of Thomas L. Markey, *Germanic dialect grouping and the position of Ingvæonic*, 1976. *Linguistics* 16. 327–330.

Nielsen, Hans Frede. 1982. Review of Rolf H. Bremmer Jr, *Frisians in Anglo-Saxon England: A historical and toponymical investigation*, 1981. In Danielsen, Niels, Erik Hansen & Hans Frede Nielsen (eds.), *Friserstudier II*, 101–109. Odense: Odense Universitetsforlag.

Nielsen, Hans Frede. 1986. Review of Ottar Grønvik, *Die dialektgeographische Stellung des Krimgotischen und die krimgotische cantilena*, 1983. *Beiträge zur Geschichte der deutschen Sprache und Literatur* 108. 65–70.

Nielsen, Hans Frede. 1991. Review of Alfred Bammesberger, *Die Morphologie des urgermanischen Nomens*, 1990. *Diachronica* 8(2). 273–276.

Nielsen, Hans Frede. 1994. Review of Orrin W. Robinson, *Old English and its closest relatives. A survey of the earliest Germanic languages*, 1992. *RASK* 1. 123–126.

Nielsen, Hans Frede. 1995. Review of Frank Heidermanns, *Etymologisches Wörterbuch der germanischen Primäradjektive*, 1993. *Kratylos* 40. 149–153.

Nielsen, Hans Frede. 1995. Review of Herbert Penzl, *Englisch. Eine Sprachgeschichte nach Texten von 350 bis 1992. Vom Nordisch-Westgermanischen zum Neuenglischen*, 1994. *RASK* 2. 139–142.

Nielsen, Hans Frede. 1995. Review of Irmengard Rauch, *The Old Saxon Language: Grammar, epic narrative, linguistic interference*, 1992. *Word* 46. 442–444.

Nielsem, Hans Frede. 1997. Review of Frans van Coetsem, *The vocalism of the Germanic parent language. Systemic evolution and sociohistorical context*, 1994. *RASK* 5/6. 209–213.

Nielsen, Hans Frede. 2003. Review of Elmer H. Antonsen, *Runes and Germanic linguistics*, 2002. *NOWELE* 42. 115–119.

Other

Hansen, Erik W. & Hans Frede Nielsen. 1983. Editorial preface. *NOWELE* 1. 3–8.

Hansen, Erik W. & Hans Frede Nielsen. 2017. Editorial epilogue: The autonomy of historical linguistics. *NOWELE* 70(2). 267–274.

Journal issues

Co-founder of the journal *NOWELE* and its supplement book series. Edited approximately 70 volumes of the journal between 1983–2017. https://benjamins.com/catalog/nowele

Co-founder of the journal *RASK* and its supplement book series; active as editor 1994–2013, about 40 issues. https://www.sdu.dk/en/om_sdu/institutter_centre/iks/forskning /forskningspublikationer/rask

Edited seven *Tværfaglige vikingesymposier* volumes: http://www.vikingesymposium.dk /symposieberetninger.htm

This bibliography does not claim to be complete. A few publications or reviews may have slipped our notice. Introductions and prefaces to volumes were generally omitted.

Ostfries.-nd. *Bau, Schuurschott* und *Tiek(e)* — drei friesische Substratnamen für Insekten
Einige lexikalische Notizen zum Friesischen

Nils Århammar

> In *Friesische Relikte im ostfriesischen Niederdeutsch* ('Frisian relics in East Frisian Low German' 2001), Ulrich Scheuermann restates the point that rural vocabulary connected with farming, such as plant, animal and insect names, often retains substrate relic forms. Among many examples, Scheuermann draws attention to the insect names *Baue* 'gadfly', *Schürschott* 'dragonfly' and *Tîke* 'beetle'. The purpose of this study is to investigate the wider distribution of these three names and their etymologies.

In seinem Handbuchartikel „Friesische Relikte im ostfriesischen Niederdeutsch" rekapituliert Ulrich Scheuermann (2001: 444f.) unter *5. Wortschatzbereiche, Erhaltungsbedingungen* einen Leitsatz der Substratforschung, nach dem insbesondere die Bereiche „bäuerlicher Wortschatz, Pflanzen- und Tiernamen, affektiver Wortschatz" reich an Relikten sind. Unter *6.1. Wortgeographische Beispiele* finden sich dann *Baue* 'Viehbremse' (Ofriesl., Jevl., dazu Wursten; CM (= Cadovius Müller) i. J. 1691 *bawen*, Pl.) und *Schürschott* 'Libelle' (Osfriesl., Wursten; wang. *schûrschot*; vgl. Allers/Århammar 1984: 67) und unter *6.2. Lautgeographische Beispiele* (a. a. O., 446) *Tîke* 'Käfer' (in den Wörterbüchern von Böhning, Doornkaat Koolman, Stürenburg; häufig in Zusammensetzungen wie *Brumm-, Dau-, Gaffel-, Mai-* und *Meßtîke*). — Zweck der vorliegenden Studie ist es nun, die weitere Verbreitung dieser drei Insektennamen und deren Etymologie zu behandeln.[1]

---

1. Bis zu seinem Tod am 10. Januar 2022 arbeitete Nils Århammar an diesem Beitrag für die Gedenkschrift Hans Frede Nielsen, den er aber nicht mehr vollenden konnte. Die drei Wortstudien, die er in seinem Aufsatz zusammenbringt, bilden in der jetzigen Form zwar mehr oder wenig abgeschlossene Einheiten, Nils hätte sie aber unter Heranziehung weiterer Literatur noch ergänzen und vertiefen wollen. Auch fehlt dem Aufsatz das Fazit, in dem die drei Wörter noch

https://doi.org/10.1075/nss.34.01arh
Available under the CC BY-NC-ND 4.0 license. © 2025 John Benjamins Publishing Company

1. Ostfries.-nd. *Bau* 'Viehbremse'

1.1 Allgemeines

Die Bezeichnungen für die 'Viehbremse' lauten in den nordwesteuropäischen Sprachen wie folgt: Dt. *Bremse* im Norden und *Breme* im Süden (im mittleren Übergangsgebiet abl. *Brame/Broame*, vgl. DWA V, 1957). — Nl. *paardevlieg* („Pferdefliege"; vgl. Goossens 1985). — Wfries. *(hynste)bau* („Pferde-"). — Engl. *gadfly* (altnord. *gaddr* 'Stachel' + „Fliege"). — Dän. *bremse.* — Norw./Isl. *brims.* — Schwed. *broms, styng* (dial. *sjungen* „der Stich"). — Finn. *paarma.* Die kleine, graue Bremse wird verbreitet als *Blinde (Fliege)* u. ä. bezeichnet.

1.2 Die Verbreitung von ingwäonisch *Bau* 'Viehbremse (Tabanus, Oestrus)' und Ableitungen

In der Nordwestecke von DWA V, SW-Blatt gibt es eine Anzahl Ableitungen von dem Wortstamm *Bau* bzw. *Bei: Bau(we)l(e), Beiel(e), Bäl/-e-* (bis ins Luxemburgische) und *Beier* (Gebiet im Norden, Streubelege im Osten), *Bärleck/Bälek* sowie im Süden *Ba(a)j(e)/-äi-* ohne Suffix (s. den Kartenausschnitt). Unter „Seltenheiten und Mehrfachmeldungen" finden sich in dem Gebiet die folgenden Formen: *Baulert, Veibauwel, Bauelt* (?); *Baier(e), deck Baier(n)* („dicke B."), *schäler/scheele Baier(n), Schellebaier/-el* („scheele B."), *dick Baien/-el, Scheelbai(en), Veibai; Bäl, Beler* u.a.m.

Auf dem NW-Blatt in der Südwestecke SO von Aachen steht dreimal das Symbol für *Beuel* (in der Legende irrtümlich in die rechte Spalte geraten). Unter „Seltenheiten und Mehrfachmeldungen" in der Nähe 1x *Beueler* und 2x *Blängdebeuel* („Blinde-") — Für das angrenzende Niederländische enthält Goossens (1985: 231)

---

einmal dialektologisch eingeordnet werden sollten. Fragen um das Ingwäonische haben Nils sein Forschungsleben lang beschäftigt. So fand sich in seinen nachgelassenen Papieren eine aus dem Jahr 1983 stammende 39 Titel umfassende Zusammenstellung von Literatur über das Ingwäonische. Bei einem letzten Gespräch im Krankenhaus hat er noch auf Theodor Frings verwiesen, von dem er zwei Titel in der o.a. Literaturliste aufführt. Frings habe die Theorie vertreten, dass das Ingwäonische nicht nur an der Nordseeküste beheimatet gewesen sei, sondern auch am westlichen Niederrhein bis nach Luxemburg gereicht habe. Dies stimme genau mit der Verbreitung von *Bauwel/Baul(e)* und den Ableitungen von diesem Etymon überein. Leider war es ihm nicht vergönnt, diesen Gedanken weiter zu untermauern. Obwohl der Aufsatz somit in mancher Hinsicht ein Torso geblieben ist, ist er doch so weit gediehen, dass wir, Ritva Århammar und Jarich Hoekstra, ihn hier noch gerne unterbringen möchten, zumal es Nils sehr wichtig war, in der Gedenkschrift für seinen langjährigen Freund Hans Frede vertreten zu sein. Wir haben den Text nur leicht lektoriert, ein paar editorische Fußnoten zugefügt und ein Literaturverzeichnis erstellt. [RÅ/JH]

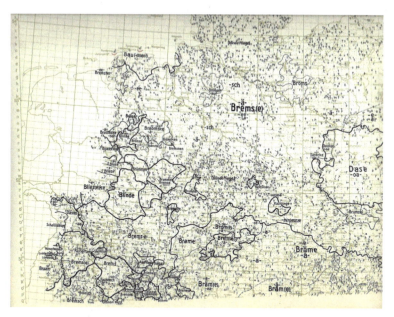

Abbildung 1. DWA V, Blatt 3 (NW-Ausschnitt)

die folgenden Angaben: (1) „de westelijke helft van West-Vlaanderen, waar globaaltoepasselijk op de paardevlieg en de (paarde)horzel de term *pauw* wordt gebruikt," (2) „het Z.O. van Oost-Vlaanderen, een areaal dat iets groter is dan het arrondissement Aalst, met *bouwel* (*baal*) of – in de onmiddellijke omgeving van Aalst – *bouwer* (*baar*)." Ansonsten ist es Goossens nur um den Typus *daas/daze* mit Ableitungen und Zusammensetzungen zu tun (mit Wortkarte).

Zu (1) vgl. L. de Bo (1892:723): *Pauw* (wvl. *Pow*), auch *Bijspauw, Heuzelpauw, Koepauw*. Zu (2) vgl. Schuermans (1883:16): *Baal, bale*. Ferner Boekenoogen (1897/1971 II: 29) in der Redensart *in de biesbauw (biezebauw) zijn* 'in de verlegenheid zitten, teneinde raad zijn' (auch sonst in Noord-Holland). Boekenoogen erläutert dazu: „*Biesbauw* beteekent oorspr. *horzel, die door zijn steken het vee aan het biezen (bijzen) brengt.* Vgl. Fris. *bou, bau, bauwe* 'horzel' (Halbertsma 1876: 470)."

Über Westerlauw. fries. *bau(we)* s. WFT. (1: 1984), 237f.) mit den Komposita *bite/hynstebau* („Biss-/Beiß-" und „Pferde-"). Dazu das Verb *bauje/bauwe* u.a.m. 'bijzen, wild heen en weer bewegen van koeien door de wei, als ze door vliegen worden gekweld'. Anders als *Tiek(e)* 'Käfer' (vgl. unter 3) hat fries. *bau(we)* in den Groninger Ommelanden keine Spuren hinterlassen.

Das Saterfriesische hat *Breemse* von der niederdeutschen Umgebung übernommen (Kramer 1992:304). Für Wangerooge überliefert B.E. Siebs (1928: 80) *blíínfliiugh*. 'Blindbremse' („Blindefliege"), ein verbreitetes norddeutsches Syn-

Abbildung 2. Legende zum DWA V, Blatt 3 (NW-Ausschnitt)

onym. Auch im Nordfriesischen hat das fries. *Bau* keine Spur hinterlassen.[2] Von den ausgestorbenen ostfriesischen Dialekten überliefert lediglich Cadovius Müller (1691) harlingerfries. *bawen* 'Pferdefliegen'. Die von mir bearbeitete Wortkarte 'Viehbremse' im DWA V (1957) zeigt auf dem NW-Blatt das geschlossene

---

2. Föhr.-amr. *Ööksenwirrem/-wörrem* 'die größere Pferdebremse' („Ochsenwurm") und *mag* 'die kleinere, graue Viehbremse' („Mücke"). Schumacher (1955: 38ff.) behandelt die verschiedenen Bedeutungen von „Mücke", hat wohl aber wegen der Lautform föhr.-amr. *mag* übersehen.

Bau(-l)(e)n-Gebiet in Ostfriesland, Harlinger Land, Jeverland, Butjardingen und Land Wursten, Streubelege auf Norderney und Spiekeroog, 4x W — S von Aurich (bis Hesel) sowie östlich von Land Wursten. Eigene Aufzeichnungen: Spiekeroog *Bau'n* (Plur.) und Land Wursten *Bau* m., Plur *Bau(d)'n*. Niedersächs. Wb. s.v. *Bau(e)* 'Bremse, Stechfliege (Tabanus)': Leer, Dykhsn. (Wtm.), Jever (Frsl.), Minssen *Baue*, Ostfr. *Bau*, *Baue*, selten *Bawe*. — *bauen*¹1. wild ziellos hin- und herrennen, blindlings daraufloslaufen (bes. vom Rindvieh).

Abbildung 3. Ausschnitt aus der DWA-Karte 'Viehbremse'

1.3 Zur Etymologie

Die früheste Gleichstellung von *Bau* mit ae. *bēaw* findet sich im Ostfries. Wb. von Stürenburg (1857:11): *Bawe, Bau* 'Pferdefliege, Bremse'. Angesl. *beaw* 'Wespe'. Demnächst sehr ausführlich im „Wb. der ostfries. Sprache" von J. ten Doornkaat Koolman (= DK) 1 (1879:117): 2 *bau, baue* und auch (selten) *bawe* 'Bremse, Stech-/Pferdefliege'. Da die Wespen hier auch *përde-immen* (Pferde-Bienen) u. hess. *beier* (von *beía* 'Biene' s. Vilmar 1883) heißen, so ist *bau* od. *bawe* identisch mit ags. *beaw* 'Wespe' u. dies wohl connex mit ags. *bev* 'Biene', [...] — *bauen* mit verschiedenen Bed.-angaben, darunter *dat fê deid niks as bauen* 'das Vieh thut nichts als umherlaufen u. rennen', resp. 'schwärmen'. DK verweist auf die Heteronyme *bîsen* und hessisch *beiern*; zur Herkunft des Letzteren führt DK (1, 135) aus:

Da hess. *beier* (Bremse) = unser *bau* ist u. davon *beiern* (umherlaufen u. rennen) gebildet ist, wie unser *bauen* von *bau*, *bawe* (Bremse) u. ferner das hess. *beier* u. unser *bau* mit ags. *beo*, ahd. *bia*, mhd. *bîe*, ndl. *bij*, *bije*, nd. *bie*, *beie* (Biene) zusammenhängt, so könnte auch das sich wohl blos auf ein frequentatives Bewegen od. das Hin- und Herbewegen u. Ziehen von Etwas beziehende „beiern" leicht von *beie*, *bije* (Biene) entstanden sein, weil eben die Bienen sehr emsige u. sehr bewegliche, hin und herfahrende Thierchen sind. [...]

Holthausen (1927:64) wird von Remmers (1993:8) wie folgt zitiert: „entspricht *bawe* bei St[ürenburg], *bau(e)*, *bawe* bei Doornkaat-Koolman und ist = ae. *beaw* 'gadfly'; dazu gehört bei D.-K. *bauen* 'hin- und herfahren, [...], schwärmen'". Bei Holthausen (1934/1974:18) lesen wir dann s.v. *bēaw* m. 'Bremse': nd. *bau*, zu lat. *fūcus* 'Drohne', s. WP. [Walde-Pokorny] II, 184. – In dem Nachfolgewerk von Walde-Pokorny (1926–1930), Pokorny (1959:163) steht s.v. (idg.) *bhouku̯os* 'summendes Insekt': Lat. *fūcus*, -ī, m. 'Brutbiene, Drohne' = ags. *béaw* m. 'Bremse', ndd. *bau* ds.

Zur Lautgleichung ae. *bēaw* ~ wfries. *bau(we)* ist ae. *dēaw* 'dew' (Campbell 1959:232) ~ wfries. *dau(we)* 'Tau (Niederschlag)' heranzuziehen.

Westfläm. *pauw* könnte sein *p*- aus dem Kompositum *bijspauw* haben. Wahrscheinlicher ist jedoch Schärfung *b*- > *p*- wie in *praam* in Belgisch-Limburg (vgl. Goossens 1985:231) neben *Braam* um Aachen herum (DWA V, NW-Blatt in der Südwestecke).

Suffixableitungen *el*/*er* liegen vor in *bouwel* (*baal*) und *bouwer* (*baar*) im Südosten von Ostflandern (Goossens 1985:231) und in *Bauwel/Baul(e)/-ow* in einem kleinen Restgebiet südöstlich von Trier (vgl. den Kartenausschnitt). Hiervon dürfte das oben genannte *Beuel* südöstlich von Aachen eine Form mit *i*-Umlaut sein.

All die anderen *Bauwel/Baul(e)* umgebenden Formen *Bai(e)*, *Baiel/-ei* und *Bäl/-e-* sowie *Beier* dürften alle zu dem ablautenden Stamm in den nordwestgerm. Wörtern für 'Biene' (vgl. oben Zitat aus Doornkaat Koolman) gehören: ae. *bēo* (e. *bee*), ahd./as. *bīa*, anord. *bý*- (dän./schwed. *bi*). Falk-Torp (1, 1910:71) verbindet dies mit der idg. Wurzel **bhî* 'beben, zittern, schwirren' und Hellquist (I, 1948:69) mit einer lautnachahmenden idg. Wurzel **bhī*, während neuere etymologische Wörterbücher wie Kluge/Seebold (2002:121) und das EWN (1, 2003:308) der Hypothese eines voridg. Substratwortes den Vorzug geben.

2. Ofries.-nd. *Schuurschott* 'Libelle, Wasserjungfer'

2.1 Allgemeines

Die Bezeichnungen der 'Libelle' lauten in den nordwesteuropäischen Sprachen wie folgt: Das von alters her verbreitetste dt. Wort ist *Wasserjungfer* (vgl. DWB 27, 1922: 2430: „jetzt allgemein verbreitet" und DWA II, 1952, Karten 53–56).[3] – Ndl. *glazenmaker* („Glaser"), *waterjuffer* (vgl. dt.). Wfries. *glêsmakker, glêsdrager* („Glasträger", 'fahrender Glaser'), *glêzebiter* („Gläserbeißer"), *bleine-/hynste-/wartebiter* („Pustel-/Pferde-/Warzenbeißer"). – Engl. *dragonfly* („Drachenfliege", *-fly* im weiteren Sinne von 'fliegenden Insekten', vgl. *butterfly*). Dän. *guldsmed* („Goldschmied"). – Schwed. *trollslända* („Troll-/Hexenspindel"). – Finn. *sudenkorento* („Wolfsstab/-(trage)stange").

Im „Handwörterbuch des deutschen Aberglaubens" (HDA 5, 1933: 1229–1240) findet sich ein sehr informativer Artikel *Libelle*, der auf Grund der europäischen Bezeichnungen des Insektes zwölf verschiedene Benennungsmotiven unterscheidet.

2.2 Afries. **skūr-/skirskot* und seine Verbreitung

Das Vorkommen dieser anscheinend ausschließlich friesischen Bezeichnung des Insekts lässt sich zunächst anhand der unter 2.1. erwähnten DWA-Karte darstellen, von der hier ein Ausschnitt mit dem ostfries.-nd. Reliktwort *Schuurschott* reproduziert wird. Südlich von Aurich erscheinen zwei Streubelege. Vgl. auch Niedersächsisches Wörterbuch s.v. *Schurr/Schūrschott* (mit Dank an Maik Lehmberg).[4] In den ausgestorbenen friesischen Mundarten ist das Wort nur im Wangeroogischen belegt: *djû schûrschot* (so auch Plur.; s. Ehrentraut 1849: 346). Das Saterfriesische hat *Peerdje* („Pferdchen") von der nd. Umgebung übernommen. Dagegen haben die Nordfriesen das friesische Wort bis heute bewahrt: wföhr. *sküürskoot*, Plur. *-skööder/-skööding* (eigene Aufzeichnung um 1960), oföhr. *skirskööd* (Schmidt-Petersen 1912: 116), amr. *skirskoot*, Plur. *-skööden* (Chr. Johansen

---

3. Bearbeitet von Liselotte Druxes-Schäfer. Ihre maschinenschriftliche Dissertation „Deutsche Synonymik der Libelle" (Druxes-Schäfer 1947) war mir nicht zugänglich. Die Beleg- und Wortliste der ungemein reichen Heteronymik füllen die zweispaltigen Petitseiten 10–19.

4. Auf der DWA-Karte 'Libelle' (Bd. 2) erscheint im südlichen Teil von Land Wursten eine Leitform *Scherschotten*. Selbst hat Nils dort um 1980 *Schuur-/Schuulschotten* aufgezeichnet. Im Niedersächsischen Wörterbuch finden sich keine *e*-Belege. Nach Auskunft von Lars Vorberger (Sprachatlas Marburg) weist der DWA-Bogen b 18 (Land Wursten) neben *Schuurschotten*, *Schulschotten* und *Libelle* auch *Scherschotten* auf. Diese Auskunft konnte Nils leider nicht mehr zur Kenntnis nehmen [RÅ].

1862:140/219), helgol. *Skiirskot, -ten* (< *Sküür-*, 19. Jhr.), festl.-nfries. *schäärschoor* und wiedingh. *skirskoor* sowie sylterfries. *skiirenskaiter* (19. Jh. MN III,1450). Ferner als fries. Relikt im Eiderstedter Nd. *Schüürschööd, -en* (Rogby 1967,114 und 237ff.).

2.3 Wortbildung und Etymologie

Wie häufig bei Tiernamen liegt hier ein sog. Bahuvrihi-Kompositum vor. Das Bestimmungswort ist das Adjektiv *schier* in der Bedeutung 'klar, glänzend', wobei hier verbreitet eine Vokalalternanz mit *-ū-* vorliegt.[5] Während afries. *ū* im Ostfriesischen als solches erhalten blieb, erfolgte im Nordfriesischen spontane Palatalisierung > /y:/, das im 19. Jh. im Helgoländischen zu /i:/ delabialisiert wurde.[6] Afries. *ī* blieb im Nordfries. erhalten bzw. wurde in geschlossener Silbe gekürzt.[7]

Das Grundwort ist afries. *skot* „Schuss", vgl. aengl. *sceot* 'schnelle Bewegung' mit der Verbalabl. *scotian* 'schnell bewegen, schleudern' = ahd. *scozon* 'schnell dahin schießen'.[8] Föhr.-amr. *skoot-* zeigt die regelmäßige Dehnung in geschlossener Silbe. Oföhr. *skööd*/eiderst.-nd. *-schööd* und festl.-nfr. *-schoor/-skoor* zeigen die Entwicklung des *-o-* in offener Silbe und intervokalischer Tenuiserweichung, sind also Verallgemeinerung der bei Insekten frequenten Pluralform. Sylt. *-skaiter* ist das Nomen agentis zu *skaiteri* 'sich beim Laufen überstürzen' = föhr.-amr. *sköödre* '(sch)wanken, torkeln', also wohl eine Neubildung zu *-skot*, wobei auch das Fugenelement *-er-* eintrat.

Wörtlich ist ostfries. nd. *schuurschott* usw. also vermutlich „glänzender Schuss" (Århammar 2013:82 unten). Vgl. HDA 5:1231a: Nach dem schillernden Glanze der Flügel: *Schille(r)bold/-bolz* u.a.[9]

---

5. Vgl. Århammar (2013:82f)., der auf die gleiche Alternanz in **rīpe ~ *rūpe* 'Raupe' hinweist. Altes *-ū-* liege wahrscheinlich auch in der föhr.-amr. *skürne* 'glänzen, glitzern' vor. Im Syltring zeigt das Wort „Schauer" sowohl die regelmäßige Lautform *sküür* (= föhr.-amr.) als auch *skiir*, diese aber nur in der Bed. 'Weile' (Möller 1916:233 + eigene Aufzeichnung); in der Bedeutung 'Fieberschauer, Geburtswehen' nur *sküür*. Bei *skiir* wird es sich um eine junge Delabialisierung handeln (vgl. das Helgoländische).

6. Vgl. Århammar (2001:750).

7. Vgl. Århammar (2001:749) und zu afries. *skīr(e)* Faltings (2010:470ff.). Zur Entwicklung zu /æ/ vor *r* im mittleren Festl.-nfr. vgl. *wäär* 'Metalldraht (ndt. *Wier*, engl. *wire*).

8. Seebold (1970:418).

9. Nicht berücksichtigt worden ist hier Hoekstra (2010:104–108), obwohl Nils diese etymologische Studie schon kannte und noch einarbeiten wollte. Im Aufsatz werden die westfriesischen Entsprechungen von ostfries.-nd. *Schuurschott* 'Libelle' aufgeführt und zwar *koweskâd* (wörtl. Kuhschatten) (WFT 11, s.v. *koweskaad*), wahrscheinlich volksetymologisch aus *koweskoat* (*-skoat* 'Schuss'), und Hylpen/Hindeloopen *schoeschoater* (Roosjen et al. 1855:93), *skoes-*

3. Ofries.-nd. *Tiek(e)* 'Käfer' und Komposita

3.1 Allgemeines

Die Bezeichnungen für 'Käfer allg.' lauten in den nordwesteuropäischen Sprachen wie folgt: Dt. *Käfer*, nl. *kever*, Engl. †*chafer* (urspr. Bed. „Kauer, Fresser"), *cockchafer* 'Feldmaikäfer'.[10] — Engl. *beetle*, dän. *bille* (urgerm. **bitulaz* zu „beißen").[11] Nl. *tor*.[12] Wfries. *krobbe*.[13] — Schwed. *skalbagge* („Schalenwidder"). — Finn. *(kova)kuoriainen* (*kova* 'hart', *kuori* 'Schale, Außenhaut').—Die Bedeutung 'Käfer allg.' können zumal als Grundwort von Komposita auch annehmen: „Fliege" (z. B. e. *butter-/dragon-/gadfly*), „Vogel" (z. B. dän. *sommerfugl* 'Schmetterling'),[14]

---

kòòter (van der Kooy 1937:47). Hoekstra verfolgt für die etymologische Erklärung dieses Wortes den Hinweis von Rogby (1967:114) auf altengl. *cusc(e)ote*, engl. *cushat* 'Ringeltaube' und die Überlegungen zu diesem Wort von Liberman (2002; 2008:43–45). Er schlägt vorsichtig ein altfries. **kūskote* 'Kuhschießer' (Insekt, das auf eine Kuh zuschießt und ihr womöglich Schaden zufügt) als Grundform für das friesische Wort für 'Libelle' vor, das dann durch Fernassimilation (*k — sk > sk — s*) und volksetymologische Abänderungen (*skū- ⤳ Schuur-, skir-*) seine unterschiedlichen überlieferten Dialektformen bekommen hat. [JH]

10. Nach Kluge/Seebold (2002:459) bezeichnete *Käfer* urspr. die Heuschrecke. Die Verallgemeinerung zu 'Käfer allg.' sei erst im 18. Jh. erfolgt, wobei älteres *Wiebel* aus dieser Bed. verdrängt wurde (zu dessen Etymologie s. Kluge/Seebold 2002:987). Vgl. Schumacher (1955:45–52) und Hellquist (II, 1948:1205) über schwed. *tordyvel*, ae. *tord-/scearnwifel*, ält. holl. *tortwevel* 'Mistkäfer' (Scarabæus)'. — Über das moselfränk. und rheinpfälz. *Bobe* 'Käfer allg.' und als Grundwort in Komposita s. Schumacher (1955:26, Karte S. 44). Dieses könnte wie festl.-nfries. (bökingh.) *pud* '(Mist)käfer' nach der plumpen gerundeten Form vieler Käferarten benannt sein (vgl. den VW-Käfer!). Zum letzten vgl. wfries./föhr.-amr. *pud* 'Kröte' (WFT 17, 2000:26 und Doornkaat Koolman 2, 1882:692f. und DWA IV, 1955).

11. Vgl. föhr.-amr. *skelbed*, sylt. *skelbeet* (< -*bite*), bökingh. *schaalbitter* (= nd. Schellbieter) 'Laufkäfer' („Schalenbiss/-beißer"). [Auch wfr. *skallebiter*, ndl. *schalle-, scharrebijter*, das aber meistens als eine volksetymologische Umbildung von franz. *escarbot* < lat. *scarabæus* aufgefasst wird (EWN). JH]

12. Auch Groninger Ommelanden und wfries. *tuorre/toarre* (WFT 23, 2007:342), föhr.-amr. *schuaren/schaasentoor* 'Mistkäfer'.

13. Auch Groninger Ommelanden. Vgl. WFT (11, 1994:358) und Spenter (1968:126) (zitiert Heeroma 1951:24). S. 26 schreibt Heeroma: *Krobbe* is wellicht op te vatten als een Ingweoonse vervorming en specialiseering van het algemeen Germaanse gevoelswoord *krop* („dik, rondachtig insekt").

14. „Sommervogel" ist eine weiter verbreitete Bezeichnung, s. HDA 7: 1238. Der Artikel „Schmetterling" umfasst die Spalten 1237–1254 mit 8. untergliederten Hauptbenennungsmotiven. Das nordseegermanische Wort ist übrigens nl. *vlinder* (EWN 4, 2009:542), wfries. *flinter* (WFT 6, 1989:129), ofries.-nd. *flinderk(e)* (Doornkaat Koolman 1, 1879:510), wang. *flinerk* (Ehrentraut 1849:345), saterl. *Flinnerke/Flitterke* (Kramer 1995:108), föhr.-amr./sylt. *flennerk* (mit *e < i*).

„Wurm" (z. B. *Bieswurm* 'Viehbremse', *Ohrwurm*[15] und *Glühwurm/-würmchen* [DWA III, 1954]) und „Zecke" (z. B. wfries. *eartyk* [WFT 4, 1987: 252], vgl. 3.2.). — Schließlich sei hier noch verwiesen auf die vorbildliche Studie von Jan Stroop (1974: 134–169) über die Bezeichnungen des 'Maikäfers' im niederländischen Sprachgebiet. Über *-tiek* und *-worm* s. S. 139f. (zu nd. *Worm* 'Käfer' s. DWA I, 1951; im Westpreußischen *Bonk* aus dem slavischen Substrat wie auch DWA V, 1957 *-bunk(e)* 'Mistkäfer' und *Bunk(e)/Bisbunk* 'Viehbremse').

3.2 Die Verbreitung der fries: Substratlautform *Tiek(e)*

Wir sind in der glücklichen Lage, dass die Verbreitung von *Tiek(e)* als Simplex und als Grundwort bestimmter Komposita auf zwei Karten dargestellt sind, die wir hier reproduzieren:

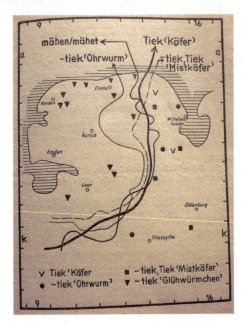

Abbildung 4. *Tiek, -tiek* (Schumacher 1955: 27), die auf den folgenden DWA-Kartenband basiert: 'Käfer' (DWA I, 1951), 'Glühwürmchen' und 'Ohrwurm' (DWA III, 1954) sowie 'Mistkäfer' (DWA V, 1957)

---

15. S. DWA III, 1954. Vgl. nl. *oorworm*, wfries. *earkrûper* („Ohrkriecher"; WFT 4, 1987: 252), engl. *earwig*, dän. *øretvist*, schwed. *tvestjärt* („Zwiesterz/-schwanz"), finn. *pihtihäntä* („Zangensterz/-schwanz").

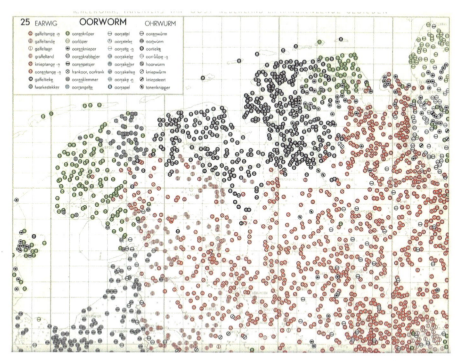

Abbildung 5. 'Ohrwurm' aus K. Heeroma (TONAG 3, 1963: 80); die Karte zeigt die Verbreitung von Groninger und ostfries.-nd. *oortiek(e)*

Zu Karte 5 schreibt Heeroma a. a. O. mit der von ihm zur Kunst entwickelten expansionlogisch-stratigraphischen Methode: „Oortiek(e) [...] is een vernieuwing aan beide zijden van de Dollart, die behoort tot de jongere laag in het Gronings-Oostfries." Das alte Wort sei nl.-nd. *oorkruper/-krüper* („Ohrkriecher"), vgl. a. a. O., 77ff.

Dr. Maik Lehmberg, Bearbeiter des Niedersächsischen Wörterbuchs an der Universität Göttingen, sandte mir dankenswerterweise die Ergebnisse der Fragebögen zu *Tiek(e)* und Komposita. Die Befragung ergab Folgendes: Für 'Maikäfer' *Brummtiek, Eckeltieke, Maitiek* und 2x *Tieke*, — für 'Mistkäfer' *Messtiek(e)* und *Peertiek(e)* (beide häufig), *Scharntiek, (Koh)schiettiek, Swarttieke* sowie 5x *Tieke*, — für 'Marienkäfer' *Sünntieke* („Sonnenkäfer") und 1x *Lütje Tiek* („Kleiner Käfer"), — für 'Kellerassel' *Müürtiek* („Mauerkäfer"), *Steentieke* („Steinkäfer"), — für 'Ohrwurm' *Ohrtiek(e)*. Dann noch übertragen: *Kleitiek* und *Smeertieke* 'Drekspatz', 'Schmierfink' (von Kindern). — Die meisten dieser Wörter sind auch enthalten im Ostfries. Wb. von G. de Vries (2000). Zur Verbreitung von *Tiek(e)* und Komposita s. die obige Kartenskizze von Schuhmacher.

Für die inzwischen ausgestorbene weserfries. Mundart der Insel Wangerooge überliefert Ehrentraut *thúrtîk* 'Mistkäfer'.[16] Die Saterländer haben aus ihrer altemsfries. Heimat *Tieke* in all dessen Funktionen mitgebracht: Minssen (1846-II,175) *tike, djû* 'so heißt jeder schwarze Käfer' und Fort (2015:621) *Tíeke, -n, ju* [= Fem.] 1. 'Zecke', 2. 'Käfer', 3. 'Küchenschabe' und 4. 'allg. Name für Käfer oder Insekt'. Das Westerlauwersche Friesland hat die Formen *tyk* [i] und *tike* mit der Bedeutung 'Zecke' mit den Komposita *eartyk* 'Ohrwurm' (neben mehreren Synonymen) und *skieppetyk* 'Schaflaus, Zecke' (vgl. WFT 22, 2006,372).

3.3 Lautgeschichte und Etymologie

Bei *Tiek(e)* handelt es sich um die ostfries. Lautform des Etymons „Zecke", Schaflaus, eine große Milbe, die sich auf der Haut von Tieren und Menschen festsetzt und deren Blut saugt. Am besten über das Wort und dessen ältere Formen orientieren die großen nationalen Wörterbücher: DWB 31, 1956:436f., WNT s.v. *teke*[III] und OED s. v. *tick*, sb.[1]. Neben ost- und westfries. *tike* stehen nd./ndl. *teke*, was auf ein westgerm. **tika/-e* mit kurzem *-i-* in offener Silbe zurückweist. Bestätigt wird dieser Ansatz durch die nordfries. Lautformen, z. B. föhr.-amr. *teg*, halligfries. *tag*,[17] ngoesh. *tääg*, bökingh. *taag* [ta:ɣ]. Bereits aufgrund dieses lautgeschichtlichen Kriteriums lässt sich also ostfries.-nd. *Tiek(e)* als ein friesisches Relikt klassifizieren. Hinzu kommt aber auch ein onomasiologisch-semantisches Kriterium: lediglich in Ostfriesland und den angrenzenden Groninger Ommelanden bezeichnet/bedeutet *Tiek(e)* 'Käfer allg.' und kommt in verschiedenen Komposita vor.

Literatur

Allers, K. & N. Århammar. 1984. Wurster Plattdeutsch. In H. E. Hansen u.a. (Hrsg.) *Jahrbuch der Männer von Morgenstern*, 43–68. Bremerhaven: Ditzen.

doi   Århammar, N. 2001. Grundzüge nordfriesischer Sprachgeschichte. In H. H. Munske u.a. (Hrsg.), *Handbuch des Friesischen / Handbook of Frisian Studies*, 744–765. Tübingen: Niemeyer.

---

16. Ehrentraut (1849:346): *thúrtîng* oder *thúrtîk*. Die erstgenannte Form geht vermutlich auf den Plural **thúrtîken* [-kɳ] zurück; *thúr-* ist wahrscheinlich = ae. *tord* 'Mist' und müsste *túr-* geschrieben werden.

17. Löfstedt (1928:170): „Der Sing. **tike* hat lautgesetzlich *tääg* (Ockh.) ergeben, während die Plur.-Form **tika* zu *tage* [tagə] werden musste." In hall. *tag* und ngoesh. *tääg* habe also Ausgleich zugunsten des Plur. bzw. des Sing. stattgefunden.

Århammar, N. 2013. Rez.: Volkert F. Faltings: Etymologisches Wörterbuch der friesischen Adjektiva (2010). *Zeitschrift für Dialektologie und Linguistik* 80(1). 77–89.

Boekenoogen, G. J. 1897/1971. *De Zaanse Volkstaal II. Zaans Idioticon.* Zaandijk: J. Heijnis.

Cadovius-Müller, J. 1691 (1986). *Memoriale linguæ Frisicæ.* Mit Zugrundelegung der in Aurich befindlichen Originalhandschrift zum ersten Male herausgegeben von Dr. L. Kükelhun. *Leer:* Leendertz.

Campbell, A. 1959. *Old English grammar.* Oxford: Clarendon.

De Bo, L.-L. 1892. *Westvlaamsch Idioticon.* Gent: Siffer.

DK = Doornkaat Koolman, J. ten. 1879 (Bd. 1), 1882 (Bd. 2). *Wörterbuch der ostfriesischen Sprache.* Norden: Braams.

Druxes-Schäfer, L. 1947. Deutsche Synonymik der Libelle. Masch.-schr. Diss. Marburg.

DWA = *Deutscher Wortatlas I-IV* 1 (1951–1955), hrsg. von W. Mitzka, *Bd. V* (1957), hrsg. von W. Mitzka und L. E. Schmidt. Gießen: Schmitz.

DWB = *Deutsches Wörterbuch von Jacob und Wilhelm Grimm*, Bd. 27 (1922), bearb. von K. von Rahder, unter Mitwirkung von H. Sickel, Bd. 31 (1956), bearb. von M. Heyne, H. Seedorf, H. Teuchert. Leipzig: Verlag von S. Hirzel; Taschenbuchausgabe (1984), München: Deutscher Taschenbuch Verlag.

Ehrentraut, H. G. 1849. *Friesisches Archiv. Eine Zeitschrift für friesische Geschichte und Sprache.* I. Oldenburg: Rudolf Schwartz. Nachdruck 1968. Wiesbaden: Sändig.

EWN = *Etymologisch woordenboek van het Nederlands.* Hrsg. von M. Philippa u.a. Bd. 1 (2003); Bd. 4 (2009). Amsterdam: Amsterdam University Press.

Falk-Torp, H. S. & A. Torp. 1910. *Norwegisch-dänisches etymologisches Wörterbuch. Teil I.* Heidelberg: Winter.

Faltings, V. F. 2010. *Etymologisches Wörterbuch der friesischen Adjektiva.* Berlin: De Gruyter.

Fort, M. C. 2015. *Saterfriesisches Wörterbuch. Mit einer phonologischen und grammatischen Übersicht.* Hamburg: Buske.

Goossens, J. 1985. Daas 'paardevlieg' en zijn varianten in de Nederlandse en Nederduitse dialecten. In H. Ryckeboer, J. Taeldeman, V. F. Vanacker (Hrsg.), *Hulde-Album Prof. Dr. Marcel Hoebeke*, 229–241. Gent: RUG. Seminarie voor Nederlandse taalkunde en Vlaamse dialectologie.

Halbertsma, J. 1876. *Lexicon Frisicum. A–Feer.* 's-Gravenhage: Nijhoff.

HDA = 1933/1987. *Handwörterbuch des deutschen Aberglaubens. Bände 5 und 7.* Hrsg. von H. Bächtold-Stäubli unter Mitwirkung von E. Hoffmann-Krayer. Nachdruck 1987, Berlin: De Gruyter.

Heeroma, K. 1951. Oostnederlandse taalproblemen. In *Mededelingen der Koninklijke Nederlandsche Akademie van Wetenschappen.* Afd. Letteren. Teil 14, Ausgabe 8. 265–307. Amsterdam: Noord-Hollandsche Uitgevers Maatschappij.

Heeroma, K. 1963. *Taalatlas van Oost-Nederland en aangrenzende gebieden.* Bd. 3. Assen: Van Gorcum.

Hellquist, E. 1948. *Svensk etymologisk ordbok. I und II.* Lund: Gleerup.

Hoekstra, J. 2010. Westerlauwerskfrysk etymologysk griemmank (V). *Us Wurk* 59. 101–120.

Holthausen, F. 1927. Ostfriesische Studien. 4. Das hochzeitsgedicht des Imel Agena von 1632. *Beiträge zur Geschichte der deutschen Sprache und Literatur* 50. 68–71.

Holthausen, F. 1934/1971. *Altenglisches etymologisches Wörterbuch.* Heidelberg: Winter.

Johansen, Chr. 1862. *Die nordfriesische Sprache nach der Föhringer und Amrumer Mundart.* Kiel: Akademische Buchhandlung.

Kluge, F. 2002. *Etymologisches Wörterbuch der deutschen Sprache.* 24. Aufl. herausgegeben von E. Seebold. Berlin: De Gruyter.

Kooy, T. van der. 1937. *De taal van Hindelopen.* 's-Gravenhage: Nijhoff.

Kramer, P. 1992. *Näi Seelter Woudebouk. Neues Saterfriesisches Wörterbuch. Nij Sealter Wurdboek. New Saterfrisian Dictionary. I (A-E).* Elst. Im Selbstverlag.

Kramer, P. 1995. *Düütsk-Seeltersk Woudelieste (Skrieuwwiese 2010).* Mildam. Im selbstverlag. https://www.seeltersk.de/deutsch-saterfriesisch/

Liberman, A. 2002. Three etymological cruces; English Chide, Clover and Cushat. In A.R. Wedel & H.-J. Busch (Hrsg.), *Verba et Litteræ: Explorations in Germanic Languages and German Literature. Essays in Honor of Albert L. Lloyd,* 59–83. Newark, DE. LinguaText.

Liberman, A. 2008. *An Analytic Dictionary of English Etymology.* Minneapolis, MN. University of Minnesota Press.

Löfstedt, E. 1928. *Die nordfriesische Mundart des Dorfes Ockholm und der Halligen.* Lund: Gleerup.

Minssen, J.F. 1846. *Mittheilungen aus dem Saterlande. Im Jahre 1846 gesammelt von Dr. Phil. Johann Friedrich Minssen. Bd. 2.* 1965 herausgegeben von P. Kramer. Ljouwert: Fryske Akademy.

MN = Nissen, M.M. 1882–1889. *Nordfrisische Wörterbuch in mehreren Dialekten Nordfrislands.* Stedesand. Unveröffentliches Manuskript. Digital in der Universitätsbibliothek Kiel: https://dibiki.ub.uni-kiel.de

Möller, P.B. 1916. *Söl'ring Uurterbok. Wörterbuch der Sylter Mundart.* Hamburg: Meissner.

Niedersächsisches Wörterbuch. Hrsg. von Albert Busch, Bd. 10: r — skrofulös. Bearbeitet von Maik Lehmberg. Kiel/Hamburg: Wachholtz Verlag 2021.

OED = Oxford English Dictionary. http://www.oed.com/

Pokorny, J. 1959. *Indogermanisches etymologisches Wörterbuch.* Bern: Francke.

Remmers, A. 1993. *Wörterbuch der ausgestorbenen ostfriesischen Dialekte. (Harlinger, Wangerooger, Brokmerländer und Wurster Ostfriesisch).* Schwelm: Manuskript.

Rogby, O. 1967. *Niederdeutsch auf friesischem Substrat. Die Mundart von Westerhever in Eiderstedt (Schleswig-Holstein). Die starktonigen Vokale und die Diphthonge. Mit 1 Karte.* (Acta universitatis upsaliensis. Studia Germanistica Upsaliensia 5). Uppsala: Almqvist & Wiksell.

Roosjen, S.O., N.D. Kroese & W. Eekhoff. 1855. *Merkwaardigheden van Hindelopen.* Leeuwarden: Eekhoff.

Scheuermann, U. 2001. Friesische Relikte im ostfriesischen Niederdeutsch. In H.H. Munske u.a. (Hrsg.), *Handbuch des Friesischen / Handbook of Frisian Studies,* 313–353 Tübingen: Niemeyer.

Schmidt-Petersen, J. 1912. *Wörterbuch und Sprachlehre nach der Mundart von Föhr und Amrum.* Husum: Petersen. Nachdruck 1969. Wiesbaden: Sändig.

Schuermans, L.W. 1883. *Algemeen Vlaamsch Idioticon.* Loven: Fonteyn.

Schumacher, Th. 1955. *Studien zur Bedeutungsgeographie deutschmundartlicher Insektennamen.* Gießen: Schmitz.

Seebold, E. 1970. *Vergleichendes etymologisches Wörterbuch der germanischen starken Verben.* The Hague/Paris: Mouton.

Siebs, B. E. 1928. *Die Wangeroger. Eine Volkskunde.* Oldenburg: Littmann. Nachdruck, 1974. Leer: Schuster.

Spenter, A. 1968. *Der Vokalismus der akzentuierten Silben in der Schiermonnikooger Mundart.* Kopenhagen: Munksgaard.

Stroop, J. 1974. *Toelichting bij de Taalatlas von Noord- en Zuid-Nederland II. Bijdragen en Mededelinngen der Dialectenkommissie 46.* (ponderboom, paardebloem, melkbocht, meikever). Amsterdam: Koninklijke Nederlandse Akademi van Wetenschappen.

Stürenburg, C. H. 1857. *Ostfriesisches Wörterbuch.* Aurich: Seyde. Unveränderter Nachdruck 1972. Leer: Schuster.

Vilmar, A. F. C. 1883. *Idiotikon von Kurhessen.* Marburg: Elwert.

Vries, G. de. 2000. *Ostfriesisches Wörterbuch. Oostfreesk Woordenbook.* Leer: Schuster.

Walde, A. & J. Pokorny. 1926–1930. *Vergleichendes Wörterbuch der indogermanischen Sprachen.* 1–3. Berlin und Leipzig: Walter de Gruyter & Co.

WFT = 1984–2011. *Wurdboek fan de Fryske taal. Woordenboek der Friese taal,* 25 Bde. Leeuwarden: Fryske Akademy/De Tille.

Towards an edition of the Hildina ballad (*Hildinakvadet*)

Michael P. Barnes
University College London

The aim of this article is to suggest and exemplify how the Shetland Norn *Hildina* ballad, collected on the island of Foula in 1774, might best be edited for the interested layman, in particular the interested Shetlander. The circumstances in which the ballad was recorded are briefly rehearsed, different ways in which the material could be edited are discussed, and previous studies and translations of the ballad are considered. Finally, stanzas 1 and 29 are given a detailed examination intended to point the way towards a full edition of the type suggested.

1. Introduction

The tour of Orkney and Shetland made by the Rev. George Low in 1774 is well known, thanks to his written account. Though compiled shortly after the tour, this account remained unpublished for over a hundred years. It finally appeared in 1879 thanks to the efforts of Joseph Anderson, who furnished the finished product with a detailed introduction describing Low's life and labours, with particular emphasis on the genesis of his manuscript of the tour (Low 1879:xiii–lxxiv). In July 1774 Low visited the remote Shetland island of Foula. During this trip his attention became at some point directed towards the inhabitants' pronunciation of Scots, and not least towards remnants of "their ancient language" which he came across — a language he terms "Norse" or "Norn" (Low 1879:105–7). Altogether the author offers three specimens of this language: (1) a "Foula Norse" version of the Lord's Prayer, (2) a list of thirty "English words translated into Norn", and (3) a thirty-five stanza "Norn" song or ballad. These linguistic fragments — the most substantial extant records of Norn — have been poured over by a number of scholars, and as early as 1900 the Norwegian philologist Marius Hægstad published a critical edition of the whole material (Hægstad 1900). In spite of this scholarly engagement, however, there exists no comprehensive edition for an English-speaking audience. Hægstad's work is written in an archaic

https://doi.org/10.1075/nss.34.02bar
Available under the CC BY-NC-ND 4.0 license. © 2025 John Benjamins Publishing Company

(to the modern eye) kind of Norwegian *landsmål*, and this may present something of a barrier even to those with a tolerably good grasp of Norwegian. Other approaches to Low's Norn material have tended to be theses or scholarly articles written to demonstrate the validity of a particular idea or theory, or simply to provide a general introduction to and overview of the subject.

2. Structure and scope

The "song" or "ballad" Low collected forms the major part of his three specimens of Norn, and is worthy of an edition on its own. But before any attempt can be made to present this material to an English-speaking readership, consideration needs to be given to precisely what is being presented. It is also essential that the editor has a clear sense of the type of audience at which the work is directed. This will determine its structure and scope. Is it, for example, intended primarily for historical linguists, or for folklorists, or the interested layman — and perhaps particularly the interested Shetlander? If the historical linguist, it might well be enough to translate and update Hægstad's 1900 edition, which after the passing of more than 120 years still forms the basis of modern treatments of the text. The very title, *Hildinakvadet* 'the *Hildina* ballad', seems to have been bestowed by Hægstad — and to have stuck. Prior to 1900 writers refer to Low's "song" or "ballad" as just that. For example, an earlier attempt by a Norwegian scholar, the historian P.A. Munch, to present and discuss the text calls it simply *kvad* 'ballad' (Munch 1838–1839:118 *et passim*). Should the edition be primarily for the folklorist, emphasis will be on parallels of theme, phraseology and metre to be found in Scandinavian balladry — and balladry more widely. If the target audience is the interested layman, the edition must not be overloaded with fine detail and technical jargon; it should provide a means for the reasonably knowledgeable and interested reader to grasp the essentials of the text — and also to comprehend the difficulties in arriving at those essentials. In the following I will try to suggest what an edition intended for this third type of reader might look like.

The edition should probably start with a brief introduction to Northern-Isles linguistic history — the arrival of settlers from Scandinavia, the establishment of their language as the chief or sole medium of communication in Orkney and Shetland, and the gradual supplanting of this language by Scots (Barnes 1998; Lindqvist 2015). There could then be a short presentation of George Low and his tour of the Northern Isles, and a more detailed account of his visit to Foula, leading to thorough discussion of his interaction with William Henry, the informant from whom he obtained the ballad. Low explains in a letter that Henry "repeated and sung the whole day" (1879: lvi), but we are left to wonder whether his recitation was limited to the *Hildina* ballad or also comprised other material. Nor does Low provide much information about the actual process of recording the ballad (beyond noting that Henry gladly received "now and then *a dram of gin*"). He claims in his manuscript of the *Tour* that he "wrote it as an old man pronounced it", and remarks that "the [...] ballad may be either written in two long line or four short line stanzas" (Low 1879: 107). As we have the text, the stanzas are in the main made up of four lines, but what Low has left us is a fair copy, and we have no idea what his original looked like. If indeed Henry "sung and repeated" the *Hildina* ballad "the whole day", one imagines what Low jotted down on paper may have been very different from the version he finally prepared for publication. His original must surely have been full of crossings out and corrections, perhaps divided into four-line stanzas, but possibly scribbled down as continuous text. There are clear indications of uncertainty about the division into stanzas in the only fair copy we have (in the manuscript of the *Tour* Low prepared for publication). It is widely held, for example, that the lines of stanzas 1 and 2 need some reorganisation in order to bring the ballad back closer to its original form (see below).

A general purpose English-language edition will also, of course, take account of earlier editions, studies and translations, and where possible weigh up the merits and drawbacks of the different solutions proffered. Because of the state of preservation of the *Hildina* ballad, however, it will often not be possible to come down firmly in favour of a particular point of view. Readers will often have to make up their own minds. To assist them, the edition should give an overview of the contributions of previous interpreters. Describing their different aims and approaches will enable readers to judge how much weight to attach to what they say. It will also introduce those less familiar with the ballad (and Norn in general) to the fairly extensive literature on the subject that has accumulated over the years. To set the scene, a brief overview of this literature is offered here.

3.   Previous studies and translations

It seems that the ballad was first published in 1805, as part of Appendix 10 to George Barry's *The History of the Orkney Islands* (Barry 1805). The text is taken from the single available source: Low's manuscript of his 1774 tour of Orkney and Shetland. Barry offers no commentary, and his printed text contains a number of misreadings. The first attempt to make some sense of the ballad was by the Norwegian historian P.A. Munch, as part of a lengthy article on the geography and history of Orkney and Shetland (Munch 1838–1839; see above). Munch takes his text from Barry. He provides it with a brief introduction and offers copious notes on the individual stanzas. In many places, however, he acknowledges his inability to understand the detail. In 1879, as noted above, Low's account of his tour through Orkney and Shetland was finally published, and at about the same time various Scandinavian scholars, headed by the Norwegian philologist Sophus Bugge, produced interpretations of the ballad. Of these, however, only Bugge's was destined to be published, and that not until some sixty years later (see Grüner-Nielsen 1939). In 1900 came Hægstad's critical edition of all of Low's Norn specimens (cf. above), and with it the starting-point of most later attempts to wrestle with the ballad he named *Hildinakvadet*. Hægstad's edition contained no translation of *Hildinakvadet*, though he did publish one separately (into *landsmål*) the following year (Hægstad 1901). What his 1900 edition offers is nevertheless impressive: a more accurate reproduction than Barry's of the relevant parts of Low's fair copy; detailed discussion of Low's wording leading to an 'amended' (*umbøtt*) text of the ballad; notes on content and phraseology; extensive comments on the language of *Hildinakvadet*; an overview of the characteristics of Shetland Norn; a concordance of all the words occurring in Low's Norn texts together with Norwegian translations; and finally photographs of those parts of Low's manuscript that contain specimens of Norn. Hægstad's work is meticulous throughout, and it is not surprising that virtually all scholars who have subsequently written on *Hildinakvadet*, or Low's other pieces of Norn, have used it as a reference point.

In 1908 W.G. Collingwood published an English verse translation of the ballad based on Hægstad's amended text. The style is archaising and will not necessarily be of help to those in search of the literal meaning of the original. In his brief introduction (p. 211) Collingwood holds out the prospect of an English translation of Hægstad's 1900 edition ("A translation [...] by G.F. Black, is in progress"), but this does not appear ever to have seen the light of day.

Six years later a translation was made into German (Poestion 1914). This is also based on Hægstad's amended text, and, like Collingwood's effort, is a verse rendering, but it follows the original more closely than Collingwood, and for those who read German it can provide some guidance to the sense of at least parts of the ballad.

A further translation, once more into English verse, is Kershaw 1921. This is of limited use to those trying to understand the original. Although based once again on Hægstad's amended text, Kershaw's rendering encompasses only the first twelve stanzas. And like Collingwood, the translator sacrifices literal sense in favour of rhyme and metre. Her diction is, however, slightly less archaic than that of the 1908 English version.

More important than these translations is Grüner-Nielsen's 1939 study. Grüner-Nielsen was a Danish folklorist, specialising in the collection and publication of ballads. His interest in *Hildinakvadet* was primarily as an example of

Scandinavian balladry and he devotes a substantial part of his article to establishing its relationship with Scandinavian ballads in general. Grüner-Nielsen also identifies many similarities of theme and diction between *Hildinakvadet* and individual examples of the genre, as well as with motifs in Old Norse literature. Of particular interest in the current context is the inclusion of a "restoration" of the text to a possible Old Norse form (pp.144–9) — a product attributed chiefly to Sophus Bugge (see above), though with input from others. Grüner-Nielsen is at pains to stress that neither he nor any of the scholars involved would claim to have returned the ballad to its original form. What is in effect a translation into Old Norse Grüner-Nielsen describes as the standardisation of the ballad through the removal of its dialect (i.e. Norn) features. For those keen to advance their understanding of the text, this "norseification" is of significance because it provides an interpretation very different from Hægstad's and with which Hægstad's can usefully be compared.

In 1950 The Viking Congress (the first in a long and continuing series) was held in Lerwick, Shetland. In the published proceedings (Simpson 1954), the "programme of meetings" notes (p. xix) that on Thursday 20th July there was a "Recital of Scaldic Poetry and Hildina Ballad" by Copenhagen's Professor of Icelandic, Jón Helgason, and its Lecturer in Faroese, Christian Matras. From Haakon Shetelig's congress diary (Simpson 1954: xxi–xxvi) we learn that it was Jón Helgason, himself a noted poet, who provided a "reading and interpretation" of the ballad (p. xxv). Unfortunately, neither text nor interpretation was published as part of the proceedings. However, a copy of the text is preserved in the Shetland Archives (Jón Helgason [1950]) to which the Archivist, Brian Smith, has kindly drawn my attention. This is presumably the text from which Jón recited, but it contains no commentary or notes at all, so it is impossible to follow the reasoning that led him to his interpretation. What he gives us is a version in which both wording and structure have been amended, sometimes fairly drastically (his text, for example, consists of only 30 stanzas as against Low's 35). But Jón's main aim seems to have been to create a written version of the ballad from which he could read aloud in close approximation to the pronunciation he thought Low's informant, William Henry, was likely to have used. There are, for example, length marks over certain vowel symbols, syllables are sometimes divided, and the character 'ø' is used to indicate the mid front rounded vowel. It is thus possible to gain some idea of the stage of development Jón considered late eighteenth-century Foula Norn to have reached. As a noted Scandinavian philologist his views carry weight. His version of the ballad needs to be taken into account by anyone seeking to compile a new edition.

Over thirty years separates Jón Helgason's version of *Hildinakvadet* from the next serious attempt to deal with the ballad. This took the form of a lengthy article by the Norwegian Eigil Lehmann, priest, poet and enthusiastic cultivator of *landsmål/nynorsk* (Lehmann 1984). He offers first a general introduction to the material, then plunges into a historical phonology of the ballad's vowels and consonants (based often on his interpretation of the text, with which not all may agree). There follows a justification for the strange Old West Norse garb in which Lehmann attempts to clothe *Hildinakvadet*. This re-working takes the form an idiosyncratic normalisation of the classical language of Scandinavia, tweaked here and there to take account of presumed innovations in Norn. Next Lehmann presents a detailed analysis of each stanza — partly, once again, justification for the forms and spellings he prefers, partly interpretation. Finally we get Lehmann's version of the complete ballad set out in two columns: column 1 contains the text written in the author's own "normalised Norse"; column 2 is headed "I norsk framburd" 'in Norwegian pronunciation' (Lehmann 1984: 53). It should be noted, though, that the text in the second column deviates from that in the first in other ways than matters of pure "pronunciation". In spite of its many idiosyncrasies, Lehmann's various attempts at interpretation are the result of considerable thought and careful analysis and deserve to be given due weight in any comprehensive future edition of the ballad.

Mention should be made at this point of a short monograph dealing with the *Hildina* ballad (Rendboe 1993). No attempt is made to analyse or interpret any part of the text, but the piece does provide a useful and readable introduction in English to Low's discovery and recording of the ballad, and to the light subsequent scholarship has been able to throw on it. The reader should, however, be warned against the over-sanguine view Rendboe expresses (in this and other works) about the longevity of Norn.

The early twenty-first century has seen a revival of interest in Norn, and not least in the *Hildina* ballad. Three contributions to *Hildina* scholarship of varying length and detail are Fischer 2010, Steintún 2016 and González Campo 2020. All three are in English, but differ considerably in their ambition and scope.

Fischer ponders the language of the ballad and wonders whether it is most closely related to Faroese or the dialects of south-west Norway. The author's primary concern, though, is with identifying similarities of diction and motif between *Hildinakvadet* and Faroese, Norwegian and Scottish balladry. Yet for those trying to understand the garbled text Low left to posterity the most useful part of this article is the "literal prose translation [...] based on Hægstad's Nynorsk recension" (p.93) which Fischer provides. For those who read Norwegian, of course, this translation offers nothing new, but it allows those who do not to gain some insight into Hægstad's understanding of the ballad. It is only a partial insight, however, for the "Nynorsk recension" is in fact Hægstad's 1901 translation, which for the sake of rhyme and metre deviates on many points of detail from the word-by-word interpretations he gives in his rigorous 1900 analysis.

Steintún's 2016 Master's thesis is a wide-ranging piece of work, despite the narrow focus implied by its title. There is a general introduction to the *Hildina* ballad and to Norn, discussion of phonological changes in Scandinavian and of the relationship of the language of the ballad to Norn as a whole, consideration of the shift from Norn to Scots in Shetland, and of much else besides. On the basis of recent photographic reproductions of the relevant pages of Low's manuscript, Steintún makes a new transcription of the ballad, and this informs his interpretation although the differences between Steintún's and Hægtad's readings are on the whole minor. He also provides a "word for word translation into classical Old Norse" (p. 64), which is to be understood as his detailed interpretation of Low's text, as well as an archaising English verse translation based on Collingwood 1908, Kershaw 1921 and an Internet version located at www.nornlanguage.x10.mx. All this leads to an amended text which differs in certain respects from Hægtad's (and forms the basis of the author's linguistic analysis of the ballad's morphological case system, which he deems to exhibit "some morphological levelling", p. 114). Steintún's work is detailed and meticulous and must be taken into account in any future edition of the *Hildina* ballad. It is particularly useful when considering the more obscure passages of the text.

Of less use is González Campo's 2020 article on *Hildina* — despite its length. This is a largely derivative piece (and one with a good few errors): it reports the results of other people's work, but contributes little in the way of fresh insights. There is a scene-setting section on the 'Context of discovery', followed by almost twenty pages on 'Scandinavian parallels' (of plot or motif), including twelve pages listing supposed 'Parallels in Scandinavian ballads'. Then comes 'Attempts at reconstruction' a reproduction in three parallel columns of Low's manuscript text of 1774, and of Hægtad's and Lehmann's amended texts of 1900 and 1984. Thereafter we have 'Attempts at translation', likewise a reproduction in columns, this time of the various translations of the ballad: Bugge's into Old Norse, Hægtad 1901, Collingwood 1908, Poestion 1914, Kershaw 1921 and Lehmann 1984. This rehearsal is rounded off with a reproduction of a verse translation by Graeme Davis (2007: 111–114) — of which more immediately below. 'Some concluding remarks' completes the article. Here González Campo advocates *inter alia* a "literary-anthropological approach" to the *Hildina* ballad. Since the author offers no reconstruction of his own and only minimal discussion of earlier efforts, this article contains little that can be fed into a new edition of the text of the ballad. Its chief use lies in the gathering together of previous texts and translations, which facilitates the making of quick comparisons.

Graeme Davis's treatment of *Hildina* I have relegated to the end of my survey. It forms a not insubstantial part of his implausible thesis that there was a Saxon settlement in Orkney and Shetland starting in the fourth century AD. It is, though, never made clear how a Norn ballad collected on Foula in 1774 advances Davis's principal idea. Of some interest in the present context is the free "long-line" verse translation of the ballad he gives, but his translation is on the whole too free to offer much help to the reader keen to get close to the meaning of the original. Davis's book is unfortunately somewhat amateurish. He prefaces his translation of the ballad by explaining that it is based on "philological methodology", a methodology which consists in looking "at Germanic roots". Yet it is impossible to see how or where this methodology informs the translation. Indeed in subsequent remarks he points out: "My own translation attempts a readable narrative, though in doing so interprets freely and should probably be regarded as a retelling of the story". So much for Davis's "philological methodology".

4. An edition for the interested layman

The compiler of an edition of the *Hildina* ballad for the lay reader has a choice between several possible models. In my view the principal aim must be to establish as far as possible the literal meaning of Low's text — the one original we have. Once the words that make up the text are understood, scholars, interpreters, poets, etc. can do with it what they will. But without a proper understanding of the basics, and of the limitations of our understanding, the way is open to confusion and error. With a view to sketching a possible method of proceeding I will now attempt a model analysis of two stanzas of the ballad, one whose meaning is relatively easy to grasp, and one that poses greater difficulty. It is my hope that those who work on *Hildinakvadet* in the future will be able to gain some inspiration from this model, even if they do not follow it directly.

Stanza 1 in Low's fair copy seems to run as follows (there can be doubts about the reading of one or two details):

> Da vara Iarlin d'Orkneyar
> For frinda sin spir de ro
> Whirdè ane skildè meun
> Our glas buryon burtaga.

With our knowledge of other forms of Scandinavian language and of the history of this type of Germanic, it is not overly difficult to explain what the stanza means, although one or two points of detail remain problematic.

Da all commentators agree is the neuter demonstrative pronoun, corresponding to ON *þat*, Faroese (Far.) *tað*, Norwegian (Norw.) *det*, Icelandic (Icel.) *það* 'that' 'it'.

There follows *vara* about which once again all agree: it is the 3rd SG past tense of the verb *vera* '[to] be'. Most print *var*, ignoring the final -*a*. Hægstad (1900:58) explains the -*a* as an epenthetic vowel, but normally a following consonant is required for the development of an epenthetic, as Far. *bøkur*, Norw. *bøker* < ON *bækr* 'books'. Possibly *vara* is a contracted form of *var hann*, where *hann* belongs with *Iarlin* and the sense is something like 'the earl of whom we speak', as in *on fruna Hildina* literally 'she the lady Hildina' (stanza 29; see below); cf. Norw. *han Per* 'Per (the one we know/are talking about)'.

Iarlin, as has just been made clear, is the noun *jarl* + the Scandinavian suffixed definite article: 'the earl'. In Faroese we find the development [rl] > [lː] > [dl] in certain cases, including *jallur* [jadlʊr] 'earl'; such a change is not reflected in Low's spelling of this word, however. We do, though, have [lː] > [dl] in, for example, *godle* < ON *gulli* [DAT.SG] 'gold' in stanza 23.

Next comes an unexpected *d* ', which has been rendered in a number of different ways by those editing or translating the ballad. Hægstad (1900:13) regards it as a mistake. He thinks Low misread an *o* ' in his original (representing a form of the ON preposition *ór* 'from' 'out of'). Most commentators seem to agree and suggest a preposition denoting movement from a place. This, however, must be considered unlikely. It is true that in *Orkneyinga saga* travel away from the Orkneys is commonly expressed as *ór Orkneyjum*, but movement is clearly not what the *d* ' *Orkneyar* of stanza 1 denotes, rather it identifies the area over which the earl rules. In ON this tends to be expressed as a compound: *Orkneyjajarl* 'Orkney islands' earl' or *Orkneyingajarlar* 'earls of the Orkney islanders'. Possibly we are dealing here with *uti/udi* an expanded form (largely literary) of the preposition *í* 'in' which can be traced back to thirteenth-century Danish (and Danish is likely, via Norwegian, to have influenced Norn, cf. Jakobsen 1928–32:cxvi–cxvii). In William Henry's recitation *udi* might well have been shortened to [d], or at least heard as [d] by Low. Lehmann (1984:24) thought along similar lines, but suggested instead *tá*, a Norwegian dialect form of *utav*, itself an expanded form of *af/av*. The age of the *Hildina* ballad is unknown, but whenever composed *í* will have been a more likely way than *af* of identifying the area over which someone's rule extended.

Whatever the preposition, we would according to the rules of ON grammar expect it to govern the dative, giving *Orkneyum* (or similar form) rather than nom./acc. *Orkneyar*. Those who translate the text into ON of course supply the expected ending, but so too does Hægstad in his *landsmål* rendering (1901:3) and also Jón Helgason [1950:1], who inserts a Norn dative plural (*Orkneyon*) in which the original final -*m* is rendered as -*n* (cf. Faroese [m] > [n] in this position). The

Towards an edition of the Hildina ballad (*Hildinakvadet*) 43

acc. (or non-inflected) form used by Henry points to a breakdown in the inherited inflectional system, perhaps not unexpected after prolonged linguistic contact with Scots.

The *for* with which line 2 begins may owe its form to Scots or perhaps Danish. The basic sense is 'before', meaning 'in the presence of' 'facing', as in Far. *hann segði einaferð fyri Niklasi, at...* 'he once said to Niklas that...'.

We would expect *for* in this sense to govern the dative, as it does in Faroese, but although *frinda* 'kinsman' might be either dative or accusative, the reflexive possessive *sin* 'his' can only be accusative (the dative is historically *sínum*), agreeing with *frinda*. Like *Orkneyar* in the preceding line, *frinda sin* suggests a breakdown in the traditional inflectional system. We can only speculate about Henry's pronunciation of *frinda*. The corresponding ON form is *frænda* [frænda]. Possibly Henry or Low, or both, have been influenced by Scots pronunciations of English *friend*.

In the following *spir de* (wrongly printed *spurd de* by Andersen 1879:108) Low has divided a single word in two. This is the 3rd person past tense form *spirde* 'asked' (cf. Far. *spurde*, Norw. *spurde, spurte*). Again we can but speculate about Henry's pronunciation. Jón Helgason [1950:1] gives the root vowel as *o* (*sporde*), but [ø], heard by Low as the neutral schwa vowel [ə], is perhaps more likely than [o].

The object of *spirde* is *ro*, presumably pronounced [roː]. This is ON *ráð* 'advice' 'counsel'. The vowel written *á* in ON was originally a long [aː]. It became rounded to [oː] in most forms of mainland Scandinavian, while in Icelandic and Faroese it ultimately developed into a diphthong, Icel. [au], Far. [ɑa]. There are indications that something like the Faroese diphthong was current in at least certain types of Norn (see below), but Low's spelling *ro* implies a pure vowel in this case. Jón Helgason [1950:1] has *rō* (where the bar over the vowel symbol clearly indicates length).

The word *Whirdè* at the opening of line 3 must from the context mean something like 'whether' 'if'. Hægstad (1900:97) recognises a reflex of ON *hvárt* 'which of two' and thus 'whether the one or the other'. The word occurs in Faroese ballads in the standardised form *hvørt*, and the pronunciation Low heard might have approximated to [hwørde], with voicing [t] > [d], a common phenomenon in Norn.

The *ane* that follows *Whirdè* can only be the 3rd person singular personal pronoun *han(n)* 'he', known from all the Scandinavian languages. It appears multiple times in the *Hildina* ballad and in a variety of forms. The lack of initial *h-* is replicated widely throughout the text, but what caused Low to add an *-e* at the end of the word is unclear. Perhaps he thought to hear something like [ejn].

Next comes the modal verb *skildè*, ON *skyldi* 'should'. In ON the root vowel is the high front rounded [y], but in both Faroese and Icelandic this is unrounded to [i]. How far such unrounding was also a general feature of Norn is unclear: ON [y(:)] can appear in many guises (cf. Hægstad 1900: 39–40).

The final word in line 3, *meun*, is puzzling. Hægstad (1900: 44), like all other commentators, recognises a word meaning 'maiden', and proposes a pronunciation [mø:n]. Whether he was thinking in terms of French orthography, and attributing (doubtless rightly) knowledge of French to Low, he does not say. The root of the relevant noun is *møy-*, *mey-* in ON, in Faroese *moy-*; the ON definite ACC.SG 'the maiden' is *meyna*, Faroese *moynna*. Whatever else, *meun* can hardly be an accusative form, presumably a further indication of the breakdown of the inherited inflectional system. The final *-n*, though, must represent the definite article. Regarding Henry's pronunciation of this word, Lehmann (1984: 25–6) disagrees with Hægstad and thinks Low's spelling implies "mè-en", pointing out that in stanza 2 *meun* is the reflex of ON *meðan* 'while', which, whatever else, can hardly have developed into [mø:n]. Jón Helgason, who has *me-un* in stanza 1 [1950: 1], seems to agree. Hægstad (1900: 44–5) lists the various different guises in which the ON diphthong *øy, ey* appears in the *Hildina* ballad, all of them spellings that according to him indicate a monophthong. He also offers examples from diplomas emanating from Orkney and Shetland in which ON *øy, ey* appears as *ø*, but this could at least in part be due to Danish or Swedish influence on the written language of the period (in which forms of Scandinavian, *øy, ey* is regularly monophthongised to [ø:]). Notwithstanding my confident assertion (Barnes 1998: 47) that stanza 1's *meun* could be represented phonemically as /mø:n/, I now wonder whether something like /me:ən/ might not be nearer the mark.

It is uncertain how the *Our* 'from' 'out of' of line 4 sounded. Hægstad (1900: 49) seems to assume [o:r], and, if correct, this may well have suggested to Low something close to his Scots pronunciation of *our*.

The following word, *glasburyon*, can only be a noun + DEF.ART, meaning 'the glass castle' or 'the glass palace'. In ON we would expect *glerborginni* (DAT governed by the preposition *ór*). East Scandinavian *glas-* has replaced Old West Scandinavian *gler-*, spirant [ɣ] has apparently developed into [j], and the DAT.FEM.SG ending of the definite article *-inni* has given way to what looks like the nominative (or generalised uninflected form) *-in*, though spelt *-on* and of uncertain pronunciation. Quite what is envisaged by a 'glass palace' has been the subject of speculation. Hægstad (1900: 84) and others compare the word to the *glæstriborg* 'gleaming fortress' 'splendid palace' of Faroese balladry, and it may be that *Hildina's glasburyon* is a re-interpretation of a related image that once existed in Norn ballads.

The infinitive *burtaga* is a compound. It is made up of the adverb *burt* 'away' (ON *braut, brott*) and the verb *taga* 'take' (ON *taka*). The spelling *taga* exemplifies the common Norn voicing of [k] to [g] in postvocalic position.

The general tendency in Scandinavian four-line ballad stanzas is for there to be end rhyme between the second and fourth lines. Clearly *ro* and *burtaga* do not rhyme. However, the first line of stanza 2 runs: *Or vanna ro eidnar fuo*, which seems unconnected with the sense of the rest of this stanza, but would serve admirably in terms of both content and rhyme (*ro~fuo*) as the final line of stanza 1. And there is still enough material in what remains of stanza 2 to make up a complete four-liner with the expected end rhyme between lines 2 and 4. This has led many commentators to assume confusion here, either by Low or Henry. Accordingly, Hægstad (1900:14) in his amended text deems *Or vanna ro eidnar fuo* to be the fourth line of stanza 1. He is then left with *Our glasburyon burtaga*, which he classes as a refrain (a common feature of many Scandinavian ballads). Most who have worked with the *Hildina* ballad have followed Hægstad, at least to the extent of re-assigning stanza 2's line 1 as stanza 1 line 4.

In this new line 4 *Or* is clearly the same preposition as *Our* in *Our glasburyon*, but with a variant spelling.

The *vanna ro* which Low writes as two words is by general consensus a compound: almost all assume this to be a reflex of ON *vandaráð* 'difficult matter' 'trouble', with assimilation [nd] > [n:], and there seems no reason to disagree with their verdict. The preposition *or* governs the dative, which in ON would yield the form *vandaráði* (SG) or *vandaráðum* (PL). In Henry's rendering of the *Hildina* ballad the dative has been replaced by an uninflected form.

The *eidnar* that follows *vannaro* can in the context hardly be anything but the 3rd SG feminine possessive 'her'. As is usual in western Scandinavian, the possessive follows the head noun (cf. Norw. *bilen min* 'my car'). The ON form corresponding to *eidnar* is *hennar*. Henry's Norn shows loss of initial [h-] before a vowel (widely documented throughout the ballad), and the change [n:] > [dn]. This latter development is well known in both Icelandic and Faroese, but occurs under different conditions in the two languages. In neither is it found after a short vowel, although this does happen in one or two west Norwegian dialects (cf. Hægstad 1900:66; Chapman 1962:197). The spelling *ei* in *eidnar* should probably not be taken to indicate diphthongisation; elsewhere in the ballad we find *ednar*, DAT *hedne*, etc.

The infinitive *fuo* 'get' is dependent on the modal auxiliary *skildè* of line 3: 'should get'. It is unclear how complete the rhyme is between *fuo* and the final word *ro* of line 2. If we follow Jón Helgason [1950:1], who has *fwō*, we can perhaps assume a pronunciation something like [fwɔ], but it is worth noting that in Faroese ON [a:] develops to [ɑa], a "balanced" diphthong in which both elements are vocalic. It is impossible to say how Henry pronounced *fuo*, but Low may in any case have heard it as [fwɔ]. English-speaking learners of Faroese tend to pronounce [ɑa] more like [wa] than the correct balanced diphthong.

To exemplify a somewhat trickier stanza, I have chosen 29. In Low's fair copy it runs thus:

> Da gerde on fruna Hildina
> On bar se mien ot
> On soverin fest, fysin (*fysin* crossed through in the manuscript)
> Fysin u quarsin sat.

Da is the neuter demonstrative pronoun as at the beginning of stanza 1.

There follows the finite verb *gerde* 'did' (< ON *gerði*). The initial consonant of this word has been subject to differing degrees of palatalisation in the Scandinavian idioms. *Hildinakvadet* itself exhibits the present plural form *yera* 'do' (stanza 20), while the initial consonant in Faroese is the affricate [tɕ-]. Just possibly, Low's *gerde* is intended to indicate affricate pronunciation, as in English *general*, German.

Like *ane* 'he' in stanza 1, the 3rd person SG feminine personal pronoun *on* 'she' has lost its initial [h-], cf. ON/Far. *hon*, Norw. *hun, ho*.

The noun *fruna*, together with *on*, forms the subject, and one would therefore expect it, as *on*, to appear in the nominative case; *fruna*, however, looks like the accusative form. Conceivably -*na* is a generalised ending, as in *Hildina*, which seems to be derived from the basic female name *Hild*. Jón Helgason amends to *fruen*.

Line 2 of stanza 29 is problematic. The subject is *On* just as in line 1, while *bar* is clearly the 3rd person past tense SG of *bera* 'carry'.

If correctly read by Hægstad, the following word, which is badly obscured by an ink splodge, is *se*, presumably dative of the reflexive pronoun 'self'. It would function here as an ethic dative (rare in English, referring to someone with an interest in or affected by an action, as in *I finally got **me** a drink*). The general sense is 'for herself' 'for her benefit', but the word is best omitted from an English translation. The Sophus Bugge ON rendering recognises here a completely different word: *svá* 'thus' (Grüner-Nielsen 1939: 148), but this can be no more than a hopeful guess.

The object of *bar* 'carried' is *mien*. Hægstad (1900: 43) sees in this a reflex of ON *mjǫðinn*, ACC.SG of the word for 'mead' + definite article. In evidence he refers to the spelling *hwetemiel* for standard ON *hveitimjǫl* 'wheat flour' in a diploma from Orkney of ca. 1425 (Marwick 1929: 223 = *Diplomatarium Norvegicum* 2, no. 691). Unfortunately the correct reading here seems to be *hwetemiøl*. Yet the con-

Towards an edition of the Hildina ballad (*Hildinakvadet*)   47

text supports Hægstad's interpretation. Hildina, who plans to burn her enemies alive in a hall, is busy plying them with drink in order to send them into a drunken stupor. However, two preceding stanzas declare that her chosen beverage was wine, not mead. It must be acknowledged that Low's *mien* is a long way from *mjǫðinn*, and there is simply insufficient evidence to determine whether or not Hægstad's suggestion might be accepted. Jón Helgason's text has *mi-en*, but with no indication of how he thought the word should be understood.

The concluding *ot* of line 2 seems to be an adverb indicating movement towards a place. This has generally been taken as a reflex of ON *at* with lengthening of the vowel in stressed position and subsequent rounding: [at] > [aːt] > [ɔːt] 'thither' 'to that place'.

The verb construction *soverin* in line 3 looks like a form of intransitive *sova* '[to] sleep' followed by the particle *inn*, but this can hardly be the case since verb and particle appear to be complemented by an object: *fysin* (see below). On contextual grounds Hægstad surmises that *sover* is a reflex of ON *svæfir* 'puts to sleep' 'lulls to sleep', but the phonetic development is hard to follow. If Hægstad is right, the particle *inn* then means something like 'into': 'brings into a state of sleep'.

The adverb *fest* (unclear in Low's fair copy and possibly to be read *fast*) means 'firmly' 'fast' (cf. *fast asleep*). Jón Helgason, on the other hand, suggests *fist*. He presumably has in mind a Norn reflex of ON *fyrst* 'first [of all]' (cf. his drastic emendation of line 4: *o kvar sin dar idne sat* 'and each [person] who sat in there' — see below).

The object of *sover*, *fysin* is written twice in Low's manuscript, but the first occurrence, at the end of line 3, has been crossed through. The repetition would, however, appear desirable for metrical reasons (cf. Jón Helgason's emendation above). To interpret *fysin* we need first to divide Low's written form into two words: *fy sin*, and then to consider the relationship between sound and spelling in English. What Low heard was almost certainly [faːi sin] or [faj sin] a reflex of ON *faði(r) sinn* 'her father'. The grammatically correct ON form would in fact be *fǫður sinn* (acc.), but we presumably have here a further example of an inflectional system in decline.

The next word is *u* (< ON *ok*) 'and', which has lost its consonant (*ok* > *og* > *o/u*; cf. Norw. *og* [ɔ(ː)], Far. *og* [o(ː)]).

The *quarsin* that follows *u* again amalgamates what are two separate words: *quar* 'each [person]' 'everyone' and *sin* the relative particle 'who', cf. ON/Icel. *sem*, Far. *sum*, Norw. *som*. The development [-m] > [-n] in unstressed position is paralleled in Faroese dative endings (cf. DAT.PL *gentum* [tɕɛɳtʊn] 'girls') — though not in *sum* — and is documented in identical circumstances in at least some types of Norn (cf. *Hildinakvadet* stanza 4 DAT.PL *londen* < ON *lǫndum* 'lands').

Finally we have the self-evident *sat* 'sat'.

The two stanzas that have been treated here can thus be rendered fairly literally into English (following what appear to me the most plausible choices where there are alternatives):

1 It was the Earl of the Orkneys
   Of his kinsman he asked advice,
   Whether he should take the maiden
   From the glass palace/
   Whether he should get the maiden
   Out of her troubles.

29 That did the lady Hildina
    She bore the mead(?) thither,
    She put her father firmly to sleep,
    Her father and everyone who sat [there].

In my view it ought to be possible to produce interpretations along these lines of all 35 stanzas of the *Hildina* ballad. Some stanzas will be as relatively straightforward as 1, others will throw up considerably greater problems than 29. In all cases the aim should be to make clear in plain English what is known, what is reasonable surmise, and what is educated guesswork. The end product should be a guide for the layman interested in understanding as much as can be understood of the original. I am the first to admit that the scope of such an edition will of necessity be limited, but as I try to make clear in the introduction, the way would then be open to folklorists, historical and comparative linguists, etc. to compile other editions better suited to their interests.

References

Barnes, M. P. 1998. *The Norn language of Orkney and Shetland*. Lerwick: Shetland Times.

Barry, G. 1805. *The history of the Orkney islands...* Edinburgh: Constable.

Chapman, K. G. 1962. *Icelandic-Norwegian linguistic relationships* (*Norsk tidsskrift for sprogvidenskap*, suppl. bind VII). Oslo: Universitetsforlaget.

Collingwood, W. G. 1908. The ballad of Hildina. *Orkney and Shetland Old-lore* 6. 211–216.

Davis, G. 2007. *The early English settlement of Orkney and Shetland*. Edinburgh: John Donald.

Fischer, F. J. 2010. 'Hildina' — a Norn ballad in Shetland. *Scottish Studies* 35. 92–105.

González Campo, M. 2020. The Norn Hildina ballad from the Shetland islands: Scandinavian parallels and attempts at reconstruction/translation. *SELIM. Journal of the Spanish Society for Medieval English Language and Literature* 25(1). 61–119.

Towards an edition of the Hildina ballad (*Hildinakvadet*)

Grüner-Nielsen, H. 1939. Den shetlandske Hildina-vise og Sophus Bugges tolkning. In H. Johannessen et al. (eds.), *Heidersskrift til Gustav Indrebø på femtiårsdagen 17. november 1939*, 139–165. Bergen: Lunde.

Hægstad, M. 1900. *Hildinakvadet med utgreiding um det norske maal paa Shetland i eldre tid* (Videnskabsselskabets Skrifter. II. Historisk-filosofiske Klasse. 1900. No. 2). Christiania: Dybwad.

Hægstad, M. 1901. Hildinakvadet. *Syn og segn 7*. 1–14.

Jakobsen, J. 1928–32. *An etymological dictionary of the Norn language in Shetland* (2 vols.). London: David Nutt.

Jón Helgason [1950] = Shetland Archives, Papers of the Shetland Folk Society, D18/3/1.

Kershaw, N. 1921. *Stories and ballads of the far past*. Cambridge: University Press.

Lehmann, E. 1984. Hildina-kvædet: ein etterrøknad og ei tolking. *Frå Fjon til Fusa 37*. 7–60.

Lindqvist, C. 2015. *Norn im keltischen Kontext* (NOWELE Supplement Series 26). Amsterdam/Philadelphia: John Benjamins.

Low, G. 1879. *A tour through the islands of Orkney and Schetland*. Kirkwall: William Peace.

Marwick, H. 1929. *The Orkney Norn*. Oxford: University Press.

Munch, P. A. 1838–1839. Geografiske og historiske Notitser om Orknöerne og Hetland. *Samlinger til det norske Folks Sprog og Historie 6*. 79–133, 475–524. Christiania: Et Samfund.

Poestion, J. C. 1914. Das Lied von Hildina. Eine shetländische Ballade. *Zeitschrift für den deutschen Unterricht 28*. 592–595.

Rendboe, L. 1993. *Shetland's Hildina ballad: its discovery and further discussions* (Pre-publications of the English Department of Odense University 68). Odense: Odense Universitetsforlag.

Simpson, W. D. (ed.). 1954. *Viking Congress, Lerwick July 1950*. Edinburgh: Oliver and Boyd.

Steintún, B. 2016. The Hildina ballad: a linguistic analysis of the case system. MA thesis, University of Bergen, Norway.

Prosodic complexity and mora counting in North Germanic

Hans Basbøll
University of Southern Denmark

This paper proposes a typology of word-prosodic complexity applied to Modern North Germanic languages, including tonal word accents in Swedish and Norwegian, and different accent systems in Danish dialects (Section 1). This is combined with an analysis of syllable weight operating in mora counting, as proposed by Trubetzkoy to account for the Danish stød. Taking the point of departure in Basbøll's Non-Stød Model, principles for mora counting in North Germanic are presented and discussed (Section 2). The paper ends by considering some synchronic and diachronic consequences of the proposals, including a discussion of prosodic variation at morpheme boundaries and of stød as a grammaticalized morpheme of singular for nouns (Section 3).

1. A typology of word-prosodic complexity, applied to Modern North Germanic

In this proposed typology of prosodic complexity, I only consider word prosody, not phrase — or utterance or sentence — prosody. My point of departure is a structuralist understanding of the linguistic sign — from Saussure (1916), in agreement with many a Glossematician's interpretation — and a Praguian distinction between segmental and prosodic phonology, see Basbøll (2023a: 318–321). The typology proposed is structural, i.e., the different *degrees* (for lack of a better term) of word-prosodic complexity are not necessary stages in any development: languages can change in word-prosodic complexity either by becoming more or less complex over time, and both directions of change are well represented in North Germanic. As the term word-prosodic complexity suggests, both morphology and phonology are concerned; thus, prosodic complexity in a purely phonological sense is not considered here (cf. Section 2.2).

In Section 1.1 the focus is on the modern Scandinavian — not including Icelandic and Faroese — standard languages: Swedish and Norwegian (Section 1.1.3)

https://doi.org/10.1075/nss.34.03bas
Available under the CC BY-NC-ND 4.0 license. © 2025 John Benjamins Publishing Company

and Danish (1.1.4). The criterion of word-prosodic complexity will be illustrated by first taking modern French (1.1.1) as an example of a language with a very simple *word* prosody, and then taking modern German (1.1.2) that in word-prosodic complexity occupies a position between French and the modern Scandinavian languages, Swedish, Norwegian and Danish.

In Section 1.2, I take word-prosodic phenomena in three Danish dialects — or dialect areas — as illustrations of different types of word-prosodic complexity (in the sense discussed in 1.1): tonal accents in East Slesvig and Als (in the eastern part of Southern Jutland), short-vowel-stød in Zealand, and the so-called West-Jutland "stød" in a large area of the western part of Jutland (Danish stød is a main topic also of Section 2).

In Section 1.3, the typology of word-prosodic complexity is applied to a selection of Danish dialects (considered in Section 1.2, as well as some others), resulting in Danish dialects representing all the possible degrees between 2 (see German in 1.1.2) and 5, i.e., one degree more complex with respect to word prosody than standard Danish (1.1.4).

The typology of word-prosodic complexity presented here is thus applied to closely related North Germanic languages in particular; other such typologies might be relevant, for example, for tone languages in Asia or Africa, etc.

1.1 Zooming in on Modern Standard Scandinavian

1.1.1 *Typology of word-prosodic complexity, degree 1: French (example)*

A simple word prosody is found in many Romance languages, such as in French, here defined as **degree 1** in complexity. In Modern Standard French, there is no consistent signaling of (single) words — as against groups of words — by prosodic or other phonological means. Furthermore, the phenomenon called *liaison*[1] shows that the word is not the relevant prosodic frame.

1.1.2 *Typology of word-prosodic complexity, degree 2: German (example)*

In Germanic languages, word prosody is typically more complex (than languages representing degree 1) due to the Germanic compound stress. If we take Modern Standard German, for example, the word-prosody is clearly more complex than that of French (Section 1.1.1), in that German has a compound stress rule, typically resulting in primary stress on the first compound member and secondary stress

---

1. A term meaning, e.g., connexion; an example of French *liaison*: *il est ici* 'he is here' pronounced with a [t], viz. as [ilɛti'si], a [t] which is not there if *est* is in absolute (utterance) final position, e.g., in *il l'est!* 'he is it/that', pronounced as [il'lɛ]. The final stress is automatic.

on the last or final member, e.g., *Dampfschiff* 'steam ship' with primary stress on *Dampf-* and secondary stress on *-schiff*. Thus, German has an added level of complexity in its word prosody as compared to French, therefore German represents **degree 2**.

1.1.3 *Typology of word-prosodic complexity, degree 3: Swedish and Norwegian*

In most forms of Swedish and Norwegian (Gårding 1977, see also Haugen 1976: 281–285), there is a further complicating factor — in addition to compound stress — in the word prosody, viz. the two tonal word accents, or 'word tones', accent 1 (acute) and accent 2 (grave).[2] Standard Swedish and Norwegian thus exhibit both the compound stress of degree 2, and an additional word-prosodic contrast which adds to the complexity in my system, so Swedish and Norwegian represent **degree 3**.

1.1.4 *Complexity scale of word prosody, degree 4: Standard Danish*

Danish has, in addition to the compound stress (of degrees 2 and 3), a word accent contrast: stød vs. non-stød. The grammatical and lexical distribution of Danish stød has many parallels with the distribution of Swedish and Norwegian accent 1 (Section 1.1.3). But the phonological restrictions of stød — relating to sonority, viz. that stød presupposes a syllable rhyme with long sonority (see Section 2.2) — make the Danish stød-non-stød contrast more complicated than the tonal accent-contrast in Swedish and Norwegian; thus, Danish represents **degree 4**. Furthermore, the fact that there can be more than one stød in a word — but only one tonal accent in a Swedish and Norwegian word — also shows that Danish is more complex with respect to word prosody: the logic is that a yes-no option (i.e., a choice between two possibilities as in Swedish and Norwegian) is simpler than a choice between more than two possibilities.

1.2 Three examples of word-prosodic complexity in Danish dialects

In his survey of Danish dialects, Ringgaard (1973: 21–26, 42–44) considers prosody (word prosody in particular) with many examples, and in his general comparison of the main dialect areas, prosody also plays an important role (pp. 44–48).

---

2. An example of contrast (a minimal pair) for tonal word accents in standard Swedish and Norwegian: [1]*tanken* 'the tank', DEF.SG of [1]*tank*, vs. [2]*tanken* 'the thought', DEF.SG of [2]*tanke*. Monosyllables do not have any contrast between accent 1 and 2, and in Haugen's analysis of Norwegian (1967) there is only one tonal accent, not two.

1.2.1 *East Slesvig and Als*

The examples below, and the notation,[3] are taken from Ejskjær (1990: 61–63), based upon Bjerrum (1948). Superscript 1 and 2 indicate two contrastive pitch accents; for vowel length, I have substituted the single dot — from the Danish (*Dania*, see Jespersen (1890)) tradition — with '∶'.

¹damb 'steam (sb.)' vs. ²damb 'steam (vb.)'
corresponding to standard Danish *damp* (with stød) and *dampe* (without stød);
¹sɛi 'tough' vs. ²sɛi 'say'
corresponding to standard Danish *sej* (with stød) and *sige* (without stød);
¹po:d 'gate' vs. ²po:d 'paw'
corresponding to standard Danish *port* (with stød) and *pote* (without stød);
¹u:ə 'out' · vs. ²u:ə 'outside'
corresponding to standard Danish *ud* (with stød) and *ude* (without stød).

Compounds can have either of the two pitch accents, but there are also examples of compounds where each of the two parts has its own pitch accent. Examples (from East Slesvig) of the three accentual types of compounds (Ejskjær 1990: 63) are: ¹kosdol̯ 'cowshed' (corresponding to standard Danish *kostald* ['kʰo(:ˀ)ˌsdalˀ], with stød), ²pan̯:ka:x 'pancake' (corresponding to standard Danish *pandekage* ['pʰanəˌkʰæːɪ̯ə], without stød), and, with two tonal accents in the same word, ²vin̯ə²ka:m 'window sills' (corresponding to standard Danish *vindueskarme* ['venduskʰaːmə], without stød).

1.2.2 *Zealand: Short-vowel-stød*

Inger Ejskjær is the expert on short-vowel-stød in Zealandic (e.g., 1969, 1990). She gives the following summary (1990: 51): "The synchronic condition for the occurrence of the short vowel stød is: disyllabic word with a short vowel followed by a plosive or a voiceless fricative (or a combination of these consonants) and an unstressed syllable". As an example, she points to ku'sginj *kusken* 'coachman', where the apostrophe (') indicates stød. Here *kusken* is a sg.def form (the sg.indef would not have this short-vowel-stød). Ejskær then goes on to formulate the rule that in the "definite singular of nouns [...] the stød occurs mechanically", e.g., hɛsd *hest* 'horse' but hɛ'sdinj *hesten* 'the horse'. Although Ejskjær (1969) attempted to give detailed rules for the distribution of vowel-stød — combining

---

3. In general, I quote the transcriptions in the sources indicated; only words in Modern Standard Danish are given in IPA, in distinct pronunciation, in a semi-narrow transcription, as used in Basbøll (2005).

phonological and morphological criteria, she concludes that the stød is often "facultative (obeying usage)" (1990:52), which is a glossematic formulation, corresponding to 'contrastive' in modern terminology.

1.2.3 West Jutland "stød"

In West Jutland — as also in the north-western part of Funen — there is, in addition to the standard Danish stød, an extra stød-like phenomenon called West Jutland "stød". It occurs in essentially mirror-image conditions when compared to standard Danish stød, i.e., very roughly, on short vowels followed by plosives *p, t, k*, and in words historically derived from words with accent 2 (i.e., old disyllables, not monosyllables), e.g., with examples from Ejskjær (1990:65):

ven̨d   corresponding to standard Danish *vent!* 'wait!' [ˈvɛnˀd̨] (with stød)
ven̨ˀd   corresponding to standard Danish *vente* '(to) wait' [ˈvɛnd̨ə] (without stød)
ven̨də   corresponding to standard Danish *vinter* 'winter' [ˈvɛnˀd̥ɐ] (with stød)
ven̨ˀdə corresponding to standard Danish *venter* 'waits' [ˈvɛnd̨ɐ] (without stød)

The main problem with the understanding of West Jutland "stød" — whose normal pronunciation is a glottal stop (which is not the case for stød in Modern Standard Danish) — is its historical and systematic relation to the Danish stød, including the interaction between segmental and prosodic aspects (e.g., the role of preglottalization/preaspiration of plosives); see the discussion in the conclusion of Ringgaard 1960 (pp. 91–110), the pioneering work on West Jutland "stød"; also, Grønnum (2023:304–306) gives a detailed discussion and evaluation of Ringgaard's experiments. In the present context of word-prosodic complexity, West Jutland "stød" is, basically, an extra layer in addition to standard stød.

1.3 Danish dialects in the typology of word-prosodic complexity

The following examples (some of which were discussed in Section 1.2) illustrate the great variation in word-prosodic complexity displayed by Danish dialects:

Degree 2: Lolland-Falster and Bornholm: no word-prosodic complexity (in our sense) apart from compound stress (as in German, Section 1.1.2).

Degree 3: Ærø (south of Funen, Kroman 1947): accent 1 and 2 are distinguished only by pitch, with no further phonological complications; whole compounds have one pitch accent (as against parts of Southern Jutland, Bjerrum 1948, see Section 1.2.1); this is reminiscent of standard Swedish and Norwegian (Section 1.1.3).

Degree 4: much of Jutland: in complexity basically like Standard Danish (Section 1.1.4).[4]

Degree 5: areas with West Jutland "stød" — if this is considered an accent (Section 1.2.3) — and parts of Zealand with short-vowel-stød in addition to standard stød, and extra stød in second parts of compounds (Section 1.2.2).

2. Mora counting in North Germanic, and the Danish stød

2.1 Trubetzkoy's moraic account of Danish stød

Trubetzkoy (1935, 1939) considered the mora, and mora counting, to be essential in the analysis of the Danish stød. In his chapter on 'Prosodische Eigenschaften' [prosodic properties] (1935: 21–29), he introduces a distinction between 'Silbensprachen' [syllable languages] and 'Morensprachen' [mora languages] (p. 25). He classifies Danish (p. 28) as a mora language with 'Stimmbruchgegensatz' [lit. voice break opposition]. In Trubetzkoy's (posthumous) main work *Grundzüge der Phonologie* (1939), he classifies the Danish stød in the section on 'Silbe und More; phonologische Auffassung der Quantität' [syllable and mora; phonological interpretation of quantity]. He claims (p. 173) that Danish stød cuts the long 'Silbenträger' [lit. 'syllable bearer', cf. 'nucleus' in modern terminology] into two parts. Trubetzkoy also claims that the (tautosyllabic) combination short vowel + sonorant, as well as a diphthong, can be the bearer of stød, just like a long vowel, which he interprets as a tautosyllabic sequence of two short vowels.

Trubetzkoy's pioneering moraic interpretation of the Danish stød is the point of departure for my phonological interpretation: Morae (μ) constitute a well-defined measure of syllable weight so that syllables, in languages with mora counting, can have 1 or 2 or 3 morae, but nothing in between. Modern Standard Danish is a language that allows mono- and bimoraic syllables, the latter only in stressed syllables (i.e., with primary or secondary stress, in a system with three degrees of stress, disregarding emphasis). Trubetzkoy expected a close correspondence between his phonological analysis and the phonetic (e.g., durational) facts. As far as the Danish stød is concerned, we know today — see Grønnum's (2023: 325–328)

---

4. The dialect examples from East Slesvig (Section 1.2.1) could be placed between degrees 3 and 4: Like Swedish and Norwegian (degree 3), but unlike standard Danish (degree 4), there are no restrictions of sonority; like standard Danish, however, but unlike Swedish and Norwegian, there can be 2 accents in one word.

recent survey of the phonetics of stød — that a moraic analysis can only be upheld in a more abstract sense: Danish is not a typical mora-language.[5] But in my view, Danish is a mora counting language in a sense to be specified in Section 2.2.

2.2 Mora counting in Danish vs. Swedish and Norwegian

The following moraic analysis of Modern Danish, viewed in contrast to the other Scandinavian languages, departs from two premises: (i) mora counting follows the phonological analysis going back to Trubetzkoy (Section 2.1), where stød is, phonologically, a signal of the second mora of its syllable (this is my formulation, not Trubetzkoy's); but (ii) this does not entail any phonetic claims regarding duration, position of particular Fo-movements, etc., thus, it is a phonological, not a phonetic, analysis.[6]

Concerning mora counting, the crucial difference between modern Danish and the other modern Scandinavian languages is — in my interpretation — the role of sonority: only sonorants can be moraic in Danish, whereas obstruents can be moraic in the other Scandinavian languages, e.g., in words like Swedish *hoppa* 'hop, vb.' with a geminate — and ambisyllabic — /p/. The contrast between 2μ- and 1μ-syllables in Danish thus lies in the sonorant material after the vowel: either a sonorant consonant or vowel length in 2μ-syllables,[7] unstressed syllables always being monomoraic.

The claim that only sonorants can be moraic in Danish — in contradistinction to Swedish and Norwegian, for example — is controversial. Thus, Vázquez-Larruscaín (2021) gives a detailed comparison between what he calls the "Light Syllable Model" = "LS-Model" (my model for the moraic structure of Modern Danish) and the "Heavy Syllable Model" = "HS-Model" (the model he favours where also obstruents can be moraic). I cannot discuss this paper here in any detail,[8] but only make my own position clear. There are many aspects of the very complicated phonological machinery he employs that I cannot accept (or

---

5. In Basbøll (1998:73) I said that a typological investigation should decide whether Danish is a typical mora-language, an atypical mora-language, or not at all a mora-language. Of course, this also depends on the definition of 'mora'.

6. The moraic analysis of Danish stød to follow has a predecessor in the concept of phonological weight, see Basbøll (1988).

7. A (phonologically) long vowel is here interpreted as /V:/, not as /VV/ as Trubetzkoy did (Section 2.1).

8. Vázquez-Larruscaín in most respects is well acquainted with my model, but sometimes misrepresents it: On p. 49, he talks as if stød-basis consists of two different conditions — stress and bimoricity — but this is for me only one condition since all unstressed syllables are, necessarily, monomoraic in my model.

discuss here), but my essential arguments for claiming that obstruents cannot be moraic in Modern Danish are: (i) phonetically and surface-phonologically, obstruents (O) in the position /VOv/ (where 'V' is short and stressed and 'v' unstressed) are short in Danish but (auditively and measurably) long in Swedish and Norwegian; (ii) Vázquez-Larruscaín's morphological arguments concerning the /t/-morpheme for ADJ neuter indef., e.g., *dybt* 'deep', *rigt* 'rich' (p. 47f) are only valid for some of the examples: e.g., *rigt* can also (commonly) be pronounced with stød, and also, e.g., the adjectives *vag* 'vague', *lav* 'low', and many others, always keep their stød in the neuter when the /t/-morpheme is added. The correct generalization lies, in my analysis, in positions in the word-structure, i.e., in morphology, not phonology (see Section 2.3.3). Thus, I do not accept the argument that all Scandinavian languages should ideally be identical as far as mora-structure is concerned, but I take the opposite position, viz. that the difference between them allows us to formulate important principles for diachronic developments.

We have seen (in Section 1.1) that there is a systematic difference — in what I called degrees of word-prosodic complexity — between Swedish and Norwegian (1.1.3) and Danish (1.1.4). From the perspective of the present section, Modern Swedish and Norwegian have moraic obstruents and can be characterized as having only bimoraic stressed syllables (e.g., both *mann* 'man' with long /n/ and *katt* 'cat' with long /t/ are bimoraic); Modern Danish, on the other hand, has both bimoraic and monomoraic stressed syllables (e.g., *mand* 'man' ['man$^?$] is bimoraic, but *kat* 'cat' ['k^{h}aḍ] is monomoraic). This analysis is well suited to account for diachronic developments. Old Norse, for example, had — in contradistinction to the Modern Scandinavian Languages — not only mono- and bimoraic syllables, but also trimoraic syllables, and all three types were found in both stressed and unstressed syllables.

This typological difference between Old Norse and Modern Swedish/Norwegian can be seen as a parallel to that between Latin and Italian; and, furthermore, the typological difference between Latin and Modern French, is in a sense a parallel to that between Old Norse and Modern Danish. These typological relations between genetically related languages invite a diachronic interpretation: the different moraic structures mirror, ex hypothesi, the diachronic evolution. This is summarized in the final table of Basbøll (1989, which also covers Finnish and Estonian); the fundamental idea is closely related to Vennemann's (1988) analysis of the evolution from Latin to the Romance languages, within his whole framework of *Preferential Laws*.

In Table 1, moraic and syllabic structures in Scandinavian languages are presented. Only the main forms of the modern languages are included; thus, Danish dialects with tonal word accents (in Southern Jutland and in southern parts of the Funish area), or without word accent (cf. Section 1.3), are not considered here. Similarly, Swedish and Norwegian dialects without tonal word accents, or with different quantity systems (cf. Kristoffersen 1999, 2011) are not included. /:/ is moraic in all the languages of the table.

Table 1. Morae in North Germanic. Table 1 is taken from a part of Table 10.1 from Basbøll (2005: 292), based upon the final table of Basbøll (1989). 'σ' stands for syllable, 'μ' for mora, and '<>' indicates Extra-Prosodicity (Section 2.3.2)

	Old Norse	(Modern) Icelandic/ Swedish/Norwegian	(Modern) Danish
number of μ in stressed (primary or secondary) σ	1 or 2 or 3	2	1 or 2
number of μ in unstressed σ	1 or 2 or 3	1	1
which types of C can be moraic?	all	all	only sonorants
word-final moraic C?	yes	yes	only in stød-syllables
length of word-final V under stress?	only /V:/	only /V:/	mostly /V:/ (in some "small" and/or foreign words /V<:>/, e.g. vi 'we')

2.3 The Non-Stød Model

Basbøll (2005, 2008) claims that stød is evidence of the second mora of a syllable. This entails that bimoraic syllables — by default — have stød. There must then be principles to account for bimoraic syllables that do not have stød. Basbøll (since 2008) has proposed two kinds of such principles, viz. Lexical Non-Stød (Section 2.3.2), and Word-structure Non-Stød (Section 2.3.3). But first I must present the relevant division of the Danish vocabulary with respect to the stød-system (Section 2.3.1).

2.3.1 Division of the Danish vocabulary with respect to stød

There is a binary division between those words (or groups of words) that are fully integrated in the stød system, and those that are not. I call the former part of the vocabulary nativelike (with respect to stød), and the latter non-nativelike.

The nativelike part typically includes loans from German (the composer *Händel* is in Danish pronounced ['hɛnˀdəl] with stød), Latin (*insula* 'island' is in Danish pronounced ['enˀsula] with stød), and Greek (*androgyn* 'androgynous' is in Danish pronounced [anɖʁoˈɡ̊yːˀn] with stød). The non-nativelike part typically includes recent loans and names from English (e.g., *Clinton*, in Danish pronounced ['kʰḷentˢʌn], PL *Clinton'er* ['kʰḷen̩tˢʌnˀɐ] with stød) and French (*Juppé*, in Danish pronounced [ɕy'pʰe], PL *Juppé'er* [ɕy'pʰeːˀɐ] with stød), and other foreign names; but in the course of time, words can change in this respect. This division of the Danish vocabulary is illustrated in Table 2.

Table 2. Lexical Non-Stød and Word-structure Non-Stød, cross-classified with respect to the nativelike and non-nativelike part of the vocabulary (from Basbøll 2012:34)

The Stød System:	Lexical Non-Stød	Word-structure Non-Stød
Nativelike:	marked	unmarked
Non-nativelike:	general	irrelevant

The moraic structure is only established when the lexeme is combined with inflectional endings, not before (see Section 2.3.2).[9]

2.3.2 *Lexical Non-Stød: Extra-prosodicity and lexical specification {–stød}*

Extra-Prosodicity (= extra-metricality) means that the final segment (including ':') of the lexeme is disregarded when the moraic structure is being decided. Thus, if a lexeme is specified for Lexical Non-Stød, the segment in the first non-V position after a short full vowel in the final syllable of the lexeme will be extra-prosodic, but this Extra-Prosodicity has consequences for the moraic structure of the word only if the lexeme is word-final (i.e., when no inflectional endings follow).

Extra-Prosodicity[10] is relevant in cases like these, but only when the lexeme is word-final: *ven* 'friend' ['vɛn] /vɛ<n>/, *hul* 'hole' ['hɔl] /hɔ<l>/, *mad* 'food' ['mað] /ma<ð>/ as against those cases: *pen* 'pen' ['pʰɛnˀ] /pɛn/, *hal* 'hall' ['halˀ] /hal/. In the following cases the final consonant will be extra-prosodic and thus non-moraic in any case, since trimoraic syllables are not permitted in (modern) Danish: *hals* 'neck' ['halˀs] /hals/, *pæn* 'nice' ['pʰɛːˀn] /pɛn/ (see Table 1).

Now I turn to Lexical specification {–stød}. There are cases of aberrant Non-Stød in lexemes which cannot be accounted for by Extra-Prosodicity since the syllables in question are undoubtedly bimoraic, e.g., English loan words like *team* ['tˢiːm] /tiːm/, *cool* ['kʰuːl] /kuːl/, *drink* ['d̥ʁɛŋ̊] /drenk/. Since stød is evidence of the second mora of its syllable, the lexical feature {–stød} is associated with the sec-

---

9. In Section 2 I only consider simplex words, i.e., words with only one root, with or without inflectional endings, and without derivatives; see, e.g., Basbøll (2005: 464–513, 2014) for complex words (compounds, derivatives, and combinations thereof).

10. In the phonemic notation (within / ... /), Extra-Prosodicity is indicated by angled brackets, moricity by underlining.

ond mora, the locus for stød (this is a phonological statement, articulatorily and acoustically the situation is more complex, see Grønnum 2023 with references). Native words like *tørst* 'thirst' ['t^{s}œ̞sd̥], *torsk* 'cod' ['t^{s}ɒːsg̊] and *barsk* 'harsh' ['b̥ɑːsg̊] are also bimoraic but lack stød, due to their evolution from short vowels followed by a voiceless /r/ [ʁ̥] (in the 19th century), i.e., they have only become bimoraic, and thus eligible for stød, quite recently (see further Section 3.3).

How is the priority decided between the two mechanisms of Lexical Non-Stød, viz. Extra-Prosodicity and Lexical specification {–stød}? Extra-Prosodicity must take priority over Lexical specification {–stød} since Extra-Prosodicity is a precondition for establishing the moraic structure, whereas Lexical specification {–stød} presupposes exactly this moraic structure since it affects the second mora. It is methodologically satisfying that the model enforces a priority, according to the principle of Ockham's razor. Furthermore, this priority inherent in the system is in accord with general linguistic arguments, since Extra-Prosodicity has wide applicability, whereas Lexical specification {–stød} accounts for exceptions. But the latter still makes predictions in my system, viz. the non-participation in morphological stød-alternations.

The principles of Lexical Non-Stød — encompassing Extra-Prosodicity and Lexical specification {–stød} — predict the moraic structure of modern Danish. Thus, in the non-nativelike vocabulary (e.g., French and English loans, foreign names, etc., see Section 2.3.1), Lexical Non-Stød accounts for ad hoc plural formations like *Clinton'er* ['kʰlenˌt^{s}ʌn^{ʔ}ɐ] with stød (from *Clinton* ['kʰlent^{s}ʌn] without stød), *Zola'er* [soˈlæːˀɐ] with stød (from *Zola* [soˈla] without stød, with a short a-vowel with a different quality than the long /aː/ in the plural form), and *Saddam'er* [saˈd̥ɑm^{ʔ}ɐ] with stød (from *Saddam* [saˈd̥ɑm] without stød). In all these cases, stød in the plural forms is a consequence of the moraic structure (which is itself predicted by the principles of Lexical Non-Stød).

2.3.3 *Word-structure Non-Stød*

This section contains a condensed version of my recent presentation of Word-structure Non-Stød in Basbøll (2023b). In a recent publication on the stød (Basbøll 2022b), I have formulated the procedure for grammaticalization of suffix positions in the form of a diagram with only yes/no-questions (binary choices), amounting to five *stages*[11] (as I now call them) shown in Figure 1:

---

11. The term *stages* has some dynamic associations, in this respect — not unintentionally — resembling my earlier use of "productivity degrees."

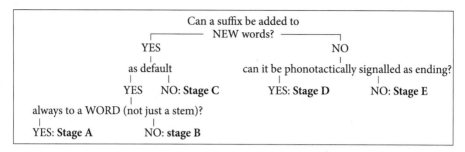

Figure 1. Diagram illustrating five *stages* A–E of suffix integration into a stem. This can apply to languages with suffixes in general. Reproduced from Basbøll (2022b)

Hypothesis on grammaticalization (phonologization) of word positions in modern Danish: The two extreme stages of Figure 1 (A vs. E) are distinguished, the three middle ones are not (B+C+D). Result: there must then be, according to the Non-Stød Model, three different suffix positions relevant for phonology and prosodic morphology in Danish word-structure: P1, P2 and P3 (plus P4 for enclitics, beyond the word proper), see Figure 2. A is *least* and E *most integrated* in the stem.

Minimum integration (position P3, stage A): PL *-er* (*bil-er* 'cars' ['b̥iːʔlɐ])
Medium integration (position P2):
    INF *-e* (*elsk-e* 'love' ['ɛlsg̊ə], stage B),[12]
    PL "Ø" (no ending): (*mus* 'mice' ['muːʔs], stage C)
    PAST *-te* (*men-te* 'meant' ['meːnd̥ə], stage D)[13]
Maximum integration (position P1, stage E): PL *-e* (*dreng-e* 'boys' ['d̥ʁæŋə])

The resulting word-structure in Danish, according to the Non-Stød Model, with positions derived from the arguments above, is shown in Figure 2.

Departing from the Danish word-structure shown in Figure 2, and employing its terminology of min-word, basic word and max-word, there are two subcases of Word-structure Non-Stød:

Subcase (1) the *penultimate syllable* of the min-word has Non-Stød
Subcase (2) a *monosyllabic* stem before a syllable has Non-Stød (domain: basic word)

---

12. Verb stems are sometimes neither normal syllables nor normal words (e.g., *krydr-e* 'spice, season' ['kʰʁydʁɐ], *cykl-e* 'go by bike' ['syg̊lə]).
13. The long vowel of *mente* ['meːnd̥ə] is a phonotactic signal that the form is polymorphemic (since vowels are short before clusters like *nt* in monomorphemic words).

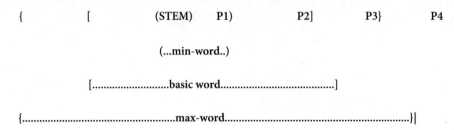

Figure 2. From Basbøll (2014: 22), cf. Basbøll (2005: 379). Word-structure in Danish based upon the three positions for the integration of suffixes. P4 is the position of the enclitic for POSS (|s|). P4 is beyond the scope for prosodic or other phonological rules

Here follow two examples illustrating Danish word-structures; the relevant part for each subcase is in bold:[14]

Subcase (1): *husenes* {[(*hus e*)] *ne*} *s* 'house+PL+DEF+POSS'
[ˈhuːsənəs] or [ˈhuːsn̥əs]   **P1:** *e*   **P3:** *ne*   **P4:** *s*
Subcase (2): *mentes* {[(*men*) *te*] *s* } 'mean+PAST+PASS'
[ˈmeːnd̥əs]   **P2:** *te*   **P3:** *s*

3. Some consequences of the proposals

In this section, I first discuss some synchronic consequences of the analyses of Sections 1 and 2, particularly related to stød-issues, viz. why all word-final long vowels in Modern Danish have stød (Section 3.1), and whether stød can be a boundary signal or function as a grammaticalized morpheme for the singular of nouns (Section 3.2). Then I turn to diachronic consequences of the analyses, viz. the evolution of /r/ in moricity, from an obstruent to a sonorant (Section 3.3, cf. Section 2.3.2), and finally I consider Jørgen Rischel's proposals on the origin of stød, seen in relation to the Non-Stød Model (Section 3.4).

---

14. Subcase (1): The PL form of the noun *hus* is a min-word since the PL suffix (an e-schwa) is not the default (which is a-schwa), and is therefore on P1, thus *hus* in PL has Non-Stød; subcase (2): the past tense of *mene* is a basic word consisting of the stem *(men)* followed by the past tense suffix *te* on P2, a verb position, therefore Non-Stød.

3.1 Why do we not find word-final long stød-less vowels in Modern Danish?

I shall now address a well-known problem in Danish phonology that has not been satisfactorily explained until now: the banning of final long stød-less vowels in Danish words.[15] According to the framework of the present paper, it will be explained by the interaction of the principles of Lexical Non-Stød (presupposing mora counting, see Section 2.3.2), viz. that the Non-Stød Model only allows one theoretically possible way a long vowel could end up without stød in this position:

a. Word-structure Non-Stød cannot apply in a word-final syllable since neither subcase (1) nor subcase (2) of Section 2.3.3 covers a final syllable, therefore
b. lack of stød in a word-final long vowel could only be due to Lexical Non-Stød, but
c. neither of the two mechanisms of Lexical Non-Stød, viz. Extra-Prosodicity and Lexical specification {–stød}, can provide a long stød-less final vowel, for the following reason:
d. Extra-Prosodicity is relevant, thus Lexical specification {–stød} is not allowed to apply (according to the logic expounded in Section 2.3.2).
e. Extra-Prosodicity is therefore the only possibility, but it will yield a short vowel (the case of *pâté, nu, vi*, etc., see Section 2.3.2).

This prediction is interesting since the ban on long stød-less word-final vowels is a robust observation but has not yet been accounted for in any principled way, to my knowledge.

3.2 Stød and non-stød as signals for morpheme boundaries or grammaticalized morphemes for number?

Can stød and/or non-stød reasonably be claimed to function as a signal for morpheme boundaries? To shed light on this question, I illustrate stød-variation at morpheme boundaries in Standard Danish with five different nouns, representing different stress- and stød-patterns, in SG.INDEF, SG.DEF, PL.INDEF, and PL.DEF, see Table 3. For each example, I give the phonetic transcriptions (IPA) of the four forms, as well as an analysis where each form is rendered, in orthography, with a

---

15. A possible counterexample is *zoo*, short-form for *zoologisk have* 'zoological garden'. The standard dictionary of modern Danish (*Den Danske Ordbog*, vol. 6: 570) gives the possibilities ['soːˀ] or ['soː], i.e., a long vowel with or without stød, respectively. The most comprehensive pronunciation dictionary (Brink et al. 1991: 1552) gives only the form with stød, but another pronunciation dictionary (Hansen 1990: 753) gives only the stød-less form (['soː] might be a reduced form of disyllabic ['soo], as in the prefix *zoo-*). It is well known that interjections and exclamations like *åh* ['ɔ(ː)], *ih* ['iː(ː)] are general violations of this structural principle.

separation of the morphemes by '+' and with indication of stød (by ' ? '); this stød-symbol could just as well be placed after the '+'. The left column specifies whether the lexeme is nativelike ('natlike') or not ('non-nat') (Section 2.3.1), and whether or not Lexical Non-Stød (LNS, Section 2.3.2) applies.

Table 3. Five different nouns in four forms. For each form a phonetic transcription (IPA) is given, together with a morphological analysis in orthographic forms where '+' separates morphemes, and with the following prosodic information added: '?' representing stød, ':' vowel length, and ''' primary stress

Lexeme	SG.INDEF	SG.DEF	PL.INDEF	PL.DEF
dreng 'boy'	['dʁæŋˀ]	['dʁæŋˀən]	['dʁæŋə]	['dʁæŋənə]
(natlike)	'dreng	'dreng?+en	'dreng+e	'dreng+e+ne
sofa 'sofa'	['so:fa]	['so:fæ:ˀən]	['so:fæ:ˀɐ]	['so:fæ:ˀɐnə]
(natlike)	'so:fa	'so:fa:?+en	'so:fa:?+er	'so:fa:?+er+ne
tal 'number'	['tˢal]	['tˢalˀəð]	['tˢal]	['tˢalˀənə]
LNS (natlike)	'tal	'tal?+et	'tal	'tal?+ene
bon 'voucher'	['b̥ʌŋ]	['b̥ʌŋˀən]	['b̥ʌŋˀɐ]	['b̥ʌŋˀɐnə]
LNS (non-nat)	'bon	'bon?+en	'bon?+er	'bon?+er+ne
paté 'pâté'	[pʰaˈtˢe]	[pʰaˈtˢe:ˀən]	[pʰaˈtˢe:ˀɐ]	[pʰaˈtˢe:ˀɐnə]
LNS (non-nat)	pa'te	pa'te:?+en	pa'te:?+er	pa'te:?+er+ne

The examples demonstrate that for many nouns, both stød and non-stød can occur at (word-internal) morpheme boundaries — whereas for many other nouns, stød occurs in all these four inflectional forms, e.g., *hal* 'hall' ['halˀ], SG.DEF ['halˀən], PL.INDEF ['halˀɐ], PL.DEF ['halˀɐnə]. In some other nouns with a bimoraic (final) syllable, such as the English loan word *mail* ['mɛɪl], there is non-stød in all the four forms: SG.DEF ['mɛɪlən], PL indef. ['mɛɪls], PL.DEF ['mɛɪlsənə] (the PL forms also occur without [s]).

The complex picture above now leads us to the second part of the question of this section, viz. whether stød and non-stød can be considered grammaticalized morphemes of number for nouns.

In an interesting new neurolinguistic study on the stød, by Hjortdal, Frid & Roll (2022) — most of which is beyond the scope of the present paper — the authors formulate a strong hypothesis that is relevant in our context of stød-variations at morphological boundaries. In their Section 3 they present a "Behavioural and event-related potential experiment" where the stimuli are "80 monosyllabic nouns, all of which can be pluralized with the suffix -*e*", i.e., schwa, half of which have stød-basis (in my terminology they are bimoraic), half of which do not (they are monomoraic). In the "General discussion" (Section 4), the authors suggest that "stød and non-stød are becoming grammaticalized as morphemes for singular and plural nouns respectively", and they repeat that statement in the "Conclusion" (Section 5). In the context of the present paper, the problem with this bold suggestion is that the stimuli used represent only one type of singular-plural variation (of nouns) with respect to stød, and that there are several others — all four logically possible combinations of stød/non-stød and singular/plural are found — some even more productive than the type investigated by Hjortdal et al. (2022); this is amply demonstrated in Basbøll (2005) and in Basbøll, Kjærbæk & Lambertsen (2011), among other works.

Even if we would accept this hypothesis with the restriction that it only applies to nouns having schwa (*-e*) as plural ending, not to plural formation generally, we would encounter a further problem: should we then posit the 'opposite' solution to the most productive noun plural pattern,[16] viz. that non-stød is grammaticalized as a morpheme for SG and stød for PL (for nouns such as SG *øl* 'beer' ['øl] without stød, *øller* 'beers, bottles of beer' ['ølˀɐ] with stød)? And what about noun plural patterns with no stød change in those four forms (such as *hal* 'hall' ['halˀ] with stød and *mail* ['mɛɪl] without stød mentioned above in 3.2)? In my view, all this makes the authors' hypothesis highly improbable.

3.3 A diachronic perspective: The evolution of Danish /r/ from obstruent to sonorant and its consequences for stød

The proposed principles for mora counting also applied in the 19th century, as in the following type of example, resulting in stød-changes in the 19th and 20th centuries when the moraic structure was changed in syllables with a short vowel followed by /r/ that had primary or secondary stress:

Diachronic stage (i): /r/ in the position between a stressed short vowel and /p t k/ was aspirated — or /p t k/ were pre-aspirated — causing /r/ to be voiceless (thus, an obstruent) and consequently non-moraic, therefore no stød (e.g., *styrk!* 'strengthen!' ['sd̥yʁ̥g̊]).
Diachronic stage (ii): /r/ is turned into a glide [ɐ], thus a sonorant and therefore moraic (Section 2.2), e.g., *tørst* 'thirst' ['tˢœɐ̯sd̥]; the glide [ɐ] can be assimilated to a neighbouring [ɒ] or [ɑ], as in *torsk* 'cod' ['tˢɒːsg̊] and *barsk* 'harsh' ['b̥ɑːsg̊] (Section 2.3.2).

---

16. Speakers of standard Danish demonstrate that they have internalized this pattern when they encounter and think up examples ad-hoc (e.g., said by a schoolteacher) like "for mange *som'er*" 'too many [instances of the relative pronoun] *som*', pronounced as PL ['sʌmˀɐ] with stød and SG ['sʌm] without stød.

Diachronic stage (iii): in the final stage, stød on the glide [ɐ̯] — and on its assimilation products [ɒː] and [ɑː] — is possible and may occur.

In several types that can be defined by a combination of phonological and morphological criteria, stød is now entering forms that previously (in the 19th century and earlier) had a voiceless and thus non-moraic /r/, e.g., imperatives (such as *styrt!* 'rush!' ['sd̥yɐ̯(ˀ)d̥], *mærk!* 'notice!' ['mæɐ̯(ˀ)ɡ̊] and *styrk!* ['sd̥yɐ̯(ˀ)ɡ̊]) and derivations with *-sel* (such as *færdsel* 'traffic' ['fæɐ̯(ˀ)səl], derived from the verb *færdes* ['fæɐ̯d̥əs] as in *færdes frit* 'move freely' ['fæɐ̯d̥əs 'fʁid̥]). How far this evolution will continue, we do not know today, but it has not ended yet.

3.4 Rischel (2001) on the origin of stød, seen in relation to the Non-Stød Model

Jørgen Rischel in his small but important semi-published paper (in Danish) on the origin of stød (2001) presents a specific hypothesis on how the interaction of the sonority hierarchy and a moraic analysis of stød can account for some decisive differences in laryngealization between different Danish dialects, and in particular for the development of stød (see also Rischel 2008 for his general "Unified Theory of Nordic *i*-Umlaut, Syncope, and Stød" in which morae play a crucial role). Most arguments in this section have been given previously in Basbøll (2008, 2022a). Rischel (2001: 21–22) says (in my translation):

> One can operate with a sonority hierarchy where V = vowel is most sonorous, then comes G = glide (2nd component of diphthongs), then S = postvocalic consonantal sonorant, and last, O = final obstruent ('+ENCL' is meant to symbolize enclitically added sonorous material), see Table 4:

Table 4. Sonority types according to Rischel (2001: 21)

I	II	III	IV
V:	VG	VS	V**
VSS	VSO		VO
VG/VS+ENCL*			

* Expansions of type II and type III
** only 'small words' with vowel shortening and the type *vindu* 'window')

Rischel exemplifies as follows, see Table 5:

Table 5. Rischel's exemplification (2001: 21–22) of the sonority types of Table 4

I	II	III	IV
V: $bo^?$, $lå^?s$ 'live', 'lock'	VG $vej(^?)$, tov 'road', 'rope'	VS (et) hul, $skud$ '(a) hole', 'shot, sb.'	V vi (pron.) 'we'
VSS $hal^?m$ 'straw'	VSO $kal(^?)k$ 'chalk'		VO kat 'cat'
VG/VS+ENCL $vej^?en$, $hul^?let$ 'the road', 'the hole'			

Type I–II may be called 'sonority-heavy', type III–IV 'sonority-light'.

Rischel's hierarchy is founded on several criteria. V, G, S and O are segment types with descending sonority in the usual sense with one reservation: V and G are both vocoids (= phonetic vowels), and it is controversial whether the difference between them, viz. syllabicity, is a part of the sonority hierarchy (see Basbøll 2005: 173–187). The four sonority types of Table 4 must be defined by a combination of criteria (I return to enclisis below in this section):

a. sonority length of the rhyme: VSS (type I) > VSO (type II); VS (type III) > VO (type IV)
b. length of the rhyme: VSO (type II) > VS (type III);
c. inherent sonority of segments: VG (type II) > VS (type III)

All three criteria are phonological, length being measured in number of phonological segments, i.e. (morpho)phonemes. What unites them is the relation between sonority and mora counting, a relation that varies geographically and diachronically, according to Rischel's typology.

Rischel continues his argument:

> Now, in the different regional variants the threshold for laryngealisation applies to different steps of the sonority hierarchy (according to modern linguistic jargon, this is a question of 'parameter setting'), see Table 6:

Table 6. Laryngealisation in Danish according to Rischel (2001: 22)

Southern Danish (and Scandinavian more generally):	no laryngealisation
Northern West Danish:	laryngealisation in type I
Northern East Danish:	laryngealisation in type I and II, but variation in the type VG ($vej^?$, tov 'street, rope')

[...]

> The normal case is that type III did not in itself get any stød, because an unchecked sonorant did not count as a mora and thus did not have the word-final falling tone. Nor did type IV get the stød. But stød as a rule occurred in three situations where the number of morae increased, viz. before *enclisis* (see type I) with the result *(et) tal*, but *tal²let*; in *hiatus* in the type *vindu²et*; and in *imperative* with the result *tæl²!* Within the framework of my [Rischel's] hypothesis, the most plausible explanation would be that, in exactly these three situations, the total word contour with a strongly falling tone has been concentrated in a syllable that would otherwise be too light; the function is as if the sonorant occurred in checked position finally in the syllable.

The three situations mentioned by Rischel to be accounted for specifically "where the number of morae increased" and where we get stød, will be analysed here according to the Non-Stød Model:

i. *enclisis*, i.e., stød in *tallet* 'the number' ['tˢal²əð], cf. SG.INDEF *tal* 'number' [tˢal] without stød. The lexeme is marked with Lexical Non-Stød, but this has no implication for the moraic structure of the word when the suffix for SG.DEF is added (the /l/ of *tal* then not being word-final), so the syllable is therefore bimoraic, hence stød (2.3.2);

ii. *hiatus*, i.e., stød in *vinduet* 'the window' ['ven̯du:²əð], cf. SG.INDEF *vindu* ['ven̯du] without stød. There is, as for all other word-final full vowels, a final vowel length marker /:/ in *vindu*. The final syllable being unstressed in the base form (SG.INDEF), this /:/ must be extra-prosodic (i.e., /<:>/, 2.3.2), yielding a short vowel in word-final position. When the DEF ending is added, /:/ is not word-final (no Extra-Prosodicity effect), and the syllable is therefore bimoraic, hence stød (and secondary stress);

iii. *imperative*, i.e., stød in *tæl!* 'count!' [tˢɛl²], cf. infinitive *tælle* ['tˢɛlə]. The verb is the only word class where the stem is not always a basic word (2.2), and in the Non-Stød Model the basic form of the verb is the infinitive. The inf. — which never ends in a consonant — can therefore not be subject to Extra-Prosodicity-effects, hence an imperative cannot be a VS-syllable with no stød. The imperatives *spil!* ['sb̥el²], *skod!* ['sg̥ʌð²], from infinitive *spille* 'play' ['sb̥elə], *skodde* 'butt (of a cigarette)' ['sg̥ʌðə], illustrate this when compared to the corresponding nouns *spil* 'play' ['sb̥el], *skod* 'butt' ['sg̥ʌð] which do not have stød; in the Non-Stød Model this is due to Extra-Prosodicity.

Rischel (2001: 23–24) concludes his discussion, with formulations I wholeheartedly endorse, as follows:

One can also change the point of departure for the description of Nordic accentuation and say – perhaps more à la Basbøll – that *lack of stød, respectively accent 2,
in polysyllables with heavy (in Danish: sonority-heavy) full syllables indicates that
phonologically, the words concerned are prototypical, completely streamlined poly-
syllabic words which also morphologically-lexically are perceived as well integrated
unified wholes.* Then we just have to add a paragraph about why we lack stød in
Danish also in monosyllables of the type *ven*.

The last paragraph asked for by Rischel (2001) is easily formulated in terms of
Extra-Prosodicity within my framework.

4. Conclusion: Hans Frede Nielsen and Jørgen Rischel on language history

In the "Introductory Prayer" to his *magnum opus* on the Early Runic Language of
Scandinavia, Hans Frede Nielsen (2000:19) refers to "a thought-provoking paper
entitled 'Har forskningen i dansk sproghistorie en fremtid?' [Does Research in
Danish Language History Have a Future?] by Jørgen Rischel [1996]". On pp. 29–30
(in the section "New vistas: Rischel and van Coetsem"), Hans Frede Nielsen
(2000) discusses several aspects of Rischel (1996), starting "Without questioning
the fundamental importance of the classical comparative method to historical linguistics, Rischel [...] emphasizes the need for a methodological and theoretical
reorientation in Danish language history (1996:14–15)." And Hans Frede Nielsen
(2000:30) ends by stating that "Finally, the time has come, according to Rischel
(1996:16), for a reanalysis of the traditional philological accounts of the sound
history (of Danish) in the light of modern linguistic theory." In my admiration of
both these great scholars – Jørgen Rischel (1934–2007) and Hans Frede Nielsen
(1943–2021) – I have tried to show in this paper how two theoretical models, viz. a
complexity scale for word prosody, and a model for moraic structure, can provide
insight on different aspects of North Germanic, synchronically and diachronically.

Acknowledgements

The present paper is based upon two recent presentations (unpublished), viz. "Prosodic variation across morpheme boundaries in Scandinavian (mostly Danish): exploring a hierarchy of
word-prosodic complexity", given at the Morphology-Workshop at the Austrian Academy of
Sciences (ÖAW), May 12, 2022; and "How to count morae in Danish: diachronic aspects of
the stød", presented at the 25th International Conference of Historical Linguistics, University
of Oxford, August 1–5, 2022. I am highly indebted to Nina Grønnum for numerous very

useful comments on the manuscript, mainly — but not only — concerning style, to Christian Becker-Christensen for a thorough critical reading and much good advice, and to three anonymous reviewers for many insightful and constructive comments and suggestions that certainly improved the paper.

References

Basbøll, H. 1988. The Modern Danish stød and phonological weight. In P.-M. Bertinetto & M. Loporcaro (eds.), *Certamen Phonologicum. Papers from the 1987 Cortona Phonology Meeting*, 119–152. Torino: Rosenberg & Sellier.

Basbøll, H. 1989. Phonological weight and Italian raddoppiamento fonosintattico. *Rivista di Linguistica = Italian Journal of Linguistics* 1. 5–31.

Basbøll, H. 1998. Nyt om stødet i moderne rigsdansk — om samspillet mellem lydstruktur og ordgrammatik. *Danske Studier 1998*, 33–86. Copenhagen: Reitzel.

Basbøll, H. 2005. *The phonology of Danish*. Oxford: Oxford University Press.

Basbøll, H. 2008. Stød, diachrony and the non-stød model. *North-Western European Language Evolution* 54/55. 147–189.

Basbøll, H. 2012. Monosyllables and prosody: The sonority syllable meets the word. In Th. Stolz, N. Nau & C. Stroh (eds.), *Monosyllables: From phonology to typology*, 13–41. Berlin: Akademie Verlag.

Basbøll, H. 2014. Danish stød as evidence for grammaticalization of suffixal positions in word structure. *Acta Linguistica Hafniensia* 46. 137–158.

Basbøll, H. 2022a. Danish Stød in the light of morae, the weight law and sonority (strength): A personal view. In P. Noël Aziz Hanna & L.C. Smith (eds.), *Linguistic preferences [Festschrift Theo Vennemann]*, 143–170. Berlin: De Gruyter.

Basbøll, H. 2022b. Morphology-prosody interaction in Danish — challenging the foundation of word-structure in Basbøll's Non-Stød Model (2008). Poster presented at the *22nd International Morphology Meeting*, Budapest, September 1–4, 2022.

Basbøll, H. 2023a. Phonology and phonetics, a recurrent theme in European structuralisms: The case of Otto Jespersen and André Martinet. In L. Cigana & F. Gregersen (eds.), *Structuralism as one — structuralism as many. Studies in structuralisms*. Scientia Danica, Series H, Humanistica. 8. Vol. 21, 317–364. Copenhagen: The Royal Danish Academy of Sciences and Letters.

Basbøll, H. 2023b. Herslund on Danish suprasegmentals: An appraisal and a comparison. In I. Baron & L. Lundquist (eds.), *Le génie des langues. In memory of Michael Herslund*, 544–559. Travaux du Cercle Linguistique de Copenhague vol. XXXVI.

Basbøll, H., L. Kjærbæk & C. Lambertsen. 2011. The Danish noun plural landscape. *Acta Linguistica Hafniensia* 43. 81–105.

Bjerrum, M. 1948. *Felstedmaalets tonale Accenter*. Aarhus: Universitetsforlaget i Aarhus. *Den Danske Ordbog*. http://ord-net.dk/ddo

Brink, L., J. Lund, S. Heger & J.N. Jørgensen. 1991. *Den store danske udtaleordbog*. Copenhagen: Munksgaard.

Den Danske Ordbog, vol. 6. 2005. Det Danske Sprog- og Litteraturselskab. Copenhagen: Gyldendal. http://ordnet.dk/ddo

Ejskjær, I. 1969. *Kortvokalstødet i sjællandsk.* Copenhagen: Akademisk Forlag.

Ejskjær, I. 1990. Stød and pitch accent in the Danish dialects. *Acta Linguistica Hafniensia* 22. 49–74.

Grønnum, N. 2023. Three quarters of a century of phonetic research on common Danish stød. *Nordic Journal of Linguistics* 46(3). 299–330.

Gårding, E. 1977. *The Scandinavian word accents.* Travaux de l'Institut de linguistique de Lund 11. Lund: Gleerup.

Hansen, P.M. 1990. *Dansk udtale.* Copenhagen: Gyldendal.

Haugen, E. 1967. On the rules of Norwegian tonality. *Language* 43. 185–202.

Haugen, E. 1976. *The Scandinavian languages.* London: Faber and Faber.

Hjortdal, A., J. Frid & M. Roll. 2022. Phonetic and phonological cues to prediction: Neurophysiology of Danish stød. *Journal of Phonetics* 94.

Jespersen, O. 1890. Danias lydskrift. *Dania* 1. 33–79.

Kristoffersen, G. 1999. Quantity in Norwegian syllable structure. In H. van der Hulst & N. Ritter (eds.), *The syllable: views and facts,* 631–650. Berlin: De Gruyter.

Kristoffersen, G. 2011. Quantity in Old Norse and modern peninsular North Germanic. *Journal of Comparative Germanic Linguistics* 14. 47–80.

Kroman, E. 1947. *Musikalsk Akcent i Dansk.* Copenhagen: Einar Munksgaard.

Nielsen, H.F. 2000. *The Early Runic language of Scandinavia. Studies in Germanic dialect geography.* Heidelberg: Winter.

Ringgaard, K. 1960. *Vestjysk stød.* Aarhus: Universitetsforlaget i Aarhus.

Ringgaard, K. 1973. *Danske dialekter. En kortfattet oversigt.* Copenhagen: Akademisk Forlag (1st edn. 1969).

Rischel, J. 1996. Har forskningen i dansk sproghistorie en fremtid? *Danske Studier* 91 [Universitetsjubilæets Danske Samfund 542]: 5–21.

Rischel, J. 2001. Om stødets opkomst. In J. Rischel & H. Basbøll (eds.), *Tre indlæg om stødet = Pluridicta* 38, 16–25. Department of Language and Communication, University of Southern Denmark, Odense.

Rischel, J. 2008. A unified theory of Nordic i-Umlaut, Syncope, and Stød. *North-Western European Language Evolution* 54/55. 191–235. Reprinted in Rischel, J. 2009. *Sound Structure in Language.* Ed. by N. Grønnum, F. Gregersen & H. Basbøll. Oxford: Oxford University Press.

Saussure, F. de. 1916. *Cours de linguistique générale.* Paris: Payot.

Trubetzkoy, N.S. 1935. *Anleitung zu phonologischen Beschreibungen.* Prague: Édition du Cercle linguistique de Prague.

Trubetzkoy, N.S. 1939. *Grundzüge der Phonologie = Travaux du Cercle linguistique de Prague* VII.

Vázquez-Larruscaín, M. 2021. Complementary length in Danish. Why not? In I. Youssef & M. Vázquez-Larruscaín (eds.), *Perspectives on Nordic Phonology: Selected papers from the Fifth Fonologi i Norden Meeting, University of South-Eastern Norway. Nordlyd* 45(1). 39–55.

Vennemann, Th. 1988. *Preference laws and syllable structure — and the explanation of sound change.* Berlin: De Gruyter.

The etymology of Old Frisian *ink* 'angry'

Rolf H. Bremmer Jr,[1,2] Sergio Neri[3,4] & Roland Schuhmann[5]
[1] Universiteit Leiden | [2] Fryske Akademy Leeuwarden | [3] Ludwig-Maximilians-Universität München | [4] Universität Basel | [5] Sächsische Akademie der Wissenschaften — Arbeitsstelle Jena

> The meaning of rarely attested Old Frisian *ink* 'angry' has never been contested in the history of Old Frisian lexicography. For its etymology, on the other hand, scholars have not yet been able to arrive at a satisfactory result. This contribution demonstrates that the adjective *ink* is related to Old Icelandic *økkr* 'lump, heavy clod; tumor, protuberance' and Modern Swedish *ink* 'blood lump, hemorrhoid (with horses)', reflexes of Proto-Germanic *enk^wa- 'swollen', related to Latin *inguen* 'groin, underbelly' and Greek ἀδήν 'gland, swelling', ultimately descending from Indo-European *h_1eng^w-ó-.

In human intercourse emotions sometimes run to such levels that an outburst eventually leads to legal action, today no less than in the medieval past, notably when anger is involved. The role of emotions, and anger in particular, in the medieval world has increasingly drawn scholarly attention, and the literature on the subject is vastly expanding. For medieval Frisia, too, the first exploratory steps have been made (Bremmer 2023). It appears that in Old Frisian the vocabulary for expressing the emotion of anger is larger than that of any other of the four basic emotions — fear, joy, grief. Words for anger include the adjectives *forbolgen* and *ovirbulgen* 'very angry' (past participles of otherwise unrecorded OFris. *belga* 'to swell'; anger increases your volume); *torn* 'anger' (derived from PGmc *$terana^n$* 'to tear'; anger tears you apart) with denominative *tornich* ADJ 'angry'; *hāst* 'precipitance; anger' (< PGmc *$haifsti$- 'violence, strife'; anger quickly leads to violence) and derivatives *hāste* ADJ 'violent; angry', *hāstich* ADJ 'idem'; *ire* ADJ 'angry' (< PGmc *$erzija$- 'gone astray'; anger makes you cross boundaries); *ink* ADJ

https://doi.org/10.1075/nss.34.04bre
Available under the CC BY-NC-ND 4.0 license. © 2025 John Benjamins Publishing Company

'angry'.[1] The etymology of most of these words is clear, but that of *ink* is still questioned. This contribution intends to settle that question.

The word *ink* 'angry' is remarkable in more than one respect. First of all, it only occurs — twice — in the Fivelgo Manuscript, so-called because it stems from the Frisian land of Fivelgo, situated north-east of the town of Groningen. This paper manuscript (Leeuwarden, Tresoar, R4), written in Old East Frisian in the second quarter of the fifteenth century after 1427, contains a number of texts that are also found in other manuscripts, which proved very helpful in establishing the meaning of *ink*. The first instance of the word occurs in one of the regulations of the *Synodical Law*:

(1)   Alsa thet is an vntyd vppehewen an paschamorn an a christusmorn in there
      tzurka, thet thi corpus dominj bretzen is an thi ompel stert is and thi prester
      bifuchten is to thes blodes vtrene, sa ister bretzen sacrilegium and emunitas;
      sa isti angel jnch.   (Buma & Ebel 1972: text VIII.29, line 4)
      'If turmoil is raised in a church on Easter morning or on Christmas morning,
      so that the *corpus Domini* is broken and the eucharistic chalice is toppled and
      the priest has been attacked until bleeding, then sacrilege has been committed
      and the immunity [of the church building] has been broken; then the angel is
      angry.'

The clause was copied and adapted to the local situation and dialect from an exemplar written in Old West Frisian. In the extant Old West Frisian redactions the last part of the clause reads: "so is di engel ire" (Buma & Ebel 1977: text IX.31, line 5); "soe is dy enghel ire" (Nijdam, Hallebeek and de Jong 2023: text XI.44, line 5); "so isti engel ire" (Sytzema 20: Apogr. 36r, line 6). From these text witnesses it can safely be concluded that *ire* = *ink* <jnch>. That *jnch* means 'angry' is also confirmed by a near-contemporary Low German translation of the Frisian text, which reads: "So is de engel Godis thoernich" ('Then the angel of God is wrathful'; Meijering & Nijdam 2018: 292, art. 31).

The other attestation of the word is found in a stipulation listed in the *Fivelgo Register of Compensations* which runs as follows:

(2)   Hwasa otherum ene bere deth mith egge ende mith orde, mith hasta hey ende
      mith jnxta mode: thio bote is bi xii scill.   (Buma & Ebel 1972: text XI.11, line 2)
      'If someone threatens another with (sword-)edge and (spear-)point, with a fren-
      zied mind and a very angry mood, the compensation is set at twelve shillings.'

---

1. For the etymologies of *hāst, ire*, and *ink*, see Faltings (2010: 250–252, 184, and 298); for the etymology of PGmc **haifsti-*, cf. Neri (2012: 20–21); for those of the other words, see, e.g., Kluge (2011), s.vv. *Balg* and *Zorn*.

The same clause in the *Hunsingo Register of Compensations* reads "mith hasta hei and bi ire mode" (Buma & Ebel 1969: text IX.16, line 2), which again strongly suggests that with *jnxta* we are dealing in the *Fivelgo Register* with a modifier denoting anger. In the latter case, however, the adjective is in the superlative degree, thus grammatically expressing the intensity of the emotion. A superlative in combination with *mode* is also used elsewhere; for example, in the bylaw of the town of Franeker, issued in 1417. There it is stipulated, amongst other things, that if someone hits another man with his fist or tears someone else's clothes apart "by irsten mode" ('in a very angry mood'), he forfeits, amongst other fines, a pound to the members of the town council (Sipma 1933:10, articles f; cf. art. h).

Lexicographers and translators have never hesitated in presenting the proper meaning of <jnch> and <jnxta>. The founder of modern Old Frisian lexicography, Karl Freiherr von Richthofen, does not yet mention the lexeme in his groundbreaking *Altfriesisches Wörterbuch* (1840), simply because he had been unable to use the texts of the Fivelgo Manuscript for his edition of *Friesische Rechtsquellen* (1840). The scoop was for Montanus de Haan Hettema, a lawyer with a great interest in medieval Frisian law. As such he had edited, if in a rather dilettante way, the texts of a number of medieval Frisian manuscripts, including that of the Fivelgo Manuscript, accompanied by a Dutch translation. Thus, the phrase "sa isti engel jnch" in passage (1) above is translated by de Haan Hettema as "dan is de engel gram" ('then the angel is angry'); he translated the relevant passage in (2) more or less adequately as "in drift en in arrenmoede" ('in temper and in desperation'; de Haan Hettema 1841:57 and 105, respectively). In a concise Old Frisian dictionary that he published towards the end of his life, de Haan Hettema glosses *jnch* as 'iratus, vertoornd' ('angered') and *jnxta* as 'iratus, vergramd' ('angered'), as if he were unaware of the superlative degree (de Haan Hettema 1874: cols. 288 and 294, respectively). In his concise Old Frisian dictionary, Holthausen (1925:54) entered the word as *jink* with the gloss 'erzürnt' ('angered').

The publication of a new edition of the Fivelgo Manuscript by Bo Sjölin in 1970 ushered in a new era for our problem. In the introduction Sjölin devotes a considerable part of his study of the language to a structuralist analysis of the writing system of the manuscript text. He is not concerned with paleography but with graphemology, dividing the graphemes into the subcategories of autographeme ('vowel') and syngrapheme ('consonant'). In Chapter 3.5.21 (p.78), Sjölin observes that <j> sometimes functions as an autographeme and sometimes as a syngrapheme. The former category is rarely attested: *j* 'you PL' 13x, *jn* 'in' 2x, *jnna* 'inside' 1x, *js* 'is' 1x (following a so-called *punctus* in the manuscript), in preposition; *knj* 'knee' 2x and *nj* 'nor' 1x, in postposition. Sjölin leaves unmentioned here that <j> for /i/ usually occurs when it preceded and occasionally when it followed

The etymology of old Frisian *ink* 'angry'   75

one or more minims.[2] The pronoun *j* 'you PL' would seem to be the exception here; in other Old East Frisian manuscripts it usually appears as *i*, a contraction of **jī* < WGmc **jīz*.

In his concordantic glossary to the Old Frisian texts in the Fivelgo Manuscript, Sjölin (1975:48) is the first to list the adjective as *ink*, again glossed as 'erzürnt'. Probably on this account, Hofmann, in his make-shift revision of Holthausen (1925), corrects Holthausen's *jink* to *ink*, while leaving the meaning unaltered (see Holzmann 1985: 54). Hofmann-Popkema (2008:246), finally, enter the adjective as *ink, inch*, as if they were unsure about the phonological status of the word.[3] Regarding the meaning, however, they remain confident and gloss the word as 'erzürnt, zornig'.

Lexicographers and translators appear to be in unison with respect to the meaning of <jnch, jnxta>; the voices of etymologists, on the other hand, turn out to be polyphonic. The first to venture an etymology was van Helten (1905:285). He suggested a link with OE *inca* 'vorwurf' ('reproach') and constructed a prototype **gi-inc* 'vorwurfsvoll' ('reproachful') to illustrate that link. The initial <j>, according to van Helten, with reference to his Old East Frisian grammar (1890:§ 90), is a spelling for *ji*, probably seen by van Helten as the palatalized result of the prefix **gi-*, the vowel of which was absorbed by the following *-i-* of *ink*. So actually, in van Helten's view *jnch* is an alternative spelling for *jinch*. For the final <ch> as a variant spelling for *c*, van Helten refers again to his grammar (§ 132, end), where he states that *ch* is a spelling variant of *c* (= [k], RHB) on the analogy of *gh* as a variant of the stop *g*.[4] What van Helten essentially meant to say was that the word was pronounced as [jɪŋk].

Van Helten's etymology was accepted by Ferdinand Holthausen (1909:149), with reference to his discussion of the etymology of OE *inca* (Holthausen 1907: 295). In the latter he stated that OE *inca* precisely corresponds to ON *ekki* 'Trauer, Betrübnis, Kummer' ('grief, sadness, sorrow'). In 1909 Holthausen added G *Unke*

---

2. In palaeography, a minim is a short, vertical down stroke used for the letters <i, m, n, u>. On <j> as an allograph of <i> in the immediate context of minims, see Derolez (2001:90). Whereas Sjölin subjected the Old Frisian texts of the Fivelgo Manuscript to a detailed — structuralist — analysis of its spelling system (pp.72–112), he remained almost completely silent on its palaeographical system (p.4). A palaeographical analysis of the script is therefore much needed.

3. As confirmed in a personal communication by Anne Popkema.

4. The convention of writing <h> after consonants, especially /t/ (cf. Bremmer 2017:13) and /k/, the latter indifferent whether realized as <c> or <k>, was adopted by Frisian scribes in all likelihood from Middle Low German, see Lasch (1914:§ 336; cf. van Helten 1890:§ 132 last paragraph). For <kh> = /k/ (rare in Old Frisian): <khinda> 'child GEN.PL', see Buma & Ebel (1965:§ 103). On the presence of Middle Low German in the Old Frisian texts of the Fivelgo Manuscript, see Bremmer (1996:9–10).

'fire-bellied toad' (L *bombina bombina*) as another cognate, so-called because of its mournful call.[5] Georg Walter (1910:23) also adopted van Helten's interpretation of *jnc = jinc* and posited a slightly more precise etymon: **gi-inkoz* — today the preferred notation is *-az* (NOM.SG.M) — related to OE *inca* 'reproach' and, with reference to Holthausen (1907), ON *ekke* 'schmerz' ('pain') < **inkon-* [sic]. Walter seems to have been unaware of Holthausen's 1909 linking OFris. *jinc* to OE *inc*. As is to be expected, Holthausen (1925) entered the adjective as *jink* and for its etymology referred to Walter (1911:23). Hofmann's 1985 revision of Holthausen (1925), finally, while correcting *jink* to *ink*, retained the reference to Walter's etymology.

More recently, *ink* 'angry' received renewed attention. First of all, it was extensively treated by Frank Heidermanns (1993:322) in his etymological dictionary of Germanic primary adjectives. Heidermanns' systematic presentation of the data is very helpful. First he presents the Germanic etymon: "(-)inka- (*e*-?) 'erzürnt' *V? (§ 59)". Question marks indicate uncertainty regarding the stem vowel and "*V?" suggests the possibility of the word being derived from a verb. In fact, it appears that an adjective is only attested for Old Frisian, and that in this *e*-grade form, it is isolated in Germanic. Its most closely related etymon would be **aikula-* (Heidermanns 1993:96–97), attested Old English *ācol* 'afraid' (see *DOE*, s.v.). Heidermanns (1993:322) also presents Holthausen's suggestion (1905:295) that OE *inca* (< PGmc **enka-*)[6] has a cognate in the *o*-grade in Danish and Norwegian *ank(e)* 'Unwille, Kummer, Klage, Seufzer, Beschwerde', but does not accept it. The stem of this Scandinavian lexeme is usually given as PGmc **ang-* (Falk-Torp 1903, s.v. *ank*), with different suffixes related to, e.g., Old Norse *angr* 'grief, sorrow' and OFris *ongost* 'fear' (cf. Heidermanns 1993:100–101; Faltings 2010:105–106).

The last time that someone attempted to etymologize OFris. *ink* was Volkert Faltings in his dictionary of Frisian adjectives (2010). This dictionary finds its origin in Faltings' growing frustration with Heidermanns' neglect of Frisian in his dictionary of Germanic adjectives (1993; cf. Faltings 1996). Indeed, one is struck by the abundance of new and relevant material that Faltings has managed to collect and analyze in his dictionary.[7] Faltings (2010:298) posits the Germanic etymon as "(-)inka- (*e*-?) 'erzürnt' *V/K?", which is almost the same as given by Heidermanns, except that Faltings adds K, to indicate that it is a primary adjec-

---

5. The oldest meaning of the German word was 'snake', though. On semantic and etymological details, see Neri (2016:237–239).

6. Actually, Holthausen (1905:295) does not give any reconstruction; the reconstruction was made by Heidermanns himself.

7. For supplementary remarks and additions, see Faltings (2012) and (2022). For reviews, see especially Liberman (2011; with a complete index of English words on pp.94–96); Popkema (2011); Århammar (2013).

tive, but originally part of a Germanic exocentric compound (G *Kompositum*). Faltings does not follow Heidermanns in connecting OFris. *ink* to PGmc *aikula-, but with Holthausen he links it to OE *inca* and ON *ekki*.[8] Further unambiguous derivation from an Indo-European root has remained unsuccessful, according to Faltings. Indeed, in the section "**Idg**" Faltings wonders whether to follow Heidermanns' suggestion that we have to do here with an old verbal adjective IE *ing-o-, provided that we are not dealing with an exocentric compound PGmc *ga-inka-, as claimed by Walter (1911:23). Or, Faltings wonders, must we even assume that the noun *inkan- 'resentment' has in predicative position been turned into an adjective? Suggestions and questions tumble on top of each other.

Well over a century, as this survey has shown, scholars have tried to find a proper etymology for OFris. *ink*, but without apparent success. One of the difficulties is clearly the initial vowel: Faltings' dictionary includes only one more adjective with *i*-: īd(a)la- (*ei*-?) 'wirkungslos' ('idle'), solely present in West Germanic and with no cognates outside Germanic. Perhaps, therefore, it is better to start from *e-. PGmc *enkᵂa- presents itself as a good possibility. It is the etymon for OIcel. *økkr* 'lump, heavy clod; tumor, protuberance' (Cleasby & Vígfusson 1957, s.v.). Ásgeir Blöndal Magnússon (1989:1221, s.v. *ökkur*) also mentions ModSwed. *ink* 'blood lump, hemorrhoid (with horses)'. The basic meaning of *enkᵂa- is 'swollen', the root of which is also present in, e.g., L *inguen* 'groin, underbelly' and Grk ἀδήν 'gland, swelling' (< IE *h₁n̥gʷ-én-, cf. Orel 2003:84, s.v. *enkwaz, and Neri [2019: 421, n. 16]). Semantically, it is a perfect fit for the emotion of anger. After all, anger makes you metaphorically increase in size, cf. "Jacob swelled with anger" (Genesis 31:36), an emotional experience that is also underlying the bahuvrihi compound OE *bolgenmod* 'enraged' (see *DOE*, s.v.) and the Old Frisian verbal adjectives *ovirbulgen* and *forbolgen*, mentioned at the beginning of this article. These past participles belong to an otherwise unattested strong verb OFris. *belga* < PGmc *belganⁿ 'to be or become angry' (< IE *bʰélǵʰ-e/o- 'to swell'),[9] related to PGmc *balg-i- m. '(leather) bag; bellows'.[10] In conclusion, then, the following reconstruction can be posited: IE *h₁engʷ-ó- (type *leubʰ-ó- 'lief, loved, desired, precious')[11] > PGmc *enkᵂa- 'swollen' > OFris. *ink* 'angry', substantivized as Swedish *ink* 'bloodlump, hemorrhoid' and Icel. *ökkur* 'swelling'

---

8. Holthausen's connection is also reported by Kroonen (2013:269), but without references.

9. For related forms in other Indo-European languages, see *LIV* (2001:73 –74) and Neri (2017:326–327).

10. For a discussion of metaphors related with anger, see, e.g., Lakoff and Kövesces (1987).

11. On this type of formation, see Nussbaum (2017:243–246); on this apophonic pattern in the Germanic substantives, see also Bammesberger (1990:59–62).

(< *'swollen body part' or similar).[12] This etymology gives a secure place within Germanic to a locally limited and, moreover, rarely attested Old Frisian adjective that, not wholly surprisingly perhaps, failed to live on after the Middle Ages.

The question could rightly be asked as to why IE *h_1eng^w-ó- > PGmc *enk^wa- 'swollen' did not lead to OFris. †*iunk* with labial mutation, as did, for example, OFris. *diunk(er)* 'dark', which is traditionally traced back to PGmc *$denk^wa$-.[13] It would seem that labial mutation in the prehistory of Old Frisian only occurred when *w* was preserved in a position that was not absolutely final. Besides *diunk*, there are further words that show the diphthongs /iū/ and /iu/ in the root. Three are not relevant here, because they contain inherited diphthongs. They are: *siūn*-'visible' in *siūn-līk* 'visible', **skiūw* 'shy, timid' (with various modern reflexes) and *triūwe* 'faithful' (cf. Faltings 2010: 451–453, 474–475, and 555–557, respectively). (1) Regarding *siūn-līk*, the immediately preceding form was **seuni-* < **sewni-* (cf. Goth *siuns* < **sewni-* < PGmc **seg^wni*-). (2) For **skiūw*, the preceding form was perhaps PGmc **skeuh^wa*-.[14] (3) Similarly, *triūwe* was preceded by WGmc **treuwa-* < PGmc **trewwa-*. In other forms, the mutating factor *u/w* did not appear in absolute final position in Proto-Frisian. This applies to words, such as OFris. *siugun* 'seven' < PFris. *sigun*, OFris. *niugen* 'nine' < PFris. **negun*, OFris. *thiukke* 'length and breadth' < PFris. **þikkwī̃*, OFris. *siunga* 'to sing' < PFris. **singwan* and WFris. *stjonke*, EFris. *stjúnk* 'to stink' < PFris. **stinkwan* (on these forms, see Hartmann 2020: 466). If we assume that OFris. *diunk* reflects a pre-form PGmc **denk^wija*- and not, as traditionally assumed, **denk^wa*-, then it is easier to account for apparent exceptions to the labial mutation rule such as OFris. *quik* (= /kwik/) 'alive' (and not †*kwiuk*) < PGmc **k^wik^wa*- (Neri 2017: 229–230), *ring* 'small, slight' (and not †*riung*) < PGmc **ring^wa*-[15] and *ink* itself, because it would imply that at the time of the labial mutation these forms had already lost their *w*-element, e.g., in the stem allomorph of the accusative singular:

	PGmc	*$k^wik^wa^n$: *$denk^wija^n$ >
(weakening of final *a^n*)	PFris.	*$kwikwə$: *$dinkwijə$ >

---

12. For the reflexes of the labiovelar phonemes in Proto-Germanic and in the Germanic daughter languages, see the bibliography in Kümmel (2007: 391–393). Further cognates are listed in Kroonen (2013: 270).

13. Cf. Bremmer (2009: §§ 51–53) and Hartmann (2020: 466) with further relevant examples of labial mutation.

14. Van der Sijs (2010), s.v. *schuw*, reconstructs **skeuh(w)a*-; Kluge/Seebold (2011) 'einzelheiten unklar' (s.v. *schiech*); *EWD* online s.v. *scheu*: '*skeuhwa-*'.

15. It is not necessary to assume, with Faltings (2010: 433), a loan-word from either Middle Low German or Middle Dutch.

(apocope of final *ə, weakening

of final *i, labial mutation)   Early OFris. *kwik   : *di^unkwə   >

(apocope of final *ə)   OFris.   quic   : diunk[16]

References

Árhammar, N. 2013. Review of Faltings (2010). In *Zeitschrift für Dialektologie und Linguistik* 80(1). 77–89.

Ásgeir Blöndal Magnússon. 1989. *Íslensk órðsifjabók*. Reykjavík: Orðabók Háskolans.

Bammesberger, A. 1990. *Die Morphologie des urgermanischen Nomens*. Heidelberg: Winter.

Bremmer Jr, R. H. 1996. Old Frisian Dialectology and the position of the Ommelanden. In Petersen & Nielsen (1996), 1–18.

Bremmer Jr, R. H. 2009. *An introduction to Old Frisian. History, grammar, reader, glossary*. Amsterdam: Benjamins.

Bremmer Jr, R. H. 2017. Language contact in medieval Frisia: Middle Low German spelling interferences in Old East Frisian manuscripts. In P. Lendinara et al. (eds.), *Le lingue del Mare del Nord/The North Sea languages*. Filologia Germanica–Germanic Philology 9. 1–18.

Bremmer Jr, R. H. 2023. 'In an overfurious mood': Emotion in medieval Frisian law and life. In E. Sebo, M. Firth & D. Anlezark (eds.), *Emotional alterity in the medieval North Sea world*, 95–124. London: Palgrave.

Buma, W. J. & W. Ebel. 1965. *Das Brokmer Recht*. Altfriesischen Rechtsquellen 2. Göttingen: Vandenhoeck & Ruprecht.

Buma, W. J. & W. Ebel. 1969. *Das Hunsigoer Recht*. Altfriesische Rechtsquellen 4. Göttingen: Vandenhoeck & Ruprecht.

Buma, W. J. & W. Ebel. 1972. *Das Fivelgoer Recht*. Altfriesische Rechtsquellen 5. Göttingen: Vandenhoeck & Ruprecht.

Derolez, A. 2001. *The palaeography of Gothic manuscript books. From the twelfth to the early sixteenth century*. Cambridge: Cambridge University Press.

de Haan Hettema, M. 1841. *Het Fivelingoër en Oldampster landregt, een oudfriesch handschrift uit de 14e eeuw, met eene vertaling*. Dokkum: Meidersma.

de Haan Hettema, M. 1874. *Idioticon Frisicum. Friesch–Latijnsch–Nederlandsch woordenboek, uit oude handschriften bijeenverzameld*. Leeuwarden: Hugo Suringar.

DOE = Dictionary of Old English A to I online. A. Cameron, A. Crandell Amos, A. diPaolo Healey et al. (eds.). Toronto: Dictionary of Old English Project, 2018.

EWD online = W. Pfeifer et al. *Etymologisches Wörterbuch des Deutschen* (1993). Digitalisierte und von W. Pfeifer überarbeitete Version im *Digitalen Wörterbuch der deutschen Sprache*. Retrieved February 2, 2023 from https://www.dwds.de

---

16. Sergio Neri is the main author of this paper from the second paragraph of page 78 to the end of page 79.

Falk, H. S. & A. Torp. 1903. *Norwegisch-dänisches etymologisches Wörterbuch*, 2 vols. Heidelberg: Winter.

Faltings, V. F. 1996. Bemerkungen und Nachträge zu Frank Heidermanns *Etymologischem Wörterbuch der germanischen Primäradjektive*. In Petersen & Nielsen (1996), 103–124.

Faltings, V. F. 2010. *Etymologisches Wörterbuch der friesischen Adjektiva*. Berlin: De Gruyter.

Faltings, V. F. 2012. Ergänzende Bemerkungen und Addenda zum *Etymologischen Wörterbuch der friesischen Adjektiva*. NOWELE 64/65. 117–138.

Faltings, V. F. 2022. Addenda zum *Etymologischen Wörterbuch der friesischen Adjektiva*, Teil II. In A. Walker et al. (eds.). *From West to North Frisia. A journey along the North Sea coast. Frisian studies in honour of Jarich Hoekstra*, 89–102. NOWELE Supplement Series 33. Amsterdam: Benjamins.

Hartmann, F. 2020. Old Frisian breaking and labial mutation revisited. *Amsterdamer Beiträge zur älteren Germanistik*. 80. 462–475.

Heidermanns, F. 1993. *Etymologisches Wörterbuch der germanischen Primäradjektiva*. Studia Linguistica Germanica 33. Berlin: De Gruyter.

van Helten, W. L. 1890. *Altostfriesische Grammatik*. Leeuwarden: Meijer.

van Helten, W. L. 1905. Zur altfriesischen Lexicologie. *Zeitschrift für deutsche Wortforschung* 7. 270–290.

Hofmann, D. & A. T. Popkema. 2008. *Altfriesisches Handwörterbuch*, with the assistance of Gisela Hofmann. Heidelberg: Winter.

Holthausen, F. 1905. Etymologien. *Indogermanische Forschungen* 17. 293–296.

Holthausen, F. 1909. Etymologien. *Indogermanische Forschungen* 25. 147–154.

Holthausen, F. 1925. *Altfriesisches Wörterbuch*. Heidelberg: Winter.

Holthausen, F. 1985. *Altfriesisches Wörterbuch*, 2nd, improved edn by D. Hofmann. Heidelberg: Winter.

Kluge, F. & E. Seebold. 2011. *Etymologisches Wörterbuch der deutschen Sprache*. 25th edn. Berlin: De Gruyter.

Kroonen, G. 2013. *Etymological Dictionary of Proto-Germanic*. Leiden: Brill.

Lakoff, G. & Z. Kövecses. 1987. The cognitive model of anger inherent in American English. In D. Holland & N. Quinn (eds.), *Cultural models in language and thought*, 195–221. Cambridge: Cambridge University Press.

Lasch, A. 1914. *Mittelniederdeutsche Grammatik*. Sammlung kurzer Grammatiken germanischen Dialekte 9. Halle/S.: Niemeyer.

Liberman, A. 2011. Review of Faltings (2010). In *Us Wurk* 60. 91–96.

LIV = Lexikon der indogermanischen Verben. Die Wurzeln und ihre Primärstammbildungen. H. Rix & M. J. Kümmel (eds.). 2nd, enlarged edition 2001. Wiesbaden: Reichert.

Meijering, H. D. & H. Nijdam (eds. & trans.). 2018. *'Wat is Recht?' De receptie van Oudfries recht in de Groninger Ommelanden in de 15e en 16e eeuw*. Gorredijk: Bornmeer.

Neri, S. 2012. "*asten*". In S. Neri & S. Ziegler, *"Horde Nöss". Etymologische Studien zu den Thüringer Dialekten*, 18–21. Bremen: Hempen.

Neri, S. 2016. *Unke*. In S. Neri, L. Sturm & S. Ziegler, *Von Hammeln, Leichen und Unken etymologische Studien zu den thüringischen Dialekten, Teil 2*, 235–239. Bremen: Hempen.

Neri, S. 2017. Wetter: *Etymologie und Lautgesetz* [2nd edn]. Perugia: Università degli Studi di Perugia. On-line publication: http://www.ctl.unipg.it/issues/CTL_14.pdf

Neri, S. 2019. Griechisch στάχυς und ἄσταχυς ‚Ähre'. In N.B. Guzzo & P. Taracha (eds.), *"And I knew twelve languages". A tribute to Massimo Poetto on the occasion of his 70th birthday*, 416–440. Warsaw: Agade Bis.

Nijdam, H., J. Hallebeek & H. de Jong (eds. and trans.). 2023. *Frisian Land Law: A critical edition and translation of the Freeska Landriucht*. Leiden: Brill.

Nussbaum, A.J. 2017. Agentive and other derivatives of 'τόμος-type' nouns. In C. le Feuvre, D. Petit & G.-J. Pinault (eds.), *Verbal adjectives and participles in Indo-European languages*, 233–266. Bremen: Hempen.

Orel, V.E. 2003. *A handbook of Germanic etymology*. Leiden: Brill.

Petersen, A. & H.F. Nielsen (eds.). 1996. *A Frisian and Germanic miscellany published in honour of Nils Århammar*. NOWELE 28/29.

Popkema, A.T. 2011. Review of Faltings (2010). In *It Beaken* 73. 188–193.

van der Sijs, N. et al. (eds.). 2010. *Etymologiebank*. https://etymologiebank.nl

Sipma, P. 1933. *Oudfriesche oorkonden*. Oudfriesche taal- en rechtsbronnen 2. The Hague: Nijhoff.

Sjölin, B. 1970–1975. *Die "Fivelgoer" Handschrift*. Vol. 1. *Einleitung und Text*. Vol. 2. *Namenregister, Glossar, synoptische Übersicht*. Oudfriese taal- en rechtsbronnen 12–13. The Hague: Nijhoff.

Sytzema, J. (ed.). 2012. *Diplomatic edition Codex Unia*. Retrieved 15 April, 2023 from https://tdb.fryske-akademy.eu/tdb/unia/Apografa.html

Walter, G. 1911. *Der Wortschatz des Altfriesischen. Eine wortgeographische Untersuchung*. Leipzig: Deichert.

Unity and diversity in basic color terms
A comparison of Germanic, Slavic, and Romance

Bernard Comrie
University of California, Santa Barbara

We develop a methodology for assessing the degree of unity versus diversity in Stage V basic color terms in Germanic, Romance, and Slavic languages. We make use of the Glottolog language list, with principled modifications, and of a notion "extended cognate set", which includes all terms derived from the same etymon plus genus-internal loans. We thus provide a solid underpinning of the intuitive observation that color term diversity is minimal in Germanic, extensive in Romance, and at an intermediate level in Slavic, as well as providing a methodology that should be more generally applicable in lexical typology.

1. Introduction and methodology

Table 1 provides a quick preliminary look at the basic color terms for the six Stage V basic color concepts (following Berlin & Kay 1969; Kay et al. 2009) in the three genera (following Dryer 1989: 267; 2013) Germanic, Slavic, and Romance.

Table 1 suggests a striking difference among the genera: Germanic languages are largely homogeneous in their lexical choices, with only English *black* immediately standing out as different. In Romance, by contrast, only GREEN is homogeneous. Slavic occupies an intermediate position.

But the preliminary impression gained from Table 1 is no more than that, and one can certainly point to problems in drawing conclusions from such a small uncontrolled set of data, e.g. the choice of Romance languages is heavily skewed toward the Iberian peninsula. A major aim of this article is to look more systematically at the Stage V basic color terms in the three genera in order to compare them on a more reliable basis. The initial impression will indeed remain valid, but in developing the methodology a number of general principles arise that should lead overall to a methodology that can be applied to other groups of languages in order to provide a broader cross-linguistic picture of variation among basic color terms. While some of the problems that arise may be specific to the languages con-

https://doi.org/10.1075/nss.34.05com
Available under the CC BY-NC-ND 4.0 license. © 2025 John Benjamins Publishing Company

Unity and diversity in basic color terms 83

Table 1. A preliminary list of Stage V basic color terms in Germanic, Slavic, and Romance languages

		BLACK	WHITE	RED	GREEN	YELLOW	BLUE
Germanic	Icelandic	svartur	hvítur	rauður	grænn	gulur	blár
	Danish	sort	hvid	rød	grøn	gul	blå
	German	schwarz	weiß	rot	grün	gelb	blau
	Dutch	zwart	wit	rood	groen	geel	blauw
	Frisian	swart	wyt	read	grien	giel	blau
	English	black	white	red	green	yellow	blue
Slavic	Russian	čërnyj	belyj	krasnyj	zelënyj	žëltyj	sinij
	Bulgarian	čeren	bjal	červen	zelen	žǎlt	sin
	Croatian	crn	bijel	crven	zelen	žut	plav
	Slovenian	črn	bel	rdeč	zelen	rumen	moder
	Czech	černý	bílý	červený	zelený	žlutý	modrý
	Polish	czarny	biały	czerwony	zielony	żółty	niebieski
Romance	Portuguese	preto	branco	vermelho	verde	amarelo	azul
	Spanish	negro	blanco	rojo	verde	amarillo	azul
	Catalan	negre	blanc	vermell	verd	groc	blau
	French	noir	blanc	rouge	vert	jaune	bleu
	Italian	nero	bianco	rosso	verde	giallo	blu
	Romanian	negru	alb	roșu	verde	galben	albastru

sidered here, and consideration of other languages might reveal other issues that need to be dealt with, nonetheless this article should be a useful starting point.

Before proceeding further, however, one might ask: Why is this an interesting enterprise, beyond investigating a particular empirical domain "because it's there"? An initial response might be that others have found this or similar questions interesting and have pointed to the lack of comparative material. Dworkin (2016a) asks whether the shifts in color terminology in Romance languages are typical of color terms cross-linguistically, without being able to point to an answer. His question is slightly different from ours — he is interested in language change, whereas we are interested in synchronically observable language variation — but clearly the two questions are related, since variation across languages in a given genus presupposes change, and change more often than not leads to diversification. The present article can therefore be seen as a first attempt to address Dworkin's concern. But more generally, much interest has arisen recently in the relative stability of different parts, grammatical and lexical, of different languages, with a major contribution being Dunn et al. (2011). While the present article tackles only a small corner of this overall enterprise, it is nonetheless hoped that it will point the way toward future extensions of such work.

1.1 Colors

This article is framed within the general approach to the cross-linguistic investigation of color terms developed by the World Color Survey (Berlin & Kay 1969; Kay et al. 2009), which we will henceforth refer to as BK/WCS. While much of the material and conclusions can readily be interpreted outside this framework, the framework nonetheless provides a coherent vantage point from which to investigate the phenomena of interest.

BK/WCS argues that there is a universal limited number of basic color concepts that moreover follow an evolutionary development. While the existence of basic color concepts, and their lexicalization as basic color terms in particular languages, has a long history predating BK/WCS, defining the notion has proven difficult. We follow Berlin & Kay (1969: 6–7) in working with a set of "ideal" operational criteria: (a) Basic color terms are monolexemic. (b) The signification of a basic color term is not included in that of any other color term — in practice, this has proven to be the most important criterion in our project. (c) The application of a basic color term is not restricted to a narrow class of objects. (d) Basic color terms are psychologically salient, e.g. (i) they tend to occur at the beginning of lists of color terms; (ii) they have stable reference across speakers and contexts; (iii) they occur in all idiolects (though our project throws some doubt on this in the case of languages that are undergoing lexical replacement for a particular basic color concept). Berlin & Kay further suggest the following criteria that can be applied in cases of remaining doubt: (e) All basic color terms should have the same distribution. (f) Color terms identical to the name of something having that color are suspect. (g) Recent foreign loans may be suspect. (h) Morphological complexity lowers the likelihood that a term is a basic color term. We have not made crucial use of (e)–(h), and indeed our database includes exceptions to (g), in particular in minority languages under heavy influence of a dominant language.

The BK/WCS approach also identifies a number of experiments (Berlin & Kay 1969: 8; Kay et al. 2009: 585–591) that can be conducted to establish a list of basic color terms: (a) Listing test: Subjects are asked to list color terms in their language, the hypothesis being that basic color terms will tend to be named early (see criterion (d-i) above). (b) Naming task. Subjects are presented with the Munsell color array, consisting of 320 color chips comprising 40 equally spaced hues and 8 degrees of brightness, plus 10 chips of neutral hue (i.e. the white —

gray — black scale); the array can be viewed at https://www1.icsi.berkeley.edu/wcs /images/jrus-20100531/wcs-chart-4x.png. For Berlin & Kay (1969), subjects were presented with a mounted array of the color chips and asked to trace the boundary of each relevant color term; for Kay et al. (2009) the chips were presented one by one in random order and the subject was asked to name the color of each chip. (c) Focus mapping task. Subjects are also asked to identify a focal value for each relevant color term. Focal values are more stable across languages than are boundaries and thus provide more reliable identification of basic color concepts.

Our interest in this article is those basic color concepts that have developed by Stage V, namely BLACK, WHITE, RED, GREEN, YELLOW, and BLUE. For the purposes of this article and the accompanying database, we write basic color concepts in capitals, though in this article — in contrast to the database — they will appear as small caps for esthetic reasons.

The languages we are interested in (for which see further Section 1.2) are languages of, or at least from, Europe, and have served communities familiar with these six basic color concepts, probably stably for a considerable length of time. Two caveats are, however, in order. First, it is important to bear in mind that what is stable is this set of basic color concepts; the basic color terms that are used to lexicalize them may well have changed over time, indeed such change is a prerequisite to the issue of unity and diversity. Second, Kristol (1980) shows that some regional Italo-Romance varieties lack a distinct term for BLUE, either using a paraphrase or subsuming this range under GREEN. None of our language reference varieties is of this type. However, the existence of such varieties indicates that BLUE is a principled limit to our investigation, i.e. we do not consider the Stage VI and VII basic color concepts in the BK/WCS framework (BROWN; GRAY, ORANGE, PINK, PURPLE); for some discussion of these terms, see Claassen (2021) and, specifically for Germanic, Majid et al. (2014). Likewise, we do not consider basic color terms beyond Stage VII that are found or have been claimed to exist in some languages, with perhaps the clearest case being Russian *goluboj* LIGHT BLUE (Davies & Corbett 1989), although a similar situation has been documented in Italian (Sandford 2012; Uusküla 2014); relevant cases are noted in the online database.

1.2 Languages and sources

The choice of the three genera Germanic, Romance, and Slavic is because each is "dense", in the sense of containing by any account at least a dozen languages, which gives ample room to study variation among languages. In addition, Germanic and Romance have roughly comparable time depths, although Slavic is younger, by a ratio of about 3 : 2. If Slavic turns out to have more variation than Germanic, as is indeed the case, then this is all the more striking given its shallower time depth.

The proposed research requires an independently compiled list of Germanic, Romance, and Slavic languages, in order to avoid biases imposed by the researcher (as is the case in Table 1). We have made use of the relevant language lists from Glottolog 4.4 (Hammarström et al. 2021), though with some principled exclusions, discussed below. The lists of languages, both included and excluded, are provided in the online database. In general, we have retained the Glottolog language names, though some have been changed for consistency or other reasons. It is important therefore to bear in mind the Glottolog code, which serves to identify each language uniquely and unequivocally within Glottolog. For comparison, the online database also gives ISO 639–3 codes, though in a few cases ISO languages and Glottolog languages do not coincide; in such cases, we have put in parentheses the ISO code for the closest ISO language, to the best of our ability.

First, we excluded extinct languages, using the Glottolog identification of a language as extinct. For many extinct languages, the relevant data are simply unavailable, i.e. either no color terms or only a subset of the six relevant color terms are known. But even for more broadly documented extinct languages, including those whose color systems have been investigated from the perspective of BK/WCS, and despite the significant advances that have been achieved by such research, it remains the case that the identification of basic color terms lacks the possibility of as solid a footing as is the case with living languages. With living languages that have not been investigated from a BK/WCS perspective, there is the possibility of carrying out such research. For extinct languages, there is not.

Second, we excluded Creole languages, which we identified on the basis of Eberhard et al. (2021). Glottolog's classification of Creoles with their lexifiers is not an uncontroversial position, since there is an alternative view going back at least to Thomason & Kaufman (1988) that Creoles do not have a single genealogical origin. Moreover, inclusion of Creoles would lead to excessive skewing in the choice of languages, given the large number of languages with English, French, Portuguese, Spanish, or Dutch as their lexifier. Finally, some Creole languages lack a distinct term for BLUE (Huber 2013), and thus fall outside the range of languages with Stage V basic color term systems that we are considering.

Third, we excluded Judeo-Italian, on the basis of the observations by Rubin (2017: 299–300) that Judeo-Italian "is not a single language", that "spoken Judeo-Italian dialects differ to varying degrees from those of their non-Jewish neighbors", and that "there is no single spoken Judeo-Italian dialect, rather one must speak of Judeo-Roman, Judeo-Piedmontese, Judeo-Venetian, Judeo-Livornese, etc." In addition, "most spoken Judeo-Italian varieties have become extinct". It is thus unclear to us which language, if any, would correspond to Glottolog's "Judeo-Italian".

Finally, we excluded Minderico, whose color vocabulary is formed largely by phrasal lexical substitution. While the expression for 'white', *brancano*, is much as in Portuguese (*branco*), and the word for 'black', *fusco*, shows a similar development of Latin *fuscus* 'dark-colored' as in Ladin, other color terms are all paraphrases of the type *a da borra de X* 'that of the color of X', e.g. *a da borra das gunilhas* 'red' (cf. *gunilha, gunilho* 'cherry') (Ferreira et al. 2015: s.vv. *branco, preto, vermelho, verde, amarelo, azul*). These potentially fail the monolexemic criterion for basic color terms in the BK/WCS approach.

This leaves 52 Germanic, 44 Romance, and 17 Slavic languages in our database.

For each language, we identified a reference variety and a source. The two procedures were often carried out simultaneously, since the choice of reference variety was often determined by the availability of sources. Except for languages lacking relevant internal variation, the choice of reference variety thus involves sampling. Where we selected a reference variety, the name of the reference variety is included in the online database after the language name and separated from it by a colon. In general, once we had selected a reference variety, we did not systematically research other varieties of the same language, though occasionally where we happened to have relevant knowledge such information is mentioned in passing. Where the reference variety itself shows minor dialect variation (e.g. dialectally conditioned phonetic variants), in general we cite only one form, occasionally more than one, with explanation in the Comment column of the database. The sampling aspect of our methodology needs to be emphasized; it was not our aim to include all possible lexicalizations of a given basic color term.

For each language, we have given an explicit source, even in cases where we might have used our own knowledge. In nearly every case this is a published source (including online publications). In each such case, the publication must be attributable, whether to an author or authors, a research institute, a community organization, etc. The only exception is Peruvian Amazonian Spanish, where we consulted with linguists familiar with the language.

Our sources vary considerably in nature. Some are studies following closely the research protocol of BK/WCS. Others are studies of color terms informed by BK/WCS, but not employing experimental methods. Others are, or include, lists of color terms, in sources ranging from academic articles to phrasebooks. We emphasize that such sources are valid for our purposes — a list of color terms in a phrasebook is in a sense a version of the Listing task mentioned in Section 1.1 — and are indeed more useful for present purposes than a more extensive source that lists many alternatives but without any indication of semantic, regional, stylistic, or other differences. The remaining sources are dictionaries. Where such dictionaries are searchable digitally and include translations from a meta-language, we proceeded primarily by searching on the meta-language terms.

With traditionally printed bilingual dictionaries that include translations from the meta-language to the target language, we used primarily these translations. With other traditionally printed dictionaries, we worked through the dictionary. Some traditional dialect dictionaries provide systematic inclusion only of lexical items that differ significantly from those of the standard language used as metalanguage, and in some such cases we included a term "ex silentio"; this is always indicated explicitly in the database. For some Germanic languages where we had access to only partially digitalized dictionaries, we included elements extracted from compounds; while certainly not methodologically foolproof, we are reasonably confident in the particular cases involved. In all cases where this was possible, as a check we also surveyed other sources for the same language, with emphasis on the same reference variety, including sources that would not in themselves meet our criteria (e.g. anonymous Wikipedia articles). Color terms are usually cited as given in our source (as indicated in the database), or in a standard transliteration where our source uses Cyrillic or Hebrew script; occasional departures from this practice for reasons of consistency, as well as remaining transcriptional inconsistencies that follow from this practice, are noted in the database. There will surely be some remaining errors of fact and questionable judgments. Where these do not involve assignment to a different extended cognate set (see Section 1.3), then the conclusions of the article will remain unchanged, although the database will need to be corrected. Where they do involve assignment to different extended cognate sets, then the quantitative analysis as summarized in Section 3 and detailed in the database will be affected, though we expect that the changes necessitated will be relatively small.

For the quantitative analysis, within each genus each language is assigned equal weight, without any consideration of possible hierarchical relations within the family tree. Although some subgroups are unproblematic, such as North Germanic or Balkan Romance, many other proposed subgroups, whether in Glottolog or elsewhere, are controversial and/or rest on weak evidence. For the problems that arise in the subgrouping of Germanic, see Nielsen (1989: 67–151). Using the database it is, of course, possible to test the outcome of any desired weighting.

1.3 Extended cognate sets

To assess the amount of variation within each basic color concept within each genus, we assign basic color terms to cognate sets, or rather extended cognate sets, the import of the added "extended" being discussed further below. The members of a given cognate set all derive from a single etymon, while members of different cognate sets derive from different etyma. In principle, the cognate sets could be given arbitrary labels, but both as a mnemonic device and to link our assignments to etymological research, we provide cognate set labels that explicitly identify the etyma, whether within the given genus (e.g. PGmc *swartaz within Germanic BLACK) or across genera in the case of loans (e.g. Gmc *blank* within Romance WHITE). Etyma are usually cited as complete words, except where we identify the cognate set by means of a stem to which derivational suffixes have been added in the individual languages, e.g. Lat. *alb-* for Romanian *albastru* BLUE, which thus contrasts with Lat. *albus* for Romanian *alb* WHITE.

The classification is thus dependent on etymological research, and while in general there is little controversy surrounding the cognate sets we appeal to, there are some exceptions, discussed in detail in Section 2, more specifically Section 2.1.5 for Germanic terms for YELLOW, and Section 2.2.3 for the Romance *r*-initial extended cognate sets for RED. On the positive side, given the extent of etymological research on the languages and genera under consideration, we can rely on etymologies rather than on look-alikes.

One departure from strict etymology is that we consider loans within a genus as if they were cognates, whence the use of the term "extended" cognate set. Thus, although the term for BLUE in our reference variety of Ladino, *blu*, is clearly a loan from some other Romance language, probably Italian, we nonetheless group it as part of the extended cognate set Gmc *blāo*. The reason for this is that it is often unclear whether a given term is a regular development from a given etymon or a loan from the regular development of that etymon in some other language in the same genus (cf. Dworkin 2016b: 583). Indeed, if an innovation is spreading across a landscape, it is not clear whether one can make even a principled distinction between treating this as a single innovation or as a series of local loans. Related to this, if two languages in a genus have both borrowed a word from another genus, we consider this as one extended cognate set, e.g. French *blanc* and Italian *bianco* WHITE both belong to the extended cognate set Gmc *blank*, even if one may be borrowed from a Franconian variety, the other from Langobardic. However, if a word is borrowed into a language of genus X from a language of genus Y, which in turn borrowed it from a language of genus X, this is considered a distinct extended etymological set, the crucial criterion being the crossing of a genus boundary; this concerns in particular English *blue*, which thus does not belong to the extended cognate set PGmc *blēwaz (Section 2.1.6).

Finally, we allow minor variants within an extended cognate set. First, this includes cases where different languages have generalized different morphophonological variants of a lexical item. Older West Germanic languages have alternation between presence versus absence of *w* in the declension of *w*-stem adjectives, e.g. Old English masculine singular nominative *geolu* 'yellow', genitive *geolwes*. Some languages have generalized the variant with a labial, e.g. German *gelb*, English *yellow*, others the variant without, e.g. Dutch *geel*. These are all considered a single extended cognate set. Second, we allow small semantic variation such as that between a basic adjective and its attenuative (diminutive), e.g. Latin *niger* 'black', *nigellus* 'blackish', reflexes of both of which constitute our extended cognate set Lat. *niger*. Romance languages point to several cases of a variable stem-final *e*, also found in Latin, with no clear consistent semantic value, as in our extended cognate set Lat. *russ(e)us* RED, which subsumes *russus* and *russeus* (Section 2.2.3). Particular cases are discussed as they occur, in the article text or in the online database.

In most cases, for a given basic color concept each language has just one basic color term (including minor variants). Occasionally, a language will have more than one basic color term, with the different terms assigned to different extended cognate sets; in such cases, the point for that basic color concept in that language is divided fractionally across the relevant extended cognate sets.

1.4 Database

The accompanying online database provides all the data on which the remainder of this article is based, with comments where applicable. On each sheet, column A provides a project-internal language identifier, column B the name of the language, where relevant followed by a colon and the name of the reference variety, column C the ISO 639–3 code, and column D the Glottolog code. On Sheet 1, columns E–J, one for each of the six basic color concepts, give the corresponding basic color term(s) for that language; column K identifies the type of source (1 BK/WCS experiment; 2 work informed by BK/WCS; T thematic vocabulary; a blank indicates some other type of source); column L provides any comments on the selection of basic color terms. On Sheet 2, column E gives bibliographic details of the source(s). Sheets 3–5, one each for Germanic, Romance, and Slavic, assign basic color terms to extended cognate sets in columns E ff. and provide the worked-out quantitative analysis. For Germanic and Romance, Sheets 3 (2) and 4 (2) provide comparable data given different choices of extended cognate set assignment, as described in Sections 2.1.5 and 2.2.3 below.

2. The data: Qualitative analysis

This section examines, for each genus, the extended cognate set for each of the Stage V color terms. Emphasis is on the establishment of extended cognate sets, although issues relating to language history are discussed in passing.

Unity and diversity in basic color terms   91

2.1 Germanic color terms

Germanic shows overall a high degree of homogeneity in its basic color terms.

2.1.1 *Germanic BLACK*

Reference varieties of nearly all languages have terms from the extended cognate set PGmc *swartaz 'black'. The exceptions are English and Scots, with reflexes of WGmc *blak-. In Old English, *sweart* was still the usual term for 'black', with *black* gradually taking over; for further details, see OED (s.v. *black* ADJ and N).

2.1.2 *Germanic WHITE*

Reference varieties of all languages have terms from the extended cognate set PGmc *hwītaz 'white'.

A historical account would also need to take account of Continental West Germanic *blank*, especially as it was sufficiently salient in the Germanic–Romance border area to be borrowed into Romance and become the most widespread extended cognate set for WHITE there (Section 2.2.2). Lexical items of this extended cognate set survive as color terms in some modern Germanic languages, e.g. Dutch *blank* 'pure white', but nowhere as basic color terms.

2.1.3 *Germanic RED*

Reference varieties of all languages have terms from the extended cognate set PGmc *raudaz 'red'.

2.1.4 *Germanic GREEN*

Reference varieties of all languages have terms from the extended cognate set PGmc *grōniz 'green'.

2.1.5 *Germanic YELLOW*

Reference varieties of all West Germanic languages have terms from the extended cognate set PWGmc (and probably PGmc) *gelwaz 'yellow'. Reference varieties of all North Germanic languages have derivatives of Old Norse *gulr*, whose relation to the West Germanic forms is unclear. According to the traditional analysis, the two would be reflexes of different morphophonological variants within Proto-Germanic; see Kroonen (2013: s.v. *gelwa- ~ *gulu-) for a recent explicit analysis along these lines. Crawford (2016), however, suggests that Old Norse *gulr* is rather an adjectival derivative from the Old Norse noun *gull* 'gold', which would make it a distinct lexical item and thus constituting a different extended cognate set. In our main quantitative analysis, we follow the traditional analysis that all forms in the Germanic reference varieties belong to the extended cognate set PGmc *gelwaz. However, we also include a computation treating the West and North Germanic forms as belonging to two different sets, for comparison.

Turning briefly to historical considerations, while reflexes of *gelwaz/gulr cover all present-day reference varieties as lexicalizations of YELLOW, in the past there has been at least competition from other lexical items, such as Old High German *falo* 'pale, yellow', Old English *fealo* 'fallow (color term), yellow'. Crawford (2016) suggests that *gulr* was not a basic color term in Old Norse. The modern convergence on reflexes of *gelwaz/gulr might thus reflect a remarkable innovatory centralizing tendency.

2.1.6 *Germanic BLUE*

Reference varieties of nearly all languages have terms from the extended cognate set PGmc *blēwaz 'blue'.

A clear exception is North Frisian, for which the reference variety (Moring) has *ween*, from Old Frisian *wêden* 'blue', an adjectival derivative of the noun meaning 'woad'. In fact, the two branches of North Frisian part company here, the Mainland dialects having reflexes of Old Frisian *wêden*, the Insular dialects terms from the extended cognate set PGmc *blēwaz (Sjölin 1969:43). Faltings (2020:141–142) argues that the West Frisian (Glottolog languages: Hindeloopen-Molkwerum Frisian, Schiermonnikoog Frisian, Terschelling Frisian, Western Frisian) and East Frisian (but not the Insular North Frisian) terms for BLUE are loans going back to Middle Dutch and Middle Low German respectively; since these are genus-internal loans, they are here, in keeping with the general methodology, still assigned to the extended cognate set PGmc *blēwaz.

English *blue*, despite its similarity to the terms in the other Germanic languages, is a loan from Norman French *blew*, itself a member of the Romance BLUE extended cognate set *blāo*, in turn borrowed from Continental West Germanic (see Section 2.2.6). For further details, see OED (s.v. *blue* ADJ and N).

2.1.7 *Germanic summary*

Germanic languages show little variation in choice of extended cognate set across languages, with the possible exception of YELLOW; the only clear exceptions are the English and Scots words for BLACK and the English, Scots, and (Mainland) North Frisian words for BLUE. At least some of the unity may reflect secondary homogenization. Significantly, this homogeneity applies equally to Germanic exclaves (Sprachinseln), despite pressure from the surrounding language. The imperviousness of exclaves to loans does not necessarily extend beyond Stage V terms, e.g. for BROWN Cimbrian has the Romance loan *kafèdat*.

2.2 Romance color terms

The account below has benefited immensely from the extensive overview provided by Kristol (1978).

2.2.1 *Romance BLACK*

Reference varieties of the vast majority of languages have terms from the extended cognate set Lat. *niger*. In Sardinian, the actual etymon is the attenuative *nigellus* 'blackish'.

The main focus of variation is the Iberian peninsula (without Catalan), from a local innovation *prẹtu, with a probable original sense 'dense' (cf. Spanish *prieto* 'dark; dense'), and a semantic development along the lines dense > dark > black. In our reference varieties this is the only basic term in Portuguese and Ladino, in the latter reflecting a genus-internal loan from Portuguese, while it stands alongside a term from the extended cognate set Lat. *niger* in Asturian and Extremaduran. The more detailed distribution, judging by other sources consulted informally, is surely more complex, though the distribution as shown in our database seems a reasonable reflection of the variation.

Terms of more restricted distribution are the following. (a) Aromanian has *laiŭ*, usually linked to Albanian *llaj* 'black (of cow or sheep)' and attributed to a Balkan substrate. (b) Standard Ladin has, in addition to a term from the extended cognate set Lat. *niger*, one from the extended cognate set Lat. *fuscus* 'dark-colored'. (c) Venetian has, in addition to a term from the extended cognate set Lat. *niger*, the term *mòro*, from Latin *Maurus* 'Moor; Moorish'.

2.2.2 *Romance WHITE*

Here there has been competition between two extended cognate sets, the inherited Lat. *albus* and the borrowed Gmc *blank*. Lat. *albus* is now very much confined to the periphery, in particular Balkan Romance and Romansh, though the spread to the Iberian peninsula beyond Catalan and to Sardinia is relatively recent.

2.2.3 *Romance RED*

If we leave aside for the moment most of the Iberian peninsula, Romansh, and Standard Ladin, then the basic color terms for RED across the Romance languages involve reflexes of three, possibly four, Latin terms with initial *r*: *rubeus* (originally referring to domestic animals), *russus, russeus*, and possibly *roseus* 'rose-colored' in Balkan Romance. The usual Latin term for 'red', *ruber*, leaves no direct descendants among Romance basic color terms.

Russus and *russeus* can be combined into a single extended cognate set Lat. *russ(e)us*. There is, moreover, complementary distribution between inherited reflexes of the two, with *russeus* in the Iberian peninsula except Catalan and in parts of eastern and southern Italy (e.g. Macerata ['ruʃʃu] RED (Raoul Zamponi, p.c.)), *russus* elsewhere, although Galician and Sardinian have no inherited reflexes of either (Kristol 1978: 156).

Latin *rubeus* and *russ(e)us* provide clearly distinct extended cognate sets, with many Romance languages having distinct formal and semantic reflexes of both, e.g., with the reflex of *rubeus* in each case first, Portuguese *ruivo* 'red (of hair)', *roxo* 'purple'; Spanish *rubio* 'fair (of complexion)', *rojo* RED; French *rouge* RED, *roux* 'russet; red (of hair)'.

Balkan Romance, e.g. Romanian *roşu*, presents a particular set of problems. The etymon Lat. *roseus* would account for both the stem vowel *o* and the following palatal consonant [ʃ] or [js], but is not otherwise attested as the etymon of the basic color term in Romance. Lat. *russeus* would likewise account for the palatal consonant, although the Balkan Romance stem vowel *o* is not the expected reflex of Latin *ŭ*, but cf. *roib* 'sorrel' < *rubeus*.

We now turn to non-*r*-initial Romance terms.

Lat. *coccinus* 'scarlet' provides lexicalizations in Romansh and Ladin (though some varieties of Ladin have terms from the extended cognate set Lat. *russ(e)us*).

The Iberian peninsula, this time including Catalan, provides substantial diversity in basic color terms for RED. In some cases, a given Glottolog language will include more than one extended cognate set. In some such cases, we have no basis not to include variants. In others, we have made a choice based on our source, though we acknowledge that in at least some such instances other sources might have let to a different outcome, and Galician provides an interesting problem case (see below). Terms from the extended cognate sets Lat *rubeus* and Lat. *russ(e)us* are rare in our reference varieties from the Iberian peninsula, restricted to Aragonese *royo* (< *rubeus*) and Spanish *rojo* (< *russeus*), although regional Western Catalan has *roig* (< *rubeus*) (*Catalan dictionary* 1993: s.v. *red*). Otherwise, two extended cognate sets equally provide the largest number of terms (Lat. *vermiculus*, Lat. *coloratus*), with Lat. *incarnatus* bringing up the rear.

Lat. *vermiculus*, the diminutive of *vermis* 'worm', appears in Late Latin with the sense 'scarlet'. It provides the basic term for RED in Portuguese, Galician, Catalan, and Mirandese. However, although now restricted to the Iberian peninsula, it was more widespread in the Middle Ages, providing the usual term for 'red' in French and Occitan, as well as Spanish — at least in the literary languages — (Kristol 1978: 159–160), subsequently dethroned by the extended cognate sets Lat. *rubeus* and Lat. *russeus* respectively.

Lat. *coloratus* 'colored' has reflexes with the specific meaning 'red' in a number of languages of or from the Iberian peninsula, in addition to being a widespread regional variant in varieties of Spanish. Our sources give it as the only term in Ladino, Extremaduran, and Fala, and as one alternative in Asturian and Peruvian Amazonian Spanish, although in the latter the status of *colorado* as a basic color term requires further investigation.

Finally, Lat. *incarnatus* 'incarnate' provides the other term for Asturian; as a color term its semantic origin is clearly 'flesh-colored' rather than theological.

The complications that can arise in the competition between different terms in languages of the Iberian peninsula can be seen in the study of Galician by Teixeira Moláns (2021:98), following BK/WCS methodology. All 24 subjects used *rojo/roxo*, a genus-internal loan from Spanish, while only two older subjects also used *vermello* (the term from our source) and *encarnado*.

2.2.4   *Romance* GREEN

Reference varieties of all languages have terms from the extended cognate set Lat. *viridis* 'green', although in Istro-Romanian this is alongside a loan from Slavic.

2.2.5   *Romance* YELLOW

Latin *galbinus* 'greenish yellow' provides by far the most successful extended cognate set in the Romance languages. It is the usual term in Balkan Romance, although Southern Istro-Romanian uses a Slavic loan, while Žejane Istro-Romanian retains the extended cognate set Lat. *galbinus*. Its occurrence in both Balkan Romance and the rest of Romance shows that the choice of *galbinus* was not restricted to a single locality, although in the rest of Romance it seems to have spread from Old French *jalne*, with Italian *giallo* probably a staging post for expansion through most of Italy, ultimately covering most of Romance except for the Iberian peninsula and some isolated pockets.

In the Iberian peninsula (without Catalan), a local formation *amarẹllu gives the extended cognate set used across all ten of our reference varieties. The form is derived from Latin *amarus* 'bitter', and has been variously attributed to bile or to a plant with a bitter taste.

Catalan and Sardinian use the extended cognate set Lat. *crocus*. In Classical Latin, *crocus* 'saffron' is a noun, with the derived adjective *croceus*, but the Romance forms suggest that in popular usage *crocus* was an adjective. The cognate *groc* is also the usual term for 'yellow' in the oldest Occitan, before being replaced by the spread of French *jaune* (Kristol 1978:297).

Romansh has a unique extended cognate set with *mellen*, possibly based on Lat. *mel* 'honey' (Wagner 1917:236–237).

Finally, three loans round out the list. Our reference variety for Istro-Romanian, Southern Istro-Romanian, has the Slavic loan *źut*; Žejane retains Romance *yåbir*. South Lucanian has a loan from Greek *kítrinos* 'yellow', and Standard Ladin has a loan from Germanic alongside *ÿal* from the extended cognate set Lat. *galbinus*. In addition, one of the Romansh traditional written languages, Lower Engadine, has the Germanic loan *gelg*, although this has not found its way into Rumantsch Grischun.

2.2.6 Romance BLUE

The extended cognate set Gmc *blāo* is by the most widespread among our reference varieties. This set is usually considered to be a loan from Continental West Germanic, although a minority opinion would derive the terms from Latin *flavus* 'yellow, pale yellow, blonde' (Woll 1975).

A first pass carried *blāo* reflexes from the Germanic-Romance border area as far as Catalonia and northern Italy, where such reflexes remain the basic color term. This first pass did give rise to an Italian reflex, *biavo*, with a variant *biado*, but this is not a basic color term in Italian, having rather the sense 'pale blue'. However, the Italian attenuative *biadetto* 'pale bluish' did make its way to Sardinia, where in the form *biaíttu* it is now the basic color term BLUE in all non-Campidanese varieties.

A second pass took the French version *bleu* [blø] into Italian, where it gave rise to two variants, *blu* and *blè*, which then spread to cover most of the rest of Italy (excluding Sardinia). Much of this second pass is quite recent, and Kristol (1979: 96–98) notes that in the 1920s the extended cognate set Gmc *blāo* was gradually moving southwards and replacing the extended cognate set Ital. *turchino* (see below), with *turchino* being stronger the further south one went, and often with discernible generation differences between older speakers with *turchino* and younger speakers with *blāo* reflexes. Ladino *blu*, in our reference variety, is a genus-internal loan, probably from Italian.

Among our reference varieties, cognates of Italian *turchino* are found in South Lucanian (data from the 1930s) and Corsican.

In the Iberian peninsula, with the exception of Catalan — for Ladino, see above — the universal term is *azul*, based originally on the noun meaning 'lapis lazuli' borrowed from Arabic, which is also the origin of Italian *azzurro* 'light blue'. The word seems to have been originally a noun, with its further development to an adjective internal to Romance. Campidanese Sardinian *asulu* is a loan from Spanish (Giacalone Ramat 1978: 171).

A number of terms are found in only one of our reference varieties. Romanian *albastru* is etymologically an attenuative of *alb* 'white'; it reflects a semantic shift paralleled in Slavic (Section 2.3.6). Megleno-Romanian *vínăt*, with cognates in some Romanian dialects, is from Latin *venetus* 'sea-blue'. Standard Ladin has *brum*, a semantic shift from the meaning 'brown'. Southern Istro-Romanian has the loan *blåv* from Croatian, while Žejane Istro-Romanian has a different loan from Croatian, *módər*. Finally, Aromanian has *njirlu*, which is usually derived from *njirlā* 'blackbird', from Latin *merula*, which assumes a semantic shift of the type black > dark blue > blue; there is also a Romanian dialectal form *mneru* BLUE from Latin *merus* 'pure', and one wonders if this may have played a role in the development of the Aromanian form.

2.2.7 *Romance summary*

Only GREEN shows near-exceptionless homogeneity in Romance, while RED, YELLOW, and BLUE show extensive variation. BLACK and WHITE occupy an intermediate position, the former as a result of conservatism (Lat. *niger*), the latter as a result of extensive spread of a loan (Gmc *blank*). The exclave Istro-Romanian has borrowed terms for YELLOW and BLUE from Slavic. Historically, Romance seems to have been characterized by "sweeps", extensive spreads of innovatory terms, with French and, to a lesser extent, Italian as points of origin.

2.3 Slavic color terms

Slavic languages show little variation in choice of extended cognate set across languages, with the notable exception of BLUE, where there is considerable heterogeneity.

2.3.1 *Slavic BLACK*

Reference varieties of all languages have terms from the extended cognate set PSl. *čĭrnŭ 'black'.

2.3.2 *Slavic WHITE*

Reference varieties of all languages have terms from the extended cognate set PSl. *bělŭ 'white'.

2.3.3 *Slavic RED*

Reference varieties of nearly all languages have terms from the extended cognate set PSl. *čĭrv(j)enŭ 'red', in Slavomolisano alongside the Romance loan *ros*.

Russian has famously replaced the inherited word with a word originally meaning 'beautiful', *krasnyj*.

Slovenian *rdeč* is etymologically the present participle of the verb *rdeti* 'to be(come) red, to blush' from PSl. *rŭdēti.

2.3.4 Slavic GREEN

Reference varieties of all languages have terms from the extended cognate set PSl. *zelenŭ 'green', in Slavomolisano alongside the Romance loan *vèrd*.

2.3.5 Slavic YELLOW

Reference varieties of nearly all languages have terms from the extended cognate set PSl. *žĭltŭ 'yellow', in Slavomolisano alongside the Romance loan *džal*.

Only Slovenian stands apart with *rumen*, from PSl. *ruměnŭ 'ruddy (of complexion), ruddy-complexioned'.

2.3.6 Slavic BLUE

In contrast to the other Stage V basic color terms in Slavic, there is no extended cognate set that can be identified as representing the Proto-Slavic term for 'blue'.

The extended cognate set found in the largest number of reference varieties is PSl. *modrŭ, but this form is completely absent from East Slavic.

Next comes PSl *sinjĭ, found as a Stage V basic color term in both East and South Slavic, although the word is also found in West Slavic as a non-basic color term, e.g. Czech *siný* 'light blue'.

PSl *polvŭ is found in two South Slavic reference varieties, although the cognate *płowy* is found in some dialects of Lower Sorbian, though not in our reference variety. The word occurs in other Slavic languages, but in senses like Russian *polovyj* 'pale yellow, sandy'. Presumably the semantic development was 'pale' > 'pale blue' > 'blue'; compare also the next paragraph and Romanian *albastru* BLUE in Section 2.2.6.

Attenuatives of PSl. *bělŭ 'white' are found in Slovak and Rusyn.

Finally, Polish alone has *niebieski*, a transparent adjectival derivative of the noun *niebo* 'sky'.

2.3.7 Slavic summary

Slavic languages are generally homogenous and have clear single Proto-Slavic etyma, except for BLUE. Otherwise, the Slovenian term for YELLOW and the Russian and Slovenian terms for RED depart from the usual Proto-Slavic etyma. The Slavic exclave Slavomolisano has borrowed terms for RED, GREEN, and YELLOW from Italian, although these are used alongside inherited terms rather than replacing them.

3. Quantitative analysis

In order to provide a measure of the amount of variation found within each basic color term within each genus, we make use of the statistical notion of entropy (h), more specifically the formula in (1).

(1) $h = -\Sigma(n \times \log_2(n))$

In this formula, n is the number of members of each extended cognate set expressed as a fraction of the total number of languages in that genus. The calculations are included in the online database, while the results are also presented in Table 2.

Table 2. Variation in basic color terms in Germanic, Romance, and Slavic

	BLACK	WHITE	RED	GREEN	YELLOW	BLUE	Median
Germanic	0.23518	0.00000	0.00000	0.00000	0.00000	0.37118	0.00000
Germanic-1	0.23518	0.00000	0.00000	0.00000	0.81128	0.37118	0.11759
Romance	0.68927	0.57463	1.93815	0.08967	1.74408	1.74126	1.21527
Romance-1	0.68927	0.57463	2.26991	0.08967	1.74408	1.74126	1.21527
Slavic	0.00000	0.00000	0.82621	0.19142	0.51156	1.95283	0.35149

In Table 2 the lines labeled without a numerical suffix are our basic analyses, while Germanic-1 separates out North and West Germanic extended cognate sets for YELLOW, and Romance-1 separates out a Balkan Romance extended cognate set Lat. *roseus* for RED. We will highlight some of the main results, concentrating on the lines labeled without a numerical suffix with asides where relevant for the other lines. Foci of diversity are clearly Slavic BLUE and Romance RED, YELLOW, and BLUE. Comparison of Romance BLACK and WHITE is interesting, as both have similar values, although in the case of BLACK this reflects conservatism, with most languages retaining reflexes of Latin *niger*, while in the case of WHITE it reflects innovation, most languages having adopted the Germanic loan *blank*, pushing reflexes of Latin *albus* to the periphery. Turning to specific colors, BLUE is indeed the focus of most variation, but this is largely because of the Slavic contribution. There is no general principle that the amount of diversity increases as one proceeds from Stage I through Stage V color terms, and little consistency across the three genera considered here — examination of more extensive sets of languages would be needed to test further possible correlations between individual colors and diversity. Turning to specific languages, we need a measure of overall diversity within a given genus, and we have conservatively selected the median. The figures provide strong confirmation of the initial hypothesis, namely that diversity is least in Germanic, most in Romance, with Slavic occupying an intermediate position. This remains unchanged even if one splits Germanic YELLOW as in line Germanic-1.

4. Conclusions

This article has demonstrated that it is possible to establish a methodology to reinforce the initial hypothesis that variation in basic color terms is minimal in Germanic, extensive in Romance, and at an intermediate level in Slavic. The general methodology should be applicable to other dense groups of languages, and to other lexical domains, though surely it will need to be refined and extended.

Acknowledgments

I am grateful to the following for consultation on the topics indicated: Stefan Th. Gries (quantitative methods); Alonso González Vázquez, Pilar Valenzuela, and Rosa Vallejos (Peruvian Amazonian Spanish); Martin Maiden (Romanian); Aaron Rubin (Judeo-Italian); and to two anonymous referees for comments on an earlier version. Needless to say, I bear sole responsibility for the use I have made (or not made) of these consultations and comments.

Abbreviations used in the article and online database

Arom.	Aromanian
Croat.	Croatian
Gk	Greek
Gmc	Germanic
Ib-Rom.	Ibero-Romance
Ital.	Italian
Lat.	Latin
OFris.	Old Frisian
ON	Old Norse
PGmc	Proto-Germanic
PSl.	Proto-Slavic
PWGmc	Proto-West Germanic
SCB	Serbian-Croatian-Bosnian
WGmc	West Germanic

Online database

The online database referred to in this chapter is available at: https://doi.org/10.1075/nss.34.05com.additional.

References

Berlin, B. & P. Kay. 1969. *Basic color terms: Their universality and evolution*. Berkeley: University of California Press.

Catalan dictionary. 1993. London: Routledge.

Claassen, S.A. 2021. Color terms across Europe: An investigation of the interaction between color terms and European language families. *RU:ts* 2. http://ruts-journal.ruhosting.nl/wp-content/uploads/2021/03/DEF-Color-terms-across-Europe-Simon-Claassen.pdf

Crawford, J. 2016. *Bleikr, gulr*, and the categorization of color in Old Norse. *Journal of English and Germanic Philology* 115: 239–252.

Davies, I. & G. Corbett. 1994. The basic colour terms of Russian. *Linguistics* 32: 65–89.

Dryer, M.S. 1989. Large linguistic areas and language sampling. *Studies in Language* 13: 257–292.

Dryer, M.S. 2013. Genealogical language list. In M.S. Dryer & M. Haspelmath (eds.): *The World Atlas of Language Structures Online*. https://wals.info/languoid/genealogy (consulted 2022-07-08)

Dunn, M., S.J. Greenhill, S.C. Levinson & R.D. Gray. 2011. Evolved structure of language shows lineage-specific trends in word-order universals. *Nature* 473: 79–82.

Dworkin, S.N. 2016a. A diachronic overview of color terms in the Romance languages: The lexical stability of the Latin color vocabulary. In J.P. Silvestre, E. Cardeira & A. Villalva (eds.), *Colour and colour naming: Crosslinguistic approaches*, 9–20. Centro de Linguística da Universidade de Lisboa / Universidade de Aveiro.

Dworkin, S.N. 2016b. Lexical stability and shared lexicon. In A. Ledgeway & M. Maiden (eds.): *The Oxford guide to the Romance languages*, 577–587. Oxford: Oxford University Press.

Eberhard, D.M., G.F. Simons & C.D. Fennig (eds.). 2021. *Ethnologue: Languages of the world*. 24th edn. Dallas: SIL International. https://www.ethnologue.com/subgroups/creole (consulted 2021-08-25)

Faltings, Volkert F. 2020. *Etymologisches Wörterbuch der friesischen Adjektiva*. Berlin: De Gruyter.

Ferreira, V., I. Schulze, P.C. Vicente & P. Bouda. 2015. *Dicionário bilingue piação-português*. Minde: CIDLeS.

Giacalone Ramat, Anna. 1978. Strutturazione della terminologia dei colori nei dialetti sardi. In V. Pisani & C. Santoro (eds.): *Italia linguistica nuova e antica: Studi linguistici in memoria di Oronzo Parlangèli II*, 163–181. Galatina: Congedo.

Hammarström, H., R. Forkel, M. Haspelmath & S. Bank. 2021. *Glottolog 4.4*. Leipzig: Max Planck Institute for Evolutionary Anthropology. https://glottolog.org/ (consulted 2021-08-25)

Huber, M. & the *APiCS* Consortium. 2013. Chapter 116: 'Green' and 'blue'. In S.M. Michaelis, P. Maurer, M. Haspelmath & M. Huber (eds.): *The atlas of pidgin and creole language structures*, 464–467. Oxford: Oxford University Press.

Kay, P., B. Berlin, L. Maffi, W.R. Merrifield & R. Cook. 2009. *The World Color Survey*. Stanford, CA: CSLI Publications.

Kristol, A.M. 1978. *Color: Les langues romanes devant le phénomène de la couleur*. Bern: Francke.

Kristol, A.M. 1979. Il colore azzurro nei dialetti italiani. *Vox Romanica* 38: 85–99.

Kristol, A.M. 1980. Color systems in southern Italy: A case of regression. *Language* 56: 137–145.

Kroonen, G. 2013. *Etymological dictionary of Proto-Germanic*. Leiden: Brill.

Majid, A., F. Jordan & M. Dunn. 2014. Semantic systems in closely related languages. *Language Sciences* 49: 1–18.

Nielsen, H.F. 1989. *The Germanic languages: Origins and early dialectal interrelations*. Tuscaloosa: University of Alabama Press.

OED = *Oxford English Dictionary*. Oxford: Oxford University Press. www.oed.com (consulted 2023-07-10)

Rubin, A.D. 2017. Judeo-Italian. In L. Kahn & A.D. Rubin (eds.): *Handbook of Jewish languages*. Rev. and updated edn, 298–365. Leiden: Brill.

Sandford, J.L. 2012. *Blu, azzurro, celeste* — what colour is blue for Italian speakers compared to English speakers? In M. Rossi (ed.), *Colour and colorimetry: Multidisciplinary contributions*, Vol. VIII B, 281–288. Rimini: Maggioli.

Sjölin, B. 1969. *Einführung in das Friesische*. Stuttgart: Metzler.

Teixeira Moláns, P. 2021. Os termos para as cores en galego: unha selva por explorar. *Revista Galega de Filoloxía* 22: 89–106.

Thomason, S.G. & T. Kaufman. 1988. *Language contact, creolization, and genetic linguistics*. Berkeley: University of California Press.

Uusküla, M. 2014. Linguistic categorization of BLUE in Standard Italian. In W. Anderson, C.P. Biggam, C. Hough & C. Kay (eds.): *Colour studies: A broad spectrum*, 67–78. Amsterdam: John Benjamins.

Wagner, M.L. 1917. Das Fortleben einiger lateinischer, bzw. vulgärlateinischer Pferdefarbennamen im Romanischen, insbesondere im Sardischen und Korsischen. *Glotta* 8: 233–238.

Woll, D. 1975. *Blau* und *blond*. Zum Ursprung zweier europäischer Farbbezeichnungen. In H. Meier (ed.): *Neue Beiträge zur romanischen Etymologie*, 342–367. Heidelberg: Carl Winter.

Of Angles and angels

Philology, history and the representation of identity

John Hines
Cardiff University

From a period of a thousand years from the first century AD to the eleventh, diverse sources in multiple languages collectively testify to the source and development of the group-name ('ethnonym') from which the familiar *Angeln, Angles, England* and *English* of modern usage derive. The complex range of early attested forms proves consistent with well-attested principles of language-use and language-change. Like any natural phenomenon, a group with an expressed and named identity will be a state of constant adaptation to circumstances, be those opportunities or stresses, and the adoption and replacement of the variants in textual history likewise conforms with historical circumstances in readily explicable ways. A comprehensive and empirically precise approach is especially important in case of the evolution from the *Anglii* to the *English*, which is of clear historical salience, and has attracted much inaccuracy and even misrepresentation.

1. Sensitive matters

Contrary to what punditry in many domains claims, 'identity politics' remains a distant runner-up to economic and environmental problems, alongside unalloyed power struggles, in the real strategic decision-making of public life. Nevertheless, commentary on current affairs, and academic studies, are now suffused with ostentatious sensitivity to all aspects of human identity and social recognition at a level too manifest to need specific illustration. A concept of 'contested heritage' has also become increasingly conventional in recent years. These perspectives merge to re-inflate and re-fuel long-standing conflicts over the status, reality and present-day relevance of recorded 'peoples' of European proto-history. It would seriously misrepresent the situation to label the ideologically charged and frequently hostile controversies over that topic of the last half-century and more as anything as moderate as 'differences of opinion'.

https://doi.org/10.1075/nss.34.06hin
Available under the CC BY-NC-ND 4.0 license. © 2025 John Benjamins Publishing Company

In the case of Iron-age to Early-medieval Britain — broadly, the last millennium BC and first millennium AD — objections to the use of the term 'Celtic' as a label for populations and their culture have come and largely gone in the course of the last quarter-century (James 1999; Collis 2003); more recently the term 'Anglo-Saxon' has been under virulent attack (Hines 2023; Naismith 2024); the concept of 'Viking' is clear but perennially awkward to explain and to justify (Price 2020, 2021; Woolf 2024). It is hard to overlook the curious fact that the imperial conquerors we know of as the Romans and the Normans have largely been exempted from this perceptual revisionism even though neither *Romani* nor *Normant* was widely or regularly used as an ethnonym within the relevant communities and periods. Where identity-related controversies have raised their heads, philology, historical lexicology and sociolinguistics can all contribute vitally to properly informed understandings of the issues involved, and ultimately, therefore, to a better grasp of the actual histories involved.

2. The earliest Latin and Greek sources for the Angles

This paper is focused on the group or people known to us as the Angles, from whose name the terms 'English' and 'England' have derived. The earliest surviving reference to this group is in Tacitus' *Germania* dating from the very end of the first century AD, precisely dated by a reference within the text to the second consulship of the Emperor Trajan of the year 98 (*Germania*: xxxvii). Tacitus included the *Anglii* within a list of seven peoples whom he could name as sub-groups of the Suebi, dwelling, from his perspective, beyond the Langobardi and therefore broadly across northern Germany (*Germania*: xl). The Suebian over-group is itself a clear example of how smaller groups nested within larger constellations in the ethnic taxonomy of the population of Germania. The landscape those seven groups inhabited is described as one of rivers and woods. The further information provided about them collectively is that they share in the cult of a goddess Nerthus, whose most sacred holy place is a grove and adjacent lake on an island in the sea. However, these lands of these peoples are, according to Tacitus, on the marges of *secretoria Germaniae* (*Germania*: xli): 'the more remote/hidden parts of Germania.'

Tacitus' form *Anglii* concurs perfectly with the widely attested Old English equivalent *Engle*, which like many ethnonyms in Old English is an *i*-stem noun that is attested only as a plural (Campbell 1959:§ 610.7; see further, Section 3, below). By default, Old English thus conceptualized and referred to the Angles — or the English, when that is the more appropriate translation — collectively, and had no direct concept of *an* Angle (male or female), for which it would had to have used the phrasal expression *Engla sum(e)*: 'one of the Angles'. Our earliest records of the term in Old English are geographically qualified references to the populations of the Middle and East Anglian kingdoms: the former as *Middilengli* in Bede's *Historia Ecclesiastica* (III.21 and V.24 s.a. DCLIII: there are manuscript variant spellings in *-ængli* and *-angli*; see Sweet 1885: 139 § 21, 147 § 24); the latter, possibly in the Tribal Hidage of much debated date and origin (Dumville 1989), but certainly no later than in the primary Parker Chronicle of the early 890s from the West Saxon court.

Around half-a-century after Tacitus composed *Germania*, the Alexandrian Greek scholar Claudius Ptolemaeus (anglicized as Ptolemy) compiled his 'Geography' (*Γεωγραφικὴ Ὑφήγησις*: 'Geographical Guide'; hereafter *Geographia*). This is datable to the 140s by a prospective reference to it as a planned work in the same author's 'Almagest', which in turn is dated by containing astronomical observations representing the period AD 125–141. There is no sign that Ptolemy had Tacitus' text to follow and to incorporate into the one chapter of his work on *Γερμανία μεγάλη*, 'Great Germania' (*Geographia*: II.xi), meaning Germania beyond the Roman Empire and in that sense barbarian and free. Ptolemy's information nonetheless agrees with Tacitus in identifying the Angles as a sub-group of the Suebi, and in locating them east of the Langobards. Where Tacitus, however, has them as just one of a list of peoples he could place rather vaguely in this area of northern Germany, Ptolemy attributed more prominent status to them: *Τῶν δὲ ἐντὸς καὶ μεσογείων ἐφνῶν μέγιστα μέν ἐστι τό τε τῶν Συήβων τῶν Ἀγγειλῶν...* ('Of the peoples within the interior, however, the greatest indeed is now that of the Suebian Angles...').

After Ptolemy, the Angles remained outside the notice of any writings or documentation that now constitute our historical sources until relatively late in the Migration Period of the fifth and sixth centuries AD. Book VIII of Procopius of Caesarea's 'History of the Wars' is primarily a supplement to the extended accounts of the Persian, Vandalic and Gothic wars of the Byzantine Emperor Justinian (r. AD 527–565), covering events of the period 551–3 and in particular the continuing conflicts with the Sasanian Persian Empire ruled by Chosroes I. Digressions in the book, however, note and emphasize the useful propensity of European barbarians to fight among themselves, and the twentieth chapter recounts the tale of warfare between the *Οὐάρνοι* (of the Continent) and the *Ἀγγίλοι* who are attributed to an island of *Βριττία*. In his introduction to the story of the conflict, Procopius indicates that Brittia is a separate island from *Βρεττανία*, and was then inhabited by three numerous peoples: the *Ἀγγίλοι, Φρίσσονες* and *Βρίττωνες*. At some unspecified but recent date a king of the Franks had sent an embassy to Justinian in which he included 'Angiloi' as evidence in support of a claim to hold rule over this island.

Procopius' long Chapter 20 proceeds with the tale of a war successfully waged on the Warnoi by a jilted Anglian princess, to reassert her honour — recording what would appear to have been a Christian exemplum exposing the wrongdoing of the Warnian prince Radigis, who had broken that engagement upon the death of his father and taken his newly widowed stepmother as wife instead. The chapter ends with a number of details on the environment of Brittia, and the mystical tale of men of the continental coast of what is now Holland and Frisia ferrying boatloads of the souls of the dead to Brittia as a nightly service.

This early Byzantine source is an amalgam of facts, misunderstandings and fable. The two islands, for instance, are most readily explained as a misrepresentation of the actual situation of Britain and Ireland. That Procopius did not identity either island with Strabo's Ἰέρνη or Ptolemy's Ἰουερνία νῆσος is remarkable, but a relevant and significant explanatory link with Ptolemy could lie in the fact that the earlier author had identified both 'Iwernia' and 'Alwion' (Ἀλουίωνος νῆσος) as νῆσοι Βρετανίκαι, 'The Britanic Islands' — a perception that occurs in none of the Latin sources concerning Britain and Ireland. Geographically, Procopius' whole chapter appears to conflate and muddle what was, in itself, realistic information concerning north-western Europe from the Frisian coastlands potentially as far as to Brittany, as well as concerning Britain and Ireland. The British settlement of the Armorican peninsula could well have given rise to a confusing duality of Britannia magna and Britannia minor. Comparable with Ptolemy in a further important detail, Procopius' Φρίσσονες retains a root vowel /i:/ that a general Continental Celtic sound-change would have produced from original /e:/, where the Early-medieval form is consistently Frēsones with the /e:/ preserved in Germanic. The earliest record of the latter spelling is in a sixth-century panegyric on the Frankish king Chilperic I composed by Venantius Fortunatus (Op. poet.: IX,1, line 75: terror [es] extremis Fresonibus atque Suebis, '[you are] a terror to the most distant Fresones and Suebi'). Ptolemy's form was Φρίσιοι rather than Φρίσσονες, the -i on the stem of which is paralleled in the Latin forms Frisii and Frisiavones (Tacitus, Germania: xxxiv–xxxv; Pliny, Natural History: IV.15; Galestin 2008).

Procopius' Warnoi are readily identifiable with the Varini included by Tacitus in his list of peoples within the Suebian over-group of Germania xl; indeed they follow the Anglii in that list. Pliny the Elder had included the Varinnae as a sub-group of the Vandili, in turn one of five principal genera that made up the Germanic peoples as a whole (Nat. Hist.: IV.xiv). It is credibly suggested that Ptolemy included the same group in his 'Geography' under the name of the Οὔρουνοι. The information provided in and between those sources on the supposed location of the Varini/Warnoi is vague in the extreme. Ptolemy placed his Wirounoi amongst 'smaller groups' (Ἐλάσσονα...ἔθνη) found between the Lesser Chauci, who are firmly assigned to territory between the Ems and the Weser in north-western

Germany, and the less specifically located Suebi. The mouth of a River Suebos is located approximately half-way between those of the Elbe and the Oder, and broadly in that area a River Warnow, debouching at Warnemünde, is one of the principal rivers in the region of Mecklenburg-Vorpommern (Greule 2014:574). Procopius seeks to place the Warnoi further west, towards the islands of Britain: north of the Danube (ὑπὲρ Ἴστρον ποταμὸν) and allegedly occupying land reaching to the North Sea on the right-hand side of the Rhine, and indeed there are further river names in more westerly parts of Germany which may contain this ethnonym (Greule 2014:584–585). A later direct linkage between this group and the Angles appears in the remarkable title of one of the *Leges Barbarorum* drawn up for Charlemagne at the very beginning of the ninth century: a set of texts that included Laws for the newly conquered Saxons and relatively recently conquered Frisians; a Law of the Chamavian Franks — a population associable with the southern Netherlands; and finally the *Lex Angliorum et Werinorum hoc est Thuringorum.* The modern German *Land* of Thüringen lies in what was probably the southern part of a larger territory of the Thuringii which had also fallen under Frankish rule by the early eighth century. The Carolingian Laws of the Barbarians were created and introduced as real and practical features of imperial governmental strategy. Their titles as preserved for us, however, deliberately referred in a learned way to older sources and used archaic terminology. What is clear, all in all, is that there was a deep-rooted tradition of an ancient association between the Angles and the Varini/Warnoi in central Europe north of the Danube. It is quite plausible that the story of the battle instigated by an insulted princess related by Procopius relocates a legend originally set somewhere broadly around the Elbe to the western Continent.

It is of especial importance in respect of the real situation around the middle of the sixth century, when Procopius reintroduced the Angles to the historical record, and therefore to an understanding of how and indeed why Angles were referred to as a people in various contexts, that a king of the Franks might at that date very plausibly claim some form of superiority or even formal overkingship in at least part of early Anglo-Saxon England (Wood 1983). That might indeed have been something such a king could more confidently and pragmatically try to insist upon in a diplomatic message to a far-distant emperor than he could have asserted and enforced in Britain itself. Without allowing the reference from the Byzantine source to the Frisians to confuse the picture unnecessarily, it is, as we shall see, potentially of considerable significance that in such circles in Merovingian Gaul, presumably both in the Frankish vernacular and in the widely spoken Latin, the preference was to refer to the new Germanic-speaking population of southern and eastern Britain collectively as 'Angles' rather than 'Saxons' — in notable contrast to what British and Gaelic sources indicate, where *Saeson/Sassenaich < Saxones* became the general name.

Set towards the end of the sixth century is the best known story involving the name of the Angles as a contemporary Germanic-speaking people: the hagiographical anecdote of how Pope Gregory the Great was inspired to organize the mission led by Augustine that re-established a bridgehead for the Roman Church and Christianity, initially in Kent, from AD 596. Bede appended the story to a summary life of Gregory in Book II.i of his 'Ecclesiastical History of the English People'; he clearly perceived it as a pleasing and pious but rather fanciful tradition rather than canonical biographical fact. He labelled it an *opinio* (perhaps best translated 'belief' in this context), unauthorized by documentary sources. Gregory saw young male slaves in the market-place in Rome: the answers to questions he asked about them stimulated a series of pontifical puns — their identities *Angli > angelici*; their homeland *Deiri > de ira Dei*; their king — *Aelli > alleluia*. In light of the evidence noted immediately above, for a pope who had spent years in Constantinople and was in regular contact with his bishops in Gaul and through them with Merovingian rulers, we can suppose that in reality Gregory would have had a wider and more realistic frame of reference to draw his thoughts to a people known of as the Angles. We shall turn to that in detail shortly.

3.   The etymology of the name in Germanic

Before doing so, however, it is appropriate to explore another dimension to the background, analysing the etymology of the name reflected in those various Greek and Latin sources as a Germanic proper noun. As noted above, this ethnonym occurs in Old English with the morphology of a plural *i*-stem noun. So regular was the use of the *i*-stem paradigm for this semantic field in Old English that names appear to have been transferred into the class: e.g. in the case of *Seaxe*, 'Saxons', alongside the *n*-stem *Seaxan* as in Old Saxon itself and Old High German; and the morphologically duplex compounding element *-waru* (*o*-stem) or *-ware* (*i*-stem) meaning 'folk', 'people' (Hogg and Fulk 2011: § 2.70; Campbell 1959: § 610.7; but cf. Eggers/Braune 1975: § 217 Anm. 2, and Hogg and Fulk 2011: § 2.70 n.4). The existence of regular i-stem ethnonyms in Gothic (e.g. *Iairasaulymeis*, 'people of Jerusalem'; *Rumoneis*, 'Romans'; *Sedoneis*, 'people of Sidon') shows that this was not an idiosyncrasy limited to Old English. As is very plausibly the case with other Latin second-declension ethnonyms pluralizing in *-ii* on either Germanic or Celtic roots, Tacitus' *Anglii* could as well reflect a Proto-Germanic or early West Germanic *ja*- or *jō*-stem group name pluralized in *-jôs* or *–jôz* respectively (as posited by Meid 1969: § 70.4; note that the circumflex accent over the vowel in these endings represents the rare but regular trimoric or 'schleiftonig' vowel). Tacitus' spelling cannot, *per se*, presuppose derivation from the Germanic *i*-stem plural in *-îz*. Philologically, though, the latter is as feasible an explanation as any alternative, and would mean, in addition, that the name had remained consistent in morphology in the language of successive generations of populations who retained or inherited this name as their own.

Turning to the root of the name, the alternative, and therefore competing, hypotheses are derivation of the name from an adjectival root **angu-*, meaning 'narrow', or from a nominal root **angula-*, meaning 'hook'. The former is the more convincing, ultimately because of its ability to fit a remarkably complex history. A *u*-stem adjective 'narrow' is represented by Gothic *aggus* and corroborated by the Latin cognate *angustus*. Old High German and Old Saxon, however, have this adjective in the form *engi*, and Old English in the form *enge*, implying that it passed across from the relatively uncommon *u*-stem to the more common *ja*-stem declension so that the root vowel was eventually subject to umlaut. It may be posited that the adjective was employed to denote the long, narrow Schlei fjord that forms the southern boundary of Angeln (see Figure 1). The derivation of ethnonyms from hydrographic features which somehow defined a group's territory via a suffix in *-l-* is reasonably well attested (Bach 1953: II, §§ 246–247; Udolph 2004: 145–146; Laur 1992: s.n. ANGELN; cf. Kuhn 1973).

Although new connecting or parasite vowels could be introduced between the stem **ang-* and the suffix *-l-* with the thematic vowels *-u-* or *-ja-* omitted (cf. Meid 1969, § 87.2–3), in the case of the name of this territory and its population we are faced only with forms that conform perfectly with derivations in which the original thematic vowels were retained before the suffix. The Greek forms recorded in the writings of Ptolemy and Procopius nicely support the existence of a root that should have passed through the sequence **angjal- > *angijal- > *angijl- > *angīl-> *angil-* (Campbell 1959: § 398.4). One cannot attach any weight to the precise forms of the medial vowels, or the accentuation, in the name-forms found in Ptolemy and Procopius. In both cases the Greek texts survive only in copies of considerably later medieval manuscripts. The diphthong ει had long since fallen together with ι in Ancient Greek (Horrocks 2010: 160–70; Holton et al. 2019: § § 2.1.1–2 and 2.4.8.1). In the spelling system using Greek script created for Gothic in the fourth century, ει is used for /iː/. All the same, Ptolemy's Ἄγγειλοι is pretty much what one could expect as a second-century Koine Greek representation of what could have been **Angijlî* or **Angīlî* in West Germanic at that date. The slightly different form in Procopius's text could simply represent a regular variant spelling, although it is also conceivable that the root **Angil-* was that of the Proto-Old High German used amongst or around the Franks who visited Justinian in Constantinople. *Angil-*, later *Engil-*, is a familiar personal name element in Old

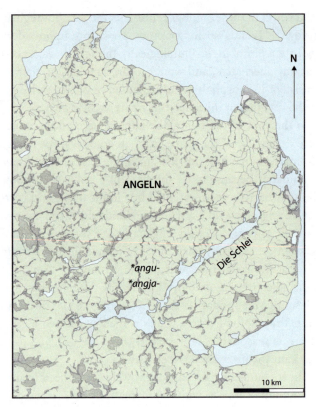

Figure 1. The landscape of the Angeln and Schwansen peninsulas, showing the Schlei. Based on the Royal Prussian Survey Map of 1877, redrawn by the author after Willroth 1992

High German, although its etymology is debated (Förstemann 1900: s.n. ANGIL; Kaufmann 1968: 35).

The few instances of this territorial name in Old English consistently show the form *Ongle* ('Widsith': lines 8 and 35; The Old English Orosius: I.1 [Bately ed. 1980: 12/31). Following Erdmann (1890: 118), in his edition of 'Widsith' Malone inferred that this was a feminine ō-stem noun with a nominative form **Ongel*, but neither Erdmann nor he really tackled the puzzle of the unstressed vowel. The one possible record of the nominative case occurs in the additions on northern European geography that precede the travelogues of Ohthere and Wulfstan in the Old English Orosius, where there is reference to *þæt land þe mon Ongle hæt*. Used transitively, the verb *hātan* can take either a complement in the nominative or an object in the accusative. Just before this in the Orosius translation, the clause *þæt land þe mon hætt seo læsse Asia* (Bately ed. 1980: 10/33) evidently implies that *Ongle* was understood to be the nominative case. At the start of the evolution of Proto-Old English from the fifth century AD, we can postulate a root *angul-* behind this form, with no umlaut-causing *i* or *j* in a following syllable. The territorial name Angeln does not show umlaut in any language, and Bede referred to *illa patria quae Angulus dicitur et ab eo tempore usque hodie manere desertus inter provincias Iutarum et Saxonum perhibetur* ('that homeland which is named Angulus, and which is reported to have remained deserted from that time to the present day in between the territories of the Jutes and the Saxons'; *HE*: I.15). The raising of *a*+nasal consonant > *o* in vernacular *Ongle* is inconsistent with a later borrowing of Latin *Angulus* (Campbell 1959: §§ 495 and 545–546).

There are several examples of Old English *Ongle* as an ethnonym too, essentially referring to 'Angles' rather than 'Englishmen', and it is plausible that this was the source of a lexeme also regularly used to refer to the region. That practice is perfectly illustrated by the one relevant of instance of a spelling *Angle* rather than *Ongle*, in the report of Ohthere's account of the trading site of Hedeby *se stent betuh Winedum 7 Seaxum 7 Angle 7 hyrð in on Dene* ('which stands between the [lands of the] Wends and the Saxons and the Angles and belongs to the Danes'; Bately ed. 1980,:16/14–15). The ethnonym *Ongle* occurs several times in the Old English Bede, and once in the Old English Martyrology in a passage on St Oswald which itself is based on the Latin text of Bede's *Historia*. Both there and in the translation of Bede's account of Oswald's death at *Denises burna*, the *Ongle* are referred to as a population instead of a closer translation of Bede's reference to *lingua Anglorum*: in *HE* III.6, the source of the relevant sentence in the Martyrology, that phrase has to be understood as meaning the English language generally, not some Anglian dialect. The same broader ('English' rather than 'Anglian') reference is required for the paraphrase of Bede's introduction to the Gregorian mission of conversion in *HE* II.1. *nostram, id est Anglorum, gentem de potestate Satanae ad fidem Christi sua industria convertit* ('by his effort, he converted our people, that is the English, from subjection to Satan to the faith of Christ'), and is represented by *to Criste he Ongle gehwyrfde mid arfæstnesse lareowdomes* ('he converted the English to Christ through the holiness of his teaching'). However the remaining five instances of *Ongle* in the Old English Bede (later on in II.1; III.1; III.28; IV.4 and V.9) refer specifically to an Anglian population, not the English comprehensively.

The first half of line 35 in 'Widsith', *Offa weold Ongle*, 'Offa ruled *Ongle*', also stands out for diverging from a formula otherwise constantly repeated in these verses with the subjects of the ruler represented by an ethnonym in the dative plural. The second half of that line, *Alewih Denum*, using the verb 'ruled' expressed in the first half of the line, illustrates this perfectly. There seems to have been some rule or perception blocking the use of a dative plural *Onglum*. *Anglum*, with the Latin stressed vowel, appears in the Parker Chronicle under the years 443 and 449 in the context of the *adventus*; after that it is in Eadgar's Fourth Law

Code of AD 962–963 that *Angle/Anglum* is rather idiosyncratically reintroduced to refer to the English population (Liebermann 1903: 206–215).

We may best understand Old English *Ongle* as an *i*-stem noun generated by transference of the toponymic root **angul-* to the standard paradigm for ethnonyms in Old English. The absence of *i*-mutation is not a problem because that sound-change did not always operate in this lexical set: cf. *Seaxe* and *Eote*, 'Saxons' and 'Jutes'. A distinction between *Ongle* as 'Angles' and *Engle* as 'English' would have been useful, although in fact the Old English Bede uses *Engle* specifically of the Angles as opposed to the Saxons in the translation of Book I.15, while the earliest instance of the phrase *Engla lond*, later 'England', occurs in the same source as a translation of *in regione Anglorum* where it refers quite specifically to Northumbrian territory bordering on Pictland (*HE*: IV.26). Had the phrase been in widespread use for 'England' then (see below), it would have been a poor choice here. In the probably mid-tenth-century 'Guthlac B' (lines 852 and 1334) the avoidance of the dative plural seems to be embedded in the phrase *on Engle*, used twice in the sense of 'in England'.

Bede must have perceived the name as he quoted it as formally identical with Latin *angulus*, 'hook', which in fact gives standard Old English *angel*, an *a*-stem masculine noun, albeit with occasional variant forms in *angil* and *angul* as well as some late evidence for the palatalization and affrication of the medial consonant group, *ancgel/ancgil* (DOE: sv. ANGEL). Around the turn of the 12th–13th centuries, Saxo Grammaticus, in his *Gesta Danorum*, identified a legendary Angul as a progenitor of both the Danes and the English, but his form was not independent of Bede, to whom he refers (*Gesta Dan.*: I.10).

The totality of the evidence does not suggest that the noun **angula-* is the actual source of the group-name, although this idea has proved tenacious (e.g. Laur 1958; Mees 2023: 7). Nor does it allow us to posit that Bede's *Angulus* was simply an educated, Latinate approximation which alone subsequently generated the regional names found in Old English, medieval German, and in Saxo's Latin. A convincing and satisfactory reconstruction of the situation is one based on the systematic variation of the medial/thematic vowel already discussed, whereby the place-name *Angeln/Angulus* retained the original *u*-stem root while the ethnonym recorded in Greek and Old English developed from the *ja*-stem variant. Such a separation is separately evident within the Old English lexicon in the differentiation of adjectival *enge* 'narrow' and adverbial *ange* 'with concern'. We can infer that the division existed by the first half of the second century AD with the innovation of the fronted medial vowel represented in the forms transmitted to Ptolemy. That would not necessarily mean that there was already then a fully regularized difference between the ethnonym and toponym, as there subsequently appears to have been. We may, however, refer to Ptolemy's estimation of the importance and magnitude of the Suebian Angles (quoted above) and note archaeological evidence of an Early Roman Iron-age culture province extending from Schleswig-Holstein over Mecklenburg-Vorpommern. The interpretation of large areas characterized by clear similarities in material cultural practice in this era in terms of 'Cultures', which in turn might speculatively be identified with the ethnographies of the contemporary Latin and Greek authors, now seems to belong to a long past era of Archaeology. It is nevertheless relevant that the archaeological record from north and east of the Elbe and along the south-western shore of the Baltic shows extensive evidence of this having been a contact zone sharing much in social structure and cultural practice in the earliest centuries of the Christian Era (well reviewed by Willroth 1992: esp. 244–248, 338–357; cf. Asmus 1938; Voß 2007; Wegewitz 1977). The relevance of this situation here is that it should also have been a broad area of communication in which alternative lexical forms referring to specific localities and populations could easily have arisen and been regularized.

Tacitus' Latin form *Anglii* tantalizingly provides no guidance on the vowel of a middle syllable that ought to have been there, and indeed poses the important challenge of explaining why that syllable is missing. Even acknowledging that 'errors' would always be likely in the transmission of the Germanic name of distant people to a Roman author, as is abundantly confirmed in the variant representations of names by Pliny, Tacitus, Ptolemy and more, the most likely explanation in terms of Latin philology is that this is an early instance of the syncope of a short medial vowel (Adamik 2016). That has no additional implications about whether the vowel was more likely then to have been *i* or *u*. It is important to be clear, too, that the Old English ethnonym *Engle* could itself just as well derive from an ancestral **Anguliz* as from a variant **Angiliz* through regular double *i*-mutation (Campbell 1959:§203). None of this, though, significantly effects the practical modelling of the etymology of the group-name and regional name as derivatives of alternate stem-forms from a prehistoric language stratum.

A source of evidence that is often overlooked is Old Welsh, where we find the ethnonym as *Eigil/Eingl*, both regular spellings for ['ɛɪŋɪl]. This appears in the archaic B-text of *Y Gododdin*, which is sufficiently early a source for us to argue that it does not appear in Welsh solely as the learned transference of a Latin proper noun, even though (Vulgar) Latin *Anglī* remains the most likely source of the lexeme in light of the weight of Roman-period Latin influence on the Welsh lexicon. The stressed initial diphthong *ei* is the product of *i*-affection of an original *a*: a form of umlaut, very similar in process to Old English *i*-mutation, although affecting only short vowels (Jackson 1953:§§ 155–157). The Old Welsh form could actually be the reflex of either *Anglī* or *Anglii*, and even directly of West Germanic **Angilīz*. A parallel and presumably quite independent phonological development is found in the regional name *Tegeingl* in north-east Wales, derived from a Roman-period 'tribal' name *Deceangli* (Rivet and Smith 1979: 331). The unstressed vowel in the second syllable of *Ei[n]gil* does not testify to the medial vowel of an original **Angilîz* as the insertion of an epenthetic svarabhakti vowel in final consonant clusters is a regular feature of Old Welsh and Old Cornish (Jackson 1953: §33).

4. Pope Gregory the Great, Angles and angels

The real primary sources for Gregory's actions aimed at bringing about the restitution of a Church subject to the Roman pontificate in Britain are letters in his own copious surviving correspondence. These texts are consistent and unambiguous in identifying the people to be converted by the name *Angli*, and the objective to be the establishment of a well structured and effective *ecclesia Anglorum*. Philologically, the Latin form *Angli* is comfortably explicable as a Latin lexeme fully consistent with Tacitus having introduced or regularized the form *Anglii* in the first century AD, with a characteristic simplification of unstressed *-iī* to *-jī* and eventually just to *-ī* or *-i* (Herman 2000: 34–35).

In the Northumbrian Church of the later seventh and early eighth centuries there was considerable interest in how and what Gregory knew of this population in the former Roman province of Britannia, and why it attracted his evangelical concern. Gregory's letters themselves, however, are very much pragmatic working documents; they do not record aspirational musings or provide anything like a journal or memoires recorded for posterity. The directly relevant letters can be grouped into correspondence with Brunhilde, the matriarch and queen mother over most of the Franks, and her favourite Bishop Syragius on the one hand (*Epistolae*: VI.57 and XI.48; IX.222), and instructions or exhortations sent to his missionary leader in Kent, Augustine, and to the king and queen who were ruling there, Æthelberht and his Frankish wife Bertha (*Epistolae*: XI.35–7, 49–57). As noted above, a Frankish view of the proto-English settlers of Britain as collectively 'Angles' is consistent with the reference to the area transmitted by Procopius, however garbled it had become. Most relevant here is Gregory's letter to Brunhilde of July 596 (*Epistolae*: VI.57) explaining the mission to south-eastern Britain, in which he refers straightforwardly to the *gens Anglorum*. Evidently he did not need to add anything to identify who or where those people are found.

In a subsequent letter to Syragius of July 599, by which time positive news had reached him from Augustine in Kent, he says that he had been contemplating a mission to the *Angli* for a long time (*diu cogitans*) — which one could interpret as meaning that the germ of the idea could be traced back to Gregory's time in Constantinople in the 580s, but which is actually so vague as to allow for practically any preferred interpretation to be put upon it (cf. Richards 1980, 238–250). Michael Richter argued (1984) that there was material in Gregory's own writings likely to have generated, over time, the pious fable of the slave boys in the market place finally recorded for posterity by Bede. A pun on *alleluia* can be found in a chapter of Gregory's *Moralia in Job* that celebrates the extension of the faith to Britain, at the edge of the world (XI.21): *ecce lingua Britanniae, quae nil aliud noverat, quam barbarum frendere, jam dudum in divinis laudibus Hebraeum coepit Alleluia resonare;* 'behold the language of Britain, which had known nothing more than to grunt barbarism, has now begun to resound with the Hebraic *Alleluia* in divine praise'. A delight in word-play is evident in a letter on the conversion of the English from Gregory to Bishop Eulogius of Alexandria (*Epistolae:* VIII.29) which refers to *gens Anglorum in mundi angulo posita,* 'the people of the Angles situated in a corner of the world', but this hardly leads even the inventive contemplative mind immediately to angels. That there is nothing to support the extremely forced pun linking a name known only to us as *Dere* with *de ira Dei* is almost reassuring given the fact that *Deiri/Deira* are not only unattested as the name of the southern sub-group of the Northumbrians and their homeland but, unlike a monophthongal root *der-,* are linguistically inexplicable in either Old English or Old Welsh (Jackson 1953: §67.6).

Within sequences of creative transmission, it is easy to see how the story of Anglian slave boys in the market place could have evolved from Gregory's genuine instruction to Candidus, his *rector* in Gaul, to consider buying Anglian *pueri* (specifically, young men of 17 or 18 years of age) to be trained as monks (*Epistolae:* VI.10). That may not actually have happened: it was one of two options for Candidus, and Augustine's mission to Kent in 597 apparently did not include native speakers of Proto-Old English (Bede, *HE:* I.23). The specific reference to Anglian slaves in the story as told by Bede in fact varies from the anonymous *Liber beati et laudabilis viri Gregorii Papae* composed at the monastery of Whitby in Northumbria, maybe as much as twenty-five years before Bede completed his *Historia.* The Anonymous Life identifies the group of young men encountered by Gregory as certain 'people of our nation', fair in form and with light hair, who had come to Rome (...*Romam venisse quidam de nostre natione forma et crinis candidate albis*). With a degree of ostentation, the author of the Anonymous Life takes the opportunity to display knowledge of the differentiation of *puer* from *iuvenis* in Latin taxonomy, which again might echo the terminology of Gregory's instructions to Candidus. The Anonymous Life also implies that Gregory interrogated the young men directly: in response to the question *cuius gentis fuissent? ... respondebent, "Anguli dicuntur, illi de quibus sumus";* producing the instant pun *"Angeli Dei!"* (of what people were they?...they replied "They are called *Anguli,* those people from whom we are." ... "Angels of God!")

The form *Anguli* here, not *Angli*, is eye-catching. It is used with near total consistency in this text (Colgrave ed. 1968, 144–145). The easy explanation is that the identification of the vernacular name for the region of Angeln at the time with Latin *angulus* was already current in the Northumbrian Church, and that supplied the base for the ethnonym. The entry on Gregory the Great in Rome's *Liber Pontificalis*, however, speaks of him having converted *gentem Angulorum* in a strong manuscript tradition that may date from as early as the first half of the seventh century, albeit in parallel with variants showing the more predictable form *Anglorum*. Unfortunately, though, it is impossible to be sure where and when the less expected form was used before the turn of the eighth-ninth centuries. For this study, the testimony to an essentially common process of derivation independently generating a Proto-Old English **Ongulî* and a Medieval Latin *Anguli* is welcome in itself. We should properly note that the lack of syncope in Old High German and the uncertain dating of high medial vowel syncope following a long initial syllable in Old English could allow vernacular forms **Anguli* and **Onguli* to be found in the 7th century. Bede, however, used the Old English ethnonym *Middilengli*, showing high-vowel syncope, and there is no occasion to force an argument for the influence of vernacular survivals of medial -*u*- on these Latin examples of *Anguli*.

For the sake of the Northumbrian legend, however, it is important to note that *Anguli–angeli* is a rather more convincing pun than *Angli–angeli*. The attribution of the eloquent 'Non Angli sed angeli, si Christiani forent!' to Gregory is apocryphal. It does not occur before the later nineteenth century, and looks like the refined product of a Victorian Latin prose composition exercise. The Anonymous Life explicitly drew attention to the parallelism of *Anguli–angeli* with the same trisyllabic rhythm, and variation of the medial vowel alone (Chapter 13). Bede was plainly embarrassed by the weakness of an *Angli–angeli* pun and has Gregory respond to the identity of the youths '...*angelicam habent faciem, et tales angelorum in caelis decet esse coheredes.*' It may be curious, then, that both the Anonymous Life and Bede were content to retain the presumably bogus ethnonym *Deiri*, although they might have been familiar with a stressed *ei* diphthong in Brythonic names — such as *Eingl*.

5. Onwards: *angelcynn* and *England*

Richter (1984) argued that, in essence, Bede generalized the Anglian ethnonym in composing a history of the English-speaking peoples — with primary attention to their religious progress as good Roman Christians — as that of the *gens Anglorum*; and that he did so, dutifully conforming to Gregory's ethnic terminology. Richter understood that to be contrary to the 'mainstream of contemporary nomenclature' which referred to 'the Germanic peoples in Britain as "Saxons"'(Richter 1984: 105–110: quotation p.107). His case, however, oversimplifies the situation with regard to the evidence for the use of the term *Saxones*, as well as that discussed above on the transmission of *Angli* and its cognates. It is certainly the case that external sources reporting on the invasion and conquest of Britannia in the fifth century, and in the case of Gildas from the first half of the sixth century, remain consistent with a later Roman paradigm in seeing *Saxones* – along with *Franci*, on the Continent – as the leading barbarian group raiding and infesting the north-western provinces of the Late Roman Empire: thus Constantius' Life of Germanus of Auxerre and the Gallic Chronicle as well as Gildas (Springer 2004: esp. 32–56; Flierman 2017: esp. 23–87).

The evidence presented above for the currency and consistency of use, in key contexts, of the term *Angli* draws attention to the real possibility of there being more of a disjunction, even a lacuna, between the historical context and provenances of those references to Saxons in Britain and a later wave of widespread use of the name *Saxones* from the mid-seventh century onwards: very often, to start with, in strongly orthodox ecclesiastical contexts (e.g. hagiographies of Columbanus, Fursey, Cuthbert and Wilfrid: cited by Richter 1984, 106). As Richter notes there too, especially remarkable is the transcript of a letter from Pope Vitalian to King Oswiu of Northumbria of AD 665 recorded by Bede (*HE*: II.29) in which the king is addressed as *rex Saxonum*, and which, being a reply to a lost letter from Oswiu to Rome, can be assumed at least in some way to reflect a style of title used by or for Oswiu himself. The quoted contents of the letter make it clear that the Pope understood Oswiu to rule, as king or overlord, the entire island of Britain. The anomalous title may indeed be explicable in the same light as those of *rex* and *regina Anglorum* used of Æthelberht and Bertha of Kent by Pope Gregory (*Epistolae*: XI.37 and 35 respectively; *HE*: I.32): these rulers were of value and interest to the papacy because they apparently held the overkingship with the title *Bretwalda*. It is proper to note that there is no primary evidence of the polities and peoples of the South, East and West Saxons being known by those specific names, either in Latin or Old English, that pre-dates the late seventh century: yet again, it may be the Tribal Hidage that is the earliest source in which the vernacular forms of those names appear. In the general absence of direct documentary records, this lack of evidence would be insignificant were it not for the fact that a change of name of the West Saxon kingdom from *Gewisse* to *Westseaxe/Occidentales Saxones* also seems to be a historical event of the late seventh century (Walker 1956; Yorke 1989: 93–94; Coates 1990). In Gregory of Tours's sixth-century *Historiae Francorum*, the term *Saxones* is used with the same automatic implication that it referred to populations settled on the Continent as that linking *Angli* with Britain in Gregory's letter to Brunhilde. Why the Saxon name should have become more widely used both sides of the Channel in the course of the seventh century is far from easily even guessed at; but it does look as if that is something that happened.

A good practical reason for the adoption and use of an 'Anglian' rather than a Saxon identity for comprehensive reference to the (eventually) Old English-speaking population of southern and eastern Britain is the disappearance of any other or 'old' Anglian population on the Continent with which it might be confused. By the end of the eighth century, the direct ancestor of the familiar compound 'Anglo-Saxon' had been developed — primarily, it would seem, to distinguish this population from the Old Saxons (*Antiqui Saxones*) in what is now north-western Germany. Paul the Deacon's *Anglisaxones* (*HL*: IV.22) conjoins the two by then 'correct' Latin lexemes. Alcuin is believed to have played a major part in drafting the report of a papal legation to England of AD 786 which reported its area of concern as *Anglorum Saxonia*, which interestingly should imply identification of the population as *Angli* but the territory as another *Saxonia* (Carella 2012). Willibald's *Vita Bonifatii* (Chapter IV) refers even-handedly to London as a site which *Anglorum Saxonumque vocabulo appellatur Lundenwich*. When, however, this compound was strategically adopted by the West Saxon court, first evidenced in Asser's 'Life of Alfred', it is the *angul-* variant that is preferred. Asser repeatedly uses the title *Angulsaxonum rex* of Ælfred, and the form recurs in several of Alfred's successors charters from the following half-century (Stevenson ed. 1904: 147–152).

The 'Anglo-Saxon' compound in the royal title began to give way to a shorter *rex Anglorum* in charters and on coins from the reign of Ælfred's grandson Æthelstan, in the later 920s; that precedes, but not by much, the appearance of the terms *Engla þeoden* and *Engla cyning* in vernacular texts (respectively 'lord' and 'king of the *Engle*'): first of all in Chronicle verses celebrating achievements of Eadmund just before the mid-tenth century and Eadgar in the 970s (Parker Chronicle: s.a. 942 and 975; cf. Molyneaux 2015 on the development of a concept of England). A curiosity is the reference in an early to mid-tenth-century macaronic poem on the earlier scholar and cleric Aldhelm as *ipselos on æðel Angolsexna byscop on Bretene*: 'the eminent and noble bishop of the Anglo-Saxons in Britain'. *ipselos* is Greek ὑφηλός, 'eminent': the whole poem creatively but ostentatiously uses vocabulary idiosyncratically (ed. Whitbread 1976). Outside of the royal title, as Sarah Foot showed and discussed in detail (Foot 1996), Ælfred's court, as the sole surviving old Anglo-Saxon kingship, determinedly fostered the use of the term *angelcynn* for 'the people of England'. However, Foot was apparently unaware then of the evidence of the Old English Martyrology for how this term was introduced as a direct translation of Bede's *gens Anglorum*, and probably from the first half of the ninth century — potentially quite early in that century (Rauer ed. 2016: 1–4; DOE: sv. ANGELCYNN; Molyneaux 2015: 201–209).

The exact form of this word is significant. *Angel-* has the Latin initial *a-*, but most importantly has to be identified with the Old English noun *angel*, 'hook', simply translating Bede's *Angulus* into the vernacular. The source of the term is thus multiply Latinate and literate. *Engelsaxo* in the early ninth-century *Vita Alcuini* (Chapter 18) may show the same influence, albeit with an initial *e-* that could reflect both Old English *Engle* and Old High German *Engil-*. One can be surprised that no variant **angulcynn* has been used in any surviving source, although the variant spelling *ongolcynn* (as well as *ongelcynn*) in the Old English Bede implies that at least one early tenth-century writer thought that it ought to have existed. *Angelfolc* occurs a couple of times, translating a plural *populi Anglorum* in the Old English Bede. *Angelþeod, ongelþeod* and *ongolþeod* are alternatives to the compound in *-cynn* that occur only in the Bedan translations, except for one eleventh-century forgery of a charter, purportedly of Æthelræd (S 914; cf. DOE: sv. ANGELÞEOD). In the eleventh century, then, the term was known, but was obsolete, and suitable for deployment to create a suitably old impression in the faked legal text.

One last fundamental lexical and cognitive shift by the early eleventh century was that from the primacy of the people as the national group designated by an ethnonym to a concept of the nation as a territory within which the state subsisted in its infrastructure and order. George Molyneaux (2015) has discussed with exemplary thoroughness and precision how the tenth and earlier eleventh centuries were a major transformative period in which an English kingdom was gradually and eventually consolidated. By Christmas AD 1027, Cnut could style himself, for the first time, as 'King of all England [and Denmark and the Norwegians/Norway and some of the Swedes]': *rex totius Angliꝫ et Denemarciꝫ et Norreganorum et partis Suavorum* and *ealles Englalandes cyning*, 'king of all England' (Liebermann 1903: 276–279: one manuscript copy of the Latin letter reads *Norregiae* rather than *Norreganorum*). The conjunction of the genitive plural *Engla* with the noun *land/lond* in the sense of 'the land of the English' had only become regular in the writing of Ælfric of Eynsham from the 990s; slightly before that, in the 980s, the West Saxon Ealdorman Æthelweard gave us the earliest surviving use of *Anglia* as a territorial name in his Latin Chronicle, albeit as synonymous with *Britannia* as a whole (*Chronicon*: 4). On the Jelling runestone of the 970s, Haraldr Gormsson is described as a king who came to rule Denmark and Norway (Barnes 2012: 71–73). Scandinavian usage was just slightly but significantly ahead of English in the association of kingship with territories. It is fitting, then, that the preference for disyllabic *England* (often *Ingland* or *Ynglond*) in fifteenth-century Chancery Standard was not a simple sound-change from the trisyllabic Middle

English *Engelond* of Chaucer and Gower, but rather the adoption of a Norse-derived variant with the pronunciation typical of a northern dialect (Fisher et al. 1984; Jordan 1934: §34.3).

6. The English

Language plays a crucial role in the conceptualization and transmission of group-identity. We have explored and observed this here, across the first millennium AD, in the case of a group traceable in records from the first century of the Christian Era that we can refer to by the modern form 'Angles'. Although his critical tone was rather severe, I concur with George Molyneaux that it was exaggerated and misleading of Sarah Foot to interpret the determined use of the term *angelcynn* by the Alfredian court in terms of the 'invention' of an English nation: linguistically, what we have traced above is a coherent and explicable series of developments whereby new usages are generated in the context of etymologically natural prior data. Concurrently, both socially and culturally — eventually politically — there is no justification for any claim that this is all, or primarily, a matter of language and discourse imaginatively marking and creating a desired reality. There was some sort of Anglian people there all along — itself part of a larger group, and also comprising several, probably many, sub-groups — until the point that the Anglian population in Britain became fully subsumed into an Anglo-Saxon, subsequently an English, population. The philological evidence allows us to explicate how this identity was, often purposefully, represented, shaped and transmitted in discourse. That means that significant generative factors were in play, but none of those is really the same as 'invention'.

There is, meanwhile, one further crucial dimension to this topic, and that is the emergence of the use of the term 'English' (OE *englisc*) to identify members of a defined group within the population. This is first evident in the West Saxon Laws of King Ine (r. AD 688–725), which include a number of clauses comparing and specifying differential conditions for the *englisc* and the *wielisc* under the law (Ine: §§ 24, 46.1, 54.2 and 74; Liebermann 1903: 88–123). This usage must derive from the primary use of the adjectival form in *-isc* to label the language: in other words, these are identities recognized on the basis of the language one spoke, which would understandably be of fundamental practical significance in legal proceedings. It is of particular interest that, in full accordance with Bede's tendency to use *lingua Anglorum* of what we would now call Early Old English generally, and to see it as a marker of group identity (e.g. *HE*: I.1 and III.6, as above), *englisc* is the name for the language; Bede occasionally refers to *lingua Saxonica* as a dialectal variant of this language (see *HE*: III.7, III.22 and IV.17; for place-names in Anglian areas cited *in lingua Anglorum, HE*: I.12, III.19 and IV.19). Note should also be taken of an intriguing group of six Mercian charters of, or deriving from, the ninth century (S183, S186, S190, S193, S271 and S1271) which use the evidently unfamiliar vernacular term *fæstingmenn*, 'tied men', and refer to it as linguistically 'Saxon' (*saxonice*) — as indeed we should classify it by dialect on phonological grounds. This is not the place, however, to pursue this peculiarity.

Ine's laws originated in the late seventh century, before the death of Erconwald Bishop of London in AD 694, but the surviving texts of the code under Ine's name are later, and clearly include alterations and interpolations. Disentangling all of the strata, let alone dating the changes, has not yet been achieved (Lambert 2017: 67–68); nevertheless the scattered placement of at least some of these clauses in the code implies that especially §§ 54 and 74 have these references as later additions. The genuine treaty between King Ælfred of Wessex and Guthrum the Danish leader of the 870s stipulates the same status for *engliscne 7 deniscne* (masculine accusative singular) in terms of compensation should one be slain (Liebermann 1903: 126–129). That amount, *viii healfmearcum asodenes goldes*, is specified using a Norse-derived unit of account (the mark), but pragmatically using refined gold as reference material in a way that actually refers to a West Saxon *wergild* tariff of 1,200 silver shillings via an exchange rate of silver:gold of 10:1 defined in the Islamic caliphate (Lyon [1969 and 1976] discusses this evidence primarily in the context of Carolingian and Scandinavian relationships; for the wider and prior context in the economic powerful Islamic world see Grierson 1960). The Parker Chronicle's use of *fresisc* and *denisc* to describe typical styles of ship-construction (s.a. AD 896) in the continuation of the annals from AD 893–914 represents the further extension of the range of these forms to material culture.

This whole body of evidence is very complicated. It is unquestionably the constant engagement of the past populations with ethnic terminology that confirms the reality of the phenomena. Carefully studied, this material allows us to understand both the interaction between language and historical processes much better, and also to indentify where and how actual creativity and agency were exercised by those who used the language in trying to describe and to control the world they found themselves in. In terms of research ethics, it is proper to emphasize these constructive and informative aspects, as well as stressing the need for well-informed, mature and balanced engagement, especially where issues have been made ideologically controversial.

Abbreviations

DOE   *The Dictionary of Old English.* Toronto: Dictionary of Old English Project.

MGH   Monumenta Germaniae Historica

S   *The Electronic Sawyer* (Online catalogue of Anglo-Saxon charters). https://esawyer.cam.ac.uk/

References

Primary sources

Æthelweard *Chronicon.* A. Campbell ed. and trans. *The Chronicle of Æthelweard.* London: Nelson, 1962.

Anonymous Life of Gregory the Great *Liber Beati et Laudabilis Viri Gregorii Papę Urbis Romę.* B. Colgrave ed. and trans. *The Earliest Life of Gregory the Great.* [University of Kansas Press, 1968] Repr. Cambridge: Cambridge University Press, 1985.

Asser W. H. Stevenson, *Asser's Life of King Alfred, together with the Annals of St Neots erroneously ascribed to Asser.* Oxford: Oxford University Press, 1904.

Bede B. Colgrave and Sir R. A. B. Mynors eds. and trans. *Bede's Ecclesiastical History of the English People.* Oxford: Clarendon Press, 1969.

Coates, R. 1990. On some controversy surrounding *Gewissae/Gewissei, Cerdic* and *Ceawlin. Nomina* 13. 1–11.

'Ealdhelm' L. Whitbread, 1976. 'The Old English poem *Aldhelm. English Studies* 57. 193–7.

Gildas *De excidio Britonum.* M. Winterbottom ed. and trans. *Gildas: The Ruin of Britain and Other Works.* Chichester: Phillimore, 1978.

Y Gododdin Sir I. Williams ed. *Canu Aneirin.* Cardiff: University of Wales Press, repr. 1979.

Gregory, Pope *Epistolae. Gregorii I Papae Registrum Epistolarum.* Vol. I *Libri I–VII,* ed. P. Ewald & L. M. Hartmann; Vol. II *Libri VIII–XIV,* ed. L. M. Hartmann. MGH Epistolae I–II. Berlin: Weidmann, 1891, 1899.

Gregory, Pope *Moralium Libri, sive Expositio in Librum B. Job.* Patrologia Latina 75–76, ed. J.-P. Migne. 1857 and 1862.

'Guthlac B' J. Roberts ed. *The Guthlac Poems of the Exeter Book.* Oxford: Clarendon Press, 1979.

Liber Pontificalis L. Duschesne ed. *Le Liber Pontificalis,* 2 vols. Paris: Ernest Thorin, 1886 and 1892.

Liebermann 1903 Fr. Liebermann, *Die Gesetze der Angelsachsen,* 3 vols. Vol. I *Text und Übersetzung.* Halle: Niemeyer, 1903.

Old English Bede T. Miller ed. and trans., *Bede's Ecclesiastical History of the English People.* Oxford: Early English Text Society, 2 vols. OS95–96, 1890–1.

Old English Martyrology C. Rauer ed. and trans., *The Old English Martyrology.* Cambridge: Brewer, 2013.

Old English Orosius J. Bately ed., *The Old English Orosius.* Oxford: Early English Text Society SS6, 1980.

Parker Chronicle J. M. Bately ed., *MS A. The Anglo-Saxon Chronicle: A Collaborative Edition*, vol. 3. Cambridge: Brewer, 1986.

Paulus Diaconus *Historia Langobardorum*. L. Bethmann and G. Waitz (eds.). MGH Scriptores Rerum Langobardorum et Italarum Saec. VI–IX. Hannover: Hahn, 1878, 12–178.

Pliny the Elder H. Rackham ed. and trans. *Pliny: Natural History Vol. II, Books 3–7*. Cambridge MA: Harvard University Press, 1942.

Procopius H. B. Ewing ed. and trans., *Procopius: History of the Wars*, 5 vols. Cambridge, Mass: Harvard University Press. Loeb Classical Library 48, 81, 107, 173 and 217 (1914–28)

Ptolemaeus, Claudius (Ptolemy) C. Müller ed., *Claudii Ptolemaei Geographia*. 2 vols. Paris: Alfred Firmin-Dinot, 1883, 1901.

Saxo Grammaticus H. Ellis Davidson and P. Fisher ed. and trans., *Saxo Grammaticus: The History of the Danes. Books I–IX*. Cambridge: Brewer, 1979–80.

Tacitus *De Origine et Situ Germanorum*. M. Winterbottom & R. M. Ogilvie eds. *Cornelii Taciti: Opera Minora*. Oxford: Oxford Univeristy Press, 1975.

Venantius Fortunatus *Opera Poetica*. F. Leo ed. MGH Auctores Antiquissimi IV. Berlin: Weidmann, 1881.

Vita Alcuini W. Arndt ed. *MGH Scriptores 15.1*. Hannover: Hahn, 1887, 182–97.

Willibald *Vita Bonifatii*. W. Levison ed. *MGH Scriptores rerum Germanicarum in usum scholarum*. Hannover: Hahn, 1905, 1–58.

'Widsith' K. Malone ed. *Widsith*. London: Methuen, 1936. (2nd ed. Copenhagen: Rosenkilde & Bagger, 1962).

Secondary sources

Adamik, B. 2016. The frequency of syncope in the Latin of the Empire: a statistical and dialectological study based on the inscriptions. In P. Poccetti (ed.), *Latinitatis Rationes: Des and Historical Accounts for the Latin Language*, 3–21. Berlin: De Gruyter.

Asmus, W.-D. 1938. *Tonwaregruppen und Stammesgrenzen in Mecklenburg während der ersten beiden Jahrhundertee nach der Zeitenwandel*. Neumünster: Wachholtz.

Bach, A. 1953. *Deutsche Namenkunde*, 3 vols. Vol. 2 *Ortsnamen*. Heidelberg: Winter.

Barnes, M. P. 2012. *Runes: A handbook*. Woodbridge: Boydell.

Braune, W. rev. Eggers, H. 1975. *Althochdeutsche Grammatik*. 13th edn. Tübingen: Max Niemeyer.

Campbell, A. 1959. *Old English grammar*. Oxford: Oxford University Press.

Carella, B. 2012. Alcuin and the Legatine Capitulary of 786: the evidence of scriptural citations. *Journal of Medieval Latin* 22. 221–56.

Collis, J. 2013. *The Celts: Origins, myths and inventions*. Stroud: Tempus.

Dumville, D. N. 1989. 'The Tribal Hidage: an introduction to its texts and their history'. In S. Bassett (ed), *The origins of Anglo-Saxon kingdoms*, 225–230. London: Leicester University Press.

Erdmann, A. 1890. *Über die Heimat und den Namen der Angeln*. Uppsala: Almqvist & Wiksell.

Fisher, J., M. Richardson & J. L. Fisher. 1984. *An anthology of Chancery English*. Knoxville: University of Tennessee Press.

Flierman, R. 2017. *Saxon identities AD 150–900*. London: Bloomsbury.

Foot, S. 1996. The making of Angelcynn: English identity before the Norman Conquest. *Transactions of the Royal Historical Society* 6. 25–49.

Förstemann, E. 1900. *Altdeutsches Namenbuch*. Bonn: Hanstein.

Galestin, M.C. 2008. *Frisii* and *Frisiavones*. *Palaeohistoria* 49/50. 687–708.

Greule, A. 2014. *Deutsche Gewässernamenbuch: Etymologie der Gewässernamen und der zugehörigen Gebiets-, Siedlungs- und Flurnamen*. Berlin: De Gruyter.

Grierson, P. 1960. The monetary reforms of 'Abd al-Malik: their metrological basis and their financial repercussions. *Journal of the Economic and Social History of the Orient* 3. 241–264.

Herman, J. trans. R. Wright. 1997. *Vulgar Latin*. University Park, PA: Penn State Press.

Hines, J. 2023. 'Anglo-Saxonists', 'Anglo-Saxonism' and 'Anglo-Saxon': trying to make some sense of things. In B. Ludowici & H. Pöppelmann (eds.), *New Narratives for the First Millennium AD? Alte und neue Perspektiven der archäologischen Forschung zum 1. Jahrtausend n.Chr.* Neue Studien zur Sachsenforschung 11. 299–313. Wendeburg: Braunschweigisches Landesmuseum.

Hogg, R.M. & R.D. Fulk. 2011. *A Grammar of Old English. Volume 2: Morphology*. Oxford: Wiley-Blackwell.

Holton, D. et al. 2019. *The Cambridge grammar of Medieval and Early Modern Greek*. Cambridge: Cambridge University Press.

Horrocks, G. 2010. *Greek: A history of the language and its speakers*. 2nd edn. Chichester: John Wiley & Sons.

Jackson, K. 1953. *Language and history in Early Britain*. Edinburgh: University Press.

James, S. 1999. *The Atlantic Celts: Ancient people or modern invention?* London: British Museum Press.

Jordan, R. 1934. *Handbuch der mittelenglischen Grammatik. 1: Lautlehre*. Heidelberg: Winter.

Kaufmann, H. 1968. *Ergänzungsband zu Ernst Föstemann Personennamen*. Munich: Fink.

Kuhn, H. 1973. Der Name. In H. Beck et al. (eds), *Hoops' Reallexikon für germanischen Altertumskunde*, 2nd. ed: sv. ANGELN, I§1. Berlin: De Gruyter.

Lambert, T. 2017. *Law and order in Anglo-Saxon England*. Oxford: Oxford University Press.

Laur, W. 1958. Angeln und die Angeln in namenkundlicher Sicht. *Jahrbuch der Angler Heimatvereins* 1958. 46–49.

Laur, W. 1992. *Historisches Ortsnamslexikon von Schleswig-Holstein*. Neumünster: Karl Wachholtz.

Liebermann, F. 1903. *Die Gesetze der Angelsachsen. Erster Band: Text und Übersetzung*. Halle: Max Niemeyer.

Lyon, S. 1969. Historical problems of Anglo-Saxon coinage — (3) denomination and weights. *British Numismatic Journal* 38. 204–222.

Lyon, S. 1976. Some problems in interpreting Anglo-Saxon coinage. *Anglo-Saxon England* 5. 173–224.

Mees, B. 2023. *The English Language before England: An Epigraphic Account*. New York: Routledge.

Meid, W. 1969. *Germanische Sprachwissenschaft: Band 3 Wortbildungslehre*. Berlin: De Gruyter.

Molyneaux, G. 2015. *The formation of the English kingdom in the tenth century*. Oxford: Oxford University Press.

Naismith, R. 2024. The Anglo-Saxons: myth and history. *Early Medieval England and its Neighbours* 51.

Price, N. 2020. *The children of ash and elm: A history of the Vikings*. London: Allen Lane.

Price, N. 2021. The Viking phenomenon: paradigms, parameters, and progress. Lecture to the Society of Antiquaries of London, 8 April 2021. https://www.youtube.com/watch?v=jvxUIw1RxO4

Richards, J. 1980. *Consul of God: The life and times of Gregory the Great*. London: Routledge & Kegan Paul.

Richter, M. 1984. Bede's *Angli*: Angles or English?. *Peritia* 3. 99–114.

Rivet, A. L. F. & C. Smith. 1979. *The place-names of Roman Britain*. London: Batsford.

Springer, M. 2004. *Die Sachsen*. Stuttgart: Kohlhammer.

Sweet, H. 1885. *The oldest English texts*. Oxford: Early English Text Society, OS 83.

Udolph, J. 2004. Suffixbildungen in alten Ortsmanen Nord- und Mitteldeutschlands. In T. Andersson & E. Nyman (eds.), *Suffixbildungen in alten Ortsnamen* 137–75. Uppsala: Acta Academiae Regiae Gustavi Adolphi LXXXVIII.

Voß, H.-U. 2007. From the Baltic to the Danube: Early Roman Iron Age warriors from Hagenow, Mecklenburg, and their relations with the Barbarian and Roman world. In A. Bliujienė (ed.), *Weapons, Weaponry and Man. Archaeologia Baltica* 8. 58–68.

Walker, H. E. 1956. Bede and the Gewissae: The political evolution of the Heptarchy and its nomenclature. *Cambridge Historical Journal* 12. 174–186.

Wegewitz, W. 1977. Zur Stammesgeschichte der Langobarden der Spätlatène- und der römischen Kaiserzeit im Gebiet der Niederelbe. *Studien zur Sachsenforschung* 1. 427–444.

Willroth, K.-H. 1992. *Untersuchungen zur Besiedlungsgeschichte der Landschaften Angeln und Schwansen von der älteren Bronzezeit bis zum frühen Mittelalter*. Offa-Bücher 72. Neumünster: Karl Wachholtz.

Wood, I. N. 1983. *The Merovingian North Sea*. Alingsås: Viktoria Bokförlag.

Woolf, A. 2024. The Viking paradigm in Early Medieval history. *Early Medieval England and its Neighbours* 51.

Yorke, B. 1989. The Jutes of Hampshire and Wight and the origins of Wessex. In S. Bassett (ed), *The Origins of Anglo-Saxon Kingdoms*, 84–96. London: Leicester University Press.

Old West Frisian *thēia**, Saterlandic *taie* and Modern West Frisian *triuwe* 'to push'

Jarich Hoekstra
Christian-Albrechts-Universität

> In this contribution I present the Frisian cognates of ModDu. *duwen* 'to push' etc. Although cognate forms of this verb are found in the older and, partly, the younger stages of all West Germanic languages, it has not, as yet, been found in Old Frisian and its modern dialects. The aim of this study is, first of all, to fill this unexpected gap and, more generally, to take a closer look at the word field of 'to push, to press' in Frisian.

In Modern Dutch *duwen* is a common verb for 'to push, to shove, to thrust'. It is actually a southern (Flemish) form that replaced the northern form *douwe* in the written language and the spoken standard language. The verb occurs as *dūwen, douwen* in Middle Dutch and as *bethūwen** 'to suppress' in Old Dutch (EWN, s.v. *duwen*). Modern German has an obsolete or dialectal verb *deuhen, dauhen* 'to press (e.g. grapes), to push' going back to MHG *diuhen* and OHG *dūhen* (EWA, s.v. *dûhen*).[1] In Modern English the verb has not survived, but in Old English it occurs as *þēowon, þȳwan* 'to press, to impel, to urge; to stab' (Bosworth & Toller 1898). Finally, the verb is found in Middle Low German as *dūwen* 'to push' (Lasch & Borchling 1956-I, s.v. *dūwen*).[2]

The etymology of the verb is not entirely clear. Some scholars attribute it to the Indo-European (extended) root **(s)teu-k-* 'stoßen, schlagen' and posit a Germanic proto-form **þūhjan* < **þunhjan* (IEW 1032, 1100). Others want to connect this same Germanic proto-form with the root of such verbs as ModWFris.

---

1. The EWA deserves praise for giving Old and Modern Frisian its rightful place, but s.v. *dûhen* it refers to a non-existent Modern West Frisian cognate *dūwe* (for details on the uncommon Dutch loanword *dowe* in Modern West Frisian, see below). This form can be traced back to the *Friesch Woordenboek* (Dijkstra 1900, 1903, 1911), which mentions *dûwe* as the word for 'to push' in the Hylpen/Hindelopen dialect (see below).

2. Kroonen (2013:551) further mentions Faroese *týggja* 'to impress on someone' as a cognate from beyond West Germanic.

https://doi.org/10.1075/nss.34.07hoe
Available under the CC BY-NC-ND 4.0 license. © 2025 John Benjamins Publishing Company

twinge, ModDu. *dwingen*, ModHG *zwingen* 'to force' (Seebold 1970: 527; Kroonen 2013: 551; EWA, s.v. *dûhen, dwingan*). Finally, there are those who argue that possible traces of *grammatischer Wechsel* (*hw–gw*) in the data and the occasional occurrence of strong inflection might point to an original strong verb of the second ablaut class, going back to **(s)teu-kʷ* with a labiovelar extension, and with several analogical formations (Blankenstein 1907, EWN).[3] As to the etymology of the verb *duwen* etc., I have nothing new to offer here, apart from bringing the Frisian cognates into play, and I will take PGmc **pūhjan* for granted here, also as the base for the Frisian forms.

Now consider the following Old West Frisian fragment from the rhyme *Fan sincte Willebrords leringha* (About Saint Willibrords teachings), that is part of the legal catechism *Haet is riucht?* (What is law?)[4] in the manuscript *Jus Municipale Frisonum* (Buma & Ebel 1977-I, 69–70):

> Aec ief him dat riocht truch God,
> dat hia mosten halda Justianus bod
> ende heet, eer se fan hem schaete,
> dat se hiara landes therwa bisette
> ende hyt him habba lete
> ende sie dat emmer toe riochte hielde
> end hij zijn ban deeroen leide,
> hoe se deerefter nen koneng deerof ne **theide**   [HRt-J II, 6]

Buma & Ebel (1977-I, 69–70) provide the following German translation:[5]

> Auch verlieh er ihnen nach Gottes Willen das Recht,
> daß sie das Gesetz des Justi[ni]anus halten mußten,
> und er verfügte, bevor sie von ihm schieden,
> daß sie, wessen ihr Land bedürfte, festsetzen dürften
> und er sie das *[Beschlossene]* behalten lassen wollte,
> und sie das immer als Recht bewahren sollten,

---

3. In many (if not all) cases the strong forms are secondary. Thus the verb *duwe* [dyvə] 'to push' (PRET *doof*, past part. *doven*) in the vernacular of the West Frisian island of It Amelân/Ameland, a Dutch dialect on a Frisian substrate, was drawn into the second ablaut class by analogy with the strong verbs *skuwe* 'to shove', *snuwe* 'to sniff' and *stuwe* 'to blow, to fly around (dust)' (cf. Oud 2016).

4. See Gerbenzon (1971a, b) on the historical background of this Old Frisian legal text.

5. English translation: He also gave them the right by God'(s will) / that they should hold Justinian's commandment / and ordered, before they separated from him, / that they should establish whatever their country needed / and he would leave that [what they decided] to them / and they should always keep that as a law, / and he would affirm it by decree, / so that afterwards no king would deprive them of it.

> und er das mit seinem Bann bekräftigen würde,
> damit nachher kein König sie dessen beraube

The last word of this text fragment is *theide*, a 3rd person singular preterite subjunctive form of a verb that has not been satisfactorily identified thus far. It is found not only in *Jus Municipale Frisonum* (J), but also in the parallel text in the *Unia* manuscript (U) (Sytsema 2012). The same text is included in the *Roorda* manuscript (Ro) and in the incunabulum *Druk* (Dr), but here different verbs are used:

hoe se deerefter nen koneng deerof ne **theide**	(J)
huse nenne[6] koningh therefter of ne **theide**	(U)
ho se deer eeffter neen koni*ng*h deer oeff ne **taghe**	(Ro)
hose deer eefter neen koni*ng*h of ne|te	(Dr)

Buma (1996) posits an infinitive **tegia* for *theide*, which he tentatively derives from OFris. *togia* 'fortschleppen' (i.e. to drag away),[7] and he translates this verb as 'fortreißen, berauben' (i.e. to tear away from, to deprive of). Both Buma's etymology and his translation are highly questionable. The infinitive ending *-ia* does not cause i-mutation, so that *togia* could never become **tegia*. Moreover, the allomorphy *teg-/tei* in infinitive and preterite would be unparalleled in Frisian and can, as far as I can see, not be accounted for. Buma seems to draw the postposition *-of* of the pronominal adverb *deerof* into the verb meaning; 'dessen beraube' as a free translation of *deerof theide* might be correct, but the verb form *theide* in itself would literally have to mean something like 'risse (3rd PERS.PRET.SUBJ of *reißen*)' (i.e. would tear).

Hofmann & Popkema (2008) probably had qualms about Buma's etymology and posited an infinitive form *teia* (with a question mark), though preserving Buma's translation. On the basis of the *Unia* text Hofmann & Popkema (2008) also provide a compound **ofteia* 'wegziehen, berauben' (i.e. to pull away from, to deprive of), without a question mark, but with the note "(oder entst[ellt] *oftiā*?)" (i.e. or corrupt *oftiā*?). A privative verb with the particle *of-* normally selects a theme argument and a source argument, the former of which receives accusative case and the latter dative case (cf. *aldeer man ene manne zijn goed ofstelt* 'whenever one steals his possessions from a man', J III, 66a). As such a verb like **ofteia* (or **oftiā*) would not match with the syntax of the sentence, in which the thema argument would be missing and the source argument (*se*) would have the wrong

---

6. The form *nenne* (ACC.SG) is odd here (but see below).

7. This translation, which is also found in Hofmann & Popkema (2008), is a bit misleading; *togia* (ModWFris. *tôgje*, Sat. *toogje*, FÖ *tööge*) simply denotes 'schleppen' (i.e. to drag, cf. Buma 1954: 132; Vries 1982: 163).

case (accusative instead of dative). Moreover, it is hard to see, how the actually attested verb form *theide* could be connected to the (strong) verb *tiā* 'to pull'. Perhaps the authors had in mind the parallel text in the *Roorda* manuscript, which shows the 3rd person singular preterite subjunctive *taghe* (instead of regular *tege*), with the stem vowel of the preterite indicative *tāch*. For the *Druk* text Hofmann & Popkema (2008) tentatively propose a verb *ofnēda* 'abnötigen' (i.e. to extort from), which is hardly convincing, either phonologically (the expected preterite would be *-natte < *-nætte < *-nǣd(i)the < *-naudithe*, not *-net(t)e*, cf. Hoekstra & Tigchelaar 2014) or syntactically (again, the theme argument is missing and the source argument should be dative, not accusative). It seems more consistent to interpret *of* as an ellipsis of *(ther)of* (both in Dr and in U),[8] *ne* as the negative particle (as in the other texts) and *tē* as the 3rd person singular present subjunctive of *tia* 'to pull' (comparable to the preterite subjunctive *taghe* in Ro).

As for *theide* in J and U, I propose to take the <th>-digraph at face value as representing an (original) /þ/ and to assume an infinitive form OWFris. *thēia** deriving from PGmc *þūhjan* 'to push' (by *i*-mutation of *ū* and subsequent unrounding to *ē*, syncope of *h* between vowel and sonorant and loss of *n* at the end of an unstressed syllable). Accordingly, the relevant passage in *Fan sincte Willebrords leringha* would (literally) translate into German and English as follows:

> damit nachher kein König sie davon drängen würde
> so that afterwards no king would push them from it

The variation in verbs in J, U, Ro and Dr might in fact suggest that the form *thēide*, which is found in the older manuscripts (J, U), where it rhymes (though imperfectly so) with *leide*, was not well understood any more and was replaced by a formally somewhat similar, but semantically antonymic and non-rhyming verb in the younger sources, viz. *tāghe* (Ro) and *tē* (Dr). The curious accusative *nenne koningh* in U might be indication that, even already in this older text version, the meaning and syntactic valency of *thēide* had become obscure.

Hypothetical OWFris. *thēia** 'to push' is corroborated by the modern Saterlandic verb for 'to push', which is *taie* (Minssen 1854: 223; Fort 2015). The Old

---

8. For the elliptic use of *of* one may compare the following passage from the Fivelgo manuscript (Sjölin 1970-I: 364):

> Sa is thach niar, thet to betriane, and sines hera hild to winnane, than eng mon him is **of** to driwane, sa fir saret alle betria welle. (F XIX, 36)
> 'Then he (the tenant) is still more entitled to compensate for it (the damage to the land or the non-payment of the tenure for the land) and to win his (land)lord's benevolence, than any man is, to drive him away from it (the land), insofar as he wants to compensate for everything'

Frisian diphthong *ēi* develops via *āi* to *ai* (sometimes *oai*) in Saterlandic, cf. Sat. *klaie* 'to mess' (*klaast/klaat, klade, klaad*) <*klāia < *klēia < PGmc *klaijan, Sat. *klaie* 'to scratch, to tickle' (*klaast/klaat, klade, klaad*) < *klāia <*klēia < PGmc *klaujan, Sat. *Lai* 'lightning' < *lāith(e) < OFris. *lēithe < PGmc *laugithō (cf. Löfstedt 1931: 155–156; Lehmann 1986: 228), also *laie* 'to lighten', and Sat. *Koai / Kai* (Skäddel/Scharrel) 'key' < OFris. *kēi, kāi*.[9] Kramer (1969) wants to connect *taie* with ModDu. *tooien* 'to adorn; to fit out', *voltooien* 'to complete', *touwen* 'to curry (hides)' < PGmc *taujan* 'to make' (cf. Kroonen 2013). Referring to the last Dutch verb, Kramer (1969: 12) writes:

> Wan wi betoanke dät me deerbi doo Fälle kneedjen däd, so ferstounde wi gliks dät et dätsälge Woud is as 'taie'. Ap gootisk rakt et dan noch 'taujan' dat 'moakje' un 'dwo' betjut. Dät is dan uk wier dätsälge Woud as 'taie', wan me betoankt dät jü Betjudinge sik annerd hääbe kon fon 'moakje' tou 'Leeder moakje' un dan tou 'kneedje'.[10]

A formal development of PGmc *taujan* > OFris. *tēia > *tāia > Sat. *taie* is certainly feasible,[11] but a semantic development from 'to curry (hides)' to 'to knead' to 'to push, to press' is rather farfetched and not attested in other Germanic languages. Derivation of Sat. *taie* from OFris. *thēia* 'to push' is clearly preferable.

If *thēia* was already becoming obsolete in Old West Frisian, it may have been partly replaced by OWFris. *trytza, thretza* 'to push, to press' (past part. *tracht*), the cognate of ModDu. *drukken*, ModHG *drücken* < *þrukkjan (Loopstra 1935: 43–44; Miedema 1979), but perhaps also by the Middle Dutch loanword *dūwa*, although this is not yet attested in Old West Frisian (see the discussion below). The verb *trytza, thretza* only occurs in the Old West Frisian charters (O) and the Snitser Recesboeken (SnR) for pressing a seal, but it may have had

---

9. In order to prevent the long diphthong *āi* from appearing in a closed syllable, Saterlandic shows the same strategies as Fering-Öömrang (cf. Hoekstra 2010: 104): In a sequence *āiC* either the second part of the diphthong is deleted (*klaat* <*klāit*) or the consonant is dropped (*Lai* < *lāi(th)*).

10. Translation: When we consider that one kneaded the hides in this process, we immediately understand that it is the same word as 'taie'. Further, in Gothic there is 'taujan', which means 'to make' and 'to do'. That is again the same word as 'taie', when one considers that the meaning may have changed from 'to make' to 'to make leather' and then to 'to knead'.

11. Kramer (1969: 12) refers to OWFris. *tāia* (past part. *tayth/taied*) 'to make, to fit out', which only occurs in the alliterative pair *tayth ende tymmeret* (J), *taied ende temmeret* (U) 'fit out and build'. This verb is traditionally derived from hypothetical *tāwia, a denominative of *tāwe* 'tool, equipment' (van Helten 1896: 58–60; Buma 1996: s.v. *taya*), but a direct derivation from *taujan* (> *tēia > *tāia*) seems to be preferable. The past participle ending -*ed* in *taied* may have been influenced by *temmeret*.

a wider use originally. Neither *thēia** nor *trytza, thretza** survive in Modern West Frisian. Modern West Frisian has a relatively young and quite puzzling verb for 'to push', viz. *triuwe* (PRET *treau*, past part. *treaun*), a strong verb of the first ablaut class, which has the additional meaning 'to hug (by pressing close to one-self)' (cf. ModHG *drücken* 'to push; to hug'). The verb *triuwe* does not appear before the early modern period (17th century) and is hard to etymologize. Some early proposals by van Helten (1894: 361), *triuwe*=Goth. *þreihan* 'to press' (also Kloosterman 1907: 72),[12] Loopstra (1935: 43), *triuwe*=OE *þrowian* 'to suffer, to endure', and Brandsma (1936: 203), *triuwe* < OFris. *thrūwa* 'to threaten', must be rejected on both formal and semantic grounds.

In the 1970s, Miedema published a series of articles in which he pointed out some possible Old Norse loanwords in West Frisian from the period of the Viking raids in Frisia or Viking rule in the Low Countries (Miedema 1972; 1978; 1979). Most of Miedema's proposals were convincingly refuted by Dietrich Hofmann, see Hofmann (1976) on OWFris. *touwerdey* 'Thursday', ModWFris. *touwer(je)* '(to) thunder'[13] and Hofmann (1979) on the family name *Jarla*. One proposal by Miedema has, however, remained uncontested until now, viz. his etymology of ModWFris. *triuwe* 'to push'. Miedema (1979) considers this word as the equivalent of Old Norse *þrífa* 'to catch, to grasp', a verb only found in the Scandinavian languages and, probably as a Scandinavian loan, in English (cf. Kroonen 2013: 547). He suggests that ModWFris. *triuwe* is a Scandinavian loanword, but leaves open the possibility that the verb is originally Frisian and, in that case, represents a common Frisian-Scandinavian lexical feature (cf. already Löfstedt (1967: 59; 1969: 32), who credits Falk & Torp (1910, 1911) for first comparing the

---

12. Van Helten draws a parallel between *triuwe* and ModWFris. *riuwe* 'to thread, to string' (OHG *rīhan* 'id.') and argues that the glide *w* in both verbs stems from a preterite plural with the stem vowel of the preterite singular (**thrēwun, *rēwun*). Even if one is not willing to accept this rather mechanical Junggrammatiker-style explanation, it might still be the case that whatever explains *w* in *riuwe* explains it in *triuwe* too. There are, however, not only formal problems. Direct cognates of Goth. *þreihan* are rare or maybe even non-existent in West Germanic; verbs that are sometimes compared with this form, like MHG *drīhen* 'to embroider', early ModDu. *driegen* 'to baste, to tack' (EWN), have rather special meanings, which might suggest another explanation.

13. Hofmann (1976) shows that *touwer* is not ON *Þór* 'Thor', but rather a form with metathesis (*thonre* > *thōre* > *tōwer*) of OWFris. *thunder-, t(h)on(d)er-, t(h)onger-* 'thunder' (ModWFris. *tonger*). Interestingly, van Helten (1896: 61) regards *touwer*, which he does not want to interpret as 'thunder', but as 'mit heftigkeit forttreibender wind' (heavily pressing wind), as a nomen agentis of the Old West Frisian cognate of ModDu. *duwen*, ODu. *bethūwen**, OE *þȳwan* etc., implicitly assuming a Germanic proto-form **þūwjan*, in which *w* would have blocked *i*-mutation. Note, however, that *ū* in open syllable would have resulted in MWFris. *ō*, not in *ɔu*, e.g. OFris. *skūva* 'to shove' > ModWFris. *skowe* (cf. also Miedema 1972: 4–6).

Scandinavian with the West Frisian verb). Miedema's etymology was adopted by the WFT (23, s.v. *triuwe*), Dyk (2008:108) accepts it in his article on the so-called Jorwert breaking (the diphthongization of front vowels before bilabial *w*) in West Frisian, and Strik (2015:288–289) takes the same tack in leading ModWFris. *triuwe* directly back to PGmc **þrīban*.

Deriving ModWFris. *triuwe* from OFris. **thrīva* (< ON *þrífa* 'to catch, to grasp'?) would be formally unproblematic (cf. ModWFris. *skriuwe* < OFris. *skrīva*, ModWFris. *bliuwe* < OFris. *blīva* etc.),[14] but from a semantic point of view it is not immediately clear how **thrīva* could assume the meaning 'to push'. Löfstedt (1967:59) takes the somewhat infelicitous meaning description 'naar zich toe halen' next to 'duwende van zich af (weg-)drukken' (i.e. to push away from oneself) in Sytstra & Hof (1925:268) literally as 'to draw towards oneself' and compares with ON *þrífa eptir e-u* 'try to grab something', *þrífa í e-t* 'to reach out for, to grasp at something'. From the context it is clear, however, that Sytstra & Hof refer here to *triuwe* in the sense of 'to hug (by pressing close to oneself)'. Miedema suggests that there is a connection to the loss of *trytza, thretza** 'to push, to press' in late Old West Frisian, the meaning of which would have been transfered to **thrīva*. It remains unclear, however, what would have triggered this semantic transfer. Moreover, even though the Old Frisian written tradition is fragmentary, one might wonder why a supposedly old loan or 'Erbwort' like **thrīva* surfaces so late in West Frisian (and only there).[15] So, apart from the question whether Old Norse loanwords in West Frisian are conceivable, the etymological equation of ModWFris. *triuwe* with ON *þrífa* is rather shaky.

Saving Miedema's original idea that the decline of *trytza, thretza** and the rise of *triuwe* are somehow related, I venture another etymology, in which *triuwe* is basically a blend of the (near-)synonyms *trytza, thretza** × **dūwa* < MDu. *dūwen*.[16] The peripheral West Frisian dialects, i.e. those in the city of Hylpen/ Hindeloopen and on the islands of Skylge/Terschelling and Skiermûntseach/ Schiermonnikoog, have all adopted the Dutch loanword: Hylpen/Hindeloopen

---

14. On the pronunciation of the diphthong *iu* (or triphthong *iuw*) in verbs like these and its development in the Modern West Frisian dialects see Hof (1933:58–61).

15. In the Fivelgo manuscript one finds *thriw-* in the pair formula *thriwan ende dregan* 'driving and carrying' (Rfi-F 117) and in the compound *thriwal wey* 'cattle track' (Rfi-F 44), where it clearly denotes 'to drive (cattle)' and where <th> is most certainly an orthographic variant of <d> (cf. Sjölin 1970:83; van Helten 1907:73).

16. Cf. Jespersen (1922:312–313): "Blendings of synonyms play a much greater role in the development of language than is generally recognized. [...] Such blends are especially frequent in words expressive of sounds or in some other way symbolical." To which extent sound symbolism (a phonaestheme *tr-/dr-* 'pressure'?) has played a role in this case, is not easy to determine (for clear cases of sound symbolic blending in Fering-Öömrang see Hoekstra 2022).

doewe [duːə] (Blom & Dyk 2019), Skylge/Terschelling *doeë* (Roggen 1976; van Wichen-Schol 1986; for older *troekje* see below), Skiermûntseach/Schiermonnikoog *deeuwe* (Spenter 1968: 303; Visser & Dyk 2002). Even in central West Frisian *dowe* was marginally found alongside common *triuwe* (WFT 4, s.v. *dowe II*).[17] This might be an indication that the Dutch loan **dūwa* intruded into late Old West Frisian and entered into competition with *trytza, thretza** (perhaps eventually reducing its range of use to the technical meaning 'to press a seal'). A formal blending of both verbs, in which *trytza, thretza** provided the onset and **dūwa* the rhyme, would have resulted in **trūwa*. The subsequent incorporation of this blend in the first ablaut class (**trūwa* ⟶ *triuwe*) was favoured by the fact that many verbs of this class end in *-(i)uwa* and in particular by the fact that nearly all of these have an initial consonant cluster containing a liquid, most often *r* (ModWFris. *driuwe* 'to drive; to force; to float', *skriuwe* 'to write', *priuwe* 'to taste', *wriuwe* 'to rub', *riuwe* 'to thread' and *bliuwe* 'to stay', *kliuwe* 'to climb', but, without a liquid, *wiuwe* 'to wave'). In these respects, *triuwe* fits perfectly in the first ablaut class.[18] The first ablaut class verb O(W)Fris. *drīva, driuwe* in its special meaning 'to compel, to force' may have been a catalyst in the attraction process, but it was probably not semantically close enough to *trytza, thretza** to be the base of the blend itself. Note that the first ablaut class has attracted a few other weak verbs, which did not have an *ī* as their original stem vowel: ModWFris. *priuwe* 'to taste' ⟵ **preuwa* < OFris. **prēva* < PGmc **prōbjan* (Spenter 1968: 305), ModWFris. *wiuwe* 'to wave' ⟵ **weuwa* < OFris. **wēva* < PGmc **waibjan* (cf. ON *veifa* 'to wave, to swing').

Blending is also claimed to have played a role in the development of the North Frisian verbs for 'to push, to press'. Next to OWFris. *trytza, thretza**, OIslNFris. **thrikka* (FÖ *trak*, Helg. *trek*) and OMainlNFris. **threkka* (SG *treeke*) < PGmc **þrukkjan*, with a geminate *-kk-*, one must assume OFris. **thrukia* < PGmc **þrukōn* (Århammar 1986: 26), with a simple consonant *-k-*.[19] This variant seems to be attested throughout the whole Frisian-speaking language area; it is con-

---

17. The Dutch dialects on a Frisian substrate spoken in a number of West Frisian cities show younger Dutch *douwe* (Duijff 1998; van Bree & Versloot 2008: 77). The 'mixed' dialect of the island of It Amelân/Ameland has *dôuwe/duwe* 'to push' as well, but next to the Frisian substrate word *trieuwe* (weak verb), which has acquired the special meaning 'to hit, to hurt sneakily (children)' here (Oud 2016). Also compare *ôftrieuwe* 'to trash, to beat up' (Burger 1944: 272, Oud 2016).

18. Verbs of the second ablaut class ending in *-ūwa* always have an *s*-cluster (without a liquid) as their onset: OFris. *skūwa* 'to shove', ModWFris. *skowe*; OFris. **stūwa* 'to blow, to fly around (dust)', ModWFris. *stowe*; OFris. **snūwa* 'to sniff', Early ModWFris. *snuwe, snouwe* [snoːwə], ModWFris. *snuve* < ModDu. *snuiven*.

19. ModIcel. *þroka* 'to endure', Faroese *troka* 'to push, to shove; to jostle' and ModSwed. *tråka* 'to work slowly and tediously; to struggle along' might go back to PGmc **þrukōn* too.

tinued by Skylge/Terschelling *troekje* (Steenmeijer-Wielenga 1972: 45, 57; Roggen 1976; Roggen 1975: 79),[20] Wangeroogic *thruukii* (FA I, 54; FA III, 226) and Harlingerlandic *truhken* (König 1911: 60) 'to push, to press'.[21] Århammar (1986: 26) suggests that the verb might also underly Moor. *krööge* 'to push, to press', FÖ *kröge* 'to strain (with bowel movements); to push; to make one's way with difficulty', Sylt. *krööki* 'to squeeze together', if these forms are derived from a blend of *krodia*[22] (Moor. *kroose*, FÖ *krööde* 'to compel to eating or drinking') × *thrukia*.[23] Matters are further complicated here by the presence of a verb *truke/truuke* 'to go fast and determined; to take a walk' in Fering-Öömrang (FÖW, s.v. *truke/truuke*), which might be an ablaut form to *thrukia* with *uu/u* < OFris. *ā* < PGmc *au* (cf. ModIcel. *þrauka* 'to endure').[24]

Taking a wide view of the word field 'to push, to press' in Frisian, one may thus conclude that a moribund verb for 'to push', *thēia**, the cognate of ModDu. *duwen* etc. (< PGmc *þūhjan*), can just be identified in Old West Frisian and survives as a relic (*taie*) in Saterlandic. The central verb for 'to push, to press' in Frisian is without any doubt OWFris. *trytza, thretza** / OInsNFris. **thrikka* / OMainN-Fris. **threkka* (< PGmc *þrukkjan*) with its byform **thrukia* (< PGmc *þrukōn*), of which traces can be found in West, East and North Frisian. The young Modern West Frisian verb *triuwe* might be a blend of OWFris. *trytza, thretza** and the Dutch loanword **dūwa*, which was attracted into the first ablaut class.

---

20. Roggen (1976) also mentions the substantive *troek* 'struggle against the wind'.

21. Perhaps Early ModWFris. *druwckje* (Gysbert Japicx) 'to press; to print' with a *d*-onset from ModDu. *drukken* belongs here as well (Brandsma 1936: 65), but note that a Dutch loanword *drukka* is already found in Old West Frisian (Hofmann & Popkema 2008), so that the form with -*je* may very well be an idiosyncrasy of Gysbert Japicx. Modern West Frisian *drukke* has been completely adapted to the Dutch verb. For 'to print' the verb *printsje* came into use in the 19th century (in the written language).

22. Cf. OWFris. *krodia* 'to hinder, to block', MDu. *croden* 'to hinder, to bother' next to OE *crēodan, crūdan* 'to crowd, to press, to drive', MDu. *crūden* 'to push (e.g. a wheelbarrow)', ModDu. *kruien* 'to push a wheelbarrow (*kruiwagen*); to drift, pile up (ice)' (Kroonen 2013: 303). Also ModWFris. *kroade* 'wheelbarrow' (MDu. *crode(wagen), crūdewagen*), *kroadzje* 'to push a wheelbarrow', *bekroadzje* (refl.) 'to bother'.

23. NG *krooge/krååge* has the generalised stem vowel of the 2nd and 3rd person singular present, the preterite and the past participle. In this dialect *u* in open syllabe became *oo/åå* before an *a* of the following syllable, *öö* elsewhere (Löfstedt 1931: 112–119; Århammar 1986: 26).

24. Clement (1853: 80) records a verb *truuke* 'bei Tisch nötigen mit zu essen oder mehr zu essen' (to compel to join the dinner or to eat more) in Öömrang.

Acknowledgements

For helpful comments on a draft of this paper I thank Siebren Dyk, Patrick Stiles, Arjen Versloot and Oebele Vries.

References

Århammar, N. 1986. Etymologisches um den 'Stress', mit einem Exkurs zum älteren Einfluß des Niederländischen auf das Nordfriesische. In H.L. Cox, V.F. Vanacker & E. Verhofstadt (eds.), *Wortes anst — Verbi gratia*. Donum natalicium Gilbert A.R. de Smet, 19–28. Leuven: Acco.

Blankenstein, M. van. 1907. Duwen. *Tijdschrift voor Nederlandse Taal- en Letterkunde* 26. 70–73.

Blom, G. & S. Dyk. 2019. *Graet Hylper Wordebook. Woordenboek van het Hindelopers*. Ljouwert: Afûk.

Bosworth, J. & T. Northcote Toller. 1898. *An Anglo-Saxon dictionary*. Oxford: Clarendon Press. (+ T. Northcote Toller. 1921. *An Anglo-Saxon dictionary: Supplement*. Oxford: Clarendon Press). [http://bosworth.ff.cuni.cz (last accessed 17th July 2023)]

Brandsma, W.L. 1936. *Het werkwoord bij Gijsbert Japicx*. Assen: van Gorcum & Comp.

Bree, C. van & A.P. Versloot. 2008. *Oorsprongen van het Stadsfries*. Ljouwert: Afûk.

Buma, W.J. 1954. *Het tweede Rüstringer handschrift*. 's-Gravenhage: Nijhoff.

Buma, W.J. & W. Ebel (eds.). 1977. *Westerlauwerssches Recht I. Jus Municipale Frisonum*. 2 Bde. Göttingen: Vandenhoeck & Ruprecht.

Buma, W.J. 1996. *Vollständiges Wörterbuch zum westerlauwersschen Jus Municipale Frisonum*. Ljouwert/Leeuwarden: Fryske Akademy.

Burger, H. 1944. *Avondrood. Bloemlezing en overzicht der Stadfriese, Amelandse en Bildtse letteren*. Assen: Van Gorcum & Comp.

Clement, K.J. 1853. Eigentümliche Elemente der friesischen Sprache. *Herrigs Archiv* XII. 71–81.

Dijkstra, W. 1900, 1903, 1911. *Friesch Woordenboek*. Leeuwarden: Meijer en Schaafsma.

Duijff, P. 1998. *Wurdlisten fan 'e Fryske stedsdialekten*. Ljouwert/Leeuwarden: Fryske Akademy.

Dyk, S. 2008. Jorwert breaking: A Late Old West Frisian sound change. In R.H. Bremmer Jr, S. Laker & O. Vries (eds.), *Advances in Old Frisian philology*, 91–128. Amsterdam: Rodopi.

EWA = *Etymologisches Wörterbuch des Althochdeutschen*. Bd. II, *bî — ezzo* (1998). Edited by A.L. Lloyd, R. Lühr & O. Springer. Göttingen: Vandenhoeck & Ruprecht.

EWN = *Etymologisch Woordenboek van het Nederlands*. 4.dl. (2003, 2005, 2007, 2009). Onder hoofdredactie van dr. M. Philippa et al. Amsterdam: Amsterdam University Press.

FA I, II = H.G. Ehrentraut, Mittheilungen aus der Sprache der Wangerooger. *Friesisches Archiv* I (1847/1849). 3–109, 338–406; II (1954). 1–84.

FA III = H.G. Ehrentraut, *Mittheilungen aus der Sprache der Wangerooger*. Bearbeitet und herausgegeben von A.P. Versloot. Ljouwert/Leeuwarden: Fryske Akademy (1996).

Falk, H. & A. Torp. 1910, 1911. *Norwegisch-dänisches etymologisches Wörterbuch*. Heidelberg: Winter.

Fort, M. C. 2015. *Saterfriesisches Wörterbuch*. Hamburg: Buske.

FÖW = *Fering-Öömrang Wurdenbuk. Wörterbuch der friesischen Mundart von Föhr und Amrum. Herausgegeben von der Nordfriesischen Wörterbuchstelle der Christian-Albrechts-Universität zu Kiel*. Neumünster: Wachholz (2000).

Gerbenzon, P. 1971a. Bijdrage tot het bronnenonderzoek van *Haet is riocht*. *Us Wurk* 20. 1–18.

Gerbenzon, P. 1971b. *Haet is Riocht?* (What is Law?): An Old Frisian introduction to jurisprudence, related to 'Elegantius in iure diuino'. *Bulletin of Medieval Canon Law* Ser. NS 1. 83–85.

Helten, W. L. van. 1894. Zur Lexikologie und Grammatik des Altwestfriesischen. *Beiträge zur Geschichte der deutschen Sprache und Literatur* 19. 345–440.

Helten, W. L. van. 1896. *Zur Lexikologie des Altwestfriesischen*. Verhandelingen der Koninklijke Akademie van Wetenschappen te Amsterdam. Afdeeling Letterkunde. Deel I. N°. 5. Amsterdam: Müller.

Helten, W. L. van. 1907. *Zur Lexikologie des Altostfriesischen*. Verhandelingen der Koninklijke Akademie van Wetenschappen te Amsterdam, Afdeeling Letterkunde, Nieuwe Reeks, Deel IX. Amsterdam: Müller.

Hoekstra, J. 2010. Westerlauwerskfrysk etymologysk griemmank (V). *Us Wurk* 59. 101–120.

Hoekstra, J. 2022. Eine kleine Übung in Lautsymbolik: Die Entstehung des NJ-Anlauts im Fering-Öömrang. *Nordfriesisches Jahrbuch* 57. 129–145.

Hoekstra, J. & G. Tigchelaar. 2014. *kenna ~ kanna*: the *e/a*-variation in Old Frisian and its Modern Frisian reflexes. *Amsterdamer Beiträge zur älteren Germanistik* 73. 185–200.

Hof, J. J. 1933. *Friesche dialectgeographie*. 's-Gravenhage: Nijhoff.

Hofmann, D. 1976. *Thor*, 'Donnerstag' und 'Donner' in Friesland. *Us Wurk* 25. 33–42.

Hofmann, D. 1979. Zur Herkunft des altfriesischen Geschlechtsnamens *Jarla* und des Namenselement *Jar-*. *Naamkunde* 11. 67–79.

Hofmann, D. & A. T. Popkema. 2008. *Altfriesisches Handwörterbuch*. Heidelberg: Winter.

IEW = J. Pokorny, *Indogermanisches etymologisches Wörterbuch*. Bern: Francke Verlag (19892).

Jespersen, O. 1922. *Language, its nature, development and origin*. London: Allan & Unwin.

Kloosterman, P. 1907. *Het vocalisme der beklemtoonde lettergrepen van den Metslawierschen tongval, historisch uiteengezet. Een bijdrage tot de kennis der historische grammatica van het Nieuwwestfriesch*. Groningen: Wolters.

König, E. (ed.). 1911. *Johannes Cadovius Müllers Memoriale linguæ Frisiscæ*. Norden: Diedr. Soltau's Verlag.

Kramer, P. 1969. Straie, daie, laie, taie. *Seelter Trjoue* 4(2). 12.

Kroonen, G. 2013. *Etymological dictionary of Proto-Germanic*. Leiden: Brill.

Lasch, A. & C. Borchling. 1956. *Mittelniederdeutsches Handwörterbuch*. Bd. I. Neumünster: Wachholtz.

Lehmann, W. P. 1986. *A Gothic etymological dictionary*. Leiden: Brill.

Löfstedt, E. 1931. *Nordfriesische Dialektstudien*. Lund: Gleerup / Leipzig: Harassowitz.

Löfstedt, E. 1963/1965, 1966, 1967, 1969. Beiträge zur nordseegermanisch-nordischen Lexikographie, *Niederdeutsche Mitteilungen* 19/21. 281–345; 22. 39–64; 23. 11–61; 25. 25–45.

Loopstra, J. J. 1935. *De assibilatie in de Oudfriese oorkonden*. Haarlem: Tjeenk Willink & Zoon.

Miedema, H. T. J. 1972. Thor en de Wikingen in Friesland. Oudfries **thôresdey* 'Donderdag'. *Naamkunde* 4. 1–20.

Miedema, H. T. J. 1978. Van Dublin naar Dokkum. *Naamkunde* 10. 48–80.

Miedema, H. T. J. 1979. Fries *triuwe* (Oudnoors *thrífa*) en *trytza*, twee woorden voor 'duwen, drukken'. *Taal en Tongval* 31. 56–61.

Minssen, J. F. 1854. Mittheilungen aus dem Saterlande. *Friesisches Archiv* II. 135–227.

Oud, A. G. 2016. *Groat Amelander Woa'deboek*. Bezorgd door Siebren Dyk. Ljouwert/Leeuwarden: Fryske Akademy / Afûk.

Roggen, C. 1975. Schyljelôn. Dêgeliks leven 'Om Aast' ±1800 − ±1900. *It Beaken* 37. 1–85.

Roggen, C. 1976. *Woordenboek van het Oostterschellings. Wêdenboek fon et Aasters*. Ljouwert/Leeuwarden: Fryske Akademy.

Seebold, E. 1970. *Vergleichendes und etymologisches Wörterbuch der germanischen starken Verben*. The Hague / Paris: Mouton.

Sjölin, B. 1970. *Die "Fivelgoer" Handschrift*. I. Einleitung und Text. Den Haag: Nijhoff.

Steenmeijer-Wielenga, T. 1972. *Ds. J.S. Bakker en het Westterschellingers*. Ljouwert/Leeuwarden: Fryske Akademy.

Strik, O. 2015. Modelling analogical change. A history of Swedish and Frisian verb inflection. Dissertation, University of Groningen.

Sytsema, J. 2012. *Diplomatyske útjefte Kodeks Unia* (Diplomatic edition of Codex Unia). [http://tdb.fryske-akademy.eu/tdb/index-unia.html (last accessed 17th July 2023)]

Sytstra, O. H. & J. J. Hof. 1925. *Nieuwe Friesche Spraakkunst*. Leeuwarden: van der Velde.

Visser, W. & S. Dyk. 2002. *Eilander Wezzenbúek. Woordenboek van het Schiermonnikoogs*. Ljouwert/Leeuwarden: Fryske Akademy.

Vries, O. & M. Oosterhout. 1982. *De Leeuwarder Stedstiole 1502–1504*. Grins/Groningen: S.F. Frysk Ynstitút Ryksuniversiteit Grins/Groningen.

WFT = *Wurdboek fan de Fryske taal / Woordenboek der Friese taal*. Ljouwert/Leeuwarden: Fryske Akademy (1984–2011).

Wichen-Schol, M. van. 1986. *Woddenboek fan et Westers*. Ljouwert/Leeuwarden: Fryske Akademy.

Deʒsastan

John Insley
Ruprecht-Karls-Universität Heidelberg

In 603, the Angles of Bernicia inflicted a crushing defeat on the Scots of Dálriada at a place called *Degsastan* in Bede's History. The site of the battle and the etymology of the name have been the subjects of much scholarly debate. The present paper concludes that there is not enough evidence to establish the location of the site of the battle, but that the name was formed in an English linguistic environment and denoted a stone landmark named after a man with the Northumbrian name **Deʒsa* (from Proto-Anglian **Dæʒisa*). The paper also examines the use of the *-isan*-suffix in Germanic anthroponymy and that of other hypocoristic suffixes in combination with the name element *Dæʒ-* in Old English.

In 603, the Angles of Bernicia inflicted a crushing defeat on an army led by Áedán, king of the Scots of Dálriada "in loco celeberrimo, qui dicitur *Degsa stan*, id est *Degsa lapis*" (Bede HE i. 34; Colgrave & Mynors 1969:116). Bede HE v. 24 has [ad] *Degsastanae* (Colgrave & Mynors 1969:562). The site of the battle and the etymology of the name have been the subjects of much speculation. Bede's text gives no indication of the site of the battle, though most commentators would tentatively favour Dawston Rigg in Liddesdale (Roxburghshire) (cf. Anderson 1941:152; Förster 1941:796–797; Colgrave & Mynors 1969:117 n. 4, 603; Cox 1976:19–20). The debate about the site of the battle was examined in detail by Peter Hunter Blair (1954:157–158 n. 2) and it is most apposite to quote his conclusion: "For all that has been written about the site of *Degsastan*, no advance has been made beyond the position of John Smith in 1722: 'hic locus, Bedae seculo tam celebris, hodie ignotus est.'"

In the Anglo-Saxon Chronicle, the name occurs as [æt] *Dæʒsan stane* in Mss. D and E, [æt] *Eʒesanstane* [sic! for *Deʒesanstane*] in Mss. B and C and as [æt] *Dæʒstane* in a 12th-century addition to Ms. A (Förster 1941:796). These forms indicate, as indeed Förster (1941:796) noted, that the West Saxon scribes of the Anglo-Saxon Chronicle recognized that Northumbrian *Deʒsa-* (with Northumbrian loss of inflectional *-n* as a result of weak stress, cf. Campbell 1959:189 [§ 472]) was the genitive of a personal name **Dæʒsa* or **Deʒesa*. Förster

https://doi.org/10.1075/nss.34.08ins
Available under the CC BY-NC-ND 4.0 license. © 2025 John Benjamins Publishing Company

(1941: 796–797) realized that the modern *Dawston* (or rather Scots *Dawstane*) cannot be the continuation of Bede's *Degsa stan*, because the latter would have resulted in Modern English *Daistone (or, better, *Daystone). Förster (1941: 798) reconstructs Bede's *Degsa stan* as OE **Deʒ(e)sa(n)stān*, a name with a short or hypocoristic form of a personal name as its first element. He notes that occasionally different hypocoristic variants and short forms can exist side by side. Förster (1941: 807–808) derives Scots *Dawstane from an OE *Daʒanstān 'Daʒa's stone' and interprets English *Daʒa as a short form and takes *Deʒesa to be a hypocoristic derivative of *Daʒa formed with an *-is-*suffix. He goes on to deny the existence of the *-s-*suffix in Germanic personal nomenclature, but points out that the suffixes *-isso* and *-issōn* are well attested in Celtic, where we find such names as Continental Celtic *Dubn-issus* and, with *n*-extension, *Bodu̯-issō* (ibid.; cf. also Evans 1967: 151, 197). Förster concludes that here *Deʒesa must have been formed from *Daʒa by means of a British *-isso*-suffix. He takes these names to belong to British *dago-s 'good' and compares such names as Continental Celtic *Dago-dubnus, Dago-vassus* and *Ollo-dagus* and the hypocoristic variants *Dagō, Dag-illus, Dag-idius* and the feminine *Dag-aniā* (1941: 809; for further examples and discussion, see Evans 1967: 188–189). Förster (1941: 809) derives **Deʒesa-* from a British hypocoristic form *Dag-issōn and interprets *Daʒa as the corresponding short form to an unknown full name in Celtic **Dago-*. Förster (1941: 810) takes the stone in question to have had the function of a boundary mark associated with a man who bore a British dithematic name in *Dago-* which he suggests would have been variously shortened to a simplex **Daga(n)* or *Dagān or to a suffix formation *Dagissu. He further suggests that Bede's informant(s) would have anglicized the second of these forms to **Dæʒisan-*. Subsequent *i*-mutation would have caused raising of [æ] > [e] in the stem syllable to give **Degisan-* with reducton to *Deʒsa(n)-* as a consequence of weak stress in the medial syllable.

Kenneth Jackson (1953: 612) regarded Förster's etymology as "very uncertain". Barrie Cox (1976: 19–20, s.v. DAWSTON RIGG?) quotes Förster, but cites the doubts of Peter Hunter Blair (1954). Andrew Breeze (2021: 58–59, 60–61) has proposed a monolith near Drumelzier in Tweedsdale as the site of *Degsastan*. He is of the opinion that the form *Degsastan* may be corrupt and would emend the first element to *Degui*, an Old Welsh (here, more specifically Cumbric) scribal variant of *Dewi* (David) comparable with *Osguid* for OE *Ōswiu* in the *Annales Cambriae* (Breeze 2021: 60). Breeze (ibid.) justifies this with the remark: "The termination *-ui* here having three vertical strokes, it was not difficult for an English scribe to misread the first as minuscule *s* and the two latter as *a*." Ingenious as this may be, it is nevertheless mere speculation and it must be rejected as bearing no relationship to the form given by Bede.

140   John Insley

A more promising line of inquiry is that of Olof S. Anderson (1941:73) who gave the head-form as *De(g)sa* which he took to be a derivative of the name theme *Dag-* (OE *dæʒ* m. 'day'), an element which he notes is common in 'Old German' names, such as Bede's *Dægberct* (the Merovingian king Dagobert I). May G. Williamson, who noted that Dawston Burn in Castleton parish is usually taken to be the site of the battle, suggested an unrecorded Old English personal name **Dæʒ(i)sa* as the first element of Bede's *Degsa stan* (Williamson 1942: xvi [§ xliii]). Bede's form shows *i*-mutation of [æ] > [e] (see Brunner 1965:72 [§ 96.1]) and subsequent syncope of weakly stressed medial [i] (see Brunner 1965:132–133 [§ 159c]; cf, also Anderson 1941:116, where we find the caveat "if *Degsa* is from **Dægisa*, pers. name"). This caveat is unnecessary and we can take the base to be OE (Northumbrian) **Deʒsa(n)stān* from earlier **Dæʒisanstān* (< Germanic **Dayisan + *staina-*). The word order of specific followed by generic indicates that this name was formed in a Germanic linguistic environment, in this case that of the Northumbrian dialect of Old English, though this in itself cannot be taken to indicate that the personal name is of Germanic origin. Again, though the name was formed by English speakers, this in itself is no proof that it was in a region that was actually settled by the English. On the other hand, there is enough evidence that the *-isan-* suffix was used to form hypocoristic personal names in Germanic (see the comprehensive analysis in Nedoma 2004:263–266). Among Nedoma's examples are runic **buirso** standing for pre-OHG **Būriso* on a mid-6th-century bow brooch from Beuchte in Lower Saxony (Nedoma 2004:261–264), *Flavius Hariso*, the name of an officer presumably of Erulian origin in a 4th-/5th-century sarcophagus inscription from Concordia in the Veneto (Reichert 1987:420; Nedoma 2004:265), and the name of the Visigothic king *Witiza* (Nedoma 2004:266). A feminine variant in *-isōn-* would appear to be represented by runic **hariso** (for **Harisō*) on a 3rd-century bow brooch from Himlingøje on Sjælland, though, as Marie Stoklund (1999:580) has indicated, the discovery of the masculine names **niþijo** and **wagnijo** in inscriptions from Illerup Ådal may have cast some doubt on this assumption. We also have a West Germanic *Aliso*, mentioned by Ammianus Marcellinus as the name of a *tribunus* (Reichert 1987:36), and an ablative form of uncertain gender, *Torisa*, which occurs in a letter of Ennodius (Reichert 1987:707). Nedoma (2004:265, 266) has demonstrated that it is unclear whether these two names are hypocoristic formations of the *-isan-/-isōn-* type. *Torisa* can be interpreted as a simple short form of a name in *Thoris-*, such as *Thorisarius* (Gothic **Þaúris-harjis*), in which case it would not be a true hypocoristic suffix formation of the *-isan-/-isōn-*type.

A clear English parallel to the first element of *Deʒsastan* is provided by the Oxfordshire place-name BENSON < OE **Benesinʒtūn* 'estate named after Benesa' (Gelling 1953–54:116; Watts 2004:50). The base of the personal name **Benesa* would be PrimOE *Bæn-isan-, a hypocoristic form of an original byname belonging to OE *bana* m. 'killer, slayer'. A strongly inflected name containing an -s-suffix is *Tilisi*, a hypocoristic form of names in *Til-*, such as *Tilberht, Tilfrið, Tilrēd*, etc., which occurs in the 9th-century part of the Durham *Liber Vitae* (Insley & Rollason 2007:184 [A.4.162]). Other suffixed pet-forms of dithematic names in *Dæʒ-* are also on record. A hypocoristic form of names in *Dæʒ-*, OE *Dæʒel*, forms the first element of DAYLESFORD in Gloucestershire (Smith 1964–65, Pt. 1: 217). Smith (1964–65, Pt. 1: 69) interprets DAGLINGWORTH in Gloucestershire as 'enclosure of the people of Dæggel or Dæccel'. He takes OE *Dæʒʒel* to be a hypocoristic form of such names as *Dæʒbald* or *Dæʒhelm* and regards OE *Dæccel* as a similar -el-derivative of the OE *Dæcca* suggested for the first element of DAGENHAM Essex (ibid). Watts (2004:177) wisely drops the second of these alternatives and prefers to take the first element of DAGLINGWORTH to be OE 'Dæggel'. Early spellings of DAGLINGWORTH given by Smith (1964–65, Pt. 1: 69) include the following: *Daglingworth, -yng-, -wurth* c. 1150, 1273, 1323, 1324 *et freq* to 1535, *Dagelingwurth, -yng-, -worth* 1248, 1268, 1287, 1291 *et freq* to 1365. <-g-> at the end of the first syllable of the medieval spellings of DAGLING-WORTH could appear to stand for original geminated [ɣɣ]. A reflex of the simplex [ɣ] would have formed a diphthong [aʊ] with the preceding [a] in Middle English, this then being represented by <aw>, and would have resulted in the Modern English form *Dawlingworth* (see Jordan 1968:115 [§§ 111, 112]). If we were concerned with a diminutive *-ila(n)-suffix, we might expect *i*-mutation of [æ] > [e], though before consonant groups and geminates, there was a strong tendency to eliminate the umlaut and to restore [æ] by analogy with related non-mutated forms (cf. Campbell 1959:76 [§ 194]). However, an *-ila(n)-suffix would have induced palatalization of [ɣ]. Presupposing a velar suffix, we can take the first element of DAGLINGWORTH to be OE *Daʒʒol(a) < Germanic *Dayɣ-ula(n)-. We would have to start with a Germanic simplex form *Daya, a short form of dithematic names in *Daya-* (cf. Latino-Gothic *Dagalaifus*). This *Daya* would have then been subject to expressive consonantal gemination of [ɣ] > [ɣɣ] followed by the acquisition of a velar hypocoristic suffix. To judge by the early spellings, reduction of the geminated [ɣɣ] > [ɣ] must have taken place in early Middle English after the diphthongization of [a] + [ɣ] > [aʊ] which was early in the south-west Midlands (cf. Jordan 1968:115 [§§ 111, 112]). A velar -ula-suffix is also contained in [signum manus] *Theabul* 697 or 712 (contemporary or original) S 19 Ms. 1 and in *Utol episcopus* (bishop of Hereford) 799 × 801 (original) S 1186a. *Theabul* stands for OE *Þēoful* (Insley 2003:382a), while *Utol* is a hypocoristic side-form of *Utta*, a short form of dithematic names in *Ūht-* (see Ström 1939:78–79).

Much effort has been expended on attempts to ascertain the site of the battle of *Deʒsastan*. It has been shown to be a fruitless endeavour because Bede's text simply does not give us precise details. The name is a different matter. Morphologically, it is clearly an Old English formation and it is best interpreted as denoting a stone landmark named after a man with the unrecorded Old English (Northumbrian) personal name *Deʒsa from Proto-Anglian *Dæʒisa.

References

Anderson, O. S. 1941. *Old English material in the Leningrad manuscript of Bede's Ecclesiastical History* (Skrifter utgivna av Kungl. Humanistiska Vetenskapssamfundet i Lund/Acta reg. societatis humaniorum litterarum Lundensis 31). Lund: C. W. K. Gleerup/Leipzig: O. Harrassowitz/London: Humphrey Milford/Oxford: Oxford University Press).

Bede HE = Bede's *Historia Ecclesiastica Gentis Anglorum*.

Breeze, A. 2021. 603: Carnage at 'Degsastan' by Wester Dawyck, Borders. In A. Breeze, *British battles 493–937: Mount Badon to Brunanburh*, 49–62. London: Anthem Press.

Brunner, K. 1965. *Altenglische Grammatik. Nach der angelsächsischen Grammatik von Eduard Sievers*, 3. Aufl. Tübingen: Niemeyer.

Campbell, A. 1959. *Old English grammar*. Oxford: Clarendon.

Colgrave, B. & R. A. B. Mynors (eds.). 1969. *Bede's ecclesiastical history of the English people*. Oxford: Clarendon.

Cox, B. 1976. The place-names of the earliest English records. *Journal of the English Place-Name Society* 8. 12–66.

Evans, D. E. 1967. *Gaulish personal names. A study of some Continental Celtic formations*. Oxford: Clarendon.

Förster, M. 1941. *Der Flußname Themse und seine Sippe. Studien zur Anglisierung keltischer Eigennamen und zur Lautchronologie des Altbritischen* (Sitzungsberichte der Bayerischen Akademie der Wissenschaften. Philosophisch-historische Abteilung, Jahrgang 1941, Band I). Munich: Verlag der Bayerischen Akademie der Wissenschaften.

Gelling, M. 1953–54. *The place-names of Oxfordshire* (English Place-Name Society 23–24). Cambridge: Cambridge University Press.

Hunter Blair, P. 1954. The Bernicians and their northern frontier. In N. K. Chadwick (ed.), *Studies in early British history*, 137–172. Cambridge: Cambridge University Press.

Insley, J. 2003. Pre-conquest personal names. In H. Beck, D. Geuenich & H. Steuer (eds.), 2003. *Reallexikon der germanischen Altertumskunde*, 2. Aufl., Bd. 23. 367–396. Berlin: De Gruyter.

Insley, J. & D. Rollason. 2007. A.4. English monothematic names. In D. Rollason & L. Rollason (eds.). 2007. *The Durham Liber Vitae*. London. British Library, MS Cotton Domitian A VII. Volume II: Linguistic Commentary, 165–187. London: British Library.

Jackson, K. H. 1953. *Language and history in Early Britain. A chronological survey of the Brittonic languages first to twelfth century A.D.* Edinburgh: Edinburgh University Press.

Jordan, R. 1968. *Handbuch der mittelenglischen Grammatik*: Lautlehre, 3. Aufl. Heidelberg: Winter.

Nedoma, R. 2004. *Personennamen in südgermanischen Runeninschriften* (Studien zur altgermanischen Namenkunde I, 1, 1). Heidelberg: Winter.

Reichert, H. 1987. *Lexikon der altgermanischen Namen*, 1. Teil: Text (Thesaurus Palaeogermanicus 1. Band). Vienna: Verlag der österreichischen Akademie der Wissenschaften).

S = Sawyer, P. H. 1968. *Anglo-Saxon charters. An annotated list and bibliography* (Royal Historical Society Guides and Handbooks 8). London: Royal Historical Society (The Electronic Sawyer: http://www.esawyer.org.uk/searchfiles/index.html), cited by number and accessed 12 June 2023.

Smith, A. H. 1964–65. *The place-names of Gloucestershire* (English Place-Name Society 38–41). Cambridge: Cambridge University Press.

Stoklund, M. 1999. Himlingøje § 2. Runologisches. In H. Beck, D. Geuenich & H. Steuer (ed.), 1999. *Reallexikon der germanischen Altertumskunde*, 2. Aufl., Bd. 14. 579–580. Berlin: De Gruyter.

Ström, H. 1939. *Old English personal names in Bede's history. An etymological-phonological investigation* (Lund Studies in English 8). Lund: C. W. K. Gleerup/London: Williams & Norgate, Ltd./ Copenhagen: Levin & Munksgaard — Ejnar Munksgaard.

Watts, V. (ed.). 2004. *The Cambridge dictionary of English place-names. Based on the collections of the English Place-Name Society*. Cambridge: Cambridge University Press.

Rasmus Rask and Vilhelm Thomsen
The Danish godfathers of Finnish linguistics

Petri Kallio
University of Helsinki

This paper is a tribute not only to Hans Frede Nielsen but also to all the other Danish linguists on behalf of all the Finnish linguists. Namely, Finland would hardly have become a "superpower" in Uralic studies without the boost of the two great Danish Indo-Europeanists, Rasmus Rask and Vilhelm Thomsen, who were instrumental in launching the two 19th-century comparative linguistic revolutions in Finland: Palaeogrammarian and Neogrammarian. While Rask served as a role model for the earliest Finnish Uralicists A. J. Sjögren and M. A. Castrén, Thomsen started the modern era in Finnic and Sámi studies, inspiring the foremost Finnish Neogrammarians E. N. Setälä and J. J. Mikkola.

Prologue

This story mainly takes place in the Grand Duchy of Finland, an autonomous part of the Russian Empire from 1809 to 1917. Before 1809 the leading superpower in comparative Uralic linguistics was no doubt Hungary (see e.g. Sajnovics 1770; Gyarmathi 1799). By 1917, however, Finland had taken the lead, thanks to the fact that Finland was a part of the Russian Empire where almost all the Uralic languages were spoken, whereas the only Uralic language spoken in the Austro-Hungarian Empire was Hungarian itself. Yet this was not the only explanation: Finland also received an unexpected helping hand from Denmark.

Rasmus Rask

As is well-known, "Denmark has always been a superpower in linguistics" (Kortlandt 1995: 91). Needless to say, "always" here means 'since the beginning of linguistic science', but then again one of its beginners was Rasmus Kristian Rask (1787–1832). Although he started as a scholar of North Germanic languages (see

https://doi.org/10.1075/nss.34.09kal
Available under the CC BY-NC-ND 4.0 license. © 2025 John Benjamins Publishing Company

especially Rask 1811), his interests soon covered the rest of Indo-European as well as several non-Indo-European languages such as Finnish and Sámi (a.k.a. Lapp). In this connection, I do not need to repeat his achievements outside Uralic studies since there are already numerous excellent biographies including those by our honouree (Nielsen 2003, 2008).[1]

The reason why Rask became interested in Finnish and Sámi is evident: Forest Finnish and Kven Finnish as well as South Sámi, Ume Sámi, Pite Sámi, Lule Sámi, North Sámi, and Skolt Sámi were among the domestic languages of the Dano-Norwegian union before its dissolution in 1814. Instead of Norway, however, he travelled to Sweden in 1812 in order to study Finnish and Sámi because back then Sweden was well ahead of Norway in both Finnish and Sámi studies. As a result, Finnish and Sámi were much more prominent in his magnum opus *Undersögelse om det gamle Nordiske eller Islandske Sprogs Oprindelse* (1818) than its title would ever suggest.[2]

Yet Rask's Finnish and Sámi studies had barely begun. During his 1816–1823 linguistic expedition as far as India and Ceylon he spent most of March 1818 in Turku, the only university town in Finland at the time. His Finnish teacher was the leading Fennist of the era Gustaf Renvall (1781–1841) whom Rask in turn familiarized with modern lexicography and grammatology, as best shown by Renvall's later Finnish dictionary (1826) and grammar (1840). Meanwhile, Rask wrote but never published his own Finnish grammar entitled *Udkast-Optegnelser til en Finsk Sproglære*, which survives in its original manuscript from 1818–1819 as well as in a handwritten copy from the hand of Vilhelm Thomsen dated 1864 (Lauerma 2019).

As Renvall's linguistic work was descriptive rather than historical in approach, he was not destined to become the "Finnish Rask". If anyone deserves this title, it is Anders Johan Sjögren (1794–1855), who failed to meet Rask in person despite being in Turku at the same time. Of course, this was long before social media, not to mention that Sjögren was still an undergraduate student. According to his autobiography (published as Sjögren 1955), Rask had already left Turku for Saint Petersburg when the news about him reached Sjögren. However, his diaries (published as Sjögren 2020) reveal that he did hear the news in time (11 March 1818)

---

1. Rask is undoubtedly the most biographed Danish linguist ever (see Gregersen 2013: xxix–xxx for a bibliography), and also his Finnish connections are exceptionally well documented (see especially Häkli 2017). In order to avoid excessive references, I do not provide references to basic facts that can be found in any biography of him.

2. No such study was in fact written for nearly two centuries until Peter Schrijver's *Language contact and the origins of the Germanic languages* (2014) similarly paid closer attention to Finnish, Sámi, and other neighbouring languages.

but that he did not regard himself as worthy of introducing himself to such a world-famous scholar.[3]

Even so, Rask instantly became Sjögren's role model: what Rask had already done on the Germanic side, Sjögren intended to do on the Finnic side. Yet it took until April 1819 before he was ready to write a letter to Rask who was still stuck in Saint Petersburg. Sjögren's research plan attached with Renvall's recommendation letter was well-received by Rask who, however, was unable to promise anything concrete because in June 1819 he finally continued his expedition from Saint Petersburg towards Persia and India. Instead, Rask eagerly encouraged Sjögren to pursue his dream in Saint Petersburg where the big money was. From April 1820 onwards, therefore, Sjögren permanently lived and worked in Saint Petersburg, and the rest is history so to speak (Branch 1973; Laine 2020).

Retrospectively speaking, Sjögren is today considered a no less important pioneer in comparative Uralic linguistics than Rask in comparative Indo-European linguistics. Moreover, Sjögren also laid the foundation for ethnolinguistics and anthropological linguistics through his extensive fieldwork activities in the Russian North (1824–1829), the Caucasus (1835–1838),[4] and the Baltics (1846 and 1852). Already in his lifetime his works were expanded and perfected by his compatriot and protégé Matthias Alexander Castrén (1813–1852), but this fact does not take anything away from Sjögren. On the contrary, what Sjögren initiated, Castrén completed. Then again, both of them named Rask as their primary source of inspiration (Korhonen 1986: 42, 51).

Interestingly, the earliest Finnish Uralicists were inspired by Rask's contributions to Indo-European rather than those to Uralic. As a matter of fact, most of the latter works were only published posthumously (Rask 1834: 1–113, 1836: 330–359). Indeed, the few exceptions were not really published by himself, such as his short report in *Finnische Sprache und Literatur* (1821) which was based rather on his 1818–1819 personal letters to his friend Rasmus Nyerup (1759–1829). It seems to me that although Rask was genuinely interested in Finnish, he was also self-critical enough to realize that he could never have competed against native Finnish speakers like Renvall and Sjögren. Apparently, this was also the reason why Rask never finished his Finnish grammar either.

---

3. Even as an eminent academician, Sjögren still suffered from low self-esteem due to his humble origins. Little did the son of a village cobbler know that Rask was likewise only the son of a village tailor.

4. Sjögren travelled to the Caucasus in order to treat his health issues, but instead he ended up studying local languages such as Georgian, Kabardian, and, most of all, Ossetic (Aalto 1971: 28–30). Although he returned to Saint Petersburg half-blind and frostbitten, his sacrifice was not in vain because in 1844 the Imperial Academy of Sciences created a chair of Finnic and Caucasian studies specifically for him.

Yet there were no native Sámi speaking linguists around, and so Rask did not shelve one of his last publications, *Ræsonneret lappisk Sproglære* (1832), the modernization of *En lappisk Grammatica* (1748) by the Norwegian priest Knud Leem (1697–1774). Even today Rask's North Sámi grammar is unique in the sense that it was written by someone who by his own admission had never even seen a single speaker of the language — although during the proofreading process he was finally able to consult a native North Sámi named Hans Mortensen Kolpus (1803–1880). Rask was already severely ill from tuberculosis, but his grammar proved to be the best of its kind so far. True, it was not flawless, but the guilty party was more often Leem than Rask.

"Perhaps the most brilliant of the early linguists" (Lehmann 1967: 29) and "the greatest Danish linguist ever" (Basbøll 2005: 8) are only a few superlatives used to describe Rask, and with his North Sámi grammar he certainly lived up to his reputation. Above all he is credited for laying the foundation for modern North Sámi orthography, which at his insistence became phonemic.[5] There were also glimpses of his genius, such as his observation to equate the Finnic *l*-cases with the Sámi *al*-postpositions. This brilliant idea went unnoticed by the 19th and 20th century Uralicists until it was finally convincingly confirmed to be correct at the beginning of this millennium (see now the detailed discussion by Aikio & Ylikoski 2007, 2016).

As Rask had already immortalized himself in his early twenties thanks to his *Vejledning til det Islandske eller gamle Nordiske Sprog* (1811), it may come as a surprise that someone with achievements of such magnitude never saw his 45th birthday. No matter how much he had published, he left even more unpublished manuscripts behind,[6] some of which were instantly published as *Samlede tildels forhen utrykte Afhandlinger* (1834–1838). Around a century later, however, another three-volume collection followed, this time titled *Udvalgte Afhandlinger* (1932–1935), which also included new critical editions of his already published studies. Indeed, if anything proves that Rask has reached the highest of academic echelons, it is the existence of critical editions more typically reserved for the likes of Plato and Aristotle.

---

5. For Rask's sake I have favoured the spelling Sámi over Saami throughout this article. Regardless of the languages in question, he was always a strong advocate of phonemic orthographies, even though North Sámi ended up being pretty much the only language in whose case he instantly succeeded. For instance, it took until the 1948 orthography reform before Danish officially replaced the digraph *aa* with his favoured *å*. On the other hand, he similarly offered a more Hungarian-like orthography for Finnish (e.g. *aa* → *á*), but all such proposals were already shot down by Renvall for typographical reasons (Lauerma 2019: 195–196).

6. A contributing factor was the fact that while Rask insisted on using his own Danish orthography, the Royal Academy and other publishers insisted on using theirs, thus causing a stalemate (Gregersen 2013: xxvi).

As far as comparative Uralic linguistics was concerned, Rask's arguably most important paper was *Afhandling om den finniske Sprogklasse* written in Saint Petersburg in May 1819 (but not published until 1834:1–46). At the time when most Uralic languages remained fragmentarily documented, his Finno-Ugric language family was already as we know it today: Finno-Volgaic (Finnic, Sámi, Mari, Mordvin), Ugric (Hungarian, Mansi, Khanty), and Permic (Komi-Zyryan, Komi-Permyak, Udmurt). He specifically excluded Chuvash by instead advocating its Turkicness, something that the rest of the world figured out much later (Schott 1841; Ahlqvist 1859). On the other hand, Rask was also among the first to subdivide Finnic into North Finnic (Finnish, Ingrian, Karelian, Olonetsian) and South Finnic (North Estonian, South Estonian, Livonian).

One may now wonder why Rask left such a groundbreaking paper unpublished. First, it was written during his seven-year expedition when it was understandably more difficult for him to publish his studies than both before and after. Second, the same expedition led him to so many new languages stretching from Avestan to Sinhala that Finnish and Sámi were hardly among the first languages on his mind after returning to Copenhagen. And third, Sjögren had by now begun to publish his even more groundbreaking studies, and Rask might have come to the conclusion that his manuscript was no longer worth publishing at least without extensive rewriting. Fortunately, we have it anyway as an eternal proof that his linguistic talent was not limited to Indo-European.

Vilhelm Thomsen

If any Danish linguist followed Rask's legacy to the letter, it was Vilhelm Thomsen (1842–1927).[7] Already as a schoolboy in Jutland he read Rask's books and became interested in studying the same languages, including Finnish. Once a student at the University of Copenhagen from 1859 onwards, Thomsen read every Finnish book he could find in the Royal Library, but he also took every opportunity to speak Finnish with Finnish visitors regardless of whether they were students at the university or sailors at the harbour. As they understood him better than he did them, he found out the hard way what every student of Finnish sooner or later does: written and spoken Finnish are different.

---

7. Thomsen has always interested biographers to a far lesser extent than Rask, not least because while Rask was "a sort of feverish, increasingly intellectually dyspeptic Mozart of linguistics" (Markey 1976:xxxv), Thomsen was "the most unassuming, the most gentle of men" (Konow 1927:929). Thus, the most recent detailed biographies of Thomsen are still his obituaries (see especially Sandfeld et al. 1927).

One of these Finns was the future music lecturer Fredrik Vilhelm Illberg (1836–1904) who visited Copenhagen in summer 1861 and who generously sent Thomsen several Finnish books soon after returning to Finland. Thomsen was so grateful that he sent Illberg a lengthy letter written in flawless Finnish. Illberg was in turn so impressed that he published extracts of the letter in the newspaper *Mehiläinen* (March 1862). Therefore, Thomsen began to gain a name in Finland despite still being an undergraduate student. Soon he was contacted by the amateur comparativist Daniel Europaeus (1820–1884) who became a friend and lifelong correspondent with Thomsen (see further Kallio 2019).

Although Thomsen was eager to visit Finland early on, it had to wait until his graduation in January 1867. Then in the following May he left Denmark for Finland where his host was none other than Illberg. Together they mixed business and pleasure by travelling around Finland, Illberg collecting folk songs and Thomsen linguistic materials. Meanwhile, almost every Finnish VIP was excited to meet Thomsen: not only the Fennists Elias Lönnrot (1802–1884) and August Ahlqvist (1826–1889), but also the authors Johan Ludvig Runeberg (1804–1877) and Zachris Topelius (1818–1898). Still, Thomsen also had time to conduct fieldwork among Estonian sailors at the Helsinki harbour.

In September 1867 Thomsen briefly visited Saint Petersburg where he was guided by the Finnish Sanskritist Otto Donner (1835–1909). Incidentally, Donner later became the first Nordic professor of comparative linguistics (1875–1905), whereas Thomsen was only the second one (1887–1912). Once back in Finland, Thomsen still had a chance to meet the Norwegian Lappologist Jens Andreas Friis (1821–1896) who was visiting Helsinki. Thomsen returned to Copenhagen in October 1867, but in order to study Sámi he took a shorter trip to Norway in summer 1868 before he was finally ready to finish his doctorate.

On 23 March 1869 history was made: Thomsen defended his doctoral dissertation titled *Den gotiske sprogklasses indflydelse på den finske* (1869). Although the Neogrammarian revolution had barely begun in Indo-European studies, he already introduced the Neogrammarian methods to Germanic-Finnic loanword studies. Just as the great German Indo-Europeanists Franz Bopp (1791–1867) and August Schleicher (1821–1868) had earlier emphasized the role of sound laws in genetic linguistics, Thomsen emphasized the role of sound substitutions in contact linguistics, thus marking the rise of loanword studies as a linguistic science.

Indflydelse or more precisely its German translation *Über den einfluss der germanischen sprachen auf die finnisch-lappischen* (1870)[8] was an instant success all

---

8. The translator was no less than the German *Wunderkind* Eduard Sievers (1850–1932), "probably the most brilliant of the Neogrammarians" (Lehmann 1967: 210). Following Rask, Thomsen still spoke of *gotisk* which Sievers translated as *germanisch*. According to our honouree,

over Europe and deservedly received an award from the Bopp-Stiftung. The rising Neogrammarian generation was particularly excited by the fact that many Proto-Germanic reconstructions like *kuningaz 'king' were now independently confirmed by phonologically and semantically perfect or near perfect Finnish matches like kuningas 'king', thus demonstrating that the comparative method indeed works, contrary to what is still argued in the literature (see now Olsen 2017 for a splendid discussion).

Paradoxically, although Thomsen received raving reviews everywhere else, the Finnish scholarly community long remained strangely indifferent. Note that the only apparent exception did not really belong to the scholarly community: Europaeus wasted no time to declare Indflydelse as an epoch-making masterpiece (Finlands Allmänna Tidning, 14–17 July 1869). Contrary to some 20th century Fennists, the 19th century Fennists did not oppose loanwords for nationalistic reasons, but Ahlqvist in particular was exceptionally loanword-friendly (see especially Ahlqvist 1871). Still, he was also a Palaeogrammarian to whom the Neogrammarian Thomsen was simply too modern.

Indeed, Thomsen single-handedly began the modern era in Finnic and Sámi linguistics in general and etymology in particular. Without belittling the legacies of Sjögren, Castrén, and Ahlqvist, they still had no rigorous methods to distinguish between true cognates and coincidental lookalikes. All this was changed by Thomsen whose suggested loan etymologies remain predominantly accepted by today's etymological dictionaries (see especially Kylstra et al. 1991–2012). As a matter of fact, he would no doubt have etymologized even more Finnish words, but by then Lönnrot's monumental Finskt-Svenskt Lexikon (1866–1880) had only reached the letter I (Thomsen 1869:19).

During the 1870s and 1880s Thomsen's publications involving comparative Uralic linguistics were close to zero, the only exception being a two-page abstract (1888). Yet he was hardly angry at the Finns for his mistreatment. Rather, he simply followed his childhood hero Rask by being interested in much more than just Finnish and Sámi. For instance, Thomsen offered the strongest linguistic evidence so far for the Norman theory of Russian origins (1877), something that distracted him from publishing his 1877 study on the Indo-Iranian Palatalgesetz (not pub-

---

Thomsen's terminological choice was evidently linked to Danish anti-German sentiment particularly high immediately after the 1864 disastrous war against the German Confederation (Nielsen 2008:39). Indeed, Thomsen's personal letters sent home during his 1869–1870 European "book tour" confirm that he still felt uncomfortable in Germany (Sandfeld et al. 1927:97). Yet he also befriended several German colleagues, and especially his friendship with the Indologist Ernst Kuhn (1846–1920) proved to be lifelong (see Schmitt 1990).

lished until 1920: 303–327), hence today not known to us as Thomsen's Law (cf. Mayrhofer 1983: 137–142; Collinge 1985: 133–142).[9]

Thomsen finally made a grand comeback to comparative Uralic linguistics with his magnum opus *Beröringer mellem de finske og de baltiske (litauisk-lettiske) Sprog* (1890). No matter how highly we value his debut, this sequel was even better, although it drew less international attention due to the fact that there were of course far fewer Balticists than Germanicists, not to mention that Lithuanian and Latvian were back then largely banned from official usage. This time, however, Finland was ready: the Neogrammarian revolution had finally been launched by the Fennist Emil Nestor Setälä (1864–1935) and the Slavist Jooseppi Julius Mikkola (1866–1946), who both wrote raving reviews about Thomsen's newest masterpiece — Setälä in fact no less than three (Eyser 1912: 227).

As early as 1888 Setälä spent a few months in Copenhagen where he got to know both Thomsen and the preliminary version of *Beröringer*. Hence, Setälä's pioneering reconstruction of Proto-Finnic (1890–1891) owed a lot to Thomsen who, among other things, was the first to identify the Livonian broken tone similar to his native Danish *stød*. As usual, all this happened at the Copenhagen harbour during a 4–5 hour meeting with a Livonian sailor. Setälä was arguably the greatest Fennist of his era and perhaps of all time, although he was notorious for not always sufficiently crediting Thomsen and others. Yet this did not bother Thomsen at all, judging from the fact that he ultimately even became Setälä's father-in-law.

Setälä's friend Mikkola similarly came in touch with Thomsen in 1888. As Thomsen had already discussed Finnic-Germanic and Finnic-Baltic contacts, Setälä suggested that Mikkola should discuss Finnic-Slavic contacts.[10] As a result, Mikkola's *Berührungen zwischen den westfinnischen und slavischen Sprachen*

---

9. This is a pity indeed. Consider Thomsen's compatriot and contemporary Karl Verner (1846–1896) who still remains a household name among Indo-Europeanists, although his contributions other than Verner's Law were modest compared to those of his friend and confidant Thomsen. Incidentally, it was Thomsen who was the first to realize the importance of Verner's discovery and without whose pressure *Eine ausnahme der ersten lautverschiebung* (Verner 1877), maybe "the single most influential publication in linguistics" (Lehmann 1967: 132), might never have been published (Jespersen 1897: 5).

10. The idea did not come from Thomsen who himself had long planned to discuss Finnic-Slavic contacts before Mikkola made it unnecessary (Sandfeld et al. 1927: 107). About the same time Thomsen also shelved his original plan to discuss Uralic-Indo-Iranian contacts, allegedly "because Stackelberg took up the subject before he could do so" (Konow 1927: 932). Contrary to Mikkola, however, the Baltic German born Iranist Reinhold von Stackelberg (1860–1907) never met Thomsen's expectations, but the first exhaustive monograph on Uralic-Indo-Iranian contacts had to wait until this millennium (see now Holopainen 2019).

(1894) was the first Thomsenian loanword study made in Finland, and it was even named after *Beröringer*, as he afterwards admitted himself (1927). Later in life as a world-famous Slavist, however, Mikkola began to accuse his own debut as being too loanword-friendly, but *Die älteren Berührungen zwischen Ostseefinnisch und Russisch* (1938) ultimately proved to be a mere shadow of its groundbreaking predecessor (Aalto 1987:159).

Beröringer cemented Thomsen's position as the foremost authority on Uralic loanword studies, and even the remaining Palaeogrammarians were no longer in a position to complain. One of them was Donner who was never much of a scholar but who was rich enough to found the *Société Finno-Ougrienne* in 1883. His etymological suggestions were severely criticized in *Beröringer*, but he was not one to hold a grudge. Quite the contrary, Donner's *Société Finno-Ougrienne* was instrumental in publishing and promoting Thomsen's 1893 decipherment of the Old Turkic Orkhon inscriptions (1896, 1916). Indeed, if today any non-Finn can name one thing about Thomsen, it is this decipherment which pretty much made him a Turkologist for the rest of his career.

Thus, Thomsen spent three decades without publishing anything on comparative Uralic linguistics apart from short book reviews and encyclopaedia entries. Still, he had not forgotten Finland where he finally returned in 1912 for the first and only time since 1867. This time he was welcomed like the king of Denmark, and his whereabouts were reported on a daily basis by the leading newspapers (see e.g. *Helsingin Sanomat*, 14 September — 2 October 1912). Not everyone was happy though: the radical Fennoman pseudo-etymologist Sigurd Wettenhovi-Aspa (1870–1946) blasted Thomsen as "the chief Finnophobe" (1915:78–79). Amusingly enough, Thomsen spoke better Finnish than the native Swedish speaker Wettenhovi-Aspa ever did.[11]

Thomsen still returned to Uralic loanword studies one last time when his 1869 debut was reprinted in his *Samlede afhandlinger* (1919–1931). Thus, half a century later he wrote a postscript aptly titled *Efterskrift 1919* (1920:239–264). Despite nearing his eighties he was still fully aware of the most recent developments in the field. Hardly surprisingly he sided with his son-in-law Setälä against Tor Evert Karsten (1870–1942) who advocated much earlier and heavier Germanic influence on Finnic. On the other hand, Thomsen was also humble enough to admit that thanks to Just Knud Qvigstad (1853–1957), Karl Bernhard Wiklund (1868–1934),

---

11. Even today Wettenhovi-Aspa is perhaps the best-known etymologist in Finland, not that anyone believes in a single etymology of his. Quite the contrary, the very appeal of his etymologies rests on the fact that they are patently wrong in such a hilarious way that a professional linguist could never reproduce them, no matter how hard one tried.

and Konrad Nielsen (1875–1953), Sámi studies had made such huge steps forward since 1869 that *Indflydelse* had become outdated in this respect.

Indeed, *Indflydelse* was already updated in Thomsen's lifetime (e.g. Setälä 1913) and even more so afterwards (e.g. Kylstra et al. 1991–2012). Instead, "*Beröringer* is still the most comprehensive and significant overview of the linguistic contacts between Finnic and Baltic" (Junttila 2016:15). True, a lot has happened since his passing: Mikkola's student Valentin Kiparsky (1904–1983) already introduced structuralism to Finnish linguistics, but Jorma Koivulehto (1934–2014) also applied it to loanword studies which underwent a true renaissance (see e.g. Kallio 2015).[12] However, while Thomsen's prehistoric interpretations have now become obsolete, his loan etymologies are still rock solid (e.g. Finnish *kallio* 'rock, cliff' ← Germanic **xallijōn-* 'flat rock'; Thomsen 1869:120).

Epilogue

"All Danish linguists are, whether they are aware of this or not, pupils of Rask", as declared by one of them (Gregersen 2013:xxix). Thomsen was a prime example because he briefly studied under Rask's foremost disciple Niels Matthias Petersen (1791–1862). Thomsen in turn mentored the likes of Otto Jespersen (1860–1943) and Holger Pedersen (1867–1953) who maintained Denmark's position as a linguistic superpower (see e.g. Kortlandt 1995). Since Thomsen also acted as Setälä's supervisor, many Finnish linguists are similarly academic descendants of both Rask and Thomsen. Indeed, even I too am one of them through Setälä's student Gustaf John Ramstedt (1873–1950), grandstudent Pentti Aalto (1917–1998), and great-grandstudent Asko Parpola (b. 1941).

---

12. This renaissance did not go unnoticed in Denmark where especially the Indo-Europeanist Jens Elmegård Rasmussen (1944–2013) made frequent use of Finnic and Sámi loanword evidence when discussing Germanic phonology (e.g. Rasmussen 1983), something that was occasionally done by our honouree as well (e.g. Nielsen 1994). Namely, both were well-aware of the state of the art, relying on Koivulehto rather than Thomsen. Not least thanks to Rasmussen's inspiring teaching, this millennium has brought a host of Danish Indo-Europeanists interested in Uralic loanword studies (e.g. Hyllested 2014; Nørtoft 2015; Bjørn 2017).

References

Aalto, P. 1971. *Oriental studies in Finland 1828–1918*. Helsinki: Societas Scientiarum Fennica.

Aalto, P. 1987. *Modern language studies in Finland 1828–1918*. Helsinki: Societas Scientiarum Fennica.

Ahlqvist, A. 1859. Nachrichten über Tschuwaschen und Tscheremissen. *Archiv für wissenschaftliche Kunde von Russland* 18. 39–64.

Ahlqvist, A. 1871. *De vestfinska språkens kulturord: Ett linguistiskt bidrag till finnarnes äldre kulturhistoria*. Helsinki: Frenckell.

Aikio, A. & J. Ylikoski. 2007. Suopmelaš gielaid *l*-kásusiid álgovuođđu sáme- ja eará fuolkegielaid čuovggas. In J. Ylikoski & A. Aikio (eds.), *Sámit, sánit, sátnehámit: Riepmočála Pekka Sammallahtii miessemánu 21. beaivve 2007*, 11–71. Helsinki: Société Finno-Ougrienne.

Aikio, A. & J. Ylikoski. 2016. The origin of the Finnic *l*-cases. *Fenno-Ugrica Suecana Nova Series* 15. 59–158.

Basbøll, H. 2005. *The phonology of Danish*. Oxford: Oxford University Press.

Bjørn, R.G. 2017. Foreign elements in the Proto-Indo-European vocabulary. MA thesis, University of Copenhagen, Copenhagen.

Branch, M. 1973. *A. J. Sjögren: Studies of the North*. Helsinki: Société Finno-Ougrienne.

Collinge, N.E. 1985. *The laws of Indo-European*. Amsterdam: Benjamins.

Eyser, J. 1912. Thomsen-Bibliografi. In *Festschrift für Vilhelm Thomsen zur Vollendung des siebzigsten Lebensjahres am 25. Januar 1912*, 222–236. Leipzig: Harrassowitz.

Gregersen, F. 2013. Introduction to the new edition of Niels Ege's 1993 translation of Rasmus Rask's prize essay of 1818. In R.K. Rask, *Investigation of the origin of the Old Norse or Icelandic language*, xi–xlvii. Amsterdam: Benjamins.

Gyarmathi, S. 1799. *Affinitas linguae Hungaricae cum linguis Fennicae originis grammatice demonstrata*. Göttingen: Dieterich.

Häkli, E. 2017. *Rasmus Rasks korrespondens med språkforskare i Finland*. Helsinki: Kansalliskirjasto.

Holopainen, S. 2019. Indo-Iranian borrowings in Uralic: Critical overview of sound substitutions and distribution criterion. PhD dissertation, University of Helsinki, Helsinki.

Hyllested, A. 2014. Word exchange at the gates of Europe: Five millennia of language contact. PhD dissertation, University of Copenhagen, Copenhagen.

Jespersen, O. 1897. Karl Verner. *Tilskueren* 14. 3–17.

Junttila, S. 2016. Tiedon kumuloituminen ja trendit lainasanatutkimuksessa: Kantasuomen balttilaislainojen tutkimushistoria. PhD dissertation, University of Helsinki, Helsinki.

Kallio, P. 2015. The stratigraphy of the Germanic loanwords in Finnic. In J.O. Askedal & H.F. Nielsen (eds.), *Early Germanic languages in contact*, 23–38. Amsterdam: Benjamins.

Kallio, P. 2019. Daniel Europaeus and Indo-Uralic. In A. Kloekhorst & T. Pronk (eds.), *The precursors of Proto-Indo-European: The Indo-Anatolian and Indo-Uralic hypotheses*, 74–87. Leiden: Brill.

Konow, S. 1927. Vilhelm Thomsen. *Journal of the Royal Asiatic Society of Great Britain and Ireland* 59. 929–934.

Korhonen, M. 1986. *Finno-Ugrian language studies in Finland 1828–1918*. Helsinki: Societas Scientiarum Fennica.

Kortlandt, F. 1995. General linguistics and Indo-European reconstruction. *Rask* 2. 91–109.

Kylstra, A. D., S.-L. Hahmo, T. Hofstra & O. Nikkilä. 1991–2012. *Lexikon der älteren germanischen Lehnwörter in den ostseefinnischen Sprachen*. Amsterdam: Rodopi.

Laine, P. 2020. Suutarinpojasta Venäjän tiedeakatemian akateemikoksi: A. J. Sjögrenin ura Pietarissa 1820–1855. PhD dissertation, Tampere University, Tampere.

Lauerma, P. 2019. Observations on the Finnish grammar of Rasmus Rask. *Folia Uralica Debreceniensia* 26. 193–208.

Leem, K. 1748. *En lappisk Grammatica efter den Dialect, som bruges af Field-Lapperne udi Porsanger-Fiorden*. Copenhagen: Missionens Bekostning.

Lehmann, W. P. 1967. *A reader in nineteenth-century historical Indo-European linguistics*. Bloomington: Indiana University Press.

Lönnrot, E. 1866–1880. *Suomalais-Ruotsalainen Sanakirja: Finskt-Svenskt Lexikon*. Helsinki: Suomalaisen Kirjallisuuden Seura.

Markey, T. L. 1976. Rasmus Kristian Rask: His life and work. In R. K. Rask, *A grammar of the Icelandic or Old Norse tongue*, xv–xxxv. Amsterdam: Benjamins.

Mayrhofer, M. 1983. *Sanskrit und die Sprachen Alteuropas: Zwei Jahrhunderte des Widerspiels von Entdeckungen und Irrtümern*. Göttingen: Vandenhoeck & Ruprecht.

Mikkola, J. J. 1894. *Berührungen zwischen den westfinnischen und slavischen Sprachen*. Helsinki: Société Finno-Ougrienne.

Mikkola, J. J. 1927. Vilhelm Thomsen ja suomalainen kielentutkimus. *Virittäjä* 31. 297–299.

Mikkola, J. J. 1938. *Die älteren Berührungen zwischen Ostseefinnisch und Russisch*. Helsinki: Société Finno-Ougrienne.

Nielsen, H. F. 1994. On the dialectical split of Ingveonic West Germanic from the Early Runic language of Scandinavia. In K. Düwel (ed.), *Runische Schriftkultur in kontinental-skandinavischer und -angelsächsischer Wechselbeziehung*, 117–127. Berlin: De Gruyter.

Nielsen, H. F. 2003. Rask, Rasmus Kristian. In H. Beck, D. Geuenich & H. Steuer (eds.), *Reallexikon der Germanischen Altertumskunde* 24, 143–146. Berlin: De Gruyter.

Nielsen, H. F. 2008. Rasmus Kristian Rask (1787–1832): Liv og levned. *Rask* 28. 25–42.

Nørtoft, M. 2015. Tidlige låneord i finnopermiske sprog og deres rolle for placeringen af et germansk urhjem: Et arkæologisk-lingvistisk eksperiment. BA thesis, University of Copenhagen, Copenhagen.

Olsen, B. A. 2017. Reconstruction and realism in Indo-European linguistics. In A. Hyllested, B. Nielsen Whitehead, T. Olander & B. A. Olsen (eds.), *Language and prehistory of the Indo- European peoples: A cross-disciplinary perspective*, 107–121. Copenhagen: Tusculanum.

Rask, R. K. 1811. *Vejledning til det Islandske eller gamle Nordiske Sprog*. Copenhagen: Schuboth.

Rask, R. K. 1818. *Undersögelse om det gamle Nordiske eller Islandske Sprogs Oprindelse*. Copenhagen: Gyldendal.

Rask, R. K. 1821. Finnische Sprache und Literatur. *Jahrbücher der Literatur* 15. 14–27.

Rask, R. K. 1832. *Ræsonneret lappisk Sproglære efter den Sprogart, som bruges af Fjældlapperne i Porsangerfjorden i Finmarken*. Copenhagen: Schuboth.

Rask, R. K. 1834–1838. *Samlede tildels forhen utrykte Afhandlinger*. Copenhagen: Popp.

Rask, R. K. 1932–1935. *Udvalgte Afhandlinger.* Copenhagen: Levin & Munksgaard.

Rasmussen, J. E. 1983. Two phonological issues in Germanic. *Acta Linguistica Hafniensia* 18. 201–219.

Renvall, G. 1826. *Suomalainen sana-kirja: Lexicon Linguæ Finnicæ.* Turku: Frenckell.

Renvall, G. 1840. *Finsk språklära: Enligt den rena Vest-Finska, i Bokspråk vanliga Dialecten.* Turku: Hjelt.

Sajnovics, J. 1770. *Demonstratio: Idioma Ungarorum et Lapponum idem esse.* Trnava: Collegium Academicum Societatis Jesu.

Sandfeld, K., O. Jespersen, H. Høffding & E. N. Setälä. 1927. Vilhelm Thomsen. *Oversigt over det Kongelige Danske Videnskabernes Selskabs Forhandlinger: Juni 1926 — Maj 1927,* 87–135.

Schmitt, R. 1990. *Ernst Kuhn und Vilhelm Thomsen: Aspekte ihres Forschens im Spiegel ihrer Korrespondenz.* Copenhagen: The Royal Danish Academy of Sciences and Letters.

Schott, W. 1841. *De Lingua Tschuwaschorum.* Berlin: Veitius.

Schrijver, P. 2014. *Language contact and the origins of the Germanic languages.* London: Routledge.

Setälä, E. N. 1890–1891. *Yhteissuomalainen äännehistoria.* Helsinki: Suomalaisen Kirjallisuuden Seura.

Setälä, E. N. 1913. Bibliographisches verzeichnis der in der literatur behandelten älteren germanischen bestandteile in den ostseefinnischen sprachen. *Finnish-Ugrische Forschungen* 13. 345–475.

Sjögren, A. J. 1955. *Tutkijan tieni.* Helsinki: Suomalaisen Kirjallisuuden Seura.

Sjögren, A. J. 2020. *Allmänna Ephemerider: Dagböckerna 1806–1855.* Helsinki: Kansalliskirjasto.

Thomsen, V. 1869. *Den gotiske sprogklasses indflydelse på den finske: En sproghistorisk undersøgelse.* Copenhagen: Gyldendal.

Thomsen, V. 1870. *Über den einfluss der germanischen sprachen auf die finnisch-lappischen: Eine sprachgeschichtliche untersuchung.* Halle: Waisenhaus.

Thomsen, V. 1877. *The relations between ancient Russia and Scandinavia and the origin of the Russian state.* Oxford: Parker.

Thomsen, V. 1888. Sproglige vidnesbyrd om berøringer mellem finsk-ugriske og forskellige indoeuropæiske folkeslag. *Kort Udsigt over det philologisk-historiske Samfunds Virksomhed* 2. 123–124.

Thomsen, V. 1890. *Berøringer mellem de finske og de baltiske (litauisk-lettiske) Sprog: En sproghistorisk Undersøgelse.* Copenhagen: Blanco Lunos.

Thomsen, V. 1896. *Inscriptions de l'Orkhon.* Helsinki: Société Finno-Ougrienne.

Thomsen, V. 1916. *Turcica: Études concernant l'interprétation des inscriptions turques de la Mongolie et de la Sibérie.* Helsinki: Société Finno-Ougrienne.

Thomsen, V. 1919–1931. *Samlede afhandlinger.* Copenhagen: Gyldendal.

Verner, K. 1877. Eine ausnahme der ersten lautverschiebung. *Zeitschrift für vergleichende Sprachforschung auf dem Gebiete der Indogermanischen Sprachen* 23. 97–130.

Wettenhovi-Aspa, G. S. 1915. *Finlands Gyllene Bok I: Svar på Svenskt i Finland.* Helsinki: Suomalaisen Kirjallisuuden Seura.

Old English breaking
A parallel to Lachmann's Law

Yuri Kleiner
St. Petersburg State University

The division of the Old English diphthongs, represented in spelling as *ea* and *eo*, into 'short' and 'long' ones, reflects their origin rather than any real difference in length/quantity. The long ones stem from Gmc *au, *iu, the short ones from the *æ* and *e* before *l, r, χ* as a result of breaking. Synchronically, both types are biphonemic combinations; /V̆V̆/ before /l, r, χ/ suggests the latter's inability to form — in combination with /C/ in the rime and a short vowel as the nucleus — a syllable long by position equal prosodically to /V̆(C)V̆/. Likewise, the lengthening of the short root vowel in perfect participles in -*tus, lĕgo* — *lēctus* (Lachmann's Law), may have been a compensation of the 'consonantal deficiency' of /k/ in this position, cf. Latin *rēctē* — Umbrian *rehte*. The results of compensation were concordant with the principles of the /(C)V̄-/ = /(C)V̆C-C/ = /(C)V̆CV̆-/ equality, which was typical of the organization of a speech chain both in Latin and Old English.

1. Introduction

In its most general form, the term *breaking*, as applied to Old English, denotes the "Übergang eines kurzen *ë* in *eo*, *a* in *ea* (und *i* into *io*)" (Sievers/Brunner 1951: §§ 83–86) before *l, r, χ*+a consonant and single χ. In principle, it may signify either the fracture of a simple vowel, as Grimm's 'Brechung' implies, or an epenthesis in this position, as suggested by Koch, the critic of Grimm's "nicht glücklich" choice of the term: "*a* ist durch nachfolgende consonanten *r, h* und *l* ... veranlasst" (Koch 1870: 158). That 'diphthongization' was due to the assimilative influence of the postvocalic consonant and its 'special character' has been taken for granted (Bauer 1956: 429):

> we may well say that ... the consonant that caused breaking ... which, by the preceding digraph, is shown to be different from ordinary *r* and *l*, must have been something like a velar ... The consonants *r* and *l* in the combinations -*ear*-, -*eor*-, -*eal*-, and -*eal*- in OE ... would, in phonetic transcription, be represented by [R] and [ł], i. e. uvular *r* and velarized *l*.

https://doi.org/10.1075/nss.34.10kle
Available under the CC BY-NC-ND 4.0 license. © 2025 John Benjamins Publishing Company

To illustrate the role of the (uvular, velar, retroflex, apical, trilled, flapped, etc.) consonants as a conditioning factor of diphthongization, analogs with modern Germanic dialects have been used. Already Sievers (1901:§ 507) compared the Westphalian "'kurze Diphthonge' oder 'Brechungen'" and Old English "kurzen *eo, io*", and quite recently we can read that there are "large quantities of relatively reliable data from modern dialects of the Germanic languages which should help determine exactly what kinds of *r* forms seem to cause the various types of vocalic mutation found in early Germanic languages" (Howell 1991:21). For example, Hogg (1992:103) finds OE breaking "remarkably similar to 'L Vocalisation' in Received Pronunciation," where "/l/ is velarised (> ł) in roughly the environments we stated for Old English and then may become vowel-like, so that *milk*, for instance, is pronounced [mɪǫk] rather than [milk]". As for breaking before /rC/, he compares it with the diphthongization of long vowels before /r/, e.g., in "[biə] rather than [biːr] for *beer*", and describes it as "a very natural kind of phonetic development". As 'phonetic explanations in phonology' generally, this one disregards the status of the interacting elements, which may be different in typologically/chronologically different systems, especially those where the process in question did or did not take place.

Predominant during the entire pre-phonological period was the view that the digraph spelling reflected some sort of bipartition of vocalic segments, otherwise represented in the same environment by simple letters, e.g., *thuearm* (vs. *þuarm*), *ðearf* (vs. *ðarf*), *earm* (vs. *arm*), etc. before *r*+C., *feallan* (vs. *fallan*), *eald* (vs. *ald*), etc. before *l*+C. The distribution of graphic variants shows a certain regularity, supposedly chronological, cf., "in den alten Glossen" and "spätws. und spätkent." (Sievers/Brunner 1951:§ 84, Anm. 1; § 85), and dialectal, cf., "before *l* groups, Angl. develops *a* from West Gmc. *a.*, but W-S and Kt. have *ea*. Spellings with *a* penetrate eW-S and eKt extensively, spellings with *ea* invade Angl. only in Ru.'" (Campbell 1959:§ 258).

Whether the graphemes reflect some sort of synchronic variation or a diachronic change (the dialects belonging to one and the same stage or different stages of language evolution respectively) depends on the phonological basis of each orthographic system and, in the last analysis, on the status of the elements represented by respective spellings. According to Koch (1870:158), "1) der brechung *ea* liegt *e* oder *æ* zugrunde: *e* ist daher der hauptlaut, -- 2) *a* ist durch nachfolgende consonanten *r, h* und *l* ... veranlasst; es fügt sich daher als leisen nachschlag zu *e*". Koch's "Hauptlaut" and "Nachschlag" may correspond either to the head and the glide of a monophonemic diphthong or to members of a biphonemic combination; the problem was not to be discussed until after André Martinet's article *Un ou deux phonèmes?* (Martinet 1939) and Trubetzkoy's "rules of mono- and polyphonematic evaluation" (Trubetzkoy 1939:50–57; 1969:55–62).

2. Early phonological approaches

A phonological dimension was added to the debate on 'breaking diphthongs' after Marjorie Daunt had put forward her interpretation of *ea, eo, io* and *ie* as graphic representations of monophthongs before consonants, a retroflex *r* in *weorpan*, a velar fricative in *feoht*, etc. (Daunt 1939: 121–122, 128). The critics' main objection concerned her alleged use of the second element of the digraphs as only "a diacritical symbol qualifying the neighboring consonant" (Kuhn & Quirk 1968: 39; cf., similarly, Samuels 1952: 17). In her rejoinder, Daunt made it plain that, contrary to the position ascribed to her, she did not regard the function of the second element as purely graphical: "I have never for one moment suggested that there was *no* glide between a front vowel and a velar consonant in such forms as *bearn, seolh*, etc. Of course, there must always have been one". She compares breaking diphthongs with the vowels in English *field* (with [i]) and *milk* (with [ɪ]), where "[t]here is a definite glide to be heard (after [i] and [ɪ] — Yu. K.), but no one ... has classed the sounds in these words as diphthongs. These are conditioned diphthongs" (Daunt 1953: 49). Daunt's understanding of phonemes and variants is closest to that of the Prague Circle; in particular, her "conditioned diphthongs" correspond to Trubetzkoy's "kombinatorische Varianten/combinatory variants" (Trubetzkoy 1939: 44–45/1969: 49–50). Her examples are the same as Hogg's; the difference is that Hogg focuses on processes leading to identical results, while Daunt's focus is the status of the results of the processes. According to Daunt, the breaking diphthongs are monophonemes separate from the following consonants, i.e. glides belonging to vocalic nuclei. She does not exclude that a "glide could at any time become the stressed element," but "that does not alter the fact that for a definite period the original simple vowel was the phoneme" (Daunt 1953: 49). In other words, breaking diphthongs can, in principle, coincide with those in *dream, eac* and *beatan*, and be "not dependent ... on the neighbouring sounds" (Daunt 1939: 110), but the coincidence itself presupposes the equal status of the entire combinations, either mono- or biphonemic, which, in turn, depends on boundaries, after or between their elements. The solution requires a segmentation procedure, which Daunt has skipped, for obvious reasons: her article appeared in the same year as Martinet's and Trubetzkoy's works (see above).

3. Alternative views

Opposite to Daunt's is Stockwell and Barritt's interpretation of the products of breaking, with [æ] and [ea] as members of the same phoneme, /æ/: *ea* being a 'back allophone' of /æ/ plus an off-glide [ə], which is a part of the following consonant (Stockwell & Barritt 1951: 13). As Sherman M. Kuhn and Randolph Quirk (1968: 40) remark in this connection, "[a] description of the CONSONANTS of the early West Saxon of King Alfred's time would call for all of the graphs now recognized, plus such additional symbols as *ah* in *meaht, al* in *healt, ar* in *earm*". They add that "[t]he Anglian texts would require an even greater array of graphic symbols" and that a "description of Old English in general would have to include ... many more which occur in other dialects and texts" (Kuhn & Quirk 1968: 41). This is unlike *éa* (i.e. *ēa*), phonetically [æə], which, according to Stockwell and Barritt is /æ/ plus a phonemic off-glide /h/, which is a part of the syllabic nucleus. Kuhn and Quirk's comment on this reads: "[t]he analysis ... upon closer inspection, turns out to be wholly a matter of segmentation: *hēah* they would divide *h-ea-h*; *neaht, n-e-ah-t*".

4. Segmentation procedures

Neither Daunt's nor Stockwell and Barritt's segmentation relies on objective criteria based either on morpheme boundaries, which is the key principle of Lev Shcherba's (Leningrad/St. Petersburg) school (Zinder 1979: 37), or the syllable boundaries of Prague phonology (Trubetzkoy 1939: 50; 1969: 56). The two boundaries are not mutually exclusive. For example, in Gothic 1st class weak verbs, the suffixal *-i-* ~ *-j-* alternation (= [i] ~ [i̯] variation), before 2nd and 3rd SG endings, *-is* and *-iþ*, post-consonantally as in *sō-keis* 'you seek' and *wan-deiþ* 'he/she turns', with <-ei>=/i:/=[i]+[i̯], and syllable-initially as in *was-jis* 'you dress', <-ji>=[i̯]+[i]), depends on syllable boundary, suggesting a biphonemic character of the long vowel in the suffix+ending combination; cf., in *ja*-nouns: *hairdeis* 'a shepherd' vs. *harjis* 'an army', syllabified *hair-deis, har-jis*. A similar alternation, [u] ~ [u̯], in *taujan* ~ *tawida* 'to do' (PRES and PRET), demonstrates a biphonemic nature of /au/ and other 'diphthongs' also regarded as /V̆V̆/-combinations. Concordant with this is A.I. Smirnitsky's conclusion concerning *ei, eu, ēi, ōu, oi, ou*, etc. "usually treated as diphthongs": "if the diphthong is a unit phoneme, not a phoneme cluster, but a special complex sound unit equal functionally to simple units, monophthongs, it should be recognized that such formations [*ei, eu, ou*, etc.] are not units in the ancient system of sounds of the Indo-European languages, but ordinary combinations, similar to such as *et, ek, ēt, ōk*, etc." (Smirnickij 1946: 81).[1]

---

1. The first to point this out was Bohumil Trnka (1936).

5. Vowels and vowel combinations: Prosodic equality

In Old English, neither of the two divisibility criteria, a morphological boundary or resyllabification, is applicable to 'diphthongs', either in *neaht* and *heorð* or in *hēah* and *rēord* (corresponding to Gmc. */au eu/). It is for this reason that, as the latter's development in Old English, Smirnitsky has suggested monophthongization resulting in "phonemes in their own right, rather than combinations of phonemes", another reason being that "they are the only vocalic complexes, treated in the language on a par with simple long vowels" (Smirnickij 1946: 82).

A similar treatment can manifest itself in different ways. In Gothic, the segmentation boundary that determines the <-*ei*-> (/i:/ = [ii̯]) ~ <-*ji*-> (/ji/ =[i̯i]) alternation, (Sievers' Law) is determined, in turn, by preceding structures. In addition to syllables 'long by position', *wan-(deiþ)*, they include those with long nuclei ('long by nature'), *sō-(keis)*, and disyllabic short-vowel combinations, both in *miki-(leis)* and *dau-(þeiþ)*, 3.SG.PRES of *dauþjan* 'to kill', *daupjan* 'to baptize' — *dau-peins* 'baptism', etc., with /au/, most probably identical with that of *maujos* — *mawi* 'maiden' (GEN and NOM) and, thus, regarded as /V̆ + V̆/, or as /V̆(C)V̆/. Here, the manifestation of a "similar treatment" of long vowels and biphonemic combinations is their participation in prosodic structures with a similar behavior in speech chain, namely, /(C)V:-/ = /(C)VC-C/ = /(C)VCV-/.

In Old English, word final *l, m, n* and *r* are treated as separate syllables when root syllables are long, e.g., *sūsl* 'misery', *bōsm* 'bosom', *bēacen* 'sign' vs. monosyllabic *setl* 'seat', *fæþm* 'embrace', *þegn* 'warrior' (Sievers 1893: 127, 185), suggesting a different syllabification in the /-CR̥/ and /C-R/ groups, viz. *sū-sl — sū-sles, bō-sm — bō-smes, bēa-cen — bēa-cnes* vs. *setl — set-les, fæþm — fæþ-mes, þegn — þeg-nes*, and revealing three types of pre-boundary structures, viz. /(C)V:-/ (= syllables long by nature): *bō-, bēa-* (cf. Go. *dō-, stō-*), /(C)VC-/ (= syllables long by position): *set-, fæþ-, þeg-* (cf. Go. *wan-, was-*) and, in such forms as *wæteres* 'water' and *werodes* 'army' (both GEN.SG), syllabified *wæte-res*, and *wero-des*, a complex of two short open syllables /(C)VCV-/ identical to Go. *miki-* (for details, see Kleiner 1999).

Monophthongization did take place in Old English (/ai/ > /ā/), cf., also <stræm>, <strem> 'stream' or <tre> for more common *trēo* 'tree' documented in late OE (Minkova 2014: 176), but since Sievers' Law was still operative, the resulting monophthongs must have existed within the same /(C)V:-/ = /(C)VC-C/ = /(C)VCV-/ equality, together with the 'long diphthongs', which, in principle, could be equal prosodically to the resolved /V̆CV̆/ disyllables (*sunu*), similar to Gothic *miki-*, as well as the variant biphonemic /V̆V̆/ combinations.

In this context, questions arise concerning the status of the breaking diphthongs. According to Fourquet, "les produits de la fracture des voyelles brèves sont venus occuper dans le système des brèves la même place que les diphtongues d'origine ancienne occupaient dans le système des longues" (Fourquet 1959: 151; also in Krupatkin 1970: 62). This, in turn, goes back to the traditional interpretation of the nuclei of such pairs as *hēah — neaht*, etc. as distinguished "nur durch die Quantität" (Luick 1964: § 133). The *Quantität* corresponds to Fourquet's long and short *vowels*, being their 'distinctive feature' in terms of classical phonology. As such, the notion may be applicable to the elements of biphonemic combinations ('old diphthongs'), but not to their opposition with 'breakings', whose status remains unclear.

6. Breaking diphthongs: Evolution and regional variation

One of the arguments for the monophonemicity of the breaking diphthongs is their subsequent development: "in the overwhelming majority of cases the forms to be traced in Middle English show exactly the development to be expected of [e] and [æ], e.g. OE *earn*, ME *ern, arm*; in OE *eorþe*" (Daunt 1939: 128). Daunt (p. 129) adds:

> A late OE stage *æ* and e or *i* is always allowed in established phonology for earlier *ea, eo*, and accounted for as a monophthongization; but the point is sufficiently clear that in the great majority of cases the apparently descended forms are no different from those descended from the simple vowel in each case. In general the so-called 'short' diphthongs leave no trace.

As Kuhn and Quirk (1968: 46–47) remark:

> This view derives from some of the old treatments of English phonology, in which Old English is represented by the WS dialect of Alfred's time[2] and Middle English by the Southeast Midland of Chaucer's, the two being presented as though the later type of English were directly descended from the earlier. In point of fact, of course, the two dialects belonged to different regions as well as to different periods; Chaucer's *old* is a later form, not of Alfred's *eald*, but of an Anglian *ald*.

In other words, the later monophthongs may well be the reflexes of the OE Anglian forms, which were also monophthongal. As examples that "seem to indicate a diphthongal pronunciation," they cite place-names such as *Estharabyar, Trendelbiare, Wydebyer* (<WS *-bearu), la Hyele* <(WS *healh), Fiemham* (<WS *feam-), Vialepitte* < (WS *fealw-), Dyalediche* (<WS *Dealla-), Piarrecumbe* (<WS

---

2. Cf. Minkova (2014: 179): "The digraph spellings are fairly uniform in the 'focused' variety of late West Saxon OE, where some orthographic homogeneity can be attributed to the strong normative tendencies characteristic of the Winchester school and the stability of the Ælfrician texts".

pearroc-). etc. (Kuhn & Quirk 1968: 47). We can conclude that the modern English reflexes correspond to short unbroken vowels which coexisted with bipartite formations corresponding to OE /ea ea/.[3]

6.1 Scribal practices and their interpretation

Kuhn and Quirk (1968: 51) give the following explanation of the *ia*-spellings: "The scribe frequently reacted against the *ea*-spelling, not in order to use any symbol suggesting a monophthong, but rather to emphasize the diphthongal (that is, biphonemic — Yu. K.) character of the sound and to indicate a more palatal first element than that suggested by *e: biarn, wiarð* (also *wierð, wiearð*, PRET of *weorðan*), *cyealf, getiald* (PPL of *tellan*), *sialde* (also *syelde*, PRET of *sellan*), *sielt-*, etc.". They also point out that "the scribe frequently replaced *ea* (< WGmc. *au*) with a similar range of spellings: *biagas, dieadan, gelyafan, geliefen, lyeuum*, etc." This seems to be preferable to Stockwell and Barritt's idea of the scribes' recording (or not recording) certain "articulations" (e.g., *ea*, the back allophone of /æ/) more or less distinct in different environments (/l/ plus consonant, /r/ plus consonant, etc.) and more or less consistently reflected in spelling (Stockwell & Barritt 1953: 13).

Daunt's suggestion that "...the Irish teachers, listening as foreigners to a strange tongue and trying to write it down, would hear shades of pronunciation which the English speakers would not have heard in themselves" (Daunt 1939: 115) is absolutely plausible in principle. Somewhat doubtful, however, is that this method of the designation of allophones should have become a native orthographic tradition. It would be more realistic to admit that the use of the same digraphs for the derivatives of *au* and *iu* and the products of breaking indicates their identity not only in quality but also in quantity. This is similar, in part, to the conclusion drawn by Hogg (1992: 104):

> breaking of long front vowels [*nǣh > nēah*] resulted in diphthongs which were phonologically identical to the diphthongs developed from Germanic [e.g., *hēah*]. If we also accept that the breaking of short front vowels was phonetically parallel, so that *sæh > seah* involved epenthesis of a back glide just as in *hēah* then, given that length contrasts were maintained, breaking will have introduced the contrast between long and short diphthongs.

Hogg insists on the maintenance/introduction of contrast between long and short diphthongs, but Daunt (1939: 108) found it "a highly improbable state of affairs" that "certain spellings, *ea, eo, io, ie* ... said to represent diphthongs which exist in

---

3. Such forms are similar to those resulting from Scandinavian breaking, with *ia, io*, etc., which are "manifestly biphonemic", according to Steblin-Kamenskij (1957: 88).

164 Yuri Kleiner

two quantities, and are phonemic" be "only distinguished by the quantity of one of their elements, e.g. [e:o] and [eo], [e:a], and [εα], etc." As in other cases, her judgment is based on the analogy of existing languages: "there is, so far as my knowledge and information go, no example of 'long' and 'short' diphthongs, differentiated only by quantity, being phonemic, and it seems very unlikely that Old English had what is now non-existent" (Daunt 1939:110). This is not exactly true: in Modern Icelandic, for example, diphthongs can be long and short in the same way as simple vowels, cf. *dæma* [tai:ma] 'to judge' and *dæmdi* [taimti] 'judged' (Árnason 2003:32). In Icelandic, length depends on the structure of a syllable, /V:C/ ~ /VC:/ ("syllable leveling"). So it cannot be an analog of the Old Germanic prosody based on an absolutely different principle (see 5. above).

6.2 Manifestation of length/quantity

Daunt explains that the "distinction in quantity of the elements" would have implied lengthening of "one of their elements" (assuredly, the first one) in the reflexes of *au* and *iu* in Old English, that is, [æ:o] (vs. [eo]), [e:o] (vs. [εo]), etc. But judging by the 'vocalis ante vocalem corripitur' rule operative in some of the Germanic languages, shortening is more likely in this position, cf. in Gothic, *sēþs* 'seed' and *saian* /sɛan/ 'to sow'; *stōjan* 'to judge' and *staua* /stɔa/ 'a judge', *stauida* /stɔida/ 'judged' (D'Alquen 1974:145–154); in Old Icelandic, *bua* (= *búa*) 'to live', *nia* (= *nía*) 'nine', *tio* (= *tío*) 'ten', *trua* (= *trúa*) 'to believe'; the historically long vowels never had an apex on them in manuscripts; in poetry, such forms were treated as combinations of two short syllables, e. g. *runar* 'boars', unlike *rúnar* 'runes', with the two syllables making up a regular foot (Bugge & Sievers 1891; Benediktsson 1968:38–42). Other forms of such words e. g. *búm* (PRES.PL of *búa*), have long or, compared with *bua*, lengthened vowels, the two forms being juxtaposed as the /V̄/ and /V̆V̆/ syllables.

Nothing suggests that lengthening took place in the Old English [VV]-combinations ("long diphthongs"), so their length must have been the same as that of the short diphthongs. In this context, one may recall comment by Bülbring (1902:§ 107, Anm. 1):

> Das Längezeichen über dem ersten Element von *ēa* [ǣa̠] soll nicht etwa andeuten, dass eine Dehnung des wg. Diphthongs stattgefunden hätte, sondern dient hier ... zur Unterscheidung von der erst innerhalb des Englischen aus einfachen kurzen Palatalvokalen entstandenen Kurzdiphthongen.[4]

---

4. Cf. Minkova's remark concerning late WS [æə], [ea] and [ia]: "They are not 'long diphthongs' (though that is their traditional name), just simply diphthongs" (Minkova 2014:176).

In other words, the opposition of the 'breakings' and Längezeichen-marked digraphs reflects difference in origin or, more likely, linguists' convention, rather than linguistic reality.

7. 'Diphthongs': Prosody and meter

Among other things, the 'similarity of behavior' of monophthongs and diphthongs reflects the syntagmatic aspect of their functioning, including factors underlying verse structure. Comparing the role in verse of the syllables with the nuclei designated by respective digraphs, Campbell (1959: §38) writes:

> The symbols *ea, eo, io* were used in a great many words for sounds developed out of a monophthong. When this monophthong was long, the symbols no doubt had the same value as when they represented sounds developed out of diphthongs, e.g. *nēah* near, *ġēar* year, *nēolæċan* (Angl.) approach, *līoht* light (in weight). But in many words the symbols *ea, eo, io* represented sounds which were derived from older short monophthongs, and which were themselves equivalent to short vowels in the metrical system.

Liberman (1998: 78) discusses the word **sæh* 'saw', saying that it "constituted a light base, and after breaking this situation remained the same: *seah* (the historically recorded form) did not increase its length once **æ* changed to *ea*". But treated as /V̆ + V̆/, *ea* could well make the base heavy. For example, in

sec[g] sārigferð	— *seah on unlēofe* —	
'man sad at heart	— looked at hateful ones'	(Beowulf 2863)

seah is in a strong (alliterating) position, which requires either a syllable long by nature or position or a resolved disyllabic sequence (Suzuki 1996: 17); the latter is presumably the case with *seah*. A /VCC/ syllable, 'long by position', can occupy a lift irrespective of its nucleus. A long nucleus or a /V̆V̆/ combination before /CC/, however, would result in "overlong" sequences that do not fit in the /(C)V̄-/ = /(C)V̆C-C/ = /(C)V̆CV̆-/ equality. To avoid this would require either the shortening of the vowels or some specific paradigmatic character of the postvocalic consonants, such as those in the position of breaking, e. g., *bearm* that, too, can occupy a strong (alliterating) position, cf.,

bēaga bryttan	*on bearm scipes*	
'breaker of rings	on ship's bosom'	(Beowulf 2863)

8. The mechanism of breaking: Phonetics — phonology — prosody

Howell (1991: 8) calls pre-breaking combinations "liquid clusters (LC)", their first elements being subject to *liquid reduction* (LR), a process that "yields contextual variants which are much more vowel-like than syllable-initial variants such as the trill or flap common in /r/". That the "L's" (and h) possessed certain qualities that distinguished them from other consonants, thus occupying a special place in the (West-) Germanic languages is an established fact. The specific character of /r l h/ manifested itself throughout the history of the Germanic languages, affecting preceding vowels or, ultimately, being vocalized or disappearing. But since the processes in question took place at different periods and, obviously, under different conditions, the designation of the pre-vocalic elements involved as *phonetically* 'weak' or 'close to vowels' cannot be an explanation of their mechanisms.

According to Howell (1991: 81), LR is one of the two strategies "to mitigate the phonotactic problems inherent in liquid plus consonant sequences," *hælp* > *healp* 'helped', *ærm* > *earm* 'arm' (with a tautosyllabic second consonant). Howell's second strategy is "the insertion of an epenthetic vowel between the liquid and the following consonant, a process of resyllabification which removes the liquid from the syllable rhyme and places it in the onset of a newly formed syllable". Synchronically, the result of the two strategies is the complementary distribution of the two *r*'s paradigmatically: "vowel-like" pre-consonantal allophones of the /h/, /r/ and /l/ phonemes in *healp, earm*, etc., and prevocalic *consonantal* allophones, e. g., in *berg* > *berig* 'mountain'.[5] Not less significant for the system based on the /(C)V:-/ = /(C)VC-C/ = /(C)VCV-/ equality is the syntagmatic aspect, that is, "the nature of the interaction between vowel segments and reduced liquids" (Howell 1991: 98), so that "[t]he *segmental boundary* between a vowel and a following reduced liquid is considerable less clear than the boundary between a vowel and, say, a following trill" (Howell 1991: 82; italics mine — Yu. K.). In this context, a "vowel-like" character is an adequate enough designation of the liquids' inability (be it for phonetic reasons) to perform the main function of the consonant, which is "the production of an obstruction" (Trubetzkoy 1939: 84; 1969: 94), and to create a syllable 'long by position', in this case, substituted for by the prosodically equal /V̆V̆/ sequence.

---

5. So in Mossé (1945); according to Reszkiewicz (1953), r's in the position of breaking and prevocalically are distinct phonemes. From the point of view of syntagmatics, however, their status is of secondary importance.

9. Dialectal /VVRC/ ~ /VCC/ ~ /VCV/ variation

The results of breaking manifest themselves regularly, although not without exceptions, even within one dialect and in it, within one text, be it a short one, such as *Caedmon's Hymn*. Seventeen copies of it have been preserved, two of these, the earliest ones, are in the Northumbrian (Anglian) dialect; the texts in the Alfredian translations of the Venerable Bede's *Historia Ecclesiatica* are in late West Saxon (see Smith 1933: 1 – 41; Dobbie 1937: 1 – 48).

Table 1. Caedmon's Hymn

Northumbrian (Anglian)		West Saxon
The Moor manuscript (737)	The Leningrad/St. Petersburg Bede (746)	Alfredian translations (ca. 10th c.)
Nu scylun herȝan hefaenricæs uard,	*Nu scilun herȝa hefaenriccæs uard,*	*Nu sculon heri(ȝe)an heofonrices weard,*
metudæs **maecti** *end his modȝidanc*	*metudæs* **mehti** *end his modȝithanc,*	*meotodes* **meahte** *7 his modȝeþanc,*
uerc uuldurfadur sue he	*uerc uuldurfadur, sue he*	*weorc wuldor-fæder, swa he*
uundra ȝihuaes	*uundra ȝihuæs*	*wundra ȝihuæs*
eci dryctin or **astelidæ**	*eci dryctin, or* **astelidæ.**	*ece drihten, or* **onstealde.**
he aerist scop aelda **barnū**	*He ærist scop aelda* **barnum**	*He aerist sceop ylda* **bearnum**
....	....	....
tha middunȝeard moncynnes uard,	*tha middunȝard moncynnes uard,*	*tha middanȝeard moncynnes weard,*
....	...	....
firum fold^v frea **allmectig**	*firum foldu^v frea* **allmehtig**	*firum foldan frea* **ælmihtig**
(Dobbie 1937: 13)	(Dobbie 1937: 17)	(Dobbie 1937: 24)

'Now ought we to praise heaven's kingdom's guardian, the might of the Creator and the thought of his mind, the works of the Father of glory, how he, the eternal Lord, set up a beginning for every wondrous thing. First of all, He designed, for the children of men ...Then mankind's guardian, the omnipotent Lord ... [made] the Middle Yard for the people of the earth.'

The dialectal distribution of broken and unbroken forms is fairly consistent: *weard, weorc, onstealde, bearnm* and *meahte* in WS vs. Anglian *uard* (twice), *uerc, barnū/barnum, astelidæ* and *maecti ~ mecti*, with *e* in place of *æ* due to Anglian smoothing (Smith 1933: § 11). Fluctuation between broken and unbroken forms takes place in one and the same dialect as well, cf. in this connection, "For those who insist on minimal word pairs to determine ... oppositions, the Vespasian Psalter Gloss contains the spelling *meorde* (GEN.SG) and *merde* (preterit of *merran* 'to injure'); and in WS, the *ea* in *bearn* 'child' is distinct from *æ* in *bærn* (IMPER) 'burn'" (Samuels 1952: 22–23). Likewise, [*middun/middan*]-ȝeard is present not only in the WS Alfredian version, but also in the Moore *Hymn*, while the Leningrad/St. Petersburg version has *middunʒard*. Also, all the versions of the *Hymn*, have *all-/æll-*[mihtig] (9b), but cf., *God ælmihtig* and *Drihten eallmihting* in the Anglo-Saxon paraphrase of Latin Psalm 93, 22.

The mixing of forms in texts different both geographically and chronologically (in this case, between the 8th and 10th c.) suggests that such variation can only be synchronic, that is, taking place within the same linguistic system, rather than being a transition to a different system as it would be in the case of change (see 1. above). Bülbring's description of the phonetic aspect of the variation is as follows: "Die Brechung hat ihren Grund in der velaren, und wenigstens z. T. vielleicht labialen Artikulation bzw. Nebenartikulation, welche den brechenden Konsonanten eigen war... Wo keine Brechung eintrat, z. B. in ae. *fell, fillen, fallan*, muss diese Nebenartikulation beträchtlich schwächer gewesen sein oder ganz gefehlt haben" (Bülbring 1902: § 139). Judging by the predominance of forms with breaking, the 'Nebenartikulation' was typical of WS, resulting in /V̆V̆/ + /h, l, r+C/ and /h/#. In Anglian, monophthongs before /C₁C₂/ are an indication of 'schwächer' secondary articulation (or the lack of it) in /C₁/ (consonant proper), which, in combination with /C₂/, was responsible for 'syllables long by position'.

With or without breaking, the variation remains within the /(C)V:-/ = /(C)VC-C/ = /(C)VCV-/ equality. This is perfectly in agreement with Liberman's conclusion: "Breaking was typical of only (rather, predominant in − Yu. K.) the West Saxon dialect, and yet the factors that have brought it forth must have been present in the whole of Old English" (Liberman 1998: 78).

10.   Parallels: Lachmann's Law

It is in connection with the phonetic quality of OE /l r h/ that Liberman asks: "If Old English breaking was due to the velar quality of /l r h/ ... why this backwardness did not affect the preceding vowels three centuries earlier or two centuries later?" (Liberman 2007: 15). Meillet (1894: 299) has reconstructed the pre-consonantal velar [l] not only for Old English and Old High German, but also for Armenian, Greek and Latin. In Latin, a problem similar to OE diphthongization arises in the interpretation of the lengthening of the short root vowel in perfect participles in *-tus* (Lachmann's Law): *ăgo − āctus* 'to move', *lĕgo − lēctus, cădo − cāsus* (< *kăd-tos*) 'to fall', *fŭndo − fūsus* (< *fŭd-tus*) 'to pour', etc. (Otkupščikov 1984: 83). This lengthening has traditionally been connected with the nature of the postvocalic consonant, i.e. depending on whether "the corresponding verbal root ends in a voiced stop" (Otkupščikov 1984: 83). This, alone or in conjunction with an analogical transfer may account for some cases of lengthening, e. g., in *lĕktos > *lĕgtos > lēctus, while the short vowel in strĭctus remains unexplained.

In most examples, short and long vowels are nuclei of different types of syllables, either long by nature or position or else the /V̆CV̆/ sequence, as in Table 2.

Table 2. Syllable-quantity variation in Latin

V̆CV̆ ~ CV̄	V̆CC ~ CV̆	V̆CV̆ ~ VCC	V̆CC ~ V̆CC	V̆CC ~ CV̄
cădo – cāsus 'to fall'	fŭndo – fūsus 'to break'	fŏdio – fŏssus 'to dig'	fĭngo – fĭctus 'to touch'	(rŭmpo –) rūpi (perf.) – rŭptus 'to tear'
ĕdo – ēsus 'to eat'	fŭndo – fūsus 'to pour'	*lădo – lăssus 'to tire'	păndo – păssus 'to broaden'	
	tŭndo – tūsus 'to beat'		strĭngo – strĭctus 'to compress'	

Exceptions are forms like āctus, lēctus, etc., that is, syllables long 'by nature' due to their nuclei, on the one hand, and 'by position' because of the post-nuclear complexes, on the other. To regard such syllables as "overlong" is not necessary, since their role in the syntagmatic organization of a speech chain, for example, in verse, does not differ from other long categories, cf., lēctus (part. perf. of lĕgo),

> Ennius est lēctus salvo, tibi, Roma, Maronem
> – ∪∪ – – – – – ∪ ∪ – ∪ ∪ – ∪
> Ennius was read by you, O Rome, while Maro was alive
>
> (Martial. Epigrammaton V: 10, 7)

with lĕctus 'a coach, bed' in:, cf.,

> mollierant animos lĕctus et umbra meos
> – ∪∪ – ∪∪ – – ∪ ∪ – ∪ ∪ –
> The couch and shade had softened my spirit;   (Ovid. Amor I, 9: 42)[6]

It would be logical to conclude that the function of the long vowel in lēct-, etc. was to adjust the syllable to one of the structures in the prosodic equality, rather than add to it another, 'overlong' category. So vowel lengthening could be a kind of compensation of the consonant's inability to create a syllable long by position, by making it long by nature. How consistent was vowel lengthening in this position in different dialects (or its reflection in writing) is not clear enough; nor is

---

6. This explains why /t/ after /ēc/ in lēctus "does not add a third mora to the first syllable" (Tronskij 1960: 61).

the nature of the allophone of /k/ in this position, possibly akin to the result of the Oscan and Umbrian spirantization of *k* before *t*, "so that the combination *kt* appears as *ht* ... In Umbrian, the *h* was weakly sounded or wholly lost, as is evidenced from its frequent omission in the writing, and the preceding vowel was lengthened," e.g. O. *ehtrad*, U. *ap-ehtre*, from **ek-tro* : L. *extra*, etc.; O. *Úhtavis* : L. *Octāvius*; U. *rehte* : L. *rēctē*; O. *saahtúm*, U. *sahta, satam, sahatam* : L. *sānctus*; U. *ahtur* : L. *auctor*, U. *speture* : L. *(in-)spector*" (Buck 1904: 89).

This is not unlike Icelandic spirantization before fricatives, *slíkt* [slixˑt] 'such', *taktu* [taxˑtɤ] 'take!', *flaksa* [flaxˑsa] 'flap', similar, in turn, to the /kt/ ~ /ht/ variation in Old English. But the similarity, if any, is only that of phonetic realizations representing differently organized phonological/prosodic systems.

11. In conclusion: Phonology/prosody/typology and linguistic geography

Widely discussed at one time in connection with breaking was its spread across the area of the Germanic languages, also sub specie the influence of various Germanic dialects on one another. In terms of absolute chronology typical of the Neo-Grammarian approach, every occurrence of a phenomenon in a particular dialect/language is either the result of borrowing or a language change. Hence, there is the hypotheses of 'tribal interassociations', West Norse influence on Kentish, the dating of breaking to "before the 8th century," etc. (for examples and discussion, see Bauer 1956: 430ff). Not disputing the significance of such an approach, it does not always discern between a change and borrowing or, more importantly, change and variation (see 1 above). It should be stressed, however, that borrowing does not change the target system based on the same principles as the source one. Likewise, similar processes taking place in similarly organized systems, however distant geographically and chronologically, suggest their relationship, definitely typological and probably genetic. Whatever was responsible for the defectiveness of the first element in the postvocalic cluster, the lengthening of the vowel before it in Latin is similar to breaking in Old English (and, probably, Old Norse and Old Frisian). It will be appropriate to recall, in this connection, Hans Frede Nielsen's conclusion made when comparing breaking and back mutation in Old English, Old Norse and Old Frisian: "there are good structural grounds for believing that the diphthongization came about independently in the three languages" (Nielsen 1984: 80). There are good grounds to expand this conclusion to all typological similarities, especially those in languages connected by genetic relationship that, in our case, manifests itself in the /(C)V:-/ = /(C)VC-C/ = /(C)VCV-/ equality, being a context of numerous processes in early Indo-European languages.

References

Árnason, Kristján. 2003. The representation of vowel shortness: Icelandic once more. *Jazyk i rečevaja dejatel'nost' / Language and Language Behavior* (The Linguistic Society of St. Petersburg). Vol. 6. 27–46.

Bauer, G. 1956. The problem of short diphthongs in Old English. *Anglia* 74. 427–37.

Benediktsson, H. 1968. Nordic vowel quantity. *Acta Linguistica Hafniensia*. 11(1). 32–65.

Buck, C. D. 1904. *A grammar of Oscan and Umbrian. With a collection of inscriptions and a glossary*. Boston: The Athenæum Press.

Bugge, S. & E. Sievers. 1891. Vocal Verkürzung im Altnordischen. *Beiträge zur Geschichte der deutschen Sprache und Literatur* 15. 291–411.

Bülbring, K. D. 1902. *Altenglisches Elemenarbuch*. I. Teil: *Lautlehre*. Heidelberg: Winter.

Campbell, A. 1959. *Old English grammar*. Oxford: Clarendon.

D'Alquen, R. 1974. *Gothic AI and AU*. (Janua Lingarum. Series Practica, 151). The Hague/Paris: Mouton.

Daunt, M. 1939. Old English sound changes reconsidered in relation to scribal tradition and practice. *Transactions of the Philological Society* 38. 108–137.

Daunt, M. 1953. Some notes on Old English phonology. *Transactions of the Philological Society* 52. 48–54.

Dobbie, E. v. K. 1937. *The manuscripts of Cædmon's Hymn and Bede's Death Song. With a critical text of The Epistola Cuthberti de obitu Bedæ*. New York: Columbia University Press.

Fourquet, J. 1959. La système des éléments vocaliques longs en vieil-anglais. *Mélanges de linguistique et de philologie. Fernand Mossé in memoriam*. Paris: Didier. 148–160.

Hogg, R. M. 1992. *The Cambridge history of the English language*. Vol. I. *The Beginnings to 1066*. Cambridge, Cambridge University Press.

Howell, R. B. 1991. *Old English breaking and its Germanic analogues*. Tübingen: Niemeyer.

Kleiner, Yu. 1999. Syllables, morae and boundaries. *Interdisciplinary Journal for Germanic Linguistics and Semiotic Analysis* 4 (1). 1–17.

Koch, C. F. 1870. Die ags. Brechung. *Zeitschrift für deutsche Philologie* 2. 147–158

Krupatkin, Y. B. 1970. From Germanic to English and Frisian. *Us Wurk* 19(3). 49–71.

Kuhn, S. M. & R. Quirk. 1968. *Essays on the English language medieval and modern*. Bloomington & London: Indiana University Press.

Liberman, A. 1998. Toward a theory of West Germanic breakings. *International Journal of Germanic Linguistics and Semiotic Analysis* 3(1). 63–119.

Liberman, A. 2007. Palatalized and velarized consonants in English against their Germanic background, with special reference to *i*-umlaut. In C. M. Cain & G. Russom (eds.), *Managing chaos: Strategies for identifying change in English*, 5–36. Berlin: De Gruyter.

Luick, K. 1964. *Historische Grammatik der Englischen Sprache*. Mit dem nach den hinterlassenen aufzeichnungen ausgearbeiteten zweiten kapitel herausgegeben von Dr. Friedrich Wild und Dr. Herbert Koziol. Volume One, in two parts. Oxford; Basil Blackwell.

Meillet, A. 1894. De quelques difficultés de la théorie des gutturales indo-européennes. *Mémoires de la Société de linguistique de Paris*, 8. 277–304.

Minkova, D. 2014. *A Historical phonology of English*. Edinburgh: Edinburgh University Press.

Mossé, F. 1945. *Manuel de l'Anglais du moyen âge. I. Vieil-anglais (Grammaire, texts, notes, glossaire)*. Paris: Aubie.

Nielsen, H. F. 1984. A note on the origin of Old English breaking and back mutation. *Amsterdamer Beiträge zur Älteren Germanistik* 22. 73–81.

Otkupščikov, Yu. V. 1984. Zakon Laxmana v svete indojevropejskix dannyx. (Gipotezy i fakty) [Lachmann's Law in the light of Indo-European data. (Hypotheses and facts)]. *Voprosy jasykoznanija* 2. 83–90.

Reszkiewicz, A. 1953. The phonemic interpretation of Old English Digraphs. *Biuletyn Polskiego Towarzystwa Językoznawczego* 12. 179–187.

Samuels, M. L. 1952. The study of Old English phonology. *Transactions of the Philological Society* 51(1). 15–47.

Sievers, E. 1893. *Altgermanische Metrik*. Halle: Niemeyer.

Sievers, E. 1901. *Grundzüge der Phonetik zur Einführung in das Studium der Lautlehre der indogermanischen Sprachen*. Fünfte verbesserte Auflage. Leipzig: Druck und Verlag von Breitkoff & Härtel.

Sievers, E. & K. Brunner. 1951. *Altenglische Grammatik*. Nach der Angelsächsischen Grammatik von Eduard Sievers neubearbeitet von Karl Brunner. Zweite, revidierte Auflage der Neubearbeitung. Halle (Saale): Niemeyer.

Smirnickij, A. I. 1946. Voprosy fonologii v istorii anglijskogo jazyka [Phonological problems in the history of English]. *Vestnik Moskovskogo Universiteta* 2. 81–89.

Smith, A. H. 1933. *Three Northumbrian poems. Cædmon's Hymn, Bede's Death Song and The Leiden Riddle*. London: Methuen & Co. Ltd.

Steblin-Kamenskij, M. I. 1957. Scandinavian breaking from a phonemic point of view. *Studia Linguistica* 11(2). 84–91.

Stockwell, R. P. & C. W. Barritt. 1951. Some Old English graphemic-phonemic correspondences — *ae, ea*, and *a*. *Studies in linguistics*, Occasional papers 4. Washington, DC.

Suzuki, S. 1996. *The metrical organization of* Beowulf. *Prototype and isomorphism*. Berlin: De Gruyter.

Trnka, B. 1936. Fonologický vývoj germanského vokalísmu [Phonological evolution of Germanic vocalism]. *Časopis pro moderní filologii*. 22 (2). 155–159.

Tronskij, I. M. 1960. *Istoričeskaja grammatika latinskogo jazyka*. [*Historical grammar of the Latin language*]. Moscow: Izdatel'stvo literatury na inostrannyx jazykax.

Trubetzkoy, N. S. 1939. *Grundzüge der Phonologie*. (= Travaux du cercle linguistique de Prague 7). Prague: Cercle linguistique de Prague et Ministère de l'instruction, publ. de la République Tchéco-Slovaque.

Trubetzkoy, N. S. 1969. *Principles of phonology*. Translated by Christiane A. M. Baltaxe. Berkeley and Los Angeles, CA: University of California.

Zinder, L. R. 1979. *Obščaja fonetika* [*General Phonetics*]. Moscow: Vysšaja škola.

Relativsätze im Saterfriesischen

Stephen Laker & Pyt Kramer
Kyushu University | Fryske Akademy und Seelter Buund

The article surveys relative clauses in Saterland Frisian based on a corpus of written and spoken language. Although the spoken language tends towards short coordinated sentences rather than complex subordinate structures, relative clauses are also found with some frequency. Some relative pronouns are common (especially when they function as a subject and direct object), while other structures are rare and restricted for the most part to written texts in the corpus (possessives, direct object, and dative-type uses). Relative clauses with prepositions and free relatives are formed in different ways and evidence diachronic change over the last two centuries of the language's recorded history. Other characteristics of Saterland Frisian relative clauses include the use of *deer* 'there' following subject relative pronouns and the use of resumptive pronouns and adverbs after relative clauses.

1. Einleitung

Saterfriesisch ist eine bedrohte Sprache, die in der Gemeinde Saterland in Niedersachsen gesprochen wird. Ähnlich wie die deutsche Umgangssprache neigt das Saterfriesische zu kürzeren Sätzen ohne komplexe Subordination (Siebs 1893: 405).[1] Relativsätze, die eine Erklärung zu einem Bezugswort (häufig einem Nomen) in einem übergeordneten Satz angeben, sind jedoch nicht selten, und die Sprache weist gewisse Unterschiede zu anderen west- und nordfriesischen Dialekten auf (vgl. Hoekstra 2002). In diesem Beitrag sollen die wichtigsten Relativsatztypen des Saterfriesischen behandelt werden. Zudem wollen wir einige Besonderheiten bei der Verwendung von Relativsätzen beschreiben und auf Aspekte der dialektalen, historischen und typologischen Variationen aufmerksam machen.

---

1. Dies trifft auch für die benachbarten niederdeutschen Mundarten zu (Saltveit 1983: 285–286; Thies 2017: 325–335).

https://doi.org/10.1075/nss.34.11lak
Available under the CC BY-NC-ND 4.0 license. © 2025 John Benjamins Publishing Company

Grundlage dieser Studie bildet in erster Linie eine von Pyt Kramer erstellte Sammlung saterfriesischer Texte und transkribierter Tonbandaufnahmen, die gegenwärtig über zwei Millionen Wörter umfasst.[2] Mit Hilfe des Computerprogramms AntConc (Anthony 2022) konnten diese Quellen korpuslinguistisch untersucht werden. Die frühesten Belege von Relativsätzen stammen aus einer Übersetzung eines Abschnitts des Johannesevangeliums aus dem Jahre 1812 (s. FS = Fort 1988). Für die jüngsten Belege wurden Tonbandaufnahmen, Bücher und Zeitungsartikel aus den letzten Jahrzehnten herangezogen.[3] Alle Sprecher der verwendeten Tonbandaufnahmen wurden vor dem Zweiten Weltkrieg geboren. Sie wuchsen mit dem Saterfriesischen als Erstsprache auf, sprachen aber seit ihrer Jugend auch Niederdeutsch und Hochdeutsch. Für diese Studie haben wir zuerst ca. 2000 Relativsätze aus den schriftlichen Quellen extrahiert und dann das Korpus gezielt auf besondere Relativsatztypen durchsucht (vgl. die ähnliche Studie von Laker & Kramer 2022). Nach dem Verfassen des Aufsatzes konnte Laker während seiner Feldforschungen im Saterland (insbesondere im April 2024) noch weitere Details zu einigen Relativsatztypen ermitteln. Obwohl es sich hier nicht um eine quantitative Studie handelt, weist die Seltenheit bestimmter Strukturen bzw. ihre Beschränkung auf schriftliche Quellen darauf, dass sie wenig oder gar nicht gebraucht werden.

Unsere Studie beginnt mit einem Überblick über die Relativpronomina im Saterfriesischen (Abschnitt 2) und behandelt danach die verschiedenen Funktionen des Relativsatzes wie Subjekt (3), direktes Objekt (4), indirektes Objekt sowie Dativfunktionen (5), Possessiv (6). Weiterhin werden Relativsätze mit Präpositionen (7), Relativadverbien (8) und freie Relativsätze (9) thematisiert. Schließlich werden die Ergebnisse der Untersuchung zusammengefasst (10).

---

2. Im Folgenden sind schriftliche Quellen so wiedergegeben wie im Original. Eine Ausnahme bilden die komplexen phonetischen Transkriptionen aus Minssen 1846 (1970). Hier haben wir die Wortakzentzeichen weggelassen und aus typographischen Gründen für Langvokale Makron (¯) anstatt Zirkumflex (^) verwendet. Der Deutlichkeit halber haben wir bei Relativsätzen das Relativum (gegebenenfalls mit zugehöriger Präposition) fettgedruckt und die Bezugswörter (d. h. das Antezedens) unterstrichen. Die Audioaufnahmen wurden von Pyt Kramer mit einer Art phonologischer und teilweise phonetischer Schreibweise transkribiert, die Dialektunterschiede zwischen den Dörfern deutlich zeigt. Übersetzungen saterfriesischer Belege ins Deutsche sind von uns vorgenommen worden, es sei denn, eine deutsche Übersetzung bzw. ein Originaltext lag bereits vor (z. B. bei SS, SV, FK). Bei Bibelübersetzungen (NTP) wurde die katholische Einheitsübersetzung von 1979 verwendet.

3. Im Juni 1972 fuhr unser Honorant Hans Frede Nielsen mit seinem Kommilitonen Flemming Schroller und seinem Friesischlehrer Arne Spenter ins Saterland, um dort Tonbandaufnahmen von Sprechern des Saterfriesischen zu machen. In den letzten Jahren ist der Wert dieser Aufnahmen noch deutlicher geworden, denn heutzutage hat sich die Anzahl von Sprechern, die Saterfriesisch fließend beherrschen, wesentlich verringert. Für weitere Informationen zur Sprache empfehlen wir besonders die Website <https://www.seeltersk.de/>.

2. Das Einleitungselement der Relativsätze

Das Einleitungselement von Relativsätzen im Saterfriesischen ist meistens ein Relativpronomen, das die gleiche Form wie der bestimmte Artikel hat. Im Singular unterscheidet das Relativpronomen drei Geschlechter; die Pluralform ist unmarkiert. Anders als in anderen friesischen Dialekten, aber ähnlich wie in den meisten niederdeutschen Mundarten, gibt es zwei unterschiedliche Formen im Singular Maskulinum, und zwar die Subjektform (Nominativ) *die* und die Objektform (nicht-Nominativ, d. h. direktes und indirektes Objekt, Dativfunktionen) *dän*.[4] Alle anderen Formen sind, was den Kasus betrifft, unmarkiert.

Tabelle 1. Relativa im Saterfriesischen[5]

	Singular			Plural
	Maskulinum	Femininum	Neutrum	
Subjekt	*die*	*ju*	*dät / wät*	*do*
Nicht-Subjekt	*dän*			

Die Relativpronomina in Tabelle 1 leiten sich von den Nominativ- und Akkusativformen der Demonstrativpronomina des Altfriesischen ab.[6] Der im Altfrie-

---

4. Das Inventar der Relativpronomina ist ähnlich wie in den meisten niederdeutschen Dialekten. Die Terminologie Nominativ gegenüber Non-Nominativ entstammt dieser grammatischen Tradition (vgl. Lindow et al. 1998: 172), in dieser Studie aber werden stattdessen Subjekt und Nicht-Subjekt verwendet.

5. Der wohl aus dem Deutschen übernommene Relativmarker *wäkke* 'welche' wird hier nicht behandelt. Es finden sich allerdings einige Beispiel davon in Minssen, Bd. 3: *wécker* 110, 112, 116, 117 (2×), 119 (2×), 120, 123, 130, 136 *trugg wécker* 118, 120, 130). Die Belege sind alle aus Sachtexten (d. h. nicht aus Märchen u. dergl.) entnommen. Sie behandeln Themen wie Spiele, Apparate, Hausbau, Transport und Landwirtschaft. Ansonsten ist das Relativum *wäkke* wenig gebräuchlich. Beispiele kommen in Marron Forts Bibelübersetzung vor. Vor dem Ramsloher Rathaus steht ein zweisprachiges Informationsschild mit den Worten *Bit 1992 wude in two Meentehuuse oarbaided, wäkke in Skäddel un Roomelse studen.* Dies ist vermutlich eine Übersetzung des deutschen Textes am gleichen Schild: 'Bis 1992 wurde in zwei Rathäusern gearbeitet, welche in Scharrel und Ramsloh standen'.

6. Die Relativpronomina stammen letztlich von Demonstrativpronomina bzw. dem neutralen Fragepronomen ab: *die* (< afries. *thī* Nom. Sg. m.), *dän* (< afries. *thene* Akk. Sg. m.); *ju* (< afries. *thiu* Nom. Sg. f. und nicht von afries. *thā* Akk. Sg. f.); *dät* (< afries. *thet* Nom-Akk. Sg. n.); *wet* (< afries. *hwet* Nom-Akk. Sg. n.); *do* (< afries. *thā* Nom-Akk. Pl.); Dativ- und Genitivformen von Demonstrativpronomina, die es im Altfriesischen noch gab, sind mit Ausnahme von einigen versteinerten Resten verlorengegangen. Zu Relativsätzen im Altfriesischen s. Bremmer 2009: 54, 57 und Bor 1986, 1987a–c, 1988.

sischen noch vorhandene Unterschied zwischen dem Nominativ und Akkusativ Singular Femininum wurde jedoch zugunsten der Nominativform *ju* (meist *dju* in Quellen des 19. Jahrhunderts) aufgehoben. Weiter ist zu erwähnen, dass Singular Neutrum *dät* im Laufe der Zeit durch das Interrogativpronomen *wät* ersetzt wurde (s. hierzu 2.1). Außer den Relativpronomina gibt es auch im Saterfriesischen Relativadverbien (s. 8). Für alle diese Einleitungswörter kann Relativum als Oberbegriff dienen (s. Pittner 2007:727).

2.1 Kongruenz

Das Relativpronomen richtet sich in Numerus und Genus nach dem Bezugsnomen. Ausnahmen gibt es gelegentlich bei Lebewesen mit neutralem Geschlecht. In solchen Fällen kann das Relativpronomen entweder mit dem grammatischen (1a) oder biologischen Geschlecht (1b) übereinstimmen:

(1) a. Dan kuud <u>dät Wieuwmaanske</u>$_{NOM.SG.N}$, **dät**$_{NOM.SG.N}$ an't Spinnen was, mäd düsse krassede Wulle spinne.
'Dann konnte die Frau, die beim Spinnen war, mit dieser kardierten Wolle spinnen.' [7]   (1985/U/SV, *Finsterjen*/S. 27)

   b. Deer was bie älke Mädder <u>een Wieuwmaanske</u>$_{NOM.SG.N}$ bie, **ju**$_{NOM.SG.F}$ do Jierwen biende moaste.
'Es war bei jedem Mäher eine Frau, die die Garben binden mußte.'
        (1985/U/SV, *Dät Mjoon*/S. 141)

Es gibt zwar keine feste Regel, aber nach unseren bisherigen Beobachtungen benutzen die meisten gegenwärtigen Sprecher das neutrale Geschlecht nur dann, wenn das Relativum gleich danach oder nahe beim Bezugswort steht, sonst wird das natürliche Geschlecht bevorzugt.[8]

---

7. Zu jedem Beleg geben wir einige Metadaten an: Publikationsjahr (1985), Dialekt (= U[tende]), Quelle (S[aterländisches] V[olksleben]), Blattseite (S. 110). Weitere Informationen finden sich im Anhang.

8. In den Jahren 2023–2024 adaptierte Laker die für das Projekt „Syntax hessischer Dialekte" (SyHD) entwickelten Fragebögen für das Saterfriesische. Die Kategorien „grammatisches" und „biologisches Genus" werden in diesem Projekt teilweise behandelt (s. Leser-Cronau 2016). Mit Hilfe dieser Fragebögen konnten bis jetzt die Gebrauchstendenzen von sechs Sprechern (zwei aus Strücklingen, zwei aus Ramsloh und zwei aus Scharrel) ermittelt werden. Nur eine Sprecherin aus Scharrel bevorzugte fast immer das neutrale Relativpronomen bei *dät Wucht* 'das Mädchen' (mit *dät Bäiden* 'das Kind' jedoch nicht) in sämtlichen Relativsatztypen (mit Ausnahme von Relativa mit Possessivpronomina wie in 6.1).

Ein ähnliches Phänomen kommt auch bei manchen Kollektiva vor. Handelt es sich bei dem Bezugsnomen um ein Kollektivum im Singular, kann das Relativpronomen in manchen Fällen im Singular (2a) oder im Plural (2b) stehen:

(2) a. <u>Dät Fouelk</u>$_{\text{NOM.SG.N}}$, dät$_{\text{NOM.SG.N}}$ hier woonjen diede, ron deer fluks touzoamen, ...
   'Die Menschen, die hier wohnten, rannten da schnell zusammen, ...'
   (1985/U/SV, *Wilms Kasper twiske Hemel un Idde*/S. 110)

   b. Wail deer <u>fuul Fouelk</u>$_{\text{NOM.SG.N}}$ was, do$_{\text{NOM.PL}}$ fon't Romelster Määrked kemen wierne, ...
   'Es war eine ganze Menge Leute da, die von dem Ramsloher Markt gekommen waren, ...' (1985/U/SV, *Silme ap Seeltersk*/S. 69)

Wie bereits erwähnt, wird, was den Kasus angeht, nur im Singular Maskulinum ein Unterschied zwischen Subjekt und Nicht-Subjekt gemacht. Allerdings hat wie im Deutschen die grammatische Kategorie des Relativpronomens nichts mit dem Bezugswort des Hauptsatzes zu tun, sondern mit seiner grammatischen Rolle im Relativsatz.

In den folgenden Abschnitten werden die wichtigsten grammatischen Kategorien des Relativums behandelt und bestimmte Einschränkungen und Tendenzen bei seiner Verwendung aufgezeigt.

3. Subjekt

Das Relativpronomen ist meist das Subjekt des Relativsatzes und entspricht dem deutschen Nominativ. Der Singular Maskulinum hat eine eindeutige Subjektform, andere Relativpronomina sind unmarkiert (s. Tabelle 1).

(3) a. Owwer fon doo oolden Seelter, däär lued däälig wul <u>nit aan moor</u> fon, **die** där noch Seeltersk baalt in Näischäddel.
   'Aber von den alten Saterländern dort lebt heute wohl keiner mehr, der noch Saterfriesisch spricht, in Neuscharrel.' (1972/B94/S/7:35)

   b. <u>Ju Streeite,</u> **ju** deertruch lop, ju lop likut, wul duuzent Meeter likut ooder twooduuzend.
   'Die Straße, die dort hindurchläuft, die läuft geradeaus wohl tausend Meter geradeaus oder zweitausend.' (1972/S/B94/07:10)

   c. Do Ingewand, do Täirmen un allez moast je scheen un <u>jeedet Lood Fat</u>, **dät** der waas, wuud je zauber binunner gesoacht, wail dät aal man knap waas.
   'Die Eingeweide, die Därme und alles musste ja sauber, und jedes Stück Fett, das da war, wurde ja sauber zusammengeholt, weil das alles doch knapp war.' (1972/U/B119/51:50)

d. <u>Du Monljude</u>, **do** deer Eed greeuen hiden, do moasten deeges je wul fiu säks Aiere hääbe.'
'Die Männer, die dort [nach] Torf gegraben hatten, mussten am Tag ja wohl fünf, sechs Eier [zum Essen] haben.' (1972/U/B118/23:50)

Eine Tendenz, die auf die Subjektfunktion des Relativpronomens beschränkt ist, ist der Einschub des Wortes *deer* 'da', das bei der Übersetzung ins Deutsche oft nicht notwendig ist (s. Belege 3a, 3d) oder weggelassen werden muss (s. Belege in Fußnote 27). Ein ähnlicher Gebrauch von *da* war im Mittel- und Frühneuhochdeutschen sowie in verwandten altgermanischen Sprachen bekannt, vgl. etwa in Luthers Bibelübersetzung aus dem 16. Jahrhundert: *ich weisz das Messias komt, der* **da** *Christus heiszet* (Johannes 4, 25).[9] Vielleicht hat sich diese Verwendungsweise im Saterfriesischen einfach lange erhalten. Slofstra (2023, 2024) weist allerdings darauf hin, dass der Gebrauch von *da* nicht mit dem des heutigen Saterfriesischen und des heutigen Plattdeutschen identisch ist.

Eine weitere Tendenz, die in dieser Studie öfters zum Vorschein kommt, sieht man in (3d). Hier wird das wiederaufnehmende Pronomen *do* 'die' nach dem Relativsatz eingefügt. Die wortwörtliche deutsche Übersetzung würde wie folgt lauten: <u>*Die Männer*</u>, *die dort Torf gegraben hatten,* <u>*die*</u> *mussten am Tag ja wohl fünf, sechs Eier haben.* Resumptive Pronomen und Adverbien kommen im Saterfriesischen oft vor (s. 3b 3d, 4a; diese Verwendung beschränkt sich nicht nur auf Subjekt-Relativa) und ist im gesamten norddeutschen Raum zu beobachten (Thies 2017:299, 303).

Ähnlich wie im Deutschen, Niederländischen und anderen friesischen Dialekten wechselt das neutrale Relativpronomen *dät* mit dem Interrogativpronomen *wät* ab. Sprecher des Saterfriesischen benutzen das Relativum *wät* in folgenden Kontexten: (1) nach einem quantifizierenden Pronomen, z. B. *aal* 'all', *alles* 'alles', *niks* 'nichts', *nit* 'nicht', *wät* 'etwas'; (2) nach dem Demonstrativum *dät*; (3) nach einem substantivierten Adjektiv im Neutrum, z. B. *dät Bääste* 'das Beste', *dät Uurde* 'das Zweite'; (4) wenn das Relativpronomen gleichzeitig Objekt des übergeordneten Satzes ist (s. Abschnitt 9 zu freien Relativsätzen); (5) wenn das Relativpronomen den gesamten oder einen Großteil des übergeordneten Satzes relativiert (dies wird auch weiterführender Relativsatz und Satzrelativsatz genannt). Siehe dazu die Beispielsätze (4a–e).

---

9. Laut dem DWB (s.v. *da*) setzt man *da* „ohne weitere bedeutung, nur als verstärkung nach dem meist im nominativ stehenden pronomen relativum". Vergleichbare Sätze sind auch in älteren Stufen des Sächsischen und Niederländischen zu finden (s. Van der Horst 2008:176–178). Darüber hinaus gibt es Ansätze zu dieser Struktur im Altfriesischen (s. Bremmer 2009:57–58; Bor 1987b).

(4) a. <u>alles</u>, **wät** fuchtig leegert wädt, dät färdäärft.
'Alles, was feucht gelagert wird, das verdirbt.'   (1972/S/B188/4:50)

     b. Tjukke Goarte mäd Sierup, dät waaz je <u>dät</u>, **wät** bi de alle Ljuudene wät äkstroa was.
'Perlgraupen mit Sirup, das war ja das, was bei den alten Leuten etwas Besonderes war.'   (1972/U/B117/6:20)

     c. <u>Dät Eensichste</u>, **wät** strom inne Meente ferbeeden waas: neemens doarste deer un Huus baue un neemens doarste inne Meente woonje.
'Das Einzige, was in der Gemeinde streng verboten war: niemand durfte dort ein Haus bauen und niemand durfte in der Gemeinde wohnen.'
(1997/S/B185/50:50 [erschien auch in:
Skn, *Woo Seedelsbierch apsteen is*/S. 23])

     d. Dan studen do Strukeljer Noabere deer aal uum't Huus un häbe lusterd, **wät** deer nu wäil keem.
'Da standen die Strücklinger Nachbarn alle ums Haus herum und haben gelauscht, um zu erfahren, was da noch wohl käme.'
(1985/U/SV, *Pestoor Tronekomp*/S. 80–81)

     e. Un die is nid <u>boang weeden</u>, **wät** min Uurgrootfoar weeden is.
'Er ist nicht ängstlich gewesen, was mein Urgroßvater war.'
(1972/S/B98/67:25)

Manche Sprecher scheinen bei Neutra fast ausschließlich *wät* zu verwenden, außer wenn sich das Bezugsnomen auf Personen bezieht, wie z. B. *Bäiden* 'Kind', *Wieuw* 'Frau', *Wucht* 'Mädchen' (vgl. z. B. 1a und 2a oben; s. Slofstra & Hoekstra 2022:79). Darüber hinaus stellt Fort fest, dass vor allem Sprecher des Utender Dialekts einen noch allgemeineren Gebrauch von *wät* haben, solange es sich *nicht* auf Personen bezieht. Man sieht zum Beispiel in (5), dass *wät* anstelle von *ju* (das Bezugsnomen ist *ju Stede* 'die Stätte') verwendet wird.[10]

(5) Dät broachten wie ätter <u>en Stede</u> wai, **wät** wied genouch fon do Huze owe was.
'Das brachten wir an einen Ort, der weit genug von den Häusern entfernt war.'
(1985/U/SV, *In ju Paaskentied*/S. 64)

Ähnliche Tendenzen zur Generalisierung von *wät* als Relativum findet man in niederdeutschen Dialekten (Thies 2017:174; Brandt & Fuß 2019:100). Zudem ist sie mittlerweile in den nordfriesischen Dialekten von Fering und Mooring

---

10. „In der Utender Mundart kommt *wät* (= was) häufig als unveränderliches Relativpronomen vor, wenn das Bezugswort nicht eine Person bezeichnet [...] Ist das Bezugswort eine Person, so finden wir immer das sonst übliche Relativpronomen" (SV = Fort 1985:152). Für ein weiteres Beispiel, siehe 6f (dort ist das Bezugsnomen *do Gailtoppe* von Singular Maskulinum *die Gailtop* 'auf einem Kuhfladen wachsender Grasklumpen').

(Arfsten et al. 2019: 58; 2020: 45) zur Norm geworden, so dass man bei *wät* wohl von einer Relativpartikel sprechen kann.

4. Direktes Objekt

In den Beispielen (6) fungiert das Relativpronomen als direktes Objekt, was dem Akkusativ im Deutschen entspricht.

(6) a. Tou <u>dän lätste Breeu</u>, **dän** Ji mi tousaant häbbe un wier Ji uk twoo Siden Froagen meesaant häbbe, wol ik Jou dät wier tourääch seende un ap ju <u>Kassätte</u>, **ju** Ji deer bi lait häbbe, soo dät Ji däd beeter färstounde konnen un beeter begripe konnene ... wier tou rääch seende.
'Bezüglich des letzten Briefes, den Sie mir zugesandt haben und bei dem Sie auch zwei Seiten Fragen mitgeschickt haben, will ich Ihnen das wieder zurückschicken und [zwar] auf die Kassette [sprechen], die Sie dazu gelegt haben, damit Sie das besser verstehen können und besser begreifen können ... wieder zurückschicken.' (1997/S/B187/00:10)

b. <u>Dät Schäärsaaks</u>, **dät** hie deerfoar bruukte, doarste hie hoolde.
'Das Rasiermesser, das er dazu gebrauchte, durfte er behalten.' (1985/U/SV, *Deelbjoor*, S. 60)

c. Oaber dät is't <u>aal</u>, **wät** ik deerfon kweede kon, dan dät iz <u>dät</u>, **wät** ik mi as e Wäänt fortälle lät hääbe.
'Aber das ist es alles, was ich dazu sagen kann, denn das ist das, was ich mir als Junge habe erzählen lassen.' (1972/U/B117/35:35)

d. in Ameerikoa, kwad hi, rakt et al. <u>Maschinen, wier doo Tüwelke bäät al appe Wain fljooge</u>, **wät** wie nu däälich uk hier hääbe.
'In Amerika, sagte er, gibt es schon Maschinen, bei denen die Kartoffeln hinten auf einen Wagen fliegen, was wir nun heute auch hier haben.' (1972/S/B95/48:45)

e. Jä, no kon ik Jou nog en bitsken fortälle so fon do <u>Hontwierkere</u>, **do** wi dan früüer hier so hiden.
'Ja, nun kann ich Ihnen noch ein bisschen von den Handwerkern erzählen, die wir dann früher hier so hatten.' (1972/R/B101/59:40)

f. In do Weden wieren <u>do Gailtoppe</u>, **wät** do Bäiste nit freten hieden.
'Auf den Weiden standen die auf Kuhfladen wachsenden Grasklumpen, die die Kühe nicht gefressen hatten.' (1985/U/SV, *Luntjen*/S. 48)

Relativpronomina, die als Subjekt oder direktes Objekt des Relativsatzes fungieren, treten im Saterfriesischen am häufigsten auf. Dieser Befund steht im Einklang mit den Erwartungen der Zugänglichkeitshierarchie, wie sie in deutschen Dialekten zu finden ist (s. Fleischer 2005).[11] Vor allem sind die Verwendungen von Relativa als indirektes Objekt (einschließlich Konstruktionen, die einem freien Dativ entsprechen, s. 5.2) und Possessivkonstruktionen selten und scheinen fast ausschließlich auf die schriftlichen Teile des Korpus beschränkt. Der Umfang des Korpus macht es jedoch schwer möglich, eine vollständige Frequenzhierarchie zu erstellen.

5. Indirektes Objekt und Dativkonstruktionen

5.1 Indirektes Objekt

Im Saterfriesischen gibt es keine ausgeprägte Dativform, die zur Bezeichnung des indirekten Objekts verwendet wird (anders als im Deutschen, z. B. *dem* Dat. Sg. m./n.). Darüber hinaus sind Belege des Relativums im Saterfriesischen in der Funktion eines indirekten Objekts selten (ähnlich wie in regionalen Dialekten des Deutschen, s. Fleischer 2006: 215). Die folgenden Beispiele stammen aus schriftlichen Quellen, insbesondere aus Übersetzungen aus dem Deutschen von Gretchen Grosser:

(7) a. Uumdät do Wäänte <u>aan Moansk</u> hieden, **dän** jo alles kweede kuuden, wät hiere Haat belastede.
'Damit die Jungen einen Menschen hätten, dem sie alles sagen könnten, was ihr Herz bedrückte.' (2013/R/FK/Kap. 5, S. 69)

b. Dät is <u>ju</u>, **ju** iek mäd dän Skirrem Schutz roat hääbe.
'Das ist die, der ich mit dem Schirm Schutz gegeben habe.' (2009/R/LP/Kap. 21, S. 72)

Im Korpus finden wir kein Beispiel eines Relativums im Singular Neutrum in der Funktion eines indirekten Objekts. Das Relativum als indirektes Objekt kommt sowieso selten vor, und wenn solche Konstruktionen vorkommen, dann meist in Bezug auf Personen oder Tiere, was die Zahl der Möglichkeiten stark einschränkt.[12] Befragungen vor Ort deuten darauf hin, dass in solchen Fällen das

---

11. Die von Keenan & Comrie (1977) aufgestellte Zugänglichkeitshierarchie (auch Akzessibilitätshierarchie genannt, vgl. engl. „Accessibility Hierarchy") sieht wie folgt aus: Subjekt > direktes Objekt > indirektes Objekt > obliques Objekt > Genitiv > Vergleichsobjekt. Mit anderen Worten ist ein Relativpronomen mit Subjektfunktion zugänglicher als eines mit direkter Objektfunktion, und dieses ist wiederum zugänglicher als eines mit indirekter Objektfunktion usw.

12. Ein Beispiel für ein indirektes Objekt im Plural findet sich in Forts Bibelübersetzung: *Atterdät hie wierumekemen waas, liet hie <u>do Tjoonste</u>, do hie dät Jeeld roat hiede, ätter sik touroupe*

biologische Geschlecht bei den meisten Sprechern verwendet wird, wie etwa *Dät Bäiden, dän* (oder *ju* wenn weiblich) *iek dän Ball roat häbe* 'das Kind, dem ich den Ball gegeben habe' oder *Dät Wucht, ju iek dän Ball roat häbe* 'das Mädchen, dem ich den Ball gegeben habe' (siehe jedoch Fußnote 8 und 8c).

5.2 Dativkonstruktionen

Abgesehen von der Verwendung des Relativpronomens zur Kennzeichnung eines indirekten Objekts gibt es im Saterfriesischen noch weitere Konstruktionen, die einem Dativ im Altfriesischen (und im gegenwärtigen Hochdeutschen) entsprechen. Es handelt sich um Dativobjekte nach bestimmten Verben und um freie Dative (darunter der sogenannte possessive Dativ),[13] bei denen eine Person normalerweise durch ein Ereignis positiv oder negativ betroffen ist. Diese Dativkonstruktionen werden jedoch in der gesprochenen Sprache nur selten durch ein Relativpronomen ausgedrückt. Wenn sie vorkommen, scheinen sie weitgehend auf den schriftlichen Gebrauch beschränkt zu sein. In den meisten Fällen handelt es sich wiederum um Übersetzungen aus dem Deutschen.

(8) a. Un unnern stuude <u>aan litjen Wäänt</u>, **dän** hüünenhaftige Troonen uut do Oogene ronnen.
'Und unten stand ein kleiner Junge, dem riesige Tränen aus den Augen tropften.' (2013/R/FK/Kap. 12, S. 136)

b. un leter do keem <u>mien ouer Möie</u>, **ju** die Mon oustuurwen was, in mien Ooldenhuus ...
'und später kam meine andere Tante, deren Mann [wörtl. der der Mann] gestorben war, in mein Elternhaus ...'
(1985/U/SV, *Fugelfang in Seelterlound*/S. 39)

'Nach seiner Rückkehr ließ er die Diener, denen er das Geld gegeben hatte, zu sich rufen' (NT, Lukas 19:15) Die vorliegende Studie beschränkt sich jedoch auf Sprecher, die mit der Sprache aufgewachsen sind, daher wird dieses Beispiel hier nur am Rande erwähnt.

13. Viele Grammatiken sehen einen Unterschied zwischen dem freien Dativ (z. B. *mir ist der Ball aus den Händen gefallen*) und possessiven Dativ-Konstruktionen, wo ein Körperteil meistens verletzt wird (*ich habe mir den Arm gebrochen*). Nach der überzeugenden Analyse von Seržant (2016) sind beide Konstruktion im Grunde identisch, er nennt sie „free-affectee" Konstruktionen. Wie in vielen Sprachen ist es meist überflüssig, das eigene Körperteil mit einem Possessivpronomen zu markieren. Interessant ist jedoch die Tatsache, dass sich das Englische und auch das Niederländische in dieser Hinsicht geändert haben und normalerweise Possessivpronomina zur Markierung von Körperteilen benötigen (s. Vennemann 2002 und Van Bree 2007).

c. Deer stoant hie as 'n Bäiden, dät ju Hanne dät Buutje wächnuumen häd.
'Da stand er wie ein Kind, dem die Henne das Brötchen weggenommen hat.' (1953–1965/R/LS, #199: *Spreekwoude un Glieknisse*/#759)[14]

d. Do Amerikoaner, do ju dütske Erfiendunge in de Hounde fäl, kuden eerste 1948/49 uk binai so gau fljooge.
'Die Amerikaner, denen die deutsche Erfindung in die Hände fiel, konnten erst 1948/49 auch fast so schnell fliegen.'
(1969/R/ST, *Bääte ju Schalmuure luurt di Dood*/S. 8)

Obwohl die formale Unterscheidung zwischen Akkusativ und Dativ im Saterfriesischen sowie in anderen friesischen Dialekten und im Niederdeutschen verlorengegangen ist, hat dieser Verlust im Allgemeinen keine signifikanten Auswirkungen auf das Überleben von Konstruktionen, die einem freien Dativ im Deutschen entsprechen. Trotzdem sind Relativpronomina mit Dativfunktion im Saterfriesischen selten.

6. Possessivkonstruktionen

Wie bei den Dativkonstruktionen kommen Relativsätze, die mit einem Possessiv eingeleitet werden, selten vor. Das Possessiv kann entweder durch eine periphrastische Struktur mit einem Possessivpronomen (6.1) oder durch die Verwendung der Präposition *fon* 'von' (6.2) gebildet werden.

6.1 Possessiva mit Possessivpronomina

Im Saterfriesischen wird diese Struktur wie in Tabelle 2 gebildet. Im Singular Maskulinum wird das Objekt-Relativpronomen gebraucht. Für die Formen des Neutrums gibt es weiter unten nähere Erklärungen.

Tabelle 2. Relativsätze mit Possessivpronomina im Saterfriesischen

Singular			Plural
Maskulinum	**Femininum**	**Neutrum**	
dän sin (+ Sg. m. Substantiv)	*ju hiere*	=> Sg. m./f.	*do hiere*
dän sien (+ sonstige Substantiva)			

---

14. Auf dieses Beispiel wies uns dankbarerweise Bouke Slofstra hin.

Dieser Relativsatztyp taucht allein in den schriftlichen Quellen des Korpus auf. Die folgenden Beispiele entstammen dem *Leesebouk foar Seelterlound*:

(9) a. Min Naber, Gerd Rombrink, **den sien** Buräi nit wied fon us lig, woonde unner an de Seelter Amze.
 'Mein Nachbar, Gerd Rombrink, dessen Bauernhof nicht weit von uns liegt, wohnte unter der Sagter Ems.'
 (1953–1965/S/LS, #132: *Dät Roupgjucht ur Tiwar fon Seelterlound*)

 b. Do Doktere makje mast ock 'n Unnerscheed twiske ju „schärpe" Piene, ju man ap ju Buterside fon 't Liuend woarnimt, un ju „dumpfe" Piene, **ju hire** Urseeke gewönlik in Störrungen fon binnere Organe häd.
 'Die Ärzte machen meistens auch einen Unterschied zwischen dem stechenden Schmerz, den man äußerlich wahrnimmt, und dumpfem Schmerz, der seine Ursache gewöhnlich in Störungen von inneren Organen hat.'
 (1953–1965/R/LS, #145: *Di Smaat is 'n Fründ*)

 c. Fereenigungen, **do hiere** Apgoawe et is af do hiere Oarbeid mäd do Stroafgesetse in kontrast stounde, af sik jun ju gesetslike Ornunge af jun dän Toacht fon dät Foulkerferstounden gjuchte, sunt ferbeeden.
 'Vereinigungen, deren Zwecke oder deren Tätigkeit den Strafgesetzen zuwiderlaufen oder die sich gegen die verfassungsmäßige Ordnung oder gegen den Gedanken der Völkerverständigung richten, sind verboten.'
 (1953–1965/R/LS/#227: *Gruundgesets foar de Bundesrepublik Dütsklound fon de 23. Mai 1949/Art. 9*)

Wir konnten im Korpus keine Beispiele eines neutralen Nomens finden, dem eine solche Possessivkonstruktion folgt. Pyt Kramer, der für seine Grammatik Interviews mit Saterfriesen durchführte, erfuhr von diesen, dass bei Lebewesen mit neutralem Geschlecht ein Relativpronomen, das dem biologischen Geschlecht entspricht, gebraucht wird (Kramer 1982:24). Das heißt etwa *dät Wiu*, **ju hire** *Woain ik kooped hääbe* 'die Frau, deren Wagen ich gekauft habe', *dät Bäiden*, **dän sien** (oder: **ju hiere**) *Oolden keemen sunt* 'das Kind, dessen Eltern gekommen sind' oder *dät Swien*, **dän sien** *Nosering uutrieten is* 'das Schwein, dessen Nasenring ausgerissen ist'.[15]

---

15. Für muttersprachliche Hinweise und auch für das letzte Beispiel bedanken wir uns bei Margot Tameling. Sie meinte auch, dass im Saterfriesischen ein neutrales unbelebtes Nomen nicht durch ein Possessiv relativiert werden kann. Ein Satz wie *dän Man*, **dän sien** *Huus oubaddened is* 'der Mann, dessen Haus abgebrannt ist' ist einwandfrei, aber *******dät Huus*, **dät sien** *Dak oubaddend is* 'das Haus, dessen Dach abgebrannt ist' ist nicht akzeptabel. Stattdessen würde man sagen: *dät Huus*, **wier** dät Dak aubaddend is (siehe 7.1 für weitere Relativsätze mit *wier*).

Ähnliche possessive Strukturen gibt es auch in Niederdeutschen, Niederländischen und Westfriesischen.[16] Ein possessives Relativpronomen wie das Deutsche *dessen* oder das Englische *whose* ist im Saterfriesischen nicht belegt (vgl. jedoch westfries. *waans*, Mooring *huums, huumsen* 'wessen', s. Popkema 2006: 176; Arfsten, Paulsen-Schwarz, Terhart 2020: 46).[17]

6.2 Possessiva mit *fon*

Die Possessivstruktur mit *fon* ist eine von mehreren Relativkonstruktionen mit Präpositionen im Saterfriesischen (s. Abschnitt 7). Es gibt in der Sprache zwei Möglichkeiten, um einen präpositionalen Relativsatz zu bilden. Eine Möglichkeit ist, den Relativsatz mit *wier* 'wo' zu beginnen. Normalerweise wird die Präposition dann „gestrandet" (10a), aber auch zusammengesetzte Präpositionaladverbien kommen gelegentlich vor (10b):

(10) a. Dät was aber nit eenfach, wail <u>do grattere Wäänte</u>, **wier** do Baben **fon** in dän Kriech wierne, stuur tou remäntjen wierne.
'Das war aber nicht einfach, weil die größeren Jungen, deren Väter im Krieg waren, schwer zu bändigen waren.'
(1985/U/SV, Ju grote Schoule/S. 105)

   b. Auks sätte sik in Schäddel, Blok in Roomelse, un Käärkhof in Utänne, <u>wier ze sik älk groote Steenhuuse baudene</u>, **wierfon** dat Eene noch kuts in Schäddel bääte Auks ow Awiks Hus steen här un dät Pitsel ... Pizel hit.
'[Die Familie] Auk saß in Scharrel, Blok in Ramsloh, und Kaarkhof in Utende, wo sie sich große Steinhäuser bauten, wovon das Eine vor kurzem in Scharrel hinter Auks, oder Awiks Haus, gestanden hat und Piesel hieß.'[18]
(1999/S/B198/46:10)

---

16. Im Niederländischen und Westfriesischen kommt diese possessive Struktur allerdings nur im Singular vor (s. Popkema 2006:176 und Broekhuis 2012:400). Im Westfriesischen wird sie nicht nur mit dem Relativpronomen *dy* 'der/die' sondern auch mit dem Fragepronomen *wa* 'wer' gebildet. Diese Konstruktion ist dem Saterfriesischen und auch dem Niederdeutschen fremd (s. Thies 2017:171), vgl. westfriesisch *de man wa syn* (oder: *dy syn*) *auto oft oanriden is* oder *de man fan wa't de auto oanriden is* 'Der Mann, dessen Auto angefahren ist'. Zudem gibt es in der westfriesischen Schriftsprache das veraltete Pronomen *waans* 'wessen': *de man waans auto oft oanriden is* (s. Popkema 2006:300).

17. Mooring: *Di smas, huums süster ik frai, as måål.* 'Der Schmied, dessen Schwester ich heirate, ist wütend'. Die mit *weer* 'wo' beginnende Struktur scheint aber geläufiger zu sein: *Di smas, weer ik jü süster foon frai, as måål.* Im Saterfriesischen ist das Wort *wäls* 'wessen' nur als Fragepronomen belegt (z. B. *wäls is dät?* 'wem gehört das/es').

18. Diese alteingesessene Familie heißt auf Saterfriesisch *Auks* und amtlich *Awicks*. Weiteres zu dem steinernen Gebäude, was 'Piesel' heißt, s. Kramer 1994: s.v. *Piesel* (vgl. afries. *pīsel* 'Wohnstube').

Die andere Möglichkeit besteht darin, den Relativsatz mit der Präposition selbst zu beginnen:

(11) a. Dän Nitsmooker — so namden jo <u>dän Mon</u>, **fon dän** jo dän wuddelke Noome heel un aal nit koanden.
'Den Nichtraucher — so nannten sie den Mann, von dem sie den wirklichen Namen gar nicht kannten.' (2013/R/FK/Kap. 2, S. 31)

    b. Toufaane wierne deer in Seelterlount <u>tjo groote Familjen</u>, **fon do** immer die olste Junker hit.
'Früher waren dort in Saterland drei große Familien, von denen immer die älteste Junker hieß.' (1999/S/B198/48:55)

Laut Hoekstra (2002: 68) können mit *fon* beginnende Possessivstrukturen nur mit dem Singular Maskulinum *dän* und der Pluralform *do* verwendet werden (wie oben 11a–b). Mit anderen Worten kommt die in (11a-b) dargestellte Struktur nicht mit dem Femininum und dem Neutrum von Demonstrativa vor. Im Korpus sind keine Possessivkonstruktionen des Typs *fon ju* oder *fon dät* vorhanden, aber Beispiele gibt es in Forts Bibelübersetzung, die von Muttersprachlern als akzeptabel empfunden wurden.[19] Slofstra und Hoekstra (2022: 81) vermuten, dass die mit Präposition beginnenden Relativsätze aus dem Deutschen entlehnt wurden, was durchaus möglich ist. Beispiele gibt es bereits in den von Minssen gesammelten Sachtexten. Sie kommen jedoch nicht in den Volkserzählungen von Fokke Hamken vor, die dem gesprochen Idiom deutlich näher stehen.

Die Strukturen mit *wier… fon* und *fon* + Demonstrativum haben Parallelen im Nord- und Westfriesischen. Im Westfriesischen wird jedoch anstelle des Saterfriesischen *wier* das ältere Relativum *der* 'da' verwendet (zu Resten im Saterfriesischen s. 7.1).[20] Eine ganz ähnliche mit *wier*-beginnende Struktur wird in den Grammatiken von Fering und Mooringer Friesisch als Normalfall angegeben (Fering *huar*, s. Arfsten, Paulsen-Schwarz, Terhart 2019: 59; Mooring *weer*, s. Arfsten, Paulsen-Schwarz, Terhart 2020: 45–46).

---

19. *N Wieuw, fon ju ju Dochter fon n uunrainen Jeest biseten waas* 'Eine Frau, deren Tochter von einem unreinen Geist besessen war' (NTP, Markus 7:25) und *Glukkelk is <u>dät Foulk</u>, fon dät God die Here is* 'Wohl dem Volk, dessen Gott der Herr ist' (NTP, Psalmen 33:12).

20. Im Westfriesischen tritt *der* in Kombination mit einem nachfolgenden „Dummysubjekt" im Neutrum auf, d. h. *der't*. Diese Struktur ist im Westfriesischen bei Gegenständen obligatorisch und bei Lebewesen optional. Dagegen muss der mit Präposition beginnenden Struktur im Westfriesischen *wa* 'wer' folgen. Sie kann sich daher nur auf Personen bzw. Lebewesen beziehen (Popkema 2006: 176). Vgl. Westfriesisch *<u>it hûs</u> dêr't it dak fan ynsakke* wie 'das Haus, von dem das Dach eingestürzt war'; *it wyfke dy har* (oder: *wa har*) *baarch oft net rinne woe* oder *<u>it wyfke</u> fan wa't de baarch net rinne woe* 'Die Frau, deren Schweine nicht laufen wollen' (Popkema 2006: 176). Aus stilistischen und anderen Gründen werden im Westfriesischen manchmal Präpositionaladverbien gebraucht. In solchen Fällen benutzt man immer das *w*-Pronomen, z. B. *wêrfan* 'wovon' nicht *dêrfan* 'davon'.

7. Relativsätze mit Präpositionen

Abgesehen von den in 6 behandelten Possessivstrukturen können Präpositionen zur Angabe von verschiedenen anderen Rollen verwendet werden. Wie bereits im Abschnitt 6 erwähnt, beginnen Relativsätze mit Präposition entweder mit *wier* (früher noch *deer*), gefolgt von einer meist „gestrandeten" Präposition, oder sie beginnen mit der Präposition, gefolgt von dem bestimmten Artikel, der als Demonstrativum fungiert. Die Gründe für den Gebrauch des einen oder anderen Typs können hier nicht im Einzelnen untersucht werden, aber mit *wier* beginnende Relativsätze scheinen eher in der gesprochenen Sprache vorzukommen (s. auch Fort 2015:780).

7.1 Mit *wier* oder *deer* eingeleitete Relativsätze

Eingangs sei erwähnt, dass in saterfriesischen Quellen aus dem 19. Jahrhundert statt *wier* eher das ältere *deer* verwendet wird. Beispielsweise findet sich in den Volkserzählungen von Hermann Griep — auch Fokke Hamken genannt (1800–1871) — fast ausschließlich *deer* + Präposition (s. 12a-b).[21] In Quellen des 20. Jahrhunderts dagegen ist das *deer*-Relativum eine absolute Rarität und kommt nur noch ganz vereinzelt vor (s. 12c).

(12) a. azz hī dǟr kōm un den docter trīne hīre kronkheid fertellede, sgrē͜ū hī him <u>un rēsept</u> op, **dǟr** jan **medd** étter dō aptēke waigunge sgüll.
'als er da kam und dem Arzt Trines Krankheit erläuterte, schrieb er ihm ein Rezept auf, mit dem Jan zur Apotheke hingehen soll.'[22]

(1846/S/M3, *dócter alwīten*/S. 55)

b. <u>djū kū</u>, **dǟr** hī dō mīge **fon** krīgen hīde, wazz tīd͜üg.
'die Kuh, von der er die Harne gekriegt hatte, war trächtig.'

(1846/S/M3, *Fon 't kōl͜ōū̯, det un kerrel opfrǟten hīde*/S. 70)

c. Dan mou man <u>e grooten Swinnestaal</u> hääbe, **deer** me hunnerte un moor Swine **oun** häät.
'Dann muss man einen großen Schweinestall haben, worin man hunderte und mehr Schweine hat.' (1972/R/B98/8:10)

---

21. Wir finden nur eine Ausnahme in den Erzählungen von Fokke Hamken: *Der wazz ins änmäl un būr, dī* <u>trē sūne hīde</u>*, wīrfón dī jüngste går nigt bong wazz* 'es war einmal ein Bauer, der drei Söhne hatte, wovon der Jüngste nicht ängstlich war' (M3, *Fon den fent, dī nigt bong wazz*, S. 50). Darüber hinaus fangen freie Relativsätze auch mit *wier* an (s. Abschnitt 9).

22. Der Urgroßneffe von dem in 12a–b zitierten Hermann Griep (1800–1871) war Theo Griep (1916–2007). Er benutzte noch vereinzelt das *deer*-Relativum, aber wir finden kein eindeutiges Beispiel mit Präposition. Im folgenden Beispiel gehört die Präposition *ap* eher zum Verb: *un uk*

Zusammengesetzte Formen mit *deer* (d. h. mit *deer* beginnende Präpositionaladverbien) sind sehr selten, kommen jedoch in einigen Sachtexten bei Minssen vor:

(13) a. ūm <u>un springwurtel</u> tō krīgen, **dǟrmedd** me alle slötte ǟpen ma$_e$kje kon, mōt me sō tō wērke gunge ...
'Um eine zauberhafte Wurzel zu bekommen, mit der man alle Schlösser öffnen kann, muss man auf diese Weise zu Werke gehen ...'
(1846/S/M3, *ålrūn, spríngwurtel un sō férre*/S. 60)

b. wan dī plōg oppe grūnd sta$_e$nd, dan izz <u>det unnerste</u>, wīrop dī plog sta$_e$nd, dī sōle, <u>'n fₐaurkant$_{ü}$g stuk holt</u>, **dēron** det plōgīrzen, det inne grūnd ōnsnit, medd spīkere ōnhauen izz.[23]
'wenn der Pflug auf dem Grund steht, dann ist das Unterste, worauf der Pflug steht, die Sohle, ein vierkantiges Stück Holz, woran das Pflugeisen, das in den Grund einschneidet, mit Nägeln angehauen ist.'
(1846/S/M3, *dī plōg*/S. 119)

Seit Ende des 19. Jahrhunderts aber ist das Relativum *deer* fast vollkommen durch *wier* ersetzt worden. Im Folgenden besprechen wir einige semantische Verwendungen verschiedener Präpositionen. Diese Auflistung erhebt keinen Anspruch auf Vollständigkeit, illustriert jedoch einige oft gebrauchte Typen.

Zuerst ein Beispiel für die Verwendung der Präposition *mǟd* 'mit' in der Bedeutung von 'mit etwas' oder 'mit jemandem':

(14) Dät waas ap 'n heeten Dai un Wiendstilte, as Korls Gert so drok oungungen komm un us fertälde, dät <u>Heese Bernd</u>, **wier** hi **mǟd** touhoope waas, stuurwen waas.
'Das war an einem heißen Tag mit Windstille, als Karls Gerd so eilig ankam und uns erzählte, dass Heese Bernd, mit dem er zusammen war, gestorben war.' (1953–1965/R/LS/#241, *Fon do lääste Holloundsgungere fertälde*)

Weiter wird auch der Gebrauch eines Objekts (z. B. Werkzeug, Instrument, Gerät, Material, Tier) mit der Präposition *mǟd* 'mit' ausgedrückt:

---

was deer noch foar n tritich, fjautig Jiere <u>un Huus</u>, deer do oolde Seelter ire Kloodere in-, oan-, aphongjen hiden, wän ze inne Särke wilne 'und dort war auch noch vor dreißig, vierzig Jahren ein Haus, wo die alten Saterländer ihre Kleider ein-, an-, aufgehängt hatten, wenn sie in die Kirche [gehen] wollten' (1999/S/B198/48:20). Ein weiteres Beispiel ist: *wie kriege dät Holt deel und <u>doo oubaadende Ljüüde</u>, deer die Kriech dan weesen is schällen deer dan Holt fon häbbe* 'wir kriegen das Holz runter und die ausgebrannten Leute [d. h. die Leute, die abgebrannte Häuser haben], wo der Krieg dann gewesen ist, sollen davon Holz haben' (Tw, S. 66). Es ist möglich, dass sich das *deer*-Relativum im Scharrel am längsten erhalten hat.

23. In Minssen können beide Typen in ein und demselben Text und sogar in ein und demselben Satz vorkommen (z. B. *wīrop* und *dēron* im 13b oben). Der *deer*-Typus hat wohl zu dieser Zeit gegenüber dem *wier*-Typus an Boden verloren.

(15) Jää, där wieren <u>sukke Mutten</u>, nä. Jäi, **wier** ze soo Eed **mäd** färden un Mjuks **mäd** färden
'Ja, da waren solche Mutten [ein kleines Schiff], nicht. Ja, womit sie so Torf und Dünger transportierten.'
(1972/U/B110/27:50)

Die Quelle oder Ursache wird durch die Präposition *fon* 'von' ausgedrückt. Das *fon*-Possessiv ist eng verwandt mit diesem Gebrauch und leitet sich sicherlich davon ab, s. 6.2:

(16) <u>Steene</u>, **wier** man Huuse **fon** bauen dide, wudden in Schäddel häärstaalt.
'Steine, aus denen man Häuser baute, wurden in Scharrel hergestellt.'
(1972/U/B105/08:40)

Der Ort wird durch Präpositionen wie *oan* 'in', *unner* 'unter', *uur* 'über' usw. näher bestimmt:

(17) Do hä wie deeroan maaked faar de Bäiste <u>een litje Släipkoomere</u>, **wier** min Unkel **oan** släipe kuude, bie doo Bäiste.
'Damals haben wir dort vor den Kühen eine kleine Schlafkammer eingerichtet, in der mein Onkel bei den Kühen schlafen konnte.'
(2003/S/Tw, *Ponnen foar t Huus*/S. 52)

Präpositionen, die Teil eines Verbkomplements sind, können relativiert werden (*warten auf, froh sein über, umgehen mit* usw.):

(18) un dä rakt uk <u>dweerege Lüde</u>, **wier** du nit so gjucht **mäd** umegunge kost, do immer jun n Striek sünt.
'und es gibt widerspenstige Leute, mit denen du nicht so gut umgehen kannst, die immer gegen den Strich sind.'
(1982/S/B150/46:05)

Präpositionaladverbien wie *wiermäd, wierfon, wierap, wieruur* sind wiederum seltener, kommen aber vor allem in schriftlichen Quellen wie Übersetzungen aus dem Deutschen vor. Wie im Deutschen beziehen sie sich im Normalfall auf Unbelebtes:[24]

(19) a. Dan wudde deer noch <u>en Länspumpe</u> ounbaud, **wiermäd** man dät Water, wät noch truch do Ploanken kemen was, uutpumpje kude.
'Es wurde da noch eine Lenzpumpe eingebaut, mit der man das Wasser, das noch durch die Planken gekommen war, auspumpen konnte.'
(1985/U/SV, *Schipbau in Seelterlound*/S. 117)

---

24. Ausnahmen kommen z. B. beim *fon*-Possessiv vor, vgl. Fn. 21 oder in jüngeren Zeiten: <u>Do Wuchtere</u>, **wierfon** do maaste al 16 bit 17 Jiehre oold wieren, unnerheelten sik eenfach 'Die Mädchen, von denen die meisten schon 16 bis 17 Jahre alt waren, unterhielten sich einfach'. (GA, *Du Urkundenfälscher!*, 29. Juni 2002).

b. <u>Düsse Planet</u>, **wierfon** hie wächkoom, die kude nit ful gratter weese as man bloot een Huus groot is!
'Der Planet seiner Herkunft war kaum größer als ein Haus!'
(2009/R/LP, Kap. IV, S. 18)

c. Deerfoar stounde <u>Ommere</u> inne Gruund, **wieroun** do Kröten faale, wan jo an dän Träid loangs huupje, uum aan Uutgoang tou fienden.
'Dafür stehen Eimer auf dem Boden, in die die Kröten fallen, wenn sie an dem Draht entlang hüpfen, um einen Ausgang zu finden.'
(2009/R/GA, *Foar Poagen*/Ausgabe 21. März)

d. Wie hääbe <u>twonoomige Sträitenskildere</u> kriegen, **wieruur** wie aal bliede sunt, oaber wäl fon uus rakt sien Adresse wäil mäd: 26683 Roomelse an.
'Wir haben zweisprachige Straßenschilder bekommen, worüber wir alle froh sind, aber wer von uns gibt seine Adresse wohl mit „26683 Roomelse" an.'
(2009/R/GA, *Een Kleinod*/Ausgabe 21. Feb.)

In einigen Fällen ist ein Präpositionaladverb sicherlich vorzuziehen. Wenn man zum Beispiel den Satz (19a) anders formulieren würde, käme es zu einer großen Spaltung zwischen Relativadverb und Präposition, etwa **Dan wudde deer noch en Länspumpe ounbaud, wier man dät Water, wät noch truch do Ploanken kemen was, mäd uutpumpje kude.*[25]

7.2 Mit Präpositionen eingeleitete Relativsätze

Diese Struktur scheint weniger gebräuchlich und kommt eher in schriftlichen Quellen vor.

(20) a. Wie ferjeete oafter, <u>dät Moansken</u>, **mäd do** wie lieuwje mouten, uk mäd uus lieuwje mouten.
'Wir vergessen öfters, dass Menschen, mit denen wir leben müssen, auch mit uns leben müssen.'
(1994/R/D03/S. 58)

b. Him was dat <u>mäd sin grote Woin</u> malört, **mäd dän** hi noch wul jädden drok fierde.
'Ihm war das mit seinem großen Wagen missglückt, mit dem er noch wohl gerne schnell fuhr.'
(1977/S/MT, *Wite Muse*/Art. 12)

---

25. Im Westfriesischen kommen Präpositionaladverbien äußerst selten vor. Sie können aber aus stilistischen Gründen oder zur Vermeidung von Mehrdeutigkeit eingesetzt werden. Das Präpositionaladverb hat dann eine *w*-Form wie *wêryn't* 'worin' (s. Popkema 2006: 202).

Relativsätze im Saterfriesischen **191**

c. Man die Wäänt, dän sien Muur in't Süükenhuus lain hiede, noom sik domoals foar, dät hie in düsse Skoule, in ju hie as Bäiden so lieden hiede, uumdät hie neemens ful fertjoue kuude, leeter insen säärm Huuskoaster wäide wüül.

'Der Junge aber, dessen Mutter im Krankenhaus gelegen hatte, nahm sich damals vor, dass er in dieser Schule, in der er als Kind gelitten hatte, weil er keinem voll vertrauen konnte, später einmal selber Hauslehrer werden wollte.' (2013/R/FK, Kap. 5, S. 68–69)

d. Dät waas dät Raisejäild, ap dät jo täiwden.

'Es war das Reisegeld, auf das sie warteten.' (2013/R/FK, Kap. 7, p. 86)

Schließlich gibt es auch mit Präposition eingeleitete Relativsätze, gefolgt von der in Abschnitt 6 beschriebenen Possessivkonstruktion.

(21) a. Auks Jan, **ap dän sien** Gruund di Krätseldobbe liech, wuld [= wül et] wiete.

'Auks Jan, auf dessen Grund die Kratseldobbe [= Sumpfgebiet bei Scharrel] lag, wollte es wissen.' (1980/S/MT, *Di Krätseldobbe*/Art. 87)

b. Nogh as dälig sjo ik ju Godingbaank, unner 'ne oolde breedkrounige Linde stounden, **trough ju hire** Tacken do Sunnenstroalen schenen.

'Noch wie heute sehe ich die Godingbank, unter einer breitkronigen Linde stehen, durch deren Äste die Sonnenstrahlen schienen.'

(1953–1965/S/LS, #132: *Dät Roupgjucht ur Tiwar fon Seelterlound*)

c. gjucht fuul Sneeflokken un in dän Bäätergruund een Iersenboan, **ap ju hiere** Lokomotive aan Kristboom mäd Smuk groaide.

'recht viele Schneeflocken und im Hintergrund eine Eisenbahn, auf deren Lokomotive ein geschmückter Christbaum wuchs.'

(2013/R/FK, Kap. 12, S. 136)

In diesen mit Possessivum gebildeten Sätzen gibt die Präposition immer eine Raumrelation an.

8. Relativadverbien

Relativadverbien geben im Relativsatz Ort, Zeit, Modus oder Zweck einer Handlung an. Um einen Ort näher zu bestimmen, wird in älteren Quellen *deer* 'da' verwendet, seit dem Ende des 19. Jahrhunderts findet sich fast ausschließlich *wier* 'wo' (22a–b).

(22) a. Ettern bitsken Deege sogte hie alles bienurn un look innen Frahmd wied weylessenes Lound, **deer** hie sien ganze Vormugen med sien leepe Liewend tounigte makede.

'Nach einigen Tagen packte der jüngere Sohn alles zusammen und zog in ein fremdes, weit entlegenes Land, wo er sein ganzes Vermögen durch ein liederliches Leben verschwendete.' (1812/U/FS, *Die ferläddene Súun*/S. 26)

b. De twäide Steede, **wier** de Sproake sik nit loange heelden hät, is Schäddel.

'Das zweite Dorf, wo die Sprache sich nicht lange erhalten hat, ist Scharrel.' (1972/U/B105/08:20)

Für Zeitangaben verwendete man *wan*, manchmal auch *wier*. Für die Vergangenheit kommt sowohl *wan* als auch *as* vor (23a–b).

(23) a. Nu äiwends, **wan** wie deer faar do Finstere kemen, dan was dät maastens ju Tied, **wier** ju do Biddene in't Bääd broachte.

'Nun abends, wenn wir dort vor die Fenster kamen, war das meistens die Zeit, wo sie die Kinder ins Bett brachte.' (1985/U/SV, *Finsterjen*/S. 33–34)

b. Ätters, **as** wie dät Swimmen görich kuden, do genen wie uk in de Äi oun un in do jope Kolke.

'Nachher, als wir das Schwimmen richtig konnten, gingen wir auch in die Sater-Ems hinein und in die tiefen Kolke.' (1985/U/SV, *Tseerik*/S. 127)

Zur Angabe der Art und Weise benutzt man *wo* 'wie' (24).

(24) un so keem ik nog wier ap n Gedanke, **wo** man früüer büügelt hiede.

'und so kam ich noch wieder auf den Gedanken, wie man früher gebügelt hatte.' (1972/U/B106/39:30)

Zur Angabe des Grundes benutzt man *wieruum* 'warum' (25):[26]

(25) Dät is ock ju Urseeke **wierum** do Kurigimkure tou de Kastenimkeräi urgonge.

'Das ist auch der Grund, warum die Korbimker zu dem Bienenkasten übergingen.' (1953–1965/R/LS, #111: *Ju Kastenimkeräi*)

Abgesehen von *wan* bei zeitlichen Bestimmungen, was als Archaismus zu gelten hat, ist der Gebrauch von Relativadverbien ähnlich wie im Deutschen.

---

26. Es wäre denkbar, *wieruum* zu den Relativsätzen mit Präpositionen (Abschnitt 7) einzuordnen. Aber das Wort verhält sich insofern anders, als es nicht trennbar ist.

9. Freie Relativsätze

Freie Relativsätze haben kein Bezugswort im übergeordneten Satz. Sie können am Satzanfang oder nachgestellt im Satz erscheinen. Am Satzanfang haben freie Relativsätze normalerweise eine verallgemeinernde Funktion. Im Saterfriesischen gibt es davon drei Varianten.

Beim ersten Typ, der sowohl in älteren als auch in neueren Quellen recht häufig vorkommt, beginnt der Satz mit einem schlichten Demonstrativpronomen, das nur Singular Maskulinum oder Plural sein kann. Meistens erscheint das gleiche Pronomen im folgenden Halbsatz wieder:[27]

(26) a. **Die** ze mate, die kuud ze drinke.
'Wer sie [= Sauermilch] mochte, konnte sie trinken.'
(1985/U/SV, *Säddenjen*/S. 137)

b. **Do** naan Hid hieden, aber bloos en epen Fjuur, do maken dän Dee jüsso tougjuchte, aber jo maken dan ju Fjuurplatte scheen un kipten dän Dee deerap.
'Diejenigen,[28] die keinen Herd hatten, sondern nur eine offene Feuerstelle, machten den Teig genauso zurecht, aber sie machten die Feuerplatte sauber und kippten den Teig darauf.' (1985/U/SV, *Broodbaken*/S. 136)

c. **Do** fuul Schäipe hieden, do hieden … wieren beter deran, do hieden noch moor Mjuks.'
'Diejenigen, die viele Schafe hatten, die hatten … waren besser dran, die hatten noch mehr Dünger.' (1972/R/B100/1:13:50)

Eher selten finden sich im Korpus sogenannte halbfreie Relativsätze. Solche Sätze beginnen mit einem Demonstrativpronomen, das als Dummy-Bezugselement fungiert und dem direkt ein Relativum folgt:

---

27. Viele schon bei Minssen reichlich überlieferte Aphorismen haben dieses Muster, z. B. *dī der wet wōget, dī der wet wint* 'wer wagt, gewinnt' (M3, S. 144). Lena Terhart weist in einer e-Mail (13. Okt. 2022) darauf hin, dass Sätze mit pronominaler Verdoppelung möglicherweise als linksversetzte Sätze zu interpretieren sind. Das scheint gut möglich zu sein, allerdings kommt die Wiederholung des Pronomens im zweiten Halbsatz meistens, aber nicht immer vor, z. B. *dī der lüstert, hädd nēn rein gewīten* 'wer lauscht, hat keine reines Gewissen' (M3, S. 144), *dī ēnmāl stelt, izz altīd un dēf* 'wer einmal stiehlt, ist immer ein Dieb' (M3, S. 164), *Doo nit loope kuden, bleeuen lääsen* 'diejenigen, die nicht laufen konnten, blieben liegen [d. h. als Verwundete]' (Hermann Janssen, *Scheedstrid twiske Schäddel un Loorp*, in OH, S. 53).

28. Das Saterfriesische Demonstrativum *do* lässt sich gut durch *diejenige, die* übersetzen. Verstärkte Pronomina wie *derjenige, diejenige, dasjenige* (vgl. auch westfries. *dejinge, datjinge*) kommen im Saterfriesischen nicht vor. Es gibt allerdings eine ähnliche Struktur mit *ene*, z. B. *Dän ene, die dän Buntjer fästbiende wüül, fäl dät* [...] 'Dem einen, der den Hausierer festbinden wollte, fiel das [...]' (SS: 155; s. auch SV: 52).

(27) a. **Die die** lääste was, die sin Knikker deer ounschupped hiede, dän heerden do ganse Knikkere, do in dän Pot wierne.[29]
'Wer als letzter seine Murmel da hineingeschnellt hatte, dem gehörten die ganzen Murmeln, die in dem Topf waren.' (1985/U/SV, *Knikkerjen*/S. 46)

b. **Do, do** neen epen Fjuur moor hieden, aber deerfoar en Hid hieden, deer statten dan do Monljude iere Fäite in dän Bakougend.
'Bei denen, die kein offenes Feuer mehr hatten, aber dafür einen Herd, da steckten die Männer ihre Füße in den Backofen.'
(1985/U/SV, *Finsterjen*/S. 27)

c. **Dät, wät** in dän Hunichpüüt bie't Uuttaien uurbleeuw, koom dan in ju Hunichprässe.
'Das, was in dem Honigbeutel bei dem Auspressen übrigblieb, kam in die Honigpresse.' (1990/S/SS, *Hunich*/S. 175)

Bei halbfreien Relativsätzen ist zu bemerken, dass auch neutrale und feminine Demonstrativpronomina eingesetzt werden dürfen.[30]

Drittens gibt es Relativsätze, die mit Interrogativa wie *wäl* 'wer' oder *wät* 'was' beginnen:[31]

(28) a. **Wäl** dän hele Dai herumelopt sünner wät tou ieten, die schäl wul Smaacht häbbe.
'Wer den ganzen Tag umherläuft ohne etwas zu essen, der wird wohl Hunger haben.' (1990/S/SS, *Die Wänt mär sien träi Huunde*/S. 120)

b. **Wät** ouer Ljudene hääbe, däd doocht niks
'Was andere Leute haben, das taugt nichts.' (1972/U/B119/20:10)

Wie oben erwähnt, können freie Relativsätze auch nachgestellt oder innerhalb eines Satzes vorkommen. In solchen Fällen benutzt man auch ein mit *w-* anlautendes Relativum (s. oben 4d).[32]

---

29. Dieser Satz ist wohl zustande gekommen, weil der bestimmte Artikel mit dem Superlativ erscheinen muss (d. h. *die lääste*) und weil das erste Demonstrativum im Satz wohl keine doppelte Rolle spielen darf. Ein klares Beispiel gibt es aber noch in einem Lehrbuch: *Die, die ju Tortenploate inne Hounde häd, nimt een Stuk ou un rakt ju Ploate färe ätter dän Noaber wai* 'wer die Tortenplatte in den Händen hat, nimmt ein Stück davon und gibt die Platte an den Nachbarn weiter' (Evers 2011: 56).

30. Im Korpus fand sich kein Beleg eines halbfreien Relativsatzes mit einem weiblichen Demonstrativpronomen, aber Margot Tameling gab folgendes Beispiel (es könnte sich um eine Kuh im Stall handeln): *Ju, ju deer beefte staand, ju is juust deelfalen* 'die, die dort hinten stand, sie ist eben runtergefallen'.

31. Dieser Satztyp mit *wäl* oder *wät* ist typisch für den im Saterland gesprochenen niederdeutschen Dialekt (Fort 1997: 100).

32. Am Ende sollte bemerkt werden, dass in dieser Studie V2-Relativsätze nicht behandelt werden. Es gibt zwar Sätze, die so aussehen, z. B. *Deer waas eenmoal 'n littjet Wucht, dät hiede goar*

10. Schluss

Wie in benachbarten niederdeutschen Dialekten ist die Satzreihe der Normalfall im gesprochenen Saterfriesischen. Relativsätze oder andere Schachtelsätze kommen tendenziell weniger vor. Aus den Ergebnissen der Studie lassen sich folgende Punkte festhalten:

1. Am häufigsten begegnet man Relativsätzen, in denen das Relativum als Subjekt oder direktes Objekt fungiert, was aus Sicht der Sprachtypologie und der Nachbarsprachen zu erwarten ist (Abschnitt 3 und 4).
2. Nach einem Relativum in Subjektfunktion erscheint mit höherer Frequenz das bedeutungsarme Wort *deer* 'da' (Abschnitt 3).
3. Relativpronomina mit Dativfunktion (indirektes Objekt und freie Dativkonstruktion) kommen selten vor und sind meist auf die schriftlichen Teile des Korpus, insbesondere Übersetzungen aus dem Deutschen, beschränkt (Abschnitt 5).
4. Demonstrativpronomen + Possessivpronomen-Konstruktionen für das Possessiv kommen eher selten vor und unterliegen besonderen Regeln; man findet eher die *wier + fon* Struktur (Abschnitt 6 und Fußnote 15).
5. Präpositionale Relativsätze werden auf verschiedene Weise konstruiert; am geläufigsten ist die Bildungsweise mit *wier +* eine meist aufgesplittete Präposition; Formen mit dem älteren *deer* 'da' + Präposition kommen in älteren Quellen vor, sind aber im 20. Jahrhundert kaum anzutreffen (Abschnitt 6).
6. Normalerweise werden freie Relativsätze, die oft eine verallgemeinernde Bedeutung haben, nach altem Muster mit einem schlichten Relativpronomen eingeleitet, welches nur im Singular Maskulinum oder Plural stehen kann. Freie Relativsätze, die im Satz nachgestellt sind, beginnen mit *w*-anlautendem Pronomen (Abschnitt 9).
7. Eine weitere Tendenz ist die Wiederaufnahme des Hauptsatzes nach einem Relativsatz durch ein resumptatives Pronomen oder eine adverbiale Verbindung. Ähnliche Strukturen sind auch in niederdeutschen Mundarten zu beobachten (Abschnitt 3).

---

neen Määme un uk naan Baabe moor (anstatt: *dät goar neen Määme un uk naan Baabe moor hiede*) (1999/R/Mb, *Do Stierndoalere*/S. 5). Aber es ist oft schwierig, V2-Relativsätze von Satzreihen zu unterscheiden. Zudem gibt es Fälle von Subjektwiederaufnahme bzw. Topikalisierungen, die auch V2-Relativsätzen ähneln, diesen aber nicht entsprechen, z. B. *Un di jeelstriepede Käfer, dän waas dät hier in us wäitkoolde Klima tou koold* 'und dem gelbgestreiften Käfer, dem war das nasskalte Klima bei uns zu kalt' (Frühling 1967/R/ST, *Twäin Mon mäd gans ferschiedene Meenungen*, S. 2). Hier wären weitere Untersuchungen nötig.

Funding

Die Forschung wurde finanziell von KAKENHI #19K00607 unterstützt.

Danksagung

Wir bedanken uns bei Margot Tameling (Strücklingen) für Ihre Hilfe bei Fragen zu einigen saterfriesischen Relativsatztypen, die im Korpus nicht vorhanden waren. Auch bedanken wir uns bei Bouke Slofstra und Henk Wolf für wertvolle Hinweise und Verbesserungen und auch bei Lena Terhart, die unsere Fragen zum Nordfriesischen mit Daten von Fering und Mooring beantwortete. Für sprachliche Verbesserungen danken wir Andreas Kasjan.

Abkürzungen

B	Bandaufnahme (und für schriftliche Quellen, s. Quellenverzeichnis)
AS	Arne Spenter
FS	Flemming Schroller
FT	Franz Trenkamp
HFN	Hans Frede Nielsen
JFM	Johann Friederich Minssen
MCF	Marron Curtis Fort
PK	Pyt Kramer
TG	Theo Griep (eigene Aufnahme für Pyt Kramer)
n.z.	nicht zutreffend
U	Strücklingen-Utende (Saterfriesisch: Strukelje/Uutände)
R	Ramsloh (Saterfriesisch: Roomelse)
S	Scharrel (Saterfriesisch: Skäddel)

Quellenverzeichnis

D02 = Grosser, M. 1993. *Dööntjene un Fertälstere uut Seelterlound*. Band 2. Ramsloh.

D03 = Grosser, M. 1994. *Dööntjene un Fertälstere uut Seelterlound*. Band 3. Ramsloh.

FK = Kästner, E. 2013. *Die fljoogende Klassenruum*. Übersetzt von G. Grosser. Neckarsteinach: Edition Tintenfaß.

FS = Fort, M.C.F. 1988. *Die ferläddene Súun: der bisher älteste saterfriesische Text*. *Jahrbuch für das Oldenburger Münsterland* 20. 25–33.

GA = Grosser, M. 2000–2019. Gretchen Grossers Erzählungen im *General Anzeiger*. Zeitungsstücke bis 2012 sind online einsehbar: https://wikisource.org/wiki/Gretchen _Grosser%27s_Fert%C3%A4lstere_in_d%C3%A4n_GA

LP = de Saint-Exupéry, A. 2010. *Die litje Prins.* Übersetzt von G. Grosser, 2 Aufl. Neckersteinach: Tintenfaß.

LS = Janssen, H. (Hrsg.). 1953–1965. *Lesebouk foar Seelterlound.* Online einsehbar: https://wikisource.org/wiki/Lesebouk_foar_Seelterlound

M3 = Minssen, J. F. 1970 (1846). *Mitteilungen aus dem Saterlande,* Band 3. Hrsg. von P. Kramer. Ljouwert: Fryske Akademy.

Mb = Grosser, M. 1999. *Seelter Märchenbouk.* Ramsloh.

MT = Deddens, Th. 1977–1981. Theodor Deddens *Dööntjen ut Seelterlound* in der *Münsterlandischen Tageszeitung.*

NTP = 2000. *Dät Näie Tästamänt un do Psoolme in ju aasterlauwersfräiske Uurtoal fon dät Seelterlound, Fräislound, Butjoarlound, Aastfräislound un do Groninger Umelounde / Das Neue Testament und die Psalmen in der osterlauwersfriesischen Ursprache des Saterlandes, Frieslands, Butjadingens, Ostfrieslands und der Groninger Ommelanden.* Übersetzt von M. C. F. Fort. Oldenburg: Carl von Ossietzky Universität Oldenburg.

OH = Kramer, P. & H. Janssen (Hrsg.). 1964. *Dät Ooldenhuus. Dööntjen, Gerimsele, Räätsele, Spräkwoude un Wät tou laachjen ap Seeltersk.* Westrhauderfehn: Siebe Ostendorp.

Skn = Griep, Th & P. Kramer. 1999. *Seelter Seeken.* Mildaam.

SS = Fort, M. C. 1990. *Saterfriesische Stimmen.* Rhauderfehn: Ostendorp.

ST = Janssen, H. & P. Kramer (Hrsg.). 1966–1972. *Seelter Trjoue. Tidschrift foar alle Seelter.* [Selbstverlag]

SV = Fort, M. C. 1985. *Saterfriesisches Volksleben.* Rhauderfehn: Ostendorp.

Tw = Griep, Th. 2003. *Twiske Ticheläi un Baarenbierch: Schäddeler Geschichten.* [Selbstverlag]

Literatur

Anthony, L. 2022. *AntConc (Version 4.1.4) [Computersoftware].* Tokyo, Japan: Waseda University. https://www.laurenceanthony.net/software

Arfsten, A., A. Paulsen-Schwarz & L. Terhart. 2019. *Friesische Gebrauchsgrammatik Fering.* Vorläufige Version, Stand 31.12.2019. Bredstedt. Nordfriisk Instituut.

Arfsten, A., A. Paulsen-Schwarz & L. Terhart. 2020. *Friesische Gebrauchsgrammatik Mooringer Fraasch.* Vorläufige Version, Stand 31.12.2020. Bredstedt. Nordfriisk Instituut.

Bor, A. 1986. Relative markers in Old Frisian. *Us Wurk* 35. 57–74.

Bor, A. 1987a. Relative markers in Old East Frisian. *Us Wurk* 36. 21–48.

Bor, A. 1987b. A vexed question in Old East Frisian relative clauses. *Us Wurk* 36. 49–54.

Bor, A. 1987c. Relative markers in the Old West Frisian manuscript *Jus Municipale Frisonum. Us Wurk* 36. 71–90.

Bor, A. 1988. Relative markers in the language of '*Friese Brieven*' ... *Us Wurk* 37. 52–67.

Bremmer Jr, R. H. 2009. *An introduction to Old Frisian: History, grammar, reader, glossary.* Amsterdam: Benjamins.

Broekhuis, H. & E. Keizer. 2012. *Syntax of Dutch. Nouns and noun phrases.* Bd. 1. Amsterdam: Amsterdam University Press.

DWB = *Deutsches Wörterbuch von Jacob Grimm und Wilhelm Grimm*, digitalisierte Fassung im Wörterbuchnetz des Trier Center for Digital Humanities, Version 01/21, https://www.woerterbuchnetz.de/DWB?lemid=D00002 [Zugriff 13.10.2022].

Evers, J. 2011. *Friesischer Sprachkurs — Seeltersk*. Barßel: Sambucus.

Fleischer, J. 2005. Relativsätze in den Dialekten des Deutschen: Vergleich und Typologie. *Linguistik online* 24. 171–186.

Fleischer, J. 2006. Dative and indirect object in German dialects: Evidence from relative clauses. In D. Hole, A. Meinunger & W. Abraham, *Datives and other cases: Between argument structure and event structure*, 213–238. Amsterdam: Benjamins.

Fort, M.C. 1997. Niederdeutsch als zweite Sprache der Saterfriesen. In Faltings, V.F., A.G.H. Walker & O. Wilts (Hrsg.), *Friesische Studien III* (= NOWELE Supplement Series 18), 83–112. Odense: Odense University Press.

Fort, M.C. 2015. *Saterfriesisches Wörterbuch*, 2. Auflage. Hamburg: Buske.

Hoekstra, J. 2002. Relativisation in Frisian. In P. Poussa (Hrsg.), *Relativisation on the North Sea Littoral*, 63–76. München: LINCOM.

Keenan, E.L. & B. Comrie. 1977. Noun phrase accessibility and universal grammar. *Linguistic Inquiry* 8. 63–99.

Kramer, P. 1982. *Kute Seelter Sproakleere*. Rhauderfehn: Ostendorp. (3. Aufl. 1996, mit Verbesserungen und Ergänzungen von M. Grosser.)

Kramer, P. 1992. *Näi Seelter Woudebouk / Neues saterfriesisches Wörterbuch — New Saterfrisian dictionary. Buchstaben A–E und G.* Elst: [P. Kramer].

Kramer, P. 1994. *Lound un Noomen. Die saterfriesischen Orts- und Flurnamen in der Landschaft. Einschließlich Länder- und Gewässernamen*, Bd. 1. Mildaam: [P. Kramer].

Laker, S. & P. Kramer. 2022. Der *an't*-Progressiv im Saterfriesischen. In A. Walker, E. Hoekstra, G. Jensma, W. Vanselow, W. Visser & C. Winter (Hrsg.), *From West to North Frisia: A journey along the North Sea coast*, 197–216. Amsterdam: Benjamins.

Leser-Cronau, S. 2016. Hybrid Noun Mädchen. In *SyHD-atlas*. URL: https://www.syhd.info/ /apps/atlas/index.html#hybrid-noun-maedchen [Zugriff: 5.1.2024].

Lindow, W., D. Möhn, H. Niebaum, D. Stellmacher, H. Taubken & J. Wirrer. 1998. *Niederdeutsche Grammatik*. Leer: Schuster.

Pittner, K. 2007. Relativum. In L. Hoffmann (Hrsg.), *Handbuch der deutschen Wortarten*, 727–757. Berlin: de Gruyter.

Popkema, J. 2006. *Grammatica Fries: De regels van get Fries*. Utrecht: Prisma.

Saltveit, L. 1983. Syntax. In G. Cordes & D. Möhn (Hrsg.), *Handbuch zur niederdeutschen Sprach- und Literaturwissenschaft*, 279–333. Berlin: Erich Schmidt.

Seržant, I.A. 2016. External possession and constructions that may have it. In G. Diewald (Hrsg.), Non-central usages of datives. Sonderheft von *STUF — Language Typology and Universals* 69(1), 131–169.

Siebs, Th. 1893. Das Saterland. Ein Beitrag zur deutschen Volkskunde. *Zeitschrift des Vereins für Volkskunde* 3. 239–278, 373–410.

Slofstra, B. & E. Hoekstra. 2022. *Sprachlehre des Saterfriesischen*. Leeuwarden: Fryske Akademy. https://www.fryske-akademy.nl/fileadmin/inhoud/beelden/homepage/Kennis /Utjeften/Downloads/SPRACHLEHRE-DES-SATERFRIESISCHEN-2022.pdf

Slofstra, B. 2023. Alle dêren binne gjin partikels: Relative sinnen mei *die deer* yn Sealtersk Frysk. Handout. *Dei fan de Fryske taalkunde*, 6 Oktober 2023, Fryske Akademy, Ljouwert.

Slofstra, B. 2024. „Der da" in die USA auswandert … Sprachwissenschaftliche Analzsen von saterfriesischen Redewendungen. *Kulturland Oldenburg* 199. 28–29. https://www.oldenburgische-landschaft.de/wp-content/uploads/2021/08/240311_KO_199_web.pdf

Thies, H. 2017. *Plattdeutsche Grammatik*. 3. verbesserte Aufl. Hamburg/Kiel: Wachholtz.

Van der Horst, J. M. 2008. *Geschiedenis van de Nederlandse syntaxis*. 2 Bde. Leuven: Leuven University Press.

Van Bree, C. 2007. De possessieve datief en andere constructies opnieuw bekeken. In C. Post van der Linde & L. van Wezel (Hrsg.), *'Twai tigjus jere': Jubileumnummer van het mededelingenblad van de vereniging van oudgermanisten, uitgegeven ter gelegenheid van het twintigjarig bestaan van de vereniging*, 33–41. Amsterdam: Vereniging van Oudgermanisten.

Vennemann, Th. 2002. On the rise of "Celtic" syntax in Middle English. In P. J. Lucas & A. M. Lucas (Hrsg.), *Middle English from tongue to text: Selected papers from the Third International Conference on Middle English: Language and Text, held at Dublin, Ireland, 1–4 July 1999*, 203–234. Bern: Lang.

Anhang: Zu den Quellen (s. auch Kramer 1992)

Beleg Nr.	Quelle				Saterländer(in)				
	Kode	Jahr	Zeitstempel/ Seitenzahl/ Ausgabe	Feldforscher	Name	m/w	Geboren	Dorf
1a	SV	1985	S. 27	MCF	W. Krämer	m	1905	U
1b	SV	1985	S. 141	MCF	W. Krämer	m	1905	U
2a	SV	1985	S. 110	MCF	W. Krämer	m	1905	U
2b	SV	1985	S. 69	MCF	W. Krämer	m	1905	U
3a	B94	1972	7:35	HFN	Th. Deddens	m	1934	S
3b	B94	1972	7:10	HFN	Th. Deddens	m	1934	S
3c	B119	1972	51:50	AS	G. Pahl	m	1917	U
3d	B118	1972	23:50	AS	R. Kruse	w	unbek.	U
4a	B188	1972	4:50	TG	Th. Griep	m	1916	S
4b	B117	1972	6:20	AS	W. Krämer	m	1905	U
4c	B185	1997	50:50	PK	Th. Griep	m	1916	S
4d	SV	1985	S. 80–81	MCF	W. Krämer	m	1905	U
4e	B98	1972	67:25	FS	J. Dumstorf	m	1908	R
5	SV	1985	S. 64	MCF	W. Krämer	m	1905	U
6a	B187	1997	00:10	PK	Th. Griep	m	1916	S

Beleg Nr.	Quelle				Saterländer(in)			
	Kode	Jahr	Zeitstempel/ Seitenzahl/ Ausgabe	Feld-forscher	Name	m/w	Geboren	Dorf
6b	SV	1985	S. 60	MCF	W. Krämer	m	1905	U
6c	B117	1972	35:35	AS	W. Krämer	m	1905	U
6d	B95	1972	48:45	FS	H. Ahlrichs	m	1917	S
6e	B101	1972	59:40	FS	G. Block	m	1898	R
6f	SV	1985	S. 48	MCF	W. Krämer	m	1905	U
7a	FK	2013	Kap. 5, S. 69	n. z.	G. Grosser	w	1934	R
7b	LP	2009	Kap. 21, S. 72	n. z.	G. Grosser	w	1934	R
8a	FK	2013	Kap. 12, S. 136	n. z.	G. Grosser	w	1934	R
8b	SV	1985	S. 39	MCF	W. Krämer	m	1905	U
8c	LS	1953–65	#199, Bsp. #759	n. z.	H. Janssen	m	1888	R
8d	ST	1969	S. 8	n. z.	H. Janssen	m	1888	R
9a	LS	1953–65	#132	n. z.	H. Janssen	m	1888	R
9b	LS	1953–65	#145	n. z.	H. Janssen	m	1888	R
9c	LS	1953–65	#227	n. z.	H. Janssen	m	1888	R
10a	SV	1985	S. 105	MCF	W. Krämer	m	1905	U
10b	B198	1999	46:10	TG	Th. Griep	m	1916	S
11a	FK	2013	Kap. 2, S. 31	n. z.	G. Grosser	w	1934	R
11b	B198	1999	48:55	TG	Th. Griep	m	1916	S
12a	M3	1846	S. 55	JFM	H. Griep	m	1800	S
12b	M3	1846	S. 70	JFM	H. Griep	m	1800	S
12c	B98	1972	8:10	FS	A. Blömer	m	c.1896	R
13a	M3	1846	S. 60	JFM	H. Griep	m	1800	S
13b	M3	1846	S. 119	JFM	H. Griep	m	1800	S
14	LS	1953–65	#241	n. z.	H. Janssen	m	1888	R
15	B110	1972	27:50	AS	R. Kruse	w	unbek.	U
16	B105	1972	8:40	AS	C. Naber	m	unbek.	U
17	Tw	2003	S. 52	PK	Th. Griep	m	1916	S
18	B150	1982	46:05	TG	Th. Griep	m	1916	S
19a	SV	1985	S. 117	MCF	W. Krämer	m	1905	U
19b	LP	2009	Kap. IV, S. 18	n. z.	G. Grosser	w	1934	R
19c	GA	2009	21. März	n. z.	G. Grosser	w	1934	R
19d	GA	2009	21. Feb.	n. z.	G. Grosser	w	1934	R
20a	Do3	1994	S. 58	n. z.	G. Grosser	w	1934	R
20b	MT	1977	Art. 12	n. z.	Th. Deddens	m	1934	S

Relativsätze im Saterfriesischen   201

Beleg Nr.	Quelle				Saterländer(in)			
	Kode	Jahr	Zeitstempel/ Seitenzahl/ Ausgabe	Feld- forscher	Name	m/w	Geboren	Dorf
20c	FK	2013	Kap. 5, S. 68–69	n. z.	G. Grosser	w	1934	R
20d	FK	2013	Kap. 7, S. 86	n. z.	G. Grosser	w	1934	R
21a	MT	1980	Art. 87	n. z.	Th. Deddens	m	1934	S
21b	LS	1953–65	#132	n. z.	H. Janssen	m	1888	R
21c	FK	2013	Kap. 12, S. 136	n. z.	G. Grosser	w	1934	R
22a	FS	1812	S. 26	FT	S. Ahlrichs	m	18. Jh.	U
22b	B105	1972	8:20	AS	C. Naber	m	unbek.	U
23a	SV	1985	S. 33–34	MCF	W. Krämer	m	1905	U
23b	SV	1985	S. 127	MCF	W. Krämer	m	1905	U
24	B106	1972	39:30	AS	J. Naber	w	unbek.	U
25	LS	1953–65	#111	n. z.	H. Janssen	m	1888	R
26a	SV	1985	S. 137	MCF	W. Krämer	m	1905	U
26b	SV	1985	S. 136	MCF	W. Krämer	m	1905	U
26c	B100	1972	1:13:50	FS	H. Eilers	m	c.1920	R
27a	SV	1985	S. 46	MCF	W. Krämer	m	1905	U
27b	SV	1985	S. 27	MCF	W. Krämer	m	1905	U
27c	SS	1990	S. 175	MCF	Th. Griep	m	1916	S
28a	SS	1990	S. 120	MCF	Th. Griep	m	1916	S
28b	B119	1972	20:10	AS	G. Pahl	m	1917	U

The uses of historical phonology

Anatoly Liberman
University of Minnesota

Historical phonology was inaugurated by Roman Jakobson about a hundred years ago. Its main thrust was not only to represent sounds of speech as phonemes and variants (allophones) but to prove that sound change is goal-oriented. The "goal" consisted allegedly in striving by the system for regularity and efficiency. The present paper gives examples of how hard it is to determine and evaluate both those parameters. It examines two main concepts of phonology — distinctive feature and system — from the point of view of diachrony. It also attempts to show that the nature of the distinctive feature can sometimes be understood only by examining change, and that system, far from being the principal motor of change, often serves as a conservative force preventing disruption. System emerges as a motor and a brake at the same time. The final section of the paper deals with the Neogrammarian concept of relative chronology and purports to bring out some of its weaknesses.

> The last few decades have seen an increasing interest in historical linguistics and more especially in language change. Not only has the old dictum that diachronic studies presuppose synchronic ones been questioned but also the traditional view of how language changes.
> Erik Hansen & Hans Frede Nielsen,
> *Irregularities in Modern English*, VIII

1. The birth of historical phonology

Nowadays, *phonology* as a linguistic term seems to have replaced *phonetics*. About sixty years ago, it was still possible to encounter titles like "Scandinavian Breaking from a Phonological Point of View." At present, the phonological point of view is tacitly taken for granted as the only one possible. But while comparing the first hundred pages of such well-informed books as Alistair Campbell's *Old English Grammar* (1959) with corresponding chapters in Donka Minkova's *A Historical Phonology of English* (2014), we wonder what, except for some recently obtained data and references to post-1959 publications, with their ever-changing "perspectives" and "points of view," Campbell and even Karl Luick and Eduard

https://doi.org/10.1075/nss.34.12lib
Available under the CC BY-NC-ND 4.0 license. © 2025 John Benjamins Publishing Company

Sievers would have learned from us that is *conceptually* not simply new but worthy of consideration, what solutions would have impressed them as novel not with regard to some details but in principle. What would have made them rethink their way of looking at language history?

Revolutionary breaks with the past occurred not too long ago in biology and physics. In the humanities, Marxism, psychoanalysis, deconstruction, and so forth claim to have thrown new light on history and literature. The brightness of the light is not at issue here. In linguistics, structuralism and ever-changing generative schools have offered numerous "models." Would Sievers, Luick, and Campbell have been impressed?

The first work that used the term *historical phonology* in its title was Jakobson (1931), though his book on the evolution of Russian sounds from a broad Slavic perspective (Jakobson 1929) already contained the ideas and apparatus discussed in the later article. One encounters there such now well-known terms as phonologization, dephonologization, and rephonologization, that is, a view of sounds as phonemes, or functional units. This was a promising beginning but hardly a breakthrough.

Prague historical phonology purported to show that sound change was goal-oriented, rather than chaotic. Though this approach had great potential, the Neogrammarians, despite their often-criticized atomism, were perfectly aware of the fact that one change triggered another. Later, we will have to return to the Prague Circle's teleology and to the Neogrammarians' "atomism." If sound change is indeed goal-oriented, we would like to know, what that goal is. The earliest reference to teleology appeared in Jakobson's 1928 note.

In a 1933 article, Trubetzkoy wrote: "As a representative of the phonological 'school', I would like to show here that the development of the gutturals in the Slavic languages is not at all purposeless and its explanation lies in a striving for regularity and efficiency in the structure of the sound system" (quoted from Trubetzkoy 2001: 157). Thus (let us not forget the key words), Trubetzkoy believed that sound systems strive for regularity and efficiency. Such an approach impressed Luick (Jakobson 1975: 198). It certainly inspired André Martinet's deservedly influential 1955 book.

In his essay, Trubetzkoy showed how one change triggered another. He never said that the change was inevitable, but since it occurred, he invariably discovered the structural, systemic factor that led to it in light of regularity and efficiency. Sound system, as it is presented by Trubetzkoy and the early Jakobson, looks somewhat like a kaleidoscope: in the spirit of Saussure's *tout s'tient*, no fragment is allowed to change without affecting the entire configuration. This view of language history would, most probably, have appealed to Sievers, as it appealed to Luick, even though theory is useful only to the extent that it produces an efficient method.

2. Historical phonology and distinctive features

Few phonological concepts have attracted more attention than distinctive features. The nomenclature of such features (as long as we stay with articulatory terms) is old: monophthong ~ diphthong, voiced ~ voiceless, and so forth. It is a commonplace that the terminological apparatus of historical phonetics and phonology derives from synchrony. Hence monophthongization ~ diphthongization, voicing ~ devoicing, and the rest. Trubetzkoy's experience, codified in his *Grundzüge der Phonologie* (1939), shows how difficult it is to isolate the phonologically relevant component in the phonetically observable feature. Voiceless or aspirated? Short or checked? Labial or back? and so forth.

Perhaps in some cases historical phonology may suggest the only convincing solution. Here is a case in point. Old Germanic is believed to have had five short vowels: /i u e o a/. The familiar scheme looks so:

i u

e o

a

It is unclear whether we are dealing with the front/back or the labial/non-labial opposition, that is, whether the carriers of the distinctive feature are /i e/ (then the position of the tongue is relevant) or /u o/ (then the relevant feature is the role of the lips). Questions of this type were at the center of Prague phonology, and we know how much ingenuity was spent on solving them and how often the results looked less than fully convincing. Classical phonetics did not bother about such things: [i e] were to it front *and* non-labial, while [u o] were labial *and* back. Didn't Prague phonology needlessly complicate the situation? It probably did not.

We notice that in Germanic, palatal umlaut affected /u/ and /o/ in a similar way: /i/ and /j/ fronted them. Consequently, /i/ is "distinctively" front. Only that is distinctive which "works." As regards /a/, it was believed to have stayed outside the opposition front : back because it lacked partners and could therefore have back and front variants ("allophones"). But palatal umlaut affected /a/ too! A vowel that can be fronted should be classified as back or perhaps central, shouldn't it? Knowing full well how hard it is to agree on anything in phonological theory, I am not ready to press my point, but I would like to continue arguing, as I did in Liberman (2012), that the most cogent approach to distinctive features is the dynamic one. To repeat, that is distinctive which works: history, assimilation, and alternations make distinctive features "go out of hiding." By contrast, phonetic nuance is suggestive but hardly diagnostic with regard to theory. For instance, Russian /o/ is realized with a weak labial glide, approximately [ᵘo], even though native speakers become aware of this fact only when foreigners dispense with this glide. Yet the presence of [ᵘ] in [ᵘo] should not be used in isolating the distinctive feature: it is a symptom of the phonological arrangement, not an argument for classifying /o/ as labial rather than back. So much for the old question about how much "phonetics" is allowed to be used in phonology.

In Russian scholarship, two phonological schools have been waging a war for nearly a century. As in German (cf. *Bund* 'union' and *bunt* 'variegated'), in Russian, no opposition voiced : voiceless is allowed in final position: *prud* 'pond' ~ *prut* 'a switch', *snob* 'snob' ~ *snop* 'sheaf', *bez* 'without' ~ *'bes* 'devil', and so forth are homonyms pairwise. One school, associated with L. V. Shcherba, teaches that all such forms end in /t p s/, etc. The Moscow school (so-called) observes that, when *prud* and the rest change and the final consonant happens to be followed by a vowel (for example, *prudy, snoby* — both nouns are now in the plural — or *bezo*, a variant of the same prefix), voice comes to the surface and therefore *prut, snop*, and *bes* are phonemically /prut/, /snop/, and /bes/, unlike *prud, snob*, and *bez* with their /d b z/. Some "intermediate" solutions also exist, but they need not delay us here. As is known, Trubetzkoy solved the dilemma by introducing the concepts of the archiphoneme and neutralization, which also gave rise to a great deal of discussion (cf. Akamatsu 1988).

Decades ago, I tried to convert L. R. Zinder, an outstanding linguist and the chief proponent of Shcherba's views, to the Prague faith ([t] in *prut* and *prud*, I argued, was an archiphoneme). He listened to me with a feeling bordering on compassion and then asked: "Do you have ears?" What could I tell Professor Zinder? Today, I gravitate toward the opinion that the safest way to isolate a distinctive feature is to detect it in movement. Morphological variation, assimilation (including sandhi), and especially change make the distinctive feature manifest itself, and the researcher can notice it, because it has pried itself loose from the rest of the "bundle." A view of the distinctive feature as a dynamic entity may perhaps smooth the way toward some unity among linguists.

Ideal solutions in this area probably do not exist, because language is too complex to be reduced to a set of formulas or neat modeling. To make this point clearer, we may return to Germanic short vowels. If the outwardly counterintuitive suggestion that Old Germanic /a/ was phonemically back or at least not front despite the absence of a front partner has value, we may perhaps find an additional argument for this conclusion. In Middle English, /a:/, the long partner of /a/, became /o:/, an open vowel (old /o:/ was closed). Front /a:/ would more likely have become /æ:/ and either merged with old /æ:/ or pushed it upward. Also, when Middle English borrowed another /a:/ from Old French, it yielded /ei/ by the Great Vowel Shift, a front diphthong. Finally, prehistoric Old English underwent back mutation. The vowels /e i/ behaved like /æ/ and developed a back glide (the result was the emergence of /ea eo io/). This change again seems to confirm the idea that /e/ and /i/ were indeed distinctively front, while /o/ and /u/ were back.

Difficulties arise when we look at Old Norse. One of the changes, well-represented in Old Icelandic, was labial umlaut. One of its products was the emergence of the short-lived *labial* phoneme /ǫ/ from /a/: thus, *land* 'land' (SG) versus *lǫnd* < *landu (PL). Palatal umlaut was as active in Old Norse as in Old English, and we concluded that in Old English the phoneme /u/ was back, rather that labial. But since Old Icelandic /u/ could labialize the vowel /a/, it must have been distinctively labial! It is unlikely that in the prehistorical epoch the short vowels of Old English and Old Icelandic had different distinctive features. Like the Old English velar umlaut, the Old Norse labial umlaut happened later than the palatal umlaut (there is no disagreement on this point), but it seems improbable that between those changes a rephonologization, a change of distinctive features, should have occurred. Such a hypothesis would be self-serving and unconvincing.

Is our alternative — back or labial? front or non-labial? — wrong? What about Russian /i u e o/, especially /i/, which is so obviously front (palatal) and /o/ which is so obviously labial? I would prefer to leave this intricate question open, rather than offering a rigid and controversial solution (a complex, Janus-like feature?), but I will make my point clear: historical phonology poses (and sometimes answers) questions that synchronic descriptions fail to notice or ignore.

Historical phonology may sometimes also shed light on the changing nomenclature of distinctive features. A case in point is the development of Germanic consonants over the centuries and, among others, a search for the feature separating /p t k/ from /b d g/: aspiration or voice (here I will abstain from discussing the glottalic theory)? After /s/, the stops are both voiceless and unaspirated, so that no conclusion about the distinctive feature can be made.

Very long ago, I published an article in which I discussed this problem with reference to Modern English (Liberman 1968). Among the data surveyed there was the fact that when English speakers hear unaspirated [p], they often tend to define it as [b]. My final conclusion was cautious and uninspiring: /p t k/ are voiceless, but aspiration is their inalienable feature. At that time, it did not occur to me to propose weakness or tenseness as the sought-for feature, but reference to them would not have gone a long way.

If we begin by observing some Germanic dialect in which /b d g/ are voiced, as they are in French and Russian, and /p t k/ are voiceless and unaspirated, and move all the way to Modern Icelandic, in which /p t k/ and /b d g/ are equally voiceless and /p t k/ fully aspirated, we will observe movement from relevant voice at Point A to relevant aspiration at Point B. The distinctive feature is there, but it manifests itself in diachrony as a movable target. Perhaps historical phonology may teach us a non-trivial lesson, namely, that a distinctive feature is a dynamic entity, definable with absolute clarity only at the start and at the end of evolution.

Before returning to Germanic consonants, I would like to make a short digression. The first scholar to realize the dynamic aspect of distinctive features was Roman Jakobson, who in his book on children's language (that is, on language acquisition) and aphasia (that is, on the progressive loss of the language ability: Jakobson 1941) showed the development and disintegration not of "sounds" (vowels and consonants) but precisely of distinctive features. His postwar work took him in a different direction, though it was also envisaged in the thirties. He aimed at producing a universal picture of distinctive features, applicable to both vowels and consonants. This is what he wrote in the introduction to the volume of Trubetzkoy's correspondence:

> NT's [= Nikolay Trubetzkoy's] effort to build up a multifarious classification of phonological oppositions met with Karl Bühler's philosophical and psychological doubts..... This complex and heterogeneous scheme seemed to overlook the logical essence of *oppositions* and to hamper **the consistent dissociation of phonemes into distinctive features as their actually oppositive components** [emphasis, here in bold, added].... I finally discerned some new cues to a congruously dichotomous classification of distinctive features.... I believed that for this problem ... a joint and mutually cogent solution would be sought and attained.
>
> (Trubetzkoy 1975: xiii)

Trubetzkoy died in 1938 and said at his last meeting with Jakobson that, however interesting the idea of dichotomous phonology might be, he could not begin rethinking his theory in a new light. Jakobson succeeded in bringing out *Grundzüge der Phonologie* days before the German invasion of Czechoslovakia. There is no way to reconstruct the events that might have happened, but in retrospect it seems unlikely that the two scholars would have succeeded in bridging the gap between Trubetzkoy's views and Jakobson's dichotomous phonology.

The results of Jakobson's efforts to revolutionize phonological theory are well-known: they appeared in Jakobson, Fant, and Halle (1952) and in Jakobson and Halle (1956) and became one of the main events in postwar linguistics. In my opinion, they are a step in a wrong direction. A universal theory of distinctive features excludes a dynamic approach to them, and, if one needs oscillograms to make a point in a discourse on phonology, then phonology merges with instrumental phonetics. In the welter of linguistic activity that marked the last three decades of the twentieth century, Jakobson's dichotomous phonology was all but forgotten, and Halle, the phonologist behind Chomsky and Halle (1968), found it useful to give up the acoustic features of his earlier publications and switch to the traditional terms of articulatory phonetics. *The Sound Pattern of English* is dedicated to Jakobson, though the book owes nothing to Jakobson's earlier and later insights. Nor did he ever come to terms with generative phonology.

We can now return to Germanic. The First Consonant Shift resulted in the rephonologization of stops. According to the most traditional reconstruction, the old *b, *d, *g were voiced and marked, while *p, *t, *k were voiceless and unmarked. Once *b, *d, *g lost voice and *p, *t, *k acquired aspiration, they became marked. Acquiring aspiration was tantamount to their weakening (by definition: any loosening of the obstruction means weakening). This is how the process of lenition set in in Germanic, and once it started, it never abated. It is therefore no wonder that the distinctive feature of English /p t k/ cannot be defined: its progress has been stopped in the movement toward the "goal." In recent years, Germanic lenition has been studied in great detail by Kurt Goblirsch (1994 and 2018).

As soon as we understand the nature of the change and begin to discuss strong and weak (instead of voiced and voiceless) consonants, several processes emerge as links in a very long chain. For example, fricatives acquired voice in several positions. The reflexes by Verner's Law come to mind at once, and Verner knew that voicing was tantamount to weakening. In West Germanic, fricatives were voiced (that is, weakened!) in intervocalic position and not too rarely word initially. Luick (1964: 848) was right in viewing this voicing and voicing by Verner's Law as related but probably did not quite realize the nature of the connection. Rhotacism (/z/ > /r/) is also an instance of weakening (Liberman 2020). As time went on, another cycle of weakening yielded English forms like *is* [iz], *of* [ov], and *this* [ðis].

Historical phonology can provide a most important clue to synchronic (or general) phonology/phonetics. It shows that from the time the Germanic languages became a separate group (and here the *terminus a quo* is the First Consonant Shift), lenition, which was the defining feature of the shift, never stopped spreading. Diachrony introduces a dynamic distinctive feature. Let us not bother about a strict separation of synchrony and diachrony but do what it takes to elucidate the way language works. Lenition is also one of the forces behind the Second Consonant Shift. Affricates and spirants are weaker than stops by definition. This observation settles the question about the connection between the shifts. Both are indeed related processes.

Language change is like a river going down to the sea. No prognosis can be made about the timing or volume of the changes captured by this model, especially because language is a social institution and linguistic change is the resultant of many forces. The phonological "river" may dry up or it may be made to go uphill under the influence of some societal factors (something that is impossible in the progress of a natural river): not too rarely apocopated forms restore their endings, some forms considered as vulgar are suppressed and replaced by the forms abolished a century earlier, and so forth. It is not always possible to detect logic in what looks like and sometimes probably is linguistic chaos.

The model of a river should not be confused with reference to so-called tendencies. One could read in old books that, for example, Gothic vowels display a tendency for closed variants. Such a statement is an important-looking tautology: it only confirms the fact that where the other Germanic languages had *ě* and *ǒ*, Gothic had *ī* and *ū*. We have watched lenition at work. Jury Kusmenko (or Kuz'menko) has for years been tracing another force. The rise of the correlation of syllable cut (*Silbenschnitt*), a correlation that did not exist in Old Germanic despite Sievers's belief in it (see Liberman 1979), set in motion the consolidation of the Germanic word into an indivisible whole (first discussed in detail in Kuz'menko 1991).

3. Historical phonology, system, and teleology

System is a key word in general and historical phonology. Jakobson's teleology amounts to the thesis that sound change is goal-oriented, and we remember Trubetzkoy's statement made in 1933: "I would like to show ... that the development of the gutturals in the Slavic languages is not at all purposeless, and its explanation lies in a *striving for regularity and efficiency* in the structure of the sound system." This time, I have added emphasis to his declaration (I italicized *striving for regularity and efficiency*). It is hardly possible to define either characteristic. What makes the system of phonemes regular and efficient? Trubetzkoy's essay is a small masterpiece. He showed how the interplay of correlations and disjunctions produced symmetry in the sphere of the Slavic gutturals. An analog of the linguistic Brownian movement emerged in the form of striving toward harmony. This is the idea of teleology as all the phonologists of the Prague Circle understood it. A well-organized system, we may agree, functions better than a chaotic conglomeration of elements, even though speakers do not seem to have had any problems while the system was in flux, and a look at the history of any well-documented language shows that change never stops.

I would like to propose a thesis that complements Trubetzkoy's, namely, that system is not or at least not only a motor of change, but a bulwark against it. System prevents breakdowns in human communication and produces an illusion of stability where there is none. Hence its striving for "regularity and efficiency." It rather offsets than promotes change.

An example of how deceptive the idea of symmetry sometimes is will be found in language historians' treatment of the Great Vowel Shift in English. Old textbooks cited two theories of the change: a pushchain (the change began with the low vowels, which "pushed" the other vowels upward) or dragchain (/i:/ and /u:/ became diphthongs and "dragged" the other vowels after them). But the long vowels of late Middle English probably began to change more or less simultaneously, as a mass, chasing and displacing one another, and that process never stopped (see Liberman 1995).

Another illusion is the role of empty holes (*cases vides*) in the system. Empty holes may be filled, but their presence needn't be taken for an invitation to change. To put it differently, possibility is not tantamount to necessity. Germanic phonologists always wonder why Dutch never developed [g], a correlate of the velar fricative. The emergence of a new phoneme is a serious disruption of the status quo. Why should the system of Dutch consonants have promoted this disruption if it functions so efficiently the way it does? Why should a happy uniped grow a second leg? If /ɣ/ ever appears in Dutch, linguists will say that the empty hole promoted the change, a typical aberration of a historian's vision.

I will now cite another example from the history of English, to illustrate how system attempts to counteract change. In Middle English, lengthening affected /a e o/ followed by a single consonant but, by and large, spared /i/ and /u/ (for details and references, see Liberman 1992). This reservation is a major riddle in the history of English phonetics, and it will remain such if we keep looking upon system as a force mainly or exclusively working for regularity and neglect its role as a guardian of stability.

A clue to the history of Middle English /i u/ can be found in Middle Dutch. In that language, lengthened vowels did not merge with the former long correlates of the short ones, and Dutch linguists distinguish between old and new length. This was a most uneconomical way of dealing with the change. System failed to prevent it, but saved the language from the appearance of multiple mergers that, in the absence of støds and compensatory circumflexes, as happened in the Scandinavian languages, would inevitably have happened, and which did happen in German (as we know, German survived this minor catastrophe, but it certainly made the process of communication harder).

Icelandic, unlike Danish, Norwegian, and Swedish, had no stød or syllable accents. Nor did it ever develop compensatory circumflexes, but it made one step in the direction chosen by Dutch: old /i:/ is a closed vowel in it, while the product of lengthening is open /i:/, which foreigners often take for /e:/, though regular open /e:/ also exists. Short /u/ became /y:/. In Middle English, /i/ and /u/ lengthened rarely, and when they did, they yielded /e:/ and /o:/! However, Middle English already had two /e:/'s and two /o:/'s. Rather than producing such an overcrowded series of mid vowels or numerous mergers, system chose the least predictable way: it either made the products of lengthening return to their initial

The uses of historical phonology **211**

state or blocked the lengthening altogether. We can probably detect ingenuity and efficiency in this approach to change but hardly great regularity. Change is enforced on the sounds of speech by various factors, and system exists to fight it back and make change less disruptive. In some rare cases, it even blocks change.

In parentheses, we may note that system has several options to fight or adapt to change. Middle English tried the Dutch model but missed the Icelandic way, and it is almost clear why. Just at that time, /y(:)/ was abolished in English and, depending on the dialect, yielded /i/, /u/, or /e/. Adding new /y(:)/ would have been not impossible (an empty hole had just appeared!) but perhaps counterproductive. If it had appeared, we of course would have found an obvious explanation for it. Efficiency and regularity in sound change are sometimes the products of our wishful thinking.

My next examples are less dramatic. In Early Modern English, words like *ask*, *fast*, and *cloth* "suddenly" acquired long vowels. Perhaps this lengthening is still another byproduct of lenition. Lenition had already produced voicing in words like *exhaust* [gz], *as* [z], *vat* [v], *this* [ð], and so forth. *Clothes* also developed [ð]. Perhaps to save *ask, fast*, and other similar words from voicing (lenition), system allowed the root vowels to acquire length: better [a:sk] than [azg]!

Resisting the course of the river is, in most cases, a losing battle. Lenition will have its way wherever consonants yield to it. For example, the change of intervocalic /t/ to /d/ is well-known from American English in which *seated* and *seeded*, *writer* and *rider* (to cite only two examples) are homonyms pairwise. The European settlers brought this pronunciation to their new home from England, as evidenced by the same merger in some British dialects. Voiced /d/ from /t/ was later sometimes further weakened to /r/. The best-known example of the change in the Standard is *porridge* from *pottage* (as in *a mess of pottage*). In dialects, there are more such cases.

Luick (1964, sec. 799) correctly, as I believe, classified all such changes under lenition but ascribed them to mechanical phonetic factors. He did not ask why those (seemingly universal) factors began to weaken stops in the fifteenth and sixteenth centuries. He also cited [abl] for *apple* (1964, sec. 791.3) but again failed to ask why in a much earlier period the process known as the West Germanic gemination affected the stops not only before /j/ (which disappeared as a separate element) but also before /l/ and /r/. Why, for instance, did the word for *apple* become [æppl] and later yielded, even if sporadically, [abl] ~ [æbl]? Perhaps here we can detect some "efficiency." Lenition, with its inexorable progress, had every chance to turn Common Germanic *aplu* into Engl. [æbl], just as it turned *pottage* into *porridge* and American *seated* into *seeded*. But system fought for stability and reached a compromise: it doubled, that is, reinforced stops in certain positions and did it against the background of overwhelming lenition. As a result, the disruption became minimal.

One can read in older books that to the beginner the history of sounds often looks like an exercise in futility: a vowel is lengthened, only to be shortened; first a consonant is devoiced, only to be voiced a few centuries later, and so forth (consider [æpl] > [æp:l] and [æp:l] to [æpl] to [æbl], all such changes being caused by lenition or resistance to it!). Not only beginners feel dismayed by this kaleidoscope. But if we look on phonemes as a system, *an entity that may facilitate change but also exists to counteract it*, a few things will perhaps become less enigmatic. Moving in series and striving for symmetry is inherent in language change, and system does contribute to such processes, but at the same time it makes a sustained effort to minimize the harm produced by change. Phonetic history can be understood in its proper light only if we realize *the double role of system, which is a motor and a brake at the same time.*

4. A lesson from the above

What can historical phonology teach general phonology? (1) It is tempting to arrange phonemes in rows and series like /p t k/, /b d g/, /i u/, /e o/, and so forth and obtain distinctive features from them. This is how the oppositions voiced : voiceless (or weak : strong) or in another configuration aspirated : non-aspirated, front : back, high : low, labial : non-labial, and the rest have been produced. But those are phonetic, not structural features. Replacing articulatory by acoustic terms changes nothing in this assessment. The bulky apparatus of general phonetics is not always needed for detecting the features, referred to above as structural. Functional, active distinctive features manifest themselves in movement, and historical phonology, in addition to describing how phonemes interact, brings out the essence of the feature: *it shows what this feature can do*, in addition to just being there. Those are phonological, rather than phonetic, features, even though the terminology and nomenclature remain the same. The difference is between a bird hidden among the leaves of a tree and a bird in flight. Such dynamic features sometimes teach the researcher an unexpected lesson, namely, that a certain feature cannot be defined through a synchronic description.

(2) The foundation of a phonological description is system, which is usually understood as a neatly organized scheme of vowels and consonants. Historical phonology shows that system is not an analog of a lattice or grid striving for the most solid organization of its sections. In the process of never-ending change, system works for stability. Not only does it direct (organize, steer) change in the most logical way. It functions as a defensive mechanism against change, and, while

The uses of historical phonology   **213**

counteracting change, it is often ready to sacrifice regularity, allegedly its main characteristic. Like distinctive features, system is a dynamic entity because language never stops changing. There are periods of stability in change, but synchrony is dynamic, and that is why a many-sided description of synchrony is often indistinguishable from diachrony.

Perhaps Sievers and Luick would have found those two considerations worthy of their attention. Jakobson and Trubetzkoy might perhaps have slightly modified some of their theses concerning teleology in light of the suggestions made above.

5.   System, relative chronology, and the Neogrammarians

Modern linguistics inherited the Neogrammarian doctrine of sound change that, like a train, may either arrive too early or too late. (A more cautious approach will be found in Campbell, 1959: secs. 246–55.) In the final section of this paper, I will dispense with references to books and articles, because the changes under discussion are among the best-known in the history of Germanic, and the material is the stuff of elementary textbooks.

Old English (OE) /a:/ became Middle English (ME) open /o:/ (*stān > stǫn > stone*), while short /a/ became /a:/ before a single consonant (*apa > āpa > ape*). According to the most common conclusion one finds in the standard histories of English, the /a/ became /a:/ after the change of old /a:/ to /o:/, for otherwise, it would also have become /o:/. To put it differently, the lengthened /a:/ (from /a/) missed the train. This conclusion is unacceptable. Even if the lengthening of /a:/ had happened much earlier, system might have taken care to produce a vowel different from old /a:/, to prevent merger. And indeed, as we have seen, even though /a/ was the only vowel in the lowest row, it was, most probably, distinctively back, while the product of lengthening (/a:/ before a single consonant) was, with an equal degree of probability, front, because it later yielded the front diphthong /ei/. Also, before the Great Vowel Shift, it merged with /a:/ in French borrowings, and judging by the history of French /a/, that vowel was front in the middle period.

The history of Icelandic confirms the reconstruction proposed here. Words like *á* 'river' and *kápa* 'cloak' had /a:/ in the oldest period and later became a diphthong ([au], not [ei], as in English) by a weak analog of the English Great Vowel Shift. In contrast, in *fara* 'to go; travel' and *taka* 'to take', the short vowel that underwent lengthening before a single consonant did not become a diphthong. The idea that the Icelandic version of the Great Vowel Shift preceded the lengthening of vowels before single consonants cannot even be considered. *Taka* and *kápa* had different vowels in Old Icelandic. They have changed since that time but are still different.

The qualitative difference between the old and the new phoneme is not the only factor to be considered while reconstructing the relative chronology of sound change. An example of a different situation is the history of Engl. *chin* < *cin(n)* and *kin* < *cyn(n)*. From an articulatory point of view, [k] in *cin(n)* was of course palatalized (all consonants are palatalized before front vowels). Palatalized /k/ must also have occurred *after* front vowels in words like *pic* 'pitch' (as it does in Modern Ashkenazi Yiddish, at least in Russia) and in words like *drencan* 'to drench', the causative of *drincan* 'to drink' (cf. Old Saxon *drencian* and Gothic *dragkjan*), in which */j/ was lost but left its trace in the palatalization of /k/. The processes described above pose a question. Engl. *kin* goes back to OE *cynn(n)*, with /y/ from /u/ by *i*-umlaut (cf. Gothic *kunni*). In Middle English, /y/ became /i/; hence Modern Engl. *kin*. Why did /k/ in *cynn* avoid palatalization, that is, why didn't *kin* become *chin*? The traditional answer is well-known: "/k/ underwent palatalization only before *old* /i/." Why this reservation?

The Neogrammarian answer is predictable: by the time of *i*-umlaut, the process of palatalization had come to an end. This is a circular, self-serving explanation. It reminds one of another old idea: Middle English /i u/ became /e: o:/ before single consonants (in those words in which they changed at all) because allegedly they acquired open variants (that is, [e o]) some time before the lengthening set in. This is a classic case of begging the question! The problem of *kin* is not one of relative chronology and can be solved only from the phonological point of view. Forms like [drenk'an] (*drencan* 'drench') show that even in the earliest period of recorded Old English, /k'/ could occur not only before and after a front vowel, though its distribution was limited. However, in the epoch preceding umlaut, [k] and [k'] were the positional variants (allophones) of /k/. When *drankjan* changed to *drencen*, it became /drenk'en/.

After *kuni* /kuni/ became *cynn* /kyn(:)/, /k/ might be replaced by /k'/ (which would later have yielded an affricate) but might remain intact. This second choice was perhaps less predictable, but system opted for it and did not let *chin* and *kin* become homonyms. I will skip the reference to the suggestion that in later periods /k/ had lost its ability to become palatalized before /i/. The ability to become palatalized before a front vowel can never be lost. See also Liberman (2012) for an explanation of why we today pronounce *what you* as *watch you* but *thank you*, rather than *thanch you*, even though a speaker of Old English would have undoubtedly pronounced *thank you* so.

Perhaps the most famous case of the Neogrammarian abuse of relative chronology is Axel Kock's theory of three periods of Scandinavian umlaut. In Old Scandinavian dialects, *i*-umlaut developed according to a strange rule: in short-syllabic words, final *i* was lost, but umlaut, contrary to expectation, did not occur, while if *i* was retained, umlaut did take place. Apparently, front umlaut was not

The uses of historical phonology   **215**

a mechanical compensatory process and depended on the word's prosody. After long syllables, umlaut occurred regardless of whether /i/ was retained or lost. Axel Kock suggested that Scandinavian umlaut had three periods: in the first period, /i/ was lost only after a long syllable and caused umlaut (this part of the reconstruction is non-controversial); in the second period, /i/ was (so Axel Kock) lost after a short syllable but did not cause umlaut, while in the third period, the retained /i/ caused umlaut in both short and long syllables. This hypothesis has been discussed many times. A fully convincing explanation for the wayward history of Scandinavian umlaut has not been found, but one thing is clear: a sound change cannot be plugged in and out to make sense of enigmatic processes.

In dealing with relative chronology, we should revise part of the Neogrammarian doctrine. If a change appears to occur not later than another change, we need not conclude that it occurred before it. The two changes may happen simultaneously, and system may choose to preserve an old opposition and minimize the effect of a disruptive process. Change is not only a means to achieve symmetry. It is, as repeatedly noted above, also a conservative force that counteracts change. We owe the Neogrammarians almost everything we know about the historical phonetics and morphology of old languages. Yet we can perhaps tell them something useful after a century of phonological research and offer it to them as a sign of gratitude for their monumental achievement.

References

Akamatsu, T. 1988. *The theory of neutralization and of the archiphoneme in functional phonology.* Amsterdam: Benjamins.

Campbell, A. 1959. *Old English grammar.* Oxford: Clarendon.

Chomsky, N. & M. Halle. 1968. *The sound pattern of English.* New York: Harper and Row.

Goblirsch, K. 1994. *Consonant strength in Upper German dialects.* North-Western Language Evolution. Supplement, vol. 10. Odense: Odense University Press.

Goblirsch, K. 2018. *Gemination, lenition and vowel lengthening: On the history of quantity in Germanic.* Cambridge Studies in Linguistics 157. Cambridge University Press.

Hansen, E. & H. F. Nielsen. 1986. *Irregularities in Modern English.* Odense: Odense University Press.

Jakobson, R. 1928. O hláskoslavném zákonu a teleologickem kláskoslovi. *Časopsis pro moderní filologii* 14. 183–84. (= 'The Concept of the Sound Law and the Teleological Criterion' in *The selected writings of Roman Jakobson [SW]*, vol. 1, 1–2. The Hague: Mouton, 1962.)

Jakobson, R. 1929. *Remarques sur l'évolution phonologique de russe comparée à celle des autres langue slaves. Travaux du Cercle Linguistique de Prague* 2. (= *SW*, vol 1, 7–116.)

Jakobson, R. 1931. Prinzipien der historischen Phonologie. *Travaux du Cercle Linguistique de Prague* 4. 121–38.

Jakobson, R. 1941. *Kindersprache, Aphasie und allgemeine Lautgesetze*. Uppsala: Almquist & Wiksells (= *SW* 1, 328–401.)

Jakobson, R. (ed.). 1975. *N. S. Trubetzkoy's letters and notes*. The Hague: Mouton.

Jakobson, R., C. G. Fant & M. Halle. 1952. *Preliminaries to speech analysis*. Acoustics Laboratory, Massachusetts Institute of Technology, Technical Report 13, January.

Jakobson, R., with M. Halle (co-author of Chapter 1). 1956. *Fundamentals of language*. Janua Linguarum 1. The Hague: Mouton.

Kuz'menko, J. K. 1991. *Fonologicheskaia evolutsiia germanskikh iazykov [A phonological evolution of the Germanic languages]*. Leningrad: Nauka. (See my review in *Scandinvian Studies* 66, 1994, 231–67.)

Liberman, A. 1968. O glukhikh i zvonkikh smychnykh v angliiskom iazyke [On the voiced and voiceless plosives in Modern English]. *Inostrannye iazyki v shkole* 3. 22–30.

Liberman, A. 1979. Prephonological views on the history of English syllable accents. In H. Hollien & P. Hollien (eds.), *Current Issues in the Phonetic Sciences. Proceedings of the IPS-77 Congress, Miami Beach, Fl., 17–19 Dec. 77*. Current Issues in Linguistic Theory 9, 321–29. Amsterdam: Benjamins.

Liberman, A. 1992. A bird's-eye view of open syllable lengthening in English and in the other Germanic languages. *NOWELE* 20. 67–87.

Liberman, A. 1995. The beginning and end of the (great) vowel shift in Late Germanic. In I. Rauch & G. F. Carr (eds.), *Insights in Germanic Linguistics I. Methodology in transition*, 23–30. Berlin: De Gruyter.

Liberman, A. 2007. Palatalized and velarized consonants in English viewed against their Germanic background, with special references to *i*-Umlaut. In C. M. Cain & G. Russom (eds.), *Studies in the History of the English Language III. Managing chaos: Strategies for identifying change in English*, 5–36. Berlin: De Gruyter.

Liberman, A. 2012. Sound change and distinctive features in light of dynamic synchrony. In S. Harris, M. Moynihan & S. Hobison (eds.), *Germanic languages and literature in honor of James E. Cathey*. Medieval and Renaissance Texts and Studies 429, 1–23. Tempe, Arizona: Center for Medieval and Renaissance Studies (ACMRS).

Liberman, A. 2020. Germanic /r/ as an isogloss, rhotacism, and the West Germanic gemination. In P. J. Grund & M. E. Hartman (eds.), *Studies in the History of the Germanic Languages VIII: Boundaries and boundary-crossings in the history of English*. Topics in English Linguistics 108, 211–23. Berlin: De Gruyter.

Luick, K. 1964. *Historische Grammatik der englischen Sprache*. Stuttgart: Bernhard Tauchnitz. (A revision of the 1914–1921, 1929–1940 edition by Friedrich Wild and Herbert Koziol.)

Martinet, A. 1955. *Economie des changements phonétiques*. Berne: A. Francke.

Minkova, D. 2014. *A Historical phonology of English*. Edinburgh: Edinburgh University Press.

Trubetzkoy, N. S. 1939. *Grundzüge der Phonologie*. Travaux du Cercle Linguistique de Prague. 7. Prague.

Trubetzkoy, N. S. 1933 [2001]. On the Development of the Gutturals in the Slavic Languages. In N. S. Trubetzkoy, *Studies in General Linguistics and Language Structure*, edited by A. Liberman, with translation by M. Taylor and A. Liberman, 157–164. Durham and London: Duke University Press. First publ. in 1933 as 'Die Entwicklung der Gutturale in den slavischen Sprachen,' *Sbornik" v" čest' na Prof. L. Miletič" za sedemdesetgodišninata ot" roždenieto mu* (1863–1933). Sofia: Izdanie na Makedonskija naučen" institut", 1933, 267–79.

Turmbau auf Färöisch

Sprachverwirrung in Rasmus Rasmussens Roman *Bábelstornið*

Christer Lindqvist
Universität Greifswald

Published in 1908/09, Rasmus Rasmussen's *Bábelstornið* was the first novel in Faroese. The naturalistic work narrates the fate of two families in the period from 1815 to 1908, including their connections with the Faroese independence movement. The novel exhibits a number of features typical of their time, which are intertwined with its content in an unusual way. In a new edition published in 2011, these particular features have partly been deleted or modified, resulting in a narrative flattening. The present article attempts to shed light on a representative selection of words and passages in order to critically examine the impact this editing practice has on the Faroese self-conception of the nation's literary and linguistic history.

1. Sprach- und Literaturgeschichte — der färöische Fall in aller Kürze

Dem Umstand, dass Sprach- und Literaturgeschichte oftmals verschränkt sind, wird die Sprachwissenschaft nicht immer gerecht. So sind textimmanente Analysen durch die Literaturwissenschaft nicht selten weitaus aussagekräftiger als die einer noch so elaborierten Textlinguistik. Dennoch kann gerade der sprachwissenschaftliche Blick erhellend sein, um die literaturwissenschaftliche Bedeutung mancher Textdetails aufzuzeigen. Das trifft insbesondere zu auf die Entstehung und Tradierung literarischer Werke einer so jungen Schriftsprache wie der färöischen, die trotz der Eroberung vieler Domänen im Laufe des 20. Jh. in manchen Bereichen noch lange als eine Ausbausprache zu bezeichnen war. Das gilt vor allem auch für die färöische Literatursprache um die vorletzte Jahrhundertwende, als der erste Roman auf Färöisch, Rasmus Rasmussens *Bábelstornið*, 1908/09 erschien. Bevor aber auf einige seiner Besonderheiten eingegangen wird, soll der sprachkulturelle Hintergrund seiner Entstehung skizziert werden.

Da wegen der dänisch-norwegischen Union 1380 und des Kieler Friedens 1814 die Färöer politisch, wirtschaftlich und vor allem ab der Reformation auch

https://doi.org/10.1075/nss.34.13lin
Available under the CC BY-NC-ND 4.0 license. © 2025 John Benjamins Publishing Company

sprachlich immer enger an Dänemark gebunden wurden, entstand dort eine Diglossiesituation mit Färöisch als mündlicher Alltagssprache (Low Variety) und Dänisch als Sprache aller öffentlichen und schriftsprachlichen Domänen (High Variety). Bis auf die Aufzeichnung und Veröffentlichung einiger Balladentexte und die Übersetzungen des Matthäusevangeliums und der *Færeyínga saga* in einer weitgehend orthophonen Schreibweise existierte bis weit ins 19. Jh. so gut wie keine färöischsprachige Schriftlichkeit.

Daran änderte sich zunächst auch nicht viel, nachdem der isländische Politiker, Historiker und Philologe Jón Sigurðsson (1811–1879) zusammen mit dem dänischen Philologen und Historiker N.M. Petersen (1791–1862) die historisierende Gegenwartsorthographie im Jahr 1846 geschaffen und vom damaligen Theologiestudenten V.U. Hammershaimb (1819–1909) mit nur wenigen Anpassungen und Korrekturen als geeignet bestätigt bekommen hatten (zu alledem ausführlich in Lindqvist (2018)). Dänisch blieb weiterhin lange die dominante Sprache in den Domänen Schule, Bildung, Wissenschaft, Technik, Handel, Rechtswesen, Politik, Verwaltung, Religion, Literatur, Kultur und Medien. Hammershaimb selbst benutzte die neue Orthographie zunächst in erster Linie, um färöische Sprachdenkmäler zu veröffentlichen (Lindqvist 2018: 165–174). Es galt vornehmlich, das literarische Erbe zu dokumentieren.

Erst 1890 erschien mit *Føringatíðindi* die erste färöischsprachige Zeitung. Damit entstanden neue für aktuelle Themen und Debatten geeignete Textsorten mit einer eigenen färöischen Stilistik. Zu den ersten wissenschaftlichen Texten in färöischer Sprache gehören Artikel in der Zeitschrift *Búreisingur*, wie z.B. *Um elektriskan streym* (1902) des Pädagogen, Naturwissenschaftlers, Autors, Übersetzers, Redakteurs und Selbständigkeitspolitikers Rasmus Rasmussen (1871–1962; Abbildung 1), der 1899 zusammen mit Símun av Skarði (1842–1942) *Føroya Fólkaháskúli* gründete (Gaard 2021). Dort konnte man u.a. die neue Rechtschreibung lernen, schon bevor 1912 Färöisch in den ersten Schulklassen erlaubt und als schulische Schriftsprache 1920 obligatorisch wurde. Allerdings wurde das Färöische erst 1938 als eine mit dem Dänischen gleichberechtigte Schulsprache anerkannt. Zu den frühesten Beispielen färöischer Wissenschaftssprache gehören auch Jakob Jakobsens Einleitung des *Diplomatarium Færoense* (1907) und Rasmus Rasmussens *Plantulæra* (1910). Für das Färöische als Ausbausprache ging es indes nicht nur darum, neue Terminologien für die neu eroberten Domänen zu finden. Mindestens genauso wichtig war es, für die verschiedenen Genres einen morphologisch, syntaktisch, textgrammatisch und rhetorisch angemessenen Stil zu finden.

In ähnlicher Weise kann um die Jahrhundertwende beobachtet werden, wie einige wenige Personen um die Entstehung einer gegenwartsgerechten Literatursprache rangen. So wurden die beiden ersten färöischen Theaterstücke „schon" 1889 uraufgeführt: Rasmus Effersøes (1857–1916) Tragödie *Gunnar Havreki* und

Turmbau auf Färöisch 219

Abbildung 1. Rasmus Rasmussen (1871–1962). Foto: *Sosialurin* 2012, Nr. 12 (links);
Abbildung 2. *Tingakrossur* 1908, Nr. 43, 21.10.1908 (rechts)

Súsanna Helena Paturssons (1864–1916) Lustspiel *Veðurføst*. Mit *Yrkingar* von J. H. O. Djurhuus (1881–1948) erschien 1914 die erste färöische Gedichtsammlung. Und 1909 kam vom bereits genannten Rasmus Rasmussen unter dem Pseudonym Regin í Líð der Roman *Bábelstornið* heraus, nachdem er zuvor in der Wochenzeitschrift *Tingakrossur* vom 21.10.1908 (Nr. 43–52) bis 08.12.1909 (Nr. 1–8, 10–28, 31, 33–36, 38, 42–49) unter dem Titel *Ættarbregi* (recte: -*bregði*) erschienen war (Abbildung 2 und 3). Allerdings wurde mit Jógvan/Joen Poulsens (1900) *Bíbliusøga* schon vor *Bábelstornið* ein größeres literarisches Werk in der neuen Gegenwartsorthographie geschaffen.

Um *Bábelstornið* und seine verschiedenen Auflagen soll es im Folgenden gehen, und zwar mit einem Fokus sowohl auf die schriftliche Sprachform als auch auf Funktion und Schicksal der darin vorkommenden Entlehnungen. Das ist deswegen von besonderer Bedeutung, weil gerade diese Züge das im Roman vielfach thematisierte Verhältnis zu Dänemark reflektieren. Bei den Entlehnungen geht es vor allem um Danismen, wozu hier auch durch das Dänische vermittelte Entlehnungen aus anderen Sprachen gezählt werden. Auf diese Unterscheidung kommt es aber im Folgenden nicht an.

Abbildung 3. Anfang von *Ættarbregi* in *Tingakrossur*, Nr. 43, S. 3, 21.10.1908

2. *Bábelstornið* als naturalistischer Roman

Rasmus Rasmussens *Bábelstornið* hat Kirsten Brix (2002) aus literaturwissenschaftlicher Sicht (mit kritischer Würdigung der wenigen bisherigen Untersuchungen) ausführlich behandelt. Brix zeigt überzeugend auf, dass es sich um einen naturalistischen Roman handelt, in dem der Handlungsverlauf mit Vor- und Rückgriffen sowie thematischen Korrespondenzen komplex gestaltet ist. *Bábelstornið* erzählt von drei Generationen der beiden Familien auf den Höfen í Jógvansstovu und uppi í Stovu im Ort Dalbyrgi während eines für die Färöer besonders prägenden Zeitraums etwa von 1815 (unmittelbar nach dem Kieler Frieden) bis zur Abfassungszeit 1908. Das Ende des königlichen Monopolhandels (fär. *einahandil*) 1856 und die damit verbundene Einführung von wirtschaftlichem Liberalismus samt Freihandel bewirkte eine Transformation der Färöer von einer traditionellen Bauerngesellschaft mit feudaler Struktur zu einer modernen kapitalistischen Gesellschaft im Wesentlichen basierend auf der Fischerei-Industrie. *Bábelstornið* ist somit auch ein historischer Roman, der nach Isaksen (2017: 155) noch heute eine Sonderstellung in der färöischen Literaturgeschichte einnimmt, weil er deutlich auf politische Fragen fokussiert.

Brix (2002: 107–115) vermutet, dass Rasmussen den Roman als eine Reaktion auf die Niederlagen der Nationalbewegung in den Wahlen zum dänischen Folketing am 22. Mai 1906 und zum färöischen Løgting am 18. Juli im selben Jahr geschrieben hat. Dabei wurde vor allem ein Vorschlag zu mehr politischer, wirtschaftlicher und ökonomischer Selbstständigkeit abgelehnt, den der färöische Folketing-Abgeordnete und schillernde Nationalist Jóannes Patursson (1866–1946) zusammen mit dem dänischen Justizminister P.A. Alberti (1851–1932) und weiteren Ministern ausgearbeitet hatte. Ganz nach dem naturalistischen Programm — allerdings nicht immer ohne Wertungen der Erzählinstanz — schildert der Roman, wie im deterministischen Wechselspiel von Erbanlagen (fär. *ættarbregði*) und sozialer Umgebung diese Niederlagen zustande kamen. Die miteinander verwobenen Themen, welche die Handlung vorantreiben, sind im Wesentlichen: Politik, Wirtschaft, Eigentumsverhältnisse, Nationalismus, Vernunft, Kultur, Religion, Schule, Bildung, Sprache, Liebe, Sexualität, Erbanlagen, Geschlechterverhältnisse und -rollen. Der Roman thematisiert somit Fragestellungen, die bereits Georg Brandes 1871 in seiner legendären Vorlesungsreihe *Hovedstrømninger i det nittende århundredes litteratur* aufgegriffen und zur Agenda moderner Literatur erklärt hatte.

Der Roman ist zweigeteilt. In *Tingakrossur* erschien er unter dem Namen des ersten Teils, *Ættarbregi*, während die Buchpublikation (mit einer Auflage von 1000 Exemplaren, wovon jedoch lediglich 80 gebunden wurden (Gaard 1987: IX)) nach dem zweiten Teil, *Bábelstornið*, genannt ist. Der Romantitel bezieht sich auf den Turmbau zu Babel (Gen 11,1–9). Am zunächst auffälligsten zeigt sich dieser Bezug bei dem Haus im dänischen Stil, welches einer der Protagonisten seiner dänischen Frau, mit der er nur Dänisch redet, baut. Im übertragenen Sinne bezieht sich der Titel aber auch auf den bereits erwähnten Niedergang der Nationalbewegung bei den beiden Wahlen und auf die damit verwobene Auflösung der beiden mächtigen Familien der Höfe í Jógvansstovu und uppi í Stovu.

Für das ganze Werk kann man sicherlich davon ausgehen, dass sowohl durch die Erzählinstanz als auch durch die implizite Autorenfigur Rasmus Rasmussens eigene Stimme spricht.

3. Anpassungen und Korrekturen der Rechtschreibung, Auslassungen

Die erste Auflage (Abbildung 4) basiert auf dem Bleisatz der *Tingakrossur*-Fassung. Allerdings finden sich an einigen wenigen Stellen in der Buchfassung Änderungen wie etwa *ófatuligt, við Pæturi, bráddliga* → *ófatiligt, við Pætri, brádliga* (1. Aufl.: 30). Es hat offensichtlich eine Durchsicht vor dem Druck gegeben, wohl mit dem Ziel, dem Text eine bestimmte Form zu geben. Wer die Änderungen veranlasst hat, ist indes unbekannt. Es ist aber anzunehmen, dass sie zumindest nicht ohne Rasmussens Zustimmung erfolgt sind.

Während die zweite Auflage von 1987 ein reprographischer Nachdruck der ersten Auflage ist, die auf die bewahrte Sprachform Wert legt (Gaard 1987:XI), ist die im färöischen Verlag *sprotin* erschienene dritte Auflage von 2011 (Abbildung 5) hingegen eine "[e]ndurskoðað útgáva", d.h. eine durchgesehene Ausgabe. Entsprechend gibt es eine Reihe von Textänderungen. Die folgenden Aufzählungen sind exemplarisch und erfassen nicht das gesamte Belegmaterial.

3.1 Anpassungen an die Gegenwartsschreibung

Auf dem Weg zur heutigen Rechtschreibung wurden in der dritten Auflage manche Details geändert, die Anfang des 20. Jh. anders oder gar nicht normiert waren. Wie oft üblich bei einer durchgesehenen Auflage modernisiert die dritte Auflage *Bábelstornið* entsprechend wie z.B. in den folgenden Fällen:

(1) 1. Aufl.: Dalbyrgingar (19), vax (83), táið (91), ovnær (92), uppá (104), frøken (150, 151), rættuliga (218), Trawlarin (251, 257), sorgfyllri (222)

(2) 3. Aufl.: dalbyrgingar (23), vaks (72), tá ið (80), ov nær (80), upp á (91), frøkun (131, 131), rættiliga (190), Trolarin (218, 224) sorgfylri (194)

Dadurch geht aber gerade bei den Lehnwörtern *frøken, Trawlarin* → *frøkun, Trolarin* etwas zeittypisches Kolorit verloren.

Abbildung 4. *Bábelstornið*, 1. Aufl. 1909. Foto: *Føroya Landsbókasavn* (links);
Abbildung 5. *Bábelstornið*, 3. Aufl. 2011. Foto: *Sprotin* (rechts)

Zur orthographischen Anpassung gehören auch einige Änderungen in den dänischsprachigen Textpassagen. Dort wird entsprechend der Reform von 1948 die Substantivgroßschreibung beseitigt und <aa> durch <å> ersetzt. Allerdings erfolgt dies nicht durchgehend, wie z.B. *Naa/Naa, saa/saa* (1./3. Aufl.: 91/79, 91/79) zeigen. Ein im Roman zitierter dänischsprachiger Brief (37f./39f.) verliert dadurch an Zeitkolorit (s. Kap. 5 unten).

Gelegentlich ändert die dritte Auflage sogar korrekt Gebliebenes an der heute gültigen Norm vorbei, so z.B. bei *hebraiska* [aː] (90) → *hebráiska* [ɔaː] (79) entsprechend einer integrierten Aussprache (nur fremdsprachig vorhandenes [aː] wird damit vermieden). Die hyperkorrekte, nicht-kodifizierte Form *hebráiskur* ist aber nicht ohne Vorbild; man findet sie u.a. in der von *Det Danske Bibelselskab* herausgegebenen färöischen Bibel.

3.2   Korrektur von Schreibfehlern

Anfang des 20. Jh. war selbst für viele Gebildete die neue färöische Orthographie mit ihrem historisierenden Charakter eine Herausforderung — Dänisch war ja die übliche Schriftsprache. Rasmus Rasmussen soll erst mit 25 Jahren Schriftfäröisch gelernt haben (Gaard 1987: VI). So finden sich in *Bábelstornið* eine Reihe von Fehlschreibungen und Inkonsequenzen. Wie üblich bei einer durchgesehenen Auflage modernisiert die dritte Auflage den Text entsprechend wie etwa in den folgenden Beispielen. Die überaus seltenen Setzfehler, welche teilweise auch aus der *Tingakrossur*-Fassung übernommen wurden, wie etwa *Darmark* (1. Aufl.: 177) für *Danmark*, werden hier nicht berücksichtigt.

(3) 1. Aufl.: ættarbregi (1), pladdi, pløddi, pløddu (10, 167, 255), stedgaði, steðgaði, stegg (63, 201, 244), Brúðleyp, brúdleypið, brúðleyp (72, 128, 128), ótíggir, Ótiggini (81, 82), kødnað (82) byrtist, birtist (82, 232), míkindum (84), vælgerðandi (89), undalig, undarligt (90, 249), Í hvussi er (115), blíðliga, blídliga, Sorgblídni (122, 170, 255), kannska, Kanska (140, 245), givi (140), livukor, livukorð (162, 162), »pinta« (172), særtú, Særtú, Sær tú, særtú (187, 189, 234), tað samlaða forstandarskapi (204), »Bábulstornið«, »Bábulstornið« (205, 206, 262), trýggir (211), sæt (238), vesti (248)

(4) 3. Aufl.: ættarbregði (5), plagdi, pløgdi, pløgdu (15, 145, 221), steðgaði, steðgaði, steðg (60, 176, 213), Brúdleyp, brúdleypið, brúdleyp (68, 112/112), ótýggir, Ótýggini (71, 71), kódnað (72), birtist, birtist (72, 203), mýkindum (74), vælgerandi (78), undarlig, undarligt (79, 217), Ið hvussu er (101), blídliga, blídliga, Sorgblídni (107, 148, 222), kanska, Kanska (122, 214), givið (122), livikor, livikor (141), pynta (150), sær tú, Sær tú, sær tú (163, 189, 204), tað samlaða forstandarskapið (178), »Bábelstornið« (180, 180, 227), trígggir (185), sat (207), versti (216)

3.3 Typographische Änderungen

Die dritte Auflage greift auch in die typographische Gestaltung des Textes ein, indem in vielen Wörtern die Sperrschrift beseitigt wird. Rasmussen setzt dieses Mittel an nicht wenigen Stellen ein, um bestimmte Wörter, Wortgruppen oder Namen hervorzuheben. Dadurch erhalten beispielsweise manche Demonstrativpronomina wie *hendan* (1. Aufl.: 151) eine zusätzliche Emphase. Das alles geht in der dritten Auflage verloren. An wenigen Stellen ersetzt die dritte Auflage die Sperrschrift durch Majuskelschrift: *Hansara!* (1. Aufl.: 215) → *HANSARA!* (3. Aufl.: 188). Da sich Majuskeln seit Erscheinen der dritten Auflage vor allem in der computervermittelten Kommunikation als Merkmal für "Lautstärke" etabliert haben, erweist sich diese Änderung auch rückblickend als ungünstig.

Rasmussen verwendet an vielen Stellen in *Bábelstornið* das Mittel der erlebten Rede. Sie wird manchmal durch eingefügte Gedankenstriche rhythmisiert. Die dritte Auflage verzichtet oftmals hierauf, womit eine erzähltechnische Verflachung einhergeht.

Die erste Auflage hat vielfach eine leere Zeile zwischen zwei Absätzen, so dass eine Gliederung mit Absatzgruppen entsteht. Diese leeren Zeilen entfallen oft in der dritten Auflage, wodurch der Text an optischer Leichtigkeit verliert.

3.4 Morphologische Änderungen

Wie die folgenden Beispiele zeigen, macht die dritte Auflage vor Eingriffen in die färöische Wortbildungs- und Flexionsmorphologie nicht Halt.

(5) 1. Aufl.: hattar (55), Fáastaðnis (81), Mittskeiðis (83), ríkisligur (87), Ímillum (115), seinri, Seinni, seinni, seinni (118, 186, 248, 251), fyri mentaði menniskjur (149), hevur flógvað donsk hjørtur (167), Aldrig (167), ongastaðnis (175), til Darmark (177), Hulisligt (244)

(6) 3. Aufl.: hatta (54), Fáastaðni (71), Miðskeiðis (73), ríkiligur (76), Millum (101), seinri, Seinri, seinri, seinri (103, 162, 216, 218), fyri mentað menniskju (130), hevur fløvað donsk hjørtu (145), Aldrin (145), ongastaðni (152), til Danmarkar (155), Hulisliga (212)

Adverbableitungen mit dem mündlich verbreiteten neuen Suffix -nis (fáastaðnis, ongastaðnis) sind in der normierten Schriftsprache nicht vorgesehen und werden in der dritten Auflage durch Ableitungen mit -ni ersetzt. Bei ríkisligur wird die Wortbildungsfuge geändert, indem der nicht normkonforme Substantivstamm dem Adjektivstamm in ríkiligur weichen muss. Bei Mittskeiðis → Miðskeiðis wird das ganze Erstglied durch ein Synonym ersetzt, obwohl jenes Wort (wenn auch mit dem Vermerk „sj.“ = sjáldsamt) durchaus von der heutigen Norm (gemäß Føroysk orðabók von Poulsen et al. (1998)) gedeckt ist. Mit aldrig → aldrin wird eine dänisch anmutende (aber zumindest im älteren Altwestnordisch durchaus vorhandene) Wortform beseitigt.

Die dritte Auflage nimmt sich auch die Flexionsmorphologie vor. So wird die mündliche Part. Perf.-Form mit -aði und Neutr.Pl. -ur in fyri mentaði menniskjur durch die eher schriftsprachliche und konservative Form fyri mentað menniskju ersetzt (so auch bei Neutr.Pl. hjørtur → hjørtu). Hier kann nur unmarkiertes Neutrum menniskja gemeint sein (≠ Fem. menniskja ‚1. Menschengeschlecht; 2. Mensch (Stilwert: biblisch)‘). Mit seinni → seinri wird hingegen eine regionale Form generalisiert, während mit hattar → hatta eine schriftsprachliche Form den Vorrang bekommt.

Insgesamt geht dabei nicht wenig an konzeptioneller Mündlichkeit, zeittypischem Kolorit und wohl auch regionalen Besonderheiten von Rasmussens eigenem Färöisch selbst verloren.

3.5 Ein Sprichwort

Die dritte Auflage ersetzt an einer Stelle die Form *ljúgva* (1. Aufl.: 171) durch *lúgva* (3. Aufl.: 149). Fär. *ljúgva* ist nicht nur eine altertümliche Form, die sich in der Bibel- (z.B. Ex 19,11) und der Balladensprache (z.B. *Sigurðar kvæði* → *Triðja táttur: Högni* (FK 1 H, 128:4); *Roysingur* (FK 166 A, 9:2); *Margretu kvæði* → II. *Frúgvin Margeta* (FK 77 C, 117:4)) findet. An der relevanten Stelle in *Bábelstornið* steht das Wort in einem Sprichwort, d.h. in einem Kontext, in dem veraltete Formen durchaus vorkommen können:

(7)   Børn kundu hvørki at ljúgva/lúgva ella loyna, søgdu tey eldru

(1./3. Aufl.: 171/149)

Der heutige Wortlaut des Sprichwortes ist nach Petersen/Isholm (2003: 29): *Barnið dugir hvørki at lúgva ella loyna*. Auch Poulsen (1957: 108) hat die Verbform *lúgva*, während Hammershaimb (1849–51: 274; 1891: 315) und wohl in Anlehnung an ihn auch Evensen (1911: 432) *ljúgva* verwendet. Diese Verbform ist noch heute (seit Jacob Dahls Übersetzung 1922) auch aus Luthers Kleinem Katechismus bekannt. Bei Svabo ist das Sprichwort selbst nicht überliefert. In seinen Wörterbüchern führt er aber sowohl *ljúgva* als auch *lúgva* auf und notiert: „Ljygva er bedre" (Matras 1966: 523). Von Svabo ist „ljygva" auch in *Àniasar táttur* (FK 192 A, 43:4; Matras 1939: 403). Rasmussen kann somit das Sprichwort in der Fassung mit *ljúgva* sehr wohl gekannt haben. Ob es ihm auch in der Form mit *lúgva* geläufig war, ist kaum zu entscheiden. Ihm dürfte jedoch bewusst gewesen sein, dass es sich bei *ljúgva* um eine archaisierende Wortform handelt. Diese unterstreicht den Sprichwortcharakter sowohl formal als auch inhaltlich. Sprichwörter drücken ja nicht selten „geronnene" Menschheitserfahrungen aus, was gerade mit fossilierten Formseiten gut korrespondiert, zumal wenn wie hier auf die Aussagen Älterer hingewiesen wird. Möglicherweise ist damit auch der Versuch verbunden, Zeitkolorit der Figurensprache zu signalisieren. Auf hier greift die 3. Auflage nivellierend ein.

3.6 Auslassungen

Gelegentlich fehlen in der dritten Auflage einzelne Wörter oder gar ganze Phrasen, wodurch die entsprechenden Passagen teilweise syntaktisch defekt werden. Vor allem in der ersten Auflage kursivgesetzte — und damit inhaltlich zentrale — Stellen sind hiervon betroffen:

(8)   tað at vita *sína ætt* endurnýggjaða   (1. Aufl.: 93)

(9)   tað at vita endurnýggjaða ...   (3. Aufl.: 82)

(10) gera nakað framstig sum bóndi í Føroyum — *og tað vildi hann* — so

(1. Aufl.: 141)

(11) gera nakað framstig sum bóndi í Føroyum — — so (3. Aufl.: 123)

(12) Hví varst tú einans, *frímenska*! mítt sálareyga (1. Aufl.: 256)

(13) Hví vart tú einans, mítt sálareyga (3. Aufl.: 222)

Im letzten Beispiel ist sogar eine Neuschöpfung von Rasmussen verlorengegangen: Geschlechtsneutrales *frímenska* ist wohl zu *frímaður* gebildet. Zudem wurde die analogische (und mit dem Neuisländischen übereinstimmende) Neuerung *varst* gegen normgerechtes *vart* ersetzt.

4. Entlehnungen

Bis auf die Auslassungen bewegen sich die bisherigen Änderungen im Großen und Ganzen im Rahmen üblicher (und an manchen Stellen unbeabsichtigt entstellender) Anpassungen eines älteren Textes für eine Neuauflage. Im Folgenden geht es aber um Eingriffe, die darüber hinausgehen. Die „[e]ndurskoðað útgáva" hat nämlich auch nicht wenige Entlehnungen im Text bearbeitet.

4.1 Entfernte Markierung der Sprachschichtung

Vor allem im Erzählbericht finden sich viele — oft phonologisch, morphologisch und orthographisch angepasste — Entlehnungen verschiedener Art. Zumeist sind das Danismen oder durch das Dänische vermittelte Wörter. Vielfach setzt Rasmussen diese in doppelte Anführungszeichen. Einfache Anführungszeichen stehen, wenn die Wörter zur Personencharakteristik innerhalb einer direkten Rede vorkommen, für welche er ebenfalls doppelte Anführungszeichen verwendet. In wenigen Fällen ist das Wort zusätzlich kursiv gesetzt. Die dritte Auflage verzichtet in der Regel auf diese Anführungszeichen. Wie »*bakdyrnar*« (1. Aufl.: 101) → *bakdyrnar* (3. Aufl.: 88) zeigt, ist Rasmussen manchmal sogar sehr empfindlich gegenüber dem fremden Einfluss; es handelt sich hier um eine Lehnübersetzung von dän. *bagdør*, von der sich Rasmussen trotz der gleichen färöischen Etyma distanziert. Hier einige weitere Beispiele:

(14) 1. Aufl.: »tolerant« (87), »studeraði« (87), í »Studerikamarinum« (89), »bakdyrnar« (101), »forklárað« (104), »*forhoyr*«, »forhoyr« (105, 249), »proviant« (114), »halda útkikk« (121), »tørnaði inn« (123), »máltíðtalið« (129), »í drosku« (152), »plikt« (181), »kreditturin« (184), fyri »direktiónina« (204), »check«,

check (214, 222), tað »behagiligasta« (235), eg 'respekteri' (237), »sku« (235, 238), 'óforsigtigur' (238)

(15) 3. Aufl.: tolerant (76), studeraði (76), í studerikamarinum (77), bakdyrnar (88), forklárað (91), forhoyr, forhoyr (92, 217), proviant (100), halda útkikk (106), tørnaði inn (107), máltíðtalið (113), í drosku (132), plikt (157), kreditturin (161), fyri direktiónina (178), kekk (187, 194), tað behagiligasta (205), eg 'respekteri' (206), sku (205, 207), óforsiktigur (208)

Mit den Anführungszeichen markiert Rasmussen, dass im (damaligen) Färöisch ein passendes Wort fehlt. Die Entlehnung wird als Fremdwort gekennzeichnet und vom restlichen Text auf optische Distanz gehalten. Es wird sozusagen in Purismus-Quarantäne gesetzt. Predelli (2003) hat dieses Vorgehen „scare quotes" genannt; vgl. hierzu auch Zieseler (2024: 319–324).

Die dritte Auflage nimmt in dieser Beleggruppe ein paar orthographische Integrationen vor (*check, óforsigtigur* (1. Aufl.) → *kekk, óforsiktigur* (3. Aufl.)), verzichtet vor allem aber auf die Anführungszeichen — bis auf ein paar wohl versehentlich unveränderte Stellen: wie z.B. *í »forholdini«* (1./3. Aufl.: 169/147), *»flink«* (1./3. Aufl.: 170/148).

Dass die dritte Auflage die Anführungszeichen weglässt, mag daran liegen, dass das eine oder andere Wort inzwischen eingebürgert ist. Dennoch geht mit dem Weglassen der Anführungszeichen die optische Zweischichtigkeit des Textes und damit auch eine Kommunikationsebene verloren: Durch die Anführungszeichen führt nämlich der implizite Autor seiner Leserschaft im wörtlichen Sinne vor Augen, dass Färöisch als Literatursprache noch eine Ausbausprache ist. Diese Botschaft an die Leserschaft geht also direkt von der Textform und nicht vom Textinhalt aus. Der gedruckte Romantext der ersten Auflage reflektiert sein eigenes Medium in der Gestaltung der Schriftform.

Im folgenden Beispiel hat die Weglassung der Anführungszeichen eine weitere Folge. Einer der Protagonisten, eldri Jógvan, genießt großes Ansehen in der Bevölkerung. Von ihm heißt es:

(16) Hann var eisini ein væl upplýstur maður, og mangir søktu hansara ráð, tá ið teir liðu órætt frá hægri støðum. Tess vegna hevði honum ofta borist á orði við »øvrigheitina«. (1. Aufl. : 17)

(17) [...] ofta borist á orði við øvrigheitina. (3. Aufl.: 21)

Zeittypisch wird hier dän. *øvrighed* mit phonologisch integriertem Suffix in der Form *øvrigheitina* verwendet. In der ersten Auflage leisten die Anführungszeichen aber nicht nur die bereits genannte Distanzierung. Hier stellen sie zudem das Bezeichnete, nämlich die dänische Obrigkeit selbst, in Frage. Mit dem Weglassen der Anführungszeichen in der dritten Auflage geht dieser Effekt verloren.

4.2 Ersatzwörter

Die dritte Auflage greift noch mehr in den Text ein, indem Entlehnungen durch färöische Ablösewörter ersetzt werden. Das sieht dann etwa so aus:

(18) prestfólkini gjørdu nógv av at gera »selskap« og »middagurin« skuldi vera ríkisligur.
(1. Aufl. : 87)

(19) prestfólkini gjørdu nógv av gestaboði, og døgurðin skuldi vera ríkiligur.
(3. Aufl.: 76)

Hier sind die phonologisch und morphologisch integrierten Danismen *selskap, middagurin* (dän. *selskab, middagen*) gegen einheimisches *gestaboði* (hier in einer Dativ-PP) und *døgurðin* ersetzt worden (zu *ríkisligur* → *ríkiligur* s. Kap. 3.4). Einige weitere Beispiele:

(20) 1. Aufl.: gentakast (54), í ... hvønndagsosa (82), »andektuliga« (88), mestiparturin, Meginparturin (104, 124), »balsalinum« (115), Onei (128, 150), hetta »alminuliga« (149), stíling (158), langt tilbakar (167), ið kallast kundi »anstændigt« fyri eina »damu« (169), eg hevi fingið ein »ide« (189), ein »Check« til 500 at hevja [dän. *hæve penge*] úr einem útlendskum banka (191), kommunavalg, stórvalg, valgstríðið, valginum (211, 231, 232, 239), gera mær »undskildning« (218)

(21) 3. Aufl.: endurtakast (53), í ... gerandisosi [!] (72), við andakt (77), meginparturin, Meginparturin (91, 109), veitsluhollini (101), Ánei (113, 131), hetta vanliga (130), at stíla (138), aftarlaga (146), ið kallast kundi sømiligt fyri eina dámu (147), eg havi hugsað um eitt (165), ein kekk á 500 at taka úr einum útlendskum banka (167), kommunaval, stórval, valstríðið, valinum (185, 202, 203), geva mær umbering (191)

Mit all diesen Veränderungen wird Rasmussens Roman rückwirkend heutigen konservativen Sprachidealen angenähert. Indem an seinem Text sozusagen gerade jenes puristische Programm umgesetzt wird, wonach der Text mit seinen vielen Anführungszeichen verlangt, geht nicht nur viel zeittypische Sprache verloren. Die Dringlichkeit mancher Passagen im Text zur dänisch-färöischen Diglossiesituation erscheint dadurch weniger motiviert. Die dritte Auflage beraubt damit den Roman genau der Sprachform, in der sich eines seiner Anliegen begründet. Dadurch verliert der Text an sprachpolitischer Spannkraft.

5. Ein dänischsprachiger Brief

In *Bábelstornið* spielen mehrere Wahlen eine zentrale Rolle. Im Vorfeld der Folketing-Wahlen von 1851 erhalten Sunneva (die Gegenspielerin von eldri Jógvan) und ihr Mann Hanusar Pætur einen Brief, in dem der Landvogt (fär. *sýslumaður*) Werbung für seine eigene Kandidatur macht. Dieser Brief erscheint im Romantext als Zitat in Anführungszeichen (1./3. Aufl.: 37f./39f.).

Obwohl färöischer Muttersprachler schreibt der Landvogt selbstverständlich auf Dänisch, denn eine andere Schriftsprache für solche Belange gab es 1851 nicht. Der Brief ist in zeittypischem Dänisch mit Substantivgroßschreibung und <aa> abgehalten; z.B. *Mand, Naade* (1. Aufl.: 37f.). Die dritte Auflage hingegen verlegt die dänische Rechtschreibreform von 1948 in eine Zeit von vor der ersten Auflage, schreibt also die Substantive klein und verwendet <å>: *mand, nåde* (3. Aufl.: 39f.). Durch diesen Anachronismus geht wieder einmal zeittypisches Kolorit verloren.

Es fällt auf, dass in der ersten Auflage das Wort *Undersaatter* bei seiner zweiten Nennung mit färöischer Pluralendung steht: *Undersaattar* – und zwar abweichend von der *Tingakrossur*-Fassung. (Fär. *undirsátt* (Pl. *-ar*) ist außer in við Ánnas (1977) *Óføroysk-føroysk orðabók* lexikographisch nicht erfasst, kommt aber schriftlich und mündlich durchaus vor.) Die dritte Auflage hat dagegen zu dänisch korrektem *undersåtter* geändert. Möglicherweise soll mit der färöischen Flexion bei *Undersaattar* eine leichte Unsicherheit des Landvogts mit dem Dänischen signalisiert werden.

Eine weitere Änderung in der ersten Auflage gegenüber der *Tingakrossur*-Fassung spricht dafür, dass Rasmussen gerade auf solche Details Wert gelegt hat: Während der Brief in der *Tingakrossur*-Fassung für die Abfassungszeit (1908/1909) zeittypisches dän. *gører* enthält, wird dieses Wort in der ersten Auflage *gjører* geschrieben. Diese <gj>-Schreibung, welche eine rückgängig gemachte Palatalisierung reflektiert, wurde 1889 zu <g> reformiert. Da es aber hier um die Folketing-Wahlen von 1851 geht, hat Rasmussen für die Buchfassung – man sollte es zumindest nicht ausschließen: vielleicht sehr bewusst – eine historische Schreibweise gewählt. Die dritte Auflage lässt – vielleicht in unbemerkter Assoziation zu dän./fär. *gjorde/gjørdi, gjort/gjørt* – die Schreibung *gjører* stehen, statt zu *gør* ändern, obwohl der Text sonst der gegenwartsdänischen Norm angepasst wurde.

6. Gøtudansk – und sein Gegenteil

Da in der Zeit von *Bábelstornið* Dänisch noch gänzlich die High Variety auf den Färöern war, kommt diese vor allem dann ins Spiel, wenn die dänisch(sprachig)e Obrigkeit beteiligt ist. In solchen Fällen sprechen die Färinger sog. *Gøtudansk*, ein regiolektales Dänisch mit — je nach Beherrschung — unterschiedlich vielen färöischen Interferenzen (hierzu Poulsen 1993; Petersen 2010). Ein Beispiel hierfür ist die im Dänischen nicht vorhandene Konstruktion *gøre saa vel* (1. Aufl.: 91), das in Anlehnung an fär. *gera so væl* ‚bitte‘ gebildet ist. Wie lächerlich sich viele Färinger damals beim Dänisch-Radebrechen machten, wird im Roman u.a. anhand des Schullehrers in Kapitel III des ersten Romanteils geschildert, in dem überhaupt der dänisch(sprachig)e Schulbetrieb stark kritisiert wird.

Im folgenden Beispiel ist yngri Jógvan, eldri Jógvans Sohn, beim Pfarrer, um seinen Neugeborenen (ungi Jógvan) für die Taufe am nächsten Sonntag anzumelden. Während er wartet, zerreißt der Jagdhund des Pfarrers seine Hose. Drinnen beim Pfarrer fragt dieser nach, ob der Hund ihn gebissen habe. Yngri Jógvan verneint das, beklagt aber die gerissene Hose. Daraufhin fallen folgende Repliken (meine Unterstreichungen):

(22) »Ja det var galt nok, men det var værre om det havde været Benet« helt prestur.
»Det havde været <u>fradere</u>, thi Buxerne ere spildte men Benet havde nok <u>batnet atter</u> af sig selv.« [antwortet yngri Jógvan] (1. Aufl.: 90)

(23) »Ja det var galt nok, men det var værre om det havde været benet« helt prestur.
»Det havde været <u>fragere</u>, thi Buxerne ere spildte men benet havde nok <u>batnet atter</u> af sig selv.« [antwortet yngri Jógvan] (3. Aufl.: 78)

Zunächst zeigt sich in dieser insgesamt etwa zwei Seiten langen Passage, wie damals vielen Färingern nichts anderes übrigblieb, als sich wegen ihres schlecht beherrschten Dänisch nicht nur lächerlich zu machen, sondern dadurch auch in eine noch unterlegenere Position zu geraten, als dies ohnehin im Gespräch mit „øvrigheitin“ der Fall war.

Die in (22, 23) unterstrichenen Wörter sind für die Verständnisprobleme exemplarisch. Dän. *atter* dürfte dem Pfarrer als altertümliches Synonym von *igen* verständlich sein. Für yngri Jógvan ist das dagegen wegen fär. *aftur* [aʰtːʊɹ] eine naheliegende Wortwahl. Die beiden Wörter *fradere* und *batnet* sind hingegen echte Färoismen, die Dänischsprachigen ohne Gøtudansk- oder Färöischkenntnisse unverständlich sind. Das Supinum *batnet* ist eine direkte Übernahme von fär. *batna* ‚gesund werden‘.

Bei *fradere* scheint Rasmussen eine Leseaussprache mit [d] (oder [d̥]) — ein dänisches [ð] ist bei diesem Gøtudansk auszuschließen — zu verschriften, das sich aber im zugrundeliegenden fär. *frægari* [fɹɛːaɹɪ] ‚besser‘ nicht findet. Vielmehr handelt es sich bei *fradere* um eine Hyperkorrektur. Wegen konvergierenden Lautwandels sind die Verbindungen <æga, æða> (wie in *frægari, klæða*) homophon mit stummem <g, ð> auszusprechen. So erklärt sich, wie yngri Jógvan beim Versuch, für fär. *frægari* ein dänisches Äquivalent des gleichen Etymons zu finden, auf das nicht vorhandene Wort *fradere* kommt (vgl. dän. *klæde*, das er auf Gøtudansk mit [d/ḍ] sprechen dürfte). Hyperkorrektes <d> samt Leseaussprache setzt aber voraus, dass yngri Jógvan die Orthographie von 1846 schon beherrscht. Das ist vermutlich nicht der Fall, obwohl das geschilderte Gespräch sich um 1870 abgespielt haben dürfte. Zu diesem Zeitpunkt waren jedoch nur wenige Texte mit der neuen Orthographie erschienen. Erst mit *Føringatíðindi* ab 1890 dürfte die färöische Orthographie allmählich bekannt geworden sein. Es sieht daher so aus, als wäre Rasmussen hier ein Anachronismus unterlaufen. Mit *fragere* in der dritten Auflage wird diese Scharte ausgewetzt. Allerdings führt dies auch dazu, dass yngri Jógvans Gøtudansk weniger lächerlich erscheint.

Im folgenden Beispiel versucht yngri Jógvan, dem Pfarrer klar zu machen, wie das Kind heißen soll (meine Unterstreichungen):

(24) »Hvad skal saa Drengen hedde?« spurdi prestur [...]. (1. Aufl: 91)

(25) »<u>Hann</u> skal <u>ede</u> Jógvan vælsignaður eftir abbanum«. (1. Aufl: 91)

(26) »Hvad skal så Drengen hedde?« spurdi prestur [...]. (3. Aufl.: 79)

(27) »<u>Hann</u> skal <u>hede</u> Jógvan vælsignaður eftir abbanum«. (3. Aufl.: 79)

In *Hann skal ede* ist <nn> mit [nː] als Gøtudansk zu verstehen. Deutlicher gøtudansk ist *ede*, das dän. *hedde* und fär. *eita* kontaminiert. Die dritte Auflage behält <nn> in *Hann*, schwächt aber mit dem hinzugefügten <h> in *hede* die färöische Interferenz ab. Yngri Jógvan erscheint damit etwas dänischkundiger als in der ersten Auflage.

Relativ selten kommt das Umgekehrte von Gøtudansk vor, nämlich dass Dänischsprachige Färöisch mit entsprechenden Interferenzen sprechen. In *Bábelstornið* gibt es hierfür ein paar Beispiele, wie wenn Helga, die Frau von ungi Jógvan, ihre misslungenen und als lächerlich geschilderten Versuche unternimmt, Färöisch mit den Kindern in der Gegend zu sprechen, wobei es hier eher danach aussieht, als wäre zumindest in der ersten Auflage Dänisch die Matrixsprache (meine Unterstreichungen):

(28) ikke <u>dette</u> i <u>sjegven</u>, og heller ikke <u>gakke</u> der og pille i den rodne <u>taren</u>
(1. Aufl.: 170)

(29) ikke <u>dette</u> í <u>sjegven</u>, og heller ikke <u>gakke</u> der og pille í den rodne <u>táren</u>
(3. Aufl.: 148)

Hier geht es um fär. *detta* ‚fallen‘, *sjógv* [ɛ] ‚See‘ und *tari* ‚Tang‘. Die Form *gakke* ist eine scherzhafte Form dän. *gakke* (gebildet zum heute veralteten Imperativ dän.

gak; eventuell unter Einfluss von *gak ikke!*). Durch den Akzent auf dem *í* verhilft die dritte Auflage Helga zu einem etwas besseren Färöisch als in der ersten Auflage. Mit *taren* → *táren* (vgl. fär. *tárini* ‚die Tränen', Dat.Pl. *tárum* mit [-ʊn/-ɪn] und dän. *tåren* ‚die Träne') wird Helgas Färöisch in der dritten Auflage weitaus weniger verständlich, als es tatsächlich ist.

7. Danismen in erlebter Rede

Folgende Passage spielt sich im Jahr 1851 ab, als das dänische Folketing gewählt wurde (meine Unterstreichungen):

(30) 1. Aufl. 53–55:
Amtmaðurin stóð <u>frammanfyri kantórs</u>vindeyganum [...]. Ja nú vóru bara tveir sunnudagar <u>aftrat</u>, til <u>valgið</u> skuldi fara at <u>vera</u> — og aftur skuldu hesir — hesir »radikalis« hava fund í dag.
  Amtmaðurin hugsaði um, antin tað ikki var best at leggja niður forboð móti, at slíkar »subordinatiónir« skuldu <u>gentakast</u>, men nei, tað var [...] — Tað var tó allar hægst <u>óbetonkt</u> at lata eitt so <u>ómogið</u> fólk, sum <u>hettar</u> í Føroyum fáa rætt til at velja <u>eitt medlem til</u> fólkatingið, tað kundi jú vera heilt <u>tíðssva-</u><u>randi</u>, at kongur útnevndi <u>eitt medlem</u> fyri Føroyar. <u>Ja høgst óbetonkt, merkju-</u><u>ligt</u>, at hann, amtmaðurin, ikki var tikin meira <u>uppá</u> ráð. — Ja, ja! <u>man</u> fekk nú <u>inrætta</u> sær sum man livdi í einum konstitutionellum landi. Hann hevði einki at <u>bebreyda sær</u>, hann hevði roynt alt tað hann kundi, hann hevði tikið orðið fleiri ferðir báðar hinar sunnudagarnar fyri at talt f o r n u f t til fólkið, men hesin — Niels Winther — forrestin ein hálvstuderaður røvari [...] Men hvør var <u>hattar</u>? Amtmaðurin toygdi seg út móti vindeyganum. <u>Ja so</u> sanniliga var tað Joen Joensen úr Dalbyrgi, ná! Ja so! <u>var</u> hann komin her, tað segðist jú at hann reisti <u>landi</u> runt og agiteraði fyri Niels Winther — ein gemeinur bóndi — ja tað <u>bleiv</u> meira og meira óforstáiligt.

Mit dem Amtmann (fär. *amtmaður*) dürfte der — nicht sonderlich beliebte — Däne Carl Emil Dahlerup gemeint sein, der als höchster Repräsentant Dänemarks 1849–1861 Gouverneur der Färöer war. Die Passage ist ein ungewöhnliches Beispiel für erlebte Rede. Es werden nämlich nicht nur die üblichen Mittel zur Erzeugung von sprachlicher Unmittelbarkeit verwendet wie: erstaunte Ausrufe in Frageform (*Men hvør var hattar?*), Ausrufe (*men nei*), Indefinitpronomina (*Ja, ja man fekk nú ...*), Modalpartikeln (*tað segðist jú*), Adverbien der Emphase (*Ja so sanniliga ... ná*), wertende, nebenbei genannte Kommentare (*forrestin ein hálv-studeraður røvari*), zögerliches Suchen nach den Wörtern (*hesir — hesir »radika-lis«*).
  Rasmussen nutzt darüber hinaus auch die besondere Sprachsituation auf den Färöern, um die erlebte Rede zu gestalten. Zunächst fällt in dieser Passage die

starke Häufung von Entlehnungen auf, vor allem aber auch, dass diese anders als sonst in *Bábelstornið* nicht in Anführungszeichen gesetzt sind, wodurch sie dem Gedankengang des dänischsprachigen Amtmanns näher zu stehen scheinen. Nur zwei Wörter bleiben in Anführungszeichen, da sie innerhalb der erlebten Rede des Amtmanns als Mittel der Distanzierung gegenüber dem, was er beobachtet, stehen: »*radikalis*« und »*subordinatiónir*«. Zur erlebten Rede des Amtmanns trägt auch bei, dass Jógvan mit seinem amtlichen, d.h. dänischen Namen *Joen Joensen* bezeichnet wird. Auch im färöischen Erbwortschatz trägt der Stilwert mancher Wortformen zur Unmittelbarkeit der erlebten Rede bei: *hettar, hattar* mit *-r* und das Fugen-*s* in *tíðssvarandi* (vgl. Fem.Gen.Sg. *tíðar*) sind Formen der Mündlichkeit wie auch die Danismen *bleiv, óforstáiligt, forrestin, gemeinur*. Rasmussen verzichtet zudem nach Interjektionen auf Interpunktionszeichen (*Ja høgst óbetonkt; ja tað bleiv*) und Großschreibung (*Ja, ja! man*), um den Gedankenfluss zu unterstreichen. Was macht nun die dritte Auflage aus dieser Passage?

(31) 3. Aufl. 53f.:
Amtmaðurin stóð <u>framman fyri</u> <u>skrivstovu</u>vindeyganum [...]. <u>Ja, nú</u> vóru bara tveir sunnudagar <u>afturat</u>, til <u>valið</u> skuldi fara at <u>verða</u> — og aftur skuldu hesir — hesir »radikalis« hava fund í dag.

Amtmaðurin hugsaði um, antin tað ikki var best at leggja niður forboð móti, at slíkar »subordinatiónir« skuldu <u>endurtakast</u>, men nei, tað var [...] — Tað var tó allar hægst <u>óumhugsað</u> at lata eitt so <u>óbúgvið</u> fólk, sum <u>hetta</u> í Føroyum fáa rætt til at velja <u>ein mann á</u> fólkatingið, tað kundi jú vera heilt <u>tíðarsvarandi</u>, at kongur útnevndi <u>ein mann</u> fyri Føroyar. Ja, <u>lítið umhugsað</u>, <u>merkiligt</u>, at hann, amtmaðurin, ikki var tikin meira <u>upp á</u> ráð. — Ja, ja! <u>Man</u> fekk nú <u>innrættað</u> sær sum man livdi í einum konstitutionellum landi. Hann hevði einki at <u>brigsla sær</u>, hann hevði roynt alt tað hann kundi, hann hevði tikið orðið fleiri ferðir báðar hinar sunnudagarnar fyri at talt <u>fornuft</u> til fólkið, men hesin — Niels Winther — forrestin ein hálvstuderaður røvari [...] Men hvør var <u>hatta</u>? Amtmaðurin toygdi seg út móti vindeyganum. <u>Ja, so</u> sanniliga var tað Joen Joensen úr Dalbyrgi, ná! Ja so! <u>Var</u> hann komin her, tað segðist <u>jú, at</u> hann reisti <u>landið</u> runt og agiteraði fyri Niels Winther — ein gemeinur bóndi — ja tað bleiv meira og meira óforstáiligt.

Die dritte Auflage weicht in vielen Fällen von der ersten ab (meine Unterstreichungen). Zunächst finden sich ein paar der sonst üblichen Anpassungen an die Gegenwartsorthographie: *frammanfyri, uppá* → *framman fyri, upp á*. Ebenso finden sich einige morphologische Korrekturen: *fekk nú inrætta, landi* → *fekk nú innrættað, landið*. Diese führen auch dazu, dass eingefügte Kommata und die Verwendung von Großbuchstaben nach Ausrufezeichen den Sprachfluss etwas stockender machen: *Ja nú; Ja høgst; Ja, ja! man fekk; Ja so sanniliga; Ja so! var hann; tað segðist jú at hann reisti* → *Ja, nú*; *Ja, lítið*; *Ja, ja! Man fekk*; *Ja, so sanniliga*; *Ja so! Var hann*; *tað segðist jú, at hann reisti.* In *ja tað bleiv* ist aber kein Komma eingefügt.

Die dritte Auflage enthält aber auch darüber hinausgehende Änderungen. Die Markierung von Emphase durch Sperrstil ist weggefallen: *fornuft* → *fornuft*. Mit *hettar, hattar, tíðssvarandi* → *hetta, hatta, tíðarsvarandi* wird der mündliche Stil der erlebten Rede in einen schriftsprachlichen Stil überführt. Mit *merkjuligt* → *merkiligt* wird eine zeittypische gegen eine heute geläufigere Form ersetzt. Mit *aftrat* → *afturat* wird eine explizitere, nicht-synkopierte Form eingeführt.

In *til valgið skuldi fara at vera* → *til valið skuldi fara at verða* wird mit *valgið* → *valið* wie an anderen Stellen im Werk der dänische gegen den färöischen Wortstamm ersetzt. Außerdem wird *vera* gegen homophones *verða* ersetzt mit einer Bedeutungsverschiebung, die nur schriftlich erkennbar ist, aber mit dem Amtmann eine semantisch etwas elaboriertere Überlegung verbindet: ‚bis die Wahl sein sollte' → ‚bis die Wahl stattfinden sollte'.

Es finden sich aber auch andere Änderungen bei den Entlehnungen. Vor allem aber kommt es zum sprachpuristischen Ersatz folgender Wörter:

- *kantórsvindeyganum* (dän. *kontor*) → *skrivstovuvindeyganum*;
- *gentakast* (dän. *gentage*) → *endurtakast*;
- *óbetonkt* (dän. *ubetænkt*, fär. *ó-*, fär. *teinkja/tonkti/tonkt*) → *óumhugsað*;
- *ómogið* ‚unreif' (dän. *umoden* ‚unreif', fär. *ó-* samt <ð, g>-Verwechslung wie bei **fradere/frægari* — Wortpaare wie *bogi/boði* mit <ð/g>[j] sind homophon; vgl. auch nyn. *mogen/moden* ‚reif'; fär. *moðin* ‚vergammelt, schimmelig' ist semantisch zu weit entfernt) → *óbúgvið*;
- *eitt medlem til fólkatingið* (dän. *medlem*) → *ein mann á fólkatingið*;
- *eitt medlem fyri Føroyar* (dän. *medlem*) → *ein mann fyri Føroyar*;
- *bebreyda sær* (dän. *bebrejde*) → *brigsla sær*.

Damit reduziert die dritte Auflage die — von Rasmussen im Dienst der erlebten Rede — eingesetzte hohe Danismendichte. Außerdem wird dabei ohne Not die für erlebte Rede typische Wiederholung des Adverbs in *allar hægst* [mit <æ>] *óbetonkt*; *Ja høgst* [mit <ø>] *óbetonkt* → *allar hægst óumhugsað*; *Ja, lítið umhugsað* abgeschwächt (fär. *høgur/hægri/hægstur* — dän. *høj/højere/høj(e)st*). Bei alledem kommt hinzu, dass die vielen Anführungszeichen in der dritten Auflage so gut wie durchgehend im Romantext weggefallen sind. Damit kann deren in der ersten Auflage auffallende Abwesenheit in der erlebten Rede nun in der dritten Auflage keine besondere Wirkung mehr entfalten.

Es geht der dritten Auflage gewiss kaum darum, die raffiniert gestaltete erlebte Rede des Amtmanns zu zersetzen. Es ist wohl eher von der Intention auszugehen, Rasmus Rasmussen rückwirkend eine puristischere Sprache zuzuschreiben, als er tatsächlich hatte. Entscheidend dabei ist jedoch, dass das kausale (und wohl nicht intendierte) Ergebnis dieses Bestrebens eine Banalisierung von Rasmus Rasmussens Erzähltechnik und eine Minderung des literarischen Wertes des Romans mit sich führt.

8. Zusammenfassung

Insgesamt führt Rasmussen mit *Bábelstornið* (zumindest in der ersten Auflage) eindringlich vor Augen, wie eine jahrhundertealte Diglossie mit dem Dänischen das Färöische beeinflusst hat. Mit seinem Romantext zeigt Rasmussen nicht nur auf, dass das Färöische um die Jahrhundertwende auch als Literatursprache eine Ausbausprache ist. Mehr noch: Er setzt diesen Umstand als erzähltechnisches Mittel ein. So weist er unter anderem mit dem Einsatz von Anführungszeichen auf die Danismen hin und geht zugleich zu ihnen auf Distanz. Das korrespondiert mit vielen Themen des Romans, in dem der dänische Einfluss überhaupt kritisch gesehen wird. Rasmussen zeigt auf, in welch unterlegene Position die Färinger im Kontakt mit der dänisch(sprachig)en Obrigkeit sowohl in weltlichen als auch in religiösen Domänen geraten, wenn sie auf ihr mehr und oft genug weniger gut beherrschtes Gøtudansk angewiesen sind. Schließlich stellt Rasmussen Danismen in den Dienst der erlebten Rede Dänischsprachiger. Damit erweist sich *Bábelstornið* auch in sprachlicher Hinsicht als ein überaus elaborierter Text. Aus der ausbausprachlichen Not macht Rasmussen eine erzähltechnische Tugend.

Die dritte Auflage hingegen ist bemüht, Rasmussens Sprache heutigen, vor allem schriftsprachlichen Idealen anzupassen. Das betrifft sowohl die Wahl von konservativen Varianten beim färöischen Erbwortschatz als auch die Verwendung von Ablösewörtern statt Entlehnungen. Der Preis dafür ist hoch: Zwar wird die eigene Literaturgeschichte zu einer Geschichte, die dem einen oder der anderen vielleicht besser gefallen mag — allerdings geschieht dies auf Kosten der Wahrhaftigkeit. Außerdem wird viel von Rasmussens Schriftstellerkunst beseitigt und seinem Roman eine erzähltechnische Banalität verpasst, die ihr in der ersten Auflage gewiss nicht eigen ist.

9. Ein Vorgängerwerk

Solche rückwirkenden Revisionen des eigenen Kulturerbes im Dienste gegenwärtiger Ideale und Ziele kommen in nationalen Diskursen immer wieder vor. Und so wundert es nicht, dass *Bábelstornið* nicht der einzige färöische Text ist, der von einer solchen Revision geprägt ist. Tummas Lenvig, dessen *høvuðsritgerð* (Masterarbeit) über *Bábelstornið* 1995 erschien, hat in *Tá ið føroyskt málstrev byrjaði. — viðrák og andróður 1888–1900* einige Zeitungsartikel zur Sprachdebatte aus dem Ende des 19. Jh. gesammelt und 2009 im Verlag *sprotin* herausgegeben. Die dänischsprachigen Artikel (hauptsächlich aus *Dimmalætting*, aber auch aus *Færøsk Kirketidende*) hat er ins Färöische übersetzt, so dass die Zweisprachigkeit des Diskurses unsichtbar wird. Allein schon die Tatsache, dass die zur Verfügung stehenden Medien damals fast alle auf Dänisch waren und somit der Diskurs vielfach nicht in der Sprache geführt werden konnte, deren Durchsetzung man anstrebte, mutete widersprüchlich an und war ein zentraler Punkt in der damaligen Sprachdebatte. Genau in diese Wunde hat der Dichter J.H.O. Djurhuus mit seinem polemischen Artikel *Et Folk i Opløsning* den Finger treffsicher gelegt (im Extrablatt der *Dimmalætting* vom 12.04.1905):

> Men naar begge vore Højskolemænd [= die Gründer der *Føroya Fólkaháskúli*: Rasmus Rasmussen und Símun av Skarði] gerne ynder at meddele sig til Offentligheden paa Dansk, gør det unægteligt et nedslaaende Indtryk at maatte konstatere, at disse Grundtvigs, Lokes og Thors drabelige Repræsentanter sikkert mod deres Vilje svigter deres eget Program. Og her kan Grunden kun være manglende Evne. [...] al denne Talen og Skriven om Modersmaalets Ret [...] viser sig at være løst Mundsvejr.

Die von Djurhuus losgetretene Debatte hat nicht wenig dazu beigetragen, dass die färöischen Zeitungen dann im 20. Jh. nach und nach zum Färöischen übergingen.

Die von Lenvig wiedergegebenen Beiträge aus *Føringatíðindi* sind auf Färöisch nachgedruckt — allerdings nicht in ihrer ursprünglichen Form. Im Vorwort weist Lenvig darauf hin, "at stavsetingin er lagað eftir vanligum núgaldandi reglum, og at í einstøkum førum eru orð, bending o.a. hampað um ella rættað, har sum mett hevur verið, at tað var til bata ella var neyðugt" (Lenvig (2009:9). Es handelt sich somit auch hier um eine "[e]ndurskoðað útgáva" im Sinne der dritten Auflage von *Bábelstornið*. Entsprechend findet man Änderungen — und keineswegs nur "í einstøkum førum". Hier eine Auswahl:

– Anpassungen an die Gegenwartsschreibung (*hegar til → higartil, stedga → steðga, til fullnar → til fulnar, gekkst → gekst*);
– Korrekturen von Schreibfehlern (*vorið → vorðið, nýtur → nítur, væntar → vantar*);
– morphologische Änderungen (*longri → longur, öðruvísini → øðruvísi, aldrig → aldrin, ómerkjuligt → ómerkiligt, ídráttsmenn → ítróttarmenn, Av tí grund → Av teirri grund, seinri → seinni, dugdu at syngja → dugdu at sungið, hettar og hattar → hetta og hatta, aðrastaðnis → aðrastaðni*);
– Ablösewörter bzw. Paraphrasierungen bei Entlehnungen (*fullførdu → fullbúgvdu, fyri tann skuld → av teirri grund, fyri tann skyld → somuleiðis eisini, útleggja → umseta, eina samling → eitt savn, er ikki tvívlsmál um → er eingin*

ivingur um, Til síðst → At enda, innvirknað → ávirkan, tilgang → tilgongd, begynti → byrjaði, orðvending → áheitan);

– syntaktische Veränderungen (*sína signing → signing sína, skal uppsetast → skal setast upp, Tað vilja kannske summir siga → Summir fara kanska at siga*).

Dadurch entstehen stärker puristische Texte, wie sie für die damalige Zeit völlig untypisch waren. Außerdem verzichtet Lenvig systematisch auf die in den Originaltexten reichlich verwendete Sperrschrift, so dass der emphatische Duktus des zeittypischen Stils abgeschwächt wird. Insgesamt bekommt man bei Lenvig den Eindruck, dass die Autoren dieser Artikel mit ihrer Sprache sozusagen schon da sind, wo sie noch hin wollten. Die Dringlichkeit der leidenschaftlich angebrachten Anliegen wird damit in Frage gestellt und die Texte ihrem kulturpolitischen Kontext entfremdet.

Literatur

Internetquellen

Dimmalætting 1878–2003. ⟨https://apps.infomedia.dk/Avisportal/da/fao⟩. Rech. 2022-02-19.

Færøsk Kirketidende 1890–1906. ⟨https://apps.infomedia.dk/Avisportal/da/fao⟩. Rech. 2022-02-19.

Tingakrossur 1901–1990. ⟨https://apps.infomedia.dk/Avisportal/da/fao⟩. Rech. 2022-02-07.

Primärliteratur

Dahl, J. 1922. *Dr. Martin Luthers lítla Katekismus.* Tórshavn: H. N. Jacobsens Bókahandil.

Det Danske Bibelselskab (ed.). 2000. *Bíblia. Halgabók. Gamla Testamenti og Nýggja. Týdd ur Frummálunum.* [Keypmannahavn]: Det Danske Bibelselskab.

Evensen, A.C. 1911. *Lesibók.* Tórshavn: Hitt føroyska bókmentafelagið.

FK I–VIII = (ed.) (1941–2003): *Føroya kvæði. Corpus carminum færoensium a Sv. Grundtvig et J. Bloch comparatum. Ed. v. Napoleon Djurhuus (Vol. I, IV–VI), Christian Matras (Vol. I–IV), Michael Chesnutt/Kaj Larsen (Vol. VII), Marianne Claussen (Vol. VIII).* – Kopenhagen: Munksgaard (Vol. I–IV, VI–VII), Kopenhagen: Akademisk Forlag (Vol. V), Hoyvík: Stiðin (Vol. VIII).

í Líð, R. [= Rasmus Rasmussen] (1909): *Bábelstornið.* – Tórshavn: Prentsmiðja hjá partafelaginum "Fram".

í Líð, R. ²1987. *Bábelstornið. Inngangur og Bábelstornið endurprentað óbroytt.* Tórshavn: Emil Thomsen.

Lenvig, T. 2009. *Tá ið føroyskt málstrev byrjaði — viðrák og andróður 1888–1900.* Tórshavn: Sprotin.

Matras, C. (ed.). 1939. *Svabos færøske Visehaandskrifter*. København: Bianco Lunos Bogtrykkeri A/S.

Matras, C. 1966. *Dictionarium Færoense. Færøsk-dansk-latinsk ordbog. Af J. C. Svabo. Udgivet efter håndskrifterne af Chr. Matras. I Ordbogen*. København: Munkgsgaard.

Rasmussen, R. ³2011. *Bábelstornið*. Vestmanna: Sprotin.

Sosialurin, Nr. 12, 2012.

Sekundärliteratur

Brix, K. 2002. *Dialog i babelstårnet. Analyse af Regin í Líðs fiktive prosaforfatterskab*. Tórshavn: Fróðskaparsetur Føroya.

Gaard, G. 1987. Inngangur I. In *Bábelstornið. Inngangur og Bábelstornið endurprentað óbroytt*, R. í Líð, v–xi. Tórshavn: Emil Thomsen.

Gaard, G. 2021. *Rasmus á Háskúlanum*. [Tórshavn]: Fagralíð.

Hammershaimb, V. U. 1849–1851. Færøiske ordsprog, Nogle færøiske talemåder, Færøiske skikke og lege, Barneviser og ramser. Færøiske gåder, Færøiske folkesagn. *Antiquarisk Tidsskrift*, 271–340. [Nachdruck in Hammershaimb (1969: 153–222)]

Hammershaimb, V. U. 1891. *Færøsk anthologi. Bd. I. Tekst samt historisk og grammatisk indledning* [= *Samfund til Udgivelse af gammel nordisk Litteratur*; XV]. København: Møller & Thomsen.

Hammershaimb, V. U. 1969. *Savn úr Annaler for nordisk Oldkyndighed og Historie og Antiqarisk* [sic] *Tidsskrift*. Hrsg. v. Jóhan Hendrik W. Poulsen. Tórshavn: Emil Thomsen.

Isaksen, J. 2017. *Færøsk litteraturs historie. Fra middelalderen til det 21. århundrede. Første bind 1298–1950*. [Nivå]: Marselius.

Lenvig, T. 1995. *Fyrsta føroyska skaldsøgan. Regin í Líð: Bábelstornið. Evni og hugsjónir hennara*. Klaksvík: Egið forlag.

Lindqvist, Ch. 2018. *Untersuchungen zu den Gründungsdokumenten der färöischen Rechtschreibung. Ein Beitrag zur nordischen Schriftgeschichte* [= NOWELE Supplement Series 29]. Amsterdam/Philadelphia: John Benjamins.

Petersen, H. P. & P. Isholm. 2003. *Steinur brestur fyri mannatungu — tiltaksorðabók á føroyskum —*. Syðrugøta: Forlagið Brattalíð.

Petersen, H. P. 2010. *The Dynamics of Faroese-Danish Language Contact*. Heidelberg: Winter.

Poulsen, J. 1900. *Bíbliusøga*. Tórshavn: Føringafelag í Førjum.

Poulsen, J. H. W. 1993. Some Remarks on Gøtudanskt. *NOWELE* 21/22 (= Twenty-Eight Papers Presented to Hans Bekker-Nielsen on the Occasion of his Sixtieth Birthday 29 April 1993). 111–116.

Poulsen, J. H. W. et al. 1998. *Føroysk orðabók*. Tórshavn: Føroya Fróðskaparfelag og Fróðskaparsetur Føroya.

Predelli, S. 2003. Scare quotes and their relation to other semantic issues. *Linguistics and Philosophy* 26: 1–28.

Zieseler, L. 2024. *On the Integration of Non-Native Nouns in Faroese*. Heidelberg: Winter.

The Tienen inscription
and the dialectal position of Tungrian

Bernard Mees
Bangor University

An inscription found in the early 1980s during an excavation at Tienen in
Flemish Brabant, Flanders, appears to preserve the oldest attested Germanic
sentence from Belgium. Dating to the same period as the earliest runic texts,
the Tienen inscription is particularly interesting from the perspective of
early Germanic dialectology. Languages such as Tungrian, the Germanic
idiom spoken in the Roman Civitas Tungrorum, are rarely referred to by
historical linguists. Yet the Tienen inscription seems to preserve a short
syntactic text similar in its brevity to the earliest runic inscriptions, but
which preserves at least one dialectal feature also found otherwise in
Tungrian onomastics. Taken in the broader context provided by Tungrian
onomastic evidence, the Tienen inscription can be understood as
preserving the earliest recorded sentence in a West Germanic dialect.

Introduction

In his introductory survey *The Germanic Languages* (1989), Hans Frede Nielsen
set out the key developments in early Germanic dialectal scholarship. August
Schleicher (1860: 47–95) separated the Germanic languages out into three main
families — Gothic (or East Germanic), Nordic (or North Germanic) and *Deutsch*
(West Germanic) — and in 1924 Ferdinand Wrede advocated employing the
ancient tribal designation Ingvaeonic to refer to the common ancestor of Old English, Old Frisian, Old Saxon, Old High German and Old Dutch. In 1942, however, Friedrich Maurer separated the West Germanic languages out into three
subgroups, employing the archaeological designations North Sea Germanic, Elbe
Germanic and Weser-Rhine Germanic, proposing that each of these groups had
developed separately. In 1948 Theodor Frings similarly grouped Old English, Old
Frisian and Old Saxon together under Wrede's label Ingvaeonic, clearly distin-
guishing Old Frisian from Old Dutch by taking Old Dutch to be a non-Ingvaeonic
dialect that stemmed (as Old Low Franconian or Frankish) originally from the

https://doi.org/10.1075/nss.34.14mee
Available under the CC BY-NC-ND 4.0 license. © 2025 John Benjamins Publishing Company

area between the Rhine and the Weser. A series of linguistic developments were argued by Maurer and Frings to be common to these larger groupings — Ingvaeonic, Franconian and Alemannic/Suebian — and most of these linguistic features are reflected in the more recent assessments of West Germanic dialectology such as those of Patrick Stiles (2013) and Don Ringe (in Ringe and Taylor 2014:10–166).

None of these assessments of early Germanic dialectology employs epigraphic evidence to any great degree, in contrast to most comparable scholarship on North Germanic. Assessments of the early development of North Germanic such as those of Nielsen (2000) are substantially based on early epigraphic evidence and hence are less reliant on reconstructions of likely forms and relationships — they only employ projections from medieval linguistic evidence onto a much earlier past occasionally, rather than predominately. More focus on early German, English and Frisian runic inscriptions has appeared recently (e.g. Findell 2012, Hines 2019, Düwel, Nedoma & Oehrl 2020, Kaiser 2021, Mees 2023a), but much of the more recent work on West Germanic dialectology fails to engage with the evidence for Germanic preserved in Roman epigraphy, despite the widespread nature of the onomastic material from the Germanic-speaking provinces of the Empire. Inscriptions such as that discovered in Tienen during archaeological excavations of a settlement in the ancient Civitas Tungrorum have never been considered in previous studies of early West Germanic dialectology. Yet the Tienen inscription appears to preserve the earliest sentence recorded in a West Germanic dialect, and although a very brief text, it is of much the same length as many of the earliest runic inscriptions.

Background

Tienen lies 38 kilometres west of Tongeren, the site of the capital of the ancient Civitas Tungrorum (Figure 1). Like the Roman administrative district, Tongeren is named after the Tungri, the Germanic tribe that dominated the area in Roman times. Germanic names recorded in inscriptions from the Civitas Tungrorum have been collected by Marie-Thérèse Raepsaet-Charlier (2019) and she has also produced a summary of all the Germanic names she could find that are attested in Roman inscriptions from the two German provinces and Gallia Belgica (Raepsaet-Charlier 2011). Some Tungrian names were assessed in earlier scholarship (Much 1920:30–31, Gutenbrunner 1936:10–11, Weisgerber 1954, Krahe 1961:37–39, Neumann 1983:1071–72), but not in a systematic manner, and improved methods for dating Roman inscriptions (as well as new finds) have made assessing the onomastic material simpler. Yet it is especially finds since the

1980s such as the Tienen inscription that have put assessing the evidence for Tungrian on a much surer footing than had been possible previously, and they allow for a more confident analysis to be made of the dialectal position of Tungrian.

The Tungri are first mentioned as dwelling in Belgic Gaul in the first century by the Roman encyclopedist Pliny (*N.H.* 4, 31) and they are described by the historian Tacitus (*Germ.* 2) as the descendants of the peoples that Caesar (*B.G.* 2, 3) called the Germani cisrhenani 'the Germanic tribes on this side of the Rhine'. Germanic groups had been migrating into northern Gaul since at least the latter years of the second-last century BC and the Tungri seem to have become the leading tribe among the Germani cisrhenani after Caesar had annexed northern Gaul to the Roman Republic. Very few accounts have survived of the period between Caesar's Gallic wars of 58–50 BC and the appearance of Pliny's *Natural History* in the middle of the first century AD, but archaeologists have recently ascribed two inscribed coin issues from the period between 50 BC and AD 10 to the Tungri (Roymans and Arts 2009: 16–19) and the origins of the Roman settlement at Tongeren can be traced archaeologically to about 20 BC (Raepsaet 2013: 135).

The capital of the Tungri is recorded as *Aduaga Tungrorum* in the third-century *Antonine Itinerary* (378, 5), a form usually corrected to *Atuatuca Tungrorum* on the basis of the spelling *Atuacutum* (Ἀτουάκουτον) recorded by Ptolemy (2, 9, 6) and the similarly syncopated form *Atuaca* on the Peutinger Map (Miller 1916: 30). Caesar (*B.G.* 6, 32) also described a fortress called *Atuatuca* as the place in the territory of the Eburones where Roman forces wintered in 54/53 BC and were subsequently besieged by Ambiorix's followers, and this seems likely to have been the Iron Age fortification at Caestert on Mount Saint Peter, just south of Maastricht where the Jeker empties into the Meuse (Vanvinckenroye 2001). Tongeren is situated on the left bank of the river Jeker and it seems likely that it was a new Atuatuca, built by the Romans on the Via Belgica, the Roman road that crossed Northern Gaul from Boulogne-sur-Mer (Gesoriacum) to Cologne (Colonia Claudia Ara Agrippinensium). *Atuatuca*, the ethnonym *Tungri* and the names that appear on the early Tungrian coins are all likely to have been linguistically Tungrian expressions, and all of these names can be analysed as transparently Germanic.

The ethnonym *Germani* was associated by Rudolf Much (1936) with Old High German *gerēn, gerōn* 'to desire' (< Indo-European *$\hat{g}^her$- 'desire'), and Ancient Greek χάρμα 'source of joy, delight' and χάρμη 'joy of battle, lust of battle' are the only other cognates of Old High German *gerēn* that feature similar enlargement by *-m-* (cf. Neumann 1998, Mees 2023a: 26–27). The ethnonym Tungri, however, appears best associated linguistically with *$\flat ung$, the preterite stem of *$\flat inh$- 'to prosper', also found in the name of the *Dea Tungabis* from Pier (*AE* 2001, 1431; Nedoma 2016), while the toponym *Atuatuca* seems most immediately comparable

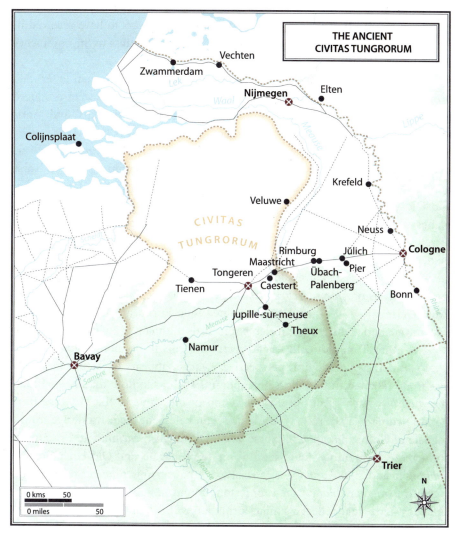

Figure 1. The ancient Civitas Tungrorum

to Old English placenames such as *Adbaruæ* 'Barrow' (Bede, *H.E.* 4,3) and *Adtuifyrde* 'Twyford' (Bede, *H.E.* 4, 28) where, as Hugh Smith (1956: I.5) noted, the locative preposition *æt* 'could be regarded as almost an integral part' of the place name. The most plausible explanation of the root *uat-* is as a cognate of Gothic *watō*, Old Norse *vatn*, Old English *wæter*, Old Frisian *weter*, Old Saxon *watar*, Old Dutch *watar* and Old High German *wazzar* 'water', without the heteroclitic *r/n* morphology, and the suffix *-uk-* is widely attested otherwise in Germano-Roman onomastics (compare *Namucum* 'Namur', a placename first attested in Merovingian sources, and the ethnonym *Sunuci*).[1] *Atuatuca* appears to have received its name 'at the water' because of the proximity of the old fortress to the confluence of the Meuse and the Jeker.

Silver quinarii bearing the genitive legend *Annaroveci* in Roman letters and bronze coins with the nominative name *Avaucia* struck on them were produced in northern Gaul after Caesar's conquest (Figure 2). Roymans and Aarts (2009: 16–17) date the two coin issues to about 50–25 BC and 25 BC–AD 10 respectively, and both of the names can be analysed as Germanic.[2] *Annaroveci* appears to represent a compound with a first element cognate to Gothic *anþar*, Old Norse *annar*, Old English *ōðer*, Old Frisian *ōther*, Old Saxon *ōthar*, Old Dutch *andar* and Old High German *andar* 'other' (< *anþaraz*) found in medieval German names such as *Andragais* and *Andregundis*, while its second element appears to reflect the theme reflected in Old Norse *vega* 'to fight' and Old High German *ubarwehen* 'to conquer' that also appears to be reflected in the medieval name *Wehileo* (Förstemann 1900: 106–7 and 1551, Mees 2023a: 48–49). Etymological analysis of *Annaroveci* suggests that Tungrian featured a development of Proto-Germanic *-nþ- > -nn-*, that it retained Indo-European *-o-* as its composition vowel,[3] and that the second element records *a*-umlaut of *wihaz > *wehaz*.

The other Tungrian coin legend *Avaucia* seems to be more regular from a West Germanic phonological perspective. *Avaucia* appears to feature the prefix *au-* 'from' retained in Old Norse compounds such as *aufusa* 'thanks, gratitude' and *auvirð* 'wretch' (Falk 1928: 339–42) and in the name of the *Aufaniae* from Bonn (Neumann 1987: 114–15), while its second element seems to derive from a cognate of Gothic *aukan*, Old Norse *auka*, Old English *ēacian*, Old Frisian *āka* 'to increase, to multiply', Old Saxon *ōkian* 'to propagate' and Old High German *ouhhon* 'to add' < *aukaną* (Mees 2023a: 49). A patronymic *Bilaucus* recorded (as a genitive singular *Bilauci*) on a tombstone found in 2002 in Jupille-sur-Meuse (*AE* 2003, 1202) may reflect a similar formation with a first Germanic theme *bil-* 'equal, even' and a second element derived from *aukaną* 'to grow'. Yet *Avaucia* appears to show that *an*-stems could be used in early Tungrian men's names, much as is typical in North Germanic. Similar morphology is attested in the Sue-

---

1. *Atuatuca* is sometimes held to be a Gaulish toponym 'lieu de la grand prophétie' (Delamarre 2019–23: II.379), but place-names typically refer to physical features. The root *uat-* also appears in the theonymic epithet *Vatvims* (with a Germanic DAT.PL ending) and *-uk-* in the obviously Germanic name *Hahuci* (GEN.SG) preserved on a shield boss from Zwammerdam (*CIL* XIII 7892 and 8510; Haalebos 1977: no. 67).

2. As with many of the other names of Tungrians, *Annaroveci* has also been claimed to be Celtic, but *Anna-* is not recorded as a root in Gaulish onomastics (Delamarre 2019–23: I.65–66).

3. The retained composition vowels are clearly not due to Latin influence as is sometimes assumed, but rather the following labial glide (Eulenburg 1904).

Figure 2. Early Tungrian coins (photos: Numismatik Naumann, Vienna, and Numismatik Lanz, Munich).

bian name *Nasva* (Caesar, *B.G.* 1, 37), that of the Batavian leader *Chariovalda*, the Marcomannic king *Catvalda* (Tacitus, *Ann.* 2, 11 and 62–63), the second-century, presumably Middle or Upper Rhenish soldier *Dagvalda* (*RIB* 1667) and the Neronian (probably Batavian) bodyguard *Silva* (*CIL* VI 37754) where the later West Germanic languages typically employ *ōn*-stems.[4]

The apparent development of *-nþ- > -nn-* in *Annaroveci*, paralleled in Old Norse *annar*, suggests that Tungrian had already begun to diverge phonologically from the other West Germanic languages in the last century BC. The Tungrian inscriptions are too early to reflect Vulgar Latin influence and there is no obvious

---

4. Wagner (1983) proposed that the endings in *-a* reflect an early loss of Proto-Germanic *-z*, but this seems unlikely given later spellings such as *Vatvims* that retain a final sibilant (< Proto-Germanic *-maz/-miz*).

reason why *-nþ- would be rephonologised to -nn- by a Gaulish-speaking mon-eyer. *Annaroveci* is preserved at a much earlier date for the breakup of Proto-West Germanic than is usually accepted by historical dialectologists, but one of the characteristic developments of the Ingvaeonic dialects is their common loss of -n- before voiceless fricatives with lengthening of the preceding vowel (e.g. in Old English *ōðer* 'the other (of two), the second', Old Frisian *ōther* and Old Saxon *ōthar*). The lowering of root vowels under *a*-umlaut is also often consid-ered a dialectal development in West Germanic as it is commoner in the southern medieval dialects than others (Ringe and Taylor 2014: 34–35). The appearance of West Germanic features in a text centuries earlier than has usually been supposed in recent assessment of early Germanic dialectology demonstrates the limitations of relying only on reconstructions from later evidence and uncritically repeating observations recycled from nineteenth-century scholarship.

Names of speakers of other West Germanic dialects begin to be attested epi-graphically from the first half of the first century AD, but the earliest example of a name that is recorded in what appears to be a grammatically Germanic form preserved in Roman characters is the graffito *Leluais* from the Roman fortress at Zwammerdam, ancient Nigrum Pullum (Haalebos 1977: no. 36). It is recorded in Old Roman cursive letters on the bottom of a Samian ware plate of the Dra-gendorff 18 type (Dragendorf 1895: table II) and it appears to be of late first-century date (Figure 3). 'Rutenian' terra sigillata of this type were manufactured in the south of Gaul and exported north, but it is not clear which tribe the Ger-manic soldier who wrote his name on the plate belonged to. A similarly dating (or slightly later) graffito on a Samian ware cup from Zwammerdam preserves a name *Batavi* 'Batavus's' (Haalebos 1977: no. 10), presumably the cognomen of a Batavian soldier stationed at the fortress. But Zwammerdam lies in the region set-tled by the Cannanefates and the graffito *Leluais* may have been inscribed by a member of another West Germanic tribe serving in the Roman army. The names attested in Roman graffiti are usually recorded as genitives (indicating possession of the object that bears them), but the ending *-ais* is clearly not Latin. Haalebos (1977: no. 36) suggests that the *s* could be an abbreviation for the military title *signifer* 'standard-bearer', but an ending *-ai* does not make much sense from a Latin or Germanic perspective either. Instead, *-ais* is comparable to the Gothic feminine *i*-stem genitive singular ending *-ais* and the Old Norse *i*-stem ending *-ar* (< *-aiz) as if the name were a masculine *i*-stem. Similar names such as *Lella* (*CIL* XIII 7899 and 8228), *Lellavus* (*CIL* XIII 7789), *Lellius* (*CIL* XIII 3980) and *Lellua* (*CIL* XIII 8411 and Nesselhauf 1937: no. 241) are attested from Luxembourg and the Rhineland, and they appear to be best explained as deriving from a redupli-cated perfect stem of *lew-* 'to cut off' (< Indo-European *leu̯H-) comparable to Greek λέλυμαι 'be freed' given that a sigmatically enlarged strong verb *leusaną 'to lose' and other derivatives of *leuH- such as *lewô 'scythe' and *lawwō 'groove' are also attested in Germanic. Deverbative *i*-stems (usually *nomina actionis* with zero-grade roots) are widely attested in Germanic and the gemination may be a sign of laryngeal metathesis.

Figure 3. The Germanic graffito from Zwammerdam (photo: Julia Chorus)

The names of Tungrian soldiers are known from a similar period, with two that are clearly Germanic being recorded on first-century tombstones. The oldest appears to date either to the middle or the end of the first century. Discovered in 1804 in Mainz (Roman Mogontiacum), it formerly featured a relief of the deceased on the lost part of the stone above the inscription, and both the angular shield depicted on what remains of the relief and the commemorative phrasing recorded on the memorial are typical of first-century finds (*CIL* XIII 7036):

> *Freioverus*
> *Veransati f(ilius)*
> *cives Tung(er) eq(ues) ex*
> *coh(orte) I Astur(um) an(norum)*
> *XL stip(endiorum) XXII h(ic) s(itus) e(st)*
> *t(estamento) f(ieri) i(ussit) h(eres) f(aciendum) c(uravit).*

> Freioverus
> son of Veransatus,
> a Tungrian tribesman, a former cavalryman
> of the First Cohort of the Asturians, 40
> years old, with 22 years of service, lies here.
> In accordance with (his) will, commissioned by (his) heir.

Freioverus is a dithematic name, featuring a first element that reflects **frija-* 'free' (perhaps with *a*-umlaut) and a second element **wira-* 'man' (with *a*-umlaut) or *wēra-* 'true'. The soldier's patronymic *Veransatus* appears to feature the same element followed by **ans-* 'god' and a dental suffix **-aþ-*. Neither name shows any sign of syncopation and the only remarkable phonological feature is the composition vowel *-o-* inherited from Indo-European attested in *Freioverus* (and *Annaroveci*) rather than the *-a-* employed in early runic inscriptions such as in the early third-century dithematic name **bidawarijaz** preserved on the Nøvling fibula (Krause and Jankuhn 1966: no. 13a).

Like the Zwammerdam form *Leluais*, many of the earliest Tungrian anthroponyms recorded epigraphically are monothematic. Another early funerary inscription that features Tungrian names is recorded on a tombstone of a soldier that was discovered in 1922 near Neuss. Uncovered along with a single-handled jug, a pot and a key that all appear to date to the late first century, the tombstone features a relief of the deceased soldier holding a military standard. Named in the inscription as a standard-bearer (*signifer*) of the Ala Afrorum, an auxiliary originally raised in Roman Africa, the funerary monument records that it was commissioned by *Tungro*, the brother of the deceased soldier. Conserved in the Clemens Sels Museum in Neuss, its dedication reads (Finke 1927: no. 304):

> *Oclatio Carvi f(ilius)*
> *signif(er) Alae Afror(um)*
> *Tungro frater h(eres) f(aciendum) c(uravit).*

> For Oclatius son of Carvus,
> a standard-bearer of the African auxiliary.
> Tungro (his) brother (and) heir commissioned (this).

Oclatius is a Roman family name, but *Carvus* and *Tungro* both appear to be Germanic forms. A Gaulish name *Carvus* is also attested (Delamarre 2019–23: I.193–94), but a Tungrian name *Carvus* seems better understood as deriving from Germanic **harwaz* 'bitter'. The same patronymic appears to be spelled as *Harvi* in an inscription from Wardt (*AE* 2006, 883) and despite the development of pejorative meanings in Old Norse *herfiligr* 'wretched' and Old English *gehieran* 'to despise', the employment of **harwaz* as an anthroponym may indicate that the adjective had a meaning such as 'tough, bitter from experience, hardy' when it was employed onomastically — after all, a similar meaning seems to be fossilised in **harska-* 'rough' (Heidermanns 1993: 282–83). *Tungro* is presumably an *ōn*-stem agentive derivative of the ethnonym *Tungri*.

Tungrian names are also attested on writing tablets preserved in the remains of the fortress at Vindolanda in Roman Britain, the earliest of which date to the late first century. The first fort at Vindolanda was built by Tungrian soldiers in about AD 85 and most of the Germanic names recorded in the letters unearthed from the site since the 1980s appear to be Tungrian (Birley 2001, Clay 2010: 173–76). From a dialectal perspective, the most important are preserved in an account of commodities found in an archaeological context of c. AD 120–30. The double-leaf tablet was found in 1987 broken into 27 fragments and the text on the tablet is preserved in three columns, all of which record Germanic names. Its first column reads (*Tab. Vindol.* 184):

> ꜵ *Uceṇi*
> —*superarias ✕ xiiii[*
> —*Tagarminis [[ꜵ]]*
> —*piper ✕ ii*
> *Ǥambax Tapponis*
> *ṣ[udari]uṃ ✕ ii*
> *Soll]ẹmniṣ[..(.)]ubar[*
> —*ampullam[*
> *[F]uṛiọ(?) Ṣṭ[ip]ọnis(?)*
> —*sudarium ✕ ii*
> —*Ammius[*
>> *]xxiix*
>> *]i*
>> *]ṃ ✕ iii;*
>> *]s*
>> *]i ✕ i s(emissem);*
>> *[su]ḅarmal ...*

century of Ucen(i)us
✓ overcoats, 14 denarii
✓ Tagarminis ...
✓ pepper, 2 denarii
Gambax son of Tappo
towel, 2 denarii
Sollemnis (?) ...
✓ a flask
Furio (?) son of Stipo (?)
✓ towel, 2 denarii
✓ Ammius ...
... 28 (?)
...
... 3 denarii and a quadrans
...
... 1 denarius, a semis and a quadrans
passing under the arms ...

Most of the names recorded in the first column appear to be Germanic, but the most interesting from a dialectal perspective is *Gambax*. Given that no root **gamb-* is attested in Gaulish onomastics, *Gambax* appears to be a syncopated form of an earlier **Gambagaz*, a derivative of **gambōną* 'to hop, to jump' enlarged by a velar suffix in a manner comparable to the early runic form **godagas** of the Valsfjord cliff inscription (Krause and Jankuhn 1966: no. 55, Mees 2023a: 114–15). *Gambax* may feature a semantic development similar to that attested in Old High German *gambar* 'vigorous' and presumably in the ethnonym *Sugambri*. *Gambax* also appears to evidence syncopation in the final syllable of a heavy trisyllabic, a development that also seems to be recorded in the Suebian ethnonym *Hermunduri* (< **Ermuna-dur-*) attested in first-century sources.

The second column features more Germanic names and continues the list of goods evidently ordered by the soldiers:

> *coturnum ✱ iii ṣ(emissem)*
> *Messor   [[......]]*
> *—sagaciam ✱ v;*
> *Luçius scutarius*
> *sebum ✱ [*
> *[U]xperus*
> *i[*
> *Agị[lis]*
> *ṣ[ebum]*
> *Hueṭịị[*
> *suḍaṛ[.] ✱ ii*
> *Tullio Carpẹnṭạri*
> *✱ xḷ ...*

buskin, 3 denarii and a semis
Messor
√ a military cloak, 5 denarii, a quadrans and an octans
Lucius the shield-maker
tallow, .. denarii
... Uxperus
...
Agilis (?)
tallow (?), ...
Hwet...
towel, 2 denarii
Tullio son of Carpentarius
40 denarii

Of the names from the second column, the most interesting from a dialectal perspective is *Uxperus*. The name is also recorded in a graffito from Vechten (*CIL* XIII 10017, 937), on a tombstone from Rimburg (Nesselhauf 1937: no. 247) and as a patronymic on a gravestone from Klosterneuburg, Pannonia (*AE* 1992, 1448), as well as in a derived form *Ucsperianus* from Jülich (*CIL* XIII 7877). The name appears to feature Germanic **uhs-*, a zero-grade cognate of **wahsijaną* 'grow' (to Indo-European **h₂ueg-s*), and the loanword **per-* 'pear' also found in the Batavian patronymic *Pero* and the second-century anthroponym *Gamuxperus* from Mainz (*CIL* XIII 7086; *AE* 1988, 906; Mees 2022). The lack of a composition vowel appears to indicate syncopation of the unaccented vowel of an etymologically heavy disyllabic initial theme, a phonological development that is also attested in the Suebian placename *Lupfurdum* (Λούπφουρδον) recorded in the mid-second century by Ptolemy (2, 11, 28), whose first element also appears to be recorded by Ptolemy in the Suebian placename *Luppia* (Λουππία). Similar syncopation is argued by Roland Schuhmann (2014: 412–13) to be reflected in the early runic name **niwajē-mariz** recorded on the Thorsberg chape (with **mariz** < **mērijaz* 'famous') which, on archaeological grounds, is likely to have been an early third-century continental Anglian or Saxon inscription (Krause and Jankuhn 1966: no. 20).

The third column in the account from Vindolanda appears to deal with an order by soldiers from a different century, but it is largely of the same form:

ↄ *Tullionis*
corrigia ✗ ii s(emissem)
—*sebum ✗ ii*
sudari(um) ✗ i
Butimas
sebum ✗ ii[
d sudar(ium) ✗ i[
]ọ *subạrmalọ*
sebum ✗ [
[C]aleḍus
Vell[---]
Veṛ[ecundus](?) ṃaliator

century of Tullio
thongs, 2½ denarii
√ tallow, 2 denarii
towel (?), 1 denarius
Butimas
tallow, 2 denarii
towel, ... denarii

...

tallow, ... denarii

Caledus

Vell...

Verecundus (?) the hammerer (?)

Some text is also recorded on the back of the tablet, but nothing semantically meaningful appears to have survived.

From a linguistic perspective the most important form in the third column is the name *Butimas*. The same name is known from an inscription excavated from a graveyard in Rotweil (Roman Ara Flavia) dated to the late first or second century (*AE* 2010, 1071h) and although it has been taken to be Celtic,[5] the first element of *Butimas* seems more regularly understood as a derivative of the apophonically remodelled root **būt-* 'to beat, to strike' (earlier **beut-* < Indo-European **bʰeud-* 'to strike') reflected in Middle High German *būzen* 'to hit' (if not just a zero-grade **but-*) while the second theme appears to be **īm-*, a cognate of the Old Norse poetic term *íma* 'strife, fight, battle' (< **īmǭ*); compare the first element of the first-century Batavian name *Imerix* (*AE* 1971, 299). The ending of *Butimas* is written as if it were a Latin consonant stem, but a similar development appears to explain the Batavian patronymic *Vihirmas* (only attested as a genitive singular *Vihirmatis*; *CIL* XIII 8771) that seems to represent a compound of **wīh-* 'holy' and **erm-* 'mighty, great' (Förstemann 1900: 470–73 and 1589–90, Mees 2023a: 51–52) with the assimilation of **erm-* to *irm-* perhaps an indication that the underlying Germanic genitive was **Wīhirmaþis*. The second element of *Butimas* appears to also feature enlargement by **-aþ-* and syncopation of the third syllable of a heavy tri-syllabic, indicating consistency in the phonological development of the Germanic names recorded on the tablet.

A final pair of inscriptions from Roman Britain that appears to preserve dialectal features of Tungrian are two dedications from the Roman fort at Birrens, Scotland. In 1776 an altar from Birrens was noted by the antiquarian and natural historian Thomas Pennant (1776: 406) which preserves a dedication that clearly features two Germanic names. It is not made clear in the dedication which military unit the commissioner of the inscription was part of, but two votive inscriptions dedicated by members of the Second Cohort of the Tungri are known from the site (*RIB* 2100 and 2107). The Roman fort at Birrens (Roman Blatobulgium) seems to have been garrisoned by the Cohors II Tungrorum between AD 155 and 180, and to have been abandoned after that date. Recorded on a white sandstone altar, 69 cm

---

5. Delamarre (2019–23: I.165) takes *Buti-* to be a cognate of the second element of the Old Irish consonant stem *Cathbad* with stem vocalism not attested otherwise in Gaulish (cf. *Buturatis, Buturicus, Buturus* etc.).

high and 36 cm wide, with decorative bolsters on its top, stepped cornices and a stepped pediment, the first of the Birrens inscriptions reads (*RIB* 2096):

Deae
Harimel-
lae sac(rum) Ga-
midiahus
arc(h)it(ectus) v(otum) s(olvit) l(aetus) l(ibens) m(erito)

To the goddess
Harimella sacred.
Gamidiahus,
the engineer, fulfilled (his) vow, gladly, willingly, deservedly.

Conserved in the Dumfries Burgh Museum, the altar was dedicated to an otherwise unknown Germanic (and hence presumably Tungrian) goddess *Harimella*. *Harimella* preserves a syncopated first element *Hari-* 'army' followed by a second onomastic theme that Much (1892) analysed as a cognate of Old Norse *mjǫll* 'snow'. Much translated the Birrens theonym as 'the one who shines (like the snow) in battle', but his etymology was questioned by Edward Schröder (1924) who compared *Harimella* to the Belgian place name *Hermalle* first attested in a Carolingian source as *Harimalla* (< Germanic **Harjamaþlą* 'army meeting place'). Yet Much (1926) criticised Schröder's derivation of the second element of the goddess's name as phonologically improbable — the dental is preserved in the early Frankish gloss *maltho* 'I declare' (albeit in a metathetic form) in a verb clearly derived from **maþlą* '(speech given at) a meeting place' and there is no other evidence for **-þl- > -ll-* at such an early date in Germanic.

Supporting Schröder's comparison with the place name *Harimalla*, Norbert Wagner (2002) compares the second element of *Harimella* to that attested in the name *Fledimella* recorded on a tombstone from Vechten (*CIL* XIII 8821) and argues that later instances of the Germanic onomastic element *mella-* such as *Mellebaudis, Mellaricus* and *Mellaridus* reflect Romanised spellings of **maþlą*. The widespread remodelling that he assumes, however, is not supported by evidence contemporary to the Birrens inscription and appears quite implausible. Yet Old Norse *mjǫll* is also employed as a woman's name and it can mean 'flour' — it appears to derive from **melaną* 'to grind', the root of Old English *melu* 'flour, meal' (< **melwą* 'ground corn'). Etymologically *Harimella* seems best understood as a bahuvrīhi 'having army flour' as if she were a goddess who was thought to provide food to hungry soldiers.[6] Roman soldiers carried hand-mills with them

---

6. *Fledimella* 'beauty-flour' (*CIL* XIII 8821) may be a reference to make-up.

in order that they could make bread and the theonym may reflect the idea that Harimella was a goddess who made sure that soldiers always had enough to eat. The connection may also be reflected in Old Norse mythology: in the Old Norse poem *Gróttasǫngr* (18–20), two giantesses, Fenja and Menja, use a magical grindstone called Grótti to grind out (*mǫlum*) an army (*herr*) to punish king Fróði — the ground out army then burns down the king's hall Lejre and kills Fróði.

The name of the engineer *Gamidiahus*, however, has proved more difficult to analyse. Theodor von Grienberger (1896: 533) proposed that it is a Celtic formation **Gamidia(v)os*, with the -*h*- indicating vocalic hiatus after the loss of **-u̯-*, whereas Moritz Schönfeld (1911: 102) took the name as featuring the Germanic prefix *ga*- 'with' and the adjective that is reflected in Old English *midde* 'middle' (< Proto-Germanic **medjaz* 'middle'). Yet *Gamidiahus* appears to preserve a suffix -*iah*- (cf. the Gallo-Roman toponymic suffix -*iac*-) without the voicing expected under Verner's law, and a more regular analysis of *Gamidiahus* would be to compare it to the Old English past participle *gemiþen* 'hidden' (< Proto-Germanic **ga-midanaz*) or the root of Old Norse *gaman* 'fun', Old English *gamen* 'sport, joy, game' and Old High German *gaman* 'fun, joy' also reflected in Old Norse *gamðir* 'amusing one'. The engineer's name can be most regularly analysed as a detoponymic 'the one from **Gamidiacum* (the settlement of **Gamidaz*)'.

Harimella is most important from a dialectal perspective in terms of the further development of syncopation in Tungrian. *Harimella* appears to show that Tungrian had lost the composition vowels of palatal diphthongs after light disyllabics by the late second century just as the medieval West Germanic languages did (cf. Old English *herebeorg* 'harbour, shelter, lodgings, quarters' and Old Saxon and Old High German *heriberga* 'army encampment, hostelry' < **harja-berg*-). Various attempts to explain away the shortening in *Harimella* have emerged over the years (most recently Harðarson 2023), but the most straightforward assumption is to accept that it evidences syncopation. Taken as a whole, the evidence for syncopation in Tungrian appears to show that it was a typical West Germanic language, featuring all the developments associated with syncopation also attested in the medieval languages by the end of the second century.

This evidence seems to contrast with the treatment of the composition vowel in another theonym attested at much the same time at Birrens. Found in about 1812, the red sandstone altar is 1.1 m tall and features decorative bolsters on its top and is conserved in the National Museum of Scotland, Edinburgh (*RIB* 2107):

> *Deae Ricagam-*
> *bedae pagus*
> *Vellav(u)s milit(ans)*
> *coh(orte) II Tung(rorum)*

v(otum) s(olvit) l(ibens) m(erito)
To the goddess Ricagambeda,
(men of) the Vellavian
district serving in the
Second Cohort of the Tungri,
fulfilled (their) vow, willingly, deservedly.

The identity of the *pagus Vellav(u)s* has been the subject of some disagreement. An inscription from Sanssac-l'Eglise appears to mention a *civit(as) Vell[av(orum)]* in the third century (*CIL* XIII 8878) and Merovingian coins struck with the legend *Vellavos* are known from the Auvergne, the home of a Gaulish tribe called the *Vellavi* (Chambon and Greub 2000: 168–69). Yet Paul Marchot (1930) argued that *Vellav(u)s* is continued in the name of a heath called *Veluwe* in North Brabant and that the *Vellavi* mentioned on the Birrens dedication were an early constituent people of the Tungri.

The proper analysis of the theonym *Ricagambeda* is also unclear, however.[7] The first element of *Ricagambeda* has generally been taken to be a form of Germanic **rīk-* 'king' or the derived adjective **rīk(ij)a-* 'rich, powerful', but the rest of the theonym has been subject to only problematic attempts to explain it. Much (in Gutenbrunner 1936: 105) compared *gambeda* to Old English *gombon* 'tribute' (cf. Old Saxon *gambra* 'tribute' and Old Norse *gamban-* 'great') and conflating Old High German *gibiotan* 'to command' (< **ga-beud-*) with Old High German *bitten* 'to ask' (< **bed-*), Elard Meyer (1891: 170) translated *-gambeda* as 'mistress', an interpretation supported by Siegfried Gutenbrunner (1936: 105–6) although Gutenbrunner suggested that *-agam-* could instead reflect a form of **aganą* 'to fear' (translating *Ricagambeda* as 'the mighty mistress of fear'). Most recently Wagner (2018) compared *gambeda* to **gambra-* 'vigorous' and translated the theonym as 'the one who efficiently and vigorously acts in favour of a ruler'. But Wagner claimed that the root of **gambra-* is an otherwise unattested adjective **gamba-* (rather than the root of the actually attested Middle High German verb *gampen* 'to hop, to jump') and he analysed *gambeda* as an equally unparalleled agent noun. A similarly enlarged Tungrian name *Gamaleda* is known from a fragment of worked stone unearthed in 1900 in Maastricht (*CIL* XIII 3613), however, that seems to derive from **gamal-* 'old' and a similar feminine ending, and the same ending is presumably attested in *Veleda*, the name of the seeress of the Bructeri who prophesised the Batavian revolt (Tacitus, *Hist.* 4, 61).

Ricagambeda may represent a form with a composition vowel retained after a heavy stem. But like Gothic *reiks*, **rīk-* 'king' is usually reflected in early West Ger-

---

7. Delamarre (2019–23: I.206) considers it Gaulish, but with 'sens obscur du deuxième terme'.

manic names as if it were a root stem. The case forms taken by names recorded in classical sources such as that of the Sugambrian *Deudorix* son of *Baetorix* (Strabo 7, 1, 4) and the Frisian king *Malorix* (Tacitus, *Ann.* 13, 54) are reflected epigraphically by that of the first-century Batavian soldier *Imerix*, but **rīk-* then fell out of popularity as an onomastic element until the end of antiquity when it reappears in Germanic names as a thematic form usually spelled *-ricus* in Latin. Gothic uses composition vowels in compounds where the first element is a consonant stem (cf. *brōþralubo* 'brotherly love' and *nahtamats* 'supper'), and a similar practice presumably applied with root stems in the early West Germanic languages. The connecting vowels of compounds with root stems as first elements seem to have been analogical, modelled on those employed by other stem-classes, but as a secondary development, the apparent composition vowel in the theonym *Ricagambeda* (if it is not merely to be understood as *Rīk-agam-beda*) cannot be used as clear evidence for the development of syncopation otherwise in Tungrian.

The Tienen inscription

During excavations of Roman Tienen in 1981–82, Flemish archaeologists discovered a ceramic dish, a low-walled plate or shallow bowl, with a two-line inscription scratched into its bottom after firing (Figure 4). Tienen was first settled during the Augustan period and later developed into a *vicus* where potters, glassblowers and other manufacturers established workshops. Tienen's pottery industry became especially important from the late first century and the *vicus* also developed into a market town where agricultural surpluses could be traded. Several tumuli have been excavated in the area and in 1998 a Mithraeum dated to the third century was discovered in the southwest periphery of the *vicus* (Martens 2012). The 1981–82 excavations occurred at a site just to the west of Tienen's main railway station, and the archaeological finds unearthed at the time are conserved in the Museum Het Toreke in Tienen where the dish has the inventory number 82.ST.10.47.

About half of the inscribed dish is lost, but it is 5.5 cm high, 22.4 cm in diameter at the rim and 22.4 cm at the base (De Clercke 1983: no. 121). The dish is of orange to yellow-white sandy clay with a grey-brown smooth surface and was one of over 200 ceramics uncovered at the site during the 1981–82 excavations. It is of a local type with curved walls also known from Tongeren (Vanwinckenroye 1967: no. 90) and is one of over a dozen ceramics of this sort discovered at Tienen. The archaeologists excavated a ceramic kiln and several loose pieces of jewellery from the settlement which date from the first three centuries AD. The dish has been dated to the late second or early third century which is the time of the height of the 'epigraphic habit' in the Roman provinces. The production of inscriptions declined markedly after the middle of the third century at the time of the imperial crisis that was occasioned by a series of civil wars, Frankish and Alemannic raids, economic disruption and hyperinflation.

The Tienen inscription is engraved in clear, Old Roman cursive letters and features only two short lines: *lubait / lupiotex* (De Clercke 1983: no. 121). The only questionable characters are the sequence ‹ai› in the first line which could be taken as an ‹n› (or even a ligature ‹an›) and the ‹p› of the second line that features a stroke at the bottom and hence could perhaps be a ligature ‹p͡l› (Welkenhuysen in De Clercke 1983: no. 121). But a sequence *lubnt* would not be expected on phonotactic grounds and reading ligatures in Roman graffiti is usually unwarranted. The ending of the second line's *lupiotex* makes it appear to be a name (Welkenhuysen in De Clercke 1983: no. 121) and the ending of the first word *lubait* seems to indicate that it is a verb. Another plate or bowl of the same low-walled type found during the 1981–82 excavations features a Latin graffito *Aviti* 'Avitus's' on its outer wall (De Clercke 1983: no. 119) and a fragment of a glazed cup similarly records *Avit[i]* (De Clercke 1983: no. 118), but none of the other ceramics found at the time preserved similar graffiti.

Figure 4. The Tienen graffito (photo: Museum Het Toreke)

The first word, *lubait*, appears to be the expected third-person singular present indicative of the weak class-III verb reflected in Old High German as *lobēn* 'to praise' and in Gothic *lubains* and Old English *lufen* 'hope' (cf. Mees 2023b). Gaulish has a similar verbal root *lub-* 'to love', but not a verbal ending *-ait*. A similar name *Lubainis* recorded on a tombstone from Namur (*CIL* XIII 3622) was linked by Much (1920: 30) with Gothic *lubains* (and compare the form *Lubainius* on a more recently discovered dedication from Krefeld; *AE* 1981, 686), but taking *lubait* as a participle or a name seems unlikely. The past participles of weak class-III verbs did not feature the medial *-ai-* of secondary formations such as Gothic *lubains* and Old English *lufen* (Ringe 2017: 286), and a past participle with *-ai-* generalised from the third-singular present (as occurs with many weak class-III past participles in Old High German) appears improbable given the woman's name *Lifðina* (cf. the weak class-III preterite stem **libd-* 'lived') recorded on another gravestone from Namur (*AE* 2004, 939). A third-person singular subjunctive present would not be expected either as the ending of such forms was probably *-ai* in Proto-Germanic, although as the late Tom Markey (p.c.) observed, second plural subjunctives and imperatives also ended in *-iþ* which might explain why the verb comes first in the inscription (Ringe 2017: 286). Given that Latin had no voiceless dental fricative (and hence no regular graphemic manner to distinguish /þ/ from /t/), *lubait* presumably stands for a Germanic *lubaiþ* with typical lack of indication of the frication (as in *Tungri, Tungro, Carvi* etc.).

Old High German also features a weak class-II verb *lobōn* 'to praise' which has cognates in Old Norse *lofa*, Old English *lofian*, Old Frisian *lovia*, Old Saxon *lofōn* and Old Dutch *lovon* 'to praise'; and compare, also, Old Norse *lof*, Old English *lof*, Old Frisian *lof*, Old Saxon *lof*, Old Dutch *lof* and Old High German *lob* 'praise' (< **lubą*). But inherited weak class-III verbs were semantically statives and factitives, unlike weak class-II verbs which were a more productive class (Ringe 2017: 204–5), and the stem of Old English *lufen* and Gothic *lubains* is the morphological equivalent of that attested in the Latin stative verb *lubet, lubēre* 'it pleases, is pleasing, is agreeable' (Kroonen 2013: 341). Three weak verbs seem to have shared the root **lub-* in Germanic: Old English has a weak class-I verb *lufian* 'to love' that appears to have been formed directly from Old English *lufu* < **lubō* 'love' and Old English *lufen* and Gothic *lubains* 'hope' seem to have been derived from a weak class-III verb **lubāną* 'to hope' which given Latin *lubet, lubēre* 'it pleases', presumably originally had a stative meaning 'to be hoping'. It seems likely that the meaning 'to praise' for Old High German *lobēn* is derived from that of the weak class-II verb *lobōn* 'to praise' rather than being inherited, and that the Tienen inscription's *lubait* indicated 'hopes' rather than 'praises'. Yet amatory texts, particularly *amo te* 'I love you', are a relatively common find on Germano-Roman personal items (cf. *CIL* XIII 10018, 14, 18 and 19b; and 10024, 41 and 43b), and a developed meaning 'loves' may also have been intended by the author of the graffito. The names *Lubainis* and *Lubainius* appear more regularly understood as meaning 'love' than 'hope' too given the common employment of the full-grade theme *leub- 'love' in Germanic onomastics.

The second line's *lupiotex* is more difficult to assess. A Roman name *Lupio* is attested in a dedication from Elten (*CIL* XIII 8705), but unless *tex* is taken as a separate word or an abbreviated name, *lupiotex* would seem best to be understood as a dithematic anthroponym (Welkenhuysen in De Clercke 1983: no. 121; Raepsaet-Charlier 2011: 228; Raepsaet-Charlier 2019: 113). A binomen *Lupio Tex()* may have been intended with the second element perhaps indicating a connection with the Texuandri, a tribe from the north of the Civitas Tungrorum mentioned by Pliny (*N.H.* 4, 17), and the size of the gap between the ‹t› and the ‹o› could indicate that *tex* was part of a separate word or name. Inscriptions that mention Texuandri are known epigraphically from Britain (*RIB* 1538), Worms (*CIL* XIII 6239) and Romania (*CIL* III 14214), with the Worms inscription showing what may be a similar abbreviation (*ci(ves) Tex[--]*), although a lacuna follows immediately after the ethnic identification in the text, and the early second-century inscription from Adamklissi records *Veldes Texu(ander)* 'Veldes the Texuandrian'. Roman names derived from Latin *lupus* 'wolf' are well known (cf. *Lupio, Lupicus, Lupinus, Lupicinus, Lupianus, Lupatus, Lupatellus* etc.), but no similar Gaulish or Germanic anthroponyms are attested. If it is a Germanic man's name, however, the first element of *lupiotex* may be cognate with *Lupia*, the ancient name of the river Lippe, or perhaps a variant of the element *luppij-* attested in the Suebian placename *Luppia*. Yet *Luppia* appears to be related to *luppijaną* 'to lift (oneself) up, to hop' and *luppō* 'flea', and without supporting evidence for some semantic development and with a geminate -*pp*-, it seems a less likely candidate for an onomastic element on both phonological and semantic grounds.

Given Latin *lūbricus* 'slippery, slimy', Albrecht Greule (2014: 317–18) explains the name of the Lippe as deriving from an *s*-mobile variant of Old English *slūpan* 'to slip, to slide' and Old High German *sliofan* 'to sneak', but the loss of the *s*- in *lūbricus* is a characteristic only clearly found in Italic, not Germanic. Hans Krahe (1959: 227–28) associated *Lupia* with a series of other river names from eastern Europe that began with *Lup*- (cf. Polish hydronyms such as *Łupawa, Łupca, Łupia, Łupka* and *Łuplanka*) and claimed that the name of the Lippe preserved an inherited *p that had not undergone Grimm's law, a solution supported by Jürgen Udolph (1994: 79–82). But *Lupiotex* may feature the name of the Lippe as its first element, much as the name *Rhenas* recorded in Cologne is clearly derived from the that of the Rhine (*AE* 2012, 976) and the name of the Meuse may be reflected in the Frisiavonic name *Masavo* from Manchester (*RIB* 577) and the Ubian form *Masuva* from Pesch (*AE* 1968, 356).

Similar medial vocalism is also recorded in other Germanic names recorded epigraphically such as the patronymic *Servofredus* borne by the Batavian soldier

Imerix who died in Ivoševci during the first century (*AE* 1971, 299) and the Sunucian name *Friomathin[i]a* attested in a funerary inscription of second- or third-century date from Übach-Palenberg (Nesselhauf and Lieb 1959: no. 188). Yet like the theonym *Ricagambeda*, the patronymic of the Tungrian soldier Chartius son of Tagadunus recorded on an undated tombstone from Wels, Noricum (*AE* 1968, 212), features the expected Germanic composition vowel. *Tagadunus* is presumably a dithematic name that features a derivative of **þag-* 'to be silent' as a first element and **dūnǫ* 'hill' as its second theme, and a similar name *Tagadunius* is recorded on a dedication to the goddess Nehalennia from Colijnsplaat (*AE* 1975, 645), with two of the altars found at the site preserving references to dates of AD 223 and 227 respectively (*AE* 1975, 652 and *AE* 2001, 1488).[8] The composition vowel employed in Germanic names recorded in Roman inscriptions is regularly written -*o*- in finds that date to the first century and the alternation between -*o*- and -*a*- in inscriptions from the late second and early third centuries presumably shows that the composition vowel inherited from Indo-European was being replaced by -*a*- in the West Germanic dialects spoken in Roman Germany and Gallia Belgica at the time.

If it is a compound name, the second onomastic theme (or element) of *Lupiotex* looks like an abbreviation or a root stem, but no form **teks, *tēks, *þeks* or **þēks* is known otherwise in Germanic. Instead, *tex* may reflect a prosodically heavy stem syncopated much as the first element of *Uxperus* seems to be, with an ending comparable to *Gambax*. In that case, *tex* is most obviously to be linked with **þēkaz* 'floating seaweed', although a form of **tehswa-* 'right' might also be a possibility. The ethnonym *Tex(u)andri* appears to reflect **tehswa-* 'right' (and the tribe appear to have lived on the right bank of the Scheldt), but a compound featuring **tehswa-* is difficult to reconcile semantically with *Lupia*. If the first element of *lupiotex* is the name of the Lippe, a cognate of **þēkaz* 'floating seaweed' might seem acceptable if the name (or compound) referred to a freshwater hydrophyte such as duckweed, hornwort or water starwort, all of which are attested as native species in the rivers of the area.

Nothing comparable to a name *Lupiotex* is known from elsewhere in Germanic, however. Instead, the Tienen inscription seems most obviously to be understood as a third-person singular verb followed by a name, with *Lupio Tex()* 'Lupio the Texandrian' a more expected form than a dithematic *Lupiotex*. A dithematic interpretation of *Lupiotex* would also not be consistent with Greule's etymology of the name of the Lippe (that would seem to require that the hydronym had a long vowel in its root) or the syncopation attested in the theonym *Harimella*. Greule's etymology could simply be wrong, however, and the altar

---

8. Meissner (2017) interprets the names in *Taga-* as Celtic, but partly Germanicised.

The Tienen inscription and the dialectal position of Tungrian **261**

to Harimella could be later than the Tienen inscription. Yet Germanic names typically reflect what John Insley (2006) calls 'onomastic dialects' and the lack of obviously comparable names in Germanic undermines the assumption that *Lupiotex* could be a dithematic name. The Tienen inscription seems to confirm a significant feature of Germanic verbal morphology, however. Along with the Tungrian names *Lubainis* and *Lubainius*, the Tienen inscription's *lubait* is evidence that inherited unstressed **ai* is continued in Tungrian without monophthongisation, and this demonstrates that the weak class-III verbs had diphthongs in their stems both in Proto-Germanic (contrary to the reconstructions employed in Kroonen 2013) and in Proto-West Germanic (cf. Ringe and Taylor 2014:24–27, Mees 2023b).

Yet the syntax of the Tienen inscription is also unexpected. In most early runic inscriptions, the subject precedes the verb, much as verb-medial word orders predominate in all of the early Germanic languages except when imperatives are employed. But verb-initial word orders are attested in the Old Germanic languages for verbs other than imperatives and the commonest form of verb-first syntax of this type is narrative inversion, a feature that usually marked 'a turning point, a transition, or a change of pace, in the prose' (Mitchell 1985:II.976). Narrative inversion is usually restricted to 'lively storytelling', but typically only appears within a longer narrative 'signalling an ongoing narrative with no change in participants' (Booth and Beck 2021:20). Rather than narrative inversion, the syntax recorded in the Tienen inscription may instead be presentational, a type of construction employed in existential expressions such as Old Norse *Eru nú hér ...* 'There are now ...' and Old English *Wæs bi eastan þære ...* 'There was to the east ...'. The syntax preserved in the graffito on the bottom of the Tienen dish may have been presentational (at least in a pragmatic sense) because the object that bears it was a gift from Lupio/Lupiotex.

The alternative is to take the verb in the Tienen inscription as an imperative. But an imperative plural would not be expected in a sentence with a singular (vocative) subject such as *Lupio* (or *Lupiotex*) and *Lupio* and *Tex()* cannot be credibly taken as different names without the appearance of a conjunction. Asyndetic orders are sometimes recorded in Old Germanic poetry and in lists (such as those of witnesses to deeds), but interpreting *lubait* as a plural seems less plausible than as a singular verb given the lack of indication of an obviously plural vocative subject. A graffito featuring an imperative addressed to an unnamed plural subject may be a possible interpretation if *Lupio Tex()* is a syntactically separate form, however, a kind of signature indicating the originator of a wish: 'May you be pleased!' or 'May you love! Lupio Tex(ander)'. Gaulish graffiti featuring invocations that the owner may love drinking are known from southern Gaul, and the Tienen inscription may represent a similar text. The Bassanac graffito *lubi rutenica onobia tiedi ulano celicnon* has been translated as 'Love the Rutenian aqua vitae! May you be prince of the banquet!' and the La Graufesenque inscription *lubi caunonnas sincera* similarly as 'Love the Caunonnian pure (wine)!' (*RIG* L-37 and L-51). Both graffiti are recorded on terra sigillata cups rather than plates and the proper translations are not completely clear, but the parallel use of a verb derived from **lub-* is striking. They suggest that the Tienen inscription is best understood as 'May you love! Lupio Tex(ander)'.

The dialectal position of Tungrian

Tungrian appears to feature several developments that may be employed to situate the dialect within West Germanic. *Annaroveci* appears to feature **-nþ- > -nn-* where Tungrian retained **-nd-* in forms such as *Andangius* (*Tab. Vindob.* 891) and it may well have been the case that cisrhenish Germanic became phonologically distinct from the transrhenine West Germanic dialects before the characteristic developments associated with the Ingvaeonic languages first emerged. Yet the syncopation in Tungrian that is first clearly attested in the Vindolanda inscriptions is paralleled not just in contemporary Suebian ethnonyms and placenames, but also in Germanic names preserved epigraphically in the two provinces of Roman Germany. Robert Nedoma (2016) takes the name of the goddess *Tungabis* as reflecting **Þung(a/i/u)-gabi-* 'splendid-giver', presumably **Þungi-gabi-* given Old English *þyng* 'progress, profit', and although haplology might be suspected in such a formation, other theonyms from the Rhineland appear to confirm the loss of composition vowels after heavy stems in Ubian. Much (1891: 321–23) similarly took the divine epithet *Saitchamim[s]* from Hoven (*CIL* XIII 7915–16) as featuring the Germanic root **saiþa-* 'magic' and an agent noun **hamja-* 'defender' (with syncopation of the composition vowel), and Gutenbrunner (1936: 250) interpreted the street address *Gantunas* in Roman Cologne (*CIL* XIII 10015 99, 105 and 115) as preserving a syncopated form of **Ganta-tūn-* 'geese-market' (although it could, again, be explained by haplology). Tungrian evidently underwent similar phonological development at much the same time, presumably because syncopation of vowels in the second and third syllables of heavy stems occurred in all the West Germanic languages in the late first or early second century.

The syncopation evident in second- and third-century inscriptions also has ramifications for the interpretation of other Tungrian names. Arend Quak (2016: 314) takes *Freioverus* as if it contains the element **wēr-* 'true' rather than **wir-* 'man' (i.e. as a copulative compound 'free and true') and *Veransatus* might similarly be understood as containing a reference to a 'true god' (rather than a 'man god'). Another name *Verveccus* attested on a memorial from Theux (*CIL* XIII

The Tienen inscription and the dialectal position of Tungrian   **263**

3612) may similarly preserve a first element *wēr- 'true' with the composition vowel syncopated, although Leo Weisgerber (1968: 246) preferred to associate *Verveccus* (somewhat irregularly) with the more obviously Celtic formation *Vervicus* (Delamarre 2019–23: II.410). The earliest evidence for lowering (and retraction) of West Germanic *ē > ā may be preserved in the Lugian ethnonym *Nahanarvali* recorded by Tacitus (*Germ.* 43), a form whose initial element can be explained as a West Germanic reflex of *nēhwa- 'near'; compare the second- or third-century epigraphic spelling *Texand(ri)* (*RIB* 1538) where Pliny records *Texuandri* and the Adamklissi inscription has *Texu(ander)* for a similar West Germanic reduction of *-hw- > h-. But examples of retained *ē are widely attested in names from Roman Germany and in inscriptions left behind by Germanic soldiers serving in Northern Britain, with forms such as *Belada* (Weiss-König 2010: 84), *Fersomeris* (*RIB* 926), *Fledimella* (*CIL* XIII 8821), *Retoma* (*CIL* XIII 8614) and *Unsenis* (*RIB* 926) representing some of the clearest instances (cf. *bēla- '(bon)fire, pyre', *mēri- 'famous', *flēdi- 'beauty', *rēti- 'fierce' and *sēhwi- 'visible'). Citing examples of retained *ē in the Malberg glosses, Quak (2016) argues that (contrary to Ringe and Taylor 2014: 10–12) the lowering and retraction of inherited *ē was relatively late in the Low Franconian dialects, and the epigraphic evidence from the Roman period supports a post-Proto-West Germanic date for *ē > ā.

Conclusion

Although very brief, the Tienen inscription appears to preserve the only attested sentence written in a West Germanic dialect spoken in the ancient Civitas Tungrorum, and along with the discoveries from Vindolanda, allows linguistic analysis of Tungrian. As the oldest West Germanic text preserved in Flanders, the Tienen inscription is important evidence for understanding the dialectal development of the Germanic languages spoken in the area, and it seems to have preserved at least one key dialectal feature of Tungrian. Most clearly, the verb records the retention of unstressed *ai and demonstrates that the stem vowel of the weak class-III verbs in Germanic was originally a diphthong. The diphthong recorded in the Tienen inscription is also otherwise consistent with similar vocalism attested in Germanic names recorded in inscriptions from elsewhere in the Civitas Tungrorum, providing key evidence for the earliest history of the Germanic dialects spoken in Belgium.

More broadly, the evidence for Tungrian is crucial for understandings of the early dialectal development of West Germanic. The development of *-nþ- > -nn- apparently recorded on the *Annaroveci* coins suggests that significant dialectal variation was already present in West Germanic in the last century BC. The Tungrian names *Gambax* and *Butimas* recorded in the second century appear to demonstrate that the syncopation of stem vowels in West Germanic began with their loss in heavy trisyllabics at a much earlier date than is usually recognised, and similarly dating forms such as *Uxperus* and *Harimella* appear to show that reduction had begun to occur in heavy disyllabics and also in light disyllabics that featured palatal diphthongs as second elements by this date. By the end of the second century, Tungrian appears to have already completed the main or principal syncopations that are common to each of the medieval West Germanic languages, indicating that West Germanic syncopation is to be dated to a much earlier period than has often been assumed. The evidence is consistent with that attested in early runic inscriptions and in Suebian forms recorded in classical sources, demonstrating that the evidence for the loss of stem vowels in Tungrian was part of a broader West Germanic reduction that appears to have begun in trisyllabics such as the first element of the Suebian ethnonym *Hermunduri*, but that Tungrian names such as *Uxperus* and *Harimella* indicate was completed before the end of the second century.

References

AE = *L'Année épigraphique*. Paris: Presses Universitaires de France, 1888ff.

Birley, A. R. 2001. The names of the Batavians and the Tungrians in the Tabulae Vindobonensis. In Th. Grünewald (ed.), *Germania Inferior: Besiedlung, Gesellschaft und Wirtschaft an der Grenze der römisch-germanischen Welt*, 240–59. Berlin: De Gruyter.

Booth, H. & Ch. Beck. 2021. Verb-second and verb-first in the history of Icelandic. *Journal of Historical Syntax* 5.1–53.

Chambon, J.-P. & Y. Greub. 2000. Données nouvelles pour la linguistique gallo-romane: les legends monétaires Mérovingiennes. *Bulletin de la Société de linguistique de Paris* 95. 147–82.

CIL = *Corpus Inscriptionum Latinarum*, eds. Th. Mommsen et al./Academia litterarum regiae Borussica (and successor bodies). 17 vols. Berlin: Reimer/De Gruyter, 1863ff.

Clay, Ch. L. 2010. *Germanic migrants in Roman Britain: A preliminary study and interdisciplinary approach*. Unpublished PhD dissertation, University of Sheffield.

Clerck, M. de. 1983. *Vicus Tienen: Eerste resultaten van een systematisch onderzoek naar een Romeins verleden*. Tienen: Museum Het Toreke.

Delamarre, X. 2019–23. *Dictionnaire de thèmes nominaux du Gaulois*. 2 vols. Paris: Les Cent Chemins.

Dragendorff, H. 1895. *Terra sigillata: Ein Beitrag zur Geschichte der griechischen und römischen Keramik*. Bonn: Georgi.

Düwel, K., R. Nedoma & S. Oehrl. 2020. *Die südgermanischen Runeninschriften*. Ergänzungsband zum Reallexikon der Germanischen Altertumskunde, 119. Berlin: De Gruyter.

The Tienen inscription and the dialectal position of Tungrian **265**

Eulenburg, K. 1904. Zum Wandel des idg. *o* im Germ. *Indogermanische Forschungen* 16. 35–40.

Falk, H. 1928. Prefiks-studier. In J. Brøndum-Nielsen et al. (eds.), *Festskrift til Finnur Jónsson 29 Maj 1928*, 339–50. Copenhagen: Levin & Kunksgaard.

Findell, M. 2012. *Phonological evidence from the Continental runic inscriptions.* Ergänzungsband zum Reallexikon der Germanischen Altertumskunde, 79. Berlin: De Gruyter.

Finke, H. 1927. Neue Inschriften. *Berichte der Römisch-Germanischen Kommission* 17. 1–107 and 198–231.

Förstemann, E. 1900. *Altdeutsches Namenbuch.* 2nd edn. Bonn: Hanstein.

Frings, Th. 1948. *Grundlegung einer Geschichte der deutschen Sprache.* Halle (Saale): Niemeyer.

Greule, A. 2014. *Deutsches Gewässernamenbuch.* Berlin: De Gruyter.

Grienberger, Th. von. 1896. Review of W. Golther, *Handbuch der germanischen Mythololologie* (Leipzig 1895). *Zeitschrift für die österreichischen Gymnasien* 47. 999–1010.

Gutenbrunner, S. 1936. *Die germanischen Götternamen der antiken Inschriften.* Halle (Saale): Niemeyer.

Haalebos, J. K. 1977. *Zwammerdam — Nigrum Pullum. Ein Auxiliarkastell am Niedergermanischen Limes* (Cingula 3). Amsterdam: Universiteit van Amsterdam.

Harðarson, Jón Axel. 2023. Das Wort für 'Heer' im Germanischen und seine Formen in komponierten Personennamen und Ableitungen. In M. Marti Heinzle & L. Thöny (eds.), *Swe gamelip ist. Studien zur vergleichenden germanischen Sprachwissenschaft. Festschrift für Ludwig Rübekeil zum 65. Geburtstag*, 227–63. Heidelberg: Winter.

Heidermanns, F. 1993. *Etymologisches Wörterbuch der germanischen Primäradjektive.* Berlin: De Gruyter.

Hines, J. 2019. Practical runic literacy in the Late Anglo-Saxon Period: Inscriptions on lead sheet. In U. Lenker & L. Kornexl (eds.), *Anglo-Saxon Micro Texts*, 29–59. Berlin: De Gruyter.

Insley, J. 2006. Early Germanic personal names and onomastic dialects. In A. J. Johnston, F. von Mengden & S. Thim (eds.), *Language and text: Current perspectives on English and Germanic historical linguistics*, 113–32. Heidelberg: Winter.

Kaiser, L. 2021. *Runes Across the North Sea from the Migration Period and Beyond: An Annotated Edition of the Old Frisian Runic Corpus* (Ergänzungsband zum Reallexikon der Germanischen Altertumskunde, 126). Berlin: De Gruyter.

Krahe, H. 1959. Eigennamen und germanische Lautverschiebung. In J. Vendryès (eds.), *Mélanges de linguistique et de philologie, Fernand Mossé in memoriam*, 225–30. Paris: Didier.

Krahe, H. 1961. Altgermanische Kleinigkeiten. *Indogermanische Forschungen* 66. 35–43.

Krause, W. & H. Jankuhn. 1966. *Die Runeninschriften in älteren Futhark.* Göttingen: Vandenhoeck & Ruprecht.

Kroonen, G. 2013. *Etymological dictionary of Proto-Germanic.* Leiden: Brill.

Marchot, P. 1930. Le pagus Vellavus. *Revue belge de philologie et d'histoire* 9. 897–98.

Martens, M. 2012. *Life and culture in the Roman small town of Tienen: Transformations of cultural behaviour by comparative analysis of material culture assemblages.* PhD Dissertation, Vrije Universiteit Amsterdam.

Maurer, F. 1942. *Nordgermanen und Alemannen: Studien zur germanischen und frühdeutschen Sprachgeschichte, Stammes- und Volkskunde*. Strasbourg: Hünenburg.

Mees, B. 2022. Batavian *Pero* and Germanic *perō 'pear'. *Amsterdamer Beiträge zur älteren Germanistik* 82. 1–14.

Mees, B. 2023a. *The English language before England*. New York: Routledge.

Mees, B. 2023b. Early epigraphic evidence for Germanic weak class-III verbs. *Beiträge zur Geschichte der deutschen Sprache und Literatur* 145. 347–64.

Meissner, T. 2017. Tagadunus und Genossen. In I. Hajnal, D. Kölligen & K. Zipser (eds.), *Miscellanea Indogermanica. Festschrift für José Luis Garcia Ramon zum 65. Geburtstag*, 471–76. Innsbruck: Institut für Sprachen und Literaturen der Universität Innsbruck.

Meyer, E. H. 1891. *Germanische Mythologie*. Berlin: Mayer & Müller.

Miller, K. 1916. *Itineraria Romana: Römische Reisewege an der Hand der Tabula Peutingeriana*. Stuttgart: Strecker & Schröder

Mitchell, B. 1985. *Old English syntax*. 2 vols. Oxford: Clarendon.

Much, R. 1891. Germanische matronennamen. *Zeitschrift für deutsches Altertum und deutsche Literatur* 35. 315–24.

Much, R. 1892. Dea Harimella. *Zeitschrift für deutsches Altertum und deutsche Litteratur* 36. 44–47.

Much, R. 1920. *Der Name Germanen*. Vienna: Hölder.

Much, R. 1926. Harimella, Harimalla. *Zeitschrift für deutsches Altertum und deutsche Litteratur* 63. 19–21.

Much, R. 1936. Das Problem des Germanen-Namens. In H. Arntz (ed.), *Germanen und Indogermanen: Volkstum, Sprache, Kultur. Festschrift für Herman Hirt*, vol. 2, 507–31. Heidelberg: Winter.

Nedoma, R. 2016. Dea Tungabis. *Beiträge zur Namenforschung* ns 51. 39–54.

Nesselhauf, H. 1937. Neue Inschriften aus dem römischen Germanien und den angrenzenden Gebieten. *Bericht der Römisch-Germanischen Kommission* 27. 51–134.

Nesselhauf, H. & H. Lieb. 1959. Dritter Nachtrag zum CIL XIII. Inschriften aus den germanischen Provinzen und dem Treverergebiet. *Berichte der Römisch-Germanischen Kommission* 40. 120–229.

Neumann, G. 1983. Die Sprachverhältnisse in den germanischen Provinzen des Römischen Reichs. In H. Temporini & W. Haase (eds.), *Aufsteig und Niedergang der Römischen Welt*, II.29.2.1061–88. Berlin: De Gruyter.

Neumann, G. 1987. Die germanischen Matronen-Beinamen. In G. Bauchhenß & G. Neumann (eds.), *Matronen und verwandte Gottheiten: Ergebnisse eines Kolloquiums veranstaltet von der Göttinger Akademiekommission für die Altertumskunde Mittel- und Nordeuropas*, 103–32. Köln: Rheinland-Verlag.

Neumann, G. 1998. Germanen, Germania, Germanische Altertumskunde. II. Sprache und Dichtung. A. Name und Namen. In H. Beck, H. Steuer & D. Timpe (eds.), *Reallexikon der Germanischen Altertumskunde*, 2nd edn, vol. XI, 259–65. Berlin: De Gruyter.

Nielsen, H. F. 1989. *The Germanic languages: Origins and early dialectal interrelations*. Tuscaloosa: University of Alabama Press.

Nielsen, H. F. 2000. *The early Runic language of Scandinavia: Studies in Germanic dialect geography*. Heidelberg: Winter.

Pennant, Th. 1776. *A tour in Scotland, MDCCLXXII, Part 2*. London: White.

Quak, A. 2016. Urgermanisches $\bar{e}_1$ im Kontinentalgermanischen. In A. Bannink & W. Honselaar (eds.), *From variation to iconicity: Festschrift for Olga Fischer on the occasion of her 65th birthday*, 311–330. Amsterdam: Pegasus.

Raepsaet, G. 2013. Ethnogenèse de la *civitas Tungrorum* et la formation de la Province de Germanie. *L'Antiquité classique* 82. 111–148.

Raepsaet-Charlier, M.-Th. 2011. Les noms germaniques: adaptation et latinisation de l'onomastique en Gaule Belgique et Germanie inférieure. In M. Dondin-Payre (ed.), *Les noms de personnes dans l'Empire romain. Transformations, adaptation, évolution*, 203–34. Bordeaux: Ausonius.

Raepsaet-Charlier, M.-Th. 2019. Onomastique et société en cité des Tongres. *Revue Belge de philologie et d'histoire* 97. 95–136.

RIB = The Roman Inscriptions of Britain, I: Inscriptions on stone, ed. R.G. Collingwood and Richard P. Wright. Oxford: Clarendon, 1965.

RIG = Recueil des inscriptions gauloises (Supplément à «Gallia» 45). Ed. P.-M. Duval et al. 4 vols. 1985–2002. Paris: CNRS.

Ringe, D. 2017. *From Proto-Indo-European to Proto-Germanic* (A Linguistic History of English 1). 2nd edn. Oxford: University Press.

Ringe, D. & A. Taylor. 2014. *The development of Old English* (A Linguistic History of English 2). Oxford: Oxford University Press.

Roymans, N. & J. Aarts. 2009. Coin use in a dynamic frontier region. Late Iron Age coinages in the Lower Rhine area. *Journal of Archaeology in the Low Countries* 1. 5–26.

Schleicher, A. 1860. *Die deutsche Sprache*. Stuttgart: Cotta.

Schönfeld, M. 1911. *Wörterbuch der altgermanischen Personen- und Völkernamen*, Heidelberg: Winter.

Schröder, E. 1924. Bunte lese II. *Zeitschrift für deutsches Altertum* 61. 59–60.

Schuhmann, R. 2014. Zur Endung runisch-altfriesisches *-u* und zur Entwicklung der Endung nom.sg.m. a-St. urgermanisches *-az*. *Amsterdamer Beiträge zur älteren Germanistik* 73. 397–419.

Smith, A.H. 1956. *English place-name elements* (English Place-Name Society 25/26). 2 vols. Cambridge: Cambridge University Press.

Stiles, P. 2013. The pan-West Germanic isoglosses and the sub-relationships of West Germanic to other branches. *NOWELE* 66. 5–38.

Tab. Vindol. = Bowman, A K. & J.D. Thomas. 1974–2003. *Vindolanda: The writing-tablets/The Vindolanda writing-tablets*. Newcastle upon Tyne: Graham, and London: British Museum Press; and A.K. Bowman, J.D. Thomas & R.S.O. Tomlin. 2010–19. The Vindolanda writing-tablets (tabulae Vindolandenses IV). *Britannia* 41. 187–224, 42. 113–44 and 50. 225–51.

Udolph, J. 1994. *Namenkundliche Studien zum Germanenprobleme*. Berlin: De Gruyter.

Vanwinckenroye, W. 1967. *Gallo-Romeins aardewerck van Tongeren*. Tongeren: Provincial Gallo-Romeins Museum.

Vanwinckenroye, W. 2001. Über Atuatuca, Cäsar und Ambiorix. In M. Lodewijckx (ed.), *Belgian Archaeology in a European Setting II*, 63–67. Leuven: Leuven University Press.

Wagner, N. 1983. Zum -a von Chariovalda und Catvalda. *Sprachwissenschaft* 8. 429–436.

Wagner, N. 2002. *Fledimella*, Harimella** und *Baudihillia*. Historische Sprachforschung* 115. 93–98.

Wagner, N. 2018. Ricagambeda. *Beiträge zur Namenforschung* ns 53. 339–42.

Weisgerber, J.L. 1954. Zur Namengut der Germani cisrhenani. *Annalen des Historischen Vereins für den Niederrhein* 155/156. 35–61.

Weisgerber, J.L. 1968. *Die Namen der Ubier.* Cologne: Westdeutscher Verlag.

Weiss-König, S. 2010. *Graffiti auf römischer Gefäßkeramik aus der Bereich der Colonia Ulpia Traiana / Xanten.* Mainz: von Zabern.

Wrede, F. 1924. Ingwäonisch und Westgermanisch. *Zeitschrift für Mundartforschung* 1. 270–84.

Der Name der Insel Thule

Robert Nedoma
Universität Wien

In the 330s or 320s BC, the Greek explorer Pytheas of Massalia undertook a pioneering voyage to northern Europe. In his report Περὶ τοῦ ὠκεανοῦ ('On the ocean'), which has come down to us only as a few excerpts quoted by later authors, Pytheas mentions the island Θούλη, which is situated in the far north, six days' sail from Britain. There is uncertainty as to the location of this island: the Faroe Islands, Iceland, or perhaps somewhere in Norway. Much effort has been spent on explaining Θούλη as a Germanic toponym but none of the proposals is conclusive. It might well be an exonym of Greek origin coined by Pytheas himself. A sound etymology in phonological, morphological and semantic respects can be presented: Θούλη = $^{*}t^h\bar{u}l\bar{e}$ seems to reflect the substantivized feminine form of the adjective PIE $^{*}d^huh_2ló$- 'smoky, steamy, misty, foggy' (: PIE $^{*}d^h\underline{u}eh_2$-, $^{*}d^huh_2$- 'produce smoke, steam') which, following the derivational pattern -o- → -i-, is the base for the noun $^{*}d^huh_2li$- f. > OI dhūli-, dhūlī 'dust, powder', cp. Lith. dúlis m., dúlė f. 'smoke, mist, fog' etc. The name Θούλη meaning 'the misty, foggy one' would have correspondences in, for example, *Fog Islands* (British Columbia, Canada) and *Eilean a' Cheò* 'island of mist' (cp. OIr. *ceó* m./f. 'mist'), the Gaelic name of the Isle of Skye.

1. Thule in den Quellen

Der erste Reisende, von dem Nachrichten über Nordwest- bzw. Nordeuropa überliefert sind, war Pytheas von Massalia (Πυθέας ὁ Μασσαλιώτης, *Pytheas Massiliensis*) zur Zeit Alexanders des Großen. Der von ihm verfaßte Periplus Περὶ τοῦ ὠκεανοῦ 'Über das Weltmeer'[1] ist als solcher nicht erhalten; wir kennen ledig-

---

[1]. Die Pytheas-Fragmente zitiere ich nach der noch immer maßgeblichen Edition von Mette 1952 (mit Lesarten). Textwiedergaben bieten ferner Roseman 1994, Bianchetti 1998 und Scott 2022 (jeweils mit Kommentar); eine deutsche Übersetzung liefert Stichtenoth 1959. Aus der umfangreichen Literatur zu Pytheas und seiner Expedition nenne ich hier nur Gisinger 1963; Timpe 1989: 325–332; Roseman 1994: 148–159; Bianchetti 1998: 27–80; Schmedt 2020: 519–521; Scott 2022: 5–23, 127–133, 138–160, 165–183.

https://doi.org/10.1075/nss.34.15ned
Available under the CC BY-NC-ND 4.0 license. © 2025 John Benjamins Publishing Company

lich ein wörtliches Zitat[2] und ein paar Paraphrasen und Erwähnungen in Werken anderer antiker Autoren. Vieles bleibt daher offen — so können über die Person des Pytheas und die näheren Umstände seiner Expedition (Zweck bzw. Anlaß, Finanzierung, Ausstattung, Ziel, genaue Route, Zeit und Dauer der Reise) nur mehr oder weniger unsichere Überlegungen angestellt werden.

Pytheas ist wahrscheinlich in den 330er oder 320er Jahren v. Chr. aus seiner Heimatstadt abgesegelt.[3] Von der karthagischen Seemacht unbehelligt durch die Straße von Gibraltar nach Gadeira (Cadiz) gelangt, folgte er der Atlantikküste entlang bis zum Vorgebirge Kabaion (wohl Pointe du Raz, Bretagne) und der Insel Uxisamē (Ouessant). Von dort setzte der Massaliote nach Britannien über, das er ganz umrundete; dies war ihm Anlaß, über eine Insel namens Thule zu berichten, die er offenbar nicht betrat. Nach der Rückkehr zum Ärmelkanal erkundete Pytheas die festländische Nordseeküste, deren Bewohner von ihm als Skythen angesehen wurden. Ob und wie weit die Reise über die Deutsche Bucht hinaus in die Ostsee führte, läßt sich nicht entscheiden. Über die Heimfahrt nach Massalia liegen schließlich keinerlei Nachrichten vor.[4]

Der Wahrheitsgehalt von Pytheas' Reisebericht wurde in der nachfolgenden antiken Literatur mehrfach bezweifelt, vor allem von Polybios und Strabo.[5] Allem Dafürhalten nach muß der Massaliote jedoch tatsächlich bis an das Europäische Nordmeer (die Norwegische See) vorgedrungen sein, denn seine Schilderungen treffen die bis dahin unbekannten Gegebenheiten des hohen Nordens ziemlich gut. Besondere Aufmerksamkeit haben die Angaben über die Insel Thule (Θούλη) erfahren:

---

2. Gemin. 6,9: ἐδείκνυον ἡμῖν οἱ βάρβαροι ὅπου ὁ ἥλιος κοιμᾶται 'Die Einheimischen zeigten uns, wo sich die Sonne schlafen legt' (Mette 1952:28); vgl. Kosm. Indik. II,80 (Mette 1952:28–29 = Wolska-Conus 1968:399).

3. Ein — freilich nicht schlagendes — Indiz ist, daß Aristoteles (gest. 322 v. Chr.) Pytheas nicht erwähnt und ihn daher offenbar nicht gekannt hat, sein Schüler Dikaiarchos dagegen schon (Polyb. bei Strab. II,4,2; Mette 1952:27).

4. Zur Rekonstruktion der Reiseroute des Pytheas s. etwa Gisinger 1963:324–351; Timpe 1989:325–330; Scott 2022:170–179 (mit Karten). In seinem Anspruch, im Osten bis zum Tanaïs (Don) gekommen zu sein (Strab. II,4,1; Mette 1952:26), greift Pytheas allerdings sehr wahrscheinlich fehl.

5. Ein Parteigänger in jüngerer Zeit ist von See (2004:113–130; 2006:416–420): auch er meint, daß „'Thule' ein rein literarisches Produkt ist" (2004:127 = 2006:419).

Der Name der Insel Thule 271

1. Thule liegt von Britannien aus eine Sechstagefahrt in nördlicher Richtung entfernt.[6]
2. Thule ist die nördlichste britische Insel und liegt am Polarkreis; sie ist die nördlichste aller erwähnten Inseln.[7]
3. Auf Thule gibt es zur Zeit der Sommersonnenwende keine oder nur kurze Nächte (für die Wintersonnenwende gilt dasselbe für die Tage).[8]
4. Thule liegt in der Nähe des gefrorenen Meeres.[9]
5. In Thule und Umgebung existiert ein Land-Meer-Luft-Gemenge, in dem alle Dinge schweben, das einer 'Meerlunge' (einer Quallenart) ähnelt und undurchdringlich ist.[10]
6. Die Bewohner der Gegenden nahe der Frostzone (und Thules?) essen Hirse, wildes Gemüse, wilde Früchte und Wurzeln; wo es Getreide und Honig gibt, gewinnen sie daraus ein Getränk.[11]

---

6. Strab. I,4,2, Plin. nat. hist. II,187 (Mette 1952:19, 33). Plinius fügt hinzu (nat. hist. IV,104; Mette 1952:32), man segle von einer großen Insel namens Berrice (mit Mainland Orkney zu identifizieren?) aus nach Thule. Seiner Angabe *sex dierum navigatione* eine einigermaßen genaue Weglänge abzugewinnen, ist aber ein schwieriges Unterfangen. Für eine Tagesetappe sind — wohlgemerkt: unter günstigen Bedingungen — vermutlich ca. 90–110 km zu veranschlagen (vgl. z.B. Kleineberg et al. 2010:104; Lelgemann 2012:338; Schmedt 2020:520 mit Anm. 17; Scott 2022:xviii, 170–177); dazu kommt noch eine mögliche Nachtstrecke. — Nach einer wohl interpolierten Passage bei Solinus (22,9 [17]; Mommsen 1895:219) dauert die Reise von den Orkaden nach Thule indessen fünf Tage und fünf Nächte.

7. Strab. II,5,8, Solin. 22,9 [11] (Mette 1952:23, Mommsen 1895:101–102); Strab. IV,5,5, Plin. nat. hist. IV,104 (Mette 1952:25, 32). Die elliptische Formulierung *ultima [omnium insularum] Thule* ist seit Verg. Georg. I,30 (Holzberg 2016:116) sprichwörtlich.

8. Mitternachtssonne zum Sommersolstitium: Plin. nat. hist. IV,104, Kosm. Indik. II,80 (Mette 1952:32, 29 = Wolska-Conus 1968:399), Solin. 22,9 [11] (Mommsen 1895:102); Pomp. Mela III,57 (Brodersen 1994:166; Abhängigkeit von Pytheas unklar). Kurze Nächte zum Sommersolstitium: Gemin. 6,9 (zwei bis drei Äquinoktialstunden; Mette 1952:28), Steph. Byz. θ,54 (vier Stunden; Billerbeck & Zubler 2011:246). An anderer Stelle schreibt Plinius (nat. hist. II,187, VI,219; Mette 1952:33 *bis*) unter Berufung auf Pytheas, wie am Nordpol herrsche auf Thule sechs Monate Tag und sechs Monate Nacht (so auch, von Plinius abhängig, Mart. Cap. VI,595; Willis 1983:209).

9. Strab. I,4,2, Plin. nat. hist. IV,104, Solin. 22,9 [11] (Mette 1952:19, 32; Mommsen 1895:102); vgl. Strab. IV,5,5 (Mette 1952:25).

10. Strab. II,4,1 (Mette 1952:26). Zum einen läßt sich nicht recht klären, wie dieses alles umschließende Band (δεσμὸν [...] τῶν ὅλων ~ *vincula rerum* Sen. Med. 376; Zwierlein 1986:138), das weder betreten noch befahren werden kann, zu verstehen ist (zur Stelle Mette 1952:7–8; Roseman 1994:127–130). Zum anderen bleibt auch dunkel, was Pytheas zu dem Vergleich mit einer 'Meerlunge' (πλεύμων θαλάττιος ~ *halipleumon* Plin. nat. hist. XXXII,149; König et al. 1995:102) veranlaßt hat.

Die auf uns gekommenen Nachrichten sind dürftig und zudem auch nicht widerspruchsfrei (keine oder immerhin kurze Nächte zur Sommersonnenwende?, aufgrund des Elementenkonglomerates unbewohnbares oder doch zu bewirtschaftendes Land?). Die geographische Lage hat man auf verschiedene Art zu bestimmen versucht und Thule auf den Shetlands, den Färöern, auf Island, in Mittel- und Nordnorwegen, Südschweden, ja sogar in Finnland vermutet.[12] Ohne hier auf Details einzugehen, muß es bei einem *non liquet* bleiben, denn keine der vorgeschlagenen Lokalisierungshypothesen läßt sich mit allen aus der Pytheas-Tradition bekannten Angaben — insbesondere zur Reisedauer, zur Lage nördlich von Britannien nahe des Polarkreises bzw. des Eismeeres und zur Landesbeschaffenheit — glatt vereinbaren. Es ist auch die Frage, ob sich Pytheas entgegen der damaligen Praxis der Küstenschiffahrt tatsächlich auf eine gefahrbringende Reise über ein ihm unbekanntes offenes Meer nach Island oder Norwegen gewagt hat; erst die Wikinger haben ca. 1.000 Jahre später den rauhen Nordatlantik planmäßig befahren.

2. Der Name Thule

Die griechischen Autoren (allen voran Strabon, Geminos, Ptolemaios, Stephanos Byzantios und Prokop) schreiben den Inselnamen durchwegs Θουλη (Θούλη), in der lateinischen Literatur begegnet *Thule* (z.B. bei Vergil, Seneca) neben häufi-

---

11. Strab. IV,5,5 (Mette 1952:25). Handelt es sich um einen Topos, den der angriffige Strabo dem Pytheas unterschoben hat? Unecht ist jedenfalls die Schilderung des Solinus (22,9 [17]; Mommsen 1895:219), nach der die Bewohner Thules Viehzucht betreiben, sich von Obst, Kräutern sowie Milch ernähren und 'Frauen gemeinsam haben'; vgl. Timpe 1989:327.

12. Von den unzähligen Versuchen der Verortung Thules nenne ich hier nur: Müllenhoff 1870:389–408 (Shetlands, nicht plausibel); Koepp 1951/52:9–10 (Westschweden, gleichermaßen nicht plausibel); Stichtenoth 1959:30, 76–78 (Finnland, unwahrscheinlich); Gisinger 1963:336–344, 365–366 (Island); Timpe 1989:327–328 (Färöer); Bianchetti 1998:61–64 (Norwegen); Cunliffe 2003:125–135 (Island); Kleineberg et al. 2010:105–112 bzw. Lelgemann 2012 (Mittelnorwegen: Smøla); McPhail 2014:251–255 (Norwegen); Schmedt 2020:520–521 (Island etwas wahrscheinlicher als Norwegen); Scott 2022:153–156 (Norwegen). Die von Agricola bei seinem Flottenunternehmen a. 83 n. Chr. von den Orkaden aus gesichtete und von ihm zu Thule erklärte Insel (Tac. Agr. 10,4; Delz & von Ungern-Sternberg 2010:8), wird eine der Shetlands gewesen sein. Auf deren Breite (scil. 63°) erscheint Thule auch bei Ptolemaios am nördlichen Rand der Ökumene (Ptol. I,7,1, II,3,32, VIII,3,3 [vier Äquinoktialstunden]; Stückelberger & Graßhoff 2017:68, 156, 775). Im 6. Jahrhundert wird Thule von Prokop auf Skandinavien allgemein bezogen (Prok. b. Goth. II,15,4 [u.ö.]; Haury & Wirth 2001:215). Adam von Bremen identifiziert Thule im späten 11. Jahrhundert mit Island (Adam Brem. IV,36 [35]; Trillmich 1961:484), und dies verfestigt sich dann in der weiteren, vor allem altisländischen Literatur zur herrschenden Ansicht (Belege bei Metzenthin 1941:108).

gerem *Thyle* (so u.a. Pomponius Mela, Plinius, Tacitus, Solinus) und seltenerem *Tyle* (etwa bei Plinius, Martianus Capella).[13] Es ist daher von Θούλη /tʰúlē/ bei Pytheas auszugehen: im 4. Jahrhundert v. Chr. gibt ‹θ› den aspirierten Okklusiv gr. (ion.-att.) /tʰ/ wieder, und ‹ου› steht für monophthongiertes gr. (ion.-att.) (/ọ̄/ >) /ū/.[14] Freilich können ‹θ› /tʰ/ und ‹ου› /ū/ auch als Substitute für die fremdsprachlichen Laute (germ.) /θ/ und /ŭ/ gedient haben.

Fast durchwegs hat man germanische Herkunft des Inselnamens angenommen; in diesem Fall kann Thule nicht mit Island identifiziert werden, das ja erst in den 870er Jahren von germanischsprachigen Nordleuten besiedelt und benannt worden ist.[15] Keine der bisher vorgebrachten Etymologien vermag indessen zu überzeugen:[16]

Hofmann (1865:15–17) verweist auf einen aus *Tumlehed* (Ort auf der westschwedischen Insel Hisingen) gewonnenen Inselnamen (aon.) *Þumla, für den er ai. *timira-* Adj. 'dunkel, finster', *tamāla-* m. 'Garcinia xanthochymus (Baum mit dunkler Rinde)' und as. *thimm* Adj. 'dunkel' (urgerm. *þemzá-) vergleicht. Die Annahme eines Ausfalls von inlautendem *m* ist allerdings schwierig,[17] und zudem sind schwundstufige *l*-Bildungen zu uridg. *temH- 'finster sein'[18] nicht bezeugt.

Much (1918:308) stellt Θούλη zu gr. τύλη (τύλη) f. 'Wulst, Schwiele, Polster' und aksl. *tylъ* m. 'Rücken, Nacken'.[19] Dabei handelt sich um schwundstufige

---

13. Belege (einschließlich der vorhin [1.] im Text erwähnten): LaN I:702; Scheungraber & Grünzweig 2014:340. — Mit der von Solinus erwähnten indischen Insel *Tylos* (Solin. 52,49 [17]; Mommsen 1895:192) hat das nordische Thule entgegen von See (2004:128–130; 2006:418) nichts zu tun.

14. Threatte 1980:238 (ΟΥ ọ̄ > ū), 469 (‹θ› tʰ); Bubeník 1983:45 (ΟΥ ou > ọ̄), 105 (‹θ› tʰ); Allen 1987:22–23 (‹θ› tʰ), 66–67 (‹υ› y), 76–77 (‹ου› ọ̄ > ū). Die betreffenden Lautwandelprozesse haben im Ionisch-Attischen bzw. in der Koine zu folgenden Zeiten stattgefunden (ungefähre Angaben, allesamt v. Chr.): ion.-att. u > y 7./6. Jh., ou > ọ̄ 6./5. Jh., ọ̄ > ū 4. Jh., tʰ > θ 2. Jh.

15. Ari Þorgilsson, *Íslendingabók*, c. 1 (Jónsson 1930:9); *Landnámabók*, c. 8 (Jónsson 1900:7 [H], 132 [S]).

16. Auf Deutungen der ältesten Forschung, die auf bloßen Anklängen beruhen (Referate: Nansen 1911:350–351 Anm. 37; Hennig 1923:115–116), brauche ich hier nicht einzugehen.

17. Im Germanischen ist *m* vor *l* keineswegs geschwunden (und erscheint einzelsprachlich zumeist sogar durch epenthetisches *b* gestützt), z.B. urgerm. *semla- Adj. 'dauernd [o.ä.]' > ae. *simble(s)* 'immer, stets, fortwährend', ahd. *simbal* 'unablässig', vgl. as. *sim(b)la* Adv. 'immer, stets', got. *simle* Adv. 'einst, vormals'.

18. Vgl. IEW:1063–1064 s.v. *tem(ə)-; EWAia I:626 s.v. *TAM^l*.

19. Mit Vorbehalt zustimmend IEW:1081; Scheungraber & Grünzweig 2014:342 („in etwa mit der Bedeutung 'Erhebung, Berg'"). Aus semantischen Gründen bleibt ein Zusammenhang mit ved. *túla-* n. 'Rispe, Wedel, Büschel' unklar (EWAia I:662). — Gutenbrunner (1939:60–61) verbindet zwei Hypothesen, indem er Θούλη mit Much und Noreen (1920:25) als 'Erhebung'

l-Bildungen zur Wurzel uridg. **teu̯h₂-* 'schwellen, stark werden';[20] die Konstruktionsbedeutung wäre dann wohl 'Anschwellung'. Selbst wenn man eine Bedeutungsverschiebung 'Anschwellung' → 'Erhebung, Höhe, Berg' akzeptiert, erhält man keinen geeigneten Benennungsbegriff für eine Insel oder eine ganze Landschaft.[21]

Dieser Einwand gilt auch für einen Vorschlag von Noreen (1920: 25), der kurzvokalisches **Þulā* ansetzt und in ved. *tulā́-* f. 'Waage, Waagebalken' eine Entsprechung erblickt; den Weg zu 'Erhebung' weist ihm zugehöriges *tulayati* 'hebt auf' (auch: 'wägt').[22] Die Primärstammbildungen zur Wurzel uridg. **telh₂-* deuten indessen auf ein semantisches Spektrum 'aufheben' (lat. *tollere*), 'tragen' (toch. B *täl⁽ā⁾-*), 'ertragen, dulden' (got. *Þulan*, aisl. *Þola*) etc.;[23] es fehlt jedenfalls bei den zugehörigen Nomina an Evidenz für eine Bedeutung '(sich) erheben' bzw. 'Erhebung'.

Hingegen meint Collinder (1936: 96–97), der Name habe urgerm. **Þoulā* gelautet, das mit Übergang von neutralem Plural zu kollektivem femininen Singular in awn. *Þaul* f. 'Klemme' (auch in *Þaular-vágr* m. 'enge Bucht, in der man leicht festsitzen kann') fortgesetzt sei; Θούλη gilt ihm demnach als 'die (engen) Fjorde'.[24] Der den germanischen Lautgesetzen widersprechende Vokalismus (*-ou-, -ā*) wird

---

faßt und mit Reuter (1938: 26–27) auf das Toponym awn. *Þulunes* verweist; namengebend sei ein „am Meere gelegenes Gebiet *Thule* 'Höhe'" in der Nähe von Bergen. Offenbar ebenfalls im Anschluß an Much, aber ohne diesen zu erwähnen, erklärt Koepp (1951/52: 17, 52) Θούλη alternativ als 'Grabhügelinsel' ("Kurzform von thul-awjū") oder 'Hügelgräberland' (Kollektivum auf -η); verwandt sei awn. *Þulr*, ae. *Þyle* (urgerm. **Þuli-* m. 'wortgewaltiger Sprecher, weiser Redner'; dazu unten), dem er eine Bedeutung 'Grabhügelsprecher, Mann vom Ahnengrab, Ahnensprecher' zumißt. Die Deutungen Koepps vermögen angesichts ihrer lautlichen, morphologischen und semantischen Beliebigkeit nicht einzuleuchten.

20. LIV²: 639–640; vgl. IEW: 1080–1085 s.v. *tēu-, təu-, teu̯ə- tu̯ō-, tū̆-*. Ob auch ae. *Þoll* 'Ruderpflock, Dolle', aisl. *Þollr* m. 'Baum, Pfosten', nhd. *Dolle* etc. (urgerm. **Þulla-* < **tul-no-*?) hierher gehören, ist aus semantischen Gründen fraglich.

21. Der Name der *Tylangii** (Avien. *ora* 674; Stichtenoth 1968: 48, 94), in denen manche Alpengermanen des 6. Jahrhunderts v. Chr. erblickt haben, bleibt jedenfalls aus dem Spiel (s. vor allem Schmeja 1968: 15–22). Auch mit dem Ethnonym *Tulingi* (Caes. b. Gall. I,25,6 [u.ö.]; Hering 1987: 11) wird kein Zusammenhang bestehen (Sitzmann & Grünzweig 2008: 285–286).

22. Dabei scheint Noreen (1920: 25) ved. *tulā́-* 'Waage, Waagebalken' als Verbalabstraktum 'das Aufheben' (→ 'Erhebung') zu *tulay°* anzusehen. Die Verhältnisse liegen jedoch umgekehrt: das Verb ist denominal gebildet.

23. LIV²: 622–623; vgl. IEW: 1060–1061 s.v. *1. tel-, telə-, tlē(i), tlā-*; EWAia I: 658–659 s.v. *tulā́-*.

24. Thule wird von Collinder in (Nord-)Norwegen lokalisiert; zustimmend Lid 1942: 52–54 (spezifische Bedeutung: 'innerster Teil eines Fjords') und Svennung 1974: 24 (Benennungsbegriff seien die "von steilen Felsenwänden begrenzten Labyrinthe" der norwegischen Küstengegenden).

indessen nicht erklärt, und für die Wiedergabe des haupttonigen Diphthongs urgerm. /au/ (eventuell [ɔu] realisiert?) wäre im Griechischen ‹αυ› /au̯/ (Quantitätskorrelation) oder ‹ωυ› /ɔ̄u̯/ (Qualitätskorrelation) zu erwarten, nicht aber gr. ‹ου›, das zu Pytheas' Zeiten bereits /ū/ repräsentiert. Auch diese Deutung muß man daher auf sich beruhen lassen.

Reuter (1938: 26–27) verweist auf das Toponym awn. *Þulu-nes* '-vorgebirge' (in *Vǫrs*, heute *Voss*, ca. 65 km nordöstlich von Bergen),[25] dessen Bestimmungselement er zu aisl. *þula* f. 'Aufzählung (in metrischer Form), Merkversreihe' stellt. Die anfechtbare Deutung (als 'Reihe' → *'Langgestrecktes') scheitert auch an der Realprobe: die heutige Kommune Voss liegt am Ende des 183 km langen Hardangerfjords und wäre von Pytheas nicht als Insel erkannt und auch nicht verkannt worden.

Schließlich sieht Grønvik (2006: 112–114) in Θούλη den Genetiv Pl. (des Antezedens) von aisl. *þulr* (= ae. *þyle*) < urgerm. **þuli-* m. in lokativischer Funktion; das Toponym bedeute 'im Land der *þulir* („Thuler")' und beziehe sich auf sozial höherstehende Männer, die über magische Kenntnisse, religiöse Macht und Ansehen verfügt hätten. Formal ist diese Erklärung zwar durchaus möglich, der Ausgang *-ē* im Genetiv Pl. der *i*-Stämme ist allerdings ein gotisches Spezifikum und tritt in den nordgermanischen (wie auch in den westgermanischen) Sprachen nicht entgegen.[26] Zudem ist die Grundbedeutung von aisl. *þulr* bzw. ae. *þyle* 'wortgewaltiger Sprecher, weiser Redner',[27] die von Grønvik postulierte Sonderbedeutung 'mächtiger religiös-magischer Spezialist' (o.ä.) kann indessen nicht erhärtet werden. Letztlich ist auch schwer zu begründen, warum es im Gegensatz zu anderen Gegenden (nur) in Thule eine signifikante Konzentration an derartigen Kultpersonen gegeben hätte, die für die Benennung ausschlaggebend gewesen wäre.

Germanische Herkunft des Inselnamens ist allerdings keineswegs zwingend. Keltischer Ursprung ist aus lautlichen Gründen nicht anzunehmen, aber Θούλη kann — was man bislang noch nicht in Erwägung gezogen hat — durchaus aus

---

25. *Landnámabók*, c. 250 / 289 (Jónsson 1900: 92 [H], 207 [S]), normalisiert: *þeir* (scil. Loðmundr und Bjólfr) *fóru til Íslands af Vǫrs af Þulunesi* 'sie fuhren von Vörs, [und zwar] von Thulunes, nach Island'. Zustimmend Jóhannesson 1956: 450. Womöglich ist die nur hier belegte Form *Þulunes* aber, wie bereits Heggstad (1930: 733) vermutet hat, verschriebenes *Þúfunes*, heute *Tunes* (Hof in Arna, Kommune Bergen).

26. Der reguläre Ausgang ist urgerm. **-ijõⁿ* > aisl. *(bekk)-ja* 'der Bäche', ahd. as. *(win)-io*, ae. *(win)-iga* 'der Freunde' gegenüber got. *(gest)-ē* 'der Gäste', dessen Herkunft wie bei den *a*-Stämmen unklar ist (vgl. jedoch Ringe 2006: 201–202).

27. Zum Charakter des aisl. *þulr* bzw. ae. *þyle* zuletzt Poole 2005 und ausführlich Tsitsiklis 2017 (Zusammenfassung ebd.: 383–384); die Annahme, daß es sich (auch) um einen 'Kultredner' handelt, wird indessen heutzutage nicht mehr weiterverfolgt. Für die Etymologie gilt: *non liquet* (Liberman 1996: 75–77).

dem Griechischen stammen;[28] in diesem Fall würde es sich um eine von Pytheas (und/oder seinen Begleitern)[29] geprägte Fremdbenennung handeln. Tatsächlich finden sich in der Pytheas-Überlieferung nicht nur (meist etymologisch unklare) einheimische Namen, sondern auch von dem/den Reisenden geprägte Toponyme wie etwa *Basileia* 'die Königliche' (scil. Insel);[30] auch Namen wie *Berrice* verraten durch ihre Endung (*-e* ← gr. *-η*) ihre griechische Herkunft.

Anschluß bietet die Wurzel uridg. $*d^hueh_2$-, $*d^huh_2$- 'Rauch, Dampf [u.ä.] machen',[31] die in thematisiertem gr. θύω 'räuchern, ein Rauchopfer darbringen, opfern', lat. *suf-fiō, -īre* 'räuchern, beräuchern' ($*d^huh_2$-ie/o-) und ksl. *dujǫ, duti* 'blasen' (Vollstufe I $*d^heuh_2$-ie/o-) etc. fortgesetzt ist.[32] Zubehör sind u.a. die beiden schwundstufigen Nominalbildungen uridg. $*d^huh_2mó$- m. > ved. *dhūmá-* 'Rauch, Dampf', gr. θῡμός ($*$'Aufwirbeln von Teilchen, Aufwallung' →) 'Gemütsbewegung, Leidenschaft, Verlangen, Mut, Lebenskraft, Geist, Verstand', aksl. *dymъ* 'Rauch, Dampf', apreuß. *dūmis* 'Rauch' (*Elbinger Vokabular*, Nr. 39), alit. *dúmas* (1) 'Rauch', lett. *dūmi* Pl. 'Rauch' bzw. lat. *fūmus* 'Rauch, Dampf, Dunst'[33]

---

28. Alles andere als plausibel ist die Vermutung von Hamp (1989:84), daß Θούλη einer vorgriechischen Substratsprache angehöre und sloven. *tlà* n. Pl. 'Grund, Boden' entspreche (*til- < *tlH-*) — wie kommt eine Insel am Rand der nördlichen Ökumene zu einem 'pelasgischen' Namen?

29. Daß Pytheas in Begleitung gereist ist, geht aus Gemin. 6,9 ἐδείκνυον ἡμῖν οἱ βάρβαροι [...] 'Die Einheimischen zeigten *uns* [...]' (Mette 1952:28; vgl. oben, Anm. 2) hervor.

30. Plinius berichtet, Pytheas habe eine der skytischen Küste vorgelagerte große Insel *Basilia* genannt (*Pytheas Basiliam nominat* Plin. nat. hist. IV,95; Mette 1952:31); der Name Βασίλεια findet sich auch bei Diodor (Diod. V,23,1; Scott 2022:36). Daß aber Basileia als 'Königsinsel' auf den sagenhaften, erst aus altisländischen Vorzeitsagas des 13. und 14. Jahrhunderts bekannten König *Guðmundr* von *Glæsis-, Glasisvellir* 'Glanzgefilde' zu beziehen sei (Gutenbrunner 1939:72: 'Bernsteingefilde'), ist ganz unwahrscheinlich.

31. Oder ist die Grundbedeutung als 'rauchig, dampfig [u.ä.] sein, (werden,) machen' zu bestimmen?

32. LIV²:158 s.v. $*d^huveh_2$- ('Rauch machen'); vgl. ferner IEW:261–263 s.v. *4 dheu-, dheuə-* ('stieben, wirbeln, bes. von Staub, Rauch, Dampf [etc.]'); EWAia I:795 s.v. *dhūmá-*; Koch 1990:667 f. (zu ksl. *dujǫ, duti*); Vine 2006:241. Wegen heth. *tuḫḫae-zi* 'rauchen' (Kloekhorst 2016:173–176; wohl < uridg. $*d^huh_2$-o-ie/o-) und *antuuaḫḫa-/antuḫša-* c. 'Mensch' (< *-en-$d^huéh_2$-ōs, Gen. *-en-d^huh_2-s-és '*der Atem in sich hat': Eichner 1979:77; Rieken 1999:191) wird wurzelschließendes h_2 angesetzt. — Fern bleibt jedenfalls ahd. *thoum, daum* m. 'Rauch, Dampf, Dunst' (urgerm. $*þauma$- < $*(s)t$°; s. EWAhd II:745–746).

33. Das Baltoslavische zeigt Akzentrückzug gemäß Hirts Gesetz: aksl. *dymъ*, alit. *dúmas* etc. < urbsl. $*dū́ma$- < $*d^huh_2mó$- (Jasanoff 2017:106, 235; ALEW:275). Für lat. *fūmus* < $*d^húh_2mo$- kann "nominalizing accent shift" angenommen werden (so Weiss 2020:108); bei einem Antezedens uridg. $*d^huh_2mó$- wäre nach Dybos Regel ($C_0VHRV́C_0\# → C_0VRV́C_0\#$; dazu zuletzt v.a. Zair 2012:132–150; Neri 2017:221–240 mit Lit.) kurzer Wurzelvokal lat. $*fu°$ zu erwarten.

Der Name der Insel Thule   277

sowie uridg. *$d^h\acute{u}h_2li$- f.[34] > ai. *dhūli-, dhūlī* f. 'Staub', mir. *dúil* f. 'Wunsch, Hoffnung' (mit vergleichbarer Bedeutungsentwicklung wie in gr. θῡμός, s. vorhin), vgl. lit. *dū́lis* (1), *dū̃lis* (2), *dūlỹs* (4) m. 'Rauch, Räuchermasse (zum Vertreiben von Bienen), Nebel', *dū́lė* f. (1) dass., lett. *dūlis* m. 'Räuchermasse (zum Vertreiben von Bienen)', dazu ferner die Weiterbildungen ai. *dhūli-kā* f. 'Nebel, Dunst, Blütenstaub', lat. *fūlī-gō* f. 'Ruß'.[35]

Für die Grundsprache ist ein Wortbildungsmodell zu sichern, bei dem mit Suffix *-(C)o-* gebildete Adjektiva als Derivationsbasen für *(C)i*-stämmige Konkreta und Abstrakta dienen;[36] Standardbeispiele sind:

(1)   uridg. *$h_2e\acute{k}r\acute{o}$*- 'scharf, spitz' (gr. ἄκρος 'spitz auslaufend, höchst, oberst', alit. *ašras* 'scharf', aksl. *̇ostrъ* 'scharf, rauh') ⇉ uridg. *$h_2\acute{o}/e\acute{k}ri$*- m. 'Scharfes, Spitzes' ~ f. 'Schärfe, Spitze' (lat. *ocris* m. 'steiniger Berg', ved. *áśri*- f. 'scharfe Kante', gr. ὄκρις f./m. 'Spitze, scharfe Kante', ἄκρις f. 'Spitze, Berggipfel');

(2)   uridg. *$d^hubr\acute{o}$*- 'tief' (toch. B *tapre*, A *tpär* 'hoch [von tief unten aus gesehen]', mir. *dobur* 'dunkel, finster') ⇉ uridg. *$d^h\acute{u}bri$*- m. 'Tiefes' ~ f. 'Tiefe' (aksl. *dъbrъ* f. 'Tal, Schlucht', nicht-gr. δύβρις 'Meer').[37]

An einzelsprachlicher Evidenz für das nur im Slavischen produktiv gebliebene Ableitungsmuster ist etwa anzuführen:

(3)   heth. *antara-* 'blau'[38] ⇉ [síɢ]*antari-* c. 'Blaues: blaue Wolle';

---

34. Anders Vine 2008: 15, 17 (*d^huh_2-l-́* als schwacher Stamm eines *d^huh_2-él-*).

35. Zu mir. *dúil* vgl. Zair 2012: 115–116. — Ob auch alb. *dëllinjë* (älter *dëllënjë*) f. 'Wacholder' als 'Räucherholz' (*d^huh_2l-ī̆nio*- n. laut Jokl 1923: 191–192; vgl. IEW: 262) hierhergehört, bleibt ganz unklar; für freundliche Auskünfte danke ich Stefan Schumacher (Wien) herzlich. Ein Kurzreferat verschiedener etymologischer Deutungen bietet Orel 1998: 63.

36. Zum Nebeneinander von *o*-Adjektiv und *i*-Deadjektivum, das in den Umkreis des Caland-Suffixverbandes gehört, gibt es einen eigenen Zweig Literatur. Zu nennen sind vor allem: Schindler 1980: 390 (dort die meisten der oben genannten Beispiele); Weiss 1996: 204–206; Nussbaum 1999: 399–400; Rieken 2006: 52–54; Weiss 2012: 346–350; Grestenberger 2014: 89, 94, 97–98; Nussbaum 2014: 304–306; Nussbaum 2022: 216–217. Das calandeske *-i-* wird von Balles (2009a: 16–22; 2009b: 9–12) als ursprünglich wortartneutraler Ausdruck für Eigenschaftskonzepte angesehen. — Im Ansatz zweier grundsprachlicher Lexeme 'ᴋᴏɴᴋʀᴇᴛᴜᴍ' (Adjektivsubstantivierung; idealtypisch m.), 'ᴀʙsᴛʀᴀᴋᴛᴜᴍ' (Adjektivabstraktum; idealtypisch f.) und nicht eines einzigen Lexems 'ᴀʙsᴛʀᴀᴋᴛᴜᴍ; ᴋᴏɴᴋʀᴇᴛᴜᴍ' folge ich Nussbaum (2014: 304; 2022: 216; vgl. Neri 2022: 742–743).

37. Scholia in Theocritum I,118c: δύβρις [...] θάλασσα (Wendel 1914: 69). Meist erkennt man δύβρις dem Illyrischen zu (so u.v.a. IEW: 267). Nach Meissner (2006: 23 Anm. 41) handelt es sich um ein Wort aus einem südslavischen Dialekt; auch dies bleibt eine unverbindliche Möglichkeit.

38. Heth. *antara-* /and°/ < uridg. *$\d{m}d^hr\acute{o}$*-; vgl. čech. *modrý* 'blau' < urslav. *$m\d{a}dru$* (< *mod^hro-).

(4) lat. *ravus* 'heiser'[39] ⇒ *ravis* f. 'Heiserkeit';

(5) air. *glan* 'klar, rein' ⇒ *glain* f. 'Klares: Glas; Klarheit';

(6) aksl. *zъlъ* 'schlecht, schlimm' ⇒ aksl. *zъlь* f. 'Schlechtigkeit'.

Diesem altertümlichen Wortbildungsmodell zufolge kann das vorhin angeführte konkretisierte Abstraktum uridg. $*d^h\acute{u}h_2li$- f. 'Rauch, Dampf, Nebel, Dunst' von einem Primäradjektiv uridg. $*d^huh_2$-*lo*- 'rauchig (rauchend), dampfig (dampfend), nebelig, dunstig' abgeleitet sein; solcherlei Bildungen haben in der Regel Suffixbetonung, also $*d^huh_2$-*ló*-.[40] Bei Substantivierung eines derartigen oxytonierten Adjektivs zeigt sich Verschiebung des Akzents auf die Wurzelsilbe: ved. *kr̥ṣṇá*-Adj. 'schwarz, dunkel' ⇒ *kŕ̥ṣṇa*- m. 'der Schwarze: schwarze Antilope', gr. λευκός Adj. 'weiß' ⇒ λεύκη f. 'die Weiße: Weißpappel, weißer Aussatz', urgerm. **barzá*-Adj. 'starr aufgerichtet, stachelig' (ahd./bair. *parr-emo* Dat. Sg. m.) ⇒ **bársa*- m. 'der Stachelige: Barsch' (ahd. *bars*, ae. *bærs, bears*) etc.[41] Ein solchermaßen substantiviertes Femininum uridg. $*d^h\acute{u}h_2leh_2$- 'die Rauchige (Rauchende), Dampfige (Dampfende), Nebelige, Dunstige' ergibt sodann lautgesetzlich gr. $*t^h\bar{u}l\bar{a}$, (ion.-att.) $*t^h\acute{u}l\bar{e}$, das onymisiert als Θούλη erscheint.[42]

Bei Aerosolen sind Gase mit festen Schwebeteilchen (Rauch) und flüssigen Schwebeteilchen (Dampf, Nebel, Dunst) zu unterscheiden. Wiederholte Brände mit weithin zu erkennender Rauchentwicklung sind für die nördlichen Breiten der damaligen Zeit nicht vorauszusetzen, und Dunst ist weniger dicht und sonach nur auf kurze Entfernungen hin zu sehen. Als Benennungsmotiv für den Namen der Insel Θούλη bietet sich daher eine wahrnehmbare Konzentration von Dampf oder Nebel an. Was die erste Möglichkeit betrifft, referiert eine Reihe landnahmezeitlicher Toponyme in Island auf die aus heißen Quellen aufsteigenden Dämpfe, z.B. aisl. *Reykja-nes* '-halbinsel, -landzunge', *Reykjar-vík*[43] '-bucht' (im Bestim-

---

39. Lat. *ravus* < uridg. $*h_3rou̯Hó$- (vgl. Vine 2006:237), das wohl zur Wurzel $*h_3reu̯H$- 'brüllen' (LIV²:306) gehört.

40. Im Griechischen war das Primärsuffix -*lo*- nur schwach produktiv; vgl. Risch 1974:107 (mit Beispielen); Probert 2006:210. Weitere Kreise haben dagegen die komplexen Suffixe -αλο-, -ελο-, -ηλο- -ιλο-, -ωλο- und-υλο- gezogen.

41. Zum oppositiven Akzentwechsel bei Substantivierung eines (attributiven) Adjektivs Brugmann 1906:27–29; Schaffner 2001:328–345.

42. Auch wenn man die sog. Laryngalbrechung (hier: uridg. $uh_2 > u\partial_2h_2 > u̯\bar{a} >$ gr. [dor.] $\bar{a}$; dazu Olsen 2009:352–353, 359) anerkennt, ergibt sich kein Problem: bei Barytonese tritt kein derartiger Lautwandel ein.

43. Ari Þorgilsson, *Íslendingabók*, c. 1 (ʀᴀᴊᴋɪᴀʀ víc A: Ms. AM 103b, fol.: 1ᵛ, Z. 18, ʀᴀɪᴋɪᴀʀ vic B: Ms. AM 103a, fol.: 1ᵛ, Z. 8; ungenau Jónsson 1930:9: *Raykiarvíc*); *Landnámabók*, c. 9 (Hss. *Reykiar*-; Jónsson 1900:8 [H], 133 [S], 266 [M]). Das Vorderglied von (normalisiertem)

Der Name der Insel Thule **279**

mungselement aisl. *reykr* m. 'Rauch', hier vielmehr 'Dampf'). Außerhalb Islands gibt es jedoch keine heißen Quellen; da die Identifikation Thule = Island aber, wie eingangs dargelegt, unsicher bleibt, ist dem Benennungsbegriff 'Nebel' der Vorzug zu geben. (Andernfalls käme 'Dampf' in Frage; vgl. vorhin.)[44] An alten Toponymen sind etwa *Nabalia* f., 1. Jh. (Fluß oder Ort im Batavergebiet) bzw. Ναβάλια f., 2. Jh. (*polis* in der Nähe des Mittelrheins) sowie *Nebra* 9. Jh. (Ort an [und Flußabschnitt?] der Unstrut; **Nabira*) anzuführen,[45] wenn diese Bildungen als (urgerm.) *Nab-* < uridg. **nob^h-* an die Wurzel **neb^h-* 'feucht, nebelig, bewölkt [u.ä.] werden'[46] anzuschließen sind,[47] vgl. gr. νεφέλη f. 'Nebel, Wolke', lat. *nebula* f. 'Nebel, Dunst, Wolke', ahd. *nebul* m. 'Nebel, Dunst' etc. (uridg. **neb^h-el-*). Die Tatsache, daß das atmosphärische Phänomen Nebel in der gesamten Toponymie Verwendung findet, ist jedenfalls trivial; ich nenne hier nur *Fog Islands* (British Columbia, Kanada), den Ortsnamen osk. *Casīnum* 1. Jh. v. Chr., heute *Cassino* (Latium, Italien; **Kas-īno-* 'Nebellandschaft')[48] und den Bergnamen *Nebelstein* (Waldviertel, Niederösterreich).[49]

---

aisl. *Reykjar-vík* ist Genetiv Sg.; der daraus hervorgegangene Name der Hauptstadt Islands, *Reykja-vík*, zeigt hingegen Genetiv Pl. — Die altisländischen Toponyme mit Bestimmungselement *Guf(u)-* (z.B. *Guf-á, Gufu-nes*) referieren nicht auf das Appellativ *gufa* f. 'Rauch, Dampf', sondern auf den Beinamen des Landnehmers Ketill Ørlygsson, *Gufa* ('Nebel' →) 'ruhige, phlegmatische, träge Person'; s. Jónsson 1907:328; Peterson 2015:153.

44. Daß sich — in diesem meines Erachtens wenig wahrscheinlichen Fall — die Benennung auf Geysire beziehen würde, kommt kaum in Betracht. Alle drei Orte, an denen heute und wohl auch früher heiße Springquellen zu finden sind, liegen in geothermisch aktiven Gebieten im Landesinneren Islands und sind vom Meer aus nicht sichtbar; für diesen Hinweis danke ich Eleonore Gudmundsson (Wien).

45. *Nabaliae* Gen. (Lok.?), Tac. hist. V,26,1 (Köstermann 1969:237). Ναβάλια Ptol. II,11,28 [13] (Stückelberger & Graßhoff 2017:230; Ναυαλία, Var. Ναβαλία Cuntz 1923:67). *Nebra: Neueri* Urkunde Ludwigs des Deutschen, Nr. 170 (a. 876, Kopie Mitte 10. Jh.; Kehr 1934:240); weitere Belege bei Udolph 2010:22.

46. LIV²: 448 s.v. *1. *neb^h-*; vgl. IEW: 315–316 s.v. *2. (enebh-): nebh-, embh-*, > *bh-*. An Nominalbildungen gehört neben **neb^h-el-* (s. oben) auch ved. *nábhas-* n. 'Feuchtigkeit, Nebel, Wolke', gr. νέφος n. 'Nebel, Dunst, Wolke' etc. (uridg. **néb^h-es-*) hierher.

47. Zu (urgerm.) *Nab-* < **nob^h-* s. etwa Udolph 2010:23–24, 37 (*Nebra* und Zubehör; 'alteuropäische' Schicht); Bichlmeier 2013:62–64; 2015:310, 322–323 (*Naab*, linker Nebenfluß der Donau; vor-ahd. **Naba-*, germanischer oder vorgermanischer Herkunft). — Die oben vorgestellte Etymologie von *Nabalia* bzw. Ναβάλια ist freilich umstritten; vgl. das Forschungsreferat bei Scheungraber & Grünzweig 2014:258–259.

48. Opfermann 2019:445, 448–449: 'Gebiet, das durch weißlich Graues (scil. Nebel) charakterisiert ist'; Zusammenstellung der Belege ebd.: 405.

49. Vgl. Pohl 1984:59 (dort auch weitere österreichische Bergnamen mit Bestimmungselement *Nebel-*); Pohl 1997:135.

Die Benennung von Θούλη als 'die Nebelige' (scil. Insel) bietet indessen keine Entscheidungshilfe in der Frage der Lokalisierung; Nebel ist in den nordatlantischen Regionen eine allgegenwärtige Witterungserscheinung. Daß die Isle of Skye,[50] die größte Insel der Inneren Hebriden, im Schottisch-Gälischen den Namen *Eilean a' Cheò* 'Insel des Nebels' trägt (schott.-gäl. *ceò* m./f. 'Nebel, Rauch', vgl. air. *ceó* m./f. 'Nebel'), ist jedenfalls von Θούλη unabhängig zu betrachten.

Nachtrag: Über den Thule-Namen hat jüngst Blažek, V. 2022. *Lingua Posnaniensis* 64.1. 7–25 gehandelt. Er referiert abwägend Etymologien aus dem Germanischen (s. vorhin); der Name gilt ihm als Beleg für die Durchführung der Ersten Lautverschiebung um 330 v. Chr. (anlautendes /θ/ < uridg. /t/).

Abkürzungen

Adam Brem.=Adam von Bremen, *Gesta Hammaburgensis ecclesiae pontificum*
Avien. ora=Avienus, *Ora maritima*
Caes. b. Gall.=Caesar, *De bello Gallico*
Diod.=Diodor, *Bibliotheca historica*
Gemin.=Geminos, *Elementa astronomiae (Eisagōgē eis ta phainomena)*
Kosm. Indik.=Kosmas Indikopleustes, *Topographia Christiana*
Mart. Cap.=Martianus Capella, *De nuptiis Philologiae et Mercurii*
Plin. nat. hist.=Plinius maior, *Naturalis historia*
Polyb.=Polybius, *Historiae*
Pomp. Mela=Pomponius Mela, *Chorographia*
Prok. b. Goth.=Prokop, *De bello Gothico*
Ptol.=Ptolemaeus, *Geographica*
Solin.=Solinus, *Collectanea rerum memorabilium*
Steph. Byz.=Stephanus Byzantius, *Ethnica*
Strab.=Strabo, *Geographica*
Tac. Agr.=Tacitus, *Agricola*
Tac. Germ.=Tacitus, *Germania*
Verg. Georg.=Vergilius, *Georgica*

---

50. Das älteste Zeugnis ist Σκιτὶς Ptol. II,3,32 (Var. Ὄκιτις, Ὄκητις; Stückelberger & Graßhoff 2017:156). Im Altisländischen heißt die Insel *Skíð*, u.a. belegt in der um 1100 zu datierenden *Magnússdrápa* des Bjǫrn krepphendi (Str. 6,2; Gade 2009: 400).

Literatur

ALEW = W. Hock et al. 2019. *Altlitauisches etymologisches Wörterbuch*. Version 1.1. Berlin: Humboldt-Universität.

Allen, S.A. 1987. *Vox Graeca. A guide to the pronunciation of classical Greek*. 3. Aufl. Cambridge: University Press.

Balles, I. 2009a. Zu den *i*-stämmigen Adjektiven des Lateinischen. In R. Lühr & S. Ziegler (Hrsg.), *Protolanguage and Prehistory*, 1–26. (Akten der 12. Fachtagung der Indogerman. Gesellschaft, Krakau 2004.) Wiesbaden: Reichert.

Balles, I. 2009b. The Old Indic cvi construction, the Caland system, and the PIE adjective. In J.E. Rasmussen & Th. Olander (Hrsg.), *Internal reconstruction in Indo-European. Methods, results, and problems*, 1–15. (XVI International Conference on Historical Linguistics, Copenhagen 2003. Copenhagen Studies in Indo-European 3.) Copenhagen: Museum Tusculanum Press.

Bianchetti, S. (Hrsg.) 1998. *Pitea di Massalia, De Oceano*. (Biblioteca di studi antichi 82.) Pisa: Istituti Editoriali e Poligrafici Internazionali.

Bichlmeier, H. 2013. Bayerisch-österreichische Orts- und Gewässernamen aus indogermanistischer Sicht. Teil 3: Zusammenfassung bisheriger Forschungsergebnisse zu altbayerischen Flussnamen sowie einige indogermanistische Anmerkungen zu den Flussnamen *Ammer/Amper* und *Naab*. In K. Simbeck & W. Janka (Hrsg.), *Namen in Altbayern. Festschrift Josef Egginger; Gedenkschrift Günter Schneeberger*, 53–68. (Regensburger Studien zur Namenforschung 8.) Regensburg: Vulpes.

Bichlmeier, H. 2015. Ein neuer Blick auf die ältesten Orts- und Gewässernamen in (Mittel-)Europa. *Namenkundliche Informationen* 105/106. 299–331.

Billerbeck, M. & Ch. Zubler (Hrsg.). 2011. *Stephani Byzantii Ethnica*. II: $\Delta - I$. (Corpus fontium historiae Byzantinae 43,2.) Berlin: de Gruyter.

Blažek, V. 2022. On chronology of the First Germanic Sound Shift (Lex Rask — Grimm). *Lingua Posnaniensis* 64. 7–25.

Brodersen, K. (Hrsg.) 1994. *Pomponius Mela, Kreuzfahrt durch die alte Welt*. Darmstadt: Wissenschaftliche Buchgesellschaft.

Brugmann, K. 1906. *Vergleichende Laut-, Stammbildungs- und Flexionslehre nebst Lehre vom Gebrauch der Wortformen der indogermanischen Sprachen*. II,1: *Lehre von den Wortformen und ihrem Gebrauch: Allgemeines, Zusammensetzung (Komposita), Nominalstämme*. (Grundriß der vergleichenden Grammatik der indogermanischen Sprachen 2,1.) 2. Aufl. Straßburg: Trübner.

Bubeník, V. 1983. *The phonological interpretation of Ancient Greek: a pandialectal analysis*. Toronto: University Press.

Collinder, B. 1936. Der älteste überlieferte germanische Name. *Namn och bygd* 24. 92–97.

Cunliffe, B. 2003. *The extraordinary voyage of Pytheas the Greek*. London: Penguin.

Cuntz, O. (Hrsg.). 1923. *Die Geographie des Ptolemaeus: Galliae, Germania, Raetia, Noricum, Pannoniae, Illyricum, Italia. Handschriften, Text und Untersuchung*. Berlin: Weidmann.

Delz, J. & J. von Ungern-Sternberg (Hrsg.). 2010. *P. Cornelius Tacitus, Libri qui supersunt*. II,3; *Agricola*. Berlin: de Gruyter.

Eichner, H. 1979. Indogermanische Chronik 25a: II. Anatolisch. *Die Sprache* 25. 72–79.

EWAhd II = A.L. Lloyd, R. Lühr & O. Springer. 1998. *Etymologisches Wörterbuch des Althochdeutschen.* II: *bî — ezzo.* Göttingen: Vandenhoeck & Ruprecht.

EWAia I = M. Mayrhofer. 1992. *Etymologisches Wörterbuch des Altindoarischen.* I. Heidelberg: Winter.

Gade, K.E. (Hrsg.). 2009. Bjǫrn krepphendi. In K.E. Gade (Hrsg.), *Skaldic Poetry of the Scandinavian Middle Ages.* II: *Poetry from the Kings' Sagas.* 2: *From c. 1035 to c. 1300.* 1, 395–405. Turnhout: Brepols.

Gisinger, F. 1963. Pytheas 1). In G. Wissowa et al. (Hrsg.), *Paulys Realencyclopädie der classischen Altertumswissenschaft. Neue Bearbeitung* 24,1, 314–366. Stuttgart: Druckenmüller.

Grestenberger, L. 2014. Zur Funktion des Nominalsuffixes *-i-* im Vedischen und Urindogermanischen. In N. Oettinger & Th. Steer (Hrsg.), *Das Nomen im Indogermanischen. Morphologie, Substantiv versus Adjektiv, Kollektivum,* 88–102. (Akten der Arbeitstagung der Indogerm. Gesellschaft, Erlangen 2011.) Wiesbaden: Reichert.

Grønvik, O. 2006. Thule — det eldste navnet på landet vårt? In H. Gørstad et al. (Hrsg.), *Historien i forhistorien. Festschrift Einar Østmo,* 111–114. (Kulturhistorisk museum, Skrifter 4.) Oslo: Kulturhistorisk museum.

Gutenbrunner, S. 1939. *Germanische Frühzeit in den Berichten der Antike.* (Handbücherei der Deutschkunde 3.) Halle/Saale: Niemeyer.

Hamp, E.P. 1989. Prehellenica. 8: *Thule, Thyle. Živa Antica* 39. 84.

Haury, J. & G. Wirth (Hrsg.). 2001. *Procopius Caesariensis opera omnia.* II: *De bellis libri V–VIII.* München: Saur.

Heggstad, L. 1930. *Gamalnorsk ordbok med nynorsk tyding.* Oslo: Det norske samlaget.

Hennig, R. 1923. *Von rätselhaften Ländern. Versunkene Stätten der Geschichte.* München: Delphin.

Hering, W. (Hrsg.). 1987. *C. Iulii Caesaris Commentarii rerum gestarum.* I: *Bellum Gallicum.* Leipzig: Teubner.

Hofmann, C. 1865. *Ueber das Lebermeer.* (Sitzungsberichte der Königl. bayer. Akademie der Wissenschaften zu München 1865,2.) München: Franz.

Holzberg, N. (Hrsg.) 2016. *Publius Vergilius Maro, Hirtengedichte/Bucolina, Landwirtschaft/Georgica.* Berlin: de Gruyter.

Horst Roseman → Roseman

IEW = J. Pokorny. 1959. *Indogermanisches etymologisches Wörterbuch.* I: *Text.* Bern: Francke.

doi Jasanoff, J.H. 2017. *The prehistory of the Balto-Slavic accent.* (Brill's Studies in Indo-European Languages & Linguistics 17.) Leiden: Brill.

Jóhannesson, A. 1956. *Isländisches etymologisches Wörterbuch.* Bern: Francke.

doi Jokl, N. 1923. *Linguistisch-kulturhistorische Untersuchungen aus dem Bereiche des Albanischen.* (Untersuchungen zur indogermanischen Sprach- und Kulturwissenschaft 8.) Berlin: de Gruyter.

Jónsson, F. (Hrsg.). 1900. *Landnamabók.* I–III: *Hauksbók. Sturlubók. Melabók.* København: Thiele.

Jónsson, F. 1907. Tilnavne i den islandske Oldlitteratur. *Aarbøger for Nordisk Oldkyndighed og Historie, Række* 2, 22. 161–381.

Jónsson, F. (Hrsg.). 1930. *Are hinn fróði Þorgilsson, Íslendingabók.* København: Levin & Munksgaard.

Kehr, P. (Hrsg.). 1934. *Die Urkunden Ludwigs des Deutschen, Karlmanns und Ludwig des Jüngeren.* (Monumenta Germaniae historica, Diplomata regum Germaniae ex stirpe Karolinorum 1.) Berlin: Weidmann.

Kleineberg, A. et al. 2010. *Germania und die Insel Thule. Die Entschlüsselung von Ptolemaios' „Atlas der Oikumene".* Darmstadt: Wissenschaftliche Buchgesellschaft.

doi Kloekhorst, A. 2016. The story of Wāšitta and Kumarbi. In Š. Velhartická (Hrsg.), *Audias fabulas veteres. Festschrift Jana Součková-Siegelová*, 165–177. Leiden: Brill.

Koch, Ch. 1990. *Das morphologische System des altkirchenslavischen Verbums.* I: Text. II: Anmerkungen. (Münchner Universitäts-Schriften, Reihe der Philosoph. Fakultät 22.) München: Fink.

Koepp, W. 1951/52. Ultima omnium Thyle. *Wissenschaftliche Zeitschrift der Universität Greifswald, Gesellschafts- und sprachwissenschaftliche Reihe* 1. 6–18, 36–57.

König, R. et al. (Hrsg.). 1995. *C. Plinius Secundus d. Ä., Naturkunde.* XXXII: Medizin und Pharmakologie: Heilmittel aus dem Wasser. Zürich: Artemis & Winkler.

Köstermann, E. (Hrsg.). 1969. *P. Cornelii Taciti libri qui supersunt.* II,1: *Historiarum libri.* Leipzig: Teubner.

LaN = Reichert, H. 1987–1990. *Lexikon der altgermanischen Namen.* I: *Text.* II: R. Nedoma & H. Reichert, *Register.* (Thesaurus Palaeogermanicus 1.) Wien: Österreichische Akademie der Wissenschaften.

Lelgemann, D. 2012. Wo lag Thule? – Geodätische Daten aus der Antike. *Zeitschrift für Geodäsie, Geoinformation und Landmanagement* 139. 335–339.

Liberman, A. 1996. Ten Scandinavian and North English etymologies. *Alvíssmal* 6. 63–98.

Lid, N. 1942. Ultima Thule. *Serta Eitremiana. Opuscula philologica. Festschrift Samson Eitrem*, 51–55. (Symbolae Osloenses, Suppl. 11.). Oslo: Brøgger.

LIV² = M. Kümmel et al. 2001. *Lexikon der Indogermanischen Verben. Die Wurzeln und ihre Primärstammbildungen.* 2. Aufl. Wiesbaden: Reichert.

doi McPhail, C. 2014. Pytheas of Massalia's route of travel. *Phoenix* 68. 247–257.

doi Meissner, Th. 2006. *S-stem nouns and adjectives in Greek and Proto-Indo-European: a diachronic study in word formation.* Oxford: University Press.

doi Mette, H.J. (Hrsg.) 1952. *Pytheas von Massalia.* (Kleine Texte für Vorlesungen und Übungen 175.) Berlin: de Gruyter.

Metzenthin, E.M. 1941. *Die Länder- und Völkernamen im altisländischen Schrifttum.* Bryn Mawr, PA [kein Verlag].

Mommsen, Th. (Hrsg.). 1895. *C. Iulii Solini Collectanea rerum memorabilium.* 2. Aufl. Berlin: Weidmann.

Ms. = Handschrift in Stofnun Árna Magnússonar í islenskum fræðum, Reykjavík. https://handrit.is

Much, R. 1918. Taunus. In J. Hoops (Hrsg.), *Reallexikon der Germanischen Altertumskunde.* IV: *Rü – Z*, 308. Berlin: de Gruyter.

Müllenhoff, K. 1870. *Deutsche Altertumskunde.* I. Berlin: Weidmann.

Nansen, F. 1911. *Nebelheim. Entdeckung und Erforschung der nördlichen Länder und Meere.* II. Leipzig: Brockhaus.

Neri, S. 2017. Wetter. *Etymologie und Lautgesetz*. (Culture Territori Linguaggi 14.) Perugia: Università degli Studi.

Neri, S. 2022. Alb. *gur* 'Stein' und uridg. *$*g^u reh_2$-* 'schwer, massiv sein'. In A. Calderini & R. Massarelli (Hrsg.), *EQO:DUENOSIO. Festschrift Luciano Agostiniani*, 731–750. (Ariodante 1.) Perugia: Università degli Studi.

Noreen, A. 1920. Nordens älsta folk- och ortnamn. *Fornvännen* 15. 23–50.

Nussbaum, A. J. 1999. **Jocidus*. An account of the Latin adjectives in *-idus*. In H. Eichner & H. C. Luschützky (Hrsg.), *Compositiones Indogermanicae. Gedenkschrift Jochem Schindler*, 377–419. Praha: Enigma.

Nussbaum, A. J. 2014. Feminine, abstract, collective, neuter plural: Some remarks on each. In S. Neri & R. Schuhmann (Hrsg.), *Studies on the collective and feminine in Indo-European from a diachronic and typological perspektive*, 273–306. (Brill's Studies in Indo-European Languages & Linguistics 11.) Leiden: Brill.

Nussbaum, A. J. 2022. Derivational properties of „adjectival roots". In M. Malzahn, H. A. Fellner & T.-S. Illés (Hrsg.), *Zurück zur Wurzel. Struktur, Funktion und Semantik der Wurzel im Indogermanischen*, 205–224. (Akten der 15. Fachtagung der Indogerman. Gesellschaft, Wien 2016.) Wiesbaden: Reichert.

Olsen, B. A. 2009. The conditioning of laryngeal breaking in Greek. In R. Lühr & S. Ziegler (Hrsg.), *Protolanguage and Prehistory*, 348–365. (Akten der 12. Fachtagung der Indogerman. Gesellschaft, Krakau 2004.) Wiesbaden: Reichert.

Opfermann, A. 2019. Zur oskischen Herkunft des Ortsnamens *Casīnum*. *Beiträge zur Namenforschung* N.F. 54. 403–456.

Orel, V. 1998. *Albanian etymological dictionary*. Leiden: Brill.

Peterson, P. R. 2015. *Old Norse nicknames*. PhD dissertation, University of Minnesota. https://hdl.handle.net/11299/172669

Pohl, H.-D. 1984. *Wörterbuch der Bergnamen Österreichs*. I: *Kurzgefaßtes Verzeichnis der österreichischen Bergnamen*. (Österreichische Namenforschung, Sonderreihe, 7.) Salzburg: Österreichische Gesellschaft für Namenforschung.

Pohl, H.-D. 1997. Österreichische Bergnamen. *Onoma* 33. 131–151.

Poole, R. 2005. Þulr. In H. Beck et al. (Hrsg.), *Reallexikon der Germanischen Altertumskunde*. 2. Aufl. XXX, 544–546. Berlin: de Gruyter.

Probert, Ph. 2006. *Ancient Greek accentuation. Synchronic patterns, frequency effects, and prehistory*. Oxford: University Press.

Reuter, O. S. 1938. Das Vorgebirge von Thule. *Forschungen und Fortschritte* 14. 26–27.

Rieken, E. 1999. *Untersuchungen zur nominalen Stammbildung des Hethitischen*. (Studien zu den Boğazköy-Texten 44.) Wiesbaden: Harrassowitz.

Rieken, E. 2006. Neues zum Ursprung der anatolischen *i*-Mutation. *Historische Sprachforschung* 118 (2005). 48–74.

Ringe, D. 2006. A sociolinguistically informed solution to an old historical problem: the Gothic genitive plural. *Transactions of the Philological Society* 104. 167–206.

Risch, E. 1974. *Wortbildung der homerischen Sprache*. 2. Aufl. Berlin: de Gruyter.

Roseman, Ch. H. (Hrsg.). 1994. Pytheas of Massalia, On the Ocean. Chicago: Ares.

Schaffner, St. 2001. *Das Vernersche Gesetz und der innerparadigmatische grammatische Wechsel des Urgermanischen im Nominalbereich.* (Innsbrucker Beiträge zur Sprachwissenschaft 103.) Innsbruck: Institut für Sprachen und Literaturen der Universität Innsbruck.

Scheungraber, C. & F. E. Grünzweig. 2014. *Die altgermanischen Toponyme sowie ungermanische Toponyme Germaniens. Ein Handbuch zu ihrer Etymologie.* (Philologica Germanica 34.) Wien: Fassbaender.

Schindler, J. 1980. Zur Herkunft der altindischen *cvi*-Bildungen. In M. Mayrhofer, M. Peters & O. E. Pfeiffer (Hrsg.), *Lautgeschichte und Etymologie,* 386–393. (Akten der 6. Fachtagung der Indogerm. Gesellschaft, Wien 1978.) Wiesbaden: Reichert.

Schmedt, H. (Hrsg.) 2020. *Antonius Diogenes,* Die unglaublichen Dinge jenseits von Thule. (Millenium-Studien zu Kultur und Geschichte des ersten Jahrtausends n. Chr. 78.) Berlin: de Gruyter.

Schmeja, H. 1968. *Der Mythos von den Alpengermanen.* (Arbeiten aus dem Institut für vergleichende Sprachwissenschaft 8.) Wien: Gerold & Co.

Scott, L. (Hrsg.). 2022. *Pytheas of Massalia. Texts, translation, and commentary.* London: Routledge.

von See, K. 2004. Ultima Thule. In K. Hoff et al. (Hrsg.), *Poetik und Gedächtnis. Festschrift Heiko Uecker,* 113–144. (Beiträge zur Skandinavistik 17.) Frankfurt/Main: Lang.

von See, K. 2006. Ultima Thule/Thule. In H. Beck et al. (Hrsg.), *Reallexikon der Germanischen Altertumskunde.* 2. Aufl. XXXI, 416–420. Berlin: de Gruyter.

Sitzmann, A. & F. E. Grünzweig. 2008. *Die altgermanischen Ethnonyme. Ein Handbuch zu ihrer Etymologie.* (Philologica Germanica 29.) Wien: Fassbaender.

Stichtenoth, D. (Übs.). 1959. *Pytheas von Marseille, Über das Weltmeer.* (Die Geschichtsschreiber der deutschen Vorzeit 103.) Köln: Böhlau.

Stichtenoth, D. (Hrsg.). 1968. *Rufus Festus Avienus, Ora maritima.* Darmstadt: Wissenschaftliche Buchgesellschaft.

Stückelberger, A. & G. Graßhoff(Hrsg.). 2017. *Klaudios Ptolemaios: Handbuch der Geographie. Einleitung, Text und Übersetzung, Index.* I–II. 2. Aufl. Basel: Schwabe.

Svennung, J. 1974. *Skandinavien bei Plinius und Ptolemaios. Kritisch-exegetische Forschungen zu den ältesten nordischen Sprachdenkmälern.* (Skrifter utgivna av K. Humanistiska vetenskapssamfundet i Uppsala 45.) Uppsala: Almquist & Wiksell.

Threatte, L. 1980. *The grammar of Attic inscriptions.* I: *Phonology.* Berlin: de Gruyter.

Timpe, F. 1989. Entdeckungsgeschichte: E[ntdeckungsgeschichte] des Nordens in der Antike. In H. Beck et al. (Hrsg.), *Reallexikon der Germanischen Altertumskunde.* 2. Aufl. VII, 307–388. Berlin: de Gruyter.

Trillmich, W. (Hrsg.). 1961. *Quellen des 9. und 11. Jahrhunderts zur Geschichte der Hamburgischen Kirche und das Reiches.* (Ausgewählte Quellen zur deutschen Geschichte des Mittelalters. Freiherr-vom-Stein-Gedächtnisausgabe 11.) Berlin: Rütten & Loening.

Tsitsiklis, K. R. M. 2017. *Der Thul in Text und Kontext.* (Reallexikon der Germanischen Altertumskunde, Ergänzungsbd. 98.) Berlin: de Gruyter.

Udolph, J. 2010. Sprachen die Nutzer der Scheibe von Nebra keltisch? *Eurasisches Magazin* 04/2010. https://adw-goe.de/fileadmin/forschungsprojekte/ortsnamen_rhein_elbe/dokumente/Publikationen_Udolph_PDF/2006-2010/404._Udolph_Nebra.pdf [Typoskript].

Vine, B. 2006. On 'Thurneysen-Havet's Law' in Latin and Italic. *Historische Sprachforschung* 119. 211–249.

Vine, B. 2008. On the etymology of Latin *tranquillus* 'calm'. *International Journal of Diachronic Linguistics and Linguistic Reconstruction* 5. 1–24.

Weiss, M. 1996. Greek μυρίος 'countless', Hittite *mūri-* 'bunch (of fruit)'. *Historische Sprachforschung* 109. 199–214.

Weiss, M. 2012. Interesting *i*-stems in Irish. In A. I. Cooper, J. Rau & M. Weiss (Hrsg.), *Multi nominis grammaticus. Studies in classical and Indo-European linguistics. Festschrift A. J. Nussbaum*, 340–356. Ann Arbor: Beech Stave.

Weiss, M. 2020. *Outline of the historical and comparative grammar of Latin*. 2. Aufl. Ann Arbor: Beech Stave.

Wendel, K. (Hrsg.). 1914. *Scholia in Theocritum vetera*. Leipzig: Teubner.

Willis, J. (Hrsg.). 1983. *Martianus Capella*. Leipzig: Teubner.

Wolska-Conus, W. (Hrsg.). 1968. *Cosmas Indicopleustès, Topographie Chrétienne*. I: *Livres I–IV*. (Sources chrétiennes 141.) Paris: Cerf.

Zair, N. 2012. *The reflexes of the Proto-Indo-European laryngeals in Celtic*. (Brill's Studies in Indo-European Languages and Linguistics 7.) Leiden & Boston: Brill.

Zwierlein, O. (Hrsg.). 1986. *L. Annaei Senecae tragoediae, incertorum auctorum Hercules [Oetaeus], Octavia*. Oxford: University Press.

Frauennamen in alten niederländischen Ortsnamen

Arend Quak
Universität Leiden | Universität von Amsterdam

Place-names with the names of women as a first element are rather rare in the early medieval Dutch speaking areas. In all we have found twenty examples and one that is not sure. Only in one of the examples do we find a term for a manor (*hof*), all others refer to rural items such as meadows, fields, and newly cultivated lands as their second element. It would seem that the combinations with female names are younger (11th–12th century) and that the absence of female names in combination with terms related to manors may have to do with the Salic laws in the Frankish areas.

1.   Einleitung

Bei der Betrachtung der überlieferten frühmittelalterlichen Ortsnamen im nieder-ländischsprachigen Gebiet lässt sich schon bald feststellen, dass Personennamen häufig als erstes Element in den Zusammensetzungen vorkommen, welche die meisten Ortsnamen bilden. Eine zweite Frage, die man sich dann stellen kann, ist, ob sowohl Männer- wie Frauennamen als erstes Element auftreten können. Das ist tatsächlich der Fall, aber es wird auch schnell deutlich, dass es an erster Stelle Männernamen sind, die dort vorkommen. Frauennamen sind hier relativ selten. So stellt z.B. auch Luc de Grauwe (2022: 309) fest, dass sich unter den Personen-namen in den flämischen Gemeindenamen nur drei von Frauen befinden.[1] Dabei werden hier Heiligennamen außer Betracht gelassen, wie etwa *Agathenkerka* [11. Jh. und später], der alte Name für das heutige Beverwijk in der niederländischen Provinz Nordholland (LNT 58). Solche Namen nehmen eine Sonderstellung ein,

---

1. Es handelt sich um folgende Namen: *Ave* in Avekapelle (S. 34), *Hluthena* in Lanaken (S. 142) und *Odila* in Oelegem (S. 186). Nach Angaben von Debrabandere u.a. (2022) handelt es sich hier um den Namen der Stifterin der Kapelle, um den Namen einer germanischen Göttin in einer hybriden Zusammensetzung und um einen Frauennamen Odila, obwohl hier m.E. auch ein männlicher Personenname Odilo nicht ausgeschlossen werden kann.

https://doi.org/10.1075/nss.34.16qua
Available under the CC BY-NC-ND 4.0 license.   © 2025 John Benjamins Publishing Company

weil sie nichts über eventuelle Besitzverhältnisse aussagen. Man vergleiche etwa auch Bierstadt, einen Ortsbezirk von Wiesbaden. Als „Birgidestad" wird es in einer Schenkungsurkun-de vom 12. März 927 erstmals erwähnt (TW 142). Der Ort ist eine Gründung irischer Mönche, die ihn nach der irischen Nationalheiligen Brigida von Kildare benannten.

Interessanter ist dann die Frage, mit welchen Elementen diese wenigen Frauennamen in den überlieferten frühmittelalterlichen Ortsnamen im niederländischsprachigen Gebiet (bis etwa 1200) zusammengesetzt sind. Dabei werden hier auch Ortsnamen in Nordfrankreich berücksichtigt, weil sie auch von (Nieder)franken gegeben wurden und trotz ihrer hybriden Form doch etwas zu diesem Thema aussagen können. In diesem Zusammenhang wurden die Ortsnamen in den beiden Ausgaben von Toponymen in den Niederlanden, Belgien und Nordfrankreich (TW und LNT) untersucht. Dabei wurden folgende Ortsnamen gefunden, die vermutlich einen Frauennamen enthalten.

2. Belege

1. **Athelhilt**, unbekanntes Gelände in der Provinz Nordholland (LNT 74): ..., *Gestichin decem uncias, Athelhilt decem uncias, Brocchingelant septem uncias,* ... [12. Jh., Kop. um 1420, Egmond]. Der Beleg findet sich in den 'Fontes Egmundenses' (Opperman 1933: 74,20–21. Vermutlich liegt hier der Genitiv eines Frauennamens vor, denn auch in einigen der unten stehenden zusammengesetzten Ortsnamen findet sich ein endungsloses erstes Element, das aus einem Frauennamen besteht (Nr. 3, 4, 6, 10, 11, 14, 15, 17, 19 und 20: Förstemann 1900: 172. Eine männliche Parallele zu diesem Ortsnamen findet sich vielleicht in: *in locis subnotatis Agilmari in pago Uelue* [950] (LNT 59).

2. **Auinęmed**, Ort bei Oudenburg, Prov. Westflanderen (TW 87): *Auinęmed* [1130]. Das erste Element dürfte ein Personenname Avina sein (so TW). Das scheint nicht ausgeschlossen, denn die Namensform *Auina* (und ähnliche Formen) ist in niederländischsprachigem Gebiet 27mal im 10.-12. Jahrhundert belegt.[2]

3. **Bertild med in Dic**, Stück Land in Vladslo, Diksmuide (TW 132): *Bertild med in Dic* [1176]. Der Name ist nach TW mit anl. *mâda* 'Heuland' (ONW) zusammengesetzt und zwar in einer nordseegermanischen Form mit /e:/. Der Personenname ist im 10. Jahrhundert zweimal in den Niederlanden belegt. Vgl. auch Förstemann (1900: 289).

---

2. Für diesen Namen und weitere in diesem Beitrag genannten Personennamen vgl. Kees Nieuwenhuis, *Namen in de Lage Landen voor 1150. Vroeg-middeleeuwse persoonsnamen in Nederland en Vlaanderen.* Vrouwennamen. (keesn.nl).

Frauennamen in alten niederländischen Ortsnamen **289**

4. **Dilentstic**, Stück Land in Wulpen, Veurne, Westflandern (TW 272): *Dilentstic* [1162, Kop. um 1225]. Nach TW handelt es sich um eine Verbindung von anl. *stukki, stikki* 'Stück Land' (ONW) mit dem Personennamen Theudalind, s. auch Nr. 7. Dieser Frauenname kommt im 8.–10. Jahrhundert im Altniederländischen 4mal vor (Förstemann 1900:1439).

5. **Ermengarde belc**, Sint-Pieters-op-den-Dijk, Brügge (TW 327): *Ermengarde belc* [1120], eine Zusammensetzung mit anl. *biluka* 'abgeschlossener Raum' (ONW). Das erste Element ist der Frauenname Irmengard, s. Förstemann 1900:478. Der Name kommt bis 1150 nicht weniger als 18 Male in den Niederlanden und Flandern vor.

6. **Gerlentstic**, Uitkerke, Brügge (TW 399): *Gerlentstic* [1177], eine Zusammensetzung von anl. *stukki, stikki* 'Stück Land' mit dem weiblichen Personennamen Gêrlind, der in den Niederlanden und Flandern zweimal im 9. und 10. Jahrhundert belegt ist (Förstemann 1900:582).

7. **Haia Hersendis**, unbekannt bei Azincourt, Nordfrankreich (TW 435): *nemus paruum* ('ein kleiner Wald') *quod dicitur Haia Hersendis* [um 1156]. Es handelt sich um eine Zusammensetzung mit afrk. *haga* 'Waldstück', vgl. anl. *haga* 'von Hecken umgebener Teil eine Waldes, etwa für die Jagd' (ONW). Auch in anderen Fällen wird dieses Appellativ mit einem Personennamen im Genitiv oder lateinisch bzw. romanisch durch eine Verbindung mit *de* kombiniert: *Haia de Blanchet, Haia Huberti* usw. (TW 435). Bei der Form *Hersindis* handelt es sich wohl in diesem Frauennamen um eine lateinische Endung, vgl. Nr. 8 und 18. Zu dieser Endung siehe jetzt ausführlich van Loon 2021:201–220. Es betrifft wohl den Namen Hereswinth, der vor 1150 4mal in den Niederlanden und Flandern belegt ist (Förstemann 1900:778).

8. **Ligardis vallis**, Pont-à-Celle et Buzet, Charleroi (TW 616): *Ligardis uallis* [1220] 'Tal der Leudigard' mit dem Frauennamen Liodegard (Förstemann 1900:1040). Auch hier liegt wohl eine lateinische Endung vor. Der Frauenname ist vor 1150 10mal in den Niederlanden und Flandern belegt.

9. **Livildenmeeth**, Ort bei Veurne, Westflandern (TW 625): *terram que Luudmed vocatur* [1154], *Le bien dit Luuldmeld, qui contenait 12 mesures* 'das Gut genannt Liefhildmeet, das zwölf *gemet* umfasst' [1154], *Liuildenmeeth* [1162, Kop. um 1225]. In De Flou IX, 1021 wurde in diesem Ortsnamen die Kombination <iui> wahrscheinlich als <uu> gelesen und daher wird dieser Ort irrig als *Luuldmeet* erwähnt. Auch hier liegt anl. *mâda* 'Heuland' (vgl. Nr. 2 und 3) vor, in Verbindung mit dem Frau-ennamen Liufhild, die hier im dritten Beleg schwach gebeugt wurde, vgl. *Liubhild* bei Förstemann (1900:1026). Der Name ist vor 1150 als *Liaueld* bzw. *Liuild* in den Niederlanden und Flandern belegt.

10. **Livosart,** Febvin-Palfart, Saint-Omer (TW 625): *Liueldsart* [(1152–74)]. Eine Verbindung des weiblichen Personennamens Liufhild (s. Nr. 10) mit lat.-rom. *exsartum* 'Rodung'.

11. **Meinburgbelc,** Lissewege, Brügge (TW 680): *terram cui nomen est Meinburg belc* [1213] mit dem Frauennamen Meginburg und mit anl. *bilûka* 'umzäunter Raum', s. oben Nr. 5 (Förstemann 1900:1074). Der Name kommt in der Form Meinburg im 10. Jahrhundert einmal in den Niederlanden und Flandern vor.

12. **Metz-en-Couture,** Arras (TW 694–95): *Mainsendis culturę* [1110], *Mainsendis cultura* [1180], *Meinsendis cultura* [1190], *Mensent couture* [1208], *Mensandis cultura* [1224] die *cultura* 'Neurodung' der Meginswind. Hier liegt im Personennamen wohl auch die lateinische Endung vor (Förstemann 1900:1079–80), s. Nr. 8. Der Frauenname kommt als *Meinsuind, Mensuind* und *Mensuit* dreimal in den Niederlanden und Flandern vor.

13. **Ogierlande,** Gits, Roeselare, Westflandern (TW 759): *de Oujardelande* [1216]. Der Ortsname ist nach TW mit dem Frauennamen Aldagard zusammengesetzt (Förstemann 1900:60). Der Name ist vor 1150 in den Niederlanden und Flandern sonst nicht überliefert.

14. **sars Tywit,** Bruille-Saint-Amand, Valenciennes (TW 889): *li sars Tywit* [1181]. Es handelt sich um eine Verbindung von rom. *essart* ('Rodung') mit dem Personennamen Theudewid, der in den Niederlanden und Flandern vor 1150 sonst nicht belegt ist, vgl. aber Teudwit (Förstemann 1900:1451). Das Substantiv lat. *exsartum* wird normalerweise mit einem Genitiv verbunden, vgl. TW 889.

15. **Schupildhem,** unbekannt in der niederländischen Provinz Nordholland (TW 902; LNT 321): *ut … decime darentur ad supra nominatam aecclesiam [scil. Beuorhem] de uillis his nominibus nominatis: Beuerhem, Gisleshem, Hegginghem, Schupildhem* [918–48, Kop. 1090–1100, Utrecht]. Nach TW handelt es sich um einen Frauennamen *Skupahildi,* aber nach LNT liegt eine Zusammenstellung mit einem unbekannten ersten Element vor. Ein erstes Element **skupa-* in einem Personennamen ist bei Förstemann nicht belegt. Wenn es sich wirklich um einen Frauennamen handelt, so wäre es einer der wenigen Belege in Verbindung mit einer Bezeichnung für ein Haus bzw. einen Hof im niederländischen Gebiet, vgl. *Wiburchoven* (TW 1070), unten Nr. 17. In Deutschland gibt es mehr Belege dafür.

16. **Tietgerdemade,** unbekannt in der Provinz Nordholland (LNT 348): *Tietgerdemade tres uncias* [12. Jh., Kop. um 1420, Egmond], eine Zusammensetzung von anl. *mâda* 'Heuland' mit dem weiblichen Personennamen *Theudgard,* vgl. *Teutgardis* bei Förstemann (1900:1429). Der Name ist vor 1150 viermal in den Niederlanden und Flandern belegt.

17. **Wiburchoven**, unbekannt in der Rheinprovinz oder in der niederländischen Provinz Limburg (TW 1070; LNT 398): *mansus ... situs est aput Wiburchouen* [um 1170–80 (aut.), ad 1118], *venundatis ... mansis ... tertio aput Wiburchouen sito* [um 1170–80 (aut.), ad 1146]. Wahrscheinlich liegt eine Zusammensetzung mit dem Frauennamen Wigburg vor (Förstemann 1900:1581; s. auch unten Nr. 18 und 19). Dieser Frauenname ist vor 1150 dreimal in den Niederlanden und Flandern belegt.

18. **Wiburgis spina**, Flobecq, Ath, Hennegau (TW 1070): *Wiburgis spina* [um 1185] 'Dornstrauch der Wiburg' mit einem Frauennamen Wigburg, s. oben Nr. 17.

19. **fossa Wiburg**, Wasserlauf in der Umgebung von Bodegraven in der Provinz Südholland (LNT 141): *a fossa Wiburg* (ev. zu lesen als Wiburge) [1134, Falsum?, Kop. 1390–1400], vgl. oben Nr. 17 und 18.

20. **Woburgmet**, Oudenburg, Oostende (TW 1086): *Woburgmet* [1171]. Nach TW handle es sich um eine Zusammensetzung von anl. *mâda* 'Heuland' mit dem Frauennamen Waldburg (Förstemann 1900:1502). In den Niederlanden und Flandern ist vor 1150 nur der Name *Walburg* zweimal belegt.

Es betrifft also für das niederländischsprachige Gebiet somit 19 sichere Frauennamen und das unsichere *Scupild*. Beim ersten Blick fällt schon auf, dass es sich bei den meisten Belegen im Hinblick auf das zweite Element um Geländebezeichnungen handelt. Eine Bezeichnung für eine Wohnung oder einen Bauernhof findet sich nicht. Es gibt nur zwei Ausnahmen: das unsichere *Schupildhem* (15) und das eventuell hochdeutsche *Wiburchoven* (17). In einem Fall steht der Name ohne Ergänzung: *Athelhilt* (1).

Am häufigsten — fünfmal — wird ein Frauenname mit dem Substantiv *mâda* 'Heuland' verbunden. Zweimal kommt *stukki* 'Stück' vor. Im Altniederländischen finden sich insgesamt vier Belege mit diesem toponymischen Element und in zwei davon handelt es sich im ersten Element um Frauennamen. Auch *biluka* 'abgegrenztes Gelände' kommt im Material zweimal mit einem Frauennamen vor. Es kommt sowohl als Appellativ wie als selbständiges Toponym vor etwa: *i belec terre* 'ein umzauntes Stück Land' [ca. 1183], *Terra Onulfi et Walteri, que Biloke nominatur* 'das Land von Onulf und Walter, das Bijloke genannt wird' [1191–1200], vgl. ONW. Auch im Frühmittelniederländischen kommt es in Verbindung mit einem Namen im Genitiv vor, vgl. *(...) in symoens belech vp doest+dilue ½. ghemet. Ende ten vppren ende in symoens. belech.½. ghemet. xiii. roeden min* [1280–1286]; *een stic lands twelke houdet zesse jmete, ende hetet badeloghen belec* [1286] (VMNW s.v. *belc*). Interessant ist hier, dass es sich bei den Belegen mit einer Personenbezeichnung im Genitiv als Attribut in zwei von den 12 Fällen um Frauennamen handelt: *een stic lands twelke houdet zesse jmete, ende hetet badeloghen belec* [1286]; *(...) Die welke tiene sceleghe siin beset vp viere line lants dat heeth verlizemoede belch jn die prochie van lopheem te ovdengheem* [1281] (VMNW) mit den Frauennamen Badeloch und (Frau) Lizemoed.

Auch mit dem lateinischen Element *exsartum* 'Rodeland, Neubruch' (Niermeyer I,525) bzw. romanisch *essars* 'id.' kommt zweimal ein Frauenname vor. Vgl. dazu auch *terra que dicitur li Essars Huon* 'das Land, das Rodeland des Hugo genannt wird' (TW 336).

In den anderen Belegen finden sich folgende Geländebezeichnungen:

1. anl. *haga* 'durch Hecken umgebenes Waldstück, das etwa für die Jagd verwendet wird'. Es kommt sowohl als Appellativ (*in omni nemore suo tam in haia quam in reliqua silua* 'in seinem ganzen Wald, sowohl im durch Hecken umgebenen Teil wie im Rest des Waldes' [1188, Kop. 1226–1250]) wie als toponymisches Element vor, vgl. *Suithardeshaghe* [889, Kop. 1251–1300] (ONW).

2. anl. *land* 'Land' wird häufig mit einer Einwohnerbezeichnung oder einem Personennamen im Genitiv verbunden. Bei den Personennamen handelt es sich fast ausschließlich um Männernamen, vgl. *in Hildebrandislant sex libras* [1101–1200, Kop. um 1420], *Hildebrandeslant* [1125–30, Kop. um 1420], *Hildebrandisland* [1125–50, Falsum 1083] unbekanntes Gebiet in der Provinz Nordholland (TW 495; LNT 180–81).

3. lat. *vallis* 'Tal', das häufig mit dem Genitiv eines Personennamens bzw. durch eine Verbindung von lateinisch/romanisch *de* mit einem Personennamen verbunden ist, vgl. *in ualle Remboldi* [1223] (TW 993).

4. lat. *cultura* 'Feld, das neu gewonnen wurde; Felder einer Dorfgemeinde' (Niermeyer I,375–76), wohl auch: 'gesamte Felder eines Bauernhofes' wie Gysseling annimmt (TW 247: "ensemble des terres arables d'un village ou d'une ferme").

5. lat. *spina* '(Dorn)Strauch'.

6. lat. *fossa* 'Deich, Damm' auch 'Grube, Grab' (Niermeyer I,588)

Es ist anzunehmen, dass die Verteilung der Frauennamen mit den Besitzverhältnissen zusammenhängt. Im untersuchten Gebiet findet sich nur ein Beleg mit einem zweiten Element, das eine Wohnung bzw. einen Hof (*Wiburchouen*, Nr. 17) andeutet, und dieser Ort könnte auch in Deutschland liegen. Dort sind solche Zusammensetzungen offensichtlich üblicher:

1. *Adalhedẹhuson* [um 1150] Ahlhausen, Ennepetal, Arnsberg (TW 41);

2. *Dagorada uilla* [786–87, Kop. um 1222] unbekannt im Bitgau oder Ardennergau (TW 254). Der Name könnte eventuell auch den Männernamen Dagarad enthalten, vgl. Förstemann 1900: 395;

3. *Geilenkirche* [1172], *Geylenkirken* [1201; (1210); 1223], *Geilenkirken* [1223], *Gelenkirken* [1225] Geilenkirchen, Aachen (TW 391). Der Name wird von TW

zum Personennamen *Gaila gestellt, aber es könnte eventuell auch zum Männernamen Geilo gehören, siehe dort das direkt vorangehende Lemma Geildorf bzw. das darauf folgende Lemma Geilinghaus;

4. *Hirisuuithuhuson* [1036, Kop. um 1150], *Heresuethehusen* [1221] Hardehausen, Scherfede, Detmold (TW 448) zu *Hariswintha;
5. *Hassuithehuson* [1036, Kop. um 1150] Haxthausen, Paderborn, Detmold (TW 459);
6. *Irminderod* [1066, Falsum um 1084], *Irminderoth* [1109; 1174], *Irmindiroth* [1181, Bulle] Irmeroth, Hennef (Sieg), Köln (TW 536) mit dem weiblichen Personennamen *Irminlind;
7. *in Liefburgahuson, in Liefburgahusoro marcon* [(1033–50), Kop. um 1150, Werden] Lieberhausen, Köln (TW 613);
8. *Rikillahusun* [1220, Kop. um 1150] bei Beberbeck, Kassel (TW 845) zum Frauennnamen Rîkhild;
9. *Siburgohusen* [1018, Kop. um 1150, Vita Meinwerki] Sieberhausen, Kohenborn, Kassel (TW 915)

Es ist anzunehmen, dass in der Periode, da die Ortsnamen entstanden, an erster Stelle Männer als Namengebende auftraten, weil sie als Haupt der Familie das Land oder den Hof in Besitz nahmen oder den Hof gründeten. Das erklärt wohl, warum im niederländischsprachigen Gebiet so selten Frauennamen in Ortsnamen auftauchen.

Das Gebiet, das hier behandelt wird, fiel wahrscheinlich unter die 'Lex Salica'. In diesem fränkischen Gesetz war der Besitz des Bodens offenbar an erster Stelle den Männern vorbehalten, vgl. „Vom salfränkischen Land aber gehe kein Erbanteil an ein Weib über, sondern das gewinne das männliche Geschlecht, d.h. in diese Erbschaft folgen die Söhne." (Pactus Legis Salicae 59 § 6 – Eckhardt 1955: 341). Fünf der 9 Belege in Deutschland stammen aus altsächsischem Gebiet, was vielleicht die abweichende Namengebung erklärt.

Bei den Verbindungen von Frauennamen mit Geländebezeichnungen kann man annehmen, dass sie jüngeren Datums sind. Das wird vielleicht dadurch bestätigt, dass alle oben genannten Belege mit Frauennamen in niederländischem Gebiet aus dem 12. und 13. Jahrhundert stammen, mit Ausnahme der unsicheren Form *Skupild*, die aus dem 10. Jahrhundert stammt. Auch alle deutschen Belege stammen aus dieser Periode, mit Ausnahme von *Dagorada uilla* (Nr. 2), wo eventuell auch ein Männername vorliegen könnte.

Literatur

Debrabandere u.a. 2022 = Debrabandere, F., Devos, M., Kempeneers, P., Mennen, V., Ryckeboer, H. & van Osta, W. (Hgg.). 2022. *De Vlaamse gemeentenamen. Verklarend woordenboek*. Tweede, grondig herziene en vermeerderde uitgave. Leuven: Davidsfonds.

Eckhardt, K.A. 1955. *Pactus legis Salicae. II, 1 65 Titel-Text* (Germanenrechte NF. Wgerm. Recht 2). Göttingen: Musterschmidt.

De Flou, K. 1914–1938. *Woordenboek der Toponymie van Westelijk Vlaanderen, Vlaamsch Artesië, het Land van den Hoek, de graafschappen Guines en Boulogne en een gedeelte van het graafschap Ponthieu*. Gent: Siffer.

Förstemann, E. 1900. *Deutsches Namenbuch*. Erster Band: Personennamen. Zweite, völlige umgearbeitete auflage. Bonn: Hanstein. (Reprint).

De Grauwe, L. 2022. "Index van Germaanse persoonsnamen". In Debrabandere u.a. 2022, 309–36.

Gysseling, M. (Hg.). 1960. *Toponymisch woordenboek van België, Nederland, Luxemburg, Noord-Frankrijk en West-Duitsland (vóór 1226)*. I–II (Bouwstoffen en studiën voor de geschiedenis en de lexicografie van het Nederlands VI,1–2), Brüssel: Belgisch Interuniversitair Centrum voor Neerlandistiek.

Künzel, R., D.P. Blok & J, M. Verhoeff (Hgg.). 1988. *Lexicon van Nederlandse toponiemen tot 1200*. Amsterdam: Meertens-Instituut.

LNT = Künzel u.a. 1988.

Van Loon, J. 2021. *Anthroponomie van Noordwest-Europa tot de twaalfde eeuw. Deel 1: vorm en beekenis van de namen*. Leuven: Peeters.

Niermeyer, J.F. & C. van der Kieft (Hgg.). 2002. *Mediae latinitatis lexicon minus*. Darmstadt: Wissenschaftliche Buchgesellschaft.

Nieuwenhuis, K. (ohne Jahr). *Namen in de Lage Landen voor 1150. Vroegmideleeuwse persoonsnamen in Nederland en Vlaanderen*. Vrouwennamen (keesn.nl).

ONW = *Oudnederlands Woordenboek* (Altniederländisches Wörterbuch) zugänglich via: ivdnt.nl

Opperman, O. (Hg.) 1933. *Fontes Egmundenses* (Werken uitgegeven door het Historisch Genootschap. Derde serie, nr. 61). Utrecht: Kemink.

TW = Gysseling 1960.

Latin *brutes, sapo, burdo*

Ludwig Rübekeil
Universität Zürich

The Germanic languages have adopted many words borrowed from Latin during the time of the Roman Empire (e.g. ModE *wine*, NHG *Mauer* < Latin *vīnum, mūrus* 'wall'). The medieval Germanic languages, on the other hand, left their traces in Romance during the time Germanic peoples settled on former Roman territory (e.g. Fr. *guerre, salle* < Franc. **werra* 'quarrel', **sali-* 'hall, house'). Yet, there is a third and older group of words which are quoted in Latin literature and inscriptions long before the Roman Empire came to an end and individual Romance languages emerged. Well known examples are *glaesum* 'amber' and *ūrus* 'aurochs'. Some of these words became established as loanwords in Latin, while the status of others is less clear. My paper focuses on three examples from this group — *brutes, sapo* and *burdo* – and the methodological and analytical implications connected to their investigation. The main questions are if and how a Germanic origin can be substantiated and what kinds of processes might have been involved.

Loans, quotes, substitutions: Latin-Germanic language contact

Hans Frede Nielsen (1998: 10) once asserted that "for the layman it can be extremely difficult to know whether a word has been borrowed or whether it is a reflex of an indigenous [...] form". Moreover, he explains that "the circumstance that it is so difficult to identify these and other items as loan words, should be ascribed not only to their very general semantic character, but also to their adherence to the morphological, prosodic and orthographic rules". His statements referred to loans in English, but can be extended to most borrowing scenarios as e.g. for Latin or Germanic. Notably, it holds true for both Latin loan words in Germanic and for Germanic loan words in Latin, the latter of which are my focus here.

https://doi.org/10.1075/nss.34.17rub
Available under the CC BY-NC-ND 4.0 license. © 2025 John Benjamins Publishing Company

The historical context

Linguistic exchange between Latin and Germanic was a logical consequence of cultural and social contacts between the speakers of Latin and Germanic. These contacts began in the 1st century BC and continuously intensified until the Roman Empire ended in the 5th century AD or even after. The contact must have taken place constantly and along the whole linguistic frontier, but the main language exchange would have occurred within the borders of the empire, i.e. in the Roman army where many Germanic speaking mercenaries earned their living. That is why some military events might have had a particular linguistic impact on the borrowing scenario, as e.g. the so-called Marcomannic wars (which involved mainly speakers of West Germanic or pre-West Germanic) in the 2nd century and the Gothic wars (East Germanic) in the 3rd century.

The special relationship between the highly organised Roman Empire and the less rigid social and military structure of the numerous Germanic societies determined the social spheres of contact and, therefore, the semantic spectrum of mutual borrowings. Loans from Latin into Germanic covered a wider range of semantic spheres, corresponding to the many cultural fields in which Rome dominated Northern Europe. Borrowings in the opposite direction were drawn from a narrower semantic spectrum than the Latin loanwords in Germanic, in accordance with the differences in the underlying cultures. Furthermore, Germanic words in Roman (mainly Latin) sources can be simple quotes, local loans or fully-fledged loanwords. Especially in the early centuries, the Germanic words quoted in Latin sources mainly relate to isolated and even random aspects of Germanic culture which must have seemed conspicuous to Roman eyes. As the contacts intensified and the dependencies became more and stronger, many terms originated from the military sphere or at least ended up in the military language, as many mercenaries from Germania served in the Roman army. The 2nd and 3rd century must have been a key period for this layer of words, as it was an era of constant military conflicts along the northern Roman borders. During this time, the conflicts evolved from local skirmishes into widespread and persistent wars and, from a Roman perspective, the middle and lower Danube emerged as the most vulnerable region. This situation definitely escalated in the 4th century, when the Huns conquered large parts of Eastern Europe, which particularly but not exclusively affected the Goths who, in the decades to come, would become even more closely connected with Rome.

The phonology of borrowing

When Romans refer to Germanic words — and even more so when they borrowed them –, these lexical items had to be made compatible with the morphological, phonological and phonotactic constraints of the Latin language. This applied both to inflectional morphology and to the scripting of some Germanic sounds which had no counterparts in Latin. Some phonemes as e.g. /r/, /s, z/, /i/, /u/ were generally replaced by their immediate Latin counterpart; they are of less interest here. The Germanic fricatives /f/, /þ/, /χ/, however, were more problematic. Scribes sometimes followed the Latin convention for writing Greek aspirates ⟨ph-th-ch⟩ and sometimes they simply spelled them as occlusives, that is ⟨p-t-c⟩. The labial fricative /ƀ/, on the other hand, changed its representation from ⟨b⟩ to ⟨v/u⟩ in correlation with the change of Lat. *v* from a bilabial approximant to a voiced labiodental fricative (Adams 2013: 183–186). An overview of the most "regular" writing correspondences of Germanic consonants in Latin is presented in Table 1 below (for a more comprehensive list, also of the vowels that will be discussed below, see Schönfeld 1911: XV–XXVII; Reichert 1987: XIX–XXVIII):

Table 1. Germanic and Latin phoneme-grapheme correlation: Consonants

/Gmc/	f	þ	χ		s	z	b/ƀ	d/d	g/g	j	w
⟨Lat.⟩	f	th/t	ch/c/h		s		b/v	d	g/ch?	i	v/b

While the scripting of Germanic consonants is quite consistent, the vowels present more problems. The Germanic vowel system has been altered and simplified by minor sound changes from Indo-European to Proto-Germanic, the main changes being the mergers of *a* and *o* and of *ā* and *ō*. The loss of short *ŏ* and of long *ā* resulted in a four-vowel system, both for the short and the long subsystems. The ensuing gaps were partly filled by other sound changes, the most crucial being the loss of nasals with compensatory lengthening (V̆N*h* > V̄*h*). This lengthening resulted in a new *ā* which was nasalized. In the same way, long nasalized *į̄* and *ų̄* developed, but not †*ǭ* and †*ę̄*, because PGmc *ě* had become *ǐ* before nasal + consonant, and *ŏ* did not exist at all after its merger with *ă*. These vowels were only re-established by breaking in Gothic and a-mutation (only of *ŭ* > *ŏ*) in Northwest Germanic.

Latin continued the five-vowel Western Indo-European system with contrastive length, but changed the Pre-Italic diphthong system more significantly towards Latin. Compared to Germanic, a little more is known about the phonetics of the short and long vowels in Latin. As can be deduced both from the interference with other languages and later developments, the long vowels, especially *ē,ī,ū,ō* had a tense articulation, while the short vowels were more on the lax side.

Not unlike Germanic, short vowels were lengthened and nasalized before *s* and perhaps *χ* (Meiser 1998: 78–79), as in *mensa* 'table', which must have been realised as [*mẹ̄sa*]. The precise phonetic character of the attested spellings often remains unclear, since Latin had similar processes but used historical writing conventions. It is unclear, for instance, whether ⟨anh⟩ in the personal name *Hanhavaldus* (±400 AD) stands for *anh* or *ą̄h* and, even more so, whether ⟨enc⟩ in the tribal name *Tencteri* (earlier) stands for *enh* or *ẹ̄h* (or even *ị̄h*).

An overview of the most regular writing correspondences of Germanic vowels is listed in Table 2 and 3.

Table 2. Phoneme-grapheme correlations: Monophthongs

/Gmc/	ă	ĕ	ĭ	ŭ	ē₁	ī	ō	ū
⟨Lat.⟩	a/o	e	i/e	o/u	e	i	o	u

Table 3. Phoneme-grapheme correlations: Nasal vowels and diphthongs

/Gmc/	ą̄	ị̄	ų̄	ai	au	ij	uw
⟨Lat.⟩	a(n)	i(n)/e(n)	u(n)	ae	au/ao	e/i	u/o

The picture becomes more complicated because Latin and Germanic changed fundamentally in the course of their histories. Runic records and other evidence indicate an early dialectal split into single branches of Germanic which quickly strengthened during late antiquity. In Latin, on the other hand, the dialectal differentiation seems to be masked by writing conventions. Here, the written and the spoken language diverged increasingly. While some consonants tended towards lenition and consonant clusters were simplified, the vowel system experienced even more restructuring in late antiquity, especially when distinctive vowel length came to be replaced with distinction in vowel quality. The linguistic reality must have been much more complex than such a simplistic description implies (for a brief introduction to Vulgar Latin, see Herman & Wright 2000; Kiesler 2018; for a more comprehensive approach, see Grandgent 1907; Stotz 1996; Adams 2013; all of them consider the role of foreign languages like Germanic). The diachronic changes had some impact on writing — even more so on how foreign sounds were written, as writing Latin was partly conserved by writing traditions and conventions. Frequently used foreign names became part of the Latin lexicon, too. If the tribal name PGmc *Swēbōz* was written *Suebi* in the 1st century AD, it was a close representation of Germanic. But PGmc *ē₁* became NWGmc *ā* during the 3rd century, so if the name is written *Suebi* in the 4th century or after, it can be safely assumed that this is due to Latin tradition and has little to no connection with contemporary Germanic.

The morphology of borrowing

The phonetic quality of sounds is not the only factor which had an influence on their spelling. The morphology of the recipient language also played an important role, as the rules of substitution are different in lexical and grammatical morphemes. Therefore, Gmc /a/ is generally replaced with Latin ⟨a⟩ in lexemes but with ⟨o⟩ in the inflectional elements of Latin o-stems. It furthermore appears as ⟨o⟩ in the linking elements of compounds like Lat. *Lang-o-bardi, Marc-o-manni, Char-io-valda* ← Gmc **Lang-a-bardōz, Mark-a-mannoz, *Har-ja-walda(z)*. Whether Germanic or Latin is responsible for the latter behaviour is debated, though the labial quality of the following consonant (*b,m,w*) seems to have had an influence. Most probably, the phonetic ranges of the /a/-phonemes in Germanic and Latin were not compatible; a Gmc positional allophone [ɔ] of /a/ might have been closest to a Lat. allophone [ɔ] of /o/ and therefore was rendered as ⟨o⟩.

Regarding morphology, both cited and borrowed words were made to fit into the stem structure of Latin inflection. This means that, as a rule, nouns from a certain Germanic stem class were integrated into a Latin stem class that seemed equivalent in some way or another. Often enough, though not always, these corresponding classes go back to the same prehistorical roots. For example, nouns of the numerous Germanic a-stem nouns were usually treated as Latin o-stems (IE *-o-*). Similarly, i-stems in Germanic and Latin seem compatible and n-stems as well. Even if the transfer is not always straightforward, most words find themselves in their corresponding classes. Whether e.g. the nominative plural of Gmc. a- and ja-stems is rendered as Lat. *-i* or *-ii*, seems in part incidental. But as a general rule, the transfer of nouns from Germanic to Latin predominantly followed these rules (most examples are proper names since these constitute the largest corpus by far; see Table 4 for an overview).

The trigger responsible for the classification could be a single case form that dominated the pragmatic use of a noun as well as the paradigmatic pattern as a whole. A view on the i-stems makes it strikingly clear how not only single forms but whole paradigms or their larger parts could be compatible (IE **gʰost-i-s* 'stranger'; see Table 5).

Unexpected behaviour is not always a slip, though. In some cases, Latin seems to confirm the existence of primary stem forms which were lost in later stages of Germanic. The frequent name element **mēri- / mērja-* 'famous', for instance, regularly appears as NOM.SG *-us* in early personal names (*Inguiomerus, Segimerus, Chariomerus*) and even with *-o-* in the front element of compounds (*Merobaudes, Merofledis, Merovechus*). What might be judged as deviation from the rule, actually indicates the existence of a primary adjective **mēra-* which later was replaced by **mērja-* as its deverbal competitor (by interference with **mēr-*

Table 4. Germanic stem classes in Latin inflection

Gmc		Lat.	Examples
-a-	→	-o-	*mundaz → mundus (Segi-), *Hauhōz → Cauci, Chauci
-ja-		-i̯o-	*Harjōz → Harii
-wa-		-u̯o-	*baðwaz → -bod(u)us (Maro-, Gundo-)
-i-		-i-	*alχiz/algiz → alcis, achlis
			*bauðiz → -baudes (Baino-, Hario-, Mallo-, Mero-)
-n-		-n-	*Gutaniz → Gutones
-ō-		-a-	*Þūsneldō → Thusnelda
-u-		-u-	*Haðu-° → Catu-
-s-		-s-	*segis- → sigis-

Table 5. I-inflection in Germanic and Latin

Gmc *gastiz 'stranger, guest'		Lat. hostis 'stranger, enemy'	
Singular	**Plural**	**Singular**	**Plural**
*gast-iz	*gast-īz	host-is	host-ēs
*gast-īz, -aiz	*gast-ijōⁿ	host-is	host-ium
*gast-ī, -ai	*gast-imiz	host-ī	host-ibus
*gast-iⁿ	*gast-inz	host-em, -im	host-ēs, -īs

jan 'make famous'; cf. Heidermanns 1993: 409). Considering this, it is less amazing that Latin records show evidence of the double adjective inflection (Rübekeil 2006: 490) or even construed new declension types on the bases of Germanic paradigms (Schönfeld 1911: XXIV–XXV; cf. Adams 2013: 375 n. 1).

The following sections will deal with three examples of loanwords in Latin for which a Germanic origin has been suggested. I will discuss the relevant issues and sketch possible new approaches.

Example 1: Lat. *brutes, brutis, bruta*

The first example, Latin *brutes* with its variants, occurs in more than 10 instances in classical sources, most of which are inscriptions (for a list of the inscriptions see Simon 2021: 313). Its meaning is primarily 'daughter-in-law' or 'younger married woman' in a more general sense. There is no convincing etymology from within Latin, where the word's initial *b-* is difficult to explain: Latin *#b-* would either go back to *du̯-* or *gᵘ̯-* (as in *bonus < duenos* or *bōs < *gᵘ̯ōu̯s*) or even to a more complex assimilation like in *bibō* < **pibō*. None of these sources are possible here. Initial IE **bʰ-*, on the other hand, would have yielded Lat. **f-*. A foreign origin and hence a loanword is therefore generally assumed. Germanic is the only language family which uses a similar word with a suitable meaning. All Gmc branches continue a word that means 'young married woman, bride' and point to a PGmc form **brūdiz* f. (Goth. *brūþs*, OS *brūd*, ON *brúðr*, OE *brȳd*, OHG *brūt* and the like).

A confounding factor in this analogy, however, is the quality of the inner dental consonant. Judging from all parallels, Lat. ⟨t⟩ renders Gmc. *þ* and not *d*. The loanword should therefore appear as †*brūdis* rather than *brūtis*. Since Gothic has devoiced its voiced fricatives by several processes (esp. final devoicing and Thurneysen's law; cf. Braune & Heidermanns 2004: 65, 82; Miller 2019: 27, 32), Gothic provenance has generally been assumed. This appears to be backed up by the epigraphical transmission which in part originates from the lower Danube and dates from the 3rd century and, thus, the time of the "Gothic wars". In a recent study, however, Simon (2021: 313–314) has questioned this explanation. As the early attestations date to the 2nd century and originate in Pannonia, he assumes that the earliest adoption of the word into Latin might have taken place in Pannonia (Superior) or even Noricum, from where the word spread to the lower Danube later on. Simon posits a primary doublet of Northwest Gmc paradigmatic stem variants **brūþi-* : **brūdi-*. Since feminine i-stems with Verner variants do exist in large numbers (see Schaffner 2001: 436–487 for a comprehensive list), this may be a convincing explanation. The enemies of Rome at the border of Pannonia Superior during the 2nd century AD, i.e. Marcomanni, Quadi, Naristi and others, originated mainly from more westerly regions. They may therefore have spoken a (pre-)West Germanic dialect (or a Northwest Germanic dialect respectively; for further thoughts, see Nielsen 2004: 24–26; cf. also Rübekeil 2017: 987; Fulk 2018: 25).

The problem though is that Germanic lacks any evidence of a variant †*brūþiz*, in particular, or a Verner-alternation in general. The Northwest Germanic languages clearly point to **brudi-*, whereas Gothic gives no positive evidence (the only attested form is ACC.SG *bruþ* in Matth. 10,35). The etymology of **brūdi-* does not offer any distinct evidence either. The ending suggests a ti-abstract noun, but other possibilities exist, and it is especially hard to agree on an Indo-European reconstruction which fits both the structure and semantics of the word (Lloyd, Springer & Lühr 1998: 403–406; Lehmann 1986: 83–84; Kroonen 2013: 79). Besides, we should keep in mind that there are loanwords in which voiced fricatives are represented by their voiceless counterparts in Latin, and for which Verner alternation does not apply. One such example is Lat. *tufa* ← Gmc **þūbōn-*, most likely a loan from Gothic (Rübekeil 2020: 191–197).

Other cases, however, where reconstructions of lost Verner variants must be taken into consideration, sound a note of caution. For instance, Lat.-Gmc *alcis* with its variant *achlis* might represent spoken **alhiz* vs. **algiz* and thus support Simon's idea (Rübekeil 2021: 234–235; also see below for the relation between Gmc. *burþīn-* and reconstructed adjective **burþa-*). If the etymology of Gmc **bruđi-* turned out to be based on IE *-t-*, this solution would be preferable.

While the morphology of the early epigraphical transmission corresponds to the Germanic i-stem, the manuscript tradition deviates from this. The first instance is a short notice by Ioannes Lydos, a writer in 6th-century Constantinople, who construes *brūta* as a feminine derivative of the personal name *Brūtus*. In his eyes, 'when Brutus had died, they honored the dead man with a public mourning and named their own wives *brutae* after him on account of their discretion' (De Magistratibus 1,33: τελευτήσαντος δὲ τὸν βίον τοῦ Βρούτου, δημοσίῳ πένθει ἐτίμησαν τὸν νεκρὸν καὶ βρούτας τὰς σφῶν γυναῖκας ὠνόμασαν ἐξ αὐτοῦ διὰ τὴν σωφροσύνην; Bandy 1983: 50–51). Obviously this folk etymology led the morphological classification into the ā-inflection which, in turn, might point to a changing lexical status: While *brūtis, -es* was perhaps still in use with Germanic speaking soldiers, *bruta* indicates its detachment from the Germanic languages, where the i-stem still applied. The fact that **βρουτίς* or *βρούτιδες* respectively still exists in middle Greek, is a strong indicator, though, that this process was confined to the literary language.

The second instance is a gloss *nurus ~ bruta* 'daughter in law' in the second Erfurt Glossary (Codex Amplonianus 2° 42, 28v; Goetz & Loewe 1894: 314), which likewise transfers the word to the Latin ā-declension. This evidence from the 9th century certainly implies scholarly interference and may appear less relevant at first. However, the sources of the second Erfurt Glossary very likely date back several centuries (EEG: s. sources: introduction). Lindsay (1921: 92) inferred a German compiler for the *nurus ~ bruta* gloss, probably because he associated the second element with OHG *brūt* 'bride'. Yet, if this layer of the second Erfurt glossary is based on an older Latin-Greek glossary, as Lindsay (1921: 79) himself assumed, the gloss *bruta* may well confirm that the explanation given by Lydos was not isolated.

Example 2: Lat. *sapo* and related

The next word pertains to the semantic domain of medicine. It can be connected with English *soap* and German *Seife* and therefore is suspected to be of Germanic origin. Finnish *saippua, saippio* is seen as a loan from Germanic and hence seems to confirm the evidence (cf. Hofstra 2011). The etymology remains unclear and disputed. If the word is based on a root *seib-* (Walde & Hofmann 1954:II, 478), Lat. *sēbum* 'tallow' could theoretically be related, even as a loan from Celtic, though it cannot be traced in the Celtic languages (see also Vaan 2008:550).

The most famous attestation comes from Pliny. He quotes a word *sapo*, denominating some sort of hair dye and which can also be used against scrofula: 'Soap also helps [against scrofula], an invention of the Gaulic people to redden the hair' (Pliny Nat. 28,191: *prodest et sapo, Galliarum hoc inventum rutilandis capillis*; Jan & Mayhoff 1897:340). It should be noted that Pliny speaks of a Gaulic invention which might imply a Gaulic word, even though he refers to its use among Germanic people shortly after. Soon after Pliny, Martial mentions *sapo*, too. The matter, albeit without mentioning the word, turns up as 'Batavian foam that changes Latian curls' (Epigrammata 8,33: *spuma Batava*; Shackleton Bailey 2012:256). This foam comes into focus again in another book, when alluding to the 'Chattian foam that lights Teuton hair' and 'Mattiac balls (pills)' to change grey hair (Epigrammata 14,26–27; Shackleton Bailey 2012:457). The latter poems are titled as *sapo* or *crines / sapo* respectively. While the main transmission here is *sapo*, the manuscripts partly show the variant *saepo* in verse 27, which might be relevant for the ongoing discussion about the linguistic origin of the word. As Martial mentions Chattians and Teutons, a Germanic background has been posited. However, with the naming of the *Chatti, Batavi* and *Mattiaci*, the ethnic background is situated along the Rhine and in the Celto-Germanic contact area. Judging by its geography, both a Germanic and a Gaulic origin of the word are plausible as is the usage in both languages.

It should be pointed out that *sapo* has had a longer and wider history in antiquity (see André 1956 for an overview). This complicates things as only a few passages claim Germanic origin compared to a majority of sources which understand the word as Gaulic. While Pliny is the first to mention the word in Latin, the Greek transmission begins shortly before Pliny with Pedanios Dioskurides, an influential Greek physician. Dioskurides mentions a word σαπάνα for the medical flower Ἀναγαλλίς 'the red pimpernel' and, like Pliny, assigns it to the Gaulic language (De materia medica 2, 178; Wellmann 1907:247). While Pliny understands *sapo* as a cosmetic product with additional medical value, Dioskurides, conversely, describes σαπάνα as a plant with mainly medical purposes. This view persists in Greek literature which, indeed, comprises mainly medical writings. Throughout the centuries, up to late antiquity, the word was used in all sorts of medical contexts, and a large part of the sources explicitly labels the product as *gallicus* 'Gaulic'. The tradition is clearly dominated by Greek literature, and it should be taken into account that Greek authors do not make much of an effort to distinguish Germanic and Gaulic people nor their language. According to André, the Greek accounts date at least one century earlier than those in Latin.

One decisive factor in determining the origin of *sapo* is its phonological structure. There are two main parameters for the etymological analysis:

1. The Germanic descendants point to a diphthong *ai*, while the transmission — except for a few cases such as Marcellus Empiricus above — is dominated by *a*. The two can not be reconciled easily.

2. The medial *p* in Germanic and in Gaulic cannot be traced back to a common phoneme in Indo-European. IE *p* would have lead to Gmc. *f* and Gaul. *ø*. Therefore, a differing Indo-European root structure must be posited for the two cases.

Both signals put together point to a language contact scenario in pre-literary times. Germanic has both a monophthong *a* and a diphthong *ai*, whereas the system of diphthongs has been simplified and restricted in the Gaulish language. Phonemic substitution or areal sound changes would therefore be a valid explanation. Gaulic shows few instances of both *oi* and *ai*, and their origin is not always clear. Pre-Celt. *oi* resulted in a monophthong *ū*, while *ai* seems to have persisted though it was rare in pre-Celtic already. The few instances of *ai* which alternate with *ē* and *ī* appear in a handful of Gaulish names like *Aedui* (if < *h_2eid^h*- 'burn') and in inflectional endings or in possible loanwords e.g. from Germanic like **gaisa-* 'spear' (cf. Evans 1967: 396; Lambert 1994: 42; Delamarre 2003: 174; Stifter 2017: 1198; the Germanic origin of **gaisa-* is mainly justified by its analysis as IE **$g^hoisó$-* though).

The origin of *sapo* was discussed several times in the last decades, in particular by André (1956) and Simon (2020). André assumed a Germanic loanword in Celtic, from which it was borrowed into Latin and which was also brought to Asia minor by the Galatian Tectosages, where it came in contact with Greek and other eastern languages. Simon postulated independent loans from a Western European substratum language that predated Celtic and Germanic; this approach is based on observations made by Schrijver (1997). Both explanations extend into prehistory: André dates the loan before ±300 BC, the time of the Celtic migration to Asia minor. The same holds true for the substratum, because at least some of the words involved would have been borrowed before Grimm's law (e.g. PBrit. **kraχar-* vs. PGmc **hraigra(n)-* 'heron'). Notably, the pair **sapō*: **saipō* shows neither Grimm's law nor Celtic loss of *p*. Therefore, both solutions, however tempting, do not solve all problems. As to the question why a substratum sound would yield *a* in Gaulic and *ai* in Germanic, substitution processes still need to be considered, which is not very different from a loan from Germanic: The diphthong in question must have had a quality in the donor language for which, in a certain period or area, Gaulic *a* was a better fit. In other times or areas, this might have produced a different result, which could possibly explain cases like **gaisa-* (but see above).

So even if we do assume that *sapo* is a loanword from Germanic, there remain unanswered questions. However, assuming it was borrowed from Germanic after the loss of loss of Celt. *p* and perhaps after Grimm's law remains the better option.

Scholars least disagree about the region where *sapo* was borrowed into Latin. As some of the early records indicate that the word was used in the Celtic-Germanic contact area along the Rhine, this must have been the area where it was adopted. From there, the Romans borrowed the Celtic variant. The manuscript variant *saepo* in Martial's Epigrammata (see above) might be an isolated reflex of the Germanic variant but can of course also be accidental.

Example 3: Lat. *burdō* 'mule'

Let me finally discuss the most puzzling noun: *burdo*, meaning either 'mule' or 'hinny' (Adams 1993: 55–60), which offers diverse and thorny obstacles when investigating its prehistory.

By the time we encounter *burdō* in the sources, it is a distinctly Latin word without any hints at a foreign origin. One eye-catching and often referred-to aspect is its appearance both as an n- as well as an o-class noun. However, as far as I can see, the latter appears only in a single Horace scholion, glossing Horaces *mannis* DAT.PL 'small Gaulic horse, pony' (in epodos 4,14: Keller 1902: 394), which by itself seems to be a loan from Gaulic or another Northern language (Walde & Hofmann 1954: II, 29–30; Ernout & Meillet 2001: 384). And the fact that even here, *burdos* is explained by *burdones* (var. *burichos*), gives the variant *burdus* less significance.

Burdo is very productive in terms of word formation and even active in wordplay. Most of the nouns are sparsely attested in later antiquity, like *burdōnārius, burdōnicus* 'mule driver', the diminutive *burdunculus* 'a plant' or *burdātio* 'tax on a field' (TLL II, 2247–2249). *Burdubasta*, a satirical name for lame gladiators of the type *bestiarii* (Petronius Satyricon 45,11; Müller 1995: 39), is predominantly regarded as a loan from an uncertain language. In fact, it is rather a pun on the words *burdo* and *bastum* 'stick, e.g. to drive a mule' (Schmeling & Setaioli 2011: 190), given the fact that the descendant of *burdo* itself means 'stick' in the Romance languages. Last but not least, *burdo* has often been connected with *buricus* 'mannus; small horse' (see the Horace scholion above), which is probably a loan, too. Etymologically, however, the two must be separated.

Despite all these affinities, *burdo* cannot be inherited on account of its initial #*b*- None of the possible sources for #*b*- are plausible in this case (see Example 1 above, *brutes* for these sources). The word has therefore generally been viewed as a loanword, though the suggested sources are problematic or at least unprovable. Besides Basque, Iberian, Illyrian, Sabellic and other etymologies, a Germanic provenance has sometimes been posited but not elaborated on (Schrader & Nehring 1929: 52; Gregoire 1937: 84). The idea of a Celtic origin has had more backing, with scholars emphasizing local and personal names on the one hand and the double declension of *burdus* and *burdo* on the other (Ernout & Meillet 2001: 78; Lloyd, Springer & Lühr 1998: 455; Evans 1966: 31). However, the related onomasticon (TLL II, 2248; Holder 1896: I: 638–639), especially the place names, are mostly found in Aquitania and on the Iberian Peninsula and therefore probably not Celtic but rather Basque or Iberian. Furthermore, they do not provide a plausible semantic nexus. Whatmough (1970: 445–446) hence stressed that there "appear to be no Keltic cognates". With these circumstances in mind, let me evaluate the idea of a Germanic provenance again.

Some of the Germanic cognates of Lat. *burdo* are clearly taken from medieval Romance dialects; MLG *burdūn*, MDu. *burdoen*, ME *burdoun* e.g. are obvious loans from OFr. *bourdon* 'mule' (cf. Lloyd, Springer & Lühr 1998: 456). It is unclear as to how the first element in Du. *bord-esel* 'carrying donkey' belongs to this list, for it might as well contain MDu. *burde, borde* 'load' (see below). MHG masc. *burd* "der ze latein *burdo haizt*" in Konrad von Megenbergs *pŭch von den naturleichen dingen* (III.A.48; Luff & Steer 2003: 176), on the other hand, resembles Lat. *burdus* and must be separated from the loans of Old French *bourdon*. Going back in time, we find OHG *burdichīn* (Steinmeyer & Sievers 1895: 450,29), as in the Horace scholion translating *mannus*. *Burdichīn* looks like a derivation from OHG *burdĭ(n)* 'burden' at first glance. This similarity is suggestive but not without problems since *-ichīn* creates diminutives, and the expected base type would therefore be an animal name. *Burdichīn* has a similar formation pattern as, for instance, *fulichī(n)*, which is a diminutive of *folo* 'foal'. Despite the vernacular formation pattern, *burdichīn* was mostly, with more implicit than explicit reasoning, seen as a loan from Latin (cf. e.g. Palander 1899: 99; Kluge 1913: 13; Walde & Hofmann 1954: II, 123; Lloyd, Springer & Lühr 1998: 455–456) and even an early loan of Gmc. **burþīn-* into Latin which was reborrowed into Germanic again (Schrader & Nehring 1929: 53), which in view of *sapo : saepo* above is not impossible.

The explanation from Latin entails several implications. If the word had been borrowed from early *burdo* or *burdus*, the expected outcome would be NWGmc **bordaz* or **bordan-* by a-mutation. If it was a borrowing from younger Vulgar Latin **bordo(n)*, the same would hold true due to Vulgar Latin lowering. Furthermore, the result would be OHG †*bort(o)* via the second consonant shift and, thus, †*burtichīn*. The ways to escape this conflict would be to posit either a younger Old High German loan directly from written literary Medieval Latin or a secondary loan from a Low German or Old Dutch dialect. The latter is quite possible because the suffix variant *-ichīn*, is usually seen as — though not exclusively —

a northern variant, as opposed to southern *-īn*, *-ilīn* (for more information, see Wilmanns 1930: 320–322; Krahe & Meid 1969: 216–217; Klein, Solms & Wegera 2009: 60–61, 135–137).

The etymological status of OHG *burdĭ(n)* is not fully clear, since two patterns are contaminated in this noun, **burþinō-* and **burþīn-* (Thöny 2013: 75; Braune & Heidermanns 2018: 288–291), of which *-īn-* is probably older. The Germanic abstracts of the *īn*-type are mostly and typically based on a-stem adjectives. In the case of Gmc **burþīn-* (Goth. *baurþei*, OHG *burdĭ(n)*; another stem **burþinjō* in OE *byrðen*), a verbal adjective, derived from the strong verb **ber-a-*, would be the most obvious contender (Lehmann 1986: 65; Lloyd, Springer & Lühr 1998: 456; Casaretto 2004: 281, 296; Braune & Heidermanns 2004: 107). This etymology, as a bonus, connects the double declension in Latin *burdus*: *burdo* to the adjective declension of the Germanic languages, which show exactly this combination of strong and weak forms side by side. However, with an expected form Gmc **burđa-* < IE **bʰr̥tó-* of the verbal adjective, the etymology faces the same problems as above: MHG *burd-* must go back to a Verner-less variant **burþa(n)-*, not "regular" **burđa(n)-*. The absence of Verner's law is the lesser problem here, since **burþa-* is required by **burþīn-* anyway, so parallel forms similar to **alþa-* : **alđa-*, **χluþa-* : **χluđa-*, **kunþa-* : **kunđa-* or **werþa-* : **werđa-* must have existed (for the processes leading to such variants see Schaffner 2001: 266–327; Casaretto 2004: 491–493). The more serious drawback of this solution, however, is the lack of a-mutation in MHG *burd*, which should appear as **bord* instead (note that Du. *bord-* is due to younger developments).

Yet there are instances of *burd-* in Old High German. It is found, for instance, in the compound *burdhaftī* 'fascinatio; magic' (Steinmeyer & Sievers 1879: 554,2; the meaning might be the result of etymological reasoning). Here it is probably derived from the adjective **burdihaft* 'ponderosus; heavily loaded' (Steinmeyer & Sievers 1882: 221,6; ms. *purdahafter*), the front element of which is either *burdĭ(n)* 'burden' or **burdi-* < **burþi-* (see below), which would not be expected to undergo Northwest Germanic a-mutation. This question is more open for *burdref*, where the lack of a linking vowel is more remarkable (Gröger 1911: 164–165). *Burdref* is cited twice in the OHG Tatian (Tatian c. 158 p. 282; Masser 1994: 575) and translates the Latin-Greek loanword *pera* 'bag, wallet for carrying provisions' and, in both occurrences, is combined with *seckil* 'saccolus; bag'. Since *ref* by itself means 'sarcina; package' (Steinmeyer & Sievers 1895: 308), the first element *burd* may belong to the semantic field of 'load' or 'bear', which would make a reasonable functional context for a mule. The same though holds true for the ON cognates *burðr* m. 'birth, lineage' and *byrð* f. 'load', which have diverged from masculine and feminine i-stems (while ON *byrðr* stands closer to Goth. *baurþei*, OHG *bur-*

dĭ(n) etymologically). Here it should be mentioned that *burðr* m. has a specified meaning 'young born animal' (ONP: s.v.), which would also be compatible

Whether *burdo/burdus* is a loanword from Germanic or another language remains far from proven in the end. The arguments in favour of a Germanic origin are admittedly quite shaky and contain multiple obstacles. These obstacles seem, however, less severe than those encountered when assuming the word to be a loanword from other languages. It is the etymology — both in terms of structure and semantics — which makes a Germanic origin and hence a borrowing from Germanic plausible.

The etymologies of *brutis* and *sapo*, in contrast, remain unclear and therefore have no bearing on the issue at stake. The main argument in favour of a Germanic origin is simply their distribution in the Germanic languages. What appears as an explanatory difficulty at first — the voiceless *t* in *brutis* and the monophthong *a* in *sapo* — on closer inspection sheds light on the sometimes complicated and often indirect pathways of adoption into Latin. Such complications underscore that there is almost never absolute certainty about the ways and modes of loanword transmission.

References

Adams, J. N. 1993. The generic use of "mula" and the status and employment of female mules in the roman world. *Rheinisches Museum für Philologie* 136. 35–61.

Adams, J. N. 2013. *Social variation and the Latin language.* Cambridge: Cambridge University Press.

André, J. 1956. Gaulois sapana, latin sapo, grec ΣΑΠΩΝ. *Études celtiques.* Persée — Portail des revues scientifiques en SHS 7. 348–355.

Bandy, A. C. (ed.). 1983. *Ioannēs Lydos. On powers, or the magistracies of the Roman State* (Memoirs of the American Philosophical Society 149). Philadelphia, PA: The American Philosophical Society.

Braune, W. & F. Heidermanns. 2004. *Gotische Grammatik. Mit Lesestücken und Wörterverzeichnis* (Sammlung kurzer Grammatiken germanischer Dialekte A.1). 20. Auflage. Tübingen: Niemeyer.

Braune, W. & F. Heidermanns. 2018. *Althochdeutsche Grammatik. 1. Laut- und Formenlehre.* 16th edn. Berlin: De Gruyter.

Casaretto, A. 2004. *Nominale Wortbildung der gotischen Sprache. Die Derivation der Substantive.* Heidelberg: Winter.

Delamarre, X. 2003. *Dictionnaire de la langue gauloise. Une approche linguistique du vieux-celtique continental* (Collection des Hespérides). 2e éd. rev. corr. et très augm. Paris: Errance.

EEG = The Épinal-Erfurt Glossary. (Ed.) M. W. Herren, D. Porter & H. Sauer. https://epinal-erfurt.artsci.utoronto.ca/. (15 March, 2023).

Ernout, A. & A. Meillet. 2001. *Dictionnaire étymologique de la langue latine. Histoire des mots.* Retirage de la quatrième éd., augm. d'additions et de corrections nouvelles par Jacques André. Paris: Klincksieck.

Evans, D. E. 1966. 'gurdonicus' Sulp. Sev. *Dial.* 1.27.2. *Studia Celtica* 1. 27–31.

Evans, D. E. 1967. *Gaulish personal names. A study of some continental Celtic formations.* Oxford: Clarendon.

Fulk, R. D. 2018. *A comparative grammar of the early Germanic languages* (Studies in Germanic Linguistics 3). Amsterdam: Benjamins.

Goetz, G. & G. Loewe. 1894. *Corpus glossariorum Latinorum*, Vol. 5: *Placidus liber glossarum. Glossaria reliqua.* Leipzig: Teubner.

Grandgent, C. H. 1907. *An introduction to vulgar Latin.* Boston: Heath.

Gregoire, H. 1937. L'Etymologie de "Caballus" ou de l'utilité du grec moderne. In *Etudes Horatiennes. Recueil publié en l'honneur du bimillénaire d'Horace*, 81–93. Bruxelles: Édition de la Revue de l'Université de Bruxelles.

Gröger, O. 1911. *Die althochdeutsche und altsächsische Kompositionsfuge mit Verzeichnis der althochdeutschen und altsächsischen Composita.* Zürich: Zürcher & Furrer.

Heidermanns, F. 1993. *Etymologisches Wörterbuch der germanischen Primäradjektive.* Berlin: De Gruyter.

Herman, J. & R. Wright. 2000. *Vulgar Latin.* University Park: Pennsylvania State University Press.

Hofstra, T. 2011. Zum niederländischen Wort "zeep" und seinen Verwandten. In G. Kroonen (ed.), *Thi Timit Lof: Festschrift für Arend Quak zum 65. Geburtstag*, 131–142. Amsterdam: Brill.

Holder, A. 1896. *Alt-Celtischer Sprachschatz. 1. A-H.* Leipzig: Teubner.

Jan, L. von & K. Mayhoff (eds.). 1897. *C. Plini Secundi Naturalis historiae libri XXXVII. Vol. 4. Libri XXIII–XXX.* Stuttgart: Teubner.

Keller, O. (ed.). 1902. *Pseudacronis Scholia in Horatium vetustiora: I. Schol. AV in carmina et epodos.* Leipzig: Teubner.

Kiesler, R. 2018. *Einführung in die Problematik des Vulgärlateins.* 2. Auflage, aktualisiert und erweitert von Volker Noll. Berlin: Niemeyer.

Klein, Th., H.-J. Solms & K.-P. Wegera. 2009. *Mittelhochdeutsche Grammatik, Teil III. Wortbildung.* Tübingen: Niemeyer.

Kluge, F. 1913. *Urgermanisch. Vorgeschichte der altgermanischen Dialekte.* 3. verbesserte und vermehrte Aufl. Strassburg: Trübner.

Krahe, H. & W. Meid. 1969. *Germanische Sprachwissenschaft. Bd. 3: Wortbildungslehre.* 7. Aufl. bearb. von W. Meid. Berlin: De Gruyter.

Kroonen, G. 2013. *Etymological Dictionary of Proto-Germanic.* Leiden: Brill.

Lambert, P.-Y. 1994. *La langue gauloise. Description linguistique, commentaire d'inscriptions choisies.* Paris: Errance.

Lehmann, W. P. 1986. *A Gothic etymological dictionary.* Leiden: Brill.

Lindsay, W. M. 1921. *The Corpus, Épinal, Erfurt and Leyden glossaries* (Publications of the Philological Society). Vol. 8. London: Oxford University Press.

Lloyd, A. L., O. Springer & R. Lühr (eds.). 1998. *Etymologisches Wörterbuch des Althochdeutschen, Band 2: bî — ezzo.* Göttingen: Vandenhoeck & Ruprecht.

310 Ludwig Rübekeil

Luff, R. & G. Steer (eds.). 2003. *Konrad von Megenberg. Buch der Natur: II. Kritischer Text nach den Handschriften.* Tübingen: Niemeyer.

Masser, A. (ed.). 1994. *Die lateinisch-althochdeutsche Tatianbilingue Stiftsbibliothek St. Gallen Cod. 56.* Göttingen: Vandenhoeck & Ruprecht.

Meiser, G. 1998. *Historische Laut- und Formenlehre der lateinischen Sprache.* 2. Auflage. Darmstadt: Wissenschaftliche Buchgesellschaft.

Miller, D. G. 2019. *The Oxford Gothic Grammar.* Oxford: Oxford University Press.

Müller, K. (ed.). 1995. *Petronii Arbitri Satyricon reliquiae.* 4. Auflage. Leipzig: Teubner.

Nielsen, H. F. 1998. *The continental backgrounds of English and its insular development until 1154.* Odense: University Press.

Nielsen, H. F. 2004. Friedrich Maurer and the Dialectal Links of Upper German to Nordic. In H.-P. Naumann, F. Lanter & O. Szokody (eds.), *Alemannien und der Norden* (Ergänzungsbände zum Reallexikon der Germanischen Altertumskunde 43), 12–28. Berlin: De Gruyter.

ONP = Ordbog over det norrøne prosasprog. Online-Dictionary. *ONP.* https://onp.ku.dk/.

Palander, H. 1899. *Die althochdeutschen Tiernamen. 1. Die Namen der Säugetiere.* Darmstadt: Otto.

Reichert, H. 1987. *Thesaurus Palaeogermanicus. Lexikon der altgermanischen Namen.* Vol. 1. Wien: Verlag der Österreichischen Akademie der Wissenschaften.

Rübekeil, L. 2006. Völker- und Stammesnamen. §1 Sprachlich-philologisch. In *Reallexikon der germanischen Altertumskunde*, vol. 32. 487–500.

Rübekeil, L. 2017. 59. The dialectology of Germanic. In J. Klein, B. Joseph & M. Fritz (eds.), *Handbook of Comparative and Historical Indo-European Linguistics* (Handbücher Zur Sprach- Und Kommunikationswissenschaft 41.2), 986–1002. Berlin: De Gruyter.

Rübekeil, L. 2020. Tufa und Armilausini: Namen und Appellativa im römisch-germanischen Sprachkontakt. *Beiträge zur Geschichte der deutschen Sprache und Literatur* 142. 185–213.

Rübekeil, L. 2021. Linguistic Labels and Ethnic Identity. In J. Harland & M. Friedrich (eds.), *Interrogating the Germanic: A Category and its Use in Late Antiquity and the Early Middle Ages*, 225–240. Berlin: De Gruyter.

Schaffner, S. 2001. *Das Vernersche Gesetz und der innerparadigmatische grammatische Wechsel des Urgermanischen im Nominalbereich.* Innsbruck: IBS.

Schmeling, G. L. & A. Setaioli (eds.). 2011. *A commentary on the "Satyrica" of Petronius.* Oxford: University Press.

Schönfeld, M. 1911. *Wörterbuch der altgermanischen Personen- und Völkernamen. Nach der Überlieferung des klassischen Altertums.* Heidelberg: Winter.

Schrader, O. & A. Nehring (eds.). 1929. *Reallexikon der indogermanischen Altertumskunde: Grundzüge einer Kultur- und Völkergeschichte Alteuropas. Band 2.* 2. verm. und umgearb. Auflage Berlin: De Gruyter.

Schrijver, P. 1997. Animal, vegetable and mineral: some Western European substratum words. In A. Lubotsky (ed.), *Sound law and analogy: Papers in honor of Robert S. P. Beekes on the occasion of his 60th birthday*, 293–316. Amsterdam: Rodopi.

Shackleton Bailey, D. R. (ed.). 2012. *Marcus Valerius Martialis. Epigrammata* (Bibliotheca scriptorum Graecorum et Romanorum Teubneriana). Editio stereotypa editionis primae. Leipzig: Teubner.

Simon, Z. 2020. Latin sāpō 'hair-dye, soap', the Germanic Words for Soap, and the Common Substrate of Celtic and Germanic. *Amsterdamer Beiträge zur älteren Germanistik* 80(4). 391–400.

Simon, Z. 2021. Brutes: Zur Herkunft eines germanischen Lehnwortes in den lateinischen Inschriften. *Glotta* 97. 309–320.

Steinmeyer, E. von & E. Sievers. 1879. *Die althochdeutschen Glossen 1. Glossen zu biblischen Schriften.* Berlin: Weidmann.

Steinmeyer, E. von & E. Sievers. 1882. *Die althochdeutschen Glossen 2. Glossen zu nichtbiblischen Schriften.* Berlin: Weidmann.

Steinmeyer, E. von & E. Sievers. 1895. *Die althochdeutschen Glossen 3. Sachlich geordnete Glossare.* Berlin: Weidmann.

Stifter, D. 2017. 68. The phonology of Celtic. In J. Klein, B. Joseph, M. Fritz & M. Wenthe (eds.), *Handbook of Comparative and Historical Indo-European Linguistics vol. II*, 1188–1202. Berlin: De Gruyter.

Stotz, P. 1996. *Handbuch zur lateinischen Sprache des Mittelalters 3. Lautlehre.* Vol. Band 3. München: Beck.

Thöny, L. 2013. *Flexionsklassenübertritte: zum morphologischen Wandel in der altgermanischen Substantivflexion.* Innsbruck: IBS.

TLL = *Thesaurus linguae latinae, editus iussu et auctoritate consilii ab academiarum quinque germanicarum Berolinensis Gottingensis Lipsiensis Monacensis Vindobonensis.* Leipzig 1900ff.

Walde, A. & J. B. Hofmann. 1954. *Lateinisches etymologisches Wörterbuch.* 3., neubearb. Aufl. von Johann Baptist Hofmann. Heidelberg: Winter.

Wellmann, M. (ed.). 1907. *Pedanii Dioscuridis Anazarbei De materia medica libri quinque.* Vol. *I: Libri I-II.* Berlin: Weidmann.

Whatmough, J. 1970. *The Dialects of Ancient Gaul: Prolegomena and Records of the Dialects.* Cambridge, MA: Harvard University Press.

Wilmanns, W. 1930. *Deutsche Grammatik: 2. Wortbildung.* 2. Aufl., unveränderter Neudruck. Berlin: De Gruyter.

Nochmals zur Metrizität der älteren Runeninschriften

Michael Schulte
University of Agder

The author presents a minimalist approach to early runic metrics by first taking the position of the Advocatus Diaboli. This means that metrical criteria of the older runic inscriptions should speak for themselves without being directly derived from or equated with later language stages and their elaborated metrical systems. The leitmotif of this analysis is the fusion and interaction of language, sentence rhythm and alliterative metrics. Not entirely unexpectedly, the Germanic long line emerges as the basic unit of Ancient Nordic metrics, since it can be relatively reliably verified in a small group of older runic inscriptions. This unit is identified as the *proto-long line* of Northwest Germanic metrics. This examination excludes inscriptions of the transitional period and the Viking Age. Thus, the focus is on the metricity of the unsyncopated, linguistically archaic runic inscriptions of the older period prior to AD 500/550. This has the advantage of systematically excluding syncopated or partially syncopated inscriptions such as the Eggja stone and the Blekinge inscriptions. Due to their linguistic status, these inscriptions will have to be subjected to a separate study.

1. Zur Methode

Die Frage, wie der metrische Status der älteren Runeninschriften zu beurteilen ist, wurde von der Forschung ganz unterschiedlich beurteilt. Dabei werden metrische Formen jüngerer, sicher dokumentierter Sprachstufen, in Sonderheit das Altnordische, gängigerweise als Beschreibungsgrundlage der urnordischen Runenmetrik verwendet (vgl. Schulte 2010: 46–47).[1] Handhabe für die metrische Deutung

---

1. In dieser Studie schließt der Begriff des „Altnordischen" die gesamte sprachliche Überlieferung des Westskandinavischen (mit dem Altisländischen) ein. Die Sprache der älteren Runeninschriften wird der nordeuropäischen Tradition folgend als „Urnordisch" bezeichnet; vgl. Krause (1971: 15); Schulte (2018: 13–16). — Die Angaben zu den einzelnen Runeninschriften werden hier auf ein Minimum beschränkt; siehe ergänzend die Corpusausgabe von Krause und

https://doi.org/10.1075/nss.34.18sch
Available under the CC BY-NC-ND 4.0 license. © 2025 John Benjamins Publishing Company

Nochmals zur Metrizität der älteren Runeninschriften **313**

bieten die aus der späteren Runenmetrik und Eddadichtung bekannten Versformen. Diese methodische Vorgehensweise dürfte aber nicht unbedingt zu einem validen Ergebnis führen. So postuliert Pascual (2016) im Anschluss an Kuryłowicz (1970) grundsätzlich eine diachrone Entwicklung der altenglischen Metrik:

> Consequently, the composition of alliterative poetry during the prehistoric period could not have been governed by the same rules that governed the composition of Old English verse during the classical period. Any argument predicated upon the assumption of static continuity in metrical history is therefore untenable.
>
> (Pascual 2016: 300)

Durchaus krass erscheint die historische Engführung, wenn ältere und älteste Runeninschriften des 3. bis 6. Jahrhunderts in Einzelpunkten (zum Beispiel der Vokalalliteration) an Snorri Sturlusons *Háttatal* (datiert 1222–1223) gemessen werden (siehe zum Beispiel Marold 2012: 72). So stellt Marold (2012: 64; Hervorhebung M. S.) in ihrer metrischen Untersuchung immerhin mit einer gewissen Einschränkung fest, dass „[d]ie bei Sievers gegebenen allgemeinen Regeln der Darstellung rhythmischer Verse [...] hier [das heißt, in Marolds Beitrag; M.S.] nur [!] ein Analyseinstrument sein [sollen], das sich in der Anwendung bewähren muss." Es bleibt hierbei aber nach einem Korrektiv zu fragen, das den gewählten Ansatz auf die Probe stellen könnte, um seine wissenschaftliche Gültigkeit zu testen. Mees (2013: 111) bemängelt an diesem Ansatz „the essential anachronism inherent in applying a system of scansion developed to explain literary material form from the tenth century and later to texts of a much earlier date."

Denn als Axiom gilt, dass das, was wissenschaftstheoretisch nicht zu widerlegen, sprich: zu falsifizieren, ist, auch nicht verifiziert werden kann. Damit ist eine wissenschaftstheoretische Beurteilung im strengen Sinne gar nicht möglich, so dass die vorgenommenen Deutungen unwiderlegbar im Raum stehen.[2] Mit Popper (1982: 54) „nennen [wir] eine Theorie nur dann falsifiziert, wenn wir Basissätze anerkannt haben, die ihr widersprechen" (vgl. Ender, Leemann & Wälchli 2012: 2). Es ist bemerkenswert, dass die Methodenfrage zur metrischen Auswertung der älteren Runeninschriften in diesem Zusammenhang nie ausdrücklich gestellt wurde, um wissenschaftstheoretischen Forderungen der Reliabilität und Validität nachzukommen und — was wichtiger ist — dem Vorwurf des Anachronismus bzw. der Ahistorizität vorzubeugen.

Jankuhn (Signum KJ mit Inschriftennummer) und die runischen Datenbanken von Kiel und Uppsala unter den entsprechenden Inschriftensignen.

2. Zur Bedeutung der Falsifikation und Falsifizierbarkeit in der Wissenschaftstheorie siehe etwa Popper (1982: 47–59 *et passim*). Man vergleiche den entsprechend hohen Status des Widerspruchsbeweises in den Wissenschaftstraditionen der Mathematik.

Auffällig ist denn auch, dass die metrischen Wertungen einzelner Interpretinnen und Interpreten durchaus unterschiedlich ausfallen und so gesehen inkompatibel sind (siehe zusammenfassend Naumann 2018: 37–59).[3] Oftmals wird auf altnordische Versformen verwiesen, besonders häufig auf die eddische Versform des *Ljóðaháttr* oder archaische Vorformen dieses altnordischen Metrums (siehe beispielsweise Nielsen 1970; 1983: 33; zu einer kritischen Wertung s.u.). Das Gros der Deuterinnen und Deuter wählt ebenso wie Marold (2012) eine altnordische Retrospektive und projiziert metrische Grunddaten vom klassischen Altnordischen zurück auf die älteren Runeninschriften. Nicht selten ist von „archaischen" oder „primitiven" Formen des *Ljóðaháttr*, des *Málaháttr* oder des *Kviðuháttr* die Rede (zum Tjurkö-Brakteaten vgl. Salberger 1956; 1962–1963: 336–338).[4] Auch werden die fünf Verstypen nach Sievers (1893: 33–35) als Beschreibungsgrundlage zugrunde gelegt (siehe etwa Marold 2012: 66). Dass dieser methodische Zugang wissenschaftstheoretisch nicht einwandfrei ist, dürfte auf der Hand liegen. Eine Gegenposition, die von Olga Smirnitskaya (1994; 2021) bezogen wurde, erkennt in den älteren Runeninschriften („the monuments of protoverse") als metrische Grundeinheit zunächst nur die „protoverse units" an, die rhythmisch den dithematischen Namenformen vom Typ *Hlewa-gastiʀ* entsprechen (vgl. Liberman 1998: 98–99).

Im vorliegenden Beitrag wird zwischen diesen beiden Extrempositionen vermittelt, indem ein minimalistischer Grundansatz zur urnordischen Langzeile, der *Proto-Langzeile*, entwickelt wird. Der metrische Ansatz einer wohlgeformen Langzeile soll hierbei als minimalistische Beschreibungsgrundlage für die älteren Runeninschriften dienen (s.u. Abschnitt 4). Denn zunächst müssen wir nüchtern feststellen, dass wir die einzelnen Versformen des Urnordischen nicht genau kennen, falls wir überhaupt eine Anzahl von elaborierten metrischer Formen voraussetzen. Wie gesagt soll in dieser Untersuchung die Gegenposition zum Hauptstrom der Forschung bezogen werden, womit zunächst als metrische Grundform nur die *wohlgeformte Langzeile* (im Sinne einer *Proto-Langzeile*) für das Urnordische anerkannt wird. Mit diesem Begriff soll eine voreilige, direkte Gleichsetzung der metrischen Strukturen mit der altgermanischen Langzeile in

---

3. Eine Extremposition bezieht Mees in verschiedenen Arbeiten (zum Beispiel 2007, 2008) mit einem isometrischen Ansatz; vgl. zurückhaltend Schulte (2010: 45) und Marold (2012: 68).

4. Krause fand in der Fluchformel von Björketorp KJ 97 Anklänge des *Málaháttr*, was aber schon angesichts der stark abweichenden Parallelversion von Stentoften nicht unbedingt überzeugend wirkt: „Vier je zweitaktige Halbzeilen, jede mit starker Nebenhebung in der Art von eddischem Málaháttr, paarweise durch Stab zusammengehalten." Marold (2012: 84–88) erwägt deshalb Björketorp gegenüber Stentoften als metrische Neuerung zu werten. Da der vorliegende Beitrag auf die unsynkopierte Sprachstufe der älteren Runeninschriften zielt, wird diese Frage hier nicht weiter diskutiert, selbst wenn eine gewisse Skepsis angebracht scheint.

den nordwestgermanischen Literatursprachen bewusst vermieden werden. Metrische Prozesse der Auflösung (*resolution*), die auch in der metrischen Phonologie eine zentrale Rolle spielen, sind ebenfalls zu berücksichtigen (vgl. Gallehus Horn B *Hlewa-* und Noleby-Stein *ragina-*). Ebenso wichtig ist mit Andreas Heusler die 'Freiheit der Füllung' als Schlüssel zum Verständnis der urnordischen Metrik, womit Marolds Annahme katalektischer Versformen oder 'verkürzter Verse' im Urnordischen unnötig wird (vgl. unten zum Anvers der Thorsberg-Inschrift KJ 20).[5] Mit Heusler:

> Wir sehen, wie wenig das Streben auf ebenmäßige Belastung der Verse geht. Schon die älteste germanische Zeile, die vom Goldenen Horn, verbindet An- und Abvers von sehr ungleicher Schwere. (Heusler 1956 [1925]: 169)

In diesem Beitrag soll daher streng synchron, das heißt systemimmanent, verfahren werden, indem die Eliminierungsmethode zum Tragen kommt (siehe Abschitt 2). Mit anderen Worten, es wird angestrebt, semi-metrische und nichtmetrische Formen von der eindeutig metrischen Versform abzugrenzen. Als Zusatzkriterium der Metrizität wird auch das visuelle Design einzelner Runeninschriften angesprochen; siehe besonders die Argumentation zum Kjølevikstein in Abschnitt 2 mit Abbildung 1.

Damit beschreitet der vorliegende Beitrag einmal den umgekehrten Weg zum Hauptstrom der Forschung, der stark an der altnordischen, altenglischen, altsächsischen und althochdeutschen Verskunst orientiert ist. Auf die am Altnordischen ausgerichtete Beschreibungsgrundlage (in Sonderheit die Sieversschen metrischen 5 Typen) wird weitgehend verzichtet, und es wird versucht, die metrischen Regularitäten der älteren Runeninschriften *eo ipso* zu erfassen. Es steht zu hoffen, dass der Erkenntnisgewinn einer systemimmanenten Analyse in diesem Beitrag deutlich zutage tritt.

---

5. Vgl. Schulte (2010: 48). Siehe in diesem Zusammenhang auch die diachrone Perspektive von Pascual (2016: 298), die am Brakteaten von Tjurkö illustriert wird: „Because prehistoric words like *walhakurne* were significantly larger than their historical counterparts, prehistoric metre allowed the composition of verses like *on* [sic] *walhakurne*, whose number of positions exceeds the limit of classical poetry."

2. Die Eliminierungsmethode

Die Eliminierungsmethode bietet sich hier an, um semi-metrische und nicht-metrische Runeninschriften von der Kerngruppe der *Runica metrica* zu unterscheiden. Wer den kleinsten gemeinsamen Nenner zur Metrik der älteren Runeninschriften sucht, wird unweigerlich auf die germanische Langzeile zurückkommen.[6] Wichtig ist zunächst der allgemeine Befund, dass Alliteration in einem Großteil der älteren Runeninschriften nachzuweisen ist (vgl. Kabell 1978: 22–31; Smirnitskaya 2021: 141). Alliterierende Runeninschriften müssen, so gesehen, mindestens zwei lexikalische Wörter enthalten, um staben zu können; es versteht sich von selbst, dass dabei Ein-Wort-Inschriften und nicht-lexikalische Sequenzen im Prinzip ausgenommen sind. Dass Alliteration in vielen Fällen frei zur Anwendung kommt, zeigen Inschriften, in denen ganz verschiedene Wortklassen miteinander alliterieren: Substantive, Adjektive, finite Verbformen und teilweise sogar Determinative (Pronomen); zu Kjølevik siehe das Folgende. Wichtig ist die Feststellung, dass nicht die Alliteration selbst, sondern der geregelte Satzrhythmus in Verbindung mit der Alliteration den metrischen Stabreimvers bildet. Liberman (1998: 99) drückt dies in seiner Rezension von Smirnitskayas Werk so aus, wobei er die metrische Form der älteren Runeninschriften durchaus nüchtern einschätzt:

> In the oldest runic inscriptions (the monuments of „protoverse"), sentence rhythm and word rhythm had not yet come together to form a single system. Only the canonization of sentence rhythm in the long line is a Germanic innovation [...].　　　　　　　　　　　　　　　(Liberman 1998: 99)

Alliteration und Satzrhytmus gehen somit Hand in Hand, um die metrische Versform zu bilden.[7] Der Kjølevikstein (KJ 75) bietet meines Erachtens ein Anschauungsbeispiel für die freie Form der Alliteration, die noch keine Wertung im Sinne einer metrischen Versifizierung erlaubt (siehe Abbildung 1). Kjølevik zeigt eine auffällige Irregularität, wenn man so will einen Schönheitsfehler, der gegen den metrischen Status spricht: die 'Anreimung' eines vorangestellten Satzfragments, das zwar am Alliterationsschema *h–h–h* teilnimmt, syntaktisch aber vom Hauptsatz zu trennen ist.[8]

---

6. Zu den Grundlagen der germanischen Langzeile siehe Lehmann (1956: 28–29); vgl. auch Smirnitskaya (1994; 2021); siehe dazu im weiteren Abschnitt 4.

7. Zur Bedeutung der Satzbetonung und des Satzrhythmus für den Stabreim siehe auch Liberman (1998: 96, 98–99).

(1) Stein von Kjølevik   (KJ 75; Datierung 375/400–520/30, nach Imer 2015b:147)

    Zeile I   **haduḷaikaʀ**

    Zeile II   **ek hagustadaʀ**

    Zeile III   **h͡l(a)aiwido magu minino**

    Hadulaikaʀ ‖ ek Hagusta(l)daʀ hlaiwido magu mīninō

    'Hadulaikaʀ (errichtete diesen Stein?).[9]

    Ich, Hagustaldaʀ, begrub meinen Sohn.'

Damit ergeben sich mehrere Einwände gegen eine metrische Wertung, zumal der postulierte Stabreim hier auf ein finites Verb fällt (vgl. Schulte 2010:50–51). Marold (2012:78–79) erwägt, die Inschrift als Kombination einer Langzeile mit einer in sich stabenden, dreihebigen Zeile zu lesen. Dabei versucht sie, die stabende finite Verbform zu rechtfertigen, indem sie voraussetzt, „dass es sich hier nur um eine mögliche 'Anreimung' handelt, die mit dem eigentlichen Stabreim der Zeile auf *m* nichts zu tun hat" (Marold 2012:79).

Derartige Deutungsversuche, die Metrizität älterer Runeninschriften (hier des Kjøleviksteines) aufrecht zu erhalten, erscheinen mir kaum tragfähig. Es wird übersehen, dass die Sinn- und Satzeinheit mit dem Alliterationsschema zusammenwirkt, um den Stabreimvers zu bilden. In Fällen wie Kjølevik ergibt sich die Alliteration schon aufgrund der alliterativen Namengebung unabhängig von der Metrik. Einzelne Satzfragmente können nicht ohne weiteres am Stabreim teilhaben. Erst im Zusammenspiel von Alliteration und Satzrhythmus entsteht die metrisch-stabende Inschrift. Abschließend fällt Kjølevik trotz aller metrischen Deutungsversuche (vor allem Marold 2012:78–79) der Status eines Grenzgängers zu, der gleich mehrere runenmetrische Irregularitäten aufweist.[10] Ebenfalls negativ fällt die Wertung von Smirnitskaya (2021:139) aus: „The obvious presence of rhythm and 'measure' in such inscriptions [i.e., Einang and Kjølevik; M.S.] is nothing else but the consequence of their formulaicity."

Wir halten fest, dass Alliteration im Gegensatz zum regelmässig durchgeführten, satzrhythmischen Stabreim den metrischen Status einer Runeninschrift noch nicht garantiert.[11] In dieser Hinsicht ist der Kriterienkatalog von Hübler

---

8. Als vorangeschaltetes, isoliertes Satzfragment ist **haduḷaikaʀ** (Zeile I der Kjølevik-Inschrift) elliptisch zu deuten, etwa im Sinne der folgenden Ergänzungen: 'H. errichtete diesen Stein', oder 'H. malte/schrieb diese Runen'.

9. Die dithematische Namenform **haduḷaikaʀ** ist nicht sicher gedeutet: *HaþulaikaR, HardulaikaR, HaiðulaikaR* oder auch *HandulaikaR*; vgl. Peterson (1994:145–146; dies. 2004:9; dazu Marold 2012:78, Fußnote 14.

10. Zum Grenzgängerstatus der Kjølevik-Inschrift vgl. Schulte (2010:50).

11. In diesem wesentlichen Punkt sind Wulf (1998) und Marold (2012:68–69) in ihrer Kritik an Hübler (1996:30–31) zuzustimmen, da Hübler den Rhythmus vernachlässigt.

Abbildung 1. Stein von Kjølevik KJ 75. Foto: James E. Knirk. Kulturhistorisk museum, Universitetet i Oslo. Lizenz: CC BY-SA

(1996: 30–31) zu eng gefasst, da er in seiner Studie den Rhythmus, speziell aber den Satzrhythmus, ausgrenzt. Hübler postuliert folgendes (zur einer kritischen Stellungnahme siehe Marold 2012: 69):

> Wegen der Unsicherheiten in der Forschung werde ich den Rhythmus nicht ausdrücklich als Kriterium anwenden. Ich beschränke mich darauf in möglichen Langzeilen zwei Hebungen pro An- und Abvers erkennen zu können. Der Rhythmus ist meiner Meinung nach zu einem nicht unerheblichen Teil subjektives Empfinden. (Hübler 1996: 37)

Die Wichtigkeit des Rhythmus wird auch von Marold (2012: 69) für *alle* metrischen Runeninschriften ausdrücklich betont, wobei sie allgemein vom Rhythmus einer potentiell metrischen Runeninschrift spricht. Aus meiner Sicht ist hierbei aber der Satzrhythmus entscheidend, da er die syntaktische Einheit des Satzes mit dem Alliterationsschema verbindet (vgl. die Gallehus-Inschrift gegenüber Kjølevik). Auf diese Weise kann die Inschrift von Kjølevik selbst mit Wohlwollen nur als semi-metrisch (mit anderen Worten als 'Borderliner') klassifiziert werden.

In diesem Beitrag werden daher Alliteration und Stabreim nicht als Synonyme verwendet. Erst wenn die Alliteration mit dem Satzrhythmus verschmilzt, entsteht eine stabende Runeninschrift. Somit sind weitere metrische Regularitäten im Spiel. Zu fragen bleibt, wie diese Regularitäten genauer zu bestimmen sind, und welche metrische Grundeinheit sie indizieren. Eingangs wurde bereits auf den zentralen Status der Langzeile hingewiesen, die Alliteration und Satzrhythmus vereint (s.u. Abschnitt 4). Angesichts der Formelhaftigkeit der älteren und ältesten Runeninschriften, ist es angängig, ein Kontinuum von alliterierenden Personennamen und Formeln hin zur metrisch-rhythmischen Versform anzusetzen (vgl. Smirnitskaya 2021:137). Wir halten fest, dass Formelhaftigkeit als Kriterium der Metrizität älterer Runeninschriften keineswegs ausreicht, und somit kein Garant für ihren metrischen Status ist (s.u. Abschnitt 5).

3. Zusatzargumente zur Metrizität

Mindestens zwei Kriterien können den metrischen Status einer Runeninschrift unterstützen und damit die vorliegende Argumentation auf der Grundlage des minimalistischen Ansatzes untermauern:

1. metrische Syntax und Verschränkung der Glieder
2. der Gebrauch rhetorisch-poetischer Figuren.

Als ein Beispiel „metrischer Syntax" kann die Inschrift auf dem Goldhorn B von Gallehus angeführt werden (siehe Abbildung 2). Wie wir gleich sehen werden, bildet die Gallehus-Inschrift eine wohlgeformte Langzeile. Die wesentliche metrisch-formale Vorgabe liegt im Alliterationsschema. Die urnordische Langzeile hat im Prinzip zwei Grundvarianten: (1) $a–a \mid a–x$ und (2) $a–x \mid a–x$. Der alliterierende Iktus im Abvers, der Anvers und Abvers zusammenbindet, ist obligatorisch. Theoretisch wäre auch ein dritter Typ (3) $x–a \mid a–x$ möglich (a bezeichnet eine alliterierende Hebung, x eine nicht-alliterierende Hebung.). Der dritte Typ $x–a \mid a–x$ ist allerdings aufgrund der Intonationsverhältnisse als irregulär zu betrachten, da der erste Iktus im Anvers lautmechanisch eine stärkere Betonung trägt als der zweite Iktus im Anvers.[12] Aus den Betonungsverhältnissen ergibt sich weiterhin, dass der vierte, druckmäßig schwächste Iktus nie den Stab trägt. Eine Besonderheit der Gallehus-Inschrift besteht weiterhin darin, dass das einleitende Personalpronomen **ek** vortonig ist, zumal es graphisch nicht mit Worttrenner abgesetzt ist (siehe die Diskussion in Abschnitt 5; dazu Schulte 2025).

---

12. Zu Einzelheiten siehe Kuryłowicz (1970:16–20); dazu Pascual (2016:291, mit Fußnote 6).

Zu den metrischen Bedingungen der urnordischen Langzeile siehe im weiteren Abschnitt 4.

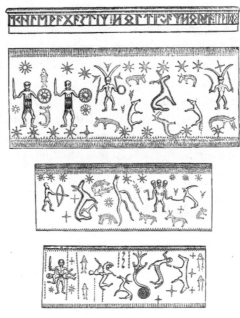

Abbildung 2. Goldhorn B von Gallehus KJ 43. Zeichnung: DR-Atlas, 15 Abb. 40. Kupferstich nach Joachim Richard Paulli 1734

(2)   Goldhorn B von Gallehus
            (KJ 43 = DR 12; Datierung 375/400–460/70, nach Imer 2015b: 88)
    ekhlewagastiʀ:holtijaʀ:horna:tawido:
    EkHlewagastiR HoltijaR | horna tawidō
    'Ich, HlewagastiR HoltijaR, fertigte das Horn.'[13]

Durchaus zentral ist die Feststellung, dass die poetische Form dieser Inschrift wahrscheinlich ihre Syntax modifiziert hat. Denn die gängige Satzstellung der älteren Runeninschriften wird mit wenigen Ausnahmen als SVO (mit weitgehend durchgeführter V2-Typologie) ausgewiesen (vgl. Eyþórsson 2012; Schulte 2018: 82–84).[14]

---

13. Die Sequenz *hlewagastir holtijar* lässt mehrere Deutungen zu. Siehe zuletzt Nedoma (2022), der einen Doppelnamen mit nachgestelltem Kurznamen *Holtijar* vorraussetzt, während die Standarddeutung von einem Patronymikon (bzw. Inkolentnamen) ausgeht. Für die Metrik ist diese Frage allerdings unerheblich.

Demgegenüber stellt Gallehus das finite Verb — wohl *metri causa* — an den Schluss des Satzes. Der Syntaktiker Þórhallur Eyþórsson (2012: 38) stellt hierzu fest: „Thus the word order in the Gallehus inscription is possibly due to the poetic nature of the text." Diese Beobachtung kann den metrischen Status der Gallehus-Inschrift, die als einwandfreies Beispiel einer metrischen Runeninschrift angeführt werden kann, noch unterstreichen. Auch Marold (2012: 70) sieht diese Möglichkeit: „Die Syntax der Inschrift [...], die gegen die Regeln das Verb an den Schluss des Satzes stellt, weist auf eine beabsichtigte metrische Gestaltung."[15]

Metrische Gestaltung weist auch die Inschrift auf dem Stein von Noleby auf (siehe Abbildung 3). In der Tat liegt hier wie beim Horn von Gallehus eine wohlgeformte Langzeile vor, wenn das metrische Phänomen der Auflösung, das heißt *Resolution*, berücksichtigt wird. Die Grundregel ist, dass der Iktus eine lange (schwere) Silbe erfordert, um den Hauptton tragen zu können, oder zwei kurze (leichte) Silben wie dies bei *ragina-* der Fall ist. Zur bimoraischen Bedingung siehe Goering (2023: 214–217); zur Metrik siehe Abschnitt 6.

(3)   Stein von Noleby   (KJ 67; Datierung 460/70–560/70, nach Imer 2015b: 191)

Zeile I   **runo fahi raginaku(n)do tojeka**

Zeile II   **unaþou ... suhurah ... susix hwatin**

Zerile III **hakuþo**

rūnō fāhi | raginakundō [...]

'eine Rune (Kollektivum) male/schreibe ich, die von den Göttern stammt. [...].'[16]

Einen Hinweis auf die Poetizität der Einleitungssequenz von Noleby gibt die Klammerstellung von *rūnō* — *raginakundō* in Verbindung mit der Initialstellung des direkten Objekts. Wie Marold (2012, 83) bemerkt, wäre die unmarkierte Prosastellung Subjekt-Verb-Objekt, das heißt SVO: *[ek] fāhi rūnō ragina-ku(n)dō* 'Ich male eine Rune, eine götterentstammte'. Auf dem Nolebystein ist nur der Teil der Inschrift versifiziert, der rhetorisch-pragmatisch hervortritt. Der Akt des

---

14. Zur selten belegten SOV-Stellung in den älteren Runeninschriften vgl. den Stein von Einang (KJ 63): **[ek go]dagastiʀ runo faihido** 'Ich, Godagastiʀ(?), die Rune (Kollektivum) malte'.

15. Andererseits ist es nicht auszuschließen, dass die Endstellung des finite Verbs (und damit die SOV-Stellung) als metrischer Archaismus deutbar ist. Die Annahme einer 'fossilisierten Syntax' (Schulte 2018: 84) erfährt dadurch Bestätigung, dass das finite Verb hier nicht am Alliterationsschema teilnimmt und auch epigraphisch vom übrigen Teil der Inschrift deutlich abgesetzt ist (siehe Abbildung 2).

16. Ob der *i*-Umlaut in der Form **fahi** durchgeführt ist, tangiert die metrische Deutung nicht, da die Stammsilbe in jedem Fall schwer ist. Zur Umlautform **fahi** = [fæ:hi] < **faihiju* siehe Schulte (1998: 112).

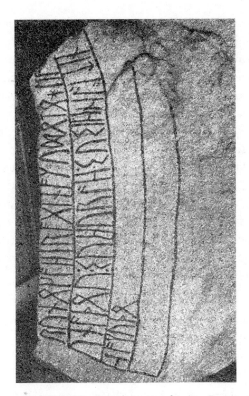

Abbildung 3. Stein von Noleby KJ 67. Foto mit retuschierten Runen: Antikvarisk-Topografiska Arkivet, Stockholm

Schreibens oder Ritzens von Runen kann in einer archaischen Gesellschaft als sakral-magischer Prozess gedeutet werden (vgl. Schulte 2021; siehe im weiteren Abschnitt 5 zu den *ek irilaR*-Inschriften).

Neben diesen plausiblen Fällen syntaktischer Stilisierung lassen sich in den älteren Runeninschriften auch einzelne poetisch-rhetorische Figuren nachweisen. Besonders zu nennen ist die Litotes, die inschriftlich auf dem Ortband von Thorsberg (frühes 3. Jhd.) belegt ist, zumindest wenn der Standarddeutung gefolgt wird.[17] Die Litotes ist als rhetorisches Stilmittel der (oftmals ironischen) Untertreibung bekannt, da sie den intendierten Ausdruck, der einen hohen Grad einer Eigenschaft bezeichnet, mittels Negation oder Privation eines Antonyms aus-

---

17. Allerdings wurde für das Ortband von Thorsberg (KJ 20) eine Vielzahl von Deutungsmöglichkeiten vorgeschlagen, die insgesamt aber das Grundfaktum einer wohlgeformten Langzeile nicht einschränken dürften; vgl. Marold (2012:73) und Nedoma (2023:31), mit dem Hinweis auf die gängige Regel, dass der hohe Extremvokal *u* vor Liquid *l* plus Geräuschlaut (hier *þ*) in der Runenschrift ausfällt (Düwel & Nedoma 2023:11).

drückt (vgl. Glück & Rödel 2016: 405). In diesem Fall wäre *niwajemāriʀ* als 'nichtschlechtberühmter', im Sinne von 'der tadellose' zu verstehen. In Anlehnung an Krauses Standarddeutung (KJ 20) dokumentiert Thorsberg die früheste bekannte Litotesformel im Altgermanischen.[18] Metrisch gesehen ist wiederum auffällig, dass eine wohlgeformte Langzeile vorliegt (vgl. Schulte 2010: 50). Mit Naumann (2010: 150) „zeigt [die Inschrift] — je nach Lesung — Stabbindung auf Halbvokal (*w* : *w*) bzw. Vokal und Halbvokal (*o* : *w*) und ist von Grønvik (1985: 191) und danach Seebold (1994: 72, Anm. 7) als regelrechte Langzeile eingestuft worden." Siehe im weiteren Abschnitt 4.

(4) Ortband von Thorsberg
(KJ 20; Datierung 210/20–250/60, nach Imer 2015b: 290)
owlþuþewaʀ || niwajemariʀ
Lesart 1: ⌈Wo⌉l*þuþewaʀ* | *ni-wajemāriʀ*
'Ullr-Diener [ist] der Tadellose (eigentlich: 'der nicht-schlechtberühmte')'.
Lesart 2: *ō[þala], W[u]lþuþewaʀ* | *ni-wajemāriʀ*
'Reichtum (Begriffsrune, eigentlich 'Odals-Besitz'): Ull-Diener [ist] der Tadellose (eigentlich: 'der nicht-schlechtberühmte')'.

Abbildung 4. Ortband von Thorsberg KJ 20. Zeichnung: Conrad Engelhardt 1869, Tafel 10,41 und Tafel 10,41a

---

18. Vgl. Naumann (1994: 494), mit Verweis auf Hübner (1930).

4. Zwischenresumee zur Langzeile in der altgermanischen Metrik

Kommen wir nochmals auf die Gallehus-Inschrift zurück. Gegenüber den eddischen Metren des *Fornyrðislag* und des *Ljóðaháttr* ist die germanische Langzeile, die wir deswegen hier als *Proto-Langzeile* bezeichnen, durch weniger Vorgaben bestimmt. Sie besteht aus zwei durch Zäsur getrennte Kurzzeilen, das heißt An- und Abvers mit je zwei Hebungen, die meist durch Senkungen (unbetonte Silben) getrennt werden (s.o. Abschnitt 3 zur Gallehus-Inschrift). Das entscheidende Kriterium ist der Stabreim, der An- und Abvers verbindet und, um mit Heusler (1956:§ 114) zu spechen, nie planmäßig „über die kürzeste, zweigliedrige Periode [...] hinaus[greift]". Träger des Stabreims sind die Hebungen (oder Ikten) der Verszeile, wobei die erste Hebung im Abvers den Hauptstab (isl. *hǫfuðstafr*) trägt und damit den Abvers an den Anvers anbindet. Die zentrale Funktion der Alliteration, die Verknüpfung des An- und Abverses zu einer metrisch-syntaktischen Einheit, hebt auch Olga Smirnitskaya deutlich hervor:

> In the short line, alliteration has a cumulative function. In the long line, the function of alliteration is to emphasize and connect words. Since alliteration spreads over the entire long line, it is the long line that should be regarded as the main metrical unit of alliterative verse.
>
> (Smirnitskaya 1994: 129; Übersetzung Liberman 1998: 95)

Die Forschung hat immer wieder das Goldhorn B von Gallehus als ein frühes runisches Beispiel dieser Versifizierung zitiert (KJ 43; zur Runeninschrift s.o. Nr. 2).[19] Jesch (2017: 185) bezeichnet den Goldschmied *HlewagastiR* als den frühesten namentlich genannten Autor einer Versform („earliest 'author' of verse (in Bredehoft's sense)"). Der Umstand, dass diese Inschrift auf einem kunstvoll gefertigten Goldhorn angebracht ist, enkräftet den Einwand, dass es sich um eine nüchterne, alltägliche Herstellerinschrift handeln könnte (vgl. Marold 2012: 70). Metrisch gesehen ist dieses Beispiel — trotz verschiedener Bedenken und Einwände (zum Beispiel Mees 2013) — als Idealform der germanischen Langzeile einzustufen.

Im weiteren ist darauf hinzuweisen, dass die Form *holtijaR* silbenmetrisch als Dreisilber mit zwei unbetonten Silben zu werten ist. Dies tangiert die metrische Analyse des Versfusses in der *Proto-Langzeile* des Urnordischen offensichtlich aber nicht. Denn diese Frage betrifft nur die Häufung der (unbetonten) Senkungssilben.[20] Derartige Probleme bestätigen meines Erachtens den hier für

---

19. Siehe mit weitgehendem Konsensus: Heusler (1956:§ 115); Lehmann (1956: 28–29); Andersen (1961: 108–113); Naumann (1998: 702–703), ders. (2010: 148–149); Schulte (2010: 48); Smirnitskaya (2021: 137–138).

20. Vgl. hierzu die Diskussion, die sich zwischen Mees (2013) und Marold (2013) entfaltet.

das Urnordische benützten Ansatz, der gegenüber dem Sieversschen Schema die „Freiheit der Füllung" (besonders in unbetonten und nebentonigen Senkungssilben) in Anschlag bringt. Die urnordische Metrik unterscheidet sich also vom Versbau des Heliand und der anderen altgermanischen Literatursprachen. Auf das Phänomen der Auflösung wird in Abschnitt 6 hingewiesen.

5. Formelhaftigkeit und Metrizität: Die *ek erilaʀ*-Mikroformel

Im Abschnitt 3 wurde gezeigt, dass poetisch-rhetorische und syntaktisch-stilistische Kriterien die Metrizität einer Inschrift unterstreichen können. Dies gilt zumindest für einzelne Inschriften wie Noleby und Thorsberg, aber selbstverständlich nur unter der Voraussetzung, dass die zugrundegelegten Lesungen und Deutungen dieser Inschriften das Richtige treffen. Auch können stabende Formeln eine wohlgeformte Langzeile bilden, wie die Noleby-Inschrift eindrucksvoll zeigt (s.u. Abschnitt 6).

Insgesamt bleibt aber zu fragen, inwieweit die Formelhaftigkeit einer Runeninschrift schon ihren metrischen Status garantiert. Wie Smirnitskaya (2021:136–147) feststellt, scheint der diesbezügliche Befund eindeutig negativ: Formelhaftigkeit ist noch kein Garant für die Metrizität einer Runeninschrift. Kabell (1978:23) stellt allgemein fest, dass „[d]er Rhythmus [der alliterierenden Inschriften; M.S.] […] derselbe [ist] wie in den nicht-alliterierenden Beispielen", und er spricht beim Amulett von Lindholm und beim Speerschaft von Kragehul (s.u. Inschrift Nr. 9 und 11) von „überflüssigen und unrhythmischen Ergänzungen". Eine zurückhaltende Wertung erscheint mir in Smirnitskayas Sinne angemessen, zumal verschiedene Irregularitäten die metrische Deutung einzelner Runeninschriften in Frage stellen.

Eine Reihe von urnordischen Inschriften weisen beispielsweise eine Erweiterung der Mikroformel *ek irilaʀ/erilaʀ* auf, die als Selbstprädikation des Runenmeisters verstanden wird.[21] Schon der Ausdruck *ek erilaʀ* (bzw. *ek irilaʀ*) ist wegen der Betonungsverhältnisse metrisch deutungsabhängig, da *ek* im Prinzip betont oder unbetont sein kann. Kabell (1978:22–23) fasst diese isolierte Mikroformel ebenso wie Smirnitskaya (2021:143) als alliterierend auf, wogegen *ek* in anderen Kontexten, beispielsweise auf dem Goldhorn von Gallehus, eindeutig vortonig, sprich: proklitisch, ist.[22] Anders demgegenüber muss zum Beispiel die

---

21. Zum Begriff der 'Mikroformel' vgl. Smirnitskaya (2021:141). Auf dieser Grundlage können wir Erweiterungen mit längeren Formeln als 'Makroformeln' bezeichnen.

zweisilbige Form **ekA** in der Inschrift von Ellestad (KJ 59, Söderköping) zumindest als nebentonig ausgewiesen werden (zu Einzelheiten siehe Schulte 2003:398).

Als grapholinguistisches Argument einer proklitischen Form *ek-* auf dem Horn von Gallehus sollte die fehlende Worttrennung zwischen **ek** und **hlewagastiʀ** angeführt werden (vgl. oben Abbildung 2).[23] Verschiedentlich wird eingewendet, dass *ek* in Initialstellung vor *Hlewagastiʀ* nicht proklitisch oder vortonig sein kann, da ein solches Pronomen zumindest im altnordischen Stabreimvers metrisches Gewicht und damit Alliteration tragen sollte; vgl. Verspaare wie *ek man jotna | ár um borna* (*Vǫlospá*, Str. 2,1–2) oder *it munuð alla | eiða vinna* (*Grípisspá*, Str. 31,1–2).[24] Allerdings stehen hier die Pronomina *ek* bzw. *it* in Initialstellung alleine als Subjekt, das heißt ohne folgendes Nominalsyntagma. Dies ist ein kontrastiver Unterschied zwischen dem Urnordischen und dem Altnordischen. Das Syntagma *ek Hlewagastiʀ Holtijaʀ* hat keine direkte Entsprechung im Altnordischen. Ich möchte außerdem einwenden, dass die Form **ik** in den Brakteatinschriften von Åsum (KJ 125) und Sønder Rind (KJ 97) durch die *i*-Schreibung Phonologisierung des *i*-Vokalismus und damit Schwachtonigkeit indiziert. Hier bietet sich ein unmittelbarer Vergleich mit dem weitgehend verallgemeinerten *i*-Vokalismus des Westgermanischen an; vgl. ae. *ic*, afries. *ik*, ahd. *ih*, mndl. *ic, icke* versus afränk. *ec/ek ~ ic/ik*, as. *ek ~ ik*.[25]

Daher erscheint mir die Annahme falsch, dass das Personalpronomen der ersten Person Singularis in Initialstellung im Urnordischen nur starktonig auftritt (zu Einzelheiten siehe Schulte 1998:96–97). Immerhin erkennt Mees (2013:114) an, dass wir verschiedene Regeln der Anakrusis in den einzelnen altgermanischen Traditionen berücksichtigen müssen (Hervorhebung M.S.): „Each of the Old Germanic metrical traditions seems to have had subtly [!] different rules concerning anacrusis and which terms may appear there." Diese *Differentia specifica* sollte aber weiter präzisiert werden, zumal die Füllungsregeln der *Proto-Langzeile* (im Sinne der vorliegenden Studie) insgesamt weniger streng sind als die entsprechenden Regeln der altnordischen oder altenglischen Literatursprachen.[26] Daher

---

22. In der traditionellen Metrik ist hier von *Anakrusis*, oder Auftakt mittels unbetonter Silbe(n) am Versanfang, die Rede. Der Auftakt wird eingehend von Marold (2013) und Mees (2013) erörtert. Siehe hierzu die grapholinguistische Auswertung der Gallehusinschrift in Schulte (2025).

23. Dieses Argument verdanke ich einem der beiden anonymen Gutachter.

24. Zu dieser Kritik siehe zusammenfassend Mees (2013:113–115).

25. Vgl. Krause (1971:§ 100.1), Nielsen (1985:164) und ders. (1989:8).

26. Auch die Möglichkeit eines ungefüllten Taktes (d.h. einer takthaltigen Leerposition) im Anvers **owlþuþewaʀ** (in Krauses Standardlesung *Wulþuþewaʀ*), aufgrund der Auflösung zweier kurzer Silben im Schlussglied *-þewaʀ*, kann diesen Befund bestätigen; vgl. auch Marold (2012:73).

scheinen mir die Beobachtungen von Suzuki (2010) und Þorgeirsson (2012) zur Anakrusis im *Fornyrðislag* und *Málaháttr* nicht unbedingt auf die unsynkopierte Sprachstufe des Urnordischen übertragbar (zum allgemeinen Faktum diachroner Entwicklungen der Alliterationsmetrik siehe Pascual 2016 am Beispiel des Altenglischen). Die Differenzierung verschiedener Intonationsmuster von *ek* + Substantiv (speziell Namenformen) wird durch Kabells und Smirnitskayas Annahme unterschiedlicher Betonungsverhältnisse der Mikroformel *ek erilaʀ* bzw. *ek irilaʀ* in unterschiedlichen sprachlichen Kontexten unterstrichen (s.u.).

In Einzelfällen muss in der Tat mit emphatischem *ek* in Initialstellung gerechnet werden (der Akut bezeichnet den Hauptton): *ék érilaʀ* (Bratsberg KJ 16), *ék áljamarkiʀ* (Kårstad KJ 52). Naumann (2010:147) unterscheidet im Anschluss an Kabell (1978:22–23) zwischen „[v]okalischem Stabreim durch Koppelung des betonten Personalpronomens *ek* an Nomen" (zum Beispiel Bratsberg KJ 16; s.u. Inschrift Nr. 5) und „Erweiterung[en] der *ek*-Formel mit deutlicher Hervorwölbung der Akzentuierung", wobei das Pronomen ausserhalb der Akzentuierung steht. Kabell (1978:22) führt diesen Unterschied der Betonungsverhältnisse weiter aus:

> [...] die Tatsache, dass die drei klaren Beispiele, die einfach *ek* + Nomen enthalten [*ek Unwōdiʀ, ek irilaʀ* [sic], *ek Aljamarkiʀ*; M.S.], alle das Nomen mit Vokal anfangen lassen, erweckt den Eindruck, dass eine Alliteration mit betontem [!] Pronomen vorliegt, also eine wesentliche Ergänzung zum bloßen Namen.
>
> (Kabell 1978:22; Hervorhebung A.K.)

Diese Deutung einer stabenden Verbindung *ek irilaʀ* steht somit dem vortonigen Pronomen *ek* in Fällen wie Gallehus und By gegenüber (zum Bystein vgl. Marold 2012:81).[27]

Zunächst seien hier die zentralen Belege mit der erweiterten Mikroformel *ek erilaʀ* bzw. *ek irilaʀ* angeführt. Bezeichnenderweise kann nur eine dieser (insgesamt 10) formelhaften Inschriften als einwandfreies Beispiel einer metrischen Runeninschrift gewertet werden: der Stein von Rosseland stellt eine wohlgeformte Langzeile dar (siehe Inschrift Nr. 7).[28] Alle anderen Inschriften sind entweder zu kurz, oder unsicher, oder sie weisen zu gravierende Schönheitsfehler

---

27. Kabell (1978:22–23) folgend nimmt Smirnitskaya (2021:141–143) unterschiedliche Betonungsverhältnisse an: unbetontes (proklitisches) *ek* setzt sie bei folgenden Kandidaten voraus: Järsberg (KJ 70), Eikeland (KJ 17a), Tune (KJ 72), Kjølevik (KJ 75), Valsfjord (KJ 55), Lindholm (KJ 29), By (KJ 71). Dagegen postuliert sie — wie Kabell (1978:22–23) — betontes *ek* in den Inschriften von Gårdlösa (KJ 12), Bratsberg (KJ 16) und Kårstad (KJ 53).

28. Zu den *erilaʀ/irilaʀ*-Inschriften siehe besonders Birkmann (1995:151–159); Grønvik (1996:53); Imer (2015a:114); Düwel (2015:274–275); Schulte (2020b:288).

auf, um den metrischen Test zu bestehen (vgl. Smirnitskaya 2021:141). In der vorliegenden Studie wird versucht, die Gruppe der metrischen Inschriften auf eine prototypische, verlässliche Kerngruppe einzuschränken. Als verbindliche metrische Regularität zeichnet sich dabei nicht unerwartet die Proto-Langzeile ab (s.o. Abschnitt 4).

(5) Fibel von Bratsberg   (KJ 16; Datierung 475–525, nach Imer 2015b: 23)
     ek̑erilâʀ
     ek erilaʀ
     'Ich, Erilaʀ.'

(6) Äskatorp- und Väsby-Brakteat
                          (KJ 128 = IK 241,1 und 241,2; Datierung Phase III; Imer 2015b:332)
     [...] uuigaʀ e͡erilar f[a]hidu uuilald
     Wīgaʀ ek erilaʀ fāhidu wīlald
     '[...] Wīgaʀ. Ich, Erilaʀ malte/schrieb das Kunstwerk.'[29]

(7) Rosselandstein   (KJ 69; Datierung 160–375/400, nach Imer 2015b:217)
     ek wagigaʀ irilaʀ agilamu(n)don
     ek Wagigaʀ irilaʀ Agilamundōn
     'Ich, Wagigaʀ, Irilaʀ der Agilamundō.'[30]

(8) Felsinschrift von Veblungsnes
                          (KJ 56; Datierung 375/400–560/70, nach Imer 2015b:316)
     ek irilaʀ wiwila[n]
     Ek irilaʀ Wiwila(n) [bzw. Wīwila(n)].
     'Ich, Irilaʀ des Wiwila.'

(9) Amulett von Lindholm   (KJ 29; Datierung 460/70–560/70)
     ek erilar sawilagaʀ ha(i)teka ‖ aaaaaaaa ʀʀʀ nnn — b m u ttt : alu :
     ek erilaʀ Sawilagaʀ haiteka   [es folgt eine nicht-lexikalische Sequenz][31]
     'Ich, Erilaʀ heiße Sawilagaʀ. [...] [apotropäisches Formelwort *alu*].'

---

29. Die Form **uuigaʀ** kann als Personenname *Wīgaʀ* (entsprechend an. *vígr* 'waffentüchtig, streitbar') gedeutet werden; vgl. Peterson (2004:34).

30. Die Form **wagigaʀ**, wohl ein Personenname, läßt ganz verschiedene phonologische Deutungen zu: entweder *Wagi(n)gaʀ* mit leichter Erstsilbe, oder *Wāgi(n)gaʀ* bzw. *Wangi(n)gaʀ* mit schwerer Erstsilbe siehe zusammenfassend Schulte (2020b:284–285). Marold (2012:75) müsste hier bei der Deutung mit schwerer Erstsilbe *Wāg-* bzw. *Wang-* eine „Spaltung der Senkung im ersten Teil" annehmen. In dieser Arbeit wird wie gesagt für das Urnordische Heuslers takthaltige Rede mit „Freiheit der Füllung" der Sieversschen Metrik vorgezogen.

31. Die Sequenz **sawilagar** ist unsicher als Personenname zu deuten, wobei die Etymologie allerdings nicht eindeutig geklärt ist; vgl. Peterson (2004:15), mit zentraler Literatur.

(10) Bystein (KJ 71; Datierung 375/400–520/30, nach Imer 2015b: 28)
ek̂ irilaʀ hroraʀ ĥroreʀ orte þat aʀina ut [...]
ek irilaʀ Hrōraʀ Hrōrēʀ ortē þat aʀina ūt [...]
'Ich, Irilaʀ, Hrōraʀ, Nachkomme des Hrōraʀ wirkte/arbeitete diese Steinplatte
heraus(?) [...]'[32]

(11) Lanzenschaft von Kragehul (KJ 27; Datierung 470–490, nach Imer 2015b: 151)
ek ẽrilaʀ̂ asugisalas m̂uĥa ĥaite [...]
ek erilaʀ A(n)sugīs(a)las mūha haitē [...]
'Ich Erilaʀ des Ansugīslaʀ heiße Mūha.' bzw. 'Ich Erilaʀ heiße Gefolgsmann
des Ansugīslaʀ.'

(12) Stein von Rakkestad [33]
(Lesung und Deutung der Eingangszeile nach Schulte 2020a: 90–91 u.
Schulte 2023c; Lesung von Zeile II und III nach Iversen et al. 2019: 63, 71–73;
Datierung 375/400–520/530)
Zeile I **ęk̲irilaʀraskaʀrunǫʀ**
Zeile II **inisni:[xxxxxxxx]ạte ʀ fạu**
Zeile III **ịnị**
ek irilaʀ Raskaʀ rūnōʀ [...]
'Ich, der Irilaʀ Raskaʀ, die Runen (malte/schrieb?). [...]'[34]

Die *ek erilaʀ*-Inschrift auf dem Stein von Järsberg umfasst drei Zeilen, die sehr
ungleich angebracht sind (siehe Abb. 5a und 5b). Denn **runoʀ waritu** ist als eigene
Zeile zu werten; siehe Jansson (1978: 37–38) und Moltke (1981).

---

32. Ob die By-Inschrift phonematischen *i*-Umlaut dokumentiert (*Hrōraʀ Hrōrēʀ* < **Hrōzijaz*)
ist für die metrische Wertung unerheblich. Zur Umlautfrage siehe Schulte (1998: 185 *et passim*).

33. Wegen der typologisch jüngeren e-Rune (ᛖ gegenüber ᚺ) kann die Inschrift von Rakkestad — ebenso wie Tune — jünger sein als der Hogganvikstein; vgl. Schulte (2020a: 89); siehe
dazu Imer (2015b: 297): Datierung von Tune: 375/400–520/30, und Imer (2015b: 122): Datierung von Hogganvik: 160–375/400. Allerdings ist dieses runographische Argument zur Form
der e-Rune höchst unsicher; vgl. die Neufunde von Svingerud (siehe Zilmer, Solheim & Vasshus
2023).

34. Die Form *Raskaʀ* 'der Rasche' ist eindeutig als Personenname bzw. Beiname zu deuten;
siehe Schulte (2020b: 290–293) und ders. (2023c) gegenüber Iversen et al. (2019).

(13) Stein von Järsberg :
  (KJ 70 = Vr 1; Datierung 520/30–560/70, nach Imer 2015b: 139)
  Zeile I /// ubaʀ h[a]ite ... h͡arabanâʀ
  Zeile II h͡ait/// ek e͡rilaʀ
  Zeile III runoʀ waritu

Ūbaʀ (Leubaʀ?) haitē h(a)rabanaʀ hait[ē] ek erilaʀ rūnōʀ w(a)ritu
'Ljúfr ('Lieber') bzw. Úfr ('Tückischer'?)³⁵ heiße ich, Hrafn heiße ich. Ich, Erilaʀ, ritze die Runen.'

Abbildung 5a. Stein von Järsberg KJ 70. Foto: Wikipedia. Lizenz: CC BY-SA 3.0

Das Charakteristikum der Formelhaftigkeit steht bei diesen *ek erilaʀ*-Inschriften außer Zweifel. Damit verbunden ist eine rhythmische Gliederung und eben eine freie Alliteration, zum Beispiel beim Namensyntagma **hroraʀ h͡roreʀ** in der By-Inschrift (siehe Inschrift Nr. 10).³⁶ Typischerweise können Inschriften wie By, Järsberg und Kragehul allenfalls als semi-metrisch ausgewiesen werden (zu Järsberg siehe Abbildung 5). Im Falle des Bysteins ist die metrisch störende Sequenz am Ende der Inschrift nicht überzeugend gelesen und gedeutet

---

35. Die erste Namenform wird zu **leubaʀ** (an. *ljúfr* 'der Liebe') ergänzt; siehe Kieler Datenbank und Samnordisk runtextdatabas, unter KJ 70. Zum Problem der Namensform **ubaʀ** auf dem Stein von Järsberg (u.a. gedeutet als Eulenname bzw. urn. *ūbaʀ* = an. *úfr* 'der Tückische'), siehe zusammenfassend Düwel (1984: 329–331), mit Literatur.

36. Zur Deutung der By-Sequenz **hroraʀ h͡roreʀ** bzw. **hroraʀ h͡rorero** siehe Schulte (2020b: 287), mit Forschungslitteratur.

Abbildung 5b. Stein von Järsberg KJ 70 = Vr 1. Foto mit retuschierten Runen: Runverkets bildsamling Vr 1

(vgl. Marold 2012: 81): Stilistisch auffällig beim Stein von Järsberg ist die formelhafte Wiederholung des finiten Verbs *haitē*, die als Epiphora gedeutet werden kann. Metrifiziert als *Ljóðaháttr*-Strophe ist der Järsbergstein aber nicht (siehe ausführlich Abschnitt 7).[37] Und auch die Eingangszeile des Rakkestadsteines kann nicht im strengen Sinne als metrisch gelten, da *ek irilaʀ raskaʀ rūnōʀ* als Verszeile (Zeile A der Inschrift gelesen nach Schulte 2000a u. 2023c)[38] syntaktisch-rhythmisch nicht vollständig ist. Zur wohlgeformten Langzeile fehlt im Abvers die vierte, nicht-alliterierende Hebung. Erst mit Ergänzung einer finiten Verbform entstünde eine potentielle urnordische Langzeile: *ek irilaʀ raskaʀ | rūnōʀ [wrītu]* ,Ich, Irilaʀ, Raskaʀ die Runen (schreibe)' allerdings nach dem abweichenden Alliterationsschema *x–a | a–x* (s.o. Abschnitt 3).

Abschließend und zusammenfassend ist das metrische Potential der *ek irilaʀ*-Inschriften durchaus begrenzt. Von den oben genannten zehn *ek irilaʀ/erilaʀ*-Inschriften erfüllt insgesamt nur eine einzige das Kriterium des metrischen Stabreimverses. Der Stein von Rosseland (Abbildung 6) bildet eine wohlgeformte

---

37. Vgl. die Kritik von Marold (2012: 79) gegenüber Nielsen (1970: 140) und ders. (1983: 30–31).
38. Zu einer anderen Lesung und Deutung siehe Iversen et al. (2019).

Langzeile, wo der Anvers *ek Wagigᴀ eriLaʀ* und der fünfsilbige Abvers *Agilamundōn* durch vokalischen Stabreim zu einer syntaktischen Einheit verbunden werden (zu dieser metrischen Wertung vgl. Marold 2012:75). Hier stabt übrigens der Halbvokal *w* in der ersten Hebung des Anverses mit Vokal, so dass sich die Stabreimform *a–a | a–x* ergibt (vgl. Heusler 1956 I:96). Außerdem kommt das Phänomen der Auflösung zum Tragen: silbenmetrisch sind die stabenden Formen *Agilamundōn* (Rosseland) und *raginaku(n)dō* (Noleby) äquivalent (s.u. Abschnitt 6).

Abbildung 6. Stein von Rosseland KJ 69. Fotoarkivet, Universitetsmuseet i Bergen

6. Alliterierende Formeln als „slot filler"

Weitere alliterierende Formeln des asyndetischen Typs sind zu behandeln.[39] Eine große Gruppe von asyndetischen Formeln bilden Wortpaare verschiedener Wortklassen, zum Beispiel bestehend aus einem Substantiv und einem Adjektiv. Die *rúnar reginkunnar*-Formel beispielsweise ist im Eddalied *Hávamál* 80,1–3, integriert, wo sie eine Halbstrophe im *Ljóðaháttr* produziert. Von den insgesamt drei Hebungen stehen zwei im Anvers und eine im Abvers.[40]

> *Þat er þá reynt, at þú at rúnum spyrr,*
> *inom reginkunnom.*
> 'Das ist nun erprobt/erwiesen, dass du von den Runen zu erfahren suchst,
> den von den Göttern stammenden.'

---

39. Zu diesem Abschnitt vgl. Schulte (2023a) im Rahmen einer Typologie der urnordischen Formelsprache.
40. Zum Text der Eddastrophe siehe Kuhn (1983:29); zur metrischen Analyse siehe Naumann (2018:45).

Ein direkter Vorläufer der Formel *rūnar reginkunnar* (wörtlich 'götterentstammte Runen'), die offensichtlich im kollektiven Gedächtnis verankert ist, erscheint im Corpus der älteren Runeninschriften vor 550/600 n.Chr. auf dem westgötländischen Stein von Noleby (Fyrunga, KJ 67) und auf dem ebenfalls westgötländischen Stein von Sparlösa (Vg 119) gegen 800 n.Chr. Allerdings wird in der Noleby-Inschrift nicht der Plural sondern der kollektive Singular gebraucht (s.o. Inschrift Nr. 3 mit Abbildung 3; zu *rūnō* siehe Schulte 2024).

(14)   a.   **runo fahi raginakudo** [...]

rūnō fāhi raginakundō [...]

'Eine Rune (kollektiv) male ich, eine von den   (Nolebystein, KJ 67)
Göttern stammende.'

      b.   [...] **rAþ | runaRþARrakiχukutu** [...]

[...] rāþ rūnaR þāR rœginukundu [...]

'[...] deute (diese) Runen, die von den Göttern   (Sparlösastein, Vg 119)
stammenden!'

Marold (2012: 83) stellt fest, dass die Noleby-Inschrift eine „metrisch einwandfreie Langzeile" mit zwei stabenden Hebungen bildet, durch die An- und Abvers verbunden werden.[41] Es liegt daher eine wohlgeformte Langzeile vor, die sie in Sievers (1893) metrischem Schema als A1/A1-Typ skandiert. Entscheidend ist, dass ein regelrecht gebauter Stabreimvers vorliegt. Im folgenden bezeichnet *H* (= Hebung) eine hauptonige stabende Hebung, während *X* eine weniger prominente (nicht-stabende) Hauptonsilbe bezeichnet. *S* (= Senkung) bezeichnet eine Schwachtonsilbe bzw. Schwachtonsilbengruppe.[42] Im übrigen beruht die Hebung (*H*) von dreisilbigem *ragina-* auf metrischer 'Auflösung' (*resolution*), die im phonologischen System des Urnordischen und der nordischwestgermanischen Literatursprachen verankert ist.[43]

rūnō fāhi | *raginakundō*
H-S X-S | *H-S X-S*

In seiner Arbeit *Revising Oral Theory* hat Acker (1998) diesen stabenden Formeltyp zusammen mit den Zwillingsformeln als *slot filler* bezeichnet. Die stabende

---

41. Siehe Marold (2011: 83, 101) gegenüber Schulte (2010: 53), ders. (2011: 10) und Naumann (2010: 150). In diesem wichtigen Punkt ist Marold eindeutig Recht zu geben.

42. Vgl. Marold (2011: 83), mit Verweis auf Sievers (1893).

43. Siehe dazu Kuryłowicz (1949) und die Stellungnahmen von Suzuki (1995) und Pascual (2016: 290–291) für das Altenglische. Der silbenmetrische Prozess der Auflösung ist auch in der nordischen Sprachgeschichte relevant; vgl. Schulte (2004).

Formel, einschließlich der Zwillingsformel, bildet die Grundlage der altgermanischen Alliterationsmetrik, was nicht nur die germanische Langzeile sondern auch die eddischen Formen des *Fornyrðislag* und des *Ljóðaháttr* einschließt (siehe ausführlich Schulte 2023a).

7. Primitive Formen des *Ljóðaháttr* im Urnordischen?

Kommen wir auf die Frage zurück, ob Vorläufer altnordischer Metren, in Sonderheit die Form des *Ljóðaháttr* (nebst archaischer Formen des *Málaháttr* und des skaldischen *Kviðuháttr*) im Corpus nachzuweisen sind. Versuche, diese Metren im Urnordischen zu identifizieren, dürften insgesamt als gescheitert gelten. Dies haben die metrischen Untersuchungen von Marold (2012) und Schulte (2010) gezeigt, die insgesamt zu einem Negativurteil kommen. Inschriften wie der Seeland-Brakteat (KJ 127), der Tjurkö-Brakteat (KJ 136), der Tunestein (KJ 72) oder gar das Goldhorn B von Gallehus (KJ 43) lassen kaum eine metrische Skandierung als frühe Formen des *Ljóðaháttr* zu, obgleich solche Deutungen wiederholt vorgeschlagen worden sind.[44] Marold (2012:75) charakterisiert Nielsens (1983:33) „archaische Form des *Ljóðaháttr*" kurz und prägnant als „äußerst unwahrscheinlich".

Ausnahmsweise sei hier eine Inschrift der Übergangszeit kurz angesprochen. Es wurde vorgeschlagen, die Eingangszeile der Stentoftener Inschrift als Folge von drei Kurzversen und einer abschließenden Vollzeile zu lesen. Somit würde eine *Ljóðaháttr*-Strophe vorliegen (siehe Nielsen 1983:44). Doch Grønvik (1996:190), Schulte (2010:56) und Marold (2012:85) bemerken Schwierigkeiten der Skandierung und kommen daher zu einem metrischen Negativurteil. Auch Lindqvist (1923:61–63) bezweifelte den metrischen Status der Eingangszeile von Stentoften, indem er diese als „stavrimslös galderform" ('stabreimlose Galderform') bestimmte. Meines Erachtens handelt es sich um rhythmisch gegliederte, alliterierende Prosa mit anaphorisch gebrauchtem Quantor niu 'neun'.[45] Neuere syntaktische Analysen, welche ein vorgeschaltetes, isoliertes Satzfragment (*nīu-*

---

44. Als Exponent der *Ljóðaháttr*-Deutung von Gallehus, Seeland II und Järsberg ist zum Beispiel Nielsen (1970) und ders. (1983:33) zu nennen. Vgl. dazu die negative Stellungnahme von Marold (2012:69) [zu Seeland II], dies. (2012:74–75 [zu Gallehus], dies. (2012:78) [zu Tune], dies. (2012:80) [zu Tjurkö] und schließlich dies. (2012:85) [zur Eingangszeile von Stentoften]. Marold stimmt meiner Negativeinschätzung hier im wesentlichen zu; siehe Schulte (2010:52) [zu Tjurkö], 53 [zu Seeland II], 55 [zu Tune], 56 [zur Einleitungszeile von Stentoften]. – Zum Stein von Järsberg siehe Abschnitt 5 mit Abbildung 5.

45. Zu den unterschiedlichen Metrifizierungsversuchen der Eingangszeile von Stentoften siehe zusammenfassend Naumann (2018:48–54).

hab⁰rumʀ nīuhangestumʀ) im Dativ annehmen, bestätigen diese nüchterne Einschätzung.[46]

(15) Eingangszeile der Inschrift von Stentoften
(KJ 96, gedeutet nach Santesson 1989; Datierung 520/30–700, nach Imer 2015b: 264)

niuhAborumʀ ‖ niuhagestumʀ ‖ hAᵽuwolAfʀ gAf j (= *jāra) ‖ hAriwolAfʀ [m]A[gi]us nu hle

nīuhab⁰rumʀ ‖ nīuhangestumʀ ‖ Haᵽuwolᵃfʀ gaf j(āra) ‖ Hariwolafʀ [m]a[giu] 's nū h[l]ē

'Mit neun Böcken, mit neun Hengsten, gab Haᵽuwolfʀ (gutes) Jahr. Hariwolfʀ ist nun Schutz für den Jungen(?).'

Die metrische Deutung des Brakteaten I von Tjurkö kann hier als ein weiteres Anschauungsbeispiel dienen (siehe Abbildung 7). Naumann (2018: 45; ders. 2010: 151) stellt im Anschluss an Salberger (1962–63) die Verbindung einer Langzeile und einer Vollzeile her und rechnet mit dem Versprinzip der 'Anreimung' (vgl. Salberger 1956):

(16) Brakteat von Tjurkö I
(KJ 136 = IK 184; Datierung: C-Brakteat, vgl. Imer 2015: 284)

wurte runoʀ an walhakurne … heldaʀ kunimu(n)diu

Wurtē rūnōʀ an walha-kurnē   Heldaʀ Kunimu(n)diu

'Er wirkte (i.e. schrieb) die Runen auf dem Welschkorn (Gold): Heldaʀ dem Kunimunduʀ.'

Den metrischen Befund fasst Naumann (2018) anschaulich zusammen:

> Die Inschrift verbürgt planvolle metrische Gliederung und Iktenverteilung und wurde zuerst von Salberger als „helming i primitiv *ljóðaháttr*" (Helming in primitivem ljóðaháttr) erschlossen (1962–63: 336ff.; 1976: 41). Handhabe von Salbergers Deutung bietet die aus Eddadichtung und späterer Runenmetrik bekannte, aber auch im Heliand vorkommende, Versverschränkung in Form von zeilenüberschreitender Stabung oder 'Anreimung' (Sievers 1893: 83f.), vgl. z.B. Hávamál 80, 1–3 in einer ljóðaháttr-Halbstrophe […].   (Naumann 2018: 45)

---

46. Der Syntaktiker Eyþórsson (2022) zieht „left dislocation" einer „Topikalisierung" der Syntagmen **niuhAborumʀ ‖ niuhagestumʀ** vor und bemerkt zur Einleitungszeile von Stentoften (Email vom 28.07.2022): „here it is argued that in these cases the first phrase stands apart from the remainder of the text (by "left dislocation"), as a separate statement, rather than being a phrase within the clause itself (involving "topicalization")."

Abbildung 7. Brakteat I von Tjurkö KJ 136 = IK 184. Zeichnung: Bildnachweis IK 184

Marold (2012:80) schließt sich meinem Negativurteil an, dass Salbergers *Ljóðaháttr*-Lesung wohl zurückzuweisen ist.[47] Beachtenswert ist Marolds Vorschlag (Marold 2012:80), die Brakteaten-Inschrift, die ja in einem Kreis verläuft, in umgekehrter Reihenfolge der Runensequenzen zu lesen: *Heldaʀ Kunimu(n)diu: wurte rūnōʀ an walhakurnē* (siehe Abbildung 7). Bei dieser Lesereihenfolge ergibt sich ein vorgeschaltetes, nicht-alliterierendes Satzfragment, das nicht im Alliterationsschema integriert ist. Diese metrische Deutung, die letztlich auf Grønvik (1987:151) beruht, wurde auch von Naumann (2018:45) aufgegriffen.[48] So gesehen ergibt sich eine wohlgeformte Langzeile mit zwei alliterierenden Stäben. Ich schliesse mich in diesem Punkt vorbehaltlos der Deutung Marolds (2012:80) an:

Heldaʀ Kunimu(n)diu || *wurtē rūnōʀ* | *an walhakurnē*
'Heldaʀ für Kunimunduʀ: er wirkte die Runen auf dem Welschkorn.'

Damit sollte gleichzeitig zur Vorsicht gemahnt werden, eddische oder sogar skaldische (das heißt, silbenzählende) Metren in die Periode der älteren Runeninschriften zu projizieren. Hier scheint bis heute der romantische Zeitgeist des 19. und frühen 20. Jahrhunderts nachzuleben, der in kühnen philologischen Rekonstruktionen gipfelte. Mithin verspürt man das ferne Echo einer älteren philologischen Tradition, die bestrebt war, eddische Dichtung auf die Sprachstufe der

---

47. Siehe Schulte (2010:52).
48. Vgl. ferner Mees (2007:216); Pascual (2016:298).

unsynkopierten Runeninschriften zu transponieren: Genzmer (1936) und Harding (1946; 1951) sind eindrucksvolle Beispiele dieser philologischen Kunst.

8. Auswertung

Ziel dieses kritischen Beitrags war es, die Spreu vom Weizen zu trennen und Kandidaten metrisch-stabender Versform im runischen Corpus zu identifizieren. Ich komme mit Smirnitskaya (1994: 2021) auf die Satzbetonung und den Satzrhythmus zurück.[49] Erst wo der Satzrhythmus mit dem Alliterationsschema verschmilzt, entsteht der regelrecht gebaute Stabreimvers, mithin die germanische Langzeile (vgl. Liberman 1998: 99). Dieses Interaktionsmuster des Urnordischen, das ich hier als *Proto-Langzeile* bezeichnet habe, garantiert den metrischen Stabreimvers. Denn die metrische Einheit ist eben auch eine Sinneinheit. Sichere Kandidaten metrischer Gestaltung im Corpus der älteren Runeninschriften sind das Goldhorn B von Gallehus, das Ortband von Thorsberg, die Steine von Rosseland und Noleby und wohl auch der Brakteat I von Tjurkö (vgl. Naumann 2018: 45).[50]

In diesem Beitrag wird diese nordwestgermanische (sprich: urnordische) Innovation als *Proto-Langzeile* bezeichnet, da sie gegenüber den altgermanischen Literatursprachen insgesamt grössere Freiheit in der Füllung der Senkungssilben aufweist. Dieses Momentum schließt die Füllung der nachtonigen Senkungssilben und wahrscheinlich auch den Auftakt (Anakrusis) ein, zumal die germanischen unbetonten Präfixe in einem Frühstadium des Nordgermanischen verloren gegangen sind.[51] Bei der metrischen Interpretation von Thorsberg ist außerdem zu erwägen, ob — durchaus in Andreas Heuslers Sinne — mit takthaltigen Leerpositionen zu rechnen ist. Denn sollte Thorsberg als Proto-Langzeile aufgefasst werden, so erfährt *-þewaʀ* Auflösung, womit uns bei der metrischen Skandierung die Senkungssilbe abhanden kommt.

Als direktes westgermanisches (genauer gesagt, voralthochdeutsches) Pendant der urnordischen Langzeile auf dem Goldhorn B von Gallehus findet sich

---

49. Überraschender Weise erkennt Smirnitskaya (2021: 141) die Versifizierung älterer Runeninschriften (insbesondere Järsberg, Kragehul, Seeland II und Gallehus) nicht an und kommt zu einem kategorischen Negativurteil: „the rhythm of a runic formula [...] does remind one of the rhythm of the L[ong]L[ine] [...] — but [...] it is no verse rhythm at all."

50. Vgl. ähnlich zurückhaltend Naumann (2010: 151), der den metrischen Status folgender Inschriften anzweifelt: Lanzenschaft von Kragehul (KJ 27), Kamm von Setre (KJ 40), Stein von Järsberg (KJ 70), Stein von Kjølevik (KJ 75) und Brakteat II von Seeland (KJ 127).

51. Dieser angenommene Nexus zwischen nordgermanischem Präfixschwund und eingeschränkter Anakrusis im Altnordischen verdient aber weitere Studien; vgl. Goering (2023: 40) mit Verweis auf Kuhn (1933) und Þorgeirsson (2012).

338 Michael Schulte

die metrische Runeninschrift auf der silbernen Gürtelschnalle von Pforzen (SG-97), die auf eine sagenhafte Auseinandersetzung aus der Wielandsage anspielt.[52] Mit Nedoma (2020:523) „[bietet] [d]er runenepigraphische Text [...] ein — literarisch nicht überliefertes — Ereigniszeugnis zur Heldensage um den Meisterschützen *Aigil* (=aisl. anorw. *Egill*) und seiner Frau bzw. Geliebten *Ailrūn* (=aisl. *Ǫlrún*, anorw. *Olrūn*)." Linguistisch vertritt diese Inschrift eine frühe westgermanische Sprachform, das heißt genauer gesprochen das Voralthochdeutsche des 6. Jhds. Metrisch auffällig ist, dass hier — wie auf dem Horn B von Gallehus — das finite Verb *gasōkun* (mit unbetontem Präfix *ga-*) in der vierten, nicht-alliterierenden Hebung steht:

(17) Gürtelschnalle von Pforzen [53]   (SG-97; Datierung: 567–600)

aigil · andi · aïlrun · ltahu · gasokun

Aigil   andi   Ailrūn   / (I)ltahu gasōkun

'Aigil und Ailrun kämpften, stritten (zusammen) an der Ilzach.'

Bereits Naumann (1998:705) erwog, dies als den „erste[n] sichere[n] Textzeuge[n] für eine regelentsprechende Langzeile auf westgermanischem Boden" zu deuten, was Feulner (2001) und Nedoma (2020:522) unmittelbar bestätigen. Dabei wird *(I)ltahu* der repräsentativen Deutung zufolge als zusammengesetztes Hydronym im lokativen Instrumental gedeutet; zum Flussnamen vgl. die *Ilz* (Nebenfluss der Donau). Die Vokalalliteration kommt durch Grønviks Substitutionsregel zustande, hier in modifizierter Form: lt steht für ḷt mit sonantischem Anlaut (</ilt/).[54] Dieser metrischen Deutung eines regelrecht gebauten Stabreimverses hat sich die neuere Forschung insgesamt konsensual angeschlossen.[55]

Weitere urnordische Kandidaten sind dagegen unsicher. Einzelne Inschriften wie die Fibel von Eikeland (KJ 17a) können bestenfalls als semi-metrisch gewertet werden, da sie das Füllungspontential der Langzeile am Schluss der Inschrift überschreiten. Dies räumt auch Marold (2012:81) ein. Im übrigen dürfte die metrische Analyse der Schnalle von Vimose (Moorfund aus Fünen, KJ 24) — trotz der positiven Einschätzung Marolds (2012) im Anschluss an Seebold (1994:64–65) — in einen hermeneutischen Zirkel münden, zumal die Deutung dieser Inschrift äußerst spekulativ ist. Naumann (2010:149) spricht in diesem

---

52. Siehe zusammenfassend Feulner (2001) und Nedoma (2020:522). Den metrischen Status von Pforzen bestätigen Schulte (2010:49), Marold (2012:95) und ferner Mees (2019), letzterer allerdings mit einigen Deutungskalkülen; siehe kritisch Nedoma (2020:523).

53. Zur Datierung vgl. Waldispühl (2013:299).

54. Siehe Nedoma (2020:518), mit Verweis auf Nedoma (2004:361).

55. Zur Metrizität von SG-97 Pforzen siehe besonders Robert Nedomas Abriss zum Stand der Forschung (Nedoma 2020:522–523); vgl. außerdem Waldispühl (2013:299).

Fall von einem „Interpretationsangebot". Als sicherer Stabreimkandidat dürfte die Vimose-Schnalle jedenfalls ausfallen.

Die metrische Form von Gallehus, Thorsberg, Rosseland und Noleby ist die des regelrecht gebauten Stabreimverses. Entgegen Marold (2012: 78–79) musste auch der Kjølevikstein aus dieser Stabreimgruppe ausgegrenzt werden, da er das wesentliche Kriterium der Satzeinheit und des Satzrhythmus nicht erfüllt. Stolpersteine der metrischen Deutung sind vor allem isolierte Satzfragmente, die zwar — streng formell betrachtet — ins Alliterationsschema integriert sein können, andererseits aber syntaktisch für sich stehen und eine elliptische Deutung nahelegen.[56]

Über den Einzelvers hinausgehende, metrische Formen sind im untersuchten Corpus durchaus unsicher. Als potentieller Kandidat einer Metrifizierung weist die relativ lange Inschrift auf dem Tunestein nicht nur „metrische Schönheitsfehler", sondern auch ein Grundproblem runologischer Art auf: Ein Teil der Inschrift ist zerstört und damit verloren; zu Ergänzungsvorschlägen siehe Marold (2012: 76). Tune wurde daher in dieser Untersuchung aus Reliabilitätsgründen ausgeklammert. Die in metrischer Sicht problematischen Inschriften von Blekinge (Stentoften und Björketorp) und Eggja wurden in dieser Studie ebenfalls beiseite gelassen, zumal sie die Sprachstufe des Urnordischen verlassen haben. Sie erfordern eine eigene metrische Untersuchung, die hier schon aus Raumgründen nicht vorgenommen werden kann; vgl. auch die zurückhaltende metrische Einschätzung in Schulte (2010: 56–57) und Naumann (2010: 151). Als unsicher werden zuletzt auch Skandierungsvorschläge betrachtet, die archaische Formen des *Ljóðaháttr* nebst anderen altnordischen Metren im runischen Corpus postulieren. Auf die Gefahr anachronistischer Deutungen im Sinne von *wishfulfilling prophecies* wurde mehrfach hingewiesen.

9. Schluss

Der minimalistische Ansatz in diesem Beitrag dürfte gezeigt haben, dass die Proto-Langzeile mit relativ großer Sicherheit als Metrum einiger weniger älterer Runeninschriften besteht. Es ist in der Tat ein *Metron ametron* (nach Feulner 2008), da es zumindest in Senkungssilben nicht die streng(er)en Versfüllungen des Altnordischen fordert. Aufs Ganze gesehen beruhen viele der vorgeschlagenen runologisch-metrischen Deutungen der älteren Forschung auf Spekulationen und einer Überbewertung der Alliteration als formeller Grundlage metrischer Versform, wie dies bei Kabell (1978), Hübler (1996) und selbst Marold (2012) zu

---

56. Wenig überzeugend daher auch Mees (2007: 220); siehe dazu Schulte (2010: 51).

bemängeln ist. Insbesondere wurde hier das Problem loser Satzfragmente, die außerhalb der syntaktischen Einheit stehen, als „Stolpersteine der Metrik" thematisiert.

Richtschnur der vorliegenden Studie ist die Sinneinheit des metrischen Alliterationsverses als Schablone von Metrik *und* Syntax (s.o. Abschnitt 2). Diesen metrische Test haben wie gesagt nur einzelne Inschriftenkandidaten bestanden.

Danksagung

Es handelt sich um die stark erweiterte und überarbeitete Fassung einer kurzen metrischen Studie, die in *Filologia Germanica* erschienen ist (Schulte 2023b). Im vorliegenden Beitrag wird die Metrizität besonders in ihrem Verhältnis zur Formelhaftigkeit beleuchtet. Der Interpretationsansatz ist stark von Smirnitskaya (2021) geprägt, ohne dass ihren Deutungen in Einzelpunkten gefolgt wird. Für konstruktive Kritik gilt mein Dank den beiden anonymen Gutachtern.

Literatur

Acker, P. 1998. *Revising Oral Theory. Formulaic Composition in Old English and Old Icelandic Verse.* New York, London: Psychology Press.

Andersen, H. 1961. Guldhornsindskriften. *Aarbøger for Nordisk Oldkyndighet og Historie* 1961. 89–121.

Axboe, M. et al. (Hgg.). 1985–1989. *Die Goldbrakteaten der Völkerwanderungszeit. Ikonographischer Katalog* (Münstersche Mittelalter-Schriften 24,1.1–24,3.2). München: Fink.

Birkmann, T. 1995. *Von Ågedal bis Malt. Die skandinavischen Runeninschriften vom Ende des 5. bis Ende des 9. Jahrhunderts* (ERGA 12). Berlin: Walter de Gruyter.

DR = Jacobsen, L. & E. Moltke. 1941–1942. *Danmarks Runeindskrifter.* 3 Bde. København: Munksgaard.

Düwel, K. 1984. Zu den theriophoren Runenmeisternamen, insbesondere in Brakteatinschriften. *Frühmittelalterliche Studien* 18, 321–333.

Düwel, K. 2015. Runenkenntnis als Oberschichtenmerkmale (mit besonderer Berücksichtigung methodischer Aspekte). In O. Grimm & A. Pesch (Hgg.), *Archäologie und Runen. Fallstudien zu Inschriften im älteren Futhark* (Schriften des archäologischen Landesmuseums 11), 265–290. Kiel & Hamburg: Wachholtz & Murmann.

Düwel, K., R. Nedoma & S. Oehrl (Hgg.). 2020. *Die südgermanischen Runeninschriften* (ERGA 119; Runische Schriftlichkeit in den germanischen Sprachen 1). Teil 1. Einleitung und Edition, Teil 2. Bibliographie, Register und Abbildungen. Berlin & Boston: Walter de Gruyter.

Düwel, K. & R. Nedoma. 2023. *Runenkunde.* 5., aktualisierte und erw. Aufl. Berlin: Springer.

Nochmals zur Metrizität der älteren Runeninschriften **341**

Ender, A., A. Leemann & B. Wälchli (Hgg.). 2012. *Methods in Contemporary Linguistics* (Trends in Linguistics. Studies and Monographs 247). Berlin & Boston: De Gruyter Mouton.

Engelhardt, C. 1869. *Vimosefundet* (Fynske Mosefund, 2). Kjøbenhavn: G.E.C. Gad.

ERGA = Ergänzungsbände zum Reallexikon der Germanischen Altertumskunde. Berlin: Walter de Gruyter.

Eyþórsson, Þ. 2012. Variation in the Syntax of the Older Runic Inscriptions. *Futhark: International Journal of Runic Studies* 2 (2011, publ. 2012). 27–49.

Eyþórsson, Þ. 2022. Exceptional Syntactic Patterns in the Early Runic Language. [Abstrakt zum Zoom-Vortrag]. *Ninth International Symposium on Runes and Runic Inscriptions, Akademie Sankelmark, Germany,* 14–19 June, 2022. Siehe URL https://www.isrri2022.uni-kiel.de/abstracts/ (Zugangsdatum: 20.07.2022).

Feulner, A. H. 2001. Metrisches zur Runenschnalle von Pforzen. *Die Sprache* 40. 26–42.

Feulner, A. H. 2008. *Theorie des „metron ametron". Zu den Grundlagen der altgermanischen Alliterationsdichtung.* Unveröffentlichte Habilitationsschrift, Berlin: Humboldt-Universität zu Berlin.

Genzmer, F. 1936. Ein germanisches Gedicht aus der Hallstattzeit. *Germanisch-Romanische Monatsschrift* 24. 14–21.

Glück, H. & M. Rödel (Hgg.). 2016. *Metzler Lexikon Sprache.* 5. Aufl. Stuttgart: Metzler.

Goering, Nelson. 2023. *Prosody in Medieval English and Norse.* Oxford: Oxford University Press.

Grønvik, O. 1985. Über den Lautwert der *ing*-Runen und die Auslassung von Vokalen in älteren Runeninschriften. *Indogermanische Forschungen* 90. 168–195.

Grønvik, O. 1987. *Fra Ågedal til Setre. Sentrale runeinnskrifter fra det 6. århundre.* Oslo et al.: Universitetsforlaget.

Grønvik, O. 1996. *Fra Vimose til Ødemotland. Nye studier over runeinnskrifter fra førkristen tid i Norden.* Oslo et al.: Universitetsforlaget.

Harding, E. 1946. [Nr. 95] En germ. hjältedikt (*Atlakviða*) i västurnord. gestalt. *Språkvetenskapliga problem i ny belysning, eller Bidrag till nordisk och germansk språkhistoria* 7. 41–55. Lund: Carl Bloms boktryckeri.

Harding, E. 1951. [Nr. 96] Trenne fornisländske eddadikter i urnordisk språkform [*Vǫlundarkviða, Hamðismál, Atlakviða*]. *Språkvetenskapliga problem i ny belysning, eller Bidrag till nordisk och germansk språkhistoria* 8. 3–48. Lund: Carl Bloms boktryckeri.

Heusler, A. 1956. *Deutsche Versgeschichte mit Einschluss des altenglischen und altnordischen Stabreimverses* (Grundriss der Germanischen Philologie 8). 2. Aufl. 3 Bde. Berlin: Walter de Gruyter.

Hübler, F. 1996. *Schwedische Runendichtung der Wikingerzeit* (Runrön 10). Uppsala: Uppsala universitet, Institutionen för nordiska språk.

Hübner, A. 1930. *Die „mhd. Ironie" oder die Litotes im Altdeutschen* (Palaestra 170). Leipzig: Mayer & Müller.

IK + Nummer = Inschrift herausgegeben in Axboe, M. et al. (Hgg.). 1985–1989.

Imer, L. M. 2015a. *Jernalderens runeindskrifter i norden. Kronologi og kontekst* (Aarbøger for Nordisk Oldkyndighed og Historie 2013). København: Det Kongelige Nordiske Oldskriftselskab.

Imer, L. M. 2015b. *Jernalderens runeindskrifter i norden. Katalog* (Aarbøger for Nordisk Oldkyndighed og Historie 2014). København: Det Kongelige Nordiske Oldskriftselskab.

Iversen, F. et al. 2019. Irilen på Øverby i Vingulmark. *Viking* 82. 63–98.

Jansson, S. B. F. 1978. *Värmlands runinskrifter* (Sveriges runinskrifter 14.2). Stockholm: Almqvist & Wiksell.

Jesch, J. 2017. Runes and Verse: The Medialities of Early Scandinavian Poetry. *European Journal of Scandinavian Studies* 47. 181–202.

Jungner, H. & E. Svärdström. 1958–1970. *Västergötlands runinskrifter* (Sveriges runinskrifter 5). 2 Bde. Stockholm: Almqvist & Wiksell.

Kabell, A. 1978. *Metrische Studien I. Der Alliterationsvers*. München: Fink.

Kieler Datenbank, Kiel: Universität Kiel; siehe URL http://www.runenprojekt-kiel.de (Zugangsdatum: 27.06.2022).

KJ + Nummer = Inschrift herausgegeben in Krause, W. & H. Jankuhn. 1966.

Krause, W. 1971. *Die Sprache der urnordischen Runeninschriften* (Germanische Bibliothek, 3. Reihe). Heidelberg: Winter.

Krause, W., mit Beiträgen von H. Jankuhn. 1966. *Die Runeninschriften im älteren Futhark* (Abhandlungen der Akademie der Wissenschaften in Göttingen. Philologisch-historische Klasse, 3. Folge, 65). 2 Bde. Göttingen: Vandenhoeck & Ruprecht.

Kuhn, H. 1933. Zur Wortstellung und -betonung im Altgermanischen. *Beiträge zur Geschichte der deutschen Sprache und Literatur* 57. 1–109.

Kuhn, H. (Hg.). 1983. *Edda. Die Lieder des Codex Regius nebst verwandten Denkmälern I.* (Germanische Bibliothek: Reihe 4). 5. Aufl. Heidelberg: Carl Winter Universitätsverlag.

Kuryłowicz, J. 1949. Latin and Germanic Metre. *English and Germanic Studies* 2. 34–38.

Kuryłowicz, J. 1970. *Die sprachlichen Grundlagen der altgermanischen Metrik*. Innsbruck: Institut für vergleichende Sprachwissenschaft.

Lehmann, W. P. 1956. *The Development of Germanic Verse Form*. Austin: University of Texas Press & Linguistic Society of America.

Liberman, A. 1998. Rez. von: Smirnitskaya, O. A. 1994. *Scandinavian Studies* 70. 87–108.

Lindqvist, I. 1923. *Galdrar. De gamla germanska trollsångernas stil undersökt i samband med en svensk runinskrift från folkvandringstiden* (Göteborgs högskolas årsskrift 29:1). Göteborg: Elander.

Marold, E. 2012. Vers oder nicht Vers? Zum metrischen Charakter von Runeninschriften im älteren Futhark. *Futhark: International Journal of Runic Studies* 2 (2011, publ. 2012). 63–102.

Marold, E. 2013. Entgegnungen zu Bernard Mees: „Early Runic Metrics: A Linguistic Approach". *Futhark: International Journal of Runic Studies* 3. 119–123.

Mees, B. 2007. Before *Beowulf*. On the Proto-history of Old Germanic Verse. *Journal of the Australian Early Medieval Association* 3. 205–221.

Mees, B. 2008. Style, Manner and Formula in Early Germanic Epigraphy. *NOWELE* 54/55. 63–98.

Mees, B. 2013. Early Runic Metrics: A Linguistic Approach. *Futhark: International Journal of Runic Studies* 3. 111–118.

Mees, B. 2019. Egill und Ǫlrún in Early High German. *Futhark: International Journal of Runic Studies* 8 (2017, publ. 2019). 151–156.

Moltke, E. 1981. Järsbergstenen, en mærkelig värmlandsk runesten. *Fornvännen* 76. 81–90.

Naumann, H.-P. 1994. *Hann var manna mestr óníðingr* – Zur Poetizität metrischer Runeninschriften. In H. Uecker (Hg.), *Studien zum Altgermanischen. Festschrift für Heinrich Beck* (ERGA 11), 490–502. Berlin: Walter de Gruyter.

Naumann, H.-P. 1998. Runeninschriften als Quelle der Versgeschichte. In K. Düwel (Hg.), *Runeninschriften als Quellen interdisziplinärer Forschung. Abhandlungen des Vierten Internationalen Symposiums über Runen und Runeninschriften in Göttingen vom 4.-9. August 1995* (ERGA 15), 694–714. Berlin: Walter de Gruyter.

Naumann, H.-P. 2010. Zum Stabreim in Runeninschriften. *Jahrbuch für Internationale Germanistik* 42. 143–166.

Naumann, H.-P. 2018. *Metrische Runeninschriften in Skandinavien. Einführung, Edition und Kommentare* (Beiträge zur Nordischen Philologie 60). Tübingen: Narr Francke Attempo.

Nedoma, R. 2004. Noch einmal zur Runeninschrift auf der Gürtelschnalle von Pforzen. In H.-P. Naumann et al. (Hgg.), *Alemannien und der Norden* (ERGA 43), 340–370. Berlin: Walter de Gruyter.

Nedoma, R. 2020. SG-98 Pforzen I. 3.2 Sprachliche Deutung [und] 3.3 Funktion der Inschrift. In Düwel, K., R. Nedoma, S. Oehrl (Hgg.). 2020. 516–523.

Nedoma, R. 2022. Zur Runeninschrift auf dem Goldhorn B von Gallehus. *Beiträge zur Geschichte der deutschen Sprache und Literatur* 144, 188–213.

Nielsen, H.F. 1985. *Old English and the Continental Germanic Languages. A Survey of Morphological and phonological Interrelations* (Innsbrucker Beiträge zur Sprachwissenschaft 33). 2., rev. Aufl. Innsbruck: Institut für Sprachwissenschaft der Universität.

Nielsen, H.F. 1989. *The Germanic Languages. Origins and Early Dialectal Interrelations.* Tuscaloosa, London: University of Alabama Press.

Nielsen, N.Å. 1970. Notes on Early Runic Poetry. *Medieval Scandinavia* 3. 138–141.

Nielsen, N.Å. 1983. *Danske runeindskrifter. Et udvalg med kommentarer.* København: Hernov.

Pascual, R.J. 2016. Old English Metrical History and the Composition of *Widsið. Neophilologus* 100. 289–302.

Paulli, J.R. 1734. *Zuverlässiger Abriss des Anno 1734 bey Tundern gefundenen Güldenen Horns.* Kopenhagen: Lynov.

Peterson, L. 2004. *Lexikon över urnordiska personnamn.* Uppsala: Uppsala universitet, Institutionn för nordiska språk; siehe URL http://www.sofi.se/1459 (Zugangsdatum: 12.07.2022).

Peterson, L. 1994. On the Relationship between Proto-Scandinavian and Continental Germanic Personal Names. In K. Düwel (Hgg.), *Runische Schriftkultur in kontinental-skandinavischer und -angelsächsischer Wechselbeziehung. Internationales Symposium in der Werner-Reimers-Stiftung vom 24.-27. Juni 1992 in Bad Homburg* (ERGA 10), 128–175. Berlin: Walter de Gruyter.

Popper, K.R. 1982. *Logik der Forschung.* 7. deutsche Aufl. Tübingen: J.C.B. Mohr. (Engl. Erstausgabe: *The Logic of Scientific Discovery.* London: Hutchinson, 1959).

RGA = *Reallexikon der Germanischen Altertumskunde*, gegründet von J. Hoops. Hrsgg. H. Beck, D. Geuenich & H. Steuer. 2. Aufl. 35 Bde. und 2 Registerbde. Berlin, New York: Walter de Gruyter, 1973–2008.

Salberger, E. 1956. Versifikatoriskt om Tjurkö-brakteaten. *Arkiv för nordisk filologi* 71. 1–13.

Salberger, E. 1962–1963. Nekrologen från Härlingstorp. *Meddelanden från Lunds universitets historiska museum* 1962–1963. 336–347.

Salberger, E. 1976. **ukiþila**. En dunkel runföljd med ett kvinnonamn. *Arkiv för nordisk filologi* 91. 33–41.

Samnordisk runtextdatabas, Uppsala, Uppsala universitet; siehe URL http://www.nordiska.uu .se/forskn/samnord.htm (Zugangsdatum: 11.07.2022).

Santesson, L. 1989. En blekingsk blotinnskrift. En nytolkning av inledningsraderna på Stentoftenstenen. *Fornvännen* 84. 221–229.

Schulte, M. 1998. *Grundfragen der Umlautphonemisierung* (ERGA 17). Berlin: Walter de Gruyter.

Schulte, M. 2003. Early Nordic language history and modern runology. With particular reference to reduction and prefix loss. In: K. Burridge & B. Blake (Hgg.), *Historical Linguistics 2001. Selected Papers from the 15th International Conference on Historical Linguistics, Melbourne, 13–17 August, 2001* (Amsterdam Studies in the Theory and History of Linguistic Science. Series IV: Current Issues in Linguistic Theory 237), 391–402. Amsterdam/Philadelphia: Benjamins.

Schulte, M. 2004. The Germanic Foot in Ancient Nordic: Resolution and Related Matters Revisited. *NOWELE* 45. 3–24.

Schulte, M. 2010. Runes and Metrics. On the Metricity of the Older Runic Inscriptions. *Maal og Minne* 2010. 45–67.

Schulte, M. 2011. Early Scandinavian Legal Texts — Evidence of Preliterary Metrical Composition? *NOWELE* 62/63. 1–21.

Schulte, M. 2018. *Urnordisch. Eine Einführung* (Wiener Studien zur Skandinavistik 26). Wien: Praesens.

Schulte, M. 2020a. Rakkestadsteinen fra Øverby i Østfold. Et nytt runefunn fra førlitterær tid. *Agder Vitenskaps-Akademi Årbok* 2019 (publ. 2020). 88–104.

Schulte, M. 2020b. Wain, Wagon, and Wayfarer. Names of Speed, Agility and Alertness in the Corpus of the Older Runic Inscriptions. *NOWELE* 73. 276–298.

Schulte, M. 2021. Magie in den älteren und jüngeren Runeninschriften? — Zum Status magischer Konzepte in der Runologie. *Filologia Germanica — Germanic Philology* 13. 307–327.

Schulte, M. 2023a. Bauprinzipien runischer Formeln. Zur Lexis und Morphosyntax urnordischer Formeln. *Beiträge zur Geschichte der deutschen Sprache und Literatur* 145.1. 1–34.

Schulte, M. 2023b. *Runica metrica*. Die metrische Gestalt der älteren Runeninschriften und ihre Grundeinheit der Proto-Langzeile. In P. Lendinara, L. Vezzosi & L. Teresi (Hgg.), *Metro e ritmo nei testi germanici medievali / Meter and Rhythm in Medieval Germanic Texts*. (Themaband Filologia Germanica — Germanic Philology 15), 223–248. Milano: Prometheus.

Schulte, M. 2023c. Geschwind wie der irilaʀ. Zum Neufund des Rakkestadsteines aus Ostnorwegen und zu den *ek Irilaʀ*-Inschriften. In W. Heizmann & J.A. van Nahl (Hgg.), *Germanisches Altertum und europäisches Mittelalter. Gedenkband für Heinrich Beck.* (ERGA 142), 211–235. Berlin & New York: Walter de Gruyter.

Nochmals zur Metrizität der älteren Runeninschriften   345

Schulte, M. 2024. Nochmals zum Runenwort urnord. *rūnō*: Ein Beitrag zur Periodisierung des Urnordischen. *Beiträge zur Geschichte der deutschen Sprache und Literatur* 146.2. 237–258.

Schulte, M. 2025. Resolution and anacrusis in Ancient Nordic: a reevaluation of the runic metrical data. In: J. Gvozdanovic et al. (Hgg.), *Historical Linguistics 2023. Selected Papers from the 37th International Conference on Historical Linguistics, Heidelberg, 4–8 September, 2023*. (Amsterdam Studies in the Theory and History of Linguistic Science. Series IV: Current Issues in Linguistic Theory). Amsterdam/Philadelphia: Benjamins [im Druck].

Seebold, E. 1994. Die sprachliche Einordnung der archaischen Runeninschriften. In K. Düwel (Hg.), *Runische Schriftkultur in kontinental-skandinavischer und -angelsächsischer Wechselbeziehung. Internationales Symposium in der Werner-Reimers-Stiftung vom 24.-27. Juni 1992 in Bad Homburg* (ERGA 10), 56–94. Berlin: Walter de Gruyter.

SG + Nummer = Inschrift herausgegeben in Düwel, K., R. Nedoma & S. Oehrl (Hgg.). 2020.

Sievers, E. 1893. *Altgermanische Metrik* (Sammlung kurzer Grammatiken germanischer Dialekte. Ergänzungsreihe, II). Halle a. Saale: Niemeyer.

Smirnitskaya, O.A. 1994. *Der Verse und die Sprache der altgermanischen Poesie* [1. Aufl.; russisches Original]. 2 Bde. Moskau: Moscow Lomonosov State University.

Smirnitskaya, O.A. 2021. *The Verse and the Language of Old Germanic Poetry*. Edited, revised and translated from Russian by I.V. Sverdlov. Arizona: Arizona State University, Arizona Center for Medieval and Renaissance Studies.

Suzuki, S. 1995. In Defense of Resolution as a Metrical Principle in the Meter of *Beowulf*. *English Studies* 76.1. 20–33.

Suzuki, S. 2010. Anacrusis in Eddic Metres *Fornyrðislag* and *Málaháttr*: Reevaluation and Reinvigoration. *Beiträge zur Geschichte der deutschen Sprache und Literatur* 132. 159–176.

Þorgeirsson, H. 2012. The Origins of Anacrusis in *Fornyrðislag*. *Beiträge zur Geschichte der deutschen Sprache und Literatur* 134. 25–38.

Vg + Nummer = Inschrift herausgegeben in Jungner, H., E. Svärdström (Hgg.). 1958–1970.

Vr + Nummer = Inschrift herausgegeben in Jansson, S.B.F. (Hg.). 1978.

Waldispühl, M. 2013. *Schreibpraktiken und Schriftwissen in südgermanischen Runeninschriften. Zur Funktionalität epigraphischer Schriftverwendung* (Medienwandel — Medienwechsel — Medienwissen 26). Zürich: Chronos.

Wulf, F. 1998. Rez. von: Hübler, F. 1996. *Alvíssmál* 8. 93–98.

Zilmer, K., S. Solheim & K. Vasshus, 2023. Runic fragments from the Svingerud grave field in Norway — Earliest datable evidence of runic writing on stone. *NOWELE* 76.2. 234–303.

Garden, town, villa and *torg*

Four emblematic words that influenced the vocabulary and semantics of European languages

Ingmar Söhrman
University of Gothenburg

> Loanwords in a language often reflect the political and cultural situation at a certain time. In this process, the influence from prestigious languages on lesser prestigious languages often makes itself felt, be it through the replacement of older words or through the introduction of new concepts. Consequently, words such as *garden, town, villa* and *torg/trg* turn up in very different languages and are often subject to semantic changes. The first two come from Germanic, *villa* is Latin and *torg/trg* is of Slavic origin. In this article, these four lexemes and their semantic pathways of change in a range of European languages are analyzed and discussed.

That the vocabulary of a language partly reflects its history and interlinguistic contacts of its speakers, be they peaceful or belligerent, is often considered evident (Boia 2022:11, 13), yet this statement is of course not the whole truth. Lexical transfer is often biased in terms of prestigious languages loaning into lesser prestigious languages, and these linguistic loans also reflect the political and cultural balance of a specific time. On the other hand, place-names often better reflect the origin of the inhabitants, although there are complications as quite a few of these have different names due to the language that is or was used, and which is the most prestigious one at a certain time. In Transylvania for instance, we find *Cluj — Kolozsvár — Klausenburg* depending on the language used. In this case, it is a question of whether you wish to use the Romanian, Hungarian or German name. The same also goes for *Vitoria* in Spain, which is *Gasteiz* in Basque, but this name is scarcely known in the rest of the world.

However, the effect of these influences underlines the importance of how sociocultural changes in any society lead to linguistic, morphological as well as semantic, changes in the languages spoken in a specific region, or in several ones, at specific times of peaceful or more warlike contacts with the surrounding peoples. It is seldom a one-directional phenomenon, and to show partly how these

https://doi.org/10.1075/nss.34.19soh
Available under the CC BY-NC-ND 4.0 license. © 2025 John Benjamins Publishing Company

changes affect even basic concepts I have taken two Germanic words — one Latin and one Slavic — that have left their marks in many European languages as examples of this phenomenon (cf. Söhrman 2017). The four words all mean 'town' and/ or 'a square' of some sort, fundamental and basic concepts of the daily life of a society. It is also enlightening to see why certain words get replaced by others, and for what reasons. These are mainly due to societal and conceptual changes, although you would think that these lexemes would stay as they are, as they refer to basic notions in a society and its vocabulary. This phenomenon also shows how a vocabulary never stays intact: there is always a circulation of words that come into a language or are created when there is a need of some kind, or words just disappear when they are not needed any more, or they may be replaced for ideological or practical reasons as the Romanian philologist Bogdan Hasdeu (1886) formulated it.

The geopolitical changes that took place as the Western Roman Empire fell apart due to strong migrating peoples like the Goths and the Franks, who often saw themselves as the successors of the Roman empire, while the Eastern Roman Empire had similar pretentions, as can be seen in the 'reclaiming' of territory on the Iberian Peninsula by the Eastern Roman emperor Justinian in the 6th century.

However, the Eastern Roman empire survived another 1000 years, although it slowly lost terrain to Slavic and Turkish, i.e., Ottoman, forces, and the expanding realms of these peoples, and then the old Roman society disappeared.

Because of these geopolitical as well as sociocultural changes, the Latin words for *town* — *urbs* and *oppidum* lost their importance and meaning, as they referred to old concepts, and a 'brave new world' arose slowly and replaced many old Roman societal and cultural structures. The *town* is, of course, a fundamental concept for a phenomenon that marks the main agglomerations of people and political and religious power. The Latin word *urbs* represented a superior category of town, cf. the idea of *urbs aeterna*, and this lexeme was mainly used for Rome and Athens as the most distinguished towns of that time, while lesser important towns were often called *oppida* (singular *oppidum*).

In Europe the idea of a town is based on the Greek πόλις, a word that originally referred to a small city-state, in particular *Athens*: "The polis is the characteristic form of Greek urban life; its main features are small size, political autonomy, social homogeneity sense of community and respect for law" (Hornblower & Spawforth 2012: 1170).

However, the lexemes that survived the downfall of the Roman Empire could be seen as semantic "offsprings" of Late Latin lexemes with a more rural and humble background, such as *civitas* and *villa*. *Civitas* was originally the social body of the citizens (*cives*) who were legally "bound together" in a certain place where they lived. Related to these two lexemes are also the words *garden* and *târg* 'square' that will be discussed further below.

If we look at these lexemes from a cognitive semantic point of view, we can see that they differentiate three basic concepts that have formed the words for the notions of town and square in most European languages. All three of them signify a place of a certain character, but two of these notions are positional and the third one is directional (cf. Söhrman 2017).

Semantically, you can see a common origin in these categories, and this origin actually is the meaning 'place', which, in this sense, implies a place that is emotionally connected to the speaker, i.e., it is not any place, but signifies **my** or **our place**. However, this place refers either to the main building and its surroundings, *villa*, i.e., 'my house' or to *town* 'originally my garden', that was owned by a Roman nobleman and where his friends, family, relatives, and servants lived as the houses in Rome and other towns were abandoned because of hard migratory and belligerent times. And these lexemes were then extended to include the neighbouring houses of the estate, and the lexeme is thus turned into 'my village' and later 'my town' (Chapelot & Fossier 1980). These two lexemes represent two subcategories of the positional meaning, one focuses on the house, e.g. *villa*, and the other one focuses on the yard in front of the house, as in *town* and also *garden*, which originally meant fence or hedge but semantically extended to the yard that was enclosed by these barriers, which, of course, is also an adequate semantic description of the origins of a castle, where the buildings were inside the fortress as in *burg, castrum* and *oppidum* (Svensson & Hering 2010; Mitre 2013: 29). The other meaning of 'place' indicates a square or some kind meeting-place where people go for commercial purposes. This square is mainly some kind of marketplace, which is a more directional concept, as people go there and, after some time, return to where they came from. As these gatherings became more and more frequent and attracted more and more people, as a consequence of all the mainly commercial activities that took place there, it was necessary to provide for the maintenance and some ground service at this meeting-place, and the place turned into a huge yard surrounded by houses. As Pirenne (1927) and Mitre (2013: 24) have pointed out, no civilization has existed where urban life has existed without external commercial contacts.

A classic definition of what a town is in a general sense was made by Gordon Childe in 1950. He described a town as the community home of an elite with an important relation to the neighbouring smaller communities of different kinds. He drew attention to certain characteristics of a town. It had to offer labour, collect some kind of tax or tithe, construct monumental buildings, define a ruling class, promote the writing and use of numbers (and schools and teaching), have

Garden, town, villa and *torg*   **349**

an artisan class, promote long distance trade, and create some kind of organic sol-idarity (Gordon Childe 1950: 3–17).

The concept of *town* as discussed by Gordon Childe helps us to distinguish a town from more rural locations such as *villages*. There are nevertheless concepts that legally and semantically lie in between town and village, such as *borough /burrow* (Gordon Childe 1950: 3–17; Thomas 2010: 10–13). The lexeme *town* is often seen as being at least partly generic, as it includes the very notion of a city, yet it is at the same time partly subordinate to the lexeme *city*. In this article *town* is used as the device term.

As a stable morphological and semantic ground for this study, I have used Darling Buck's valuable list of words in Indo-European languages to find lexemes meaning *town* and their etymologies (1949: 1307–1309). The notion of town itself is very old and has existed for thousands of years, although in Europe the concept of a town emerges, as we have seen, in Greece, but Greek πόλις refers to a small city-state as such, while ἄστυ stands for the mere urban centre, as Speake (1994: 507) explains:

> The polis was the dominant form of social and political organization in classical Greece, though certain areas such as Achaea and Aetolia were organized as 'ethnoi ('peoples') that were considered looser federal groupings of settlements within a region. [...] A polis consisted of an urban centre (asty) and its surround-ing territory (ch'ora), which formed a political, economic and social unity. The chora was normally the economic base for the state, while the asty provided the political centre.

In many languages the word πόλις is now used to refer to administrative phenom-ena, such as *politics* and *police*, and the word is also found in many toponyms, such as Constantinopolis and Alexandroupolis.

In contrast, *civitas* was originally the social body of the citizens (*cives*), who lived together and were thereby bound to each other and to the very place where they lived, and this social concept gave them certain legal rights as well as respon-sibilities, and it also gave them a recognition of their rights of citizenship. The *civitas* was thus not only the collective body of citizens, but it turned into some kind of social contract that united the inhabitants of a dwelling. This basic seman-tic meaning changed into something even more concrete, and it goes well with Gordon Childe's categories (cf. supra), and it must also be said that this kind of semantic extension is quite common in many languages, i.e., where the word for the inhabitants of a town ends up signifying the concept of the town itself. Thus the lexical development would be: inhabitants > (inhabitants') place.

We can thus see how these basic concepts and principles have given the words we use for *town*. All of them signify a place with either a positional or a directional reference. One of the positional meanings can thus be seen as the origin of the other two meanings, as it originally just means 'place', which implies a place connected to the speaker, i.e., **'the** place' or **'my** place'.

This process of semantic development can also be found in many other languages as well, such as Church Slavonic, *mesto*, where the original meaning *place* has changed into *town*. We find the same lexical situation in many Balto-Slavic languages, such as Polish *miasto*, Ukranian *misto* and Lithuanian *miestas* (cf. Russian *mesto* 'place'), and also we find it in Germanic languages, such as Dutch *staad*, German *Stadt* < *Statt* 'place', Swedish *stad* (cf. Swedish *eldstad* 'fireplace' and Danish *sted* 'place'). When *Stadt* developed into the meaning *town* in German, it returned to Swedish and replaced the old word *by* that is still found in Danish and Norwegian, even if it still exists in Swedish with the meaning of a 'small village'. There is also a semantic extension of this sememe into 'walled town' (cf. Mitre 2013:29) which, of course, was common in Europe during the Middle Ages and is also reflected in lexical variants such as German *Burg*, which can be found in many toponyms.

There are two different basic focuses of this positional meaning, one originally referred to the house, such as *villa*, while the other one focuses on the place, i.e., the yard such as *town*. In the latter case, it originally referred to the closing off of a place with a fence or a hedge, but its meaning was extended to include the place itself that was enclosed, such as the garden, and later on this lexeme was semantically extended to include the surrounding houses and other buildings and to mean the agglomeration of houses, such as a village and a town (Svensson 1997:39; Chapelot & Fossier 1980).

The word *town* derives from Old English *tūn*, and this lexeme is also found in Scandinavian *tun/tuna*, in German *Zaun* 'fence', and possibly in Celtic *dunum* (Hellquist 1957:1243; Barnhart 1995:824). In Old English *tun/tune* originally meant 'enclosure', later 'village' and 'homestead' (Svensson 1997:39–44). During the Middle Ages, it could also denote a seigneury with lord and dependent peasantry when compounded with a personal name. The word *township* was then a subdivision of the parish, such as we find in the parochial division of *Lancashire*.

In toponyms the lexeme has sometimes developed differently to -*ton* such as *Paddington* < the Saxon name *Padda* + *tun* (cf. *Tonbridge* or older *Tonebridge* and *Tunbridge Wells* in Kent which both refer to 'the town of bridges'). In Swedish we find the element in toponyms such as *Sigtuna* and *Sollentuna* — yet in Swedish *tun* can still be used as the word for the yard in front of a barn or a farmhouse (though, admittedly this meaning is rarely used today). However, it seems that it also acquired the meaning of 'fortress' at an early date, and this meaning probably dates to the late Iron Age, and it is possibly related to Celtic *dunum* as in *Lugdunum* (the Celtic god Lug's castle) > *Lyon*.

Other words for *town* in English that only remain in toponyms will not be discussed here although they often belong to the same semantic category: *castle* (Old English *castel*) in the sense 'village', 'town' from Latin *castellum* and later reborrowed from French in the sense *castle, ester* (meaning *sheepfold*), *chester* (<*cæster*) in the sense 'Roman town, city, walled town, fortification', and *wick/wīc/wich* that comes from the Anglo Saxon *-wīc*, referring to a dwelling or fortified place where trade takes place, and here both meanings 'fortified' and 'market' apply as we see in the toponym *Sandwich* (Old English *Sondwic*) 'market town on sandy soil'. Finally, we have *thorpe* 'from Germanic *þurpa* cf. Gothic *þaúrp* and Old Swedish *þorp* 'farm', 'village' (modern *torp*), and there are of course more English words for dwellings used in toponyms (cf. Svensson 1997: 21–62; Ekwall 1964).

The directional alternative indicates a meeting-place where people normally met for commercial reasons, i.e., it turned into a marketplace. And since people went there and then returned to their homes, this must be considered a more directional concept. These gatherings became more and more established and frequent and involved more people getting there and then leaving the place on a regular basis. Such a place was, and is, often situated at a crossroads or at some easily accessible place; by necessity, it had to provide certain continuous ground service for the place all the year around, and thus the permanent market came to resemble an extended yard around which more permanent buildings were constructed. Subsequently, the directional meaning lost relevance and the lexeme acquired a more positional meaning.

The main semantic difference between the positional and the directional perspectives is that on the one hand we are dealing with 'the inclusive WE vs. the exclusive THEY perspective', i.e., 'those who belong to the place and those who don't', while the directional reference reflects the coming and going of people, but these ingressive and egressive activities became more exclusive and less inclusive as time went by and as the place grew into a well-established village or town.

Thus, we see that the sememes originally referred either to a guarded place where people lived or a marketplace where people met for a limited amount of time for commercial activities. There are, of course, other aspects such as establishing a legal administration as well as a place for religious celebrations. These developed naturally as the place became more permanently inhabited, and the importance of the place grew due to an increase in commercial and military activities, as did the idea of protecting the town's people and resources as a necessary obligation for the established authorities.

However, it is interesting to see that as certain privileges and rights were given to the towns, but not to villages or other settlements (at least in many European countries), there emerged a new category of villages that were half-way to becoming towns. In English they were called *boroughs* from Germanic *Burg*, while the

Latin word *villa* that became town in French, *ville*, designates a borough in Spanish, *villa*. Curiously enough Madrid is not a town but a borough, and the Spanish capital is therefore often referred to as *La villa de Madrid*. Nevertheless, the citizens of these boroughs attained certain rights that correspond rather well to the so called *ius Latii* (Latin Rights; Encyclopaedia Britannica) which gave these people a status between that of Roman citizen and non-citizen (Speake 1994:343).

To sum up, the lexemes for *town* in Europe can be broadly divided into four etymological categories:

1. *House* with surrounding buildings and territory.
2. The semantic extension of this house, a *guarded place*.
3. Or refer to the land, i.e., *yard* (e.g. the land in front of the house).
4. And finally, the lexeme may refer to a *marketplace*.

However, we saw earlier (cf. supra) that the word for *town* linguistically may indicate the inhabitants of the place as is the case of Latin *civitatem*. Although *civis* originally means "a free member of a city" (Ernout & Meillet, 1959), the lexeme has a broader meaning, as it actually refers to the idea of a family that is consists of two free members of a town, a situation that can be considered similar to Gothic *heiwa-frauja* or Greek *oikodespotes*, both meaning 'lord of the house' (from Proto-Germanic **hīwą* and **frawjô*). In Old High German we find the lexeme *hīwo* 'husband' and *hīwa* 'wife', which is not contrary to the idea of a reference to the house itself, as this is where the family lives. It can thus be seen as a metonymic relationship.

The semantic extension 'walled place' has led to a second semantic extension to 'fortress'. In this sense the house itself and the wall around it have merged into one lexeme, as in German *Burg*, English *borough*, Icelandic and Swedish *borg*, and this word was transferred into French as *bourg* and Italian/Spanish as *burgo* from Germanic peoples (probably Franks, Goths and possibly Lombards) in the Middle Ages. It is found in many toponyms: Edinburgh, Saint Petersburg, Bourges (in France), and Burgos (in Spain). Nevertheless, in Gothic *baurgs* and in Old High German *burg/burc*, the words were used for town as these examples mentioned above clearly show.

This lexical idea is very close to the sense of the well defended and independent villa of Late Antiquity: "The country house (or villa rustica) played an important part in the Romanization of the provinces, [...]. Such villas, particularly common in the north-west provinces, functioned as self-sufficient estates and often covered a considerable acreage" (Speake 1994:61). The socio-political changes of the decaying late Western Roman Empire were, of course, fundamental to the creation of the well-defended medieval town (Barel 1981), where defence was essential for 'city-dwellers'. However, commerce, religion and art of different kinds gave the town its necessary ambiance and prestige, and it also conveyed its legal rights that were granted by a governing authority (a king, a prince or somebody else in charge of the region). In many Romance languages, Latin *civitatem* has been semantically changed to *town*, (cf. Portuguese/Galician *cidade*, Spanish *ciudad*, Catalan *ciutat*, Italian *città*, Friulan *citât*, Dolomitic Ladin *zità* and Engadin *citted*, all of which belong to (1), and so does, of course, French *ville* and Provençal *vila* (pronounced [bilo]) and Spanish *villa*. Roman-Italian influence must also have turned this word into the Albanian lexicon as *qytet*. The French influence on English has given the lexeme *city*, and English then continued to spread *city* to other Germanic languages such as Swedish, where its meaning is reduced to town centre and never refers to the whole town. Romanian *cetate* – etymologically the same word – means, and has always meant, 'fortress', and there is no indication that it should have meant 'town' because the Romanian word for this sememe is *oraş*, a Hungarian borrowing (*aros*), which was itself borrowed from Persian *var* 'castle, fortress' with the addition of an Hungarian adjectival suffix -*os*.

In Scandinavian languages the common word for *town* that refers to inhabitants is *by* from the verb *bo* 'live', and this noun is now used for *village* in Swedish (Hellquist I: 115). In Danish and Norwegian, and originally in Swedish, the word extended in meaning to *town*, and *by* was substituted with *landsby* (rural town) meaning *village*. This lexeme is also found in Icelandic *baer* (Old Scandinavian *býr*) and Faroese *býur* – and the same lexeme is also found in late Old English (Smith 1956; Svensson 1997: 58–60), as a result of Scandinavian medieval (viking) influence. Now it is mainly present in toponyms such as Carnaby, Rugby and Whitby.

In the Germanic languages 'the guarded yard' was often called *garden* (English), *Gard*, later *Garten* (German) and *gård* (Scandinavian languages). There were and still are, of course, other lexemic possibilities in Scandinavian languages such as *have/hage*, etc. During the Viking era *garðr*, later *gård/gard*, meant both 'farm' and 'town' and even 'fortress'. The meaning 'town' is nowadays only found in toponyms, such as *Midgård*, which was the name for the world (in the form of a tree as it was perceived then) where humans lived in pagan Scandinavian mythology, and *Miklagård*, the Viking name for Constantinople. Interestingly enough, this lexeme with its old meaning 'town' has been borrowed into East and South Slavic languages such as Church Slavonic *gradŭ* > *grad* (Bosnian, Bulgarian, Croatian, and Macedonian) or Russian *gorod* – *Novgorod* (with an internal vowel alternation, and in Russian toponyms it sometimes is *grad*, cf. Leningrad) as well as Belorussian *gorad* (also *goradok*). In other Slavic languages it has the meaning 'fortress', as in Czech *hrad* and Polish *gród* or Ukranian *horod* or *hrad*. These were so many in the medieval Kyivan Rus that the Vikings called this country *Garðaríki*, later *Gårdarike*, 'the country of the fortresses or fortified settlements'.

The other option 'marketplace' only appears in one Romance language, namely in Sursilvan (a Rheto-Romance variety in Switzerland; cf Söhrman 1998), as *marcau* (cf. French *marché*, Spanish *mercado* in the meaning market), but in Swedish we find *köping* (earlier *köpunger*) 'borough'. The verb *köpa* in Swedish means 'to buy', and this word has become *kaupunki* 'town' in Finnish. In this context, it is worth recalling the Old English word *čēap* and *čēping* 'market', which probably is an early Germanic borrowing from Latin *caupo* (cf. modern *cheap*). It is now only found in toponyms such as Chipping Campden.

The Slavic word *trъgъ*, originally probably **tъrg*, and *trъžište* 'market' (Udolph 2023:55–56). Old Russian *torgŭ* has most likely given Swedish/Norwegian *torg* and Danish *torv* 'square; marketplace', and, although it has not become a generic noun, it remains in many toponyms indicating their old status as marketplaces such as *Turku* (Finland), *Târgoviște* (Wallachia's old capital) and possibly *Trieste* (Italy). 'Bookfair' is also called *târg de cărți* in Romanian, and this word is used for market and square in many Slavic languages.

Comparing all these words and notions we can, of course, classify them into different semantic categories, but we can also see how people have influenced each other over time even when it comes to the fundamental vocabulary of their languages. That Roman influence has rubbed off on the Romance languages and other European languages is evident, but we have also seen how there has been, and still is, a vast cultural and linguistic exchange between Slavic, Romance, and Germanic peoples, and all around the North Sea, the Baltic Sea as well as the Mediterranean many such semantic and linguistic changes have taken place. Finally, we can also see how a Latin word passes on to Arabic to return to Europe in a different shape in Maltese, where the common word for *town* is *blet*, which seems unconnected to and does not make sense in other European languages. However, this is a misconception because it comes from Arabic *balad*, and this lexeme is probably a pre-Islamic loanword from Latin *palatium* 'palace'. It could be seen as some kind of return to sender, and this lexeme does, of course, belong to the category of walled places that later turned into a town. Word borrowings are anything but unilateral and the intention of this article was to show the complexity of cultural contacts and influences throughout history even when it comes to old basic vocabulary that refers to the historic and present situation.

References

Barel, Y. 1981. *La ciudad medieval. Sistema social-sistema urbano.* Madrid/Paris: Inst. de Estudios de Administración Local.

Barnhart, R. K. 1995. *The Barnhart concise dictionary of etymology. The origin of American English words.* New York: Harper Collins.

Boia, L. 2022. *Romänii şi Europa, o istorie surprinzatoare.* Bucureşti: Humanitas.

Buck, C. D. 1949. *A dictionary of selected synonyms in the principal Indo-European Languages.* Chicago & London: The University of Chicago Press.

Chapelot, J. & R. Fossier. 1980. *Le village et la maison au Moyen Âge.* Paris : Hachette. Available at: http://cnrtl.fr/definition/bled.

Ekwall, E. 1964. *Old English wīc in Place-Names.* Uppsala: Uppsala universitet.

Encyclopaedia Britannica, Available at: http://global.britannica.com/EBchecked/topic/308669/jus-Latii.

Gordon Childe, V. 1950. The Urban Revolution, *Town Planning Review* 21. 3–17.

Hasdeu, B. P. 1886. *Etymologicum magnum Romaniae*, vol 1, Bucureşti: Editura Socecu.

Hellquist, E. 1957. *Svensk etymologisk ordbok.* 2 vols. Malmö: Gleerup.

Hornblower, S. & A. Spawforth. 2012. *The Oxford classical dictionary*, 4th edn. Oxford: Oxford University Press.

Mitre, E. 2013. *Ciudades medievales europeas. Entre lo real y lo ideal.* Madrid: Cátedra.

Pirenne, H. 1927. *Les villes du Moyen Âge, essai d'histoire économique et sociale.* Bruxelles: Lamertin. Available at: 021477613_000_f[1].pdf

Smith, A. H. 1956. *English Place-Name Society. English place-name elements.* Cambridge: Cambridge University Press.

Söhrman, I. 1998. Romansh. In G. Price (ed.), *Encyclopedia of the languages of Europe*, 388–393. Oxford: Blackwell.

Söhrman, I. 2017. Why the lexemes *urbs* and *oppidum* did not survive and how they were substituted in Europe. In A. García Leal & C. E. Prieto Entrialgo (eds.), *Latin vulgaire – latin tardif, XI Congreso Internacional sobre el Latín Vulgar y Tardío (Oviedo, 1–5 de septiembre de 2014)*, 599–608- Olms: Weidmann.

Speake, G. 1994. *A dictionary of ancient history.* Oxford/Cambridge, MA: Blackwell.

Svensson, A-M. 1997. *Middle English words for "town". A study of changes in a semantic field.* Gothenburg Studies in English 70. Göteborg: Acta Universitatis Gothoburgensis.

Svensson, A.-M. & J. Hering. 2010. From Germanic 'fence' to 'urban settlement': On the Semantic Development of English town. In R.A. Cloutier, A.M. Hamilton-Brehm, & W.A. Kretzschmar, Jr (eds.), *Studies in the History of the English Language V: Variation and Change in English Grammar and Lexicon: Contemporary Approaches*, 187–206. Berlin: De Gruyter.

Thomas, A. R. 2010. *The evolution of the ancient city. Urban theory and the archaeology of the fertile crescent.* London: Rowman & Littlefield.

Udolph, J. 2023. *Namen – Zeugen der Geschichte.* Heidelberg: Winter.

The Loveden Hill Urn
Its second runic sequence and an afterthought

Gaby Waxenberger
Niedersächsische Akademie der Wissenschaften zu Göttingen | Ludwig-Maximilians-Universität München

The Loveden Hill Urn (ca. AD 450–550) carries an inscription in Pre-Old English that continues to challenge interpretation. Several scholars view it as three short sequences separated by word dividers. A reliable reading of the whole inscription is problematic because some of the runes in the third sequence cannot securely be identified. The first sequence may be a personal name, but the second sequence offers more than one possibility of interpretation. After discussing these possibilities, the most probable interpretation of the first two sequences is suggested. In an 'Afterthought' (Section 6) a new interpretation of the inscription as a whole is proposed. Contrary to previous interpretations, this reading suggests that the text is a funeral formula.

1. Introduction

Most scholars see the text on the Loveden Hill Urn as three lexemes separated by word dividers (see Section 3). A reliable interpretation of the whole inscription is difficult because some of the runes in the third sequence cannot satisfactorily be identified. Most scholars regard the first sequence as a personal name, but it is not entirely certain which gender it represents; the second sequence presents more than one possibility of interpretation.

What the inscription as a whole is trying to convey has not been solved, and since there are only two funerary urns in the Pre-OE Runes Corpus (Pre-OERC) and none in the Old English Runes Corpus (OERC), the scope for comparison is very limited.[1] This is probably why Ray Page (1987: 33) asked: "what on earth is a writer likely to have cut on a cremation urn?". Robert Nedoma (2016: 20) writes that he:

---

1. See Nedoma (2016: 5) for "runiform characters" on urns from Loveden Hill.

https://doi.org/10.1075/nss.34.20wax
Available under the CC BY-NC-ND 4.0 license. © 2025 John Benjamins Publishing Company

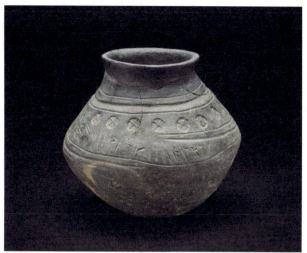

© The Trustees of the British Museum

Figure 1. The Loveden Hill Urn A.11/251

Would favour something like 'Sithæbad incised the runes' (a writer's formula), or 'Sithæbad made the urn' (a producer's formula), but apparently neither can be meant here. So it seems we should think of some kind of funeral inscription, yet this is a mere guess that cannot be confirmed sufficiently. We have to be content with a non liquet.

According to Hines (2019: 33 Footnote 3), however, the pot "need not have been made specifically as a cinerary urn, so that the name inscribed on it and the individual whose remains were buried in it could have been different people."

Although the third sequence on the Loveden Hill Urn seems undecipherable, I shall focus primarily on the suggested solutions for the second sequence. Before doing so, the two inscriptions on Early Anglo-Saxon urns, the Loveden Hill Urn and the Spong Hill Urns,[2] will be compared.

The Loveden Hill Urn and the three Spong Hill Urns (C1224, C1564, C2167) are close in their datings,[3] and also geographically not far apart (see below Map 1), but they contain different messages. The inscriptions on the Spong Hill Urns were made using a stamp, and are therefore identical on all three pots. The inscription on the Loveden Hill Urn is incised; more importantly, it is overtly personal-

---

2. See *RuneS Database*: https://www.runesdb.de Spong Hill Urn.
3. The Spong Hill urns have been dated to ca. AD 425–475 (Hills & Lucy 2013: 166;187;229ff.; C. Hills personal communication 8/9/2018; Hines 2019: 58). "Urns 1224, 1564 and 2167 make up stamp group 3, assigned to phase B at Spong Hill. Middle – late fifth century. Very approx. 430/475" (C. Hills personal communication 8/9/2018).

ized, as it contains a name. We do not know whose name it is, because the other two sequences are not clear; it may be the name of the deceased, or that of the bereaved, or somebody else (e.g., the maker's name). In contrast with the Loveden Hill inscription, Spong Hill's stamped **alu** is not overtly personalized although it may denote or characterize certain individuals or a certain group of people who are somehow associated with the formula word **alu**.

Map 1. The corpus of Pre-Old English inscriptions

1. The object: Urn A.11/251

A small blackware, angular biconical cremation urn (A.11/251) was unearthed in 1961 (Parsons 1999:55) in the Anglo-Saxon cemetery at Loveden Hill, Hough-on-the-Hill, Lincolnshire (Hills 1991:54). The excavation was led by Dr Kenneth R. Fennell, who submitted his results as a not otherwise published Ph.D. thesis to Nottingham University in 1964 (Odenstedt 1980:24 Footnote 2).

There is no agreement on the origin of the urn. For Fennell (Odenstedt 1980:24) it is not a local product, whereas Chadwick Hawkes & Page (1967:23) consider it of "Anglo-Saxon" make. According to Hills (1991:54), the "likelihood is that all the pots [= from Spong Hill and Loveden Hill] were made in England".

2. The datings

The urn was previously dated to ca. AD 450–550, "but perhaps more probably before 500" by Hills (1991:54, 51). Based on Hills' & Lucy's (2013) assessment that it belongs to Spong Hill Phase B, it has been dated to ca. AD 450–500 by Breay & Story (2018:67). Hines (2019:58) described the urn as "[n]ot closely datable by associated grave goods, form or decoration" and would not assign any more specific dating than some time within the 5th and 6th centuries to it, although both the very beginning and the very end of that range would be extremely unlikely (pers. comm. 12/1/2024). Hills, conversely (pers. comm. 24/2/2023), suggests it could be considered closer to Phase A, and therefore suggests a mid-fifth century date.

3. The ornaments and the inscription

3.1 The ornaments

Three incised grooves run around the upper part of the urn (see above Figure 1). There is a row of 17 cross-in-circle stamp impressions below the lowest groove. These impressions do not form a closed circle but leave an area, in which five to six (or possibly seven) runes could have been placed.[4] The inscription, however, was obviously too long for the free space; it therefore continued below the impressions. Two grooves running around the urn start below the stamps and above the inscription until it ends. The grooves continue to run around the urn until they reach the beginning of the inscription. There they run below the inscription from rune no. 1 to rune no. 12.

---

4. See *RuneS Database* https://www.runesdb.de Loveden Hill Urn.

These two grooves merge into one line at approximately the second set of the perpendicular lines ‖. This single line merges with another line below it approximately between rune numbers 13 ↑ and 14 ⅎ.

3.2   The inscription

The first two runes, no. 1 **s** and 2 ∫, are higher up than runes no. 3 þ, 4 ⅎ, and 5 **b**. Starting with rune no. 6 ⅎ, the runes are somewhat shorter in length so that they fit in between the stamp impressions and the line below them. There is no agreement on whether the runes (e.g., Parsons 1999: 55; Nedoma 2016: 5) or the decoration (e.g., Findell & Kopár 2017: 116) was cut first.

Some have claimed that the runes of the inscription are not carefully cut (Page 1973: 184; Odenstedt 1980: 25; Nedoma 1991–1993: 115, 2016: 5; Parsons 1999: 55),[5] and that they are poorly "spaced, and uneven in size" (Page 1973: 116, 1999: 114). In fact, some of the runes (see Figure 2) are difficult to identify and it is therefore problematic to assign them to known graphemes and phonemes. The double lines between the sequences of the runes are unanimously considered to be word dividers (e.g., Odenstedt 1980: 25; Parsons 1999: 56).

The double staves of some runes have led to different explanations (e.g, Odenstedt 1980: 25–28; Parsons 1999: 58; Nedoma 2004: 234; 2016: 14, 18–20). In my opinion, the double staves may be due to the carver's (broken) tool, a view supported by Dr. Ernst Taayke (pers. communication 29/6/2021; see below and also Waxenberger (forthcoming) with details).

3.2.1   *Datings and the sound values of runes* ⅎ *(nos. 4, 6)[6] and* ∫ *(no. 2)*

If the dating of ca. AD 450–500 is taken as a basis, the inscription linguistically belongs to the Pre-OE Phase 1 (ca. AD 425–500: Waxenberger 2019: 67). If, however, the dating ca. AD 450–550 is considered more likely, it may be either from Pre-OE Phase 1 (ca. AD 425–500) or from early Pre-OE Phase 2 (Pre-OE Phase 2 = ca. AD 500–575/625:[7] Waxenberger 2019: 67). Before ca. AD 575/610[8] the rune

---

5. Odenstedt (1980: 25), for example, thinks that "the inscription is obviously not the work of a skilled rune-master." Nedoma (1991–1993: 115) points out the irregularities of the size and shape of the runes as well as the intervals between the individual characters.

6. For rune ⅎ no. 14 (in my count no. 15) see below Section 6.

7. ca. AD 575/625 means the dating of the Harlingen solidus; this is when the phonemic split of short Pre-OE /a/ into the new phonemes Pre-OE /a/ and /æ/ probably happened (Waxenberger 2019: 72).

8. This is the date bracket between the earliest and latest dating of the **skanomodu** *solidus*, on which the new rune *āc* ⅎ **a** occurs for the first time (Waxenberger 2019: 68).

ᚨ denoted both the allophones [a(:)] and [æ(:)] of Pre-OE /a(:)/ (Waxenberger 2019:72).

Hines' (2019:58) caution over dating covers an even longer period, up to the quarter-century AD 575–600; this is the earliest phase in which the new rune *āc* ᚪ /a(:)/ has been documented (Waxenberger 2019:72). In that case, rune ᚨ of the inscription should denote the new phoneme /æ(:)/ but not the new phoneme /a(:)/, which should be represented by the new rune *āc* ᚪ **a**.

Table 1. Overview of the sound values of rune ᚨ in the period of ca. AD 425–600

Datings of the Loveden Hill Urn	Pre-OE Phase 1: ca. AD 450–500	Pre-OE early Phase 2: ca. AD 500–550	Pre-OE late Phase 2: ca. AD 550–575/625
ca. AD 450–500	Rune ᚨ denotes [a(:)], [æ(:)] of Pre-OE /a(:)/		
ca. AD 450–550	Rune ᚨ denotes [a(:)], [æ(:)] of Pre-OE /a(:)/	Rune ᚨ denotes [a(:)] and [æ(:)] of Pre-OE /a(:)/	
ca. AD 400–600	Rune ᚨ denotes [a(:)], [æ(:)] of Pre-OE /a(:)/	Rune ᚨ denotes [a(:)] and [æ(:)] of Pre-OE /a(:)/	The period from ca. AD 575–600: earliest phase in which *āc* ᚪ /a(:)/ and *æsc* ᚨ /æ(:)/ are documented.

To be on the safe side, my analysis of the inscription is based on the proposed datings of ca. AD 450–550, even though the most recent specialist archaeological opinion speaks for a mid-fifth century date (Hills: see Section 2). In the period of ca. AD 450–550, the rune ᚨ could still represent the allophones [a(:)] and [æ(:)] of Pre-OE /a(:)/. The sound value of rune no. 2 ᛁ may be /ī:/ or possibly /i:/.

The first element, sᛁᚦᚨ-, has generally been accepted as the successor of **senþa-*, a widely attested root meaning 'journey', 'military expedition'. The phonological development may have been **senþa* > **sinþa-* > **sīþ-*[9] > **sīþ-* (cf. Nedoma 2004:436; 2016:14); an intermediate stage with a lengthened and nasalized /ī:/ must have emerged in the process of Anglo-Frisian compensatory lengthening. In

---

9. Nedoma (2016:14 Footnote 36) comments that "$\tilde{V}NS > \bar{V}S$ has very likely taken place before the Loveden Hill inscription was engraved" and therefore he posits "*Sīþ-* rather than *Si(n)þ-* with non-realized nasal before obstruent (substitution $C_oVNT \rightarrow C_o\tilde{V}T <C_oVT>$ is a well-known runographic practice [...])".

my opinion, it could be this intermediate stage that is represented by the *yew* rune ᛡ. If this is the case, a Pre-OE /iː/ phoneme (< Gmc */iː/) and also a Pre-OE /ī:/ (< */ɪ+nasal+{f,s,θ}/ and */ɪ+ŋ+x/; Waxenberger 2010: Chapter 3) phoneme may be posited for this phase.

3.3 Transliteration

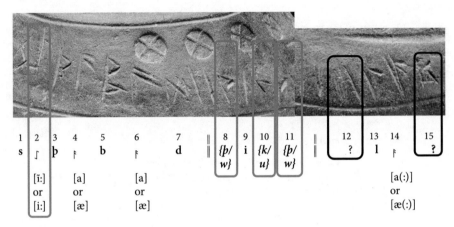

Figure 2. The inscription and transliteration of the Loveden Hill Urn Legend: Unusual/uncertain runes are put in grey frames; runes that have not been unambiguously deciphered occur in black frames

I leave the runes ᚠ and ᛡ in my transliteration; the possible phonetic realizations are presented in my transcription below the runes in question.[10]

3.4 The second sequence (rune nos. 8–11)

Due to the uncertainty of some of the runes, this sequence offers multiple possible combinations:

1. *þikþ* = Odenstedt (1980): see below
2. *þikw* = Eichner (1990): see below
3. *þiuw* = Bammesberger (1991): see below

---

10. The following graphic conventions are used in this article: Runes are transliterated in lower-case and bold letters. Uncertain runes are given in italics. Uncertain runes that allow for more than one interpretation are placed in braces { } and the individual interpretations are separated by slashes. Phonemes are put between slashes / /, and square brackets [ ] are used for allophones. Graphemes are denoted by angled brackets < >. The word dividers, ‖, are kept in the transliteration.

The Loveden Hill Urn   **363**

4. *þiuþ* = Looijenga (2003: 282): see below
5. *wiuþ*
6. *wiuw*
7. *wikþ* > *wik* (> OE *wīc* 'dwelling place') + *þ*: see Section 6.
8. *wikw* > *wik* (> OE *wīc* 'dwelling place') + *w*

Elliott (1989: 50) presents the drawing and transliteration in Figure 3, which clearly reveal his misinterpretation of rune no. 11 as "(?u)". Rather, the rune in question is either a *w* ᛈ or a *þ* ᚦ.

ᛈ ᛁ ᚲ ᚪ

w i c (?u)

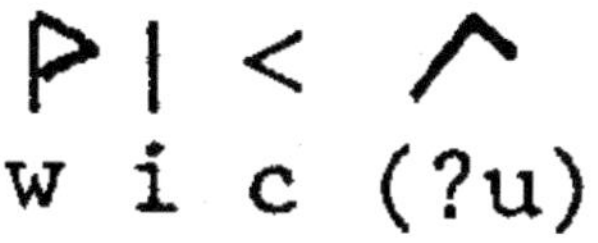

Figure 3. Elliott's (1989: 50) drawing and transliteration of the second sequence (runes nos. 8–11)

In Parsons's (1999: 57) opinion, combinations no. 1, 2, 7 and 8 (see above) have not "yet been justified in a compelling way." Combinations no. 5 and 6 make no lexical sense, while combinations no. 7 and 8 offer **wik-**, which may be the precursor of OE *wīc* 'dwelling place', but would then leave the following single rune, either *þ* (no. 7) or *w* (no. 8) unexplained (but see Section 6). Possibilities no. 1–3 are discussed in the following section.

Odenstedt (1980: 29f.) proposed option no. 1. He interprets *þicþ* as the 3rd. PERS.SG.PRES of the OE class V strong verb *þicgan* 'to get; to receive'. He regards the -*c*- instead of the rune **g** in *þicþ* as possibly the result of a "PrOE development *þiʒiþ* > *þiggiþ* (with analogical velar *gg*) > *þigþ* > *þicþ*." His suggestion is based on Luick's (1921: § 690) assumption that, in forms with a back vowel following the palatalized/assibilated *ċg* [dʒ] (e.g., OE *þicgan, þicgaþ*), velar *g* was "reintroduced in PrOE after the -*j*- (which had caused palatalization and assibilation) had been lost". Moreover, he assumes that the form of the 3rd PERS.SG *þiggiþ* would develop to *þicþ* after -*i*- was syncopated and *g* was either assimilated to *c* before *þ*, or it is simply a spelling mistake.

Bammesberger (1991: 126) has convincingly demonstrated that Odenstedt's interpretation *þicþ* (for Angl. *þigeþ*/WS *þigþ*) is not possible because of Odenstedt's assumption that *þiggiþ* (Gmc *þig-jan*, a strong class V verb with a *j*-present) could appear "with analogical velar gg". Additionally, Odenstedt's postulated form would be the West Saxon and not the Anglian variant, as the unstressed vowel was generally preserved in the latter dialect.

Bammesberger (1991: 126f.) rightly questions the relevance of an inscription of the type 'X receives bread' on a cremation urn. He accepts the general assumption that runes nos. 1–7 represent a personal name and interprets runes nos. 12–14 as *hlæ* referring to a 'grave' (see also Eichner 1990: 325). For runes nos. 8–11, he evaluates Fred Robinson's "(per litteras)" suggestion *þiuw* (= possibility no. 3 above). Bammesberger sees no "major difficulty" in interpreting rune no. 11 as *w*, since "*þ* and *w* are hard to distinguish anyway"; the shape of rune no. 10, however, "is somewhat unexpected if it stands for *k* [see 3.3 Figure 2, GW]. Robinson's suggestion simply means that ᚾ was cut in obliquely." According to Bammesberger, Robinson's interpretation of *þiuw* (= OE *þēow* masc. *wa*-stem) is "not immediately convincing". Regular phonological continuation of Gmc **þegwaz* would produce OE *þēo* as the nominative singular, "but *w* from oblique cases and the plural could readily be reintroduced in *þēow*." However, Bammesberger states that *i* is "not regularly to be expected in this paradigm" and therefore prefers to consider *þiuw* as the feminine belonging to **þegwa-*; the sense of 'female servant' is found in OE as *þēowu* "(with varying representation of the stressed syllable)"; Gothic, Old Saxon and Old High German forms suggest Gmc **þegwī* for the feminine. According to Bammesberger, it "seems reasonably clear" that **-gw-* led to **-w-*; the geminate **-ww-* in the paradigm **þiwī/þiwwjō* (< **þewī/þewijō*) could be levelled from the oblique cases into the nominative, therefore *þiww-ō* "may be the immediate starting-point for OE *þiuw* > *þēow(u)*."

Bammesberger (1991: 128) then suggests taking the forms *sʒþæbæd* ‖ *þiuw* ‖ *hlæ*[11] ('Sʒþæbæd' ‖ 'female servant' ‖ 'tomb') as nominatives, with *hlæ* 'tomb' referring to the vessel and *þiu* characterizing the vessel in question as one of a female servant.[12]

Option no. 2 of those listed above is offered by Eichner (1990: 325). For the runes no. 8–10, he suggests the personal pronoun (2nd PERS.SG) in the accusative *þic* followed by *w* representing a whole word "(wihiþ?)" and he translates "*Siþæbald* w(eiht) dich. Grabhügel (*hlæw...*)" ('*Siþæbald* consecrates you. Burial mound'). This possibility is unusual because rune no. 11 *w* would stand for a whole word and would be the only attestation of this kind in the Pre-OE and OE Runic Corpus. Although listing the Germanic equivalents (OFris. *wīa*, OS *wîjan*, OHG *wīhen*, ON *vígja* 'consecrate') for Eichner's reconstruction "wihiþ?", Hines (2019: 32) points out that this verb is not attested in Old English; however, this does not mean that it could not have existed in the "dialectal diversity among the early [...] settlers in Britain", as Hans Frede Nielsen (1998: 78) puts it.

---

11. See Brunner (1965: § 173 note 1) for the loss of -*w* in the NOM and ACC.SG.

12. Bammesberger (1994: 24) quotes a personal message from Robinson (18. February 1992): "But mightn't *Hlæ* be a personal name, perhaps incomplete?", suggesting the following rendering: "'*Siþæbæd*, the servant-girl of *Hlæ...*'".

Looijenga (2003: 282) considers possibility no. 4 above, "*þiuþ* 'good'", and interprets the second sequence as "'grave (of) S. (the) good', or 'S., (a) good grave'". From all these possibilities Bammesberger's interpretation seems to me the most probable. However, before drawing any conclusions, I wish to discuss sequence 1 of the inscription.

4. Sequence One (runes nos. 1–7) in the inscription

The first sequence of the inscription is generally viewed as a dithematic personal name. While the first element is relatively unproblematic, Nedoma (2016: 14–18) critically discusses the possibilities that have been suggested concerning the second element. Depending on the interpretations of the runes ᚠ as **a**, **æ** or **l**, he examines four possibilities.

4.1 Rune ᚠ (no. 6 and no. 4) rendering "/æ̆/" in Nedoma's phase "Pre-OE II" (Nedoma 2016: 14)

The sound value /æ̆/ may have been developed from the following sources.

4.1.1 *This would result in an interpretation Sīþæbæd; a female anthroponym*

-*bæd* would here be related to OE *beadu* 'fight, battle, war' (< Gmc *badwō-); the zero-ending (instead of the NOM.SG ending -*u*) is "most probably due to reasons of name rhythm" [Nedoma 2016: 15].

4.1.2 *Gmc *-badu- (u-stem) in second constituents of anthroponyms is "almost entirely restricted to male names" (for exceptions, see Nedoma 2016: 15)*

The number of attestations from early medieval England is small but sufficient (Nedoma 2016: 16). The prerequisite for the root vowel -*æ*- in -*bæd* is explained by Nedoma (2016: 17) as the change of the *u*-stem noun *-*badu* to the class of the *a*-stems ("*-*badu* → *-*bad(a)*") when occurring as a second element in names (*Sīþæ-bæd*). Additionally, restoration of *a* < *æ* did not happen because of the lack of a back vowel at the end, hence -*bæd*.

4.2 Rune ᚠ (no. 6 and no. 4) denoting "/ẵ/" in Nedoma's earlier period "Pre-OE I" (Nedoma 2016:17)

This would yield masc. *Sīþabad*. However, Nedoma (2016:17f.) states "that *a*, as connecting vowel of a Pre-Old English composite name, is hard to explain, since the expected form of a fifth or sixth century compound would be *(Sīþ)-æ-(bad)*." Moreover, he emphasizes that the loss of unaccented *æ* "(after heavy as well as after light syllable) takes place after *i*-umlaut, [...] which means it should not occur until late 6th century or about 600, a chronological framework into which the Loveden Hill inscription would clearly fit."

Nedoma (2016:18) thus sees *Sīþæbad* as "precisely the Pre-Old English form that one would choose as a continuant of the dithematic male name PGmc (transposition) **Senþa-badu*".[13] The apocope of *-u* was common in West Germanic dithematic names: it seems that rhythmic differences between the structures **Sígiwolf* (masc. *a*-stem) and **Sígi-frìþu* (masc. *u*-stem) were levelled in favour of the more frequent type **Sígi-frìþ*. Nedoma (2016:18) points out that this is supported by the fact that light syllable *u*-stems (e.g., **badu-*, **friþu-*, **haþu*) dropped their thematic vowel when used as second elements in Old English (and also Old High German) anthroponyms. For these reasons Pre-OE **Sīþæbad* (< **Sīþæbadu* < **Sinþa-baduz*) can be regarded as a "correct name form" (Nedoma 2016:18).

4.3 Lastly, rune no. 6 is considered to be the rune ᛁᛚ and not the rune ᚠ

In this case, a vowel rune would have to be inserted "somewhere in the string *-bld*" and in Nedoma's (2016:19) opinion, *Sīþæb(a)ld* is the only reasonable result. According to him, this means that we would be dealing with the "name element pair **-balþa-* ~ **-balda-* 'bold, brave, confident, strong'" (corresponding to the adjectives OIcel. *ballr*, OHG *bald* on the one hand and to OIcel. *baldr* on the other). The second element *-bald* is confirmed by "WFranc. *Sendebaldus* 10th c. and Langob. *Sendebaldus* 10th c.". Nedoma (2016:19) thinks that Pre-OE *Sīþæb(a)ld* would be a perfect masc. name from an onomastic point of view, but not from an epigraphical one because it requires emendation.

From his principal alternative interpretations of the sequence of runes nos. 1–7 (4.1.1 and 4.1.2 above), Nedoma (2016:19) decides on the second, based upon the premise of a "deliberate rune writer", who differentiated between the two vowels, by using ᛁᚠ for *a* and ᚠ for *æ*, and the rules of name rhythm, which explain Pre-

---

13. Nedoma (2016:18) finds its continuation in "West Franconian or Hispano-Gothic *Sendebadus*" (a. 875) and also in "Hispano-Gothic *Sende-*, *Sendo-*, *Sindovadus*" (10th cent.).

OE *-bad* (< *-badu*). Nedoma (2016: 19) does not follow up on his first alternative, namely the use of ᛁᚠ and ᚠ for *æ* and the "inflection class shift" (*-badu* → *-bad(a)* > *-bæd*).

4.4 Another possibility

I would like to discuss a third possibility. In my opinion, the rune ᚠ denoted the allophones [a(:)] and [æ(:)] of Pre-OE /a(:)/ at least up to or shortly prior to AD 575 (Waxenberger 2019; see also 3.2.1). I also think that the carver used a broken tool, meaning the tip of the tool was split or rather became split in the carving process, as can be inferred from runes no. 6 ᚠ, 14 ᚠ and possibly no. 12, which I do not consider an **h** rune (Waxenberger 2016: 354).

I contacted Dr Ernst Taayke, a specialist in earthenware, to ask for his expert advice on this matter. He finds my suggestion that the carver may have used a tool with a split tip plausible because this would explain the double lines.[14] He also points out that some rune-staves show pointed and narrow lines at the top, but wider ones towards the bottom. For him this also means that the tool was not pointed (pers. comm. 29/6/2021).[15]

Table 2 gives an overview of the possibilities discussed by Nedoma (2016) and the additional possibility proposed in Section 4.4.

---

14. Our first contact was a personal meeting at Noordelijk Archeologisch Depot, Nuis, NL in 2015. Afterwards we communicated by e-mail. Dr Taayke's e-mail (29 June 2021): " (...) Ihre Vermutung, daβ der Ritzer ein zweispaltisches Gerät benutzt hat, finde ich jetzt plausibel. Man kann damit schmale und (wenn man es schief hällt) auch breite Furchen ritzen. Auf dem Foto des BM's meine ich auch bei den aufrechten Trennlinien eine gewisse Doppeltheit zu sehen. (...)"

15. In the same e-mail Dr Taayke also comments on the state of the clay: "Die Magerung besteht aus Sand (vielleicht auch feinem Gesteinsgrus) und liegt dicht an der Oberfläche. Die Oberfläche scheint mir ziemlich trocken gewesen zu sein. Dennoch sind die Furchen an sich recht, sie wurden nicht oder nur sehr leicht abgebogen von dem Sand, obwohl das Mikroskop-Bild leichte Beschädigungen aufweist. Das deutet hin auf schnelle Bewegungen." 'The temper is sand (or possibly fine stone-grit), which is very close to the surface. The surface seems to have been rather dry. However, the sand does not cause any (or rather only small) deviation of the grooves, although the microscope photography shows minor damages, which indicate that the carver cut the inscription with rapid movements.'

Table 2. Possibilities of interpreting runes no. 1–8 (= sequence 1)

Possibilities discussed by Nedoma (2016)			Additional possibility
Sīþæbæd (see 4.1.1)	*Sīþæbæd* (see 4.1.2)	*Sīþæbad* (*Sīþabad*; see 4.2)	*Sīþæbæd* and *Sīþæbad* are theoretically possible (see 4.4)
Rune ᚠ (no. 6 and no. 4) render Pre-OE /ǣ/		Rune ᚠ (no. 6 and no. 4) denoting /ā̆/	Rune ᚠ (no. 6 and no. 4) denotes both allophones [a(ː)] and [æ(ː)]
fem. anthroponym	masc. anthroponym	masc. anthroponym	Theoretically, it could be a fem. or a masc. anthroponym
-*bæd* (< Gmc **badwō-* 'fight, battle, war'; OE *beadu*)	-*bæd* (< Gmc **-badu*; *u*-stem)	-*bad* (< **badu*; *u*-stem) *a*, as connecting vowel of a Pre-Old English composite name, is difficult to explain, because it should be -æ-, hence (*Sīþ*)-*æ*-(*bad*).	
Zero-ending most probably due to name rhythm.	Zero-ending **-badu* → **-bad(a)*	Zero-ending apocope of –*u* was common in West Germanic dithematic names	

5. Summary and conclusion

As the discussion has shown, the linguistic analysis of the name does not offer an unambiguous solution. Sometimes, archaeology supports a linguistic result or suggestion, but in this case archaeology also fails to lead us to an unequivocal result as the grave goods, a pair of iron tweezers and a bone gaming counter, are "not conclusively gender-specific, although iron tweezers are statistically more likely to have accompanied a cremated male", according to Hines (2019: 33 footn. 3), from which he concludes that there is "no real linguistic or archaeological case" for the name in the Loveden Hill inscription to be identified as "a unique feminine variant". Although Bammesberger (1991: 128 footn. 9) states that the exact shape of the name can "hardly be determined", he interprets the inscription as "*s₃þæbæd* ‖ *þiuw* ‖ *hlæ* 'S₃þæbæd' ‖ 'female servant' ‖ 'tomb'".

Bammesberger (1991: 128) considers the three sequences as nominatives suggesting a "kind of inventory." The narrative to go with it would be that "the household of $S_3þæbæd$ had commissioned a number of urns" for the ashes of deceased members. Bammesberger's scenario also explains the missing funerary inscription (see above Section 1). Summing up, I would like to highlight the following points:

1. The pot carries three runic sequences
2. In the third sequence of the inscription runes nos. 12 and 15 have not satisfactorily been identified (Waxenberger 2016).
3. Sequence no. 1 is a name, but its gender is not clear.
4. Sequence no. 2: linguistically, nothing speaks against Bammesberger's interpretation 'female servant'.
5. If Bammesberger's (1991: 128) scenario is accepted, there is no need for a funerary inscription, because the text represents an inventory.
6. Comparing the Spong Hill Urns with the Loveden Hill Urn, we are faced with two totally different text-types of which neither are typical funerary inscriptions such as known from other epigraphic cultures, where the name of the deceased is found on the urn.

In light of all this, the following interpretation, in two slightly different variants (male or female personal name in sequence one), would be possible:

s ᛋ þ ᚠ b ᚠ d ‖ þ i u w ‖ ?

For sequence two, Bammesberger's proposal 'female servant' is feasible. The gender of the personal name in sequence one, s ᛋ þ ᚠ b ᚠ d, depends on the interpretation of rune ᚠ (Figure 2: no. 6) as [a] or [æ] and can thus be interpreted as a male or female name.

1. The personal name as the male variant
   Sīþæbad ‖ *þiuw*   ‖
   (masc. pers. name)
   'Sīþæbad' ‖ 'female servant' ‖
2. The personal name as a female variant
   Sīþæbæd ‖ *þiuw*   ‖
   (fem. pers. name)
   'Sīþæbæd' ‖ 'female servant' ‖

Decoding and interpreting the third sequence could shed light on the gender of the personal name, because for archaeological reasons it may be doubted that the ashes of a female servant are in the urn: namely that the associated grave goods are more frequently associated with osteologically identified males than with females.

However, both of these interpretational variants are based upon the premise that the inscription is divided into three individual sequences separated by two word-dividers. In the following section, I would like to suggest a different way of parsing.

6. Afterthought

In my view (Waxenberger 2016: 355; see also 4.4), the first rune of the putative sequence three is not a single-barred **h H** rune,[16] but may be the rune **u ᚢ** with an extra line to its left. This extra line may have been caused by a broken or split tool.

© The Trustees of the British Museum

Figure 4. Rune no. 12 in Figures 1 and 2

With all due caution, I would like to suggest the following interpretation. If a rune **u** is allowed for, the sequence may be seen as ***ulF?***.[17] As rune **F** could have rendered the allophones [a(:)] and [æ(:)], the third sequence may be transliterated as ***ul{a/æ}?***

I cannot unambiguously identify the last rune/s of the third sequence. As pointed out above (see Section 3.2), the double lines between the sequences of the runes have unanimously been seen as word dividers. The first set of double lines (between sequences 1 and 2) is beyond doubt a word divider as it separates the name from the rest of the text. But is the second set of double lines also a word divider or might it be an unfinished rune, such as **e ᛖ**? If so, the carver only cut the two vertical staves, but did not put in the twigs between them. Dr Taayke stated that the carver must have cut the runes with rapid movements. Allowing for this possibility, the text would not consist of three, but only of two sequences: rune nos. 1–7 (*Sīþæbad/Sīþæbæd*) and rune nos. 8–17, which would read (Figure 5):

---

16. Therefore, interpretations such as *hlāf* 'bread', *hlāw* 'mound' or *hlǣ* 'grave' or *Hlǣ* a personal name are problematic (Waxenberger 2016: 355).

17. The question mark stands for one or more runes that cannot unambiguously be identified at the end of this string.

Figure 5. The inscription and a new transliteration of the Loveden Hill Urn

1	2	3	4	5	6	7	‖	8	9	10	11	12	13	14	15	16	17
s	ʃ	þ	f	b	f	d	‖	w	i	k	þ	*[M]	∩	l	f	i	k
[ī:]		[a]		[a]								*[e] u			[a(:)]		
or		or		or											or		
[i:]		[æ]		[æ]											[æ(:)]		

The shape of what would appear to be a final rune or runes at the end of this sequence is completely puzzling. There is a vertical stave which I read as **i** (no. 16), followed closely, and indeed touched at the bottom, by what looks at first sight like a tripartite **s** ⌇ similar to rune no. 1 (Figure 5) but reversed in direction.

Figures 6a and 6b, however, give another, arguably better view. The upper two lines of this hypothetical **s** ⌇ do not meet at an angle (Figure 6a), suggesting that this graph may rather be a **k** rune (Figure 6b), as also found as rune no. 10 (Figure 5).[18]

Perhaps at first, the carver attempted to cut rune no. 17 as **k** in line with the other runes and in the same direction: see Figure 5, above, for rune no. 10 and compare with Figure 6c, below. But for some reason,[19] (s)he may have stopped and started anew at a lower point.[20]

My interpretation of [a] for rune f (no. 15: see above Figure 5) is possible within the time-frame of ca. AD 450–550 (see above 3.2.1). In this period Gmc */aɪ/ had not yet developed to Pre-OE /a:/ (Waxenberger 2019: 72 Table 5 scenario 2). Based on these considerations, I transliterate runes nos. 8–17 as **wikþ*[e]ulaik**. This sequence may be interpreted as *wīk þeulaik*

---

18. See the 3D model: https://sketchfab.com/3d-models/loveden-hill-cremation-urn-exc1963-40c9c2593e0848349bec3a55bfa7d491.

19. As Dr Taayke pointed out, the temper is close to the surface and was rather dry (see Footnote 15), which may have made cutting difficult at this point. Cutting runes in a convex surface may also have contributed to this difficulty. Additionally, the rapid movements (see above Section 6 and Footnote 15) pointed out by Dr Taayke may mean that the carver was in a hurry.

20. It should not go unnoticed that the cut on the left-hand side in the Figures 6a, 6b, and 6c belongs to rune no. 15 (and may be a miscut): see Figure 5 rune 15.

© The Trustees of the British Museum

Figure 6a. Runes nos. 16 **i** and 17 the hypothetical **s** ⟨ in my count: See above Figure 5

© The Trustees of the British Museum

Figure 6b. Runes nos. 16 **i** | and 17 **k** > in my count: See above Figure 5

Runes no. 8–10 would be OE *wīc* 'dwelling place' and runes no. 11–17 may denote a name with the elements OE *þēo(w)* 'servant' (see Bammesberger in 3.4 and also Bammesberger 1990: 67f., 35) and OE *lāc* 'battle, struggle'; 'offering, sacrifice'; 'gift, present' (Bosworth & Toller 1882–1898: 603). <*eu*> in *þ*[e]u* would be the early spelling, which was still used as late as in early Old English for later OE *ēo* (cf. Waxenberger 2023: 270f.).

If the second set of parallel lines is not a word divider but a defective or unfinished rune, there must be a reason why there is a word divider or marker only after the first sequence and not somewhere in the string of rune no. 8–17. It may be assumed that there was a need to visually separate *Sīþæbad* from the

© The Trustees of the British Museum

Figure 6c. The possibly intended shape of rune no. 17 in my count: See above Figure 5

rest of the inscription. These separation marks make clear that the urn is Þeulaik's dwelling place and not Sīþæbad's. Sīþæbad may have been the commissioner, the carver or the bereaved. In this context the female name Sīþæbæd (see above 4.1.1) may also be taken into account because the iron tweezers and a bone gaming counter would then not have accompanied Sīþæbæd's remains, but Þeulaik's. As said above, I consider this name a male personal name with the first element OE þēo(w) 'male servant' and a second element OE lāc in male names (e.g., Hygelāc (Beowulf), Gūthlāc: Müller 1901: 126). While OE lāc is common as a second element in Old English dithematic personal names (Müller 1901: 126f.), I have not found attestations of OE þēo(w) as a first element in dithematic names. Nevertheless, it is well attested as a second element in Old English (e.g., Ecġþeow, Onġenþēow in Beowulf) and in Old High German, where as a first element it is difficult to separate from theuda- (Förstemann 1900: 1457–1459). My tentative interpretation and translation is as follows:

Sīþæbad / Sīþæbæd ‖ wīk þ*[e]ulaik

Sīþæbad / Sīþæbæd (male PN) (female PN)	‖	wīk	þ*[e]ulaik (male PN)
'Sīþæbad / Sīþæbæd	‖	dwelling place [for]	þeulaik (OE Þēolāc)

Regarding the text-type of the Loveden Hill Urn, the pattern of the underlying formula system may be:

1. A simple maker formula (= name: *Sīþæbad* / *Sīþæbæd*) combined with a funeral formula (the deceased's present place and his (or her) name) or alternatively the text may be represent
2. A complex funeral formula consisting of the bereaved, the deceased's present place and his (or her) name.

Acknowledgements

My heartfelt thanks go to Dr Ernst Taayke for his most valuable expertise on pottery and to Prof. Dr Alfred Bammesberger, Prof. Dr. John Hines and PD Dr Kerstin Kazzazi for reading the manuscript and making important suggestions to improve this paper.

References

3D Model of the Loveden Hill Cremation Urn. Created by D. Powlesland. https://sketchfab .com/3d-models/loveden-hill-cremation-urn-exc1963- 40c9c2593e0848349bec3a55bfa7d491

Bammesberger, A. 1990. *Die Morphologie des urgermanischen Nomens*. Heidelberg: Winter.

Bammesberger, A. 1991. Three Old English runic inscriptions. In A. Bammesberger (ed.), *Old English Runes and their Continental Background*, 125–136. Heidelberg: Winter.

Bammesberger, A. 1994. The development of the runic script and its relationship to Germanic phonological history. In T. Swan, E. Mørck, O.J. Westvik (eds.), *Language change and language structure, older Germanic languages in a comparative perspective*, 1–25. Berlin: De Gruyter.

Bosworth, J. & T.N. Toller. 1882–1898. *An Anglo-Saxon dictionary: Based on the manuscript collections of the late Joseph Bosworth*. Edited and enlarged by T.N. Toller. Oxford: Oxford University Press.

Breay, C. & J. Story. (eds.). 2018. *Anglo-Saxon kingdoms: Art, word, war*. London: The British Library.

Brunner, K. 1965. *Altenglische Grammatik: Nach der angelsächsischen Grammatik von Eduard Sievers*, 3. Aufl. Tübingen: Niemeyer.

Chadwick Hawkes, S. & R.I. Page. 1967. Swords and Runes in South-East England. *The Antiquaries Journal* 47. 1–26.

Eichner, H. 1990. Die Ausprägung der linguistischen Physiognomie des Englischen anno 400 bis anno 600 n. Chr. In A. Bammesberger, A. Wollmann. (eds.). *Britain 400–600: Language and History*, 307–333. Heidelberg: Winter.

Elliott, R.W.V. 1989. *Runes, An introduction*. 2nd edn. Manchester: Manchester University Press.

Fennell, K.R. 1964. *The Anglo-Saxon cemetery at Loveden Hill (Hough-on-the-Hill) Lincolnshire and its significance in relation to the Dark Age settlement of the East Midlands*. Ph.D dissertation, University of Nottingham, England.

Findell, M. & L. Kopár. 2017. Runes and commemoration in Anglo-Saxon England. *Fragments* 6. 110–137.

Förstemann, E. W. 1900. *Altdeutsches Namenbuch, 1: Personennamen.* 2. völlig umgearbeitete Aufl. Bonn: Hanstein; Nachdr. 1966: Fink Verlag München; Georg Olms Verlag Hildesheim.

Hills, C. 1991. The archaeological context of runic finds. In A. Bammesberger (ed.). *Old English runes and their Continental background,* 41–59. Heidelberg: Winter.

Hills, C. & S. Lucy. 2013. *Spong Hill part IX: Chronology and synthesis.* Cambridge: McDonald Institute for Archaeological Research.

Hines, J. 2019. Practical runic literacy in the late Anglo-Saxon period: Inscriptions on lead sheet. In U. Lenker, L. Kornexl. (eds.), *Anglo-Saxon micro-texts,* 29–59. Berlin: De Gruyter.

Looijenga, T. 2003. *Texts & contexts of the oldest runic inscriptions.* Leiden, Boston: Brill.

Luick, K. 1921. *Historische Grammatik der englischen Sprache:* Band I, 1. Abteilung. Leipzig: Tauchnitz.

Müller, R. 1901. *Untersuchungen über die Namen des nordhumbrischen Liber Vitae.* Berlin: Mayer & Müller.

Nedoma, R. 1991–1993. Zur Runeninschrift auf der Urne A.11/251 von Loveden Hill. *Die Sprache* 35. 115–124.

Nedoma, R. 2004. *Personennamen in südgermanischen Runeninschriften.* Heidelberg: Winter.

Nedoma, R. 2016. The personal names on the Loveden Hill urn and the Watchfield case fitting. *NOWELE* 69. 3–37.

Nielsen, H. F. 1998. The Continental backgrounds of English and its Insular development until 1154. Odense: University of Southern Denmark Press.

Odenstedt, B. 1980. The Loveden Hill runic inscription. *Ortnamnssällskapet i Uppsala Årskrift.* 24–37.

Page, R. I. 1973. *An introduction to English runes.* London: Methuen.

Page, R. I. 1987. New runic finds in England. In *Runor och runinskrifter.* Föredrag vid Riksantikvarieämbetets och Vitterhetsakademiens symposium 8–11 september 1985, 185–197. Stockholm: Almqvist & Wiksell.

Page, R. I. 1999. *An introduction to English runes,* 2nd edn. Woodbridge: The Boydell Press.

Parsons, D. 1999. *Recasting the runes, the reform of the Anglo-Saxon Futhorc.* Uppsala: Institutionen för nordiska språk.

RuneS Database https://www.runesdb.de

Waxenberger, G. 2010. *A phonology and edition of Old English runic inscriptions with an analysis of the graphemes,* unpublished habilitation thesis, University of Munich.

Waxenberger, G. 2016. Graphemes: (Re)construction and interpretation. In P. Cotticelli & A. Rizza. (eds.), *Variation within and among writing systems, concepts and methods in the analysis of ancient written documents,* 353–370. Wiesbaden: Reichert.

Waxenberger, G. 2019. Absolute chronology of early sound changes reflected in Pre-OE runic inscriptions. *NOWELE* 72. 60–77.

Waxenberger, G. 2023. The date and provenance of the Auzon/Franks Casket revisited: a linguistic and runological perspective. In G. Waxenberger, K. Kazzazi & J. Hines. (eds.), *Old English runes: Interdisciplinary perspectives on approaches and methodologies,* 267–296. Berlin: De Gruyter.

Waxenberger, G. Forthcoming. *The edition of the Pre-Old English inscriptions:* ca. AD 425–650.

Subject index

The subject index lists important subject areas, linguistic terminology, and the names of early historical sources and inscriptions.

A

Ablaut 24, 127, 131, 133–134
Ablösewort 228, 236–237
accent 50, 52–54, 58, 69, 109, 210, 233, 276
accesibility hierachy 181
Adam von Bremen, *Gesta Hammaburgensis* 272
Adamklissi inscription 259, 263
adjective 26, 57, 72, 74–78, 90, 95–96, 98, 109, 178, 248, 254–255, 269, 299, 200, 277–278, 302, 307, 332, 366
adverb 45, 47, 128, 178, 233, 225
adverbial 112
Æthelweard *Chronicon* 119
affricate, affrication 46, 112, 208
agent noun See *nomen agentis*
Akzentwechsel 276, 278
alliteration 316–339
allograph 75
allomorphy 78, 128
allophone 159, 163, 166, 170, 202, 204, 214, 299, 361–362, 367–368, 370
alternation, Alternanz 26, 89, 160–161, 260, 301, 353
anakrusis 326–327, 337
analogy 75, 127, 141, 164, 256, 301, 363
Anglian smoothing 167
Anglo-Saxon Charters 118, 121
Anglo-Saxon Chronicle 138
Annales Cambriae 139
Anonymous Life of Gregory the Great 115–116
Antonine Itinerary 242
aphasia 207
apocope 79, 366, 368
apophonic pattern 77, 252

archiphoneme 205
Äskatorp bracteate 328
aspiration 65, 204, 206, 208, 212, 297
Asser, *Life of King Alfred* 118
assibilation 363
assimilation 45, 65–66, 157, 204–205, 252, 301, 363
attenuative 90, 93, 96, 98
Auflösung 315–337
Auftakt 326, 337 See also Anakrusis
Avienus, *Ora maritima* 274

B

bahuvrihi 26, 77 See also compound
Bede, *Historia Ecclesiastica* 105–120, 138–140
Bedeutungsverschiebung 234, 274
Beowulf 165, 373
Beuchte brooch 140
Birrens inscription 252–255
blend 132–133
borrowing 89, 91–93, 96–98, 111, 170, 186, 205, 213, 219, 227–228, 234–237, 295–297, 299, 304–306, 353–354
Bratsberg Fibel 328
breaking 132, 157–170, 202, 297
Brokmer manuscript 75
Bystein inscription 329

C

Caedmon's Hymn 167
Caesar, *De bello Gallico* 242, 245, 274
Carolingian Laws 107, 121

cluster 61, 114, 133, 160, 166, 170, 298
cognomen 246
Colijnsplaat dedication 260
collective noun 177, 274, 321, 333
combinatory variant 159
compensatory processes 210, 215, 297, 361
composition vowel 244, 248, 254, 256, 260, 262–263
compound 21, 24, 26–30, 51–55, 59, 77, 88, 118–119, 132, 244, 260, 256, 262, 299, 307, 350, 366
Concordia sarcophagus inscription 140
conditioned diphthong 159
congruence 176
Constantius, *Life of Germanus of Auxerre* 117
contact 2–4, 43, 108, 145, 151, 153, 236, 295–296, 303–305, 346, 348, 354, 367
creole 86

D

Danismus 227–236
dative 42–43, 45–47, 111–112, 128–129, 175, 181–183, 229
decipherment 152, 362
declension 89, 108–109, 300, 302, 306–307
definite article 42, 44, 46, 53, 175, 194
Dehnung See lengthening
delabialisation 26
demonstrative pronoun 175, 178, 186–187, 193–194, 224
devoicing 204, 212
dichotomous phonology 207
diglossie 218, 229, 236

digraph 129, 147, 157–158,
162–163, 165
diminutive 90, 94, 305–306
Diodor, *Bibliotheca historica* 276
distinctive feature 162, 202–213,
298
dithematic name 139, 141, 248,
314, 317, 366, 368, 373
dominant language 84
dragchain 210
Druk incunablum 128–129
dummy (subject) 186, 193
Durham, *Liber Vitae* 141
Dybos Regel 276

E
Eadgar's Fourth Law Code 111
ek erilaʀ-Mikroformel 325–331
empty hole *See* gap
enclisis 67–68
Entlehnung *See* borrowing
entropy 99
epenthesis 157, 163, 273
Erbwort(schatz) 132, 233, 236
Erfurt Glossary 302
exclave 92, 97–98
expanded form 42
extension 127, 139, 349–350, 352
extra-prosodicity 58–69

F
fieldwork 3, 146, 149, 174,
199–201
First Consonant Shift 208
Fivelgo Manuscript 73–75, 129,
132
Fontes Egmundenses 288
free-affectee construction 182
Fremdwort 228
Fugenelement 26

G
Gallehushorn 315, 318–321,
324–327, 334, 337–339
Gallic Chronicle 117
gap 126, 207, 210–211, 259, 297
Geminos, *Elementa astronomiae*
270–271, 276
gender 140, 176, 356, 368–369
generative 5, 203, 208

genitive 75, 89, 119, 128, 161, 167,
175, 180, 234, 244, 246, 252, 276,
279, 288, 290, 292
Genus *See* gender
Gildas, *De excidio* 117
glottalic theory 206
Glottolog 82, 86, 88, 90, 92, 94
glottal stop 54
Y Gododdin 113
Gøtudansk 230–233, 236
grade (zero/full) 76, 247,
251–252, 259, 276
graffiti 246–247, 257–258,
261–262
grammatischer Wechsel *See*
Verner
grapheme 74, 158, 297–298, 360,
362
Great Vowel Shift 205, 208, 213
Gregory of Tours, *Historiae
Francorum* 117
Gregory, Pope, *Epistolae* 114–117
Gregory, Pope, *Moralium Libri*
115
Grimm's Law 259, 304–305
Grønviks Substitutionsregel 338
Guthlac B 112

H
Haet is riucht? catechism 127
heteroclitic *r/n* 243
hiatus 68, 254
Himlingøje brooch 140
Hirt's Law 276
homophone 231, 235
Hunsingo manuscript 74
hypercorrection 223, 232

I
i-affection 113
idiolect 84
Illerup Ådal inscriptions 140
imperative 66, 68, 232, 258, 261
infinitive 2, 45, 68, 128
influence 42, 44, 84, 113, 116, 119,
130, 152, 157, 170, 208, 227, 232,
236, 244–245, 299, 346, 353–354
interference 231, 232, 297, 299,
302
ISO 86, 90

J
Järsbergstein 330–331
Jelling runestone 119
Jus manuscript 127–128

K
Kjølevikstein 317–318
Klosterneuburg gravestone 251
Kompositum *See* compound
Kongruenz *See* congruence
Kosmas Indikopleustes,
Topographia Christiana
270–271
Kragehul lance-shaft 329

L
labial mutation (Frisian) 78–79
Lachmann's Law 168–170
La Graufesenque inscription 262
language acquisition 207
Langzeile 312–340 *See also*
Protolangzeile
Laryngalbrechung 278
Lautgleichung 24
Lautnachahmung 24
Laws of King Ine 120
l-cases 147
left dislocation 335, 193
Leges Barbarorum 107
Lehnübersetzung 227
Lehnwort *See* loan word
lengthening 26, 47, 157, 164,
168–170, 210–214, 246,
297–298, 361
lenition 208–209, 211–212, 298
Leseaussprache 231–232
Lex Salica 293
levelling 40
Lev Shcherba's school
(Leningrad/St.Petersburg)
school 160, 205
lexical specification 59–63
liason 51
Liber Pontificalis 116
ligature 257
Lindholm amulet 328
Linksversetzung *See* left
dislocation
litotes 322–323
Livonian broken tone 151
Ljóðaháttr 332, 334

Subject index 379

loan(word) 59, 64, 78, 89, 92–93, 95–99, 130–133, 149–150, 152–153, 222, 251, 295–308, 354
Loveden Hill urn 356–374
lowering 246, 263, 306
L vocalisation 158

M

Martial, *Epigrammaton* 169
Martianus Capella, *De nuptiis* 271
Matrixsprache 232
merger 205, 210–211, 213, 297, 352
meta-language 87–88
metaphor 77
minority language 84
monolexeme 84, 87
monophthongization 161, 204, 261
mora 50–69
Munsell color array 84
mutation *See* umlaut

N

names *See* personal names, place-names, -*nym*
Namur tombstone 258
nasalization 297–298, 361
neogrammarian 144, 149–151, 202–203, 213–215
Neubildung 26
Neuss funerary inscription 248
neutralization 205
Nolebystein 321–322, 333
nomen actionis 247
nomen agentis 26, 131, 255
-*nym See also* personal names, place-names
    anthroponym 248, 251, 259, 365–366, 368
    antonym 322
    ethnonym 103–119, 242, 244, 248, 250, 260, 263–264, 274
    homonym 205, 211, 214
    hydronym 259–260, 338
    patronym 248, 251–252, 259–260, 320
    theonym 253–256, 260
    toponym 112, 142, 144, 269–280, 291, 351

O

Ockham's razor 60
Ohthere's account 110–111
Old English Martyrology 111, 118
Old English Orosius 110
Old West Frisian charters 130
Old Turkic Orkhon inscriptions 152
orthography 44, 64, 147, 158, 162–163, 218, 223, 232, 296
Ortsnamen *See* place-names
Ovid *Amor* 169

P

palaeogramarian 144
palatalization 26, 46, 75, 112, 141, 214, 230, 363
palatal consonant 94
palatal diphthong 254, 264
Parker Chronicle 105, 111, 118, 121
Paulus Diaconus, *Historia Langobardorum* 118
personal names 109, 139, 140, 142, 287–293, 299, 306, 319, 328–329, 356, 365, 369–370, 373
personal pronoun 43, 46, 319, 326–327, 364
Personennamen *See* Personal names
Peutinger map 242
Pforzen Gürtelschnalle 338
phonemic split 360
phonotactics 166, 257, 297
Place-names 112, 121, 140, 162, 243–244, 251, 253, 259, 262, 287–293, 326, 346
Pliny, *Naturalis historia* 106, 113, 242, 259, 263, 271, 273, 276, 303
Polybius, *Historiae* 270
Pomponius Mela, *Chorographia* 271
postposition 128, 147
preaspiration 54
Preference Laws 57
prefix 63, 75, 205, 244, 254
preglottalisation 54
preposition 42, 44–45, 174, 183, 185–192, 195, 243
primary stress 52, 55, 58, 64–65
Prague Circle 159 160, 203–205, 209

Procopius, *De bello Gothico* 105–107, 19, 114, 272
prosody 50–69, 157, 161–170, 215, 296
Proto-Langzeile (proto-long line) 314, 324, 326, 328, 337
Ptolemy, *Geographica* 105–106, 109, 112–113, 242, 251, 272, 279, 280
pushchain 210
Pytheas fragments 269–280

R

Rakkestadstein (Øverby) 329
raising 111, 139
reborrowing 306
Rechtschreibreform 229
Rechtschreibung 218, 222
reduplication 246
reference variety 85–98
reflexive possessive 43
reflexive pronoun 46
relative adverb 190–192
relative clause 173–195
relative pronoun 65, 173–195
Relativsatz *See* relative clause
Relikt(wort) 19, 25–26, 30
relative particle 180
rephonologization 203, 208, 246
resolution 315, 321, 332, 333
resumption 178, 195
resyllabification 161, 166
retraction 263
rhotacism 208
rhyme 37, 40, 45, 52, 67, 127, 129, 133, 166
Rimburg tombstone 251
Roorda manuscript 128–129
Rosselandstein 328, 332
Rotweil graveyard inscription 252

S

sandhi 205
Saxo Grammaticus, *Gesta Danorum* 112
Schärfung 24
Schriftsprache, written language 44, 126, 134, 185, 217–238
Schwundstufe, zero-grade 147, 251–252, 273, 276
Second Consonant Shift 208

semantic development 98, 259, 350

short diphthongs 162–164

shortening 42, 66, 139, 164–165, 254, 212, 315

Sievers' Law 161

Silbenschnitt See *syllable cut*

simplification 114, 297–298, 304

s-mobile 259

Snitser Recesboeken 130

Solinus, *Collectanea rerum memorabilium* 271–273

sonority 52, 55–56, 66–67, 69

source argument 128–129

Sparlösastein 333

spelling 5, 39, 42–47, 75, 105–106, 109, 113, 119, 141, 147, 157–158, 162–163, 167, 242, 245, 253, 263, 298–299, 363, 372 *See also* Rechtschreibung

Sperrschrift 224, 238

spirantization 170

Spong Hill urns 357–359, 369

Sprachinsel See exclave

stability 84, 162, 209–213

Stentoftenstein 334–335, 339

Stephanus Byzantius, *Ethnica* 271

Sprichwort 226

Strabo, *Geographica* 106, 256, 270–272

Stabreim See alliteration

structuralism 50, 75, 105, 203

Substantivgroßschreibung 223, 230, 234

Substantivierung 276, 278

substitution 87, 149, 166, 295, 299, 304, 353, 361

substrate 19, 24, 28, 93, 127, 133, 276, 304

suffix 20, 60–62, 64, 68, 76, 89, 99, 109, 138–141, 160, 225, 228, 243, 248, 250, 254, 277, 306, 353

superlative 74, 147, 194

syllabification 160–161

syllable cut 209

symmetry 209, 212, 215

syncope 66, 113, 116, 129, 234, 140

synonym 25, 30, 119, 132, 225, 231, 319

stød 50–69, 151, 210

T

Tacitus, *Agricola* 272

Tacitus, *Germania* 104–106, 142, 263, 279

target language 88

Tenuiserweichung 26

thema argument 128

thematic vowel 109, 112, 366

Thomsen's Law 151

Thorsberg chape 323, 337

Thurneysen's Law 301

Tienen inscriptions 240–264

Tjurkö bracteate 335–336, 337

/t/-morpheme 57

toponym See names

Tribal Hidage 105, 117

U

Übach-Palenberg funerary inscription 260

Unia manuscript 128

Umlaut 111, 215, 329 *See also* labial mutation

a-~ 244, 246–247, 297, 306–307

back ~ 170, 205

i- ~ / palatal ~ 24, 109, 111, 113, 128–129, 131, 139–141, 204, 206, 214, 321, 329, 366

Old Norse labial ~ 78, 206

Nordic / Scandinavian ~ 66, 214–215

Old English velar ~ 206

unrounding 44, 129

V

V2-Satzstellung 194–195, 320–321

Valsfjord cliff inscription 327, 350

Väsby bracteate 328

Veblungsnes Felsinschrift 328

Venantius Fortunatus, *Opera Poetica* 106

verb 126–134

modal ~ 44–45

privative ~ 128

strong ~ 77, 127, 129, 131 133–134, 246, 307, 363

weak ~ 160, 257–258, 261, 263

Vergilius, *Georgica* 271

Verner alternation / variation 127, 208, 301–302, 307

Verner's Law 151, 208, 254, 307

Vespasian Pslater gloss 167

Vindolanda inscriptions 248–249, 251, 262–263

Vita Alcuini 119

Vokalalliteration 313

voicing 43, 45, 204, 206, 208, 211–212, 254

Vokalalternanz 26

Vollstufe See grade

W

weakening 78–79, 208 *See also* lenition

Wels tombstone 260

Wenkersätze 3

West Germanic gemination 211

Widsith 110–111

Wiederaufnahme See resumption

Willibald, *Vita Bonifatii* 118

World Color Survey 84